S0-EDJ-753

GOVERNMENT AND ECONOMIC CHOICE

GOVERNMENT AND ECONOMIC CHOICE
An Introduction to Public Finance

Thomas F. Pogue and L. G. Sgontz
University of Iowa

HOUGHTON MIFFLIN COMPANY   BOSTON
Dallas   Geneva, Illinois
Hopewell, New Jersey   Palo Alto   London

This book is dedicated to Mike and Rob, Paul and Julie.

Copyright © 1978 by Houghton Mifflin Company. All rights reserved. No part of this work may be reproduced or transmitted in any form or by any means, electronic or mechanical, including photocopying and recording, or by any information storage or retrieval system, without permission in writing from the publisher.

Printed in the U.S.A.

Library of Congress Catalog Card No.: 77–75157

ISBN: 0–395–25112–5

CONTENTS

PREFACE

The broad purpose of this text is to examine the role of government in economic decision making, a role that is pervasive and important in all modern societies. This introductory text is suitable for upper-division undergraduate courses in public finance and public policy. The text may also appeal to students in such related areas as political science, urban planning, and public administration.

We consider traditional public finance questions, but we treat those questions differently than do other texts. Basic to our approach is a careful distinction between government and other social institutions. We define government as the institution that exercises the power of enforcement in a society — the power to deprive persons of life, limb, and liberty. Then we show how government's potential for improving resource-allocation and income-distribution decisions rests upon its use of police power. The fundamental advantage of government, in comparison with other institutions of collective choice, is that police power can be used to lower the real cost of making and implementing economic decisions. But this power can be abused. So, in examining the economic roles of government, the central question is whether and how police power is and can be used to promote the economic objectives of a society.

Public finance texts have traditionally shown that under fairly realistic conditions markets will fail to allocate resources efficiently and distribute incomes equitably. Then they show that *costless* and *optimal* government action can remedy these market failures. In this fashion, they establish an economic rationale for government. In contrast, we recognize that government action is *not* costless and that governments may *not* respond optimally to market failures. Therefore, the empirical question of whether government action does in fact improve upon the outcomes generated by market processes must be answered on a case-by-case basis, after considering the nature and the costs of the action. That is, the choice between government and market mechanisms for making economic decisions is a choice between imperfect alternatives. And, while government has a potential for improving the welfare of its constituents by playing an active role in economic decision making, it may worsen outcomes in particular instances.

This book also differs from other texts in several other respects. First, the decision, implementation, and transactions costs implicit in governmental and other modes of collective action are directly incorporated into the analysis. The distribution of the costs and gains of government action among members of the community is also explicitly considered. In contrast, other texts postpone the question of cost distribution to chapters on taxation. This latter point is significant because *in practice* the desirability of a specific government action is seldom assessed without giving attention to the distribution among members of the community of the costs and gains from the action.

Second, our discussion of fiscal federalism comprises a relatively large portion of the book, reflecting the fact that fiscal federalism is more than a "special" topic. It is a fundamental aspect of government in the United States and virtually all modern nations. Analyses of the economic effects of government must be altered significantly to take into account the complications that arise when, instead of a single government, there are multiple units and levels of government. Also, state and local government activities are quantitatively as important as those of the federal government.

Third, we give more than the customary amount of attention to alternatives to budgetary (tax-expenditure) actions, such as direct regulation and standard setting by government and action through nongovernmental mechanisms of collective choice.

Chapter 1 reviews the basic economic choices that any society must make and defines the objectives that might govern and be used in evaluating those choices. We include this chapter because students without previous training in economics often take the undergraduate public finance course and because students who have taken previous economics courses profit from a brief review of basic economic concepts and issues.

Beyond this introductory chapter, Chapters 2–9 and 20 provide the essential elements of an introductory course and a basis for understanding and evaluating the actual and potential roles of government in the U. S. economy. Chapter 2 defines government and presents statistics to show not only the current magnitude and scope of government budgetary activity in the United States but also how that activity has evolved during the twentieth century. Chapters 3–6 examine the economic rationales for government activity. Chapters 3 and 4 develop geometrically the demand-value and supply-cost relationships that characterize market equilibrium and optimal resource allocation. These same geometric tools are used extensively in subsequent chapters so that analyses and arguments are developed within the same framework and couched in the same terms throughout the book. We believe that students should invest the necessary time and effort to understand the use of these tools and that such investment will pay off in a quicker and fuller understanding of the analyses of subsequent chapters.

Chapters 7 and 8 look at decision-making processes and tools — benefit-cost and cost-effectiveness analyses and PPBS in Chapter 7, voting rules and processes in Chapter 8. The main purpose of Chapter 7 is to provide students with a clear understanding of what is involved in designing policies that are optimal by traditional efficiency and/or equity criteria and of the costs and difficulties of doing so. Chapter 8 shows how simple democratic political processes may be used to obtain information, albeit imperfect, about preferences, and why political decision making leads to efficient outcomes only in very special circumstances.

Of the remaining "basic" chapters, Chapter 9 discusses the principles and issues involved in the choice of measures used to finance government activities. In Chapter 20, we take into account the fact that virtually all modern systems of government are multilevel and multiunit, and we consider the cases for and against decentralization of government's economic activities.

Chapters 11–19 and 21–23 can most readily be dropped or included, according to the preferences of the instructor and the constraints of time. Chapters 11–15 are basically traditional economic analyses of income, sales and consumption, and wealth and property taxation. Chapters 16–19 examine the role of fiscal policy in stabilizing the economy. Chapters 21 and 22 discuss the problems of fiscal federalism and some of the proposed "solutions" thereto. Chapter 23 uses the analyses and data presented in earlier chapters to evaluate current budgetary policies and to suggest how these policies might be altered to achieve results that are more consistent with specified equity or efficiency criteria.

This brief survey of what we know about the effects of U.S. government provides some support for the view that it is used to promote efficiency in resource allocation and equity in income distribution. But it also suggests that government may be used to promote special interests, as individuals and groups seek more at the expense of others and try to impose their will upon others regarding income distribution and other matters.

It should not be surprising that government is used in both ways. Once the police power of the state exists, and regardless of the reasons for creating the institutions of government that exercise and apply that power, individuals are likely to try to use the power for their own purposes. In some instances, the interests of many persons may be promoted by a particular government action. If no one is hurt and someone is helped by the action, it is said to be a Pareto improvement. In other instances, the action may benefit few at the expense of many. The former cases are usually thought to be appropriate uses of police power, while the latter are not. But in all cases, government is being used to serve the interests of a person or persons.

How should we react to evidence that particular government policies fail efficiency and equity tests? A common reaction is that government *must* do better and that the perverse outcomes *ought* not occur, with the main prescription for improvement being a change in the personnel making the decisions. That is, a common view is that results will be different (better?) if different people make the decisions — if others are elected to legislative and executive offices. While this view cannot be totally discounted, it fails to recognize that undesirable policy outcomes may be a reflection of the structure of the rules and procedures followed in the decision-making process. If such is the case, a change in and improvement of policy outcomes will require a change in the basic institutions of government — tax systems, electoral processes, legislative and executive roles, etc. Such institutional changes probably cannot be made unless the general population and electorate understand not only the roles that government might play in our economy but also the roles that it actually does play. It is this need that justifies the study of the subject matter of this book.

Our colleagues William Albrecht and Gary Fethke reviewed the manuscript and made many constructive suggestions that improved the final product. We also wish to express our thanks to Charles B. Knapp of the University of Texas, John Eric Fredland of the U. S. Naval Academy, Donald H. Skadden of the University of Michigan, Byron L. Johnson of the University of Colorado–Denver, Wallace E. Oates of Princeton University, and William A. McEachern and Ryan C. Amacher of Arizona State University for their helpful suggestions and comments on the text content. Special thanks go to Kathleen Mego Sgontz, who helped proof the manuscript and relieved the tedium with a wonderful sense of humor.

T.F.P.
L.G.S.

GOVERNMENT AND
ECONOMIC CHOICE

The purpose of Part One is to show how public finance fits into the general area of economics and to introduce the central issues and questions regarding government's role in the economy. Every society must decide how to use its scarce resources and how to distribute the resulting supply of goods and services among its members. Chapter 1 first describes those economic choices. Chapter 2 then defines government and discusses, in general terms, the role that government plays in economic decision making. Chapter 2 also presents expenditure and revenue statistics for United States federal, state, and local governments to show the current magnitude and scope of United States governmental activity and how it has evolved during the twentieth century.

PART ONE

INTRODUCTION

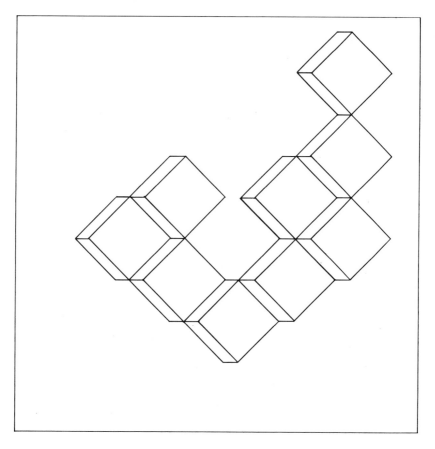

CHAPTER ONE

ECONOMIC SYSTEMS
AND ECONOMIC CHOICE

Scarcity is an inescapable fact of life. The resources available to produce the goods and services that satisfy human wants are limited relative to those wants. Choices must be made, and some wants must go unsatisfied.

Those decisions, or choices, that are forced by scarcity are the main concern of economics. More specifically, economists seek to explain how individuals, groups, and societies do or should make decisions about the use and distribution of scarce resources. Decisions about resource use (*allocation*) determine what and how goods and services are produced. Distribution decisions determine each person's share of the income and wealth of society. And, to a large extent, a person's income and wealth determine his or her role in economic decision making.

The role of government in this economic decision making is the main concern of this book, which derives from the obvious fact that the activities of government affect the functioning of our economy in many ways. Governments spend to provide goods and services and make transfer payments. To finance this spending they collect taxes, borrow money, and sell services and assets. They also regulate nongovernment producers and set and enforce property rights and rules of exchange.

In most modern economies, these economic activities of government are extensive and are growing in scope and significance. In the United States, federal, state, and local governments purchase goods and services amounting to 20 percent of the gross national product, employ 19 percent of the employed labor force, and collect taxes that are over 30 percent of gross national product. Chapter 2 provides more detail on the magnitude and scope of government spending and taxation in the United States, but even these few statistics dramatically illustrate the need to study government's role in our economy.

The questions that we will ask about that role form an outline of our study: What are the functions of an economic system? What is government? How do particular government activities affect the functioning of the economic system? Is there an economic rationale for some or all government activities? How should governments act if they are to assure that the economic system functions to achieve particular objectives? Can an economic system function without some or all activities of government? If so, under what conditions do particular activities improve the functioning of the system? What do we mean by improve? Are government institutions and activities presently consistent with the achievement of specified economic objectives? In particular, modern industrial societies are currently looking to government for the solution of a variety of problems: Poverty, pollution, rising crime rates, and racial discrimination. Why do we look to government for solutions to these problems? Why not depend on private industry and initiative? Can we realistically expect government to deal effectively with these problems?

Before considering these and other questions, however, we will clarify the nature of economic decisions, discuss and define the economic goals or objectives that we might wish to achieve through the functioning of the economic system, and define government. This and the next chapter are concerned with these matters.

THE NATURE OF ECONOMIC SCARCITY

Economic scarcity exists because available resources and technology place a limit on the quantities of various goods and services that can be produced. There is a limit to the size of and hours worked by the labor force. Workers have specific training, education, and skills, and they must work with available technology, capital (tools), and natural resources. Since economic resources are scarce, so are the things they produce. This limited output of goods and services is sufficiently low that all human wants cannot be satisfied.

The notion of a limit to the output of goods and services is often represented by what is called the economy's *production possibility frontier*, which is fixed at any particular time. A production possibility frontier for an economy in which there are only two goods, X and Y, is shown in Figure 1–1 as the line *ab*. The economy can produce *oa* units of Y per year and no X, or *ob* units of X and no Y. More generally, it can produce any combination of X and Y that lies in the area *oab*. But choice of one point precludes having any other point. We would expect a society to prefer some point on the frontier, the line *ab*, because at any interior point more of one good can always be obtained without reducing the availability of the other good. The points on the frontier are said to be *technologically efficient*.

OPPORTUNITY COST

It is clear from the preceding discussion that economic resources are not only scarce; they also have alternative uses. Thus, the production of any one good or service entails an *opportunity cost*. For example, in deciding to allocate resources to the production of, say, color television sets, society forgoes the opportunity of using those resources to produce something else. The opportunity cost of color television sets is the value of the other goods and services those resources could have produced. Or, in the two-good world of Figure 1–1, the opportunity cost of X is the Y that must be given up if more X is to be produced. For example, if the economy is producing at point e, then the total opportunity cost of the *od* units of X being produced is *ca* units of Y; the total opportunity cost of the *oc* units of Y being produced is *db* units of X. At point e, an increase in X of ΔX entails a loss in Y of ΔY. Thus the *marginal* opportunity cost of X is $-\Delta Y/\Delta X$, which is equal to the absolute value of the slope of *ab* at point e if ΔX is sufficiently small.

FIGURE 1–1
PRODUCTION POSSIBILITIES OF AN ECONOMY

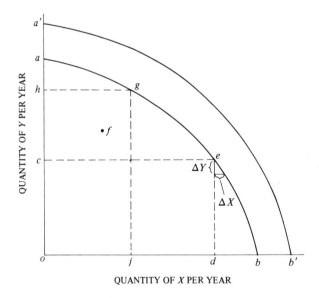

QUANTITY OF *X* PER YEAR

Similarly, the marginal opportunity cost of Y at point e is the inverse of the absolute value of the slope of ab at point e. Note that the marginal opportunity cost, or simply the marginal cost, of either X or Y generally depends on the quantity of X and Y being produced — the slope of ab changes as the outputs of X and Y change.

Opportunity costs are zero if resources are unlimited. In this happy event people can have everything they want, and the consumption of one good does not require the sacrifice of anything else of value. Similarly, the opportunity cost of a good, say a color television set, is zero if the resources used in its production are useless in the production of anything else; that is, nothing is lost in using those resources to turn out color television sets.

If there is unemployment of resources, then the economy is not on the frontier ab, but is at some other point, such as f. In this case, it might seem that the marginal costs of both X and Y are zero, since the output of one can be expanded without reducing the output of the other. But such is not the case because the use of unemployed resources to expand the output of one commodity precludes their use to expand the output of other valuable commodities. Unemployed resources can be put to work in a variety of ways. And a choice must be made among alternative public policy measures that increase total production and employment through increases in private or government spending.

For example, during the 1960–1961 recession in the United States, total output was estimated to be $50 billion below capacity, with unemployment nearly 7 percent of the labor force. The Kennedy-Johnson administration decided to increase production and employment by inducing an increase in private consumption and investment expenditures. This was the rationale for the federal tax cut of 1964 and the accommodating monetary policy of the Federal Reserve System. Others argued for increasing government expenditures on roads and public transportation, low-income housing, job training, or education instead. Regardless of the merits of these arguments, the general point is that choices have to be made. In weighing the alternatives, judgments must be made about their opportunity cost. And the judgments must be made whether resources are fully employed or not, so long as unemployed resources can be put to use through public policy measures that increase either private or government spending.

LIMITED INCOMES

Resource scarcity not only limits the output of goods and services, it also limits incomes. Limited incomes are a reflection of scarcity, not the cause of it. This is readily seen if we recognize that the price one person pays for a good is income to other persons — the persons whose scarce resources were used in producing the good. Alternatively, the value of all the goods and services produced in an economy during some period is also the amount of income received by the persons whose resources were employed in producing those goods and services. For example, suppose the economy produces at point e in Figure 1–1. The value of output and the incomes received by the economy's resource owners are both equal to $p_X(od) + p_Y(oc)$, where p_X and p_Y are the prices of X and Y respectively, and od and oc are the respective outputs of X and Y. Clearly, both incomes and the output of goods and services are limited by resource scarcity.

Prices are commonly stated in money terms, and the *level* of prices determines the *level* of money incomes. For example, if both p_X and p_Y are doubled, then *money* incomes and the *money* value of output are doubled. But *real* output and *real* incomes (the available supply of goods and services) are unchanged by this inflation of prices. Stated differently, increasing money incomes by increasing the prices paid for a given supply of resources (land, labor, and capital) will not eliminate scarcity — there will be a corresponding increase in product prices and no increase in *real* incomes.

These income concepts are actually employed in national income accounting. Table 1–1 shows U.S. national income and product for 1975. Note that the value of goods and services produced (gross national product) equals the total of incomes received (gross national income).

Incomes are commonly stated in money terms. But we should understand that a person's (or nation's) income, as the term is used in this book and by other economists, includes what is called *non-money income* — the value of goods and services that ordinarily are not bought and sold in the marketplace and therefore do not have a dollar price tag. The value of a person's leisure time, the recreational value that people derive from the use of a river, lake, or public park, and the value of clean air are examples of non-money income.[1] An economic good or service is basically any good that requires scarce economic resources for its production and therefore has a nonzero opportunity cost, whether the good is market-traded or not. Real income, in turn, consists of the value of all economic goods and services produced during some accounting period.[2]

---

1 The national income accounts shown in Table 1–1 do not include most types of non-money income. (A major exception is the imputed rental value of owner-occupied housing, which is included in GNP.) Also, the *costs* of governmentally provided goods and services (parks, police protection, etc.) are included, but their *value* is not.

2 See William Nordhaus and James Tobin, "Is Growth Obsolete?" *Economic Growth, Fiftieth Anniversary Colloquium* V (New York: National Bureau of Economic Research, 1972), who construct a measure of economic welfare (MEW) as an alternative to GNP. They explain why an ideal measure of economic welfare would include non-money income from all sources, as well as making allowances for environmental "disamenities" that result from pollution and "regrettable" uses of resources for purposes of national defense and war.

TABLE 1–1

U.S. GROSS NATIONAL PRODUCT AND GROSS NATIONAL INCOME, 1975
(BILLIONS OF DOLLARS)

Gross national product		
Personal consumption expenditures		963.8
Durable goods	128.1	
Nondurable goods	409.8	
Services	426.0	
Gross private domestic investment		182.6
Nonresidential fixed investment	148.5	
Residential structures	48.7	
Change in inventories	− 14.6	
Net exports		21.3
Government purchases of goods and services		331.2
Total		1,498.9

Gross national income		
Compensation of employees		921.4
Wages and salaries	801.6	
Other	119.8	
Proprietors' income [a]		83.3
Nonfarm	58.7	
Farm	24.6	
Rental income of persons [b]		21.1
Corporate profits [a]		100.7
Net interest		81.6
Other income and adjustments		290.8
Total		1,498.9

a With inventory valuation and capital consumption adjustments. Corporate profits
for the fourth quarter of 1975 are preliminary.

b With capital consumption adjustment.

Source: U.S. Department of Commerce, *Survey of Current Business* (March 1976).

Real income as defined here cannot be measured accurately at present.
Nevertheless, non-money income may be as important to peoples' well-
being as money income. And the effects of government policies on non-
money income should not be neglected by analysts and decision makers in
favor of the more readily measured effects of money income. In particular, a
policy that increases non-money income while decreasing money income
may increase individual welfare. For example, air or water pollution control
may reduce manufacturing output and money incomes, while increasing

non-money incomes (cleaner air, better health, more recreational opportunities), with the net effect of an improvement in individual welfare.[3]

There are many ways of distributing or rationing the goods and services (real income) produced from scarce resources. And, just as the production of one good occurs only at the expense of producing some other good, one person's use of goods usually means less for somebody else.[4] Suppose an economy can produce $500,000,000,000 worth of goods per year. If one household consumes $5,000 worth per year, $499,999,995,000 worth of goods are left for everyone else. The $5,000 of goods consumed by one household cannot be consumed by others. And if one household consumes more, others must consume less. Given this definition of income, determining the distribution of goods and services is equivalent to determining the distribution of income.

GROWTH AND SCARCITY

Up to this point we have been dealing with a static economy. But even if we allow for economic growth, we still face scarcity. Economic growth may be defined as *the expansion of the available quantity of goods and services.* More precisely, it is the outward movement of the production possibility curve — from *ab* to *a'b'* in Figure 1–1 (p. 6). Economic growth occurs as the quantity or quality (or both) of available resources increases and as technology improves (as the quantity of goods and services obtainable from given resources increases). Suppose, for example, that an economy that produced $500 billion in one year was able to produce $520 billion the next year because of improvements in technology, an increase in the labor force, and greater investment. Given that $20 billion more of goods can be produced, we must decide what *additional* goods shall be produced. And we must also decide about income distribution: Who will get the additional goods? Growth does not eliminate scarcity; it merely alters the limits imposed by scarcity. However, growth may make economic scarcity a less serious matter by expanding capacity enough for basic needs to be met.

Population growth that leads to growth in the labor force may in turn lead to economic growth. In this case, although the economy's capacity to produce has increased, the demands placed upon it are also likely to be greater

3 These possibilities are discussed more fully in Chapters 4 and 5.

4 The exception to this statement arises when goods are public, in which case consumption or use is *nonrival.* For example, one person's use of a national park does not preclude another person's use, at least until crowding begins. The concept of *public good* is defined in Chapter 3, and its implications for resource allocation are discussed in Chapter 4.

because of the increase in population. Therefore, growth in *per capita* output, rather than in total output, is often used as the index of increases in the economic welfare in a society.[5]

MAJOR ECONOMIC DECISIONS

The resource allocation and income distribution decisions forced by scarcity are commonly placed into several categories. The resource allocation decisions of particular interest are those involving choice between (1) consumption and investment goods, (2) labor and leisure activities, and (3) private- and public-sector output. Concern with income distribution decisions often focuses on the distribution of income (1) to owners of factors of production (labor, land, and capital), (2) to households in various income classes, and (3) to members of different generations. Let us look at these decisions more closely.

RESOURCE ALLOCATION

Consumption-investment Goods and services are said to be consumed when their economic value is depleted.[6] Correspondingly, *consumer goods* are those goods that lose their economic value during the period in which they are produced, while *investment goods* have value beyond their period of production. If we define a period to be one year, then bread is a consumer good, while large electrical generators and houses are investment goods. Investment goods are thus more durable than consumer goods in that they retain economic value for a longer time after they are produced.

The division of total output between consumption and investment goods (or services) is of interest because the capacity of an economy to produce in any particular period depends on the investments of previous periods. That is, investment generates economic growth. Investment goods take a variety of forms, some tangible, some intangible: machines, buildings, training of the labor force (human capital), research and development (improved technology).

The consumption-investment choices are depicted in Figure 1–2. The

---

5 For a discussion of the pros and cons of population growth and economic growth, see the essays in Mancur Olson, Jr., and H. H. Landsberg, eds., *The No-Growth Society* (New York: Norton, 1973).

6 However, they usually are not physically consumed, because most human activities do not destroy matter. The exceptions are nuclear fission and nuclear fusion, processes that "convert" matter to energy.

FIGURE 1-2
CONSUMPTION-INVESTMENT POSSIBILITIES

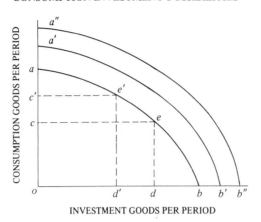

area *oab* represents the feasible combinations of consumption and investment during some given period. If investment is zero, then consumption can
be *oa;* if all output is in the form of investment goods, consumption is zero
and investment is *ob.* If consumption is maximized, the capital stock and
productive capacity of the economy will be depleted and economic growth
will be negative. Thus, if productive capacity is to be maintained, some investment goods must be produced to replace those that are worn out, and
some investment in the form of repair and maintenance must be made.
Since the economy's productive capacity also depends on the size and skills
of the labor force, investment in human capital through formal education
and job training is required to maintain capacity. Similarly, maintenance of
environmental quality and the economy's natural resource base is required if
capacity is not to be depleted. Investment in excess of the rate required for
maintenance of capacity is called *net investment.*

Since investment goods have value in future periods and may enhance
production possibilities in future periods, the choice between consumption
and investment may be thought of as the choice between *present and future
consumption.* More consumption today means reduced investment and
lower potential consumption in future periods. For example, in Figure 1-2,
if investment was *od* and current consumption was *oc,* the production possibility curve for the next period would be *a"b".* With more current consumption and less investment, say point *e'* the outward shift of the production
possibility curve would be less, to *a'b'.*

Although we may recognize that investment decisions are made in the
private sector, we may not easily see that such decisions are made in the

public sector as well. Indeed, a major share of government expenditures for goods and services is investment spending that affects present and future generations. Expenditures for dams, highways, education, fire engines, and police cars are but a few examples of government investment expenditures.

Labor-leisure We have defined *income* as the value of all goods and services produced, including non-money income, such as the value of leisure. However, that leisure has economic value and is part of a person's real income is often overlooked. Instead, the typical view is that individuals' economic well-being depends only upon the quantity of market-traded goods they can obtain. If this view is correct, people should spend more time working so they can acquire more goods and services produced in the market. Nothing is sacrificed if leisure is valueless.

However, both leisure and market-traded goods usually have economic value and each has an opportunity cost. The opportunity cost of leisure is the value of other goods and services that are given up when individuals opt for leisure rather than work. In money terms, the opportunity cost of one hour of leisure is $10 for a person who earns $10 an hour. If a person chooses one more hour of leisure, it cannot be said that his or her economic well-being is reduced because the person has less money income. In fact, if a person chooses more leisure and less work, that choice must make the person better off.[7]

The value of leisure is typically not recorded in social accounts, such as the gross national product. Because of this, an increase in the ratio of leisure to work time may show up as a slow down in the growth of a nation's money income.[8] However, if possible, what should be recorded is that the composition of output (leisure and other goods) changes over time. And if individuals prefer more leisure to other goods, the production of more leisure will increase their welfare. One of our concerns in this book is how government activity affects choices between work and leisure.

Private- and public-sector output A matter of great concern to many people is the division of resources between the private (or market) sector and the government (or public) sector. Some people believe that there is "too much" production by the government, which is the same thing as "too little" production in the private sector. Others believe that the reverse is true. Still

---

7 Of course, individuals can make mistakes and later regret certain choices.

8 Nordhaus and Tobin estimate the value of leisure at $775.5 billion in 1965 (current prices). For the same year, they estimate the value of other nomarket activity (not included in GNP) at $321.4 billion ("Is Growth Obsolete?" p. 47).

others believe that the division of output between the market and government sectors is satisfactory but that the composition of public-sector output is not — too much is spent for some functions and not enough for others. These differences of opinion reflect different subjective estimates of the relative values of public- and private-sector output.

The opportunity cost of public-sector output is sacrificed private-sector output.[9] The private-sector output sacrificed for government-produced goods may be either investment goods or consumer goods; the gain in government-produced goods may be consumer goods or investment goods.

Later chapters deal with such questions as: When should government produce goods and services? What is an optimal division of resources between the private and public sectors? Can the cost and benefits of alternative resource uses be quantified, and can this information serve as a guide to governmental decision making? Which political institutions or constitutional rules will assure better public-private sector allocation than would others?

INCOME DISTRIBUTION

Owners of factors of production   Interest in the distribution of income to owners of labor, capital, and land has a long history. Numerous theoretical analyses and many empirical studies have been devoted to explaining and documenting the distribution of income to these factor categories.[10] In some economies, such as the United States, a large share of investment decisions are nongovernmental. And interest in income distribution arises, in part, from the question of whether changes in the *functional distribution of income* affect the rate of investment and economic growth. The answer to this question is complicated because investment is undertaken not only to increase physical capital, but also to produce human capital. Hence, part of the national income that might be classified as labor income should more properly be classified as human capital income. Government activity can affect the allocation of investment between these two forms of investment, as well as the overall rate of investment.

Concern for equity in the distribution of income also leads to interest in

---

9 If the resources used by government *are not* and *would not* be employed by the private sector, then their opportunity cost would be zero. But such is usually not the case. Even if the resources are currently unemployed by the private sector, government policies could induce their private employment.

10 See Martin Bronfenbrenner, *Income Distribution Theory* (Chicago and New York: Aldine-Atherton, 1971).

the functional distribution of income. The ownership of physical property is unevenly distributed in market economies and is therefore a source of inequality in the distribution of personal income. The distribution of human capital investment may also affect the *size distribution of income*. For example, people's incomes usually correlate with their level of education.

Households in various income classes   Figure 1–3 is one way of looking at income distribution. It shows the percent of the population that receives various percentages of total personal income. The diagonal line, where the percent of population and percent of total personal income received are the same, represents perfect equality in the distribution of income. Departure from perfect equality is shown by the dotted line, which is more representative of reality. The broken line, known as the *Lorenz curve*, shows low-income persons receiving a percent of total income that is less than their percent of the population, and high-income groups receiving a share of total income that exceeds their share of the population. The distribution decision

FIGURE 1–3
**LORENZ CURVE OF INCOME DISTRIBUTION IN
THE UNITED STATES, 1974**

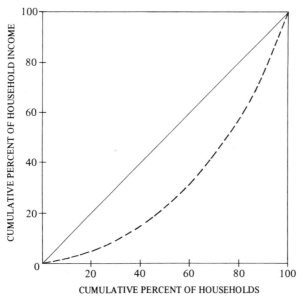

CUMULATIVE PERCENT OF HOUSEHOLDS

Source: U.S. Census Bureau, *Current Population Reports*, Series P-60, No. 100 (August 1975).

faced by society can, in part, be seen as a question of how close the dotted line in Figure 1–3 should be to the diagonal line.

Government policy may affect the size distribution of income through its influence on the functional distribution of income. Or it may affect the size distribution of income in other ways, such as taxing the nonpoor and transferring income to the poor.

Members of different generations   Still another choice concerns the distribution of income among generations of the population. The decision to reduce present consumption and increase investment is not only a resource allocation decision, as discussed above, but it may also be an intertemporal income distribution decision. Any generation that does not consume all of its capital bequeaths that accumulated capital to the following generation, thus increasing the latter's income. Similarly, a decision by the present generation to conserve natural resources increases the well-being of future generations, as does raising children, financing education, providing health care, etc. In the other direction, the younger generation may care for the older generation when the latter is no longer productive and needs income support.

Governmental activity affects the intergenerational distribution of income in many ways. For example, one generation may be taxed to finance education expenditures that increase the lifetime income of the generation being educated. If government capital expenditures such as roads and dams are financed by taxes rather than by borrowing, current generations subsidize future generations. By contrast, when workers are taxed to finance Social Security payments to the retired generation, there is a transfer of income from the younger to the older generation.

In concluding this discussion of basic economic decisions, it should be emphasized that such decisions must be made by all societies. The system, or mechanism, by which these decisions are made is termed an *economic* system. Economic systems vary from society to society at a point in time, and they vary over time. But they always remain mechanisms for making the basic economic decisions. Thus, in comparing economic systems, we do not compare what they *do*, since they all do the same thing. Instead, we try to determine *how they differ* in their manner of making the basic economic decisions and whether some systems produce decisions that are better by some criteria than do other systems.

With this in mind we will, in the next section, discuss some of the criteria employed in judging and comparing economic systems in general, and the role of government in those systems in particular.

ECONOMIC GOALS AND CRITERIA

Assumptions about the economic objectives of society necessarily underlie any meaningful analysis of the economic role of government. In this section we will discuss the goals or objectives that are commonly employed in such analyses, attempting to indicate the bases for and the arguments against each goal. To presume a goal in the analysis of the effects of government is not to say that the goal is desirable — it need merely be a goal that is of concern to someone or some group. The desirability of a goal is not determined through economic analysis. Such analysis can only explore the consequences of pursuing a goal or specify the policies appropriate to the pursuit of a goal.

Economic goals are usually classified into two general categories: equity and efficiency.

EFFICIENT ALLOCATION OF RESOURCES

There *probably* would be general agreement in most societies that resources should be used as effectively as possible to promote the welfare of the members of that society. In the language of economics, this is the objective of *economic efficiency*, or what is also called *Pareto optimality*. The allocation of resources is said to be economically efficient when each person's welfare is at a maximum, *given* the welfare levels of all other members of the community. In other words, an efficient allocation is one that cannot be altered to make some person(s) better off without making other persons worse off.

In the two-good world depicted in Figure 1-1 (p. 6), economic efficiency requires that the outputs of X and Y be at levels associated with one of the points on the production possibility frontier. Otherwise, more X or more Y could be produced and distributed to one or more persons without reducing the quantities of X and Y available to any person. When an economy is thus operating on its production possibility frontier, it is said to be *technologically efficient*.

But economic efficiency also requires that the economy operate at the point on the frontier that produces the *bundle of commodities* (quantities of X and Y) that is most valuable to the people who are the users or consumers of the goods. For example, point e on the production possibility frontier of Figure 1-1 is economically efficient if no other point on the frontier is preferable in the judgment of *any* person, given the total amounts of X and Y each person can consume with his or her income or resources. In this event, no individual or group of individuals is willing to make the substitutions of X for Y or Y for X that are required to reach another point. Specifically, if some other point, say *g*, is produced instead of *e*, then Y in the amount of *ch* is gained and X in the amount of *jd* is lost. Point *e* is efficient if no individual or group of individuals is willing to give up *jd* of X in order to obtain *ch* of Y — no one is willing to pay the opportunity cost of this expansion in the output of Y. And the same is true for every other possible change in the outputs of X and Y. Of course, this is not to say that individuals would not like to have more X (or more Y), if it were free or less costly.

It is readily seen that the efficient outputs of X and Y depend in part on the distribution of income, since the amount of X (or Y) that each person is willing to sacrifice to obtain another unit of Y (or X) is likely to depend on the quantities of X and Y available to the person. For example, if Y is a commodity that is basic to life, such as food or housing, and X is a luxury good, such as yachts or private ski lodges, then the efficient allocation of resources with a highly unequal distribution of income might be a point such as *e* in Figure 1–1, while point *g* would be efficient with a more equal distribution.

Economic efficiency is thus grounded in the principle of *consumer sovereignty*, which requires production of those goods and services that people (consumers) value most highly. Consumers determine the values of alternative goods and services. Moreover, the importance of any particular consumer in this valuation process depends on that consumer's share of income and wealth. Consumers with relatively little income play a small role and vice versa.

It should be clear that the attractiveness of economic efficiency, which in effect weights each person's preferences by his or her share of income, as an economic objective may depend on the fairness of the distribution of income. If a person feels that a society's distribution of income is very unfair, then the objective of economic efficiency may not be attractive because it gives relatively little weight to the preferences of those persons who have little income. However, it is important to understand that there is an efficient allocation for every distribution of income. Therefore, in principle, it is possible to have both a fair distribution of income *and* economic efficiency. Moreover, if the pursuit of efficiency does not in itself make the distribution of income more inequitable, one might argue that efficiency should be an important objective of rich and poor alike. Allocative efficiency means that each person receives the most valuable bundle of goods and services that can be obtained *with the income available to each person*. Thus, if resource allocation is efficient, a person's welfare can be increased only by increasing that person's share of income, not by deviating from the principle of economic efficiency — unless such deviation can be shown to shift the distribution of income in favor of that person.

Economic efficiency is equally unappealing to people who wish to deny consumer sovereignty. The objective of economic efficiency presumes that each person should be the sole judge of whether his or her production and consumption activities enhance or diminish his or her welfare. This objective would not be embraced by anyone who believes that the consumption preferences of households are frivolous or foolish and that resource allocation decisions are best made by "experts" or by "enlightened" citizens or their representatives.

Finally, the real world is uncertain and nonstatic. And it is difficult to define efficiency criteria and determine when they are met. Thus, efficiency objectives and criteria may not provide a workable basis for policy making.

Because of the difficulties of determining what would be an efficient allocation of resources, policy makers may seek "Pareto improvements," which are allocative changes that make some better off but hurt no one. Economic efficiency, or Pareto optimality, is achieved only when a society has made all allocative changes that qualify as Pareto improvements.

EQUITABLE DISTRIBUTION OF INCOME

The preceding section discusses the idea of *equitable distribution of income* but does not define it. What does it mean to say that a particular distribution is or is not equitable? There is undoubtedly significant disagreement about the answer to this question, with opinions ranging from absolute equality in incomes to whatever income distribution is determined by individual effort and luck. Economists are no more equipped to say how incomes should be distributed than anyone else, but they can say something about the *economic effects* of achieving particular equity objectives by one means or another. For example, the economic effects of equalizing incomes (absolutely) will be different from the effects of guaranteeing households a minimum income, say of $3,000 per year. And redistributing incomes through a negative income tax may have different effects from instituting a system of children's allowances.

Our purpose here is not to state how income should be distributed but to raise the question and suggest, in broad outline, how answers to the question vary. Allocation and distribution decisions are necessarily interdependent. This interdependence is apparent in many ways. An allocation of more resources to education will increase some people's productive capacities and incomes and alter the distribution of income. Private business firms compete with each other in hiring factors of production and in selling goods to consumers for profit. Households compete with each other in purchasing goods and in supplying their labor services and other resources to business firms. In such a system, resources are allocated to the production of those goods that consumers are able and willing to purchase, at a price that enables a firm to compete for productive resources and earn a satisfactory profit. And consumer purchases depend on household incomes, which in turn depend on the amount of labor services and other resources households have to offer for sale and on the price (wages, interest rates, rents) these resources can command in the market.

ADDITIONAL RELATED GOALS

Economic stabilization   The goals of full employment and price stability are commonly referred to as *stabilization objectives*. They are usually considered in addition to and independent of the objectives of efficiency in the allocation of resources and equity in the distribution of income. But full employment and price stability can be viewed as particular aspects of the more general efficiency and equity objectives. Alternatively, they are instruments by which these more fundamental objectives are achieved.

In the event of unemployment some resources simply are not allocated to the production of anything, and incomes are distributed among the population in a different pattern than would prevail under conditions of full employment. Thus, concern about unemployment derives from dislike of the waste (inefficiency) implicit in unemployment and the hardships caused by the loss of income to the unemployed.

Inflation is of concern because of its effects on the distribution of income and the allocation of resources. Some people gain from inflation; others lose. Inflation may increase speculative buying and hoarding of goods, exports may fall and imports rise, the structure of investment may be altered, etc. Thus, inflation usually causes a change in the allocation of resources — a worldwide shift in allocation if international trade is affected.

Economic growth   Although economic growth, like stability, is sometimes considered as a distinct objective of economic activity, it too is an aspect of the general objectives of efficiency in resource allocation and equity in income distribution. This becomes clear when we recognize that investment expenditures influence economic growth and that society must determine the allocation of resources between investment and consumption goods. Efficiency is one criterion that is employed in judging whether provision for the future is satisfactory. But equity criteria may also be used in deciding how much growth (investment) will take place and in distributing the costs and benefits of growth within and among generations of the population.

CONFLICT AMONG GOALS

The objectives of efficiency and equity are not always compatible. In the language of economics, there is sometimes a *trade-off* between efficiency and equity. This trade-off is reflected in such arguments as "policies to raise the incomes of the poor will impair work incentives," "subsidizing the incomes of farmers with price supports will lead to the production of surplus commodities," "progressive tax rates on income will reduce the rate of saving," etc.[11] Whether these particular arguments are valid, or whether the effects feared are significant, are different questions. The point is that it may not be possible to achieve some goals without sacrificing others.

For example, consider the military draft policy that exempts people in certain occupations because they are considered more valuable, or efficient, in the civilian sector than people in other occupations. Although a system that allows exemptions from military service may be more technologically efficient than a strict lottery, the income distribution and other effects may not be considered fair because all people are not equally subject to the risks and dangers of war. If people are to be drafted, there are those who would prefer to eliminate exemptions and thereby sacrifice efficiency for equity.

SUMMARY AND PLAN OF STUDY

Economic scarcity forces choices about the allocation (or use) of scarce resources and about the distribution of limited incomes. All societies must make these choices. But systems for economic decision making may vary among societies and over time. This book looks at the role of government in the economic decision making of modern societies such as the United States. In defining and evaluating that role, we assume that the economic objectives of society are allocative efficiency and distributive equity.

Chapter 2 defines government and looks at the magnitude and scope of government spending and taxation in the present-day United States. Why government? is the question considered in Chapters 3–6, which discuss the rationales for a government role in economic decision making, while also exposing some of the difficulties and pitfalls involved.

How these decisions are (or might be) made is the main topic of Chapters 7 and 8. Chapter 7 also discusses the information needed and the procedure that must be followed if we are to determine whether particular government policies promote economic efficiency.

11 See Arthur M. Okun, *Equality and Efficiency: The Big Trade-off* (Washington: Brookings, 1975), for a full discussion of these trade-offs.

Once a decision is made to undertake particular government activities, the question of how they should be financed must be considered. Chapters 9–15 look at the reasons for and economic effects of alternative financing measures, focusing on the main forms of taxation. Detailed discussion of government borrowing as a means of financing government spending is deferred to Part Five, especially Chapter 19.

Governments are major demanders of goods and services and major employers of people. As such, governments affect aggregate demand for goods and services, aggregate employment, and the price level (rate of inflation). That is, intentionally or otherwise, the budgetary decisions of government affect aggregate economic activity and may either reinforce or dampen fluctuations and instability in aggregate private-sector activity. This has lead to the recognition that fiscal (budgetary) policies may serve a *stabilization* function. Chapters 16 and 17 present the rationale for and discuss the mechanics of fiscal stabilization. Chapter 18 looks at our experience with fiscal stabilization and presents a number of suggestions for improving budgetary or fiscal policy as a stabilization tool. Government borrowing and the accumulation of public debt may be a consequence and key element of fiscal stabilization, so Chapter 19 looks at the economic effects of public debt.

Our system of government is not unitary; it is a multiunit, or federal, system. While all modern nations do not have the same federal, state, and local structure of government as the United States, most nations do have a system that is decentralized to a degree, with more than one level of government. Chapters 20–22 examine the economic advantages and disadvantages of a multilevel, multiunit system of government (fiscal federalism). These chapters also discuss current problems of fiscal federalism in the United States and the solutions that have been proposed for those problems.

The remaining chapter examines the overall effect of government in the United States and points out ways in which our system might be improved. That is, this last part of the book makes use of the tools and insights gained in the preceding parts to evaluate the budgetary (fiscal) policies of the three levels of government of the United States.

SUPPLEMENTARY READINGS

Albrecht, William. *Economics*, Chap. 1. Englewood Cliffs, N.J.: Prentice-Hall, 1974.

Lipsey, Richard G., and Steiner, Peter O. *Economics*. 3rd ed. Chap. 1–3. New York: Harper & Row, 1972.

CHAPTER TWO

GOVERNMENT AND THE
ECONOMY: AN OVERVIEW

What is *government?* What roles does it presently play in the U.S. economy? In answering these questions, this chapter first defines government and discusses, in general terms, its effects on the economy. The remainder of the chapter describes the current budgetary policies of U.S. federal, state, and local governments and discusses the evolution of those policies over recent decades. No attempt is made to explain that evolution or to assess the efficiency and equity implications of present and past tax and expenditure policies. Instead, the chapter presents statistics that reflect the budgetary impact of those activities in which U.S. governments are engaged. These statistics raise and give significance to the questions about the rationales for and effects of government that we consider in the remainder of this book.

GOVERNMENT AS AN ELEMENT IN THE ECONOMIC SYSTEM

To speak of government's role in economic decision making, we must first define government. Why do we commonly label certain institutions "government"? What distinguishes government from other segments of a modern economic system? Does it have a unique role to play in economic decision making? If so, why?

A government is similar in many respects to other institutions of modern societies. Its activities are managed by a bureaucracy that is not unlike those that manage modern corporations. A government buys resources in the marketplace just like businesses and individuals. It provides goods and services free of charge or at a (usually) subsidized price, as do private philanthropic institutions (churches, charities, colleges).

Government, as an institution, is commonly referred to as a *mechanism for collective choice*. Government decisions are collective in the sense that there is a group (collective) agreement about the action to be taken (alternative to be chosen). In contrast, markets are mechanisms for individual choices; that is, the outcomes are usually the results of the choices and decisions of individual buyers and sellers. With markets, no collective or group decision is made about what is to be done (that is, how resources are to be allocated and incomes distributed), although all members of the group may participate as individual buyers or sellers in the decision making that determines the overall outcome. That government decisions are collective distinguishes governments from markets but not from some other social institutions. For example, country clubs, fraternities, religious organizations, and producer and consumer cooperatives are all institutions for making collective decisions.

Although government has characteristics in common with other social institutions, it differs from them in one important respect. It exercises the police power in a society — the power to deprive persons of life, liberty, and property. Government is the ultimate locus of power.[1]

The exercise of police power is significant in economic decision making because government can confront people, businesses, and other organizations with choices that other institutions cannot. For example, government can confront economic decision makers with the choice of either paying their taxes, honoring their contracts, and recognizing the property rights of others (do not steal) *or* going to jail (with some probability). Markets, on the other hand, can confront a person with the choice of either paying the price or doing without the good or service. That is, markets confront decision makers with choices among goods and services, alternatives that do *not* include incarceration or loss of life or property. The choices private clubs and cooperatives present similarly differ from government's. Private organizations confront their members with the choice of paying dues or being dismissed, ostracized, or otherwise denied the benefits of membership. Thus, we can say that the hallmark or defining characteristic of government is its exercise of the police power in a society.

Of course, some activities of government do not involve the use of its police power. When government buys, sells, or borrows in the market it does not employ police power. And if government were only involved in these activities, it would not be distinct from other institutions, such as large corporations. But government must employ the police power in the majority of its activities in order to raise taxes to finance its expenditures, define and enforce property rights and rules of exchange, and regulate industry.

1 Anthony Downs, *An Economic Theory of Democracy* (New York: Harper & Bros., 1957), pp. 22–23.

GOVERNMENT AND COERCION

Market exchanges are sometimes said to be voluntary, while transactions with government are involuntary. That is, in the marketplace, individuals are "free" to buy or not buy, sell or not sell, while they "must" pay their taxes and abide by government rules, regulations, and laws. Thus, government is said to have the *power to coerce*, to force choices, in contrast with other institutions such as the market.

But that view is oversimplified, if not incorrect, because there is an alternative to paying taxes and complying with government rules — the fines and imprisonment that are imposed for not paying taxes or not following the rules. Therefore, if people pay taxes, we can infer that they choose to do so and are not coerced into doing so.

We could, on the other hand, point out that while there appears to be a choice involved in tax payment, there is in fact no choice: The alternative to payment is so undesirable, it is not chosen. But this reasoning conflicts with the reality: People do in fact elect nonpayment and the associated risk of fines and imprisonment, as is shown by the trial and conviction of people for tax evasion. In addition, people who are unhappy about their tax payments can sometimes move to a more suitable political jurisdiction (a different school district, city, county, state, nation). Or, they can work through the political process or engage in revolutionary activity to change the basic tax structure.

All these alternatives are, of course, costly and otherwise undesirable. But they are not necessarily more costly and unattractive than the alternatives presented in the market. For example, the market confronts the coal miner in Appalachia with two fairly unattractive alternatives: Either mine coal and bear the high risks of mining accidents and black lung disease *or* accept the much lower standard of living that would be provided by alternative employment or welfare payments and charity.[2] Neither alternative is particularly attractive, just as the alternatives of paying taxes or risking imprisonment are unattractive. Therefore, if we argue that government coerces people into particular behavior because the alternatives of imprisonment and fines are highly undesirable, we must also argue that the market, along with the forces that determine a person's skills and wealth, coerces people into taking relatively unattractive types of employment.

Another argument states that persons may be bound by collective governmental decisions even when the decisions adversely affect their welfare, while market decisions in which an individual is directly involved usually do

2 The miner may have other alternatives, for example, seeking employment outside of Appalachia, which involves the costs of moving and dislocation. In addition, the record shows that the alternatives available in other places are not distinctly superior to the coal mining–welfare alternatives.

not make that individual worse off. Again, this difference between governments and markets is more apparent than real. Persons are bound by adverse governmental decisions only in the sense that compliance is the lesser of two evils: Compliance is relatively attractive in comparison to the alternative of risking fine and/or imprisonment for noncompliance. But individuals are also bound by their market decisions, some of which make them worse off, even though they may have expected otherwise at the time of decision. In addition, the resource allocation and income distribution decisions that are made through the market process may adversely affect particular individuals.[3] Such adverse impacts are likely to derive from the market decisions of others, while the market decisions in which an individual is a direct participant are likely to enhance the welfare of that individual.

GOVERNMENT AND RESOURCE USE

Regardless of whether government coerces or whether it is more coercive than markets, there is the question of whether the police power can be used constructively. The answer is yes: There is at least the *potential* for this power to be used to enhance individual welfare. In our exploration of the role of government in economic systems, we will see that through the exercise of police power, government can bring about distributive and allocative outcomes that would otherwise not be attainable. More importantly, we will see that in some circumstances the exercise of police power and the resulting alteration of economic decisions may promote a society's economic objectives. In particular, and paradoxically, we will see that the welfare of *all* members of a community can sometimes be increased if economic decisions are altered by the threat of incarceration or other applications of the police power.[4]

The main reason such an outcome is possible is that a government's use of the police power economizes on the use of scarce resources. For example, resources are reallocated when taxes are collected and the revenues are used to finance the provision of services to a community. The taxes paid by members of the community cause them to reduce their demands for such goods and services as housing, entertainment, transportation, etc. The resources released by this reduction in private demand are then absorbed by

3 For example, a shift to smaller cars caused by higher gasoline prices and a concern about air pollution would reduce the demand for steel and adversely affect the incomes of steelworkers and the owners (stockholders) of steel companies.

4 For example, the members of a community may each be better off if they pay taxes to support the provision of particular services to the community. However, for reasons given in Chapter 4, such tax payments may not be forthcoming in the absence of a threat such as "pay your taxes or go to jail."

the government's expenditure of the tax revenue. This process of resource reallocation, which may make the community better off, requires the use of scarce resources (in addition to the resources that are reallocated). The resources consumed in the process of making and implementing economic decisions may be less if the police power is used to tax and spend, than if resources for the provision of the community services are obtained by voluntary contributions or by an agreement among community members that is not enforced by the police power.

As another example, consider nonprofit organizations, such as the March of Dimes, that solicit and collect revenues to support medical research. The collection process employed is costly: Labor, time, and communication and transportation services are absorbed in the process. Indeed, 20 to 50 or more percent of the revenues may be consumed, so that $1.25 to $2.00 might be collected for every $1.00 actually directed into medical research. In contrast, through taxation and the use of the police power, government can collect and divert a dollar into medical research at a cost that is probably less than $1.10. That is the sense in which the use of police power economizes on the use of scarce resources.

This potential for saving scarce resources provides an *economic rationale for government.* That is, we might hypothesize that institutions capable of exercising police power (governments) would be created as means of using scarce resources more efficiently. This possibility will be dealt with in more detail in Chapters 3 and 4. But, although there is an economic rationale for government, there may be other reasons for the creation of government. And, while government's use of the police power has the potential of saving resources, such may not in fact be the case.

Without scarcity, there would be no need for economic choice and, correspondingly, no economic rationale for government. Even with scarcity, an economic rationale is lacking if the scarcity does not lead to interpersonal conflicts of interest about the use and distribution of the scarce resources. And even then government (the police power) may not be called for if the conflicts of interest can be resolved by means other than the exercise of police power. Thus, while the economic rationale for government is based on scarcity, scarcity does not imply the existence or the need for government.

Furthermore, the potential for economizing on resource use by using the police power depends on the ethical and moral codes of a society and the motivations of individuals in their dealings with others. Conflicts of interest that grow out of economic scarcity can, of course, be resolved through the use of the police power in economic decision making. But if individuals were to see themselves as "their brother's keeper" and abide by the "golden rule," the use of police power to enforce contracts and property rights would be greatly reduced. Similarly, the less "materialistic" the values of a society

are, the less severe would be the conflicts of interest growing out of economic scarcity.

EFFECTS OF GOVERNMENT

Having defined government, let us consider, in general terms, the economic
effects of government activities. Virtually all government activities affect
resource allocation and income distribution in several distinct ways. First,
such activities may directly alter the allocation of resources or the distribution of income. Second, they may affect the so-called constraints on the
economy — rules of contract and exchange, tastes, and technology. Third,
they may produce indirect effects as individuals and firms adjust their resource allocation and income distribution decisions in response to government activities. These various effects may or may not be intended.

Government activities may be usefully classified as (1) law making and
regulatory and (2) budgetary. Of course, law-making and regulatory activities
have a budgetary impact, but they also have distinct economic effects of
their own. For example, a law that requires a license to be issued before a
person can enter a particular occupation may influence the flow of resources
into that occupation and the incomes of those entering the occupation.[5] A
law or regulation that places a ceiling on rental payments affects the real incomes of landlords and tenants and the incentives to construct rental housing. Antimonopoly laws may affect prices, output, and the real incomes of
consumers and factory owners.

Economic analysis of the law-making and regulatory functions of government is obviously important, but they are not our primary concern. Other
applied areas of economics analyze the economic effects of these activities.
Our concern is with government budgetary activities, although we will be
concerned with law-making and regulatory activities to the extent that they
either require budgetary decisions or constitute alternatives to government
spending.

Budgetary activities of government involve raising and spending money
(1) to secure resources that are then used to provide goods and services
and (2) to redistribute incomes. These are called *resource-using* and *income-
transfer* activities, respectively. Fire protection is an example of the resource-using function, and unemployment compensation is an example of
the income-transfer function.

Government budgetary decisions can affect resource allocation and income distribution both directly and indirectly. For example, government

---

5 Examples of such laws are those requiring licenses for realtors, barbers, and stockbrokers. Ap-
prenticeship requirements for persons entering the building and construction trades may have
similar effects.

provision of fire protection directly affects resource allocation by securing labor and having fire houses built and equipment manufactured. By reducing the extent of fire damage and the number and size of insurance claims, provision of fire protection indirectly affects the amount of resources used for insuring property against fire damage. The distribution of incomes is influenced by the way the benefits from fire protection are distributed among households and firms and how the service is financed. If a property tax finances the fire protection, a person who owns vacant land suffers a reduction in real income. That is, she or he pays taxes on the land but derives little benefit from fire protection. On the other hand, others may experience an increase in real income because they receive benefits from government services that exceed the taxes they pay. The resulting redistribution of incomes may or may not be consistent with our notions of fairness.

Similarly, the construction and maintenance of dams that provide irrigation facilities increase agricultural output and may thereby raise the incomes of farmers in the irrigated regions. If taxes are levied on the general population to finance the construction of the dams, there is a redistribution of income from the general population to those farmers.

To carry out its activities, government secures resources by conscription, as in the case of the military draft, or by purchase. And it obtains funds to purchase resources by money creation, borrowing, taxation, or the sale of goods and services. Each method of securing resources affects the allocation of resources differently. For example, the Department of Defense may either draft people for the armed services or compete for personnel in the market just as private businesses do. By and large, those who would serve in a voluntary army because salaries were attractive would not be those who would serve by conscription. Thus, private-sector output would be different if, by conscription, a football player were drafted but, by purchase, an engineer enlisted. Alternative means of financing defense spending also have different effects. If, for example, the financing required to support a volunteer army were obtained by increasing income taxes, such factors as work incentive, choice of occupation, saving, and investment would be affected. If higher tax rates discourage effort, people may choose lower paying but less onerous occupations, to be a butcher, for example, rather than a surgeon. If such reallocations do in fact occur, the net effect of conscription and lower income taxes would be a lower private-sector supply of football players and butchers relative to engineers and surgeons than would be the case with a volunteer army and higher income taxes.

CONSTITUTIONAL BASIS OF BUDGETARY POLICY

Government, as defined above, exercises the police power in a society. Included in this power, as we have shown, is the power to tax and spend. In the United States, government's power to tax and spend is defined and limited by state and national constitutions.

The federal government derives its basic power to tax and spend from Article 1 of the U.S. Constitution, which grants Congress the power "to levy and collect taxes, duties, imposts and excises, to pay the debts and provide for the common defense and general welfare of the United States." The Constitution also requires that taxes be uniformly applied throughout the United States. That is, the federal government must tax whatever it taxes (income, product sales, etc.) in the same way in each state. Thus production of particular products cannot be taxed at lower rates in some states as a means of encouraging economic development.

The Constitution also requires that all direct taxes levied by the federal government be in proportion to the population of the states. Taxes collected from a state with one million people would have to be one-half as great as taxes collected from a state with two million people. This "apportionment" rule was the basis for the 1895 Supreme Court decision that an income tax would be unconstitutional. A proportional income tax, for example, would take more taxes *per person* from states with relatively high-income residents than from states with relatively low-income residents. The outgrowth of this court decision was the Sixteenth Amendment, which specifically authorizes an income tax even though it may conflict with the apportionment rule. Since the Sixteenth Amendment, the federal government has been able to levy virtually any tax that might appear reasonable on economic grounds, with two exceptions: (1) the previously noted prohibition of regional variation in federal tax rates for purposes of economic development and (2) the prohibition of taxes on exports.

The federal Constitution imposes few constraints on the taxing power of state governments. The primary restrictions relate to trade: Neither exports nor imports may be taxed, and state taxation may not interfere with interstate or foreign commerce. Also, states may tax only those activities that take place within their jurisdictions, and they must treat residents and nonresidents the same way.

State constitutions place widely varying constraints on state government taxation. For example, in some states income taxation or government borrowing is constitutionally prohibited. Similarly, local governments differ in their power to tax, with such power being derived from the states. That is, state governments determine the rules under which local governments may tax. Thus constitutional considerations are more likely to be important in tax policy decisions at the state and local levels than at the federal level.[6]

6 For a summary of state constitutional tax provisions, see Commerce Clearing House, *State Tax Handbook*.

AMOUNT AND GROWTH OF GOVERNMENT EXPENDITURES

There are various ways to measure the influence and scope of government in an economy. Here, we look mainly at measures of the budgetary activity of government in the United States. A measure of the extent to which government diverts goods and services from private to government use is government purchases of goods and services relative to gross national product (GNP). GNP measures the total market value of private and government purchases of goods and services. A measure of the extent to which government redistributes income among persons through the mechanism of transfer payments is the amount of government transfers in relation to total personal income. Personal income is one measure of income received by individuals, although some sources of income are not included in personal income (such as capital gains and income-in-kind).

It is important that we understand that these indices are imperfect measures of the influence of government on the economy. As we have seen in the preceding section, government influences resource allocation and income distribution in ways that are not measured by revenues and expenditures.

GOVERNMENT VERSUS PRIVATE PURCHASES
OF GOODS AND SERVICES

In 1975 United States governments at all levels (federal, state, and local) purchased $339 billion of goods and services (see Table 2–1), which was

TABLE 2–1
U.S. GOVERNMENT EXPENDITURES, SELECTED YEARS, 1929–1975
(BILLIONS OF DOLLARS)

	1929	1940	1950	1960	1970	1975
Total federal expenditures	2.6	10.0	40.8	92.8	204.5	357.8
Purchase of goods and services						
(including wages)	1.3	6.0	18.4	52.9	96.5	124.4
National defense	—	2.2	14.1	44.9	75.1	84.3
Civilian	—	3.8	4.3	8.0	21.4	40.1
Transfers	0.7	1.5	14.4	23.7	63.3	148.9
Grants-in-aid	0.1	0.9	2.3	6.1	24.5	54.4
Net interest	0.4	0.7	4.5	7.0	14.6	23.5
Total state and local expenditures	7.8	9.3	22.3	50.6	132.1	227.5
Purchase of goods and services	7.7	8.0	19.5	47.1	122.5	214.5
Transfers	0.2	1.3	3.5	5.1	14.1	23.1
Net interest	0.5	0.6	0.3	0.7	−0.5	−5.7

Source: U.S. Department of Commerce, *U.S. Income and Output* (1929–1965), and *Survey of Current Business* (July issues).

TABLE 2–2

U.S. GOVERNMENT PURCHASE OF GOODS AND SERVICES AS A PERCENT OF
GNP, SELECTED YEARS, 1929–1975

	1929	1940	1950	1960	1970	1975
Total purchases of goods and services	8.7	14.0	13.3	19.5	22.4	22.4
Federal	1.2	6.0	6.5	10.5	9.9	8.2
National defense		2.2	5.0	8.9	7.7	5.6
Civilian		3.8	1.5	1.6	2.2	2.6
State and local	7.5	8.0	6.8	9.5	12.5	14.2

Source: U.S. Department of Commerce, U.S. *Income and Output* (1929–1965), and *Survey of Current Business* (July issues).

22.4 percent of GNP (see Table 2–2). Of that total, federal government expenditures ($124.4 billion) accounted for 8.2 percent of GNP, and state and
local expenditures ($214.5 billion) amounted to 14.2 percent. These sums
do not represent the actual production of goods and services by government
because many government expenditures are for goods and services produced
by the private sector. The value added to production by government is
measured by payments made to government employees. In 1975 this sum
was $178.5 billion, or about one-half of government purchases of goods
and services.

From 1929 to 1975, total government purchases of goods and services
increased from 8.7 percent to 22.4 percent of GNP (Table 2–2). Federal
purchases have usually been less than state and local purchases. Because a
large share of federal purchases is for defense purposes, federal civilian
purchases are much lower than state and local purchases. Indeed, increased
defense purchases account for most of the increase in federal purchases relative to GNP.

GOVERNMENT TRANSFER PAYMENTS

In 1975 federal, state, and local transfer payments were $172 billion (Table
2–1), or 13.8 percent of total personal income, exclusive of net interest paid
on public debt (see Table 2–3). The amount of transfers has grown considerably over the years, up from 1 percent of personal income in 1929. The federal government accounts for the greatest amount of transfer payments, with
most of the transfers occurring under the Old-Age, Survivor's, Disability, and
Health Insurance (OASDHI) program.

GOVERNMENT VERSUS PRIVATE EMPLOYMENT

Another measure of government's role in the economy is the proportion of
the employed labor force working for government (see Table 2–4). In 1975

TABLE 2-3
U.S. GOVERNMENT TRANSFERS TO PERSONS AS A PERCENT OF PERSONAL
INCOME, SELECTED YEARS, 1929-1975

	1929	1940	1950	1960	1970	1975
Excluding net interest[a]						
Total	1.0	3.6	7.8	7.2	9.5	13.8
Federal	0.8	1.9	6.3	5.9	7.8	12.0
State and local	0.2	1.7	1.5	1.3	1.7	1.8
Including net interest[a]						
Total	2.1	5.2	10.0	9.1	11.3	15.2
Federal	1.3	2.8	8.3	7.7	9.6	13.8
State and local	0.8	2.4	1.7	1.4	1.7	1.4

a Interest payments by government are regarded as transfer payments in the national income
accounts. But, since this practice is currently in dispute, the transfer data are presented both
ways.

Source: U.S. Department of Commerce, *U.S. Income and Output* (1929-1965), and *Survey of Current
Business* (July issues).

TABLE 2-4
U.S. GOVERNMENT EMPLOYMENT AS A PERCENT OF TOTAL EMPLOYMENT,
SELECTED YEARS, 1900-1975[a]

Year	Federal	State and local	Total government
1900	—	—	4.4
1920	—	—	7.1
1930	1.8	5.8	7.6
1940	3.1	6.7	9.8
1950	5.9	6.8	12.7
1960	7.0	8.9	15.9
1970	7.2	9.8	19.2
1975	5.6	13.8	19.4

a Government employment and total employment include armed forces plus civilian employment.

Source: For 1900-1970, U.S. Census Bureau, *Historical Statistics of the U.S., Colonial Times to 1970*; for
1975, *Statistical Abstract of the U.S., 1976*.

government employed over 19 percent, including armed services personnel. That figure represents a more than fourfold increase since 1900. The
proportion of employed persons working for state and local governments
exceeds that of the federal government. And, since the 1960s, the relative
increase in government employment has occurred at the state and local
levels of government.

FEDERAL VERSUS STATE AND LOCAL EXPENDITURES

Until the 1940s, state and local government expenditures exceeded federal
government expenditures (see Table 2–5). The relative expansion of the federal sector since then reflects (1) increased defense spending, (2) increased
federal income transfers, and (3) increased federal aid to state and local governments.

There are economic reasons for the traditional view that provision for national defense is a responsibility of the federal government rather than of

TABLE 2–5

**PERCENT OF TOTAL U.S. GOVERNMENT EXPENDITURES BY LEVEL OF
GOVERNMENT, SELECTED YEARS, 1902–1975**

	Total expenditures								
	1902	1927	1934	1940	1944	1950	1960	1970	1975
Federal grants included in federal expenditures [a]									
Federal	35.3	31.2	46.1	49.5	91.3	63.7	64.3	62.5	61.1
State and local	64.7	68.8	53.9	50.5	8.7	36.3	35.7	37.5	38.9
Federal grants included in state and local expenditures [b]									
Federal	35.3	30.4	38.3	45.1	90.4	60.3	59.7	55.5	52.1
State and local	64.7	69.6	61.7	54.9	9.6	39.7	40.3	44.5	47.7

	Civilian expenditures								
	1902	1927	1934	1940	1944	1950	1960	1970	1975
Federal grants included in federal expenditures [a]									
Federal	26.7	27.4	43.4	45.2	61.2	51.0	47.3	49.8	53.0
State and local	73.3	72.6	56.6	54.8	38.8	49.0	52.7	50.2	47.0
Federal grants included in state and local expenditures [b]									
Federal	26.7	26.4	35.2	40.4	57.1	46.2	40.4	40.5	42.2
State and local	73.3	73.6	63.8	59.6	42.9	53.8	59.6	59.5	57.8

a Federal grants are included in federal expenditures and subtracted from state and local
expenditures.

b Federal grants are subtracted from federal expenditures and included in state and local
expenditures.

Source: For 1902–1970, data based on U.S. Census Bureau, *Historical Statistics of the U.S., Colonial Times
to 1970*; for 1975, U.S. Census Bureau, *Governmental Finances, 1974–1975*.

TABLE 2–6

U.S. FEDERAL GRANTS AS A PERCENT OF STATE AND LOCAL SPENDING, SELECTED YEARS, 1929–1975

Year	Percent
1929	0.1
1940	9.7
1950	10.3
1960	12.1
1970	18.5
1975	23.9

Source: U.S. Department of Commerce, *U.S. Income and Output* (1929–1965), and *Survey of Current Business* (July issues).

state and local governments. Therefore, the relative expansion of the federal government in this area need not be viewed as an encroachment on state and local government functions.

Federal income transfers to persons (excluding interest payments) have increased from 0.8 percent of personal income in 1929 to 12 percent in 1975 (see Table 2–3). State and local transfers are far lower, and they have remained fairly constant (relative to personal income) since 1940. There are economic reasons for having the federal government assume primary responsibility for income transfers (see Chapter 20). And if there is a consensus that increased transfers are desirable, it is not surprising to observe this change in the role of the federal government.

Federal aid to state and local governments has increased from 0.1 percent of state and local spending in 1929 to 24 percent in 1975 (see Table 2–6). Such federal aid was 15.2 percent of federal expenditures in 1975, but only a negligible fraction in 1929. Should these expenditures be classified as federal or as state and local? To the extent that federal aid replaces state and local revenues but does not alter the public services provided by state and local governments, there has been a change only in the method of financing governments. To the extent that federal aid changes the composition or level of state and local government spending, the increased role of the federal government may be viewed as "good" or "bad." A larger role for the federal government is justified if federal aid finances government outputs that have national benefits, and if individual preferences for these outputs have increased over time. Then state and local governments serve merely as administrative agents of the federal government. The rationale for federal aid to state and local governments is discussed more fully in Chapter 22.

EXPENDITURE COMPOSITION AND TRENDS

The amount and composition of spending by all governments and by each level of government are shown in Tables 2–7, 2–8, and 2–9. Broad categories of spending are summarized in Figure 2–1. For all governments combined, the largest categories of spending are health and income maintenance (31 percent), national defense and defense related functions (19 percent), and education (17 percent). At the federal level, 71 percent of all expenditures are for health, income maintenance, and defense expenditures. Health and income maintenance programs account for the majority of federal expenditures (44 percent), with the OASDHI program receiving the largest share.

The majority of state and local spending is for education (33 percent), with the bulk going to elementary and secondary education. In 1975, $61 billion was spent for elementary and secondary education, and $22 billion

TABLE 2–7

FEDERAL, STATE, AND LOCAL GOVERNMENT EXPENDITURES, TOTAL AND RELATIVE, SELECTED YEARS, 1902–1975

	1902	1927	1940	1950	1960	1975
Total expenditures (billions)	$1.7	$11.2	$20.4	$70.3	$151.3	$556.3
Percent of total expenditures [a]						
National defense and related [b]	18.4%	10.7%	10.3%	30.7%	35.2%	19.4%
Education	15.4	20.0	13.8	13.7	12.8	17.1
Health and income maintenance [c]	6.3	7.4	14.7	17.9	18.1	31.3
Community services and development [d]	10.2	8.6	6.1	4.3	4.2	6.0
Transportation [e]	11.8	18.5	12.5	6.4	7.4	5.1
Natural resources [f]	1.0	1.8	13.4	7.1	5.6	2.9
General control and administration	10.5	4.7	3.6	2.2	1.9	2.1
Interest on debt	5.8	12.0	7.6	6.9	6.2	5.9
Other [g]	20.2	16.2	18.0	10.7	8.8	10.3

a Percents may not total 100 because of rounding.

b National defense, international affairs, and veterans services not classified elsewhere; space research and technology

c Health, hospitals, public welfare, OASDHI, unemployment compensation, and other

d Police and fire protection, sanitation and sewerage, recreation, housing and urban renewal

e Highways, air, and water transportation

f Includes agricultural program

g Utility, liquor stores, postal services, and other

Source: For 1902–1960, U.S. Census Bureau, *Historical Statistics of the U.S., Colonial Times to 1970*; for 1975, U.S. Census Bureau, *Governmental Finances, 1974–75*.

TABLE 2–8
U.S. FEDERAL GOVERNMENT EXPENDITURES, TOTAL AND RELATIVE,
SELECTED YEARS, 1902–1975

	1902	1927	1940	1950	1960	1975
Total expenditures (billions)	$0.6	$3.5	$10.1	$44.8	$97.2	$340.7
Percent of total expenditures[a]						
National defense and related[b]	53.5%	33.8%	20.8%	47.3%	54.1%	31.6%
Education	0.7	0.5	3.4	6.2	1.6	4.8
Health and income maintenance[c]	1.4	3.3	8.3	14.7	17.7	36.2
Housing and urban renewal	—	—	0.4	0.3	0.3	0.7
Transportation[d]	3.8	9.8	11.9	2.5	4.5	2.4
Natural resources	1.4	3.2	24.8	9.6	6.1	3.5
Interest	5.1	21.6	8.9	9.8	7.9	7.1
Financial administration and control	5.9	3.2	1.8	1.1	0.8	1.0
Postal service	22.0	20.1	7.9	5.1	3.8	3.7
General revenue sharing	—	—	—	—	—	1.8
Other	6.1	4.3	11.9	3.1	3.2	7.0

a Percents may not total 100 due to rounding.

b National defense, space research and technology, international affairs, and veterans service not classified elsewhere

c Health, hospitals, public welfare, OASDHI, unemployment compensation, and other

d Highways, air, and water transportation

Source: For 1902–1960, U.S. Census Bureau, *Historical Statistics of the U.S., Colonial Times to 1970*; for 1975, U.S. Census Bureau, *Governmental Finances, 1974–75*.

was spent for higher education. The next largest categories of spending at the state and local levels are health and income maintenance (18 percent), community services and development (10 percent), and highways (8 percent).[7]

The share of total government expenditures for health and income maintenance has increased since the 1900s. In 1975 this category accounted for 31 percent of all expenditures. National defense expenditures have fluctuated with hot and cold wars, but defense declined in relative importance

7 As we saw earlier, a considerable amount of state and local government expenditures are financed from federal aid funds. Table 2–9 includes all state and local spending, whether financed from own funds or federal aid.

TABLE 2–9

STATE AND LOCAL GOVERNMENT EXPENDITURES, TOTAL AND RELATIVE,
SELECTED YEARS, 1902–1975

	1902	1927	1940	1950	1960	1975
Total expenditures (billions)	$1.1	$7.8	$11.2	$27.9	$61.0	$266.2
Percent of total expenditures [a]						
Education	23.3%	28.6%	23.5%	25.8%	30.7%	33.0%
Highways	16.0	23.2	14.0	13.6	15.4	8.5
Health and income maintenance [b]	8.9	6.5	15.7	16.8	13.4	17.7
Community services and development [c]	15.5	11.9	10.7	10.4	10.3	9.9
General administration	12.9	5.3	5.0	3.6	3.4	3.2
Interest on the debt	6.2	7.5	5.8	1.8	2.8	3.3
Utility and liquor store	7.5	6.3	11.8	9.7	8.4	6.5
Insurance trust funds	0.6	1.4	6.1	8.6	6.6	6.9
Natural resources	0.8	1.3	1.9	2.5	2.0	1.6
Other	8.9	8.1	5.6	7.5	6.2	9.5

a Percents may not add to 100 because of rounding.

b Health, hospitals and public welfare

c Police and fire protection, sanitation and sewerage, recreation, housing and urban renewal

Source: For 1902–1960, U.S. Census Bureau, *Historical Statistics of the U.S., Colonial Times to 1970*; for 1975, U.S. Census Bureau, *Governmental Finances, 1974–75*.

in the 1970s.[8] Other noteworthy trends include: an increase in the share of expenditures for transportation (mainly highways) in the 1920s and an overall decline since then; a long-term decline in relative expenditures for natural resources since 1940; fluctuating total expenditures for education, but a relative increase at the state and local levels since 1940; increased expenditures for housing and urban renewal programs and the enactment of the revenue-sharing program by the federal government in the 1970s; a long-term decline in the share of expenditures for administration and support of the postal service.

INTERNATIONAL COMPARISONS

Table 2-10 shows government expenditures as a percent of GNP for selected countries for the years 1967–1969. As a share of GNP, total government

8 Veterans' services claimed a large proportion of expenditures classified as defense and defense related in the years 1902, 1927, and 1940 (e.g., 46 percent of defense and defense-related expenditures were for veterans' services in 1902).

FIGURE 2–1
CATEGORIES OF U.S. GOVERNMENT EXPENDITURES
AS A PERCENT OF TOTAL EXPENDITURES

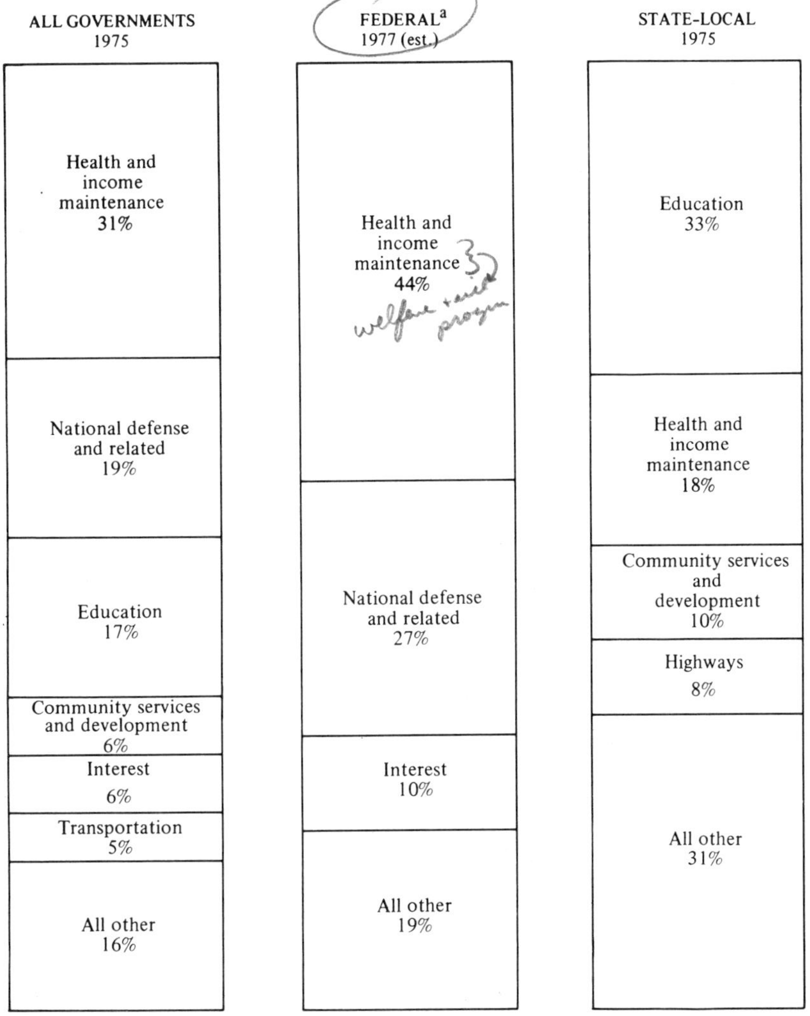

ALL GOVERNMENTS 1975	FEDERALª 1977 (est.)	STATE-LOCAL 1975
Health and income maintenance 31%	Health and income maintenance 44%	Education 33%
National defense and related 19%	National defense and related 27%	Health and income maintenance 18%
Education 17%	Interest 10%	Community services and development 10%
Community services and development 6%	All other 19%	Highways 8%
Interest 6%		All other 31%
Transportation 5%		
All other 16%		

ªCategories for federal expenditures in 1977 are not strictly comparable with categories for all governments' and for state and local governments' expenditures for 1975.

Source: For 1975, Tables 2–7 and 2–9; for 1977, *The Budget of the U.S. Government, Fiscal Year 1977.*

expenditures in the United States are lower than in all but four of the countries shown. Similarly, the United States ranks low in expenditures for civilian goods and services and for transfers to households. However, the United States spends proportionately more on defense than the other countries.

TABLE 2–10
MAJOR COMPONENTS OF PUBLIC EXPENDITURES AS PERCENT OF GNP,
SELECTED COUNTRIES, 1967–1969 AVERAGES

	Total public expenditures	Current goods and services		Current transfers to households
		Civilian	Defense	
Group I				
U.S.	31.7	11.9	9.0	6.1
Canada	33.6	12.0	3.1	9.9
Japan	19.4	—	—	4.3
France	37.0	8.7	3.7	16.6
Germany	36.5	12.4	3.4	13.8
Italy	34.2	9.6	3.8	14.3
U.K.	38.0	12.6	5.4	8.4
Total	32.0	11.2	6.5	8.2
Group II				
Austria	36.7	13.3	1.3	13.1
Belgium	35.7	11.1	2.8	13.5
Denmark	36.1	15.0	2.6	10.6
Finland	33.7	14.8	1.6	7.9
Iceland	28.3	9.0	0.0	8.3
Ireland	30.0	12.0	0.8	7.5
Luxembourg	—	10.8	1.0	15.2
Netherlands	43.9	12.4	3.4	16.6
Norway	39.4	14.3	3.5	11.4
Sweden	40.5	16.9	3.9	11.4
Switzerland	27.7	9.5	2.2	8.2
Total	36.7	13.2	2.7	12.0

Source: Organization for Economic Co-operation and Development, *Expenditure Trends in OECD Countries, 1960–1968*, table 16, p. 67.

REVENUE SOURCES AND TRENDS

Total taxes collected by all levels of government in the United States increased from 11 percent of GNP in 1929 to 30.8 percent in 1975. Total personal taxes as a percent of personal income rose from 3.1 percent to 13.5 percent over the same period (see Table 2–11). These statistics do not, however, reveal the true burden of taxation. First, taxes may influence the growth of real incomes over time, as may government expenditures. Second, taxes may distort economic choices and impose burdens in excess of actual taxes paid (see Chapter 9). Third, the income statistics do not include all sources of income to individuals. Excluded items include the value of leisure, household production, gifts, inheritances, and capital gains.[9]

9 See Chapter 10 for a comprehensive definition of income.

TABLE 2-11
U.S. TAXES AS A PERCENT OF INCOME

	1929	1940	1950	1960	1970	1975
Total taxes as a percent of GNP	11.0	18.0	24.1	27.8	30.9	30.8
Personal taxes as a percent of personal income	3.1	3.3	9.1	12.7	14.4	13.5

Source: U.S. Department of Commerce, *The National Income and Product Accounts of the U.S.*
(1929–1965), and *Survey of Current Business* (July issues).

CURRENT REVENUE SOURCES

Figure 2–2 shows the revenue sources of all governments and of each level
of government. The individual income tax is the most important source of
governmental revenue, followed by insurance trust revenues. These revenues are obtained mainly from the federal payroll tax and are earmarked for
the Social Security system. Tied for third place are charges (for government-
supplied services) and consumption-related taxes (sales and gross receipts).
Property taxes and corporation income taxes are the other important revenue
sources.

The federal government relies mainly on the individual income tax, the
tax on labor income (the payroll taxes included in the social insurance category), and the corporation income tax. The principal sources of revenue for
state governments are consumption-related taxes and aid from the federal
government. These account for over half of state government revenues. Individual income taxes, contributions to insurance trust funds, and charges
make up most of the remainder of state government revenues.

The main source of local government revenue is aid from the federal and
state governments. Intergovernmental revenue and property taxes together
account for a little more than 70 percent of local government revenues.

REVENUE TRENDS

An important trend at the federal level has been the increase in relative importance of the individual income tax since the 1900s although it has not
increased since 1960 (see Figure 2–2 and Table 2–12). In addition, the corporation income tax and sales-related taxes have declined in relative importance since 1927. These trends are due to successive reductions in taxes on
income and sales and to increases in employment (payroll) taxes. Employment taxes have increased over the years because of the growth of the Social
Security and health insurance system.

At the state level (see Table 2–13), the shares of revenue from federal aid
and from income and general sales and gross receipts taxes have increased

FIGURE 2–2
U.S. GOVERNMENT REVENUES AS A PERCENT OF TOTAL REVENUES

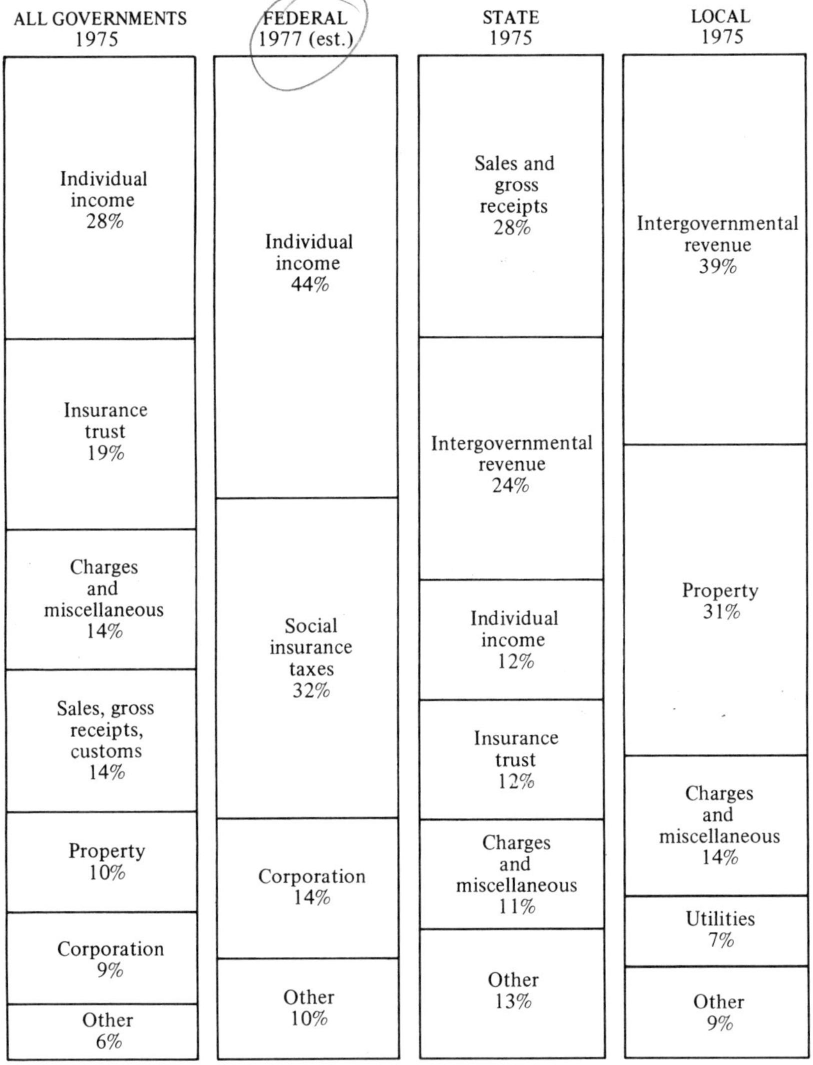

ALL GOVERNMENTS 1975	FEDERAL 1977 (est.)	STATE 1975	LOCAL 1975
Individual income 28%	Individual income 44%	Sales and gross receipts 28%	Intergovernmental revenue 39%
Insurance trust 19%		Intergovernmental revenue 24%	
Charges and miscellaneous 14%	Social insurance taxes 32%	Individual income 12%	Property 31%
Sales, gross receipts, customs 14%		Insurance trust 12%	
Property 10%	Corporation 14%	Charges and miscellaneous 11%	Charges and miscellaneous 14%
Corporation 9%			Utilities 7%
Other 6%	Other 10%	Other 13%	Other 9%

Source: For federal government, *The Budget of the U.S. Government, Fiscal Year 1977*; for all governments and state and local governments, U.S. Census Bureau, *Governmental Finances, 1974–1975*.

TABLE 2–12
U.S. FEDERAL GOVERNMENT REVENUES, TOTAL AND RELATIVE,
SELECTED YEARS, 1902–1975

	1902	1927	1940	1950	1960	1975
Total revenue (billions)	$0.7	$4.5	$7.0	$43.5	$99.8	$303.9
Revenue sources as percent of total revenue [a]						
Individual income tax	—	19.6%	14.3%	36.1%	40.8%	40.3%
Corporation income tax	—	28.0	15.7	24.1	21.5	13.4
Sales and gross receipts taxes and customs	74.6%	24.4	30.0	17.9	12.6	6.9
Death and gift taxes	—	2.0	5.7	1.6	1.6	1.5
Other	3.2	1.0	4.3	0.9	0.6	0.9
Charges and miscellaneous	21.4	22.2	18.6	11.3	10.1	10.5
Insurance trust revenues	—	1.6	11.4	8.0	12.7	26.5
OASDHI	—	—	7.1	4.8	10.7	24.9

a Percents may not total 100 because of rounding.

Source: For 1902–1960, U.S. Census Bureau, *Historical Statistics of the U.S., Colonial Times to 1970*; for 1975, U.S. Census Bureau, *Governmental Finances, 1974–75*.

since 1902. Other revenue sources have fluctuated or declined in importance.

For local governments (see Table 2–14), there has been a decline in the relative importance of the property tax. This trend has been offset by an increase in state and federal aid and the use of alternative local revenue sources. The largest part of nonproperty tax revenues is aid from state governments.

SUMMARY

There is no question that government's role in the U.S. economy has increased in importance during the twentieth century. A greater role for government has the potential for improving or worsening individual welfare. It is important, therefore, that we understand the effect of government policies and the conditions under which government can effectively promote economic welfare. The purpose of the remainder of this book is to develop such understanding.

TABLE 2–13
U.S. STATE GOVERNMENT REVENUE, TOTAL AND RELATIVE,
SELECTED YEARS, 1902–1975

	1902	1927	1940	1950	1960	1975
Total revenue (billions)	$0.2	$2.2	$5.7	$13.9	$32.8	$154.6
Revenue sources as a percent of total revenue [a]						
Intergovernmental revenue	4.7%	7.3%	12.2%	17.3%	22.7%	24.4%
Individual income tax	—	3.3	3.5	5.0	10.3	12.2
Corporation income tax	—	4.3	2.7	4.2	4.2	4.3
Sales and gross receipts tax	14.6	20.7	33.3	33.8	30.7	28.0
Property tax	42.7	17.2	4.6	2.2	1.2	1.0
Motor vehicle and operator license	—	14.0	6.8	5.4	3.4	2.5
Other	24.0	15.3	8.2	6.4	4.2	3.8
Charges and miscellaneous	13.0	11.6	6.0	6.5	10.7	10.7
Liquor store revenues	—	—	4.9	5.8	1.9	1.4
Insurance trust revenues	1.1	6.2	18.8	12.9	10.6	11.6

a Percents may not total 100 because of rounding.

Source: For 1902–1960, U.S. Census Bureau, *Historical Statistics of the U.S., Colonial Times to 1970*; for 1975, U.S. Census Bureau, *Governmental Finances, 1974–75*.

TABLE 2–14
U.S. LOCAL GOVERNMENT REVENUE, TOTAL AND RELATIVE,
SELECTED YEARS, 1902–1975

	1902	1927	1940	1950	1960	1975
Total revenue (billions)	$0.9	$6.3	$7.7	$16.1	$37.3	$159.7
Revenue sources as percent of total revenue [a]						
Intergovernmental revenue	6.1%	9.5%	24.7%	27.3%	27.1%	38.8%
Individual income tax [b]	—	—	0.2	0.4	0.7	1.6
Sales and gross receipts tax	—	0.4	1.7	3.0	3.5	4.1

TABLE 2–14 (cont.)

	1902	1927	1940	1950	1960	1975
Property tax	68.3	69.8	54.5	43.5	42.4	31.3
Other	8.8	1.5	2.3	2.4	1.9	1.4
Charges and miscellaneous	10.3	12.7	6.6	9.9	12.9	14.4
Utilities and liquor store revenues	6.7	7.3	9.1	11.2	9.9	7.0
Insurance trust revenues	—	0.6	0.8	1.7	1.5	1.4

a Percents may not total 100 due to rounding.

b Includes minor amounts of corporation income tax.

Source: For 1902–1960, U.S. Census Bureau, *Historical Statistics of the U.S., Colonial Times to 1970*; for 1975, U.S. Census Bureau, *Governmental Finances, 1974–75*.

SUPPLEMENTARY READINGS

Davie, B.F., and Duncombe, B.F. *Modern Political Arithmetic: The Federal Budget and the Public Sector in National Income Accounts.* New York: Holt, 1970.

Facts and Figures on Government Finance. New York: Tax Foundation, various issues.

Fried, Edward R., Rivlin, A. M., Schultze, Charles L., Tetters, Nancy H. *Setting National Priorities: The 1974 Budget.* Washington, D.C.: Brookings, 1973.

Kendrick, M. Slade. *A Century and a Half of Federal Expenditures.* Occasional Paper no. 48. New York: National Bureau of Economic Research, 1955.

Levy, Michael E. *The Federal Budget: Its Impact on the Economy.* New York: Conference Board, 1974.

Musgrave, Richard A. *Fiscal Systems.* New Haven, Conn.: Yale, 1969.

Pluta, Joseph E. "Growth and Patterns in U.S. Government Expenditures: 1956–1972." *National Tax Journal,* 27 (March 1974): 71–92.

Pryor, Fredric L. *Public Expenditures in Communist and Capitalist Nations.* Homewood, Ill.: Irwin, 1968.

Tussing, A.D., and Henning, John A. "Long-Run Growth of Non-Defense Government Expenditures in the United States." *Public Finance Quarterly,* 2 (April 1974): 202–222.

U.S. Congress, Joint Economic Committee, *Federal Expenditure Policy for Economic Growth and Stability,* November 5, 1957, part 1.

The main purpose of Part Two is to describe and explain the economic arguments for and against the use of government mechanisms to affect resource allocation and income distribution. That is, we address the questions: What role should government play in the economy? And why?

Chapter 3 treats the relatively simple and unrealistic case in which all goods are private goods and there are no externalities. Chapters 4 and 5 move toward reality by showing how government action may promote efficiency when there are public goods and externalities. (The terms private goods, public goods, and externalities are defined at the beginning of Chapter 3.) Chapter 6 examines government's role in the distribution of income.

PART TWO

ECONOMIC RATIONALES FOR GOVERNMENT

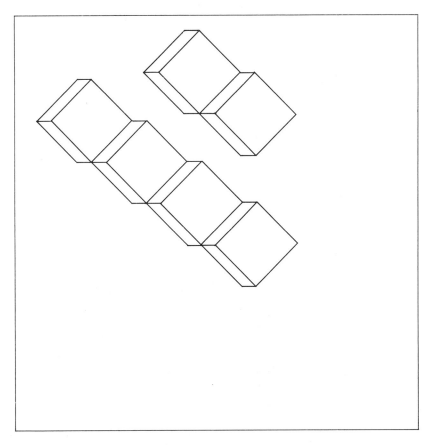

CHAPTER THREE

A PRIVATE GOODS ECONOMY

What is the role of government in an economy in which all goods are private (as opposed to public) and there are no externalities? To answer this question, we must first define *private* and *public goods* and explore the role of government in the creation and maintenance of markets. Then, we can examine, in some detail, the conditions under which equity and efficiency objectives may be promoted by government intervention in a market economy. We will see that even if there are no public goods and externalities, the achievement of efficiency and equity objectives generally requires government action. However, the opposite result is also possible: Particular government actions, such as artificial barriers to entry or trade, may inhibit efficiency.

Subsequent chapters examine the role of government when there are public goods and externalities in the economy.

PRIVATE GOODS, PUBLIC GOODS, AND EXTERNALITIES

Private goods yield utility (satisfaction) only to the person consuming the good. When one person consumes a private good, it is denied to others. Only the person who drinks a cup of coffee, for example, benefits from the consumption of that cup of coffee. And the coffee consumed by one person cannot be consumed by anyone else.[1] The space in which a person parks her or his car gives satisfaction only to the person whose car is parked there at the time. And during that time, the space is denied to others. Thus, private goods are said to be *rival* in consumption.

1 When coffee is purchased, the two parties in the exchange may benefit from the *exchange*. The discussion refers only to the benefits from *consumption*.

A *pure public good* is defined as a *good such that one person's consumption of the good does not reduce the amount available to others*; that is, consumption of a public good is *nonrival*. So, the total supply available to the community can be made available to each person in the community. For example, a television signal that is available to one person can be made available to all persons in the area within range of the signal. And one viewer's use of the signal does not reduce the amount of entertainment for other viewers. A dam that controls flooding benefits everyone in the flood region, and the benefit enjoyed by one property owner does not reduce the benefit available to other property owners.[2]

Many other goods have some of the characteristics of public goods; national defense, the deterrent effect of police protection, mosquito abatement, knowledge, and street lighting are examples. But there are few "pure" public goods like a television signal. A community swimming pool may, for example, be viewed as a public good, until it becomes congested. When the pool is not crowded, its use is equally available to everyone in the pool. And one individual's swim does not interfere with swimming by others. But, when the number of swimmers becomes large enough that they interfere with each other, one person's swim makes swimming less valuable or pleasant for others. Despite this qualification, the definition we have given of a public good is useful as a contrast to the concept of a private good.

These definitions do not, however, say anything about the *institutional arrangement* for making decisions about producing either public or private goods. In other words, a good can be public but not be produced by the government—for example, television signals. Similarly, a private good may be produced by the government—for example, public housing or electricity, such as that supplied by the Tennessee Valley Authority. A major objective of this book is to examine the effects of alternative institutional arrangements (governmental or market) for making decisions about the production and distribution of both public and private goods.

Externalities occur when either the utility that a person derives from a given set of goods and services or a firm's real costs of production depend directly on the consumption or production decisions of other persons or firms. For example, the landscaping and care of one's home may affect the welfare

---

2 That is not to say that everyone benefits equally. Flooding may be less likely in some locations than others, and individuals may evaluate flood control differently. And, although the total supply of a public good can be made available to each member of a community, such need not be the case. For example, television signals may be scrambled so that they are unusable by those who do not purchase unscrambling equipment. And some people may be excluded from having the good.

of one's neighbors. How individuals choose to maintain the pollution-control equipment on their cars affects the level of air pollution in their communities and the welfare of all the community members. Whether and how cities and firms treat wastes that are dumped into a river may affect the welfare of individuals who live downstream and the production costs of the downstream firms that use the river's water. Externalities can be positive (favorable to affected parties) or negative (unfavorable).

These are examples of "real," rather than "pecuniary," externalities. *Pecuniary externalities* arise when the consumption and production decisions of some people affect the prices paid or received by others. For example, if people use more electrical power for air conditioning, the price of electricity is likely to rise, increasing the costs of producers who use electricity. Such cost increases are pecuniary externalities because the producers are still able to get the same output from given inputs. A toaster factory, say, must now pay more for electricity, but it does not need more electricity and other inputs to manufacture toasters. In other words, its real costs of production are not changed.[3] A *real* externality would arise when, for example, upstream producers and consumers pollute the river that the factory draws water from for cooling and other purposes in the manufacture of toasters. Then the pollution (externality) increases the factory's *real* costs of production because it must use real resources (power, equipment) to purify the water before using it in the manufacturing process. More inputs are thus needed to produce the factory's output, the additional inputs in this example being those required for water purification.

Pecuniary externalities do not prevent the achievement of efficient resource allocation because they arise as prices change in response to changes in the relative scarcities of products and resources. As we shall see in this chapter, such price changes, rather than being undesirable, are the means by which markets signal the need for resource reallocation. In contrast, real externalities may cause inefficiency precisely because they are not reflected in prices. So our concern is primarily with real rather than pecuniary externalities.

Public goods and externalities are not unrelated. Externalities may affect a

---

3 An excellent example of a pecuniary externality arises in connection with coal mining. Under the Federal Coal Mine Health and Safety Act of 1969, coal miners suffering from black lung disease qualify for cash and medical care benefits financed by general funds from the U.S. Treasury. These benefit payments represent a pecuniary externality from coal mining because mining leads to black lung disease, which in turn leads to a transfer of income from federal taxpayers to persons suffering from the disease. Transfers to miners and their widows were $72 million per month in March 1975. Social Security Administration, *Social Security Bulletin*, 38, No. 9 (September 1975): 80, table Q–26.

large number of people in a uniform manner, in which case the externality is essentially a public good (or public "bad"). For example, education increases the skills and general welfare of the person being educated and may, in addition, make the person a better citizen. That is, the person's behavior in the political process may be more wise and informed, and an informed and educated electorate may make better political decisions. Since such decisions affect everyone, the education of each person produces an external benefit that accrues to the members of the community and the nation in which the person resides. This external benefit is a public good that is jointly produced along with the private goods (marketable skills) resulting from education. Similarly, air pollution generated by an iron mill's smoke and the exhaust of automobiles are public bads that are produced jointly with private goods (iron and private transportation).

However, some externalities can also be private goods and bads. The dandelion seeds that blow from my lawn to my neighbor's are a negative externality and a private bad because the bad is not available to other members of the community once the seeds settle in my neighbor's lawn. Similarly, the honey produced from the nectar from my flowers is a positive externality and a private good that accrues to the beekeeper whose bees feed on my flowers.

This chapter assumes that externalities do not arise, an obvious but temporary abstraction from reality that is remedied in Chapter 5.

PROPERTY RIGHTS AND RULES OF EXCHANGE: PREREQUISITES OF MARKET ACTIVITY

A market is an arrangement whereby resources and goods (property) are exchanged among households and business firms. Rules of exchange and the way in which property rights are defined and enforced have an important bearing on the existence and functioning of markets. And, as will be explained, there are both equity and efficiency arguments for a government role in the definition and enforcement of rules of exchange and property rights.

Ownership, or *property rights*, determine what owners are permitted by law to do with their property or with title to their property.[4] A property right is the *right to use a scarce economic resource in specified ways*.

These rights may be sold to others, but generally others may not use the resource owned by a particular person without the latter's permission. This

4 Property rights are not of property — land, buildings, etc. They are the rights of the owners of property.

permission is usually obtained by paying a price or providing compensation to the owner. For example, in most modern societies, taking or using a person's property without compensation is stealing and illegal. But a person can legally purchase property or the right to its use for a mutually agreeable price. Nobody can lawfully be made a slave, although a person can exchange labor services for an income. In reality, property rights are not always well defined, and thus markets sometimes operate inefficiently.

The process of defining and enforcing property rights and rules of exchange uses resources. In particular, the definition of property rights generally involves the settlement of disputes about who has the right to control the use of scarce resources and who has a right to the goods and services produced through use of these resources. Such disputes, or conflicts of interest, are resolved by bargaining, negotiation, threats, bluffing, or outright use of force, all of which are activities that use scarce resources — labor, materials, and often life itself. Likewise, property rights, once defined, are maintained and enforced by activities that use scarce resources.[5] What, then, are the equity and efficiency arguments for government involvement in these activities?

In terms of efficiency, government may be able to resolve the conflicts of interest more economically than would private attempts to settle disputes on a case-by-case basis. If a person's ownership claim to a particular resource is backed up only by the resources and strength at the command of that individual, then others would likely be tempted to dispute the claim. The individual "owner," as well as those who dispute that ownership claim, would then be likely to expend scarce time and other resources, either in protecting the claim (on the one side) or in trying to deny ownership or steal (on the other side). With government backing of ownership claims, resources are likewise expended. But such resource use could be less because government can use police power to threaten sanctions that will deter most people from violating a given set of property rights and rules of exchange. That is, government is able to issue such a threat as: "Anyone violating government-authorized (legal) ownership claims or rules of exchange will be arrested and subjected to specified penalties." Thus the resources expended to protect one claim could also serve to protect any other government-backed claim.[6]

---

5 For example, locks, street lighting, night watchmen, criminal justice activities, and the system of civil law all absorb scarce resources for the purpose of enforcing property rights and contracts.

6 The enforcement of property rights and contracts, therefore, approximates a public good, as we defined it above. In this case, the public good is the deterrence created by government's threat to prosecute and penalize all violators of property rights and contracts. The quantity of

In the absence of such government-sanctioned rights, more resources would likely be devoted to both thievery and the protection of property, with fewer resources being allocated to the production of goods and services. Moreover, there would be less incentive to engage in production and exchange because of the fear that one's product might be stolen or an exchange agreement might be violated. The total income of society would be lower; on the average, individuals would be worse off than with government-enforced ownership rights, contracts, and rules of exchange. In other words, the economy would have a lower production possibility frontier without such government activity than with it.

A second argument for a governmental role in the settlement and enforcement of property rights is that a more equitble distribution of income and wealth — control over the use of scarce resources — can be obtained. If government and the police power of the state are not employed in settling such distributional conflicts, then the weak are at the mercy of the strong. The resulting distribution of income and wealth would be inequitable in the eyes of many.[7]

In sum, government can use the police power to resolve distributional conflicts with fewer resources than would otherwise be required. And it also can bring about rules of exchange and a distribution of resource ownership that are ethically more pleasing — more equitable. But, government may not, in practice, live up to this potential. And the gains from a governmental role in these areas would depend on the ethics and morals of the members of the community. If, for example, all abided by an ethical standard that forbade stealing and urged people to care for the poor, then the gains from governmental intervention would be small.

RESOURCE ALLOCATION IN A SIMPLE MARKET ECONOMY

In a pure market economy, government does not employ its police power to tax and spend or to otherwise set outputs or to manipulate prices. Instead, the role of government in the allocation of resources and the distribution of

---

this good that is made available to one member of the community is also available to other members. While the deterrent effect of such threats is a public good, the actual use of the police and court system to apprehend and punish the perpetrators of particular crimes is not a public good, since the use of the system to deal with a particular crime reduces its ability to deal with other crimes.

7 In the absence of governmentally defined and enforced rights, the prevailing situation might be much like that of the "Old West," where the fast guns, the physically strong, and the wealthy ruled.

income is solely one of defining and enforcing property rights and rules of exchange. Will such a market system allocate resources efficiently when all goods are private? [8]

To begin answering this question, let us consider a very simple economy in which

1. Only private goods are produced.

2. Households allocate their income, which they receive from the use of their resources in production, so as to maximize their welfare or utility.

3. Resource owners use their resources in the production of goods so as to maximize their net income.

4. The utility that each person derives from the availability of economic goods depends only on the quantities of such goods that are available to him or her, and not on the quantities available to others.

5. There are enough producers and consumers of each good that no producer or consumer has control over prices; instead, each perceives the price of each good as given and independent of his or her own decisions.

When the fifth assumption is met, markets are said to be purely *competitive*.

VALUE AND DEMAND

How do individuals divide their purchases among various goods? To maximize their utility (or satisfaction), individuals expand their purchases of a particular good, say X, as long as the additional X adds more to their utility than the loss of other goods, necessitated by the additional purchases of X, detracts from their utility. [9] In other words, each person demands that quantity of X for which the utility of the last unit of X purchased just equals the utility of other goods that must be given up to have the X. For example, if the price of a unit of X is $2, the utility of the last unit of X is just equal to the utility that could have been gained if the $2 had been spent on other goods.

An individual who so behaves has a *demand curve* such as dd' in Figure 3-1. This curve shows how the amount an individual is willing to pay for another unit of X changes as the quantity of X consumed changes. In other

8 Recall that efficiency results when resources are allocated so that it is impossible to improve the welfare of one person without reducing the welfare of another. An efficient allocation is also termed *Pareto optimal*. The criterion of economic efficiency presumes that in the consumption of goods, each person is the best judge of her or his own welfare.

9 Given limited resources, a decision to consume more X is a decision to produce and consume less of other goods.

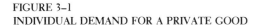

FIGURE 3–1
INDIVIDUAL DEMAND FOR A PRIVATE GOOD

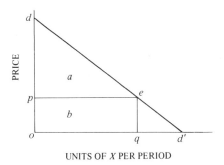

UNITS OF X PER PERIOD

terms, *dd'* shows the *marginal value* of X (expressed in dollars) for each quantity of X consumed by the individual. When the individual is consuming no X, the marginal value is relatively high; the individual is willing to pay *d* for the first unit of X. But as the consumption of X increases, the marginal value of X falls, reaching zero when the individual's consumption of X is *d'*. To maximize utility, the individual buys that quantity of a good for which price just equals marginal value. In Figure 3–1, if the price is *p*, then price equals marginal value, and utility is maximized when *q* units are purchased.

This marginal value of a good generally depends on the amounts of other commodities that are available to the individual, which depend in turn on the individual's income and the prices of other goods. As a general rule, the demand curve shifts to the right if the individual's income is increased, indicating that the individual uses some of his increased income to purchase additional X.

The economic value placed upon goods by consumers reflects their subjective appraisal of the usefulness of those goods in satisfying wants. A measure of the value of a good to consumers is the price they pay for it. If an individual pays $5 for one more unit of some good (say a spaghetti dinner), then that good must be worth at least $5 to that person. In fact, however, the good may be more valuable than $5 to the individual. If so, purchase and consumption of the good creates *consumer surplus*.

For example, someone with a severe case of pneumonia may pay only $50 for the penicillin shots that cure the disease; yet, if necessary, that person would pay much more to be cured. Polio vaccine usually sells for less than $5, yet many people would pay much more for the protection that it provides. From these examples, we can see that consumer surplus may be large relative to an individual's total spending on a commodity. The existence of consumer surplus indicates that the value of a particular good may not be accurately measured by the price people pay for it.

Let us look again at Figure 3–1 for an illustration of the concept of consumer surplus. From the definition of the demand curve, we know that the value of the first unit of X is d, the value of unit q is p, etc. If the price is p and the individual therefore buys q units to maximize utility, then the total value to the individual of the quantity q is given by the areas a and b. But the amount paid for q units is $p \times q$ dollars, which is only the area b. Since the amount paid falls short of the total value (the amount the individual is willing to pay), the individual enjoys a consumer surplus represented by area a.[10]

By adding the demands of individuals, the total demand by the community can be determined. The DD' curve in Figure 3–2 shows total, or community, demand when only two consumers, A and B, make up the community. The community demand curve is obtained by the horizontal summation of the individual demand curves, d_A and d_B. For each price, DD' shows the quantity demanded by all of the members of the community. For example, at price p, the quantity demanded by the community is

FIGURE 3–2
MARKET (COMMUNITY) DEMAND FOR A PRIVATE GOOD

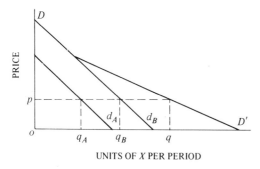

UNITS OF X PER PERIOD

10 In this chapter and throughout the book we assume that the marginal value and demand schedules of individuals are the same, so that the area under the demand curve and above the price line (area a in Figure 3–1) measures consumer surplus. This area is not always an exact measure of consumer surplus, since demand and marginal value curves need not coincide. However, this area is a good approximation of consumer surplus if the income effects of product price changes are relatively small. See William S. Vickrey, *Microstatics* (New York: Harcourt, Brace & World, 1964), pp. 66–76; or James M. Buchanan, *The Demand and Supply of Public Goods* (Chicago: Rand McNally, 1968), pp. 39–46

q, with A and B consuming q_A and q_B, respectively. So, the marginal value of X is p for *each* member of the community. Also, $\hat{p}$ is the marginal value placed upon X by the community.[11] If less (more) than q is produced, the marginal value to the community exceeds (is less than) the price of p because either A or B or both must consume less (more) than they would wish to consume at a price of p.

COST AND SUPPLY

In a market economy the goods demanded by households are produced by private producers who wish to *maximize profits*. In determining the profit-maximizing output, producers must compare the extra revenue obtained by producing more units with the extra cost of producing those units. The additional cost of producing one more unit of a good is called *marginal cost*, and the extra revenue received from selling one more unit is called *marginal revenue*. Profits will increase if the extra cost of producing more units is less than the extra revenue received.

In competitive markets, a producer's marginal revenue is the price of the good. If the price of the good is $1, the sale of an additional unit increases revenue by $1. The profit-maximizing producer therefore expands production so long as price exceeds marginal cost; when output is at the point where price equals marginal cost, profits are maximized.

With producers behaving this way, the supply of a good is a function of its marginal cost. The quantity supplied by each firm is that for which price equals marginal cost, and the total quantity supplied to the market is the sum of the amounts supplied by individual firms. This *market supply* relationship is shown by the curve S in Figure 3–3. The marginal cost of producing X is shown to increase as production increases; production increases only if the price of the good rises (other things being equal). At price p, producers maximize profits at q, the quantity at which price equals marginal cost. If less than q is produced, marginal revenue (price) exceeds marginal cost, and profits can be increased by expanding production to q. If production is expanded beyond q, profits decline because marginal cost exceeds marginal revenue.

Such a supply schedule of a competitive industry, in addition to showing the relationship between market price and quantity supplied, reflects the value of the other goods that could have been produced with the resources

---

11 We have assumed that the good has value only to the individual who consumes it. Therefore, the marginal value of X to the community is simply the value placed on the marginal unit of X by the individual who consumes it.

FIGURE 3–3
MARKET SUPPLY OF A PRIVATE GOOD

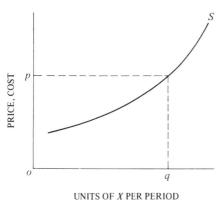

used to produce each successive unit of X. As we have seen before, resources have alternative uses; in a fully employed economy, if more resources are used to produce one good, fewer resources are available to
produce other goods. To say that the marginal cost of good X is $1 is to say
that the goods that could have been produced with the resources used to produce one more unit of X have a maximum value of $1. That is, the oppor-
tunity cost of one more unit of X is $1 worth of other goods. Therefore, if
another unit of X is to be produced by competitive suppliers, it must sell at a
price that equals or exceeds its marginal cost ($1), which in turn implies that
consumers of X must value the additional X at least as highly as they value
the other goods that must be given up to produce it.

DEMAND AND SUPPLY EQUILIBRIUM

We have seen how consumers demand more of a good, X, if and only if the
marginal value of X exceeds its price, while producers supply more X if and
only if the price of X exceeds its marginal cost. Consumers will not be satisfied with the amount consumed unless price equals marginal value, and
producers will wish to change the amount produced unless price equals
marginal cost. That is, neither producers nor consumers will be in *equilibrium* unless the amount produced is such that the marginal value (MV) to
consumers and the marginal cost (MC) to producers are both equal to price
(p): $MC = p = MV$. In such a case the quantity demanded by consumers will
equal the quantity supplied by producers. When the interaction of buyers
and sellers (consumers and producers) in the market establishes a price and

quantity of X such that this condition is met, the market is said to be in equilibrium.

Figure 3–4, with demand curve D and supply curve S, depicts equilibrium in a market at a price of p and a quantity of q. If the price is above p, say p', there is surplus production (q'' minus q'), in which case competition among producers to sell the surplus will force price down. The surplus is eliminated because the decline in price increases the consumption and decreases the production of X until quantity demanded equals quantity supplied. If price is below p, there is a shortage; competition among buyers will force price to p and quantity to q.

Although we have so far discussed demand and supply in terms of one good, X, we have indirectly taken the demand for and supply of other commodities into account. Since the demand curve for X in Figure 3–4 shows the community's willingness to give up other commodities in order to have more X, the community's demand for these other commodities is taken into account in establishing D. Similarly, since the supply curve (S) shows how much of other commodities must be given up to obtain successive increments of X, the supply of other commodities is implicitly determined when the supply of X is determined. Therefore, the market for X usually will not be in equilibrium unless these other markets are in equilibrium.

CHARACTERISTICS OF MARKET EQUILIBRIUM

Producing an output other than q in Figure 3–4 is nonoptimal in the sense that it must make some persons worse off in their own judgment than they

FIGURE 3–4
EQUILIBRIUM IN THE MARKET FOR A PRIVATE GOOD

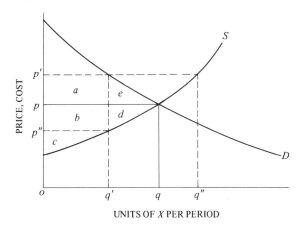

UNITS OF X PER PERIOD

are with the output of q. Recall that the marginal value of X is measured along the demand schedule D in Figure 3–4, and that the supply schedule S measures the value of the other goods that are foregone with successive increases in the output of X. Therefore, at an output less than q, say q', the marginal value of X (p') exceeds the value of alternative goods (p''). And the welfare of consumers would be increased by moving from q' to q. Moreover, the move from q' to q need not make producers (all suppliers of resources) worse off.[12] An expansion of production from q' to q would occur because consumers are willing to cover the cost of the additional X; resource owners would supply more resources to the production of X because price exceeds marginal cost.

Similarly, if output exceeds q, say q'', marginal cost exceeds marginal value, and the welfare of consumers can again be increased by moving to q. In addition, producers and resource owners are worse off at q'': Consumers are not willing to cover the cost of producing q'' and producers incur losses at that level of output.

We can state this idea differently. When the market for X is in equilibrium at some quantity, q, no individual or group of individuals is willing to make the sacrifice of other commodities required to expand the output of X beyond q, while no individual or group of individuals is willing to make the sacrifice of X required to expand the output of other goods beyond the level associated with an X output of q. The market equilibrium output in this case is Pareto optimal, or economically efficient.

An example may help to show why resource allocation is Pareto optimal when price (p) equals marginal value (MV) and marginal cost (MC). Let us consider an economy with two goods, X and Y. Let us also assume that marginal cost is constant and therefore equal to average cost in the production of both goods. In other words, the supply and marginal cost schedules are horizontal, as shown by the S curves in Figure 3–5.

The markets for X and Y in Figure 3–5 are in equilibrium at prices of $40 for X and $20 for Y, with 150 units of X and 200 units of Y being produced. With those marginal costs, twice as many resources are required to produce 1 unit of X as are needed for 1 unit of Y. Suppose the output of X is reduced by 10 to 140 units, allowing the output of Y to increase by 20 to 220 units.

12 *Producer surplus*, the difference between producer receipts and costs, is equal to the areas $a + b + c$ when output is q'. With output of q, producer surplus is the areas $b + c + d$. Producer surplus thus falls by the area $a - d$, and producers are possibly worse off. But note that consumers gain in consumer surplus the amounts represented by areas $a + e$; consumers always gain more from the expansion in output than producers lose. There is a net gain of areas $e + d$ to be distributed among producers and consumers. Therefore, producers *need not* lose from the expansion if they are compensated by consumers for their net loss of producer surplus.

FIGURE 3–5
EFFICIENT OUTPUT OF TWO PRIVATE GOODS

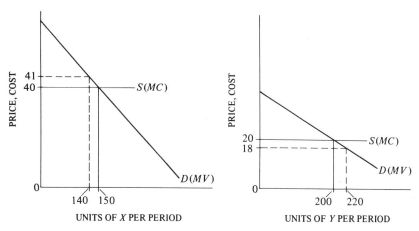

UNITS OF X PER PERIOD   UNITS OF Y PER PERIOD

The value to households of the foregone X is $405 (10 units at an average value of $40.50 per unit). The value of the additional 20 units of Y is $380 (20 units at an average value of $19 per unit). There is a $25 net loss in the value of output by this reallocation of resources, and the welfare of society is reduced.

Stated differently, with outputs of 140 units of X and 220 units of Y, reallocation of resources to restore equilibrium would increase the value of output by $25. Some or all households could be made better off without harming others. In a competitive market, this outcome would occur as follows: With 140 units of X being produced, firms want to expand production because price (marginal revenue) is above marginal cost; as output expands, price will fall until equilibrium is reached at $40. The reverse is true for the firms producing Y.[13] The resources required to increase production of X by 10 units are obtained by reducing the output of Y by 20 units. The reader can construct the reverse example to show that the value of total output falls if the output of X is increased from the equilibrium value of 150 units and the output of Y is correspondingly decreased.

As we saw earlier, a competitive market supplies the optimal quantity of a product (under the assumptions of page 54). What we will now see is that it

[13] The producers of Y lose money when output is 220 units because that many units can be sold only at a price of $18, that is, at a loss of $2 per unit. So, the hypothesized deviations from the market equilibria would not persist.

does so at *minimum* opportunity cost. That is, no actual or potential supplier of a product can supply an additional unit at a cost below the prevailing market price. Why? If price should exceed marginal cost for any supplier, then that supplier could make additional profit by offering to sell at
slightly below the market price, thereby bidding away the business of other,
higher cost suppliers. Production will therefore always be undertaken by producers who have the lowest costs. *Cost minimization* becomes necessary for
survival. Producers will also seek ways of lowering costs because the individual producer takes the market price as given and concludes that lower costs
will mean higher profits.

The conclusion that a market-determined allocation of resources may be
economically efficient is an important one. It is the basis for the widespread
belief that a "free enterprise," market economy is socially desirable. A market allocation that is efficient is indeed desirable because no participant in
the market process can be made better off without giving the participant a
larger share of society's income and wealth. Unfortunately the conditions
under which a market allocation is efficient (listed on page 54) are often
not met, and markets "fail" in ways that are discussed fully in this and
subsequent chapters.

EFFICIENT RESOURCE ALLOCATION AND THE DISTRIBUTION OF INCOME

The economically efficient allocation of resources depends on how the ownership of resources is distributed among individuals. Therefore particular
outputs may be efficient (Pareto optimal) for one distribution of resource

FIGURE 3–6
INCOME DISTRIBUTION AND EFFICIENCY

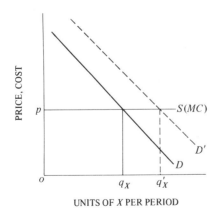
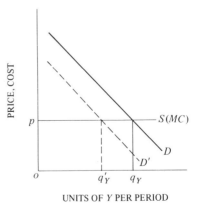

ownership, while other outputs would be efficient for another distribution of ownership.

More specifically, to construct a market demand schedule, a distribution of income must be assumed because a change in the distribution of income will usually change the demand for goods. Any distribution of income is, however, consistent with efficiency in resource allocation. Figure 3–6 shows how changing the distribution of income affects demand. Suppose that X represents necessities, food, housing, etc., and Y represents luxuries, yachts, Cadillacs, etc. Given a particular distribution of income, efficient outputs of X and Y are q_X and q_Y. If some income of the rich is now transferred to the poor, the demand for X increases and the demand for Y falls, as shown by the demand curves D'. Resources also shift — out of Y production into X production — until new and efficient output levels are established at q'_X and at q'_Y.

RESOURCE ALLOCATION IN A MARKET ECONOMY: SOME COMPLICATIONS

We have seen how an idealized market economy can allocate resources efficiently, with the efficient allocation depending on the distribution of income. Unfortunately real-world market systems do not correspond with this ideal and generally do not achieve an efficient allocation of resources. In this section we will see why markets may fail even when all goods are private goods and there are no externalities.

DECREASING COST

So far our analysis has assumed that the marginal cost of producing a good either is constant or increases as production expands. However, if marginal and average costs fall as production expands, then costs are said to be decreasing. And the conclusion that competitive markets operate to allocate resources efficiently must be modified.

Decreasing costs occur when there are high "overhead" or "fixed" costs, for example, in transportation, hospitals, postal services, and power generation. Since these are key sectors in any modern economy, it is important we understand how decreasing costs can inhibit allocative efficiency.

The marginal cost (MC) and average cost (AC) schedules of a decreasing-cost industry are shown in Figure 3–7, as is the industry demand curve D. To make this discussion more concrete we will think of Figure 3–7 as the market for electric power in a particular geographic area. To supply even a small amount of power requires large investments in generation and distribution systems. The cost per kilowatt hour of supplying a small amount of

FIGURE 3–7
DECREASING COST AND EFFICIENCY

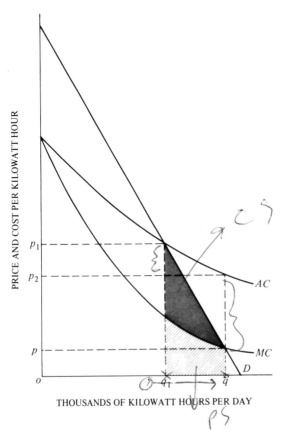

THOUSANDS OF KILOWATT HOURS PER DAY

power is relatively high. Additional output requires additional outlays for fuel, personnel, and equipment, as shown by the MC curve. However, as the AC curve shows, the unit cost (the cost per kilowatt hour) declines as output increases because the initial, or fixed, costs of the generation and distribution system are spread over more units of output. As long as marginal cost either declines or is constant as output increases, average cost will decline and exceed marginal cost.[14]

14 Of course *diminishing returns* may set in if output is sufficiently great, in which case marginal costs will increase as output increases and will eventually exceed average costs. However, in decreasing-cost industries, total demand for the product is met *before* output reaches this level.

Until the output of electric power in this market reaches q, where marginal cost and price are equal, there are potential welfare gains from increasing output. Why? Until q units are produced, the value of an additional unit of X to consumers exceeds its cost of production. In particular, even though consumers are willing to purchase only q_1 units at the price p_1, some consumers are willing to pay less than p_1 but more than the cost of producing additional units. And this is so until output reaches q, where price equals marginal cost.

But profit-maximizing producers will not sell q units at a price of p. To do so would be to lose income in the amount represented by the area $(p_2 - p) \times q$, where p_2 is the *break-even* price when q units are sold. (Price must equal average cost for the firm to break even.) Moreover, consumers will not pay a price of p_2 for q units. For the market to clear *and* for producers to break even, price and output must be p_1 and q_1, respectively, where average costs are just covered, including an allowance for normal profits.[15] In other words, the fundamental problem posed by decreasing costs is that profit-maximizing producers will not increase output to the point where all potential welfare gains are realized.

The potential welfare gain to be obtained by increasing output to q from the break-even quantity, q_1, can also be shown by comparing consumer and producer surpluses at the two output levels. In Figure 3–7 the gross gain in consumer welfare obtained by increasing output from q_1 to q is measured by the two shaded areas. The increase in cost is shown by the diagonally shaded area. The net gain in consumer welfare is the difference between these two amounts, or the darkly shaded area. How might this potential consumer welfare gain be realized?

Discriminatory pricing   One possible mechanism is discriminatory pricing, which involves charging different prices to some consumers than to others. *Perfect* price discrimination occurs when each consumer is charged as much as he or she is willing to pay for each unit; that is, the price paid equals marginal value *for each unit consumed.* And the total revenue received by the supplier for a given quantity is the total value placed on that quantity by the consumers. If perfect price discrimination is costless, the profit on each unit sold is equal to the difference between the marginal

---

15 Normal profits are part of the cost of production. Profits are normal when they are just sufficient to keep existing resources in an industry.

In the example in Figure 3–7, a single producer (monopolist) of the good would charge a price higher than p_1, but it is not necessary to presume monopolistic price determination to show that in the decreasing-cost case output may be inefficient if the good is privately produced for profit. Monopolistic pricing is discussed in the next section.

value of the unit, as given by the demand curve, and the marginal cost of
the unit. Profit continues to increase with increases in output as long as MV
exceeds MC, and profit is maximized when MV = MC. In Figure 3–8 profit
is maximized at q units, with total revenue being represented by the areas
a + b + c, total costs by area c and profits by areas a + b. Thus, with *costless*
and perfect price discrimination, profits are maximized when all potential
welfare gains are exhausted, which stands in sharp contrast to the earlier
conclusion that with no price discrimination, profit-maximizing firms will
fail to realize all potential welfare gains.

While perfect price discrimination is rarely possible, departures from uniform pricing (under which each buyer pays the same price) are often feasible
and may promote efficiency. For example, a bus system may have unused
seats except in *peak-load* or *rush-hour* periods. If so, the fare for periods
other than the rush hours could be reduced to encourage travel during those

FIGURE 3–8
PERFECT PRICE DISCRIMINATION IN A DECREASING-COST INDUSTRY

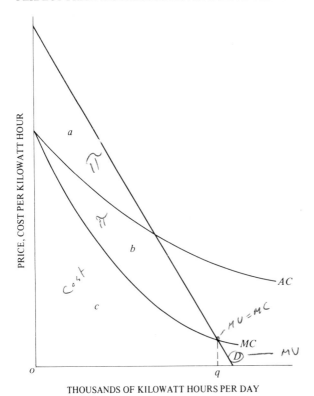

THOUSANDS OF KILOWATT HOURS PER DAY

periods. If the number of riders increases enough in response to the reduced fare, then total revenue increases. Any such revenue increase is unlikely to be offset by a cost increase, since the cost of carrying more passengers when buses are not full is very low. That is, price discrimination (charging different fares to different riders) may increase the net revenues and the financial viability of the bus system. Such pricing is often called *peak-load pricing*.

Another approach to price discrimination is to charge a per unit price equal to marginal cost and make up the resulting deficit with a lump-sum charge to each user. Bridges, parking facilities, water, and electricity are examples of goods that may be financed by such *two-part* pricing. For the electric power example of Figure 3–7, the price per kilowatt hour would be set at $MC = p$. The resulting deficit to be made up by the lump-sum charges would be $q \times (p_2 - p)$. If there are 1,000 users (homes and businesses) of electricity, then the lump-sum charge could be set at $[q \times (p_2 - p)] \div 1,000$. Each user would pay that charge rather than go without electricity should the charge be less than the user's consumer surplus from the purchase of electricity at a price of p. The lump-sum charge need not be the same for each user. It could be greater for businesses than for households. However, to achieve efficiency, the lump-sum charge should not deter use by any business or household that is willing to pay a price of p per unit for the electricity; that is, the lump-sum charge should not exceed any user's consumer surplus.

When feasible, peak-load and two-part pricing, as well as other forms of imperfect price discrimination, promote efficiency in decreasing-costs situations without government subsidy and the distortions that are likely to result from taxation to finance the subsidy. In addition, consumers bear the costs of providing the goods and services.

Discriminatory pricing, even the imperfect sort we just discussed, is not feasible in many instances. Or it may be too costly to implement in others. To discriminate among consumers, a producer must know (within limits) the marginal value each consumer, or class of consumers, attaches to the good. Such knowledge is not available without cost, if it is available at all. In addition, price discrimination will not work if goods can be bought and resold. For example, if a firm attempts to charge class A consumers $10 and class B consumers $5, the latter customers would, if possible, buy for the A's and sell at a price between $5 and $10. That resale activity would tend to drive the price to $5, thus frustrating efforts at price discrimination.

Our conclusion to this point is that when there are decreasing costs of production, potential welfare gains are not realized by a market system, unless discriminatory pricing is feasible and relatively inexpensive. For example, in Figure 3–7 (p. 64) the potential welfare gain to be obtained through discriminatory pricing is the darkly shaded area. But such action is commonly too costly because the welfare gains obtained from increased output are exhausted by the costs of carrying out the discriminatory pricing necessary to realize those gains through market processes.[16] So markets fail (to be efficient) because of the costs of discriminatory pricing.

Government policies   When discriminatory pricing is not feasible, government can conceivably improve upon the results of market processes with either of two basic policies: (1) government can employ its police power to set prices or (2) government can undertake to produce the commodity. In the first case, government can, for example, require that the price be set at p in Figure 3–7. Consumers would thus demand q units, and producers would incur losses of $(p_2 - p) \times q$. These losses would then have to be offset by a subsidy to the producers of an equal amount, with the revenue required for the subsidy being obtained by taxation — that is, through the exercise of the government's police power. In the second case, the government could produce q units and sell them at a price of p. This would incur a loss of $(p_2 - p) \times q$ to the government, which would again have to be obtained through taxation. In either case, the consumer welfare gain represented by the darkly shaded area, which was not realized through market processes, would be realized by government action. Of course, the net welfare gain to society would be less by the amount of the cost of the government action.

But the problems posed by decreasing costs are not eliminated by having government undertake production; the pricing dilemma remains. With either private or government production, a uniform (nondiscriminatory) price set to cover all costs restricts output below the level of efficiency, while marginal cost pricing requires a tax-financed subsidy. The U.S. Postal Service illustrates this very well. Although the service has been changed from a government production to a public-enterprise format, the problems of what rates to charge and how much subsidy to provide remain.[17] And note that the need for subsidy has been a factor with both arrangements.

16 Also, price discrimination may be regarded as unfair because the producer succeeds in charging "what the traffic will bear." Thus, a policy that promotes efficiency, such as price discrimination, may fail on equity grounds.

17 Another pricing issue often arises when there is government production; namely, the question of whether the government-produced good should be sold at a subsidized price, even below marginal cost, as a means of assuring that low income persons have "necessary" services, such as public transportation, power, water, and housing. This approach to helping the poor can be and is opposed on the grounds that poverty should be attacked directly, by redistributing income. Also, if government-provided goods and services are to be sold at a price below cost, should not privately produced necessities (bread, clothing) also be sold at less than cost? We consider these questions in more detail in Chapter 6.

Desirability of government action Use of government's police power to increase output may not be desirable, even if it is feasible. One reason is that government action is not without cost and those costs may exceed the consumer welfare gains obtained. One component is the cost of regulation, which is the cost of requiring firms to set a price equal to marginal cost (the price of p in Figure 3–7). Regulation costs include both information costs — for determining the marginal cost of the product, X, at various output levels — and the costs of enforcing the marginal-cost pricing rule. Added to these are the costs of taxation to provide the subsidy and the costs of distributing the subsidy.[18] Taxation costs arise whether government regulates and subsidizes production or produces the product itself.

It is also possible that under either government regulation and subsidy or government ownership the cost of producing the product will increase. That is, cost curves may shift upward. One reason is that workers' and managers' incentives to minimize costs may be weakened once they recognize that losses will be offset by a subsidy. An open-end subsidy that covers all losses greatly weakens incentives to minimize costs. In particular, an open-end subsidy reduces the firm's incentive to change technology (innovate) so as to reduce average cost; any reduction in costs reduces the subsidy rather than increasing the producer's profits. In contrast, a fixed-amount subsidy leaves intact the profit-maximizing firm's incentive to minimize costs. Also, price regulation blunts the incentive to reduce costs if, as is usually the case, a cost decrease forces a price decrease. Similarly, with government ownership, costs may increase unless workers or managers stand to gain directly and monetarily when costs are reduced. Such is typically not the case with government enterprises, although it could be. Any such increase in production costs in response to government action obviously reduces the potential welfare gains from such action.

However, if the welfare gains from government action exceed all those costs of government action, *then* the action is justified on efficiency grounds.[19] On the other hand, if the costs of action exceed the potential

---

18 Included in the costs of taxation is the *excess burden* of taxation, which we discuss more fully in Chapter 9. Excess burden is basically the difference between the amount of a person's tax payment and the amount of the cash payment to the person that would be required to restore his or her welfare level to that prevailing before the tax. In other terms, the cost of the subsidy is not necessarily measured by the amount of taxes paid. The real cost may be greater because people incur costs as they attempt to avoid or minimize taxes. For example, suppose a subsidy to producers in a decreasing-cost industry is financed by a tax on commodity Y, which is likely to cause some persons to buy less Y to avoid the tax. In doing so, those persons may reduce their welfare. This decrease in individual welfare is part of the real cost (burden) of taxation; it is a burden in excess of the taxes paid to finance the subsidy.

19 This conclusion is subject to the additional qualification that there may be offsetting imperfections in other markets. See Richard G. Lipsey and K. Lancaster, "The General Theory of the Second Best," *Review of Economic Studies* 24 (December 1956): 11–32.

welfare gains realized, then we must conclude that the market allocation was efficient; there is no way that government action can improve the welfare of some without decreasing the welfare of others. The question of whether the market-determined output is efficient is empirical; it is a question that cannot be answered without determining whether government can generate consumer welfare gains that exceed the cost of government action.

Even if government action is judged appropriate on efficiency grounds, it may nevertheless be regarded as undesirable for another reason: It may be unfair. Such might be the case if the distribution of the taxes required to finance the subsidy is unfair. For example, the taxes might fall heavily on the poor, or they might be collected from those who do not benefit from the expanded output of X. In contrast, with the private production and sale of X, those who consume or use X always pay for its cost of production.[20]

We have been discussing why government action that succeeds in achieving the efficient level of output may be inappropriate. But there is also the possibility that government action will not result in production of the efficient quantity. In particular, there may be overproduction of X when either private production is subsidized or public production is undertaken. *Overproduction* simply refers to production in excess of the amount for which (1) marginal value equals marginal cost and (2) consumers are willing to pay the full cost of production. When there is overproduction of some commodity, X, consumers value the excess output of X *less* than they value the other commodities that they have to give up in order to have this excess amount of X.

Overproduction is illustrated in Figure 3–9. The triangle *abc* represents the gross welfare gain obtainable by increasing output to *q* from the market-determined level of q_1. The small rectangle in the triangle represents the costs of government action required to bring about the output expansion. There is, thus, a net gain from the government action equal to the area of *abc* minus the area of the rectangle, *if* government action does indeed achieve the output of *q*. But the actual outcome of government action may be either a larger or smaller output. If the output is less than *q*, say q_2, then the net welfare gain is reduced by the amount of the small triangle *dec*. If output exceeds *q*, say q_3, then the net gain is reduced by the area of triangle *cfg*, which is the difference between the cost of the excess units of X and their value. Each unit of X in excess of *q* reduces the net welfare gain

20 Recall that this discussion assumes that externalities are absent. This equity issue can be viewed differently. The revenues obtained by full-cost (average-cost) pricing are in lieu of a tax to provide a subsidy. One can therefore ask whether they represent a fair tax. See William S. Vickrey, "Economic Efficiency and Pricing," in Selma Mushkin, ed., *Public Prices for Public Products* (Washington, D.C.: Urban Institute, 1972), p. 59.

FIGURE 3–9
WELFARE LOSSES FROM OVER- (UNDER-) PRODUCTION

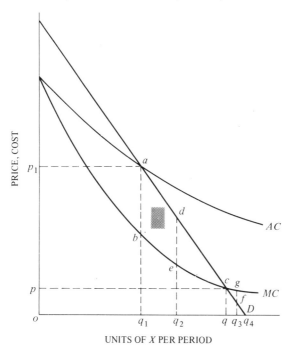

UNITS OF *X* PER PERIOD

because the cost of producing each unit, given by the MC curve, exceeds the value of the unit, given by the D curve. If overproduction is sufficiently great, then government action can actually result in a welfare loss, even though an "optimal" policy of producing *q* units and setting a price of *p* would have produced a welfare gain.

Overproduction is possible because government can use its police power to divert resources into the production of X. In contrast, private producers can obtain resources to produce X only if they can sell this X for enough to cover the opportunity cost of those resources. With government, overproduction may occur because people do not associate tax increases with spending increases. That is, they do not think that their tax payments will be increased by an increase in the output of a government-provided good. People thus see the marginal cost of the government-provided good as being zero, and they demand additional output as long as marginal value exceeds marginal cost (zero). In Figure 3–9 there would be a demand by some or all voters for additional output until output reached q_4, where the marginal value of output is zero.

NONCOMPETITIVE MARKET STRUCTURES

In the preceding discussion we presumed that suppliers (producers) are price takers; that is, they view the price they receive as being independent of the quantity they produce and offer for sale. However, when there is a single seller, when there are a few sellers, or when' sellers can differentiate their product sufficiently, sellers see prices as being dependent on the quantities they supply. When such is the case, market structures are said to be *noncompetitive*, and characterized by monopoly, oligopoly, or monopolistic competition.

When the firm sees its price decreasing as it increases its supply, marginal revenue and price are no longer the same. Marginal revenue is less than price, and the difference between the two widens as more output is sold.[21] The profit-maximizing market output will not be such that marginal cost equals marginal value (price), the condition for efficient resource allocation. Instead, market output is that for which marginal cost equals marginal revenue, which is less than the marginal value of the good and the price consumers pay.

To illustrate, the curve DM in Figure 3–10 shows the monopolist's marginal revenue, which is less than the price as given by the demand schedule DD'. To maximize profits, the monopolist expands production so long as marginal revenue exceeds marginal cost, shown by the MC curve, and therefore produces q_1, where marginal revenue equals marginal cost and the price is p_1. However, at p_1, the marginal value of X to consumers exceeds its marginal cost. And welfare could be improved by increasing output to q, where price is equal to marginal cost and marginal value. So the monopolist produces less than the efficient output *if all buyers are charged the same price*. However, with costless and perfect price discrimination, price and marginal revenue are equal; the monopolist maximizes profits at the efficient output, q in Figure 3–10.

---

21 That statement assumes that all consumers are charged the same price; i.e., there is no price discrimination. To illustrate, suppose the demand for a product is such that consumers value the first unit at $10, the second at $9, the third at $8, etc. Without price discrimination, if 1 unit is sold, both price and total and marginal revenue are $10. If 2 units are sold, the price must be $9, since consumers value the second unit at only $9; therefore, total revenue is $18. The increase in total revenue from selling the second unit, which is marginal revenue, is $18 − $10 = $8. Marginal revenue is thus less than price because the price of *all* units must be lowered as the quantity sold increases. Similarly, if 3 units are sold, the price must be $8; and, total revenue and marginal revenue are $24 and $24 − $18 = $6, respectively.

In contrast, with perfect price discrimination, each unit is sold at a price equal to the value placed on it by consumers. If 1 unit is sold, both price and marginal revenue are $10; if 2 units are sold, total revenue is $10 + $9 = $19 and marginal revenue is $9, which is also the price of the additional unit. Similarly, if 3 units are sold, total revenue is $10 + $9 + $8 = $27 and marginal revenue and the price of the third unit are both $8.

FIGURE 3–10
OUTPUT AND PRICE UNDER MONOPOLY

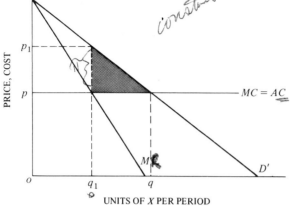

Other noncompetitive market structures, such as oligopoly, may also result in inefficient output. In general terms, with noncompetitive market structures the output of goods is usually inefficient because producers maximize profits at an output level where price and marginal value exceed marginal cost.

In addition, with noncompetitive markets, producers may fail to minimize the cost of the output that they do produce because they do not have to maximize profits and minimize costs to survive. For example, company airplanes and plush offices entail costs that may be unnecessary from a production standpoint but are incurred for the personal benefit of managers.[22]

The outcome with noncompetitive markets is similar to the outcome with decreasing-cost industries in that market-determined output will usually be below the efficient level. In both cases, government, through the exercise of police power, may improve consumer welfare if it can bring about an efficient level of production through either price regulation or government ownership. With monopoly or oligopoly, there is the additional alternative of making the market structure more competitive (through antitrust policies) so that price falls and output moves closer to the efficient level. When producers fail to minimize costs (that is, fail to be technologically efficient)

22 There is considerable debate about whether production costs are lower with competitive than noncompetitive market structures. See F. M. Scherer, *Industrial Market Structure and Economic Performance* (Chicago: Rand McNally, 1973).

because they face little competition, it is less clear what government might do. Antitrust policies might be helpful if they bring cost-cutting competition. Or taxation of producers could force them to minimize costs in order to survive, although it would be difficult to determine the proper level of taxation. Or, if government production is chosen as the means of correcting the problem, the difficulty of devising incentives for efficiency in the government enterprise must be faced.

Another problem arises with the government-enterprise solution to monopoly: Government may also price as a monopolist, causing prices to be higher and quantities to be lower than is required for efficiency. Pricing to generate profits from government enterprises provides government with nontax revenue. Examples of such revenue-raising monopolies in the United States are government-operated utilities (electric power and water), liquor stores, and lotteries. Profits from government enterprise are, of course, the major source of government revenues in socialist countries.

Any of these policies for dealing with the inefficiencies resulting from noncompetitive markets will be costly to implement and enforce, and these costs will partially or even fully offset the welfare gain from increased production. With either regulation and subsidy or government ownership there is also the potential cost of overproducing and financing the resulting losses through taxation. With the "antitrust" solution, however, overproduction will not occur. That is, since private firms cannot finance losses via the power to tax, a welfare loss from overproduction would not occur. On the other hand, if market structures fall short of perfect competition despite government antitrust policies, there may be underproduction.[23] As in the case of decreasing costs, when all costs and equity considerations are weighed against the potential welfare gains from government action, it is not clear a priori whether such action can improve upon the outcomes of noncompetitive markets.

MONOPOLY PLUS DECREASING COSTS

Monopolists' costs may be constant or increasing (constant cost is shown in Figure 3–10). Under those conditions government regulation that forces marginal-cost pricing and increases output to q does not cause losses that must be offset by a government subsidy. But monopoly and oligopoly are

---

23 Also, regulation redistributes income from the monopolist or oligopolist to consumers, which may or may not be fair. If such redistribution is considered unfair, the government may want to compensate the monopolist for any losses. In principle, the taxes used to compensate can be collected from the consumers who gain from the output expansion and still leave the consumers better off, since the consumers' gain exceeds producers' losses by the shaded area in Figure 3–10. In practice, the taxes collected to compensate may themselves impose an excess burden, or welfare loss.

likely to occur in conjunction with decreasing costs. In which case marginal-cost pricing will generate losses, and a government subsidy will be required.

The ethical drug industry illustrates most of the problems arising when monopolists' costs are decreasing. Consider costs arising in the discovery and production of a new drug capable of limiting the progress of cancer (or a vaccine for a contagious disease). Typically, large costs must be incurred to discover the drug and test its effectiveness.[24] These are fixed, or "sunk," costs that arise before even one unit of the drug can be sold. Let us suppose these costs are $1,000,000. Once the costs are incurred, however, additional units may be produced at very low cost, say $1 per unit. The marginal cost of production would thus be $1 per unit, as shown by the MC curve in Figure 3–11. But considering all costs — discovery, testing, and production — the average and marginal cost of the first unit is $1,000,001. After 1 unit is produced, the marginal cost drops to $1, while average total cost declines gradually, as shown by the AC curve, reaching $2 when output reaches 1,000,000 units. The demand curve for the drug is D. The output for which price equals marginal cost and potential welfare gains from increasing output are exhausted is 566,667 units.

But that output will not be produced if discovery and production of the drug are undertaken by a private firm. A private firm will produce at most 500,000 units and charge at least $3 per unit. Selling more would force the price below average cost and generate a loss, as would selling at any price less than $3 per unit. Also, if the demand for the drug is inelastic and the firm has a monopoly on its production, the firm can increase its profits by increasing its price above $3 and selling less than 500,000 units. This outcome is likely because the demand for effective drugs tends to be inelastic, at least in the lower range of prices. And drug producers are often monopolists by virtue of their rights as patentholders. For example, in Figure 3–11, if the firm is a monopolist and maximizes profits, it will sell 283,333 units at $9.50 per unit for a total profit of $1,408,330. And a possible, if not likely, outcome of market production of drugs will be high profits for successful drug producers and drugs selling at many times their marginal cost of production. This picture coincides fairly well with what we know about the ethical drug industry.[25]

---

24 For an analysis of discovery and innovation in the ethical drug industry, see Edwin Mansfield, John Rapoport, Jerome Schnee, Samuel Wagner, and Michael Hamburger, *Research and Innovation in the Modern Corporation* (New York: Norton, 1971), chap. 8.

25 The profits calculated in the example tend to overstate the drug firm's true profits because it may incur research and testing costs for drugs that never reach the market. The example shows what happens when the drug producer "wins" in its research "gamble" to produce a new drug. The gains from such wins must be reduced by the losses from efforts that fail if we are to have a true picture of the firm's profits.

FIGURE 3–11
OUTPUT AND PRICE UNDER MONOPOLY AND DECREASING COST

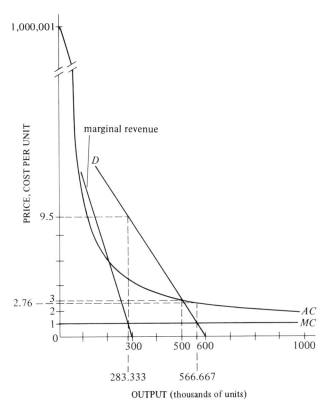

OUTPUT (thousands of units)

The underproduction by the monopolist, the 283,333 versus 566,667 units in Figure 3–11, may be divided into two components: (1) the difference between 500,000 and 566,667 units that is due to decreasing costs and (2) the difference between 283,333 and 500,000 units that is due to profit maximization by a monopolist.

The second source of underproduction may be eliminated by price regulation. If government enforces a price ceiling of $3 per unit, then the firm will be forced to produce 500,000 units just to break even. But such action entails costs: those for obtaining the information required to set the ceiling price and those for enforcing the ceiling.

An alternative policy might be to eliminate the monopoly power by not granting a patent to the firm that discovers and tests the drug. This would permit other firms to produce the drug. And, since they have not incurred the costs of discovering and testing the drug, they could sell it at a price that equals the drug's marginal cost of $1 per unit. As the market price approaches $1, output and sales expand and potential welfare gains from expanding output are eliminated. This alternative policy would seem to be ideal from an efficiency viewpoint. But it is basically unworkable because without patent protection firms would not undertake to discover and test drugs because they could never recover the costs of doing so.

One way to obtain output in excess of 500,000 units would be a government subsidy of $1.76 per unit, with the requirement that the drug sell at a price of $1. Then 566,667 units would be sold, and the total government subsidy would be $1,000,000. Another approach would be for government to undertake the discovery and testing of drugs and then license (at no charge) private firms to produce them.[26] In the present example, the competitive market price would approach $1 and output of the drug 566,667 units. The government subsidy would again be $1,000,000, in the form of the discovery and testing costs that it has incurred but not recovered. In addition, as we noted earlier, the costs of government regulation and subsidy will exceed the amount of the subsidy.

What do we learn from this example? First, the problems posed by monopoly and decreasing cost are of more than academic interest. The high profits of drug producers (relative to other industries) and the high prices of drugs (relative to their cost of production) may be direct reflections of these problems.[27] Second, we can respond to these problems with any one of several government policies. Each policy involves the use of the police power to either control prices or tax. But such government actions are not costless, and they will invariably have distributional consequences that favor some at the expense of others. Even when we look at a specific and realistic case, there is no obvious, appropriate government policy response to the monopoly and decreasing cost problems. Without information about the magnitude and distribution of costs and welfare gains from government action, we cannot even conclude that action is better than no action.

MERIT GOODS

We have so far presumed that consumers will demand the "right," or "socially desirable," amount of each good *if they are confronted with prices that*

---

26 If the government charges a license fee sufficient to cover the discovery and testing costs, that fee will have to be $2 per unit and the market price and output will have to be $3 and 500,000 units, respectively. The purpose of government action, which was to increase output beyond 500,000 units, would thus be defeated.

27 For comparisons of the profits of drug producers with other industries, see *R and D Intensity in the Pharmaceutical Industry: A Composite Profile of Six Major Companies* (Washington, D.C.: J. J. Friedman and Associates, September 1973).

accurately reflect the good's opportunity cost. This view that the consumer is always right is sometimes called the *doctrine of consumer sovereignty.* But it is not fully accepted in any society. Societies invariably attempt to interfere with at least some individual choices on the grounds that people should have more (or less) of some goods than they would freely choose at prices equal to opportunity cost. Goods for which it is thought that consumption should be encouraged are called *merit* goods; goods having the opposite characteristic may be called *nonmerit* goods.

By definition, perfect markets will not optimally supply merit and non-merit goods. And the objective of social policy is interference with and mod-ification of market decisions *even though markets are perfect in the sense we discussed above.* The basis for such intervention, which often involves gov-ernment, may be the presumption that individuals lack the information to act in their own interests. Or it may be the presumption that consumers' tastes are inappropriate and should not be responded to.

Examples include government restriction of the supply of particular com-modities (alcohol, drugs, gambling), government requirements that people attend school for a specified number of years, and government subsidy of the supply of specific commodities (education, low-cost housing).

From these examples it might seem that merit and nonmerit goods are simply those that generate external costs or benefits. Certainly goods that are often termed *merit* (or *nonmerit*) may also give rise to external costs or benefits, as occurs when an intoxicated person drives a car. However, in the case of merit and nonmerit goods, the rationale for interference with indi-vidual choices is that consumption of the commodity is either good (merit) or bad (nonmerit) for the person who consumes or uses the good, regardless of whether other persons are also favorably or unfavorably affected. That is, the merit-good motive for interference does not require the existence of ex-ternal costs or benefits.

Merit goods may also be provided for distributional reasons. People may wish to make minimum levels of necessary goods and services (housing, education, and medical care) available to everyone. But they may not wish to redistribute money incomes so that each person *can* and *will* obtain these levels; doing so would involve too much income equality and therefore too much equality in the availability of other, less necessary, goods and services. That is, people may not care that poor people are deprived of movies, televi-sion, vacations, and nonbasic items of food and clothing. But they may care very much if the poor are deprived of the basic necessities of life.

Merit and nonmerit goods provide a rationale for a government role in resource allocation *even if markets are perfect and there are no externalities and public goods.* In contrast, the governmental roles we discussed earlier rest on market failure — because of decreasing costs, monopoly, etc. The main difficulty with the merit-good rationale is that it presumes the existence of an "elite" group of persons who are better able to make decisions for other people than the people themselves.[28]

INCOME DISTRIBUTION IN A MARKET ECONOMY

The income that a person receives in a market economy depends largely upon the amount of resources (labor, capital, land) that he or she owns and the price he or she can obtain for the resources. Like the prices of goods, the prices of resources depend on demand and supply. But in this case the producers are the demanders and the households are the suppliers. Resource prices determine in turn the incomes of resource owners.

But the incomes of individuals are not derived solely from the value of the resources they own. Some people may have inherited wealth or have received gifts or have had a windfall change in the value of their assets. Such sources of income are "unearned" in that they are not a reward for productive effort. In other words, they are not derived from current production and are largely a matter of chance. To receive what is generally considered a satisfactory income in a market economy, individuals must be productive and have the capacity to earn income, or they must be lucky and receive adequate fortuitous income. If some individuals are neither productive nor lucky, they must rely on charitable contributions from friends and relatives.

However, voluntary efforts to reduce poverty are frustrated by the *free-rider* problem. Each nonpoor person may well want to raise the income of the poor but may not voluntarily transfer income to the poor. Why? Because the nonpoor person believes that his or her efforts will be ineffectual or that the charitable contributions of others will be sufficient. *With all nonpoor people thinking and acting that way, voluntary contributions will not reduce poverty to a level that the nonpoor in fact prefer.* The government can eliminate free riders by using its police power to tax and transfer income. And individuals may want to submit to this kind of governmental activity because they recognize that the free-rider problem is an obstacle to achieving an equitable distribution of income. Of course, government activities that redistribute income and wealth need not make the distribution more equitable, but there is the possibility of doing so.

In Chapter 6 we will deal more fully with the issues of income and wealth distribution. At this point, we need only recognize that government can

28 For further discussion of the concept of merit goods, see Lester C. Thurow, "The Economics of Public Finance," *National Tax Journal* (June 1975): 193; and Kenneth J. Arrow, "Values and Collective Decision Making," in Edmund S. Phelps, ed., *Economic Justice* (Baltimore: Penguin, 1973), especially pp. 125–126.

alter the market-determined distribution, which is likely to be viewed as inequitable by many people. In addition, as we noted above, some initial distribution of income and wealth, determined in part by government action, is
required for market activity, even though market activity subsequently modifies the initial distribution.

SUMMARY

Perfectly competitive markets achieve an efficient allocation of resources if
there are no public goods and externalities and if costs are not decreasing.
An efficient allocation of resources exists for each distribution of income,
and a change in the distribution of income will usually change what constitutes an efficient allocation of resources. Thus, if income is distributed very
unequally, allocative efficiency may call for the production of luxury goods,
while the basic needs of the poor go unmet. Such an outcome may be distasteful, but it is not an argument against efficiency. It argues, instead,
against the income inequality that gives rise to the distasteful pattern of
demand and output.

Market processes are likely to result in underproduction of commodities
when markets are imperfectly competitive or when unit production costs are
decreasing. The exception occurs when discriminatory pricing is feasible
and at a sufficiently low cost. Otherwise, market processes fail and there is
potentially a welfare gain from government action that increases output.
However, government action to realize this gain may be undesirable for
three reasons: First, there may not be a *net* welfare gain from government
action because the action is too costly. Second, even if a net welfare gain is possible, it may not be achieved if government overproduces or
underproduces. Indeed, the result may be a welfare loss if government-
induced overproduction is sufficiently great. Third, with market-determined
output, those who consume a good pay for its production, even though the
output level may be less than optimal. But with government-determined
output, there is the possibility that the costs of producing a good may be un-
fairly distributed — for example, to nonbeneficiaries or to the poor. In the
final analysis, whether government should try to remedy market failure in
decreasing-cost and imperfectly competitive market situations is an empirical
question that can not be answered without information about the costs and
equity consequences of such action. The information needed to reach a
judgment on this question is typically not available. Policy makers and society therefore face the dilemma of either living with the probably inefficient
outcome of market processes or taking government action that may either
improve upon or be inferior to the market outcome on efficiency or equity
grounds.

In the case of merit and nonmerit goods, government may intervene in market processes even though there is no presumption that markets have failed to meet consumer demands and allocate resources efficiently. The purpose of this intervention is to prevent consumers from exercising free choice, presumably because consumers will fail to act in their own interests. This basis for government intervention is paternalistic, if not elitist, because it presumes that some person (or persons) can better choose for other persons than the persons themselves.

Markets and other nongovernment institutions for economic decision making cannot operate well without a system of property rights (a distribution of income and wealth) and rules of exchange. And perhaps the most fundamental and widely accepted economic role for government is that of defining and enforcing property rights. Through the use of the police power of the state, property rights and rules of exchange can be defined and enforced, conceivably in a manner that is both more equitable and less costly than would be the case in the absence of government. Because market-generated distributions of income can be unsatisfactory, there is a continuing need (or role) for government redistribution activities. A government role in the redistribution of income and in the definition and enforcement of property rights and rules of exchange may be desirable even if markets are perfect and there are no public goods and externalities.

SUPPLEMENTARY READINGS

Bator, Francis. "The Anatomy of Market Failure." *Quarterly Journal of Economics*, August 1958, pp. 351–379.

Bohn, Peter. *Social Efficiency*, chaps. 1, 2. New York: Wiley, 1973.

Dorfman, Robert. *The Price System*. Englewood Cliffs, N.J.: Prentice-Hall, 1964.

CHAPTER FOUR

AN ECONOMY WITH PUBLIC GOODS

What allocation and distribution problems arise if public as well as private goods exist in an economy? Building on the analysis of Chapter 3, we see that when there are public goods, there is a potential for improving allocative and distributive outcomes through government action. But government action may also worsen outcomes, and so we must look at the conditions under which such action will be beneficial rather than harmful. We will see that the desirability of a policy or action depends on both the magnitude of the net gains from the action and the distribution of those gains among members of the community.

To demonstrate the potential economic role of government, we will first show how much of a public good will be supplied by a market system and then ask how changing this market-determined supply via government action affects the welfare of the members of a community.

MARKET SUPPLY OF PUBLIC GOODS

How will a market system allocate resources to the production of a public good? How does the presence of a public good alter the conclusions of Chapter 3 about the market's efficiency in allocating resources? To answer these questions, let us again construct demand and supply curves for a good, X, and examine the characteristics of market equilibrium. The assumptions of Chapter 3 are retained, except that X is a public rather than a private good.[1]

The supply curve, $S(MC)$, for X is the same as in the private goods case.[2]

1 Public goods are defined in Chapter 3, p. 48.

2 See Chapter 3, p. 57.

FIGURE 4-1
MARKET OUTPUT OF A PURE PUBLIC GOOD

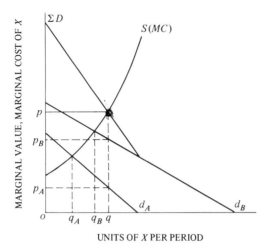

UNITS OF X PER PERIOD

The individual demand curves for the public good X are also unchanged in definition and interpretation from the case in which X was a private good. The demand curves for two individuals, A and B, are shown in Figure 4-1 (d_A and d_B, respectively). If they are the only individuals in the community, what is the community's demand curve?

The community demand curve shows the marginal value of X to the community — the value of the other goods that persons in the community, taken together, are willing to give up for an additional unit of X. Since any unit of X can be made available to every member of the community without reducing the amount available to any member, the marginal value to the community is the *sum* of the individual marginal values. This is shown by a curve ΣD in Figure 4-1. For example, to determine how much the community values the qth unit of X, we note that A and B place values on the qth unit of p_A and p_B, respectively. Hence, the value to the community is $p_A + p_B = p$. Other points on ΣD are determined in a similar fashion.[3]

3 The curve ΣD for a public good is similar to the market, or community, demand curve for a private good in that both show the marginal value of the good to the members of the community. In the case of public goods, and in contrast with private goods, the expressed, or *effective*, demand of the members of the community may not be that for which marginal value equals price. As we shall see later, the effective demand for public goods depends upon the mechanism of collective choice. For this reason ΣD is sometimes called a *pseudo demand curve*.

DEMAND AND SUPPLY EQUILIBRIUM

How much X will be provided, given demands and supply as we just defined them? In Figure 4–1, A's marginal value of X exceeds the marginal cost of X for quantities up to q_A units, while B's marginal value exceeds marginal cost for quantities up to q_B units. So, the maximum that A would purchase at a price equal to marginal cost is q_A, while this maximum for B is q_B.

However, if A should first purchase q_A units, then those units would also be available to B, who would then be willing to purchase only $q_B - q_A$ additional units. Similarly, if B should purchase q_B units, then A would purchase nothing. So, each person's purchases of the good affects the other's willingness to purchase it.

In no case is either A or B willing to bear the full cost of extending output beyond q_B, although B as an individual would demand and pay for an output of q_B. Therefore we might expect the market-determined output of X to be at least as great as q_B. The exception to this conclusion arises if A and B behave strategically, each waiting for the other to purchase, each hoping thereby to minimize their own outlays. In this case, the output of X for the community could be zero.

Such strategic behavior is a small-group phenomenon. In a large group, each person's decisions have little impact on others. A person therefore has little to gain by deferring purchases of a commodity that would be beneficial in the expectation that the delay might induce others to purchase more than they would otherwise purchase. Our examples include only two persons for the purpose of making the graphs simple and easy to read. But the main concern of our analysis is the large group case, so we assume that strategic behavior does not occur.

Given that market output is at least as great as q_B in the absence of a strategic behavior, is it possible that it will exceed q_B? To answer that question, first note that in Figure 4–1 the marginal cost of X exceeds the marginal value of X to either A or B when the output of X exceeds q_B: No *person is willing to pay the full cost of producing an additional unit.* And, for *any* person to demand a quantity greater than q_B, the price to the person must be less than the marginal cost of X. Therefore, for market output to exceed q_B, the supplier must charge a price to each buyer that is less than the marginal cost of X. That is, the supplier must recover the cost of producing each unit of X from more than one buyer.

If such pricing is feasible and costless, the supplier can charge prices p_A and p_B to A and B, respectively, with the result that both A and B demand q units of output. And the sum of the prices paid by the two persons equals the marginal cost of X at q, while the price to each buyer is equal to the buyer's marginal value of X at that output. A market output of q is an equilibrium output when pricing is costless; at outputs less than q, the sum of the prices that people are willing to pay for an additional unit of X (the sum of the marginal values of X as given by ΣD) exceeds its cost, while the sum of these prices falls short of the marginal cost of X at outputs in excess of q.

To price in this manner, suppliers must be able to exclude some persons (those who do not pay) from consumption of a particular unit of X, while making the unit of X available to other persons (those who pay). To see why, note that if a supplier charges A a price of p_A and then meets A's demand of q units, then q units are also available to B because X is a public good. Consequently, B has no incentive to pay any of the cost of producing X unless suppliers can artificially exclude B from consuming the X that has already been produced for A.[4] If such exclusion is possible, then B can be induced to pay up to p_B per unit for q units and suppliers cover their costs. However, if B cannot be excluded, then revenues fall short of costs and an output in excess of q_B is not possible.

The same reasoning applies if B makes the initial purchase or if A and B make simultaneous purchases. In the case of simultaneous purchases, they each would soon see that they can enjoy the X purchased by the other, and therefore would reduce their own purchases *unless* the producer has the capability of excluding the nonpurchaser. That is, in the absence of exclusion, each person will attempt to be a free rider. As an example, let us consider the provision of television programming to a community. Producers sell television programs to some or all members of the community. If this programming is transmitted unscrambled over the entire area of the community, people will quickly realize that they can enjoy the programs without paying. However, by scrambling the signals and selling devices to unscramble them, the producer is able to exclude nonpayers, and a pure public good (television signals) becomes marketable.

This exclusion capability is not costless,[5] so output may not be expanded, even if it is technically feasible to do so. The value of the additional output to the community may fall short of the cost of producing the additional X *and* the exclusion costs. In the television program example, the exclusion costs are the costs of the scrambling and unscrambling devices.

Even if exclusion costs are sufficiently low that market output exceeds q_B, it may not reach q. For the market output to be q, suppliers must not only be able to exclude nonpayers from the consumption of X but also be able to

---

4 This problem does not arise for outputs of X less than q_B because the producer can collect the full cost of producing X from a single person. That is, B will purchase and producers will supply q_B units even if A is a free rider. In contrast, for output to exceed q_B neither person can be a free rider.

5 As explained later, the cost of excluding nonpayers generally depends on legal institutions and the distribution of property rights.

charge a price to each person that is equal to his or her marginal value of X.
For producers to obtain and utilize such information about individual preferences is costly, if not impossible. In other words, suppliers must employ
discriminatory pricing, which, as we saw in Chapter 3, is difficult and
costly.[6]

What conclusions can we reach about the market output of a public
good? First, in the absence of strategic behavior, market output should be at
least as great as the maximum output that any one person in the community
is willing to purchase unaided by others (q_B in Figure 4–1). This output
could be zero or nearly so in the case of such goods as national defense or
television "specials" that are very costly per unit. Figure 4–2 shows this zero
output case, where marginal cost exceeds the marginal values of both A and
B for the first unit of production. Second, market output may exceed q_B if

FIGURE 4–2
A HIGH-COST PUBLIC GOOD WITH ZERO MARKET OUTPUT

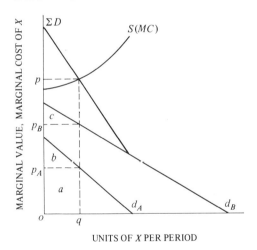

UNITS OF X PER PERIOD

---

6 Moreover, when exclusion is not feasible, the information needed for discriminatory pricing
is even more difficult and costly to obtain than in the private-good–low-exclusion-cost example
in Chapter 3. If nonpayers are not excluded, individuals lack an incentive to reveal their true
preferences (willingness to pay) for X. If asked directly, they will tend to understate their
marginal value in order to minimize the price they pay, provided they believe that their
payment will depend on their answer. If they believe their payment for the good will not
depend on their answer, then they will overstate their demand, asking for additional X as long
as it has any value at all — as long as the marginal value of X is positive. And, even if preferences would be revealed by a survey, surveys are costly. Alternatives to direct questioning are
also costly and likely to provide imperfect information.

the cost of excluding nonpayers is sufficiently low; but it would never exceed q, even in the case of zero exclusion costs. Third, for market output to reach this maximum (q), the price to each buyer must be equal to his or her marginal value of X at q, which is p_A for A and p_B for B. Such pricing usually means that each person cannot be charged the same price. Because discriminatory pricing is costly, a market output of q has to be viewed as extremely unlikely.

In the preceding analysis we presume that individuals act *independently* in the market place; that is, they adjust independently to market prices. The market equilibrium thus determined can be termed an *independent adjustment* equilibrium.

EFFICIENCY OF MARKET EQUILIBRIUM

In the absence of strategic behavior, individuals acting independently in the market determine an output of a public good that has as a lower limit the maximum output that any *one* person is willing to pay the full cost of providing (q_B in Figure 4–1). The upper limit is the amount for which the good's marginal value to the community just equals its marginal cost (q in Figure 4–1). Because of high exclusion and information costs, the market-determined output for most public goods usually will be at the lower end of this range. Is this output level (q_B) economically efficient?

To answer this question, let us first note that extending output beyond q_B produces a potential welfare gain for both A and B or, more generally, for all members of the community. The reason is that until the output of q is reached, the value that A and B *together* place on additional units of X (shown by the ΣD curve) exceeds the cost of additional units (shown by the S curve). Therefore, for outputs less than q it is conceivable that the cost of producing each unit of X can be distributed among members of the community in such a way that members each pay something less than they are willing to pay. That is, the welfare of each member of the community can conceivably be increased by collective action that expands the output of X to q and distributes the costs of output expansion in such a way that no one is made worse off. Such action is collective in that the costs of additional X are shared and there must therefore be some collective or group decision about cost sharing and the additional amount of X to be produced. Collective action may, but need not, involve government. If such collective action is both feasible and costless, then q is economically efficient and a market-determined output of less than q is inefficient.

In contrast, for outputs in excess of q, there is no way to distribute the cost of the additional X without causing some people to pay more than they are willing to pay. *Correspondingly, extending output beyond* q *can never be consistent with economic efficiency because it necessarily makes some person worse off.*

Is q the economically efficient level of output if the collective action required to extend output from q_B to q is not costless, as seems likely?[7] The answer is yes if two conditions are met. First, the value that the community places on the additional X must now exceed *both* the cost of collective action and the cost of producing the additional X. Second, the collective-action costs must either not depend on the output of X (i.e., they must be lump sum) or, if they do, they must be zero for the marginal unit of X (the qth unit).

These two conditions are met in the cases depicted in Figures 4-3 and 4-4. In Figure 4-3 collective-action costs are lump sum, in an amount represented by the shaded rectangle.[8] The welfare gains ignoring collective-action costs are represented by the area of triangle *abc*. The net gain from extending output to q is the difference between the area of triangle *abc* and the area of the shaded rectangle. This difference is positive for the case of Figure 4-3. However, it could be negative for every mechanism of collective action, in which case q_B would be economically efficient. Otherwise, q would be economically efficient, if collective-action costs are lump sum.

In Figure 4-4 the costs of collective action depend on the amount by which output is extended. These variable costs of collective action should be added to the marginal cost of producing X to obtain the full costs of obtaining additional units of X. The result is a new marginal cost curve, such as $S''S'$ in Figure 4-4. The difference between $S''S'$ and SS' represents the variable cost of collective action, which is zero at q. For the case illustrated, the net welfare gain from extending the output of X to q is positive, equal to the difference between the area of triangle *abc* and the shaded area under the $S''S'$ curve. However, this difference could be negative, in which case q_B is efficient because someone must suffer a net welfare loss if output is expanded beyond q_B.

In Figure 4-5 the costs of collective action are again variable, but they are

7 We will discuss the nature of the costs of collective action and some of the factors that determine them later in this chapter.

8 This and subsequent discussions assume that costs and benefits accrue within a single period, which greatly simplifies exposition and allows us to capture the essence of the problem. In reality, however, some costs of collective action may be one-time costs, e.g., the cost of writing and passing a statute that enables the collective action to take place. Such one-time costs are in the nature of an investment that can be allocated over the period that represents the time horizon of policy makers, in which case the one-time costs are included in the per period costs of collective action. Alternatively, the investment represented by these one-time costs can be compared to the present value of the net welfare gains it generates. If this present value exceeds the one-time costs, then the investment in setting up a means of collective action is efficient.

FIGURE 4–3
WELFARE GAINS FROM COLLECTIVE ACTION
WHEN COLLECTIVE-ACTION COSTS ARE LUMP SUM

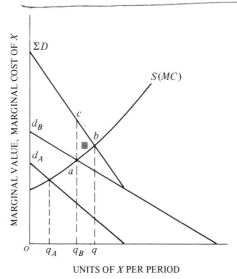

UNITS OF X PER PERIOD

FIGURE 4–4
WELFARE GAINS FROM COLLECTIVE ACTION
WHEN MARGINAL COLLECTIVE-ACTION COSTS APPROACH ZERO

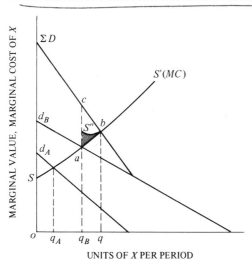

UNITS OF X PER PERIOD

FIGURE 4–5
WELFARE GAINS FROM COLLECTIVE ACTION
WHEN MARGINAL COLLECTIVE-ACTION COSTS ARE POSITIVE

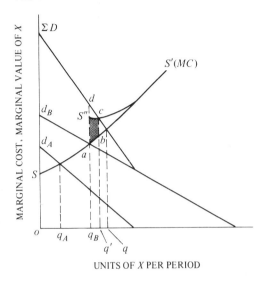

UNITS OF X PER PERIOD

not zero at q. In this case, q is not efficient. Instead, q' is efficient because the marginal value of X to the community (shown by the ΣD curve) equals the marginal cost of producing X *plus* the marginal cost of collective action to extend the output of X beyond q_B (as shown by $S''S'$). The community's net gain from acting collectively to extend the output of X is the difference between the area *abcd* and the shaded area under the $S''S'$ curve. If marginal costs of collective action are large enough that the $S''S'$ curve intersects the ΣD curve at or to the left of point d, then q_B is efficient.

Whether q is efficient when positive costs of collective action are allowed depends on whether the collective action produces a net welfare gain once costs of action are considered and on whether the marginal cost of collective action is positive at q. It is thus an empirical question whether the market equilibrium output is inefficient. We must therefore know the marginal value of X to the community, the marginal cost of X, and the costs of collective action. Without such information, we cannot state that a market process of resource allocation will result in an inefficient output of the public good, X. Stated differently: *We cannot say that the market fails to allocate resources efficiently to the production of a public good unless we can show that there exists a mechanism of collective action by which resources can be reallocated (e.g., by increasing the output of* X*) so as to make some members of the community better off and none worse off. This statement is valid even if the market allocation results in none of the public good being produced.*

It might be possible to drop the requirement that no one be made worse off by collective action in favor of a less restrictive requirement that the net welfare gains (inclusive of costs of collective action) of the gainers exceed the net welfare losses of the losers. But even if this suggestion were followed, the preceding conclusion still stands: Whether the market fails when there are public goods is still an empirical question. However, collective action may be less costly to undertake in this second case because the action no longer has to be such as to harm no one. Consequently, the conclusion that markets fail and collective action is justified may be reached more frequently.

In the preceding analysis we presumed that the market is as effective as a market can be in realizing consumer welfare gains. That is, the market structure is competitive and therefore not in itself a factor that prevents efficiency. As we saw in Chapter 3, and as we shall see later in our discussion of externalities, markets do not always perform as well as they might. And the improvement of market mechanisms therefore may be an alternative to nonmarket collective action.

COSTS OF COLLECTIVE ACTION

In the preceding discussion we saw that the nature and magnitude of collective-action costs determine whether the market output of a public good is efficient. In this section we will define more carefully the costs of collective action, and look at some of their determinants.

An increase in the supply of a public good beyond the market-determined output requires the implementation of a group or community agreement or contract to (1) increase the output of the public good and (2) share in some specified way the costs of doing so. Each member of the community may benefit from and therefore has an incentive to reach such an agreement. However, members each have an incentive to try to minimize their contributions to the costs of expanded output (to be a free rider) because their benefits from the expanded output are not necessarily dependent on their particular contributions. Paradoxically, people serve their own self-interests by both making and subsequently breaking the agreement. The agreement is not self-enforcing. Because of this conflict of interest, reaching an agreement is essentially a collective bargaining process. And reaching and enforcing an agreement to expand output usually will not be costless; there will be costs of collective action.[9]

---

9 Of course, decision making through market processes also absorbs resources (involves costs). Businesses gather information, for example, through market surveys, and expend resources debating and deciding upon plans. Likewise, consumers use time and resources in deciding how much of each good they will buy. But these decision-making costs of businesses and consumers tend to be reflected in the market prices of products.

The costs of collective action through government take a variety of forms in the present-day United States. The direct costs of making and enforcing collective decisions are the costs of operating the legislative, executive, and judicial branches of federal, state, and local governments.[10] Nongovernmental costs of collective action include the resources absorbed by the lobbying, consumer interest, and research groups that advocate, oppose, and generate information about public policies. Nongovernment costs also include the costs that individuals and businesses incur as they comply with collective decisions as, for example, with tax laws or pollution control regulations. Taken together, these costs of collective action (CCA) fall into two categories:

1. Negotiation costs, which are the costs of reaching an agreement about the amount of a public good and the sharing of its costs.

2. The costs of implementing, enforcing, and complying with the agreement, called *enforcement costs* for convenience.

NEGOTIATION COSTS

Negotiation costs arise because there are many ways to share the cost of producing a public good. Moreover, there is no obvious and necessary link between a person's share of the cost and the benefits that person derives from the public good. Consequently, a decision to produce some amount of a public good and share the production costs will entail the use of resources to communicate and bargain, as individuals each try to make the agreement as advantageous as possible from their own points of view or, at a minimum, try to assure that the agreement is one that does not reduce their own welfare. Negotiation costs are exemplified by the resources used in the political process by which Congress and state legislatures arrive at agreement on laws, funding of public activities, etc.

Included in negotiation costs are information costs. Information is needed about the preferences of the various members of the community and the costs of producing the good. Ideally, what is needed is knowledge of the individual demand and cost schedules depicted in Figure 4–1. This information is needed to determine how much of other goods people are willing to give up and must give up to have additional units of the public good.

We can see why negotiation costs arise by referring to Figure 4–2 (p. 86). We have already seen that one way of sharing the cost of producing q units of X is to charge p_A to A and p_B to B, with the total cost to A and B being

10 A rough estimate of these costs are the general control and administration expenditures of government, which are about 2 percent of the expenditures of all levels of government.

$p_A \times q$ and $p_B \times q$, respectively. But this is only one of an infinite number of ways of sharing the cost of the efficient output level, because both A and B are willing to pay more for q. Recalling the concept of consumer surplus, we can see that A is willing to pay not only $p_A \times q$, which is the rectangular area a, but the amount of the triangular area b as well. And B is willing to pay the amount of area c, as well as $p_B \times q$. The more one person pays, the less the other has to pay. Resolving this conflict requires the use of resources and adds to CCA. The efficient level of output of X is thus consistent with any number of cost-sharing arrangements or distributions of real income between A and B.[11] We made the point that efficiency does not depend upon a particular distribution of income in Chapter 3 in connection with the production of private goods. This principle holds for public goods as well.

ENFORCEMENT COSTS

Once an agreement is negotiated, it must be implemented. Even if every person gains from the agreement, that is, even if people each value the goods received more highly than the income (resources) given up as their share of the costs, voluntary compliance may not be forthcoming. To see why, let us suppose a particular person reneges and does not contribute all of his or her agreed-upon share of the costs. In particular, suppose that the person reduces that contribution by an amount equal to the cost of 1 unit of the good, with the result that the total supply of the public good is reduced by 1 unit for that person and everyone else in the community. The person who reneges thus loses an amount equal to his or her marginal value of the good and gains an amount equal to the reduction in the contribution, which is the marginal cost of the good. If other persons do not alter their contribution because of one person's reneging, that is, if the agreement does not break down when one person fails to comply, then the person who reneges gains on balance. This is so because, if an agreement is reached to expand output beyond the market output, the marginal value of the good to any one person would be less than its marginal cost. Therefore, each person sees a potential gain from being a free rider and reneging on the agreement *if* the person thinks that his or her action will not induce others to do likewise. Each person's self-interest is served by making the agreement, but an individual's self-interest may also appear to be served by breaking the agreement. Of course, if everyone reasons in this manner, the agreement breaks

11 In this example we have assumed no *income-feedbacks*. That is, we assume that different cost-sharing arrangements (real incomes) will not influence the positions of A's and B's demand curves.

down. Compliance must then be enforced, and enforcement costs must be incurred.·

Having defined CCA, we now can determine what factors influence them and how CCA may differ for governmental and nongovernmental mechanisms. While CCA may depend on a variety of factors, we will discuss only three of the more important ones: (1) exclusion costs, (2) group size, and (3) self-interest.

EXCLUSION COSTS

High exclusion costs, which prevent realization of welfare gains through market processes, also entail high CCA. We have already noted that information about preferences for goods is obtained as persons exchange goods in the market place. For example, if a person buys an apple for thirty cents but does not buy an orange that is also priced at thirty cents, we can conclude that an apple has greater value to the person than an orange and that an apple is at least as valuable as thirty cents' worth of other goods and services, while an orange is not. Preferences are therefore said to be revealed by market exchanges. But this means of obtaining such information for public goods is usually not employed because exclusion is either too costly or infeasible. Among the other mechanisms employed are survey questionnaires. But, as we noted earlier, people may not reveal their true preferences.[12] Preferences may also be revealed as people vote on particular proposals to supply public goods and share in the production costs. But in those cases also, the information obtained will be costly.

Similarly, high exclusion costs contribute to high CCA because agreements, once negotiated, cannot be enforced by exclusion of those who do not comply. In other words, the free-rider problem we discussed earlier arises if and because the person who would renege and be a free rider can not be excluded from the public good provided by the contributions of other members of the group.

Exclusion can be inherently costly and difficult. Or it can be difficult because property rights are not assigned and enforced. For example, scrambling television signals can prevent those who do not purchase or rent the unscrambling devices from viewing programs; exclusion of nonpayers from the use of this public good is possible. However owners of television station

---

12 When exclusion costs are so high as to prohibit exclusion, the quantity of a public good available to each person is the total quantity available to the community. In other words, each person's consumption of the public good cannot be made contingent on his or her payment for the good. Therefore, the person has no incentive to reveal his or her preference (willingness to pay) for the good. See note 6 in this chapter.

franchises typically are not permitted to scramble signals, and the sale of television programs to viewers is therefore not feasible. Exclusion is therefore not feasible because of the way in which the property rights of television franchise owners are defined.

The general conclusion we can draw from this example is that government may influence exclusion costs and CCA as it defines and enforces property rights (or fails to do so). In other terms, government may improve the potential for welfare-enhancing exchanges among individuals by clearly defining and enforcing property rights. This possibility is readily and widely recognized in the case of private goods. But it also exists in the cases of public goods and, as we shall see in the next chapter, externalities.

GROUP SIZE

An agreement is more easily reached and enforced when the interested parties each see their benefits as depending on their contributions to costs. Each individual is motivated both to negotiate an agreement and to make cost contributions as called for by the agreement. This connection between the contribution of each individual and the success of the agreement is most easily established when the group is small. The necessity of a contribution from each individual is more apparent as group size diminishes. In the extreme case of the two-person group, contributions from both parties are obviously required, for example, in going from q_B to q in Figure 4–1. In addition, it is easier (less costly) to detect and bring pressure to bear (for example, contributors may threaten to withdraw their support) on noncontributors in the small group. For these reasons, noncontribution, or free riding, tends to increase as group size increases; as group size increases individuals each view their own participation as increasingly less relevant to the outcome. Therefore, CCA are likely to be an increasing function of group size.

Group size can be effectively reduced to two by requiring unanimous support for any decision to increase supply of the public good; that is, the agreement is automatically voided if anyone fails to contribute.[13] Otherwise, in the large group case, the potential free rider must either be excluded from benefits or induced to contribute, by "moral suasion," through the exercise of the state's police power or by other means. All these actions entail costs. Moreover, the costs of dealing with the free-rider problem without the use of the police power increase as group size increases.[14]

13 Such agreements are costly to negotiate because individuals each have an incentive to withhold their approval of the agreement in an attempt to better their own positions.

14 For further discussion of these notions, see Mancur Olson, Jr., *The Logic of Collective Action* (Cambridge, Mass.: Harvard, 1965).

SELF-INTEREST

In the preceding discussion of CCA, as well as in the analyses of market failure in this and Chapter 3, we presumed that self-interest is the main guide to individual behavior. In pursuit of their self-interests, individuals may fail to reveal their true preferences and willingness to pay for public goods and attempt to be free riders by failing to enter into or comply with a collective agreement to provide public goods. This pursuit of self-interest is clearly a major source of collective action costs.

A behavior alternative would be for people to each voluntarily reveal their true preferences and voluntarily comply with agreements to provide and pay for public goods. One motivation would be the recognition that if everyone would behave in this manner, CCA would be lower and there would be a net welfare gain to be shared by all. That is, CCA would be lower if individuals, rather than being guided by their narrow self-interests, were to act as they would have everyone else act.

This suggests that in dealing with the problems posed by public goods, a society might well consider whether its members can be educated to "act as they would have everyone else act." Such a policy might be a useful supplement to the collective actions, discussed above, that involve the use of the police power of the state. Certainly there is evidence that people are not always guided by self-interest. For example, in a large group a person's single vote is unlikely to affect the outcome of an election, while the act of voting involves a cost of time and other resources. So, in a narrow sense, a person has little to gain by voting. The payoff to voting has to be that people feel they have "done their duty," "behaved as responsible citizens," "acted as they would have others act," etc. Similarly, some people undoubtedly pay their taxes and abide by other collective decisions because it is the "right thing to do," and they would continue to do so in the absence of the threat of fines and incarceration.

Our present purpose is not to quarrel with the view that individuals pursue their self-interest. This view appears, in fact, to be the appropriate basis from which to develop an accurate analysis and understanding of individuals' economic behavior. Instead, our purpose is to suggest (1) that the problems arising from the existence of public goods are aggravated by the pursuit of self-interest and (2) an alternative behavior rule — act as you would have everyone else act — would entail lower CCA.[15]

---

15 This behavior rule would also eliminate or reduce the seriousness of the externality problems to be discussed in Chapter 5. For example, automobile drivers each impose air pollution costs on themselves and others. And each person would prefer that others take actions to reduce the pollutants emitted by their automobiles. So individuals would take action to limit emissions by their own automobiles if they were to follow the rule "act as you would have everyone else act."

GOVERNMENT VERSUS NONGOVERNMENT MODES OF COLLECTIVE ACTION

The conditions under which markets fail and welfare gains from collective action are possible depend on technology and the nature of goods and services produced and demanded by individuals in a community. The conditions are not a function of the social organization and institutions of a society. In other words, these conditions occur in socialist as well as capitalist societies.

Although there may be potential welfare gains from collective action, such action need not involve government and the use of the police power of the state. Whether a government or nongovernment mechanism of collective action is appropriate depends in part on the net welfare gains obtainable with each mechanism. And the differences in net welfare gains associated with each mechanism depend in turn on *differences* in the costs of collective action.

Even if there is a potential for realizing welfare gains without adversely affecting any individual in the community, the *actual* realization of such gains may leave some individuals worse off. And the possibility that an individual may be called upon to give more in support of collective activity than she or he receives in benefits is an important deterrent to such activity. So the desirability of alternative means of collective action also depends on the manner in which each distributes the cost and gains of the action. Whether collective action is in fact undertaken may depend upon the ability of the group to distribute the gains from such action among enough people to assure support.

In short, choice among alternative mechanisms for collective action requires information about both the magnitude and distribution of the net welfare gains obtained with each mechanism. Therefore we will consider in this section whether and why government action may produce greater net welfare gains and a "better" distribution of such gains than other modes of collective action. If we should conclude that both the magnitude and distribution of net welfare gains are inferior for government, as opposed to nongovernment, action, then there would be no economic argument for a government role in decision making about the output of public goods.

Several factors enter into the choice between government and nongovernment modes of collective action to produce and finance the output of a public good: (1) costs of collective action, (2) production costs, (3) optimality of response, and (4) distribution of the costs.[16] We will discuss each of these in turn.

16 Risk is sometimes suggested as an appropriate factor in this choice. Specifically, government action is sometimes advocated on the ground that government can take risks that private firms and individuals cannot. The advantage of government action is presumably that the risk can be spread more broadly. However, it is not clear why government action is preferable to private action with a private insurance mechanism for pooling risk.

COSTS OF COLLECTIVE ACTION

In terms of ascertaining individual preferences and obtaining information about the costs of supplying a public good, both government and private organizations have the same options: (1) election or appointment of persons to make certain decisions, (2) informal discussion and formal debate, (3) surveys of opinion, and (4) direct voting on particular proposals. Each option entails costs that must be incurred *if* information about preferences and costs is to be collected and analyzed. And there is no reason a priori for expecting these information costs to be lower for government than for nongovernment mechanisms of collective action.

In contrast, government may have a cost advantage in its unique power to enforce agreements. In this respect, the fundamental difference between government and nongovernment mechanisms is that government has a monopoly on police power. People are more likely to comply with collective decisions as the cost of noncompliance increases. Using the police power, government can confront persons with relatively costly alternatives to compliance: incarceration, fines, moving to a different political jurisdiction, or revolution. Nongovernment mechanisms, such as clubs and cooperatives, enforce by moral suasion, advertising, monitoring for and publicizing violations, etc.[17] Thus government is a less costly means of collective action if enforcing an agreement by threatening fines and imprisonment for noncompliance absorbs fewer resources than the processes of persuasion, monitoring, ostracizing, etc., used by nongovernment organizations. Such may indeed be the case, since the police power required to back up one threat (enforce one agreement) can also be used to back up other threats.[18]

However, not everyone may gain from the use of the police power to enforce agreements. That is, even if there is a potential for realizing welfare gains without adversely affecting any individual in the community, the actual mechanism by which gains are realized may leave some persons worse off. With the police power, there is less need to take account of individual preferences because most people will comply with decisions rather than go to jail, even though they are called upon to contribute more in support of a collective activity than they receive in benefits.

This ability to ignore some preferences suggests that government may have an advantage in terms of the cost of negotiating an agreement. Information costs and therefore negotiation costs may be lower with government decision making because some preferences can be ignored, but not because

17 Nongovernment mechanisms impose costs that range from the trivial to the significant. The cost of withdrawing from the Jaycees is, perhaps, simply the disapproval of the remaining members. The cost of withdrawing from a labor union may be foregone earnings and the expense of a job search, moving, etc.

18 Recall the related discussion in Chapter 3, p. 52.

it is less costly for government to obtain the information about preferences if it wishes to do so. In the extreme case of a dictatorship, decisions about output and cost sharing can be made somewhat arbitrarily, although not entirely.[19] With representative democracy, individual preferences must be given more weight, and information costs will be higher than with totalitarian governments. Nongovernment organizations will have even higher information costs for any given activity because they can ignore member preferences only at the risk of triggering withdrawal of dissatisfied individuals. Such withdrawal usually is less costly to an individual than is failure to comply with government decisions. Of course, the fact that some preferences can be ignored, with the result that some persons will pay more than they receive from some collective activities, may argue against choosing government as a mechanism for collective decision making.

Government's relative advantage in enforcing agreements is likely to be greater for large groups than small groups. As the number of persons involved increases, people each become more and more likely to think that the final outcome will be unaffected by their own actions. For example, the number of us who would benefit from the discovery of a cure for cancer is certainly very large, and we would each be willing to pay something toward the support of research activities aimed at the discovery of a cure. However, we each also know that total research effort is unlikely to be affected by our individual contributions; therefore, there is the persistent tendency for each of us to forego voluntary contributions because our benefit from the research will be largely independent of our individual contributions. In contrast, if the number of individuals who stand to gain from collective action is very small, individuals are each likely to perceive their own support of the activity as critical to the outcome. And the likelihood of nongovernment, voluntary collective activity becomes greater.[20]

Similarly, the cost of excluding individuals from the benefit of a collective action will also influence the likelihood that it will be a government activity. If the exclusion is not costly, then any individual who does not voluntarily support the collective activity can be denied the benefits of the activity. Therefore a voluntary cooperative organization may undertake the activity. The government power to compel support is not needed. However, if individuals cannot be excluded from benefits or if the cost of doing so is prohibitive, government action, with its power to compel support, may be needed to realize the potential welfare gains from the collective action.

19 Even dictators must take some account of preferences since a government that goes against overwhelming sentiment may face revolution.

20 For example, television transmission to the residents of a small, geographically isolated community; or fire fighting services in a small community supplied by a volunteer fire department (club) rather than government.

PRODUCTION COSTS

So far we have implicitly assumed that both government and nongovernment means of providing public goods have the same production costs. However, both the manner of producing a good and its cost may depend on whether government is involved. For example, people can take measures as individuals to protect their lives and property, such as putting locks on their homes, placing valuables in vaults, and carrying firearms. The cost and quality of protection thus obtained is likely to differ from that provided through community police protection. Similarly, private control of mosquitoes will involve different techniques (yard sprays, screened porches, etc.), have different results, and entail different costs from tax-financed, public measures (aerial spraying, draining ponds, etc.).[21]

OPTIMALITY OF RESPONSE

Regardless of whether welfare gains are realized through government or nongovernment mechanisms, the net gains fall short of the potential by the amount of the CCA. In addition, realized welfare gains may be less than potential gains because the response is nonoptimal. For example, the actual output of the public good may be expanded, but either not far enough or too far. So a third consideration in choosing between government and nongovernment mechanisms is whether the output response is likely to be optimal.

The potential for overexpansion is perhaps greater for government, because individuals' decisions to comply with or support the agreed-upon output expansion with their contributions is not made on the basis of the gains that they perceive from the expansion. Instead, decisions are related to the costs (incarceration, fines) that people associate with nonpayment of taxes — noncompliance. So individuals may be induced to support output in excess of the efficient amount at which marginal social benefits just balance marginal social costs. That is, in the case of the large group, the benefits from paying taxes or otherwise complying with a collective agreement are essentially the benefits derived from the prevention of the punishment and costs associated with noncompliance, because the availability of the additional output is not conditional upon any single individual's contribution.[22] In contrast, with nongovernment mechanisms, each person's contribution tends to be related to perceived benefits from the expanded output of the good, not just the perceived benefits of compliance per se. And the likelihood of production at less than the efficient level is perhaps greater.

21 For further discussion, see Gordon Tullock, "Social Cost and Government Action," *American Economic Review*, 59, No. 2 (May 1969): 189–197.

22 Recall the related discussion in Chapter 3, p. 70.

COST DISTRIBUTION

Although resource reallocation is the basic reason for a collective action, some income redistribution almost invariably occurs in practice. This redistribution may or may not be desirable, depending on one's judgment about what constitutes an equitable distribution of income. Generally, government and nongovernment mechanisms have different distributive consequences. Nongovernment mechanisms have a greater chance of imposing costs on those who benefit from and are willing to pay for the output expansion. Or, at least, they have little potential for imposing costs in excess of perceived benefits. In contrast, governments may impose costs on nonbeneficiaries, a fact that may or may not be an advantage in particular circumstances.

SUMMARY

A decision to take collective action to expand the output of a public good beyond the market-determined output should take account of (1) costs of collective action (CCA), (2) the likelihood of nonoptimal (inefficient) adjustment of output, and (3) income redistribution effects. Whether collective action in any form, and government action in particular, is warranted (on equity or efficiency grounds or both) depends on these three factors as well as on the potential welfare gains. It is an empirical question that cannot be answered in general, but must be answered on a case by case basis.

The costs of providing public goods must be distributed among members of the community. Doing so determines each person's net benefits from government action. Increasing the costs borne by one person reduces the net benefits of that person while increasing the net benefits of other persons. So people are likely to disagree about the distribution of the costs of government. This conflict of interest may prevent action to increase the efficiency of resource allocation. And if it does not, it surely increases the costs of collective action.

SUPPLEMENTARY READINGS

Bowen, Howard R. *Toward Social Economy*, chap. 18. New York: Rinehart, 1948.

Buchanan, James M. *The Supply and Demand of Public Goods*, chap. 2, 3. Chicago: Rand McNally, 1968.

Burkhead, Jesse, and Miner, Jerry. *Public Expenditure*, chap. 2. Chicago and New York: Aldine, 1971.

Demsetz, Harold. "The Exchange and Enforcement of Property Rights." *Journal of Law and Economics* 7 (October 1964): 11–31.

————. "Contracting Costs and Public Policy." In *The Analysis and Evaluation of Public Expenditures: The PPB System*, Vol. 1, p. 167. U.S. Congress, Subcommittee on Economy in Government of the Joint Economic Committee, 91st Cong. Washington: 1969.

McKean, Roland N. *Public Spending*. New York: McGraw-Hill, 1968.

Samuelson, Paul A. "Diagrammatic Exposition of a Theory of Public Expenditures." *Review of Economics and Statistics* 37 (November 1955): 350–356.

CHAPTER FIVE

EXTERNALITIES

Externalities are pervasive and significant phenomena in modern societies.[1] There are, for example, external benefits from education:[2] children gain from having educated parents; society benefits insofar as education reduces crime, social unrest, and unemployment and welfare costs; society benefits from an educational system that inculcates acceptable social values, improves communication, and strengthens democratic institutions; etc. On the external cost side are the many forms of pollution and other disamenities. Although data on pollution costs are approximate, the available estimates indicate that such costs may be substantial.[3] One study estimates that in the United States the cost of urban disamenities — pollution, litter, congestion, noise, etc. — is about 8 percent of average family disposable income.[4]

In the first part of this chapter we will see how markets may fail to achieve efficient resource allocation when externalities are present and how such failure depends on the costs of collective action, the laws governing property rights, and the liabilities for external costs. How property rights and external cost liabilities should be assigned is a question of equity. So, both equity and efficiency issues almost always arise when attempts are made to control externalities. In the second part of the chapter we will examine government's

---

1 The concept of externality was defined in Chapter 3, p. 49.

2 See Burton A. Weisbrod, "Education and Investment in Human Capital," *Journal of Political Economy*, 70, No. 5 (1962), Part 2 (Supplement): 106–123.

3 For a review of studies estimating pollution damage costs, see Anthony C. Fisher and Frederick M. Peterson, "The Environment in Economics: A Survey," *Journal of Economic Literature*, 14 (March 1976): 1–33.

4 William D. Nordhaus and James Tobin, "Is Growth Obsolete?" *Economic Growth* (New York: National Bureau of Economic Research, 1972), p. 54.

role in adjusting for externalities. This second part is not intended to show that government is the appropriate institution for dealing with all externality problems; it shows instead the efficiency and equity implications of different mechanisms for controlling externalities.

EXTERNALITIES AND MARKET FAILURE

To see how externalities affect the efficiency of market allocation, let us consider a case in which the production of a commodity, say iron, generates air pollution that adversely affects the welfare of the people in the surrounding community. The cost of iron thus has two components: (1) the cost of the labor, machines, iron ore, coal, and other inputs directly required to produce the iron; and (2) the costs borne by members of the community in the form of air pollution damages.

Looking at Figure 5–1 we see that the marginal cost (MC) schedule shows how the first category of costs varies as the output of iron varies. The social marginal cost (SMC) schedule shows the additional costs, both direct and air pollution costs, associated with additional units of output. The vertical difference between the two schedules represents the pollution damages associated with each unit of iron production. Pollution damages are defined as the amounts that all persons affected by the pollution would pay to eliminate the pollution. For example, the shaded area of Figure 5–1 represents the amount that those damaged by pollution would pay to have pollution reduced from the level associated with iron output of q' to the lower pollution level associated with q.

The market demand schedule for iron is D. Given these demand and cost schedules, firms will produce q' units to be sold at price p', if (1) markets are competitive, (2) pollution is legal, (3) firms do not have to compensate anyone damaged by the air pollution, and (4) those damaged by pollution do not bribe firms to produce less. Under these assumptions, the competitive market equilibrium price and quantity are p' and q', respectively.[5]

Although an output of q' is the competitive market equilibrium, there is a potential welfare gain for all persons to be obtained by reducing output. To see why, note that the air pollution cost associated with the q' unit of output is the distance ef. Those damaged by pollution would be better off if they were to pay any amount less than ef to producers to induce them not to

---

5 The market is in equilibrium at p' and q' because to the left of q' price exceeds private marginal cost; competitive suppliers will increase output in an attempt to capture the profit represented by the excess of price over marginal cost. On the other hand, if output exceeds q' units, then marginal cost exceeds price; suppliers will reduce output because a loss is incurred on each unit produced in excess of q'.

FIGURE 5–1
SOCIAL COST, MARKET EQUILIBRIUM, AND EFFICIENCY

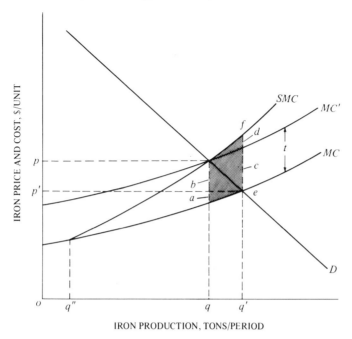

IRON PRODUCTION, TONS/PERIOD

produce the q' unit. Any such payment would also make the producers better off since they earn zero profit on the q' unit. Therefore there is potential welfare gain for all parties if the q' unit is not produced. Similarly, for all units in the range q to q', the pollution damages per unit exceed producer and consumer surplus per unit; those who are damaged by pollution would gain enough from reducing the output to more than compensate the producers and consumers of iron for the reduced output. If output is reduced from q' to q, pollution damages fall by the amount represented by the area $a + b + c + d$. Producer and consumer surplus taken together fall by area $a + b$. The potential net welfare gain is thus the area $c + d$.[6] Reducing output below q cannot increase the welfare of all persons (both those damaged

6 We can state this conclusion differently: At the competitive equilibrium output of q', the social marginal cost of iron — the cost that an additional unit of iron production imposes on all members of society — exceeds the marginal value of iron (the price of iron) to iron users because the air pollution costs are external to and therefore ignored by producers in their output decisions. And this is true for all outputs in excess of q. Therefore, if output is reduced to q, there is a potential gain that could be distributed so as to increase the welfare of all members of society.

by pollution and the producers and consumers of iron) because the reduction in pollution damages is less than the fall in producer and consumer surplus. That is, although iron production continues to generate external costs when output is limited to q, such external costs are not *Pareto relevant* because their elimination must make someone worse off.[7]

Reversing the preceding argument establishes that markets may also fail to achieve efficient allocation when external benefits are associated with a production or consumption activity. But in the case of external benefits, the tendency is for the scale of the externality generating activity to be too small. For example, a vaccination for a contagious disease (flu, smallpox, measles) directly benefits the person vaccinated. But it also reduces the ability of the virus to survive and spread among other members of the population and thereby reduces the likelihood that others will contract the disease. This risk reduction is valuable to both vaccinated and unvaccinated persons because vaccines are rarely 100 percent effective. The external benefits of vaccination provide a rationale for public subsidy of the cost of vaccinations, sometimes making them available free of charge, and laws that require vaccination, such as the smallpox vaccination that has been required for entry into public schools.

EFFICIENT ADJUSTMENT FOR EXTERNALITIES

The reasoning in the preceding discussion is typically used to support the conclusion that markets will fail to achieve allocative efficiency when there are externalities. Another conclusion that is sometimes drawn from that same analysis is that externalities require and justify government intervention in allocation decisions if efficiency is sought. But such is not always the case, as we will see in this section. Although external costs and benefits may arise in a variety of ways, we will, in this section, focus on air and water pollution as specific examples of external costs. The analysis for other externalities would be essentially the same.

It will be helpful if we think of pollution control or, more generally, the reduction of external costs as an activity. In the iron production example of the preceding section, pollution control can be achieved by reducing the scale of the pollution generating activity (iron production). Pollution control may also occur as production and consumption processes are altered; for example, scrubbers and filters may lessen air pollution emitted by an iron mill. The value of such pollution control activity is the reduction in the

---

7 For further discussion of Pareto-relevant and irrelevant externalities, see James M. Buchanan and W.C. Stubblebine, "Externality," *Economica*, 29 (November 1962): 37–84.

pollution damages that it brings about. As the degree of control increases, the total damages from pollution decrease, but the total costs of controlling pollution increase. So society may choose to bear fewer pollution costs (damages) by bearing more pollution control costs, but it cannot escape both costs.

The value of an additional unit of control is likely to diminish as total control increases. This relationship is illustrated by the curve *AB* in Figure 5–2, which shows the marginal value of air pollution control — the dollar amounts that all of the members of a community are willing to pay for incremental reductions in pollution (marginal increases in air quality). Alternatively, reading from right to left, *AB* shows the marginal cost of pollution — the minimum incremental loss (damage) that the community incurs as a result of increases in pollution. For the iron production example of Figure 5–1, the vertical distance between the *MC* and *SMC* curves, which ranges from zero at iron output of *q″* to *ef* at iron output of *q′*, represents these pollution damages. The curve *CD* in Figure 5–2 shows the marginal cost of reducing pollution when the *least-cost* means of controlling pollution are used. This marginal cost is the value of the goods and services given up for incremental increases in pollution control — the value of output sacrificed by producing more pollution control devices or producing less of the

FIGURE 5–2
EFFICIENCY IN POLLUTION CONTROL

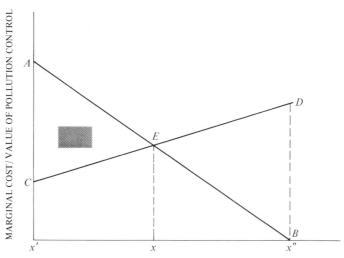

AIR QUALITY MAINTAINED DURING PERIOD (degree of pollution control)

pollution causing output or both.[8] The marginal cost of control increases as the amount of control increases because it becomes increasingly difficult to reduce pollution as the amount of pollutants in the air diminishes. Movement from left to right on the horizontal axis of Figure 5–2 indicates that air pollution damages are decreasing and air quality is increasing because more goods and services are being sacrificed to reduce pollution. To keep the geometry simple, the two curves of Figure 5–2 are assumed to be (1) unaffected by the distribution of the gains from and costs of pollution control and (2) stable over time.

The amount of control provided to the community if people each act independently to maximize their own gain from pollution control is x'. A control level of x' does not mean that no measures are being taken to limit pollution. Instead, at x' no individual is willing to pay the *full* cost of increasing pollution control by an additional unit.[9] For Figure 5–1, this independent adjustment level of control is that associated with iron output of q'. At x'' (in Figure 5–2) all damages from pollution have been eliminated; the marginal value of additional control is zero. The corresponding point in Figure 5–1 is q''.

How much pollution control is efficient? The answer depends on the CCA and the laws that specify the rights of each person to use resources such as air and water, as we will now see. We will begin with the relatively unrealistic case in which CCA are zero.

ZERO COSTS OF COLLECTIVE ACTION

By zero CCA we mean that the net gains from pollution control can be realized without cost through nongovernment modes of collective action. Also, these net gains can be distributed among members of the community in any desired fashion without cost.

Legal pollution   When pollution is legal, the rights to use scarce resources such as air and water are assigned in a particular way. In effect people are given a property right that entitles them to use resources as they see fit, without regard and liability for the costs or damages imposed upon others.

---

8 For the iron production example, if control is achieved by reducing the output of iron, then the marginal cost of control is measured by the incremental loss of producer and consumer surplus that occurs when the output of iron is reduced. This marginal cost is thus the vertical distance between the MC and D curves of Figure 5–1. This vertical distance increases as iron output is reduced below the q' level.

9 This statement rules out strategic behavior by people in the provision of control up to the level of x'.

The community restricts no person's use of air and water; no person is given the right to limit or restrict any other person's use.[10] With this legal arrangement, those who are damaged by pollution bear both the burdens of showing that pollution is undesirable and the costs of any measures taken to limit pollution.[11]

Such an assignment of property rights establishes a status quo at x' in Figure 5–2, which corresponds to q' in Figure 5–1. Control will not exceed x' unless those damaged by pollution arrange for and pay the full costs of pollution control. In Figure 5–2, the aggregate amount that all persons in the community are willing to pay for an additional unit of control exceeds its costs for control levels less than x; the marginal benefit from pollution control exceeds the marginal cost of pollution control in the range x' to x. Given that CCA are zero, it will clearly pay those damaged by pollution to extend control to x but not farther. Those whose activities cause pollution are made no worse off by such an increase in control, because the cost is borne by those damaged by pollution. The move to x is a Pareto improvement, and x is Pareto optimal. In other terms, at x the combined costs of pollution and pollution control are minimized and the community gains from control are maximized. And, because CCA are zero, the members of the community can and will negotiate and enforce an agreement to provide control at the x level without government action.[12] In this case, government action is not required to achieve efficiency.

But extension of control beyond x' does require collective action in that

10 The status quo that prevailed in the United States before 1950 might be described that way, as could the situation that continues to prevail in many instances of pollution.

11 For the iron production example, if pollution is legal, the iron producers are, in effect, given ownership of the air, which they may use as they see fit. And air pollution from iron production can be reduced only if such reduction is either costless or profitable for the producers.

12 In the example of iron production in Figure 5–1, the agreement would be one in which iron producers reduce their output to q in exchange for side payments (bribes) from those damaged by pollution. This payment could be set at t for each unit that the industry's output falls below the q' level. Since producers lose this payment when they sell a unit, the cost of selling a unit increases by t. Producers maximize profits (inclusive of bribes) by reducing output from q' to q because, for the units between q' and q, they make more by not producing the unit and accepting the bribe than by producing and selling the unit. In other terms, the industry receives area $a + b + c$ in bribes and foregoes the area a in profits that would have been earned had the units been produced and sold. The net gain to producers is the area $b + c$, while those damaged by the pollution gain an amount represented by area d. Both producers and those damaged by pollution are better off as a result of this system of bribes, and the air pollution costs of iron production are said to be "internalized." Consumers of iron lose consumer surplus equal to area b, but this loss is less than the producers' gain. So there is the potential for compensating consumers, while leaving producers a net gain of c.

the marginal control cost must be shared if the persons damaged by pollution are to be made better off. The reason is that when control exceeds x', the marginal cost of control exceeds the value that any one person places on additional control. So pollution control is a public good of the kind we discussed in Chapter 4. The benefits of this good are shared by all of those who are damaged by pollution. The amount of pollution control will usually be less than optimal unless there is some collective action to provide and share the costs of that control.

In some instances only a few persons may be damaged by pollution. But in most instances of air and water pollution, and of external costs in general, many parties are damaged. Hence pollution control or the reduction of external costs generally requires collective action by a large group.

Illegal pollution   Let us now assume that air pollution is illegal unless persons who are damaged by pollution are compensated. The effect of this law is to make each member of the community a co-owner (or equal stockholder) of the air, with any decision regarding its use requiring approval by all owners. Persons and firms whose activities have a potentially damaging effect on others have the choice of either preventing the damage or compensating fully all damaged parties. With this legal arrangement, those who cause pollution bear the burden of justifying pollution and the costs of compensating those damaged by any pollution that occurs.

That assignment of costs establishes a status quo at x'' in Figure 5–2 (corresponding to q'' in Figure 5–1), the point at which all pollution damages are eliminated. A control level of x'' is required unless those who bear the cost of control (and would therefore benefit from a reduction in control) take action to reduce control and to compensate those damaged by the consequent increase in pollution.

Since CCA are zero, polluters will act to reduce control from x'' to x because, in the range from x to x'', the incremental payment to those damaged by pollution, given by the AB curve, is less than the marginal cost of pollution control, given by the CD curve.[13] However, if control is reduced below x, the saving of control costs is more than offset by the required increase in compensation payments to those damaged by the resulting

13 In Figure 5–1, illegal pollution means that the iron industry's marginal cost curve is SMC, rather than MC, because it now has to pay the pollution damages associated with each unit of output. If the cost of executing the compensation payments is zero then the industry maximizes profits at q. (Of course, the compensation payments themselves will be positive; what are presumed to be zero are the additional costs of arranging compensation — the costs in time, labor, and materials of processing the claims of damaged parties.)

increase in pollution. An absolute prohibition of pollution would be inefficient because it would not allow realization of such cost savings.

In brief, for the case of zero CCA, the efficient level of control is the same (x in Figure 5–2) whether pollution is legal or illegal. And this efficient level will be provided without government intervention.[14]

NONZERO COSTS OF COLLECTIVE ACTION

The CCA incurred in pollution control efforts and, more generally, in the adjustment of resource allocation to account for externalities, are the costs of operating the bargaining, or political (governmental), process of deciding on and implementing a policy. These costs may be roughly divided into information, transactions, communication, and enforcement costs. In this section, we presume, as is surely the case, that these costs are not zero. We will consider two basic questions: What is the efficient (Pareto-optimal) degree of control if allocation and distribution decisions are costly to make and implement? How is the efficient degree of control affected by the distribution of the combined costs of collective action, pollution control, and pollution?

In answering these questions we will follow the procedure of the preceding section, assuming first that pollution is legal and that all costs are assigned to those who are damaged by pollution and who therefore benefit from control. Then we will assume that the costs are assigned to those who cause pollution, by requiring that they (polluters) either compensate those damaged by pollution or prevent pollution damages.

Legal pollution   The marginal value (AB) and the marginal cost (CD) curves of Figure 5–2 are reproduced in Figure 5–3. At x' the community is placing no restrictions on individuals' use of air, and those damaged by pollution are taking no action to increase control. No laws or contracts are being made and enforced. So, to achieve the x' level of control, the community need incur no *transactions* and *enforcement costs*.[15] But such costs are surely positive for greater control levels. *Information* and *communication costs* need not be zero even at x'; such costs can be incurred in the process

14 For further discussion of zero CCA, see R. H. Coase, "The Problem of Social Cost," *The Journal of Law and Economics*, 3 (October 1960): 1–44.

15 *Transactions costs* are those costs of making payments to and collections from parties to a decision to provide control in excess of the independent adjustment level of x' and thereby distributing the costs of control in a particular fashion. *Enforcement costs* are simply the costs of assuring that all parties comply with any such agreement.

FIGURE 5-3
THE LEGALITY OF POLLUTION AND EFFICIENCY IN POLLUTION CONTROL

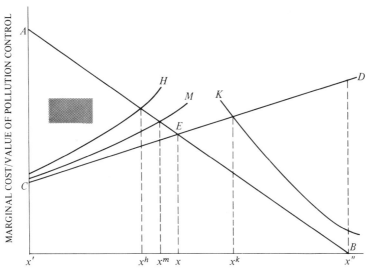

AIR QUALITY MAINTAINED DURING PERIOD (degree of pollution control)

of making a decision to "do nothing" — that is, to leave control at the x' level.[16] However, the information and communication costs of reaching and implementing a decision to provide pollution control in excess of x' are surely as great as the costs of reaching a decision to do nothing. So, with legal pollution, CCA are plausibly at a minimum at x'.

It is also likely that one or more components of the CCA will increase as the chosen control level increases. For example, increasing the control level generally requires control of more instances (sources) of pollution, as well as more intensive control of each source. And, as the control level increases, more individuals may be involved in a collective bid for a further increase in control. Hence, more detailed and accurate information about the costs and

16 *Information costs* arise in obtaining knowledge about the individual and community costs associated with alternative allocative and distributive outcomes. Information costs are negligible if the community is willing to make and accept arbitrary decisions. For example, with legal pollution, information costs are zero if the community is willing to accept the x' control level without comparing it to alternatives. But information is surely needed and information costs are surely positive if the community seeks to minimize the aggregate costs of pollution, pollution control, and collective action, either with or without a constraint on the distribution of those costs.

benefits of control and more communication among affected parties may be required.

CCA generally depend, not only on the level of control, but also on the manner in which the level of control is brought about. For example, pollution control decisions might be made by a private (nongovernment) Clean Air Committee, with increased control being financed from the voluntary contributions of those damaged by pollution. Alternatively, community government could decide upon the level of control and finance the control with a tax. The CCA associated with these two approaches are unlikely to be equal.

Furthermore, CCA depend on how CCA and pollution control costs are distributed among those who benefit from control. For example, such costs might be distributed arbitrarily, the likely result being that some individuals would be made worse off by an increase in control, even though the aggregate gain from the increase exceeds the aggregate cost. Preventing this outcome would require a different and probably more costly distribution mechanism — one that takes account of the value that each individual places on increased control and therefore entails greater information and transactions costs.

The effects of CCA on the choice of pollution control levels are illustrated in Figure 5–3. The *potential* welfare gain from increasing control beyond x' is maximum at x and equal to the area of triangle ACE. To increase control from x' to x in such a way that no one is worse off will entail CCA. If these CCA are lump sum and less than the area of triangle ACE — equal to the shaded rectangle, for example — then x is efficient. So the same degree of control, x, may be efficient with both zero and nonzero CCA. But such need not be the case since x' is efficient if CCA are lump sum and exceed the area of triangle ACE.

But as we noted above, CCA, instead of being lump sum, are likely to increase as the degree of control increases. If so, the efficient degree of control may lie between x' and x. To illustrate, let us suppose that increasing control *in such a way that no one is worse off* involves marginal CCA, as given by the vertical distance between the H and CD curves of Figure 5–3. Some or all members of the community can be made better off without making anyone worse off by extending control to x^h but no further. For control levels below x^h, the marginal cost of control *plus* the marginal CCA fall short of the marginal benefits from control, given by AB. For control levels above x^h, the opposite is true.

Of course, there are many ways of acting collectively to increase control, some of which may make some persons worse off even though aggregate gains exceed aggregate costs. Suppose one such mechanism involves CCA as represented by the curve M. M is likely to lie below H because CCA are likely to be lower when costs and gains do not have to be distributed so that no one is worse off. *Given a decision to use this mechanism*, the optimum degree of control is x^m.

Thus, we see that when CCA are neither lump sum nor zero, the optimum degree of control may depend on the mode of collective action, which may depend in turn on how we wish to distribute both the costs of pollution control and the CCA. That is, what is efficient cannot be determined until a judgment is made about what is equitable (about the distribution of costs). We also see that when pollution is legal, the efficient degree of control with nonzero CCA is less than or equal to the efficient degree for zero CCA, falling in the range x' to x in Figure 5–3. In neither case is the complete elimination of pollution efficient.

Illegal pollution   When pollution is illegal, a status quo is established at x''. A reduction in control from this point entails lower pollution-control costs, higher compensation payments to those damaged by pollution, and CCA in the amount required for the community to reach and implement an agreement to reduce control.

If CCA were zero, the maximum gain from reducing pollution control would be the area of triangle BDE. Hence, when any method of reducing pollution control without making someone worse off involves CCA that are lump sum and greater than the area of triangle BDE, x'' is efficient. However, if such CCA are lump sum and less than the area of this triangle, then x is efficient. If CCA are not lump sum but, instead, increase as control is reduced below the x'' level, then control in the range x to x'' may be optimal. For example, if the marginal CCA for reducing control are given by the vertical distance between AB and K, then x^k is efficient. The reason is that the marginal cost of controlling pollution for control levels greater than (less than) x^k is greater than (less than) marginal compensation payments (given by AB) plus the marginal CCA required to make those payments. In general, when CCA are nonzero, the efficient degree of control will fall in the range x to x''.[17]

GOVERNMENT MECHANISMS OF ADJUSTING FOR EXTERNALITIES

In the preceding section we explored the issues involved in making a decision about the control of externalities. In this section we will look at some of

17 In Figure 5–1, the efficient level of iron production will fall in the range q to q' when the costs of arranging payments to producers are nonzero and pollution is legal. In contrast, with illegal pollution, if the cost of executing compensation payments is positive, the producers may not produce as much as q and will never produce more than q. In either case, the external costs are internalized.

the mechanisms by which government might control externalities, assuming that is desirable. That is, we will see how government mechanisms of control (taxes, regulations, subsidies) work, assuming that both the mechanism of control and the degree of control have been determined, presumably after taking account of the factors we discussed in the preceding section.

DEFINITION AND ENFORCEMENT OF PROPERTY RIGHTS

We have seen that externalities do not result in inefficiency *if* property rights are defined and CCA are sufficiently low. Thus government may, in some cases, prevent inefficiency by clearly defining and enforcing property rights. For example, suppose a small lake has historically been used for fishing, swimming, and waste disposal by persons and businesses located on the surrounding land. When that area was sparsely populated, these uses were not competitive. But population and economic activity have increased to the extent that the waste disposal will soon make the lake unsatisfactory for other uses (fishing and swimming). If the lake belongs to no one, then action to limit waste disposal is unlikely, since no person has a right to demand such limits. However, if the lake belongs to those persons who own the surrounding land, then landowners and lake owners can each act to prevent use of the lake in ways that are incompatible with their own interests. If the number of owners is small, they may be able to reach some agreement about use that preserves water quality. Such agreement is facilitated by government enforcement of each person's property rights. That is, the fact that one owner may sue other owners for damages in government-operated civil courts acts as a spur to agreement and prevents the group of owners from overlooking the interests of any particular owner. But direct government intervention in or sponsorship of such an agreement may not be necessary — if the number of owners is small.

Unfortunately, most instances of pollution involve large numbers of persons and therefore large CCA. Included in these costs are the costs to both plantiffs and defendants of determining, through the judicial process, how the external costs are to be dealt with. Also, when many people are involved, those damaged by pollution may fail to file law suits to limit pollution because people each wait for someone else to act, knowing that they will benefit when others successfully press for pollution control. The present activities of private environmental protection groups such as the Sierra Club illustrate this approach to pollution control and point up the problems. The legal actions of such groups are expensive and time consuming, and the benefits of any reduction in environmental damage that they achieve are widespread. But one person's benefits do not depend on his or her contributing to defray the cost of the action. And people may fail to give financial support to the environmental defense group, even though they value the results obtained.

For these reasons, definition and enforcement of property rights is not sufficient to prevent inefficiency. Other mechanisms must be sought.

TAX ON OUTPUT

Since the production and consumption of commodities generate pollution, a straightforward means of limiting pollution would be to reduce such production-consumption activities by taxing them. In the iron production example of Figure 5–1 (p. 105), a tax on iron output of t per unit would shift the producers' marginal cost curve from MC to MC', causing output to fall to q and price to rise to p. With the fall in q would come a decrease in pollution. Similarly, a tax on automobiles would tend to reduce their numbers and thereby reduce air pollution from that source.

The costs of reducing pollution in this manner would be borne by those who generate the pollution — the consumers and producers of iron and automobiles — in the form of higher consumer prices and lower producer incomes. The revenues from such a tax could be used to compensate those damaged by the pollution that remains or for general purposes of government.

The main disadvantage of taxing output is that it provides no incentive for reducing pollution damage by changing production processes — e.g., by placing filters on smokestacks or by designing autos that produce less pollution. Also, there is the problem of determining the appropriate tax rate, which may change over time as the damages from pollution change and as the costs of and demands for products change.

TAX ON EMISSIONS AND EFFLUENTS

Rather than tax the product output of the pollution-generating activity, government could directly tax the pollution output — in our examples, the amount of air pollutants emitted in the production of iron or from automobiles. Such a tax would encourage the producers to reduce pollution by reducing output or changing the process of production so that less pollution is generated. An emissions tax would raise the iron producers' costs and therefore result in lower output and a higher price for the product. Similarly, an emissions tax on autos would encourage production of low-emission cars, even though such cars might be more expensive. The price of cars would tend to rise on the average and their number would tend to fall. However, to achieve a given degree of control, an emissions tax would raise price and reduce output less than would a tax on output. With an emissions tax, some control would likely be obtained by changing the production process so that less pollution is generated per unit of output (per ton of iron produced or per mile driven). Like the output tax, the emissions tax places the burden of control on those who generate the pollution. Again, a major difficulty would be that of determining the level of the tax. Also, monitoring emissions (to determine how much tax is due) would likely be more difficult than monitoring product output.

STANDARDS AND REGULATIONS

With either of the preceding taxes, the reduced level of pollution is determined by producers and consumers as they decide how to adjust to the taxes. Such a level may or may not reach some desired standard, and would usually do so only if the tax rates were determined with a particular standard in mind. As an alternative to taxes, government could set and enforce pollution standards and attempt thereby to directly control the level of pollution. Standards could apply to the emissions by the producer or to the quality of the air surrounding the place of production, or to both.[18] The cost of complying with the standards would be borne by the producers or their customers or by both, just as was the case with taxation. The major difficulties with standards are those of first determining the standard and then enforcing it. Enforcement requires government monitoring of emissions or air quality or both.

POLLUTION PERMITS

Government could create and sell "permits" to pollute, while prohibiting pollution unless a permit is purchased. For example, a pollution permit might entitle its owner, say an iron producer, to allow one ton of a particular gas or dust to escape into the atmosphere each month. The number of permits issued would be determined by the air (or water) quality that is

---

18 Standards and regulations may also be used to control externalities arising out of urban blight and decay. The value of a particular property (home or business) in an urban area depends on the types and qualities of nearby properties. When Bob Ritter maintains or improves his property, his neighbor Joan Klein also benefits, while Klein loses if Ritter allows his property to fall into disrepair. Clearly, the maintenance and improvement of urban property generates external benefits, and the failure to do so generates external costs. Similarly, the compatibility of uses of neighboring properties affects their values; residential properties have lower value if neighboring properties include factories, high-traffic commercial activities, etc. Local governments, by establishing and enforcing zoning laws and building codes, can prevent one property owner from imposing external costs on another. Such laws are an approach to the control of the environmental pollution produced by urban decay and blight.

sought. If the desired air quality standard can be met even though 1,000 tons of particulate are dumped into the air of a city each month, then permits that allow dumping of a total of 1,000 tons per month could be sold to producers in that city. Only owners of the permits would be allowed to dump wastes into the air.

Owning such a permit would be advantageous because the producer would be allowed to operate with less expenditure on pollution control (e.g., less elaborate and expensive filtering and cleaning of the smoke by-products of production would be necessary). Producers would bid for permits, with the amount of their bids depending on the amount of pollution control costs that would be saved by owning a permit. For example, if a producer would have to spend $10,000 annually to prevent the escape of one ton of particulate per month, then the producer would presumably bid up to $10,000 for an annual permit to dump particulate into the air at the rate of one ton per month. The limited supply of permits would be purchased by those producers who would incur the greatest cost in controlling pollution. And the reduction of pollution is achieved at *least-cost*.

This "permit" approach to pollution control is compatible with the standard-setting approach. Indeed, it presumes the setting of standards for air (or water) quality. So it meets with all of the problems of setting and enforcing standards. But it does introduce flexibility from the polluter's point of view, since no polluter is required to reduce pollution by a specified amount. Instead, each polluter is required to either cease polluting or purchase a permit to do so.

SUBSIDIES AND PUBLIC PRODUCTION OF POLLUTION CONTROL

All of the mechansims we have discussed so far have one thing in common: They impose the costs of reducing pollution on those who generate pollution by their production or consumption activities. In contrast, public subsidies to encourage pollution control and public production of pollution control (as occurs when cities treat waste water from homes and industries to reduce water pollution) place pollution control costs on taxpayers. Taxpayers are unlikely to generate pollution in proportion to their payment of taxes, and the subsidy and public production mechanisms of control tend to be more advantageous for those who pollute. Recall our earlier discussion of the legality of pollution and the assignment of property rights in air (or water): Public subsidies and production of pollution control, in effect, assign the rights to use air (water) to those who pollute. That is, they imply that pollution is legal.

Subsidies may take the form of direct grants to or tax breaks for producers that install specified pollution control equipment. Or they may take the form of publicly financed research aimed at discovering production processes that produce less pollution. Subsidies may be used in conjunction with standards, in which case standards are imposed but government pays part of the costs of meeting those standards. For example, the federal government imposes standards on sewage treatment by cities and provides federal grants for construction of sewage treatment facilities.

The major disadvantage of subsidies and public production is that they offer no monetary incentive for the reduction of pollution at its source by changing processes. For example, if government pays for a pollution control device for each new car, then car producers have no incentive to produce cars that are inherently less polluting and consumers have no incentive to demand such cars. In contrast, with a tax on emissions, producers or consumers or both stand to gain if emissions are reduced by altering automobile design, fuel, etc.

SUMMARY

Externalities may cause market failure. In the absence of collective action, the external costs generated by production or consumption activities are likely to be excessive in that there are potential welfare gains to be obtained if they are reduced. However, complete elimination of external costs is usually not justified on efficiency grounds — some externalities are not Pareto relevant.

The reduction of external costs is essentially the production of a public good if many people are affected by the externality. The full realization of the potential welfare gains will therefore require collective action and its associated costs. Whether there is a net welfare gain from reduction of these external costs depends on the magnitudes of the potential welfare gain and the CCA. Whether government is the best means of collective action depends on the factors we identified in the discussion in Chapter 4 of government's role in providing public goods. Although we did not consider the case of external benefits explicitly, the same conclusions apply, except that collective action would aim at increasing output of external benefits.

In the simple but generally unrealistic case that CCA are zero, assignment of property rights and of liabilities affects the efficient solution only if it affects marginal values and marginal costs through its implicit effects on the distribution of income. That is, pollution control of x in Figure 5–2 (p. 107) is efficient regardless of how the costs of pollution and pollution control are distributed — regardless of liability rules and the settlement of property rights.[19] Moreover, as Coase has shown, once the property rights are assigned (that is, liabilities for damages are determined), members of the com-

---

19 This statement assumes that the AB and CD curves in Figure 5–2 are not affected by the difference in the distribution of costs and gains associated with the two laws.

munity will always take those actions required to assure the efficient degree of control.[20]

CCA may be low or zero when a small group of people is affected by the externality. If so, government definition and enforcement of property rights (so that there is a basis for exchange among the externality affected parties) may be sufficient to achieve efficiency. In any case, assignment of property rights is a necessary condition for such exchange. In cases of small-group externalities or, more generally, when CCA are zero, government may play the same role that it plays in the case of private goods. Direct government intervention in allocation decisions will not be required for economic efficiency. Instead, government need only define and enforce property rights and liability rules.

Of course, the way in which property rights are defined does affect the distribution of income. With legal pollution, the real income of polluters is higher and the real income of those damaged by pollution is lower than with illegal pollution. But once a law is established, any potential for improving the welfare of some persons without harming others will be realized if CCA are zero. And equity in the distribution of income can be accomplished without sacrificing efficiency. Efficiency and equity objectives do not conflict in this case; distributional equity is in effect a free good.

In the more realistic case of positive CCA, the efficient amount of reduction in external costs — pollution control — varies with assignment of property rights (the legality of pollution) and the magnitude of CCA. *The efficient degree of control is likely to be less when pollution is legal than when it is illegal*. For the example of Figure 5-3, the efficient degree of control is less than or equal to x when pollution is legal, and greater than or equal to x when pollution is illegal, assuming in both cases that CCA are nonzero.

Even though the efficient degree of control may depend on the assignment of property rights and the CCA, efficiency can be achieved, in principle, with either assignment. Neither assignment of property rights can be labeled inefficient; one law (legal pollution) is not in general superior to the other (illegal pollution) on efficiency grounds. This conclusion suggests that the assignment of property rights and the laws governing externalities (such as pollution) can be determined on other grounds than efficiency, e.g., distributional equity and the limitation of long-term risk to life on the planet. Given judgments and decisions about the latter issues, an efficient degree of control exists.

Different judgments about distribution or risk will, of course, entail different laws and different resource allocations. For example, a decision to make pollution illegal without compensation (because of distributional, risk,

20 Coase, "The Problem of Social Cost," pp. 1–44.

or other considerations) would likely mean a reduced output of those commodities, the production or consumption of which generates external costs. Such an outcome need not be inefficient. But this example does illustrate that distributional equity and risk limitation are not free goods.

Government mechanisms to improve resource allocation when externalities are present may take several forms: taxes, subsidies, standards and regulations, and the definition and enforcement of property rights. These mechanisms differ in how they distribute the cost and gains from action, as well as in their effects on resource allocation. They also differ in the incentives that they provide for the control of external costs at their source. When government places a tax upon or limits (through standards and regulations) the extent of external cost generating activities, it places the burden of controlling or limiting the external costs on those who generate them. In addition, taxes that are related to the amount of external costs generated provide a financial incentive for the discovery of production and consumption processes that generate lower external costs. In contrast, subsidies do not usually provide such incentives. And they may shift some or all of the burden of reducing external costs away from those who generate them.

SUPPLEMENTARY READINGS

Buchanan, James M., and Stubblebine, W. C. "Externality." *Economica* 29 (November 1962): 371–384.

Coase, R. H. "The Problem of Social Costs." *Journal of Law and Economics* 3 (October 1960): 1–44.

Dales, J. H. *Pollution, Property, and Prices.* Toronto: University of Toronto Press, 1968.

Dorfman, Nancy S., and Snow, Arthur. "Who Will Pay for Pollution Control?—The Distribution by Income Class of the Burden of the National Environmental Protection Program, 1972–1980." *National Tax Journal*, Vol. 28, No. 1 (March 1975): 101–116.

Dorfman, Robert, and Dorfman, Nancy S., eds. *Economics of the Environment.* New York: Norton, 1972.

Freeman, A. Myrick, III; Haveman, Robert H.; and Kneese, Allen K. *The Economics of Environmental Policy.* New York: Wiley, 1977.

Kneese, Allen V., and Schultze, Charles L. *Pollution, Prices, and Public Policy.* Washington: Brookings, 1975.

Mishan, E. J. "The Postwar Literature on Externalities: An Interpretative Essay." *Journal of Economic Literature* 9 (March 1971): 1–28.

CHAPTER SIX

DISTRIBUTION OF
INCOME AND WEALTH

How should the goods and services that are produced by a society be distributed among its members, both present and future? To answer this question is to specify the distribution of income and wealth in a society. In the preceding chapters we have considered government's role in distributional decisions when the main policy objective is efficiency in resource allocation. In Chapter 3 we examined the case for a major government role in the settlement of some distributional issues by defining and enforcing property rights. In Chapters 3 and 4, we saw that any government action to alter the allocation of resources produces costs and benefits that must be distributed among persons in some fashion.

In this chapter, we will examine government's role in decision making about the distribution of income and wealth when explicit distributional objectives are sought. In the first part of the chapter we will discuss criteria that might be used to evaluate and guide the modification of an existing distribution of income. In the second part, we will consider mechanisms for redistributing income.

DISTRIBUTION CRITERIA

The distribution of income — the distribution of goods and services produced by an economic system — depends on a number of factors: the distribution of ownership of land, labor, and capital resources; the demand for and supply of those resources; the distribution of private and government transfer payments; the distribution of government-supplied goods and services; and the distribution of taxes. The demands for and supplies of resources depend, in turn, on many factors: discrimination according to race, age, or sex; resource mobility; licensing arrangements; unions; price regulation; etc. To judge whether the existing distribution of income is fair or equitable, we need criteria, or principles, of distributive equity. Such criteria are also necessary to guide redistribution if the existing distribution is judged unsatisfactory.

PARETO-OPTIMAL DISTRIBUTION

One distribution criterion is that of *Pareto optimality*: The distribution of income is Pareto optimal if income cannot be redistributed without making someone worse off.[1] Applying the Pareto criterion to income redistribution, income would be redistributed if doing so made someone better off but no one worse off. In the case of poverty reduction, this criterion requires that the preferences of the rich be respected; any transfer that makes the rich or the poor worse off is unacceptable. With intergeneration transfers, the preferences of both the working and retired populations must be respected.

This distribution criterion treats income redistribution essentially as an economic good, which may be either private or public. A transfer of income from A to B is a private good if the transfer increases the utility of A or B or both, but no one else. A mother, say, gives money to her son and both feel better off. The utility of A is increased by the act of giving or by making B better off or by changing the behavior of B. The utility of B is also increased, or he would not accept the gift. But B does not necessarily take satisfaction from the *act* of charity by A. Instead, the utility of B is increased because his income is higher.

A transfer of income from A to B is a public good if the transfer increases the utility of individuals in addition to A and B. The utility of C may increase if A transfers income to B; if so, the transfer is a good that is available to both A and C. More generally, rich persons may feel better if the economic well-being of the poor is increased or if the negative externalities associated with poverty, such as crime and disease, are reduced. If so, then a transfer from any rich person to poor persons increases the utility and serves

1 For additional discussion of the notion of Pareto-optimal distribution, see Harold M. Hochman and James D. Rodgers, "Pareto-Optimal Redistribution," *American Economic Review*, 59 (September 1969): 542–557; and comments on their article by Richard A. Musgrave and R. S. Goldfarb, in *American Economic Review*, 60 (December 1970): 991–1002. See also, Lester C. Thurow, "The Income Distribution as a Pure Public Good," *Quarterly Journal of Economics*, 85 (May 1971): 327–336; R. J. Zeckhauser, "Optimal Mechanisms for Income Transfers," *American Economic Review*, 61 (June 1971): 324–334; and E. J. Mishan, "The Futility of Pareto-Efficient Distribution," *American Economic Review*, 62 (December 1972): 971–976.

the interests of all rich persons. The transfer is a public good for the rich as a group.[2] In terms of intergeneration transfers, the members of the younger generation may feel better if members of the older generation have sufficient income in retirement.[3]

NON-PARETO CRITERIA

Other criteria than the Pareto rule can be used to judge income distribution. And these may result in redistribution that overrides individual preferences. Through the tax and expenditure powers of government, the rich may be required to transfer income to the poor whether the rich like it or not. Similarly, the working population can be required to transfer income to the retired generation. There are several reasons why members of society may support such an approach.

Equity   Redistribution may be justified on the grounds that it is required for equity or fairness in the distribution of income. It may be judged unfair that some individuals have substantially higher incomes than other members of society, especially if the cause of low incomes is low productivity due to circumstances beyond the control of individuals, such as age and physical or mental disability.

While people may agree with the general notion that incomes should be distributed fairly, they differ in their views about what is fair. One view is that there should be a floor under incomes, with everyone having enough income for "basic" necessities. This view underlies the definition of the *poverty-line incomes* estimated and published by the U.S. government. Families and individuals having less than the poverty line incomes are classified as poor, the implication being that poor individuals and families should receive more income than they are presently receiving. Of course, there is a disagreement about whether the government's official poverty-line incomes are too high or too low. But there is substantial agreement with the notion that there should be an income floor. Table 6–1 shows the number of poor, as defined by poverty-line incomes, for selected years.[4]

2 L. L. Orr explains interstate differences in the level of benefit payments under the Aid to Families with Dependent Children (AFDC) program with an analysis that treats these transfers as a public good. See his "Income Transfers as a Public Good: An Application to AFDC," *American Economic Review*, 66, No. 3 (June 1976): 359–371.

3 The amount of such intergeneration transfers is likely to depend on whether the younger generation believes it will receive similar transfers durings its retirement years.

4 The poverty estimates in Table 6–1 are in terms of money income after government cash transfers and before taxes. In-kind transfers (food stamps, Medicare, Medicaid, public housing)

TABLE 6-1
SELECTED CHARACTERISTICS OF PERSONS BELOW THE POVERTY LEVEL[a]
(IN MILLIONS OF DOLLARS)

	1959	1970	1975[b]
Number of poor persons	39.5	25.4	25.9
65 years and over	5.5	4.8	3.3
White	28.5	17.5	17.8
Black and other races	11.0	7.9	8.1
In families with male head[c]	29.1	14.3	13.6
In families with female head[c]	10.4	11.2	12.3

a The poverty level is defined as about three times the estimated cost of a nutritionally adequate diet. It is adjusted for family size, sex of family head, number of children, farm and nonfarm residence. Adjustments are made for changes in the consumer price index.

b Not strictly comparable with earlier years because of revised procedures.

c Includes unrelated individuals.

Source: U.S. Census Bureau, *Statistical Abstract, 1976.*

Another view suggests that, instead of establishing an absolute income floor incomes should not be allowed to fall below some percentage of the average or median income in the nation. Poverty is seen as a relative concept, varying among nations with different real-income levels and within a nation over time. Tying poverty levels to an average of incomes means that the incomes of the poor should grow as the nation's real income grows.

Still other views are that equity requires equal incomes, or a limitation of inequality, or an upper limit on the level of income. For example, John Rawls has argued that inequality should be permitted only if it increases the lowest income received by any person in a society — that is, only if it improves the life prospects of the least favored member of society.[5]

James Tobin argues that rather than being concerned about inequality per se, people are concerned about the distribution of specific commodities. He labels as *specific egalitarianism* the view that "specific commodities should be distributed less unequally than the ability to pay for them."[6] Such commodities would include food, housing, and education — "the basic necessities of life, health, and citizenship," in Tobin's terminology. Specific

to the poor are not included in income. The implications of this exclusion from income are discussed on page 129.

5 John Rawls, A *Theory of Justice* (Cambridge, Mass.: Harvard, 1971).

6 James Tobin, "On Limiting the Domain of Inequality," *Journal of Law and Economics,* 13 (October 1970); reprinted in Edmund S. Phelps, ed., *Economic Justice* (Baltimore: Penguin, 1973), pp. 263–277.

egalitarianism reflects a desire to extend and assure basic rights to specific commodities and amenities of life.[7]

Redistribution programs to achieve equity in any of the senses we have mentioned are also frequently evaluated in terms of their vertical and horizontal equity. *Horizontal equity* is achieved when households in the same circumstances are treated equally. This criterion is usually interpreted to mean that households with the same income and needs should receive the same transfers or pay the same taxes to support transfer programs.[8] *Vertical equity* is accomplished when the households in unequal circumstances are treated unequally but "appropriately" so. In defining vertical equity, many would agree that households with lower incomes and higher needs should receive larger transfers than households with higher incomes and lower needs. Beyond this, the question of how transfers should vary with income and needs is subject to considerable debate.

Income may also be redistributed between present and future members of a society. The incomes available to future members of a society — to posterity — depend on current decisions regarding investment in renewable capital (buildings, machines, labor, training, reforestation, etc.); research and other efforts to increase knowledge and improve technology; and use of nonrenewable natural resources. The question of what is an equitable intertemporal distribution of income is met most directly in conservation decisions that set aside or otherwise preserve natural resources for future use. But the question also arises in those decisions that determine the overall rate of investment and economic growth. Relatively little attention has been given to the question of what criteria should guide decisions about intertemporal distribution of income, although such criteria are implicit in conservation and growth policies and in debate about those policies.

Political equality and stability   Income redistribution may be viewed as a means of achieving political equality and stability, rather than as a means of achieving a desired distribution of income. Unequal distribution of income gives some individuals more power in the political process than others. Although the rich and poor alike may have one vote in representative government, the rich have more resources to finance the election of their

---

7 See also, Arthur M. Okun, *Equity and Efficiency: The Big Trade-off* (Washington: Brookings, 1975), p. 112; and Lester C. Thurow, "Cash Versus In-Kind Transfers," *American Economic Review*, 64, No. 2 (May 1974): 190–195.

8 Other notions of "same circumstances" might be employed. Specifically, the wealth or consumption or both of the household could be taken into account in determining its circumstances, either in addition to or in lieu of income. The question of whether households' wealth and consumption should be considered when assessing horizontal and vertical equity is discussed in Chapter 9.

candidates to office, to propagate their political ideas and preferences, and to influence and obtain positions within government. Inequalities in the distribution of income may also alienate large segments of the population and encourage behavior inimical to social and political stability.[9] The costs of such instability may exceed the cost of policies to redistribute income.

Cost of preserving inequality A related and pragmatic reason for limiting income inequality is that resources must be used to protect the relatively privileged position of higher income persons. Such use of resources is readily apparent in all modern societies. Private spending for locks, fences, night watchmen, etc., and public spending for police, courts, etc., would very likely be necessary even in a society in which incomes were distributed equally. But it seems equally likely that such private and public expenditures would be greater if there were extreme income inequality. If such is the case, then by limiting inequality, this use of resources can be limited.

Economic incentives and limits to redistribution Distribution criteria may also be concerned with the interaction of income distribution and economic incentives. It is commonly recognized and stressed that policies to redistribute income may have adverse incentive effects, thereby reducing saving and work effort and the aggregate income of society. Less attention is given to the positive productivity effects of raising the incomes of the poor and the possibility that income inequalities may create adverse economic incentives. A person with low productivity has little incentive to work long and hard if a decent standard of living is unattainable through such efforts. And the possibility of the loss of accumulated savings or other wealth because of an expensive illness in the family or other catastrophic episodes may reduce incentives to save.[10]

Related to the incentive effects of redistribution is the question of whether there is a limit to redistribution. Specifically, redistribution of income may reduce the total income available for division among the rich and poor. If so,

9 Studies of the "causes" of crime often show a direct relationship between crime rates and measures of income inequality and poverty. See Thomas F. Pogue, "The Effect of Police Expenditures on Crime Rates: Some Evidence," *Public Finance Quarterly*, 3, No. 1 (January 1975): 14–44, and the many references cited.

10 Some have suggested that transfers to the poor may change their tastes; the poor may become "hooked" on income, with the result that the poor may eventually become tax-paying rather than welfare-receiving citizens. If so, donors may reasonably view transfer payments as investments, the return on which will be the future tax payments of the current welfare recipients. For further discussion along these lines, see Jonathan Kesselman, "An 'Internality' Case for Efficient Transfers," *Public Finance Quarterly*, 2, No. 3 (July 1974): 313–321.

the potential for redistribution may be limited because, at some point, further redistribution may reduce the incomes of the poor as well as of the rich.[11]

DISTRIBUTION OF WEALTH

So far we have dealt only with the distribution of income. Should we also be concerned about the distribution of wealth? If so, what criteria should govern the redistribution of wealth? Since income and wealth are highly correlated — those with great wealth tend to have high incomes and vice versa — we might argue that there is no need for separate consideration of the distribution of wealth. Indeed, in may instances wealth generates income; income is a flow accruing to wealth holders. However, this correlation is not perfect, partly because income, as it is usually defined and measured, does not include all accruals to wealth holders. And wealth, as it is usually defined and measured, does not include human capital (wealth), which generates income in the form of wages, salaries, and the earnings of professionals (doctors, lawyers).

Much concern about the distribution of wealth reflects a belief that inequality in the distribution of wealth results in inequality in the distribution of income. From this perspective, redistribution of wealth is a means of limiting income inequality. And limits on intergeneration wealth transfers are means of preventing the perpetuation and compounding of income inequality. Thus, criteria for wealth redistribution can be derived from income distribution objectives and the relationship between wealth and income distribution.

WHY GOVERNMENT REDISTRIBUTION?

While such nongovernment organizations as the Red Cross, Salvation Army, and various religious charities can and do redistribute income, a case can be made for government redistribution guided by either Pareto or non-Pareto criteria.

We can readily see that redistribution based on non-Pareto criteria, which makes some people worse off, is unlikely to take place without the application of government's police power. Non-Pareto redistribution is motivated

11 See the related discussion on the limits to taxation in Chapter 9. Rawls suggests that inequality in the distribution of income be reduced until that point is reached — until further reductions in inequality actually reduce the incomes of the poor (*Theory of Justice*). Okun discusses in detail this trade-off between greater equality and higher incomes of the poor and the aggregate income of society (*Equity and Efficiency*). This trade-off is also the concern of Edgar K. Browning, "How Much More Equality Can We Afford?" *The Public Interest*, 43 (Spring 1976): 90–110.

TABLE 6-2
PERCENT OF AGGREGATE MONEY INCOME RECEIVED BY INCOME RANK,
SELECTED YEARS

Income rank	1947	1955	1965	1975[a]
Lowest fifth	5.1	4.8	5.2	5.4
Second fifth	11.8	12.2	12.2	11.8
Middle fifth	16.7	17.7	17.8	17.6
Fourth fifth	23.2	23.4	23.9	24.1
Highest fifth	43.3	41.8	40.9	41.1
Highest 5 percent	17.5	16.8	15.5	15.5

a Not strictly comparable with earlier years because of revised procedures.

Source: U.S. Census Bureau, *Statistical Abstract* (1975, 1976).

by the judgment that the distribution of income in the absence of government intervention is undesirable by one or more of the criteria we discussed above. Is such in fact the case in the United States? We cannot answer that question, but we can present statistics that show how income is distributed. Table 6-1 shows the number of persons with incomes below the poverty-line incomes, while Table 6-2 shows the distribution of income among all income classes.

According to Table 6-2, there is substantial inequality in the distribution of money income and only a slight change in inequality over the 1947-1975 period. However, these statistics do not give an entirely accurate picture of what has been happening to the distribution of income. One reason is that they are based on money income before taxes. Browning has adjusted the income distribution statistics to reflect some items of in-kind income and some taxes. His adjusted measures show somewhat less inequality and a trend toward greater equality during the 1952-1972 period.[12] But even with those adjustments, the distribution of income remains quite unequal; the

12 Edgar K. Browning, "The Trend Toward Equality in the Distribution of Net Income," *Southern Economic Journal*, 43 (July 1976): 912-923. Browning makes adjustments for in-kind income, educational benefits, leisure, and income and payroll taxes. But over the 1952-1972 period he makes no adjustments for capital gains, underreporting of money income, farm income in kind, fringe benefits, imputed income from owner-occupied housing, or general government expenditures. For additional discussion of the interpretation and limitations of income distribution statistics, see Morton Paglin, "The Measurement and Trend of Inequality: A Basic Revision," *American Economic Review*, 65 (September 1975): 598-609; Edward C. Budd, "Postwar Changes in the Size Distribution of Income in the U.S.," *American Economic Review*, 60 (May 1970): 247-260; Robert J. Lampman, "Measured Inequality of Income: What Does It Mean and What Can It Tell Us," *Annals of the American Academy of Political and Social Science*, 409 (September 1973): 81-91; and idem, "What Does It Do for the Poor? — A New Test of National Policy," *The Public Interest*, No. 34 (Winter 1974): 66-82.

top and bottom quintiles received income shares of 31.9 and 12.6, respectively, in 1972.

Regardless of whether the distribution of income is ethically pleasing, government redistribution may be desirable and even necessary when a Pareto-optimal distribution is sought. The reason is, as we noted above, income redistribution may be a public good. And when income redistribution is a public good, the level of private contributions may not be efficient for the reasons we discussed in Chapter 4. Individuals may make private transfers directly to the poor or to the aged, or they may make voluntary contributions to an organization that dispenses funds or goods to them. However, the total of these private transfers may be inefficient (less than the amount that maximizes the welfare of the givers) because of the free-rider problem and the cost of formulating and enforcing cost-sharing arrangements among the givers. The free-rider problem arises because one person's contribution to financing poverty reduction is insignificant, in which case that person has an incentive to conceal her or his preferences and withhold his or her contributions. If others with similar preferences do make transfers, then that person's utility will increase because the lot of the poor or the aged is enhanced or negative externalities are removed or both. If others do not make transfers, the individual's own contribution will have little effect.

To obtain transfers in optimal amounts it is necessary to determine the amounts that individuals would in fact be willing to contribute toward redistribution, and to then enforce payment on that basis. But such efforts are costly; and the government, through the use of its police powers to collect taxes, has an advantage over private efforts to effect transfers. And givers may submit willingly to government action with the expectation that such an arrangement will result in a more efficient level of transfers. However, as we noted in Chapter 4, the gains from government action may be offset in part or in full by the costs of the action. There may also be too much redistribution (in the Pareto sense) because government may either be unaware of or ignore some of the preferences of the givers and tax them more than they prefer.

REDISTRIBUTION MECHANISMS

Government may alter the distribution of income in several ways. We will be concerned with three redistribution mechanisms. Two fall into a class that is fiscal and take the form of tax and expenditure policies that provide (1) cash or in-kind subsidies (transfers) to particular persons and (2) goods and services to the population at large. The third mechanism falls into a class that attempts to alter the distribution by altering the constraints and conditions governing market exchange.[13]

13 See Tobin, "Limiting the Domain of Inequality," pp. 452ff., for additional discussion.

TRANSFER PROGRAMS

Governments may give cash or goods to specified classes of the population, financing the gifts by taxation. Such gifts are called *cash* and *in-kind transfers,* respectively. Both the collection of taxes to finance the transfers and the transfers themselves alter the distribution of income. The net effect of a transfer program is the sum of the two effects. Examples of in-kind transfers are food, medical care, and housing. In-kind transfers may be effected by distributing "vouchers" that can be used to purchase only specified commodities; the Food Stamp Program is such a voucher system. Cash transfers of income include welfare payments and Social Security benefits.

Cash versus in-kind transfers   The question of whether transfers should be "in kind" or "in cash" seemed to be a fairly settled issue until recently. The traditional argument is that cash transfers are superior on efficiency grounds because recipients know better than the grantor what combination of goods best satisfies their wants. In-kind transfers, by providing a particular good, may prevent substitution among commodities and may leave recipients worse off than if they could choose freely among goods.

In some cases, cash and in-kind transfers have the same effect on welfare. If a person wishes to spend at least $100 a month on food, a transfer of $100 worth of food stamps is equivalent to a $100 cash grant and it will not alter the recipient's choices. However, if a person would prefer to spend $90 for food and $10 for a pair of shoes, the in-kind transfer would seem less desirable. Of course, transfer recipients are better off with in-kind transfers than without any.

That traditional analysis ignores the preferences of the giver regarding the form of the transfer. However, if the wishes of the grantor (taxpayer) are to be considered, the form of the transfer may matter. With the Pareto criterion, grantor preferences do matter, and in-kind transfers may be required to maximize the utility of the grantors. This would be the case if grantors are not adversely affected by poverty per se but by the effects of poverty, such as poor housing, unsanitary conditions, inadequate clothing, and malnutrition.[14]

An attitude of paternalism may also underlie grantor preference for in-kind transfers. Grantors (taxpayers) may view the poor as being less able or willing to make wise choices than persons of other income classes and thus want to restrict the choices of the poor or to choose for them.[15]

14 Recall the discussion of specific egalitarianism, p. 125.

15 That such restrictions impair the dignity and self-respect of the recipients is a cost of in-kind transfers that must be weighed against any gain in grantor satisfaction. In practice, no transfer program is likely to satisfy fully the wishes of both grantors and recipients.

Intergeneration transfers   In addition to redistributing income among income classes, governments may redistribute income among age groups or
generations of the population. Publicly financed education redistributes income from the older to the younger generation: The older generation pays
taxes to increase the value of human capital and enhance the lifetime income of the younger generation.[16] The kind of taxes employed to finance
education may or may not have the desired effect upon the distribution of
income among the generation paying the taxes, and the education itself may
either perpetuate or improve the distribution of income among the generation receiving the education. If regressive taxes are used to finance education, then the poor give up proportionately more of their income than
higher income persons. From the benefit side, if publicly supported educational institutions are attended primarily by children of high income persons, as is definitely the case in institutions of higher education, existing inequality in the distribution of income may be perpetuated or even increased
by educational policy.[17]

Income can also be redistributed from the working (younger) generation
to the retired population. Transfers to the older generation may be either
private or public. With public transfers as provided by the Social Security
system and retirement programs for government employees, payments are financed with taxes on the working population, which in turn receives payments during its retirement years. The support accorded any retired generation, however, is not necessarily actuarially related to the taxes the retired
population contributed during its working years to the preceding generation.
Instead, the taxes paid and benefits received with an income transfer system
may be a political decision that is modified from time to time. A generation
receives a net transfer if its tax payments plus the earnings that would have
been received had those tax payments been invested are less than the ac-
tuarial value of benefits received in retirement and vice versa.

PROVISION OF GOODS AND SERVICES

Governments may provide goods and services to increase the efficiency of
resource allocation. Although not usually viewed as a redistribution mechanism itself, except in a few cases (education, training, and housing), such
activity may affect the distribution of income in two ways: (1) as taxes are
collected to finance provision and (2) as the goods and services are distributed among the population. Specifically, when people receive goods from

16 Education presumably yields external as well as private benefits.
17 Such is the conclusion of a study by W. Lee Hansen and Burton A. Weisbrod, *Benefits,
Costs, and Finance of Public Higher Education* (Chicago: Markham, 1969).

government, their real incomes, or command over goods and services, is increased by the value of the goods received. Countering this positive effect are the taxes paid by the recipients. For example, a dam that is built by the government may increase the real incomes of those whose property is subject to flood damage. The income gain for these property owners is the value of the flood control provided by the dam, minus the taxes they pay to build the dam. However, the project reduces the real income of taxpayers who reside outside the flood plain and derive no benefit from the dam.

Goods may be provided to businesses as well as to individuals — highways, police and fire protection, etc. Such goods are called *intermediate* goods in that they are used in the production of marketed goods and, as such, they have value. This value ultimately accrues to individuals, either in their capacities as consumers of the goods produced, or in their capacities as suppliers of the market goods. Government provision of goods thus affects the distribution of income even if the goods are provided to businesses (producers) and not directly to individuals.

The effects of government provision of goods and services upon the distribution of income may or may not be intended. Of particular interest is the effect on the distribution of income by income class. A common view is that the net burden, defined as "taxes paid minus the value of goods and services received," should be either proportional or progressive, rather than regressive. If the effect is proportional, relative household incomes are not disturbed because the combined effect of taxes and expenditures are the same fraction of each person's income. With a progressive distribution of the net burden there is a redistribution of income from high to low income persons, while the opposite is true with a regressive distribution.

It is difficult to determine the net burden of taxes and government expenditures because adjustments of market prices to taxes and expenditures may change the distribution of income. People who are legally liable for payment of a tax may shift part or all of the tax to other people and thereby bear a burden that is less than their tax payment. Others may be burdened by taxes even though they pay no tax. For example, people who abstain from consuming a taxed item and pay no taxes on the item are nevertheless burdened by the tax because it distorted their choices. This burden is relevant in calculating net burdens. In Chapter 9 we will discuss the questions of tax and expenditure incidence more fully.

MANIPULATION OF MARKET PRICES

Government can also redistribute income by altering market prices through (1) regulation or control of prices, outputs, and entry into markets and (2) subsidies, tariffs, and taxes. Prices that affect sources of income (wages, interest, rent) and uses of income (product prices) can be manipulated. Although there may be exceptions, price manipulation generally is a less satisfactory device for changing the distribution of income than income-transfer programs. In addition, price manipulation is more likely to lead to a misallocation of resources than income transfers. We will consider a few examples of price manipulation.

Minimum wages   An important example of price manipulation is that of placing a floor under wage rates in specified occupations. *Minimum wage* laws may indeed increase the wages of some persons. But it is likely that employment of workers whose wage rate has been raised will be reduced. Minimum wage laws tend to increase labor costs and prices in those industries where the wage rate was below the legal minimum. An increase in price in turn reduces the quantity demanded of the product and the number of workers employed. Even if the demand for the product does not fall, an increase in the wage rate may induce employers to economize on labor cost by marginally substituting capital for workers. These workers who lose their jobs suffer reduced incomes until they find new jobs. When they find jobs, the jobs may not be covered by minimum wage legislation and, thus, pay lower rates than the former jobs. Indeed, it is unlikely that the real wage of displaced workers in their new employment would be equal to the minimum wage, since they presumably were unemployed because their productivity did not, according to the market, justify the minimum wage.[18]

To the extent that minimum wage legislation reduces employment or lowers the wage rate of displaced workers, the incomes of some low-income persons (those not displaced) are improved at the expense of other low-income persons. In other words, there is a redistribution of income among low-income persons. There is also some redistribution from higher- to lower-income persons to the extent that higher wages lead to higher prices for products bought by high-income persons and to the extent that higher wages are financed by reducing profits destined for higher-income persons.

18 While some decrease in employment is a plausible result of minimum wage laws, it is not a *necessary* consequence. If the productivities of low-income workers are upgraded sufficiently as wages are increased through minimum wage laws, then labor costs and product prices need not rise in the affected industries. If product prices do not rise, then demand and employment need not be curtailed. Also, if higher wage payments under minimum wage laws have only the effect of reducing profits, thus redistributing income from capital to labor, then minimum wage laws need not lead to higher prices and lower employment. But this outcome is unlikely because profit recipients must accept lower incomes and not offset any of the higher labor costs by either reducing employment or increasing product prices.

In any case, there is no assured redistribution of income from high- to low-income persons, because the direction and magnitude of redistribution depends upon market responses to the wage increase. Even if the market adjustments entail no adverse distributional effects, minimum wage legislation does nothing for poor persons who either are unable to work or derive income from other sources. Minimum wage legislation affects only low-income workers covered by the legislation, and some of those individuals may end up worse off.

Subsidies and tariffs   Government subsidies and tariffs alter the distribution of income in favor of particular classes of income recipients. Although subsidies and tariffs are often received and paid by businesses, they ultimately affect the distribution of income among individuals. Subsidies and tariffs are typically rationalized as means of achieving objectives other than or in addition to the redistribution that occurs. For example, subsidies of domestic producers and tariffs on foreign producers are rationalized as means of promoting domestic employment and as national defense and security measures because they reduce U.S. dependence on foreign suppliers. Our present merchant marine subsidies are rationalized on national defense and security grounds, as are proposals for energy independence.

Subsidy and tariff policies aimed at altering market prices may have undesirable or unpredictable effects on the distribution of income. Agricultural price-support subsidies redistribute income from poor and rich consumers and taxpayers to poor and rich farmers.[19] Tariffs on imports increase the income of employees, landowners, and capital owners in the protected industries at the expense of consumers. Those who benefit from tariffs may be rich or poor, and those who pay higher prices may be rich or poor.

As another example, rather than set minimum wages, government may subsidize wage rates by paying a fraction of the employer's cost of hiring particular classes of labor. The wage rate paid by the employer does not increase with a wage subsidy as it does under a minimum wage law. Instead, it falls, and firms will likely increase rather than reduce employment. Although this policy is superior to the minimum wage approach, it too does not assist the nonworking poor.

Education and training subsidies may also alter the distribution of income

19 Since agricultural subsidies were based on the amount of the farmer's output, larger farmers have received the lion's share of the subsidies. The larger farmers are also the higher-income farmers in most instances, so the redistribution was from taxpayers to higher-income farmers. Ceilings have been placed on the amount of "price-support" payments that an individual farmer may receive, thus lessening the pro-rich bias of the agricultural price-support programs.

by affecting labor productivity and, hence, the prices at which labor is sold.[20] Subsidies may range up to 100 percent, and they may depend upon the income of the person and be in the form of loans or direct payments.

To the extent that they are effective, educational and work-training programs have two advantages. First, by increasing the productivity and employability of workers, they enable previously uneducated and untrained persons to earn a satisfactory income rather than receive transfer payments. Second, to the extent that such policies offset imperfections in the market for human investments, the total real income of society will be greater than otherwise. Of course, some such investments may not "pay off," i.e., the rate of return may be zero, negative, or less than returns on other investments. In such cases, transfers would, in a narrow sense, be more efficient than education and training subsidies. However, subsidies may be preferred on other grounds.

Supply restriction   Government may also alter the distribution of income by restricting the supply of particular products or factors of production. As a result, the product or factor sells at a higher price than would otherwise be the case, and producers and factor owners receive higher incomes. Usually supply restriction occurs with the acquiescence of, if not at the request of, the affected producers and factor owners. The police power of the state is used to create factor or product cartels by limiting entry or output or both. For example, the entry of persons into professions and occupations may be restricted by licensing and training requirements. Such requirements are usually rationalized as serving consumer and public interests, and they may, to a greater or lesser degree. But the requirements also increase the prices of the services involved — legal, medical, barber, etc. As another example, the U.S. government has restricted farm output and increased prices of farm products, not by restricting the entry of persons into farming, but by restricting land use through crop acreage allotments.[21]

Figure 6–1 illustrates how supply restrictions increase prices and income. Suppose the market demand for and supply of wheat are D and S, respectively. With a free market, the price and output of wheat are p and q, respectively. Gross farm income from wheat production is $p \times q$. However,

---

20 The way in which subsidized education is financed also affects the distribution of income.

21 For additional discussion see Anne Krueger, "The Political Economy of the Rent Seeking Society," *American Economic Review*, 64, No. 3 (June 1974): 291–303. She argues that people will use resources in trying to bring about restrictions on economic activity that generate economic rents. And they will use resources in competing for the benefits of the restrictions. Such competition occurs when imports of particular commodities are limited and importers compete for import licenses. Competition may take the form of bribes to the officials who dispense the licenses, or it may occur as an open bid if the licenses are marketed (auctioned).

FIGURE 6-1
INCOME REDISTRIBUTION THROUGH SUPPLY RESTRICTION

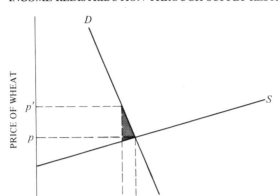

BUSHELS OF WHEAT PRODUCED PER YEAR

if government restricts output to q' through acreage allotments, price rises to p' and quantity falls to q'. Gross farm income with acreage controls, $p' \times q'$, exceeds the free market gross farm income if the demand for wheat is price inelastic, as is the case in fact. Although farmers gain from this supply restriction, consumers lose because they pay more for less wheat. Moreover, consumer losses exceed farmer gains by the amount of the shaded area; the acreage controls prevent an efficient allocation of resources between wheat production and other uses.

In particular instances, supply restriction may redistribute income in a way that is consistent with equity criteria. But more likely than not, it simply increases the incomes of particular population groups who have been successful in obtaining government help in forming factor or product cartels. Some individuals are necessarily made worse off by supply restrictions, and the losses of the losers will exceed the gains of the gainers, as was the case with the wheat example.

There are also other ways in which government can directly and indirectly affect prices and wages and, thus, the distribution of income. When the Federal Reserve System manipulates the money supply and interest rates in an attempt to regulate aggregate economic activity, it affects the real incomes of both borrowers and lenders. Similarly, effective wage and price controls, whether mandatory or voluntary, affect incomes. With both monetary and wage-price controls, the direct concern of policy is the regulation of aggregate demand and the price level, with the income redistribution that occurs being a side effect. Federal, state, and local government regulation of utility and transportation industries affects the distribution of income: Such control affects both the prices that consumers pay for electricity, gas, water, telephone service, and transportation and the incomes that producers receive from producing such services. With such regulation, a major concern of policy is distribution, with the objective being a "fair" return to producers and "fair" prices for consumers.

SUMMARY

Two general reasons are advanced for government action to alter the market-determined distribution of income. First, income redistribution is a public good; and private efforts at redistribution will be inefficient because of the free-rider problem. Second, the market-determined distribution of income is unacceptable for ethical and other reasons. In the first case, redistribution is based on the preferences of taxpayers, with the objective being a Pareto-optimal distribution of income. In the second case, the preferences of taxpayers who finance the transfers need not be considered.

Of the mechanisms used to redistribute incomes, income transfers have the greatest potential for achieving the objective of raising the incomes of the target population, while minimizing resource allocation effects. Other policies will miss some groups of the target population and have unpredictable or undesirable market effects.

Transfers may take the form of cash or goods and services, with the choice depending on whether the sovereignty of taxpayers or income recipients is to be respected.

SUPPLEMENTARY READINGS

Aaron, Henry J. *Why Is Welfare So Hard to Reform?* Washington, D.C.: Brookings, 1973.

Browning, Edgar K. *Redistribution and the Welfare System.* Washington, D.C.: American Enterprise Institute for Public Policy Research, 1975.

Buchanan, James M. "Social Insurance in a Growing Economy: A Proposal for Radical Reform." *National Tax Journal* (December 1968): 386–395.

Fried, Edward R.; Rivlin, A. M.; Schultze, Charles L.; and Teeters, Nancy H. *Setting National Priorities: The 1974 Budget,* Chaps. 3, 4. Washington, D.C.: Brookings, 1973.

Hochman, Harold M., and Rodgers, James D. "Pareto-Optimal Redistribution." *American Economic Review* 59 (September 1969): 542–557.

Rawls, John. A *Theory of Justice*. Cambridge, Mass.: Harvard, 1971.

Thurow, Lester C. "Cash Versus In-Kind Transfers." *American Economic Review* 64, No. 2 (May 1974): 190–195.

————. "The Economic Progress of Minority Groups," *Challenge* 19, No. 1 (March-April 1976): 20–29.

————. *Generating Inequality: Mechanisms of Distribution in the U.S. Economy*. New York: Basic Books, 1975.

————. "Toward a Definition of Economic Justice." *Public Interest* 31 (Spring 1973): 56–80.

Tobin, James. "Raising the Income of the Poor." In K. Gordon, ed., *Agenda for the Nation*. Washington: Brookings, 1969.

Weisbrod, Burton A. "Collective Action and the Distribution of Income: A Conceptual Approach." In Robert H. Haveman and Julius Margolis, eds. *Public Expenditures and Policy Analysis*. Chicago: Markham Publishing Company, 1970.

Preceding chapters show that social costs and benefits must be balanced at the margin if an efficient allocation of resources is to be achieved. They also show that in many situations, such a balance cannot be achieved with nongovernment institutions and mechanisms (markets, private cooperatives, clubs). In addition, income and wealth-distribution objectives generally will not be achieved with nongovernment mechanisms.

Part Three deals with the feasibility of and problems met in government action to achieve allocation and distribution goals. Chapter 7 explores the potential for, and problems of, formal systems of economic analysis: benefit-cost; cost-effectiveness; and programming, planning, and budgeting systems. It shows that such analyses are usually incapable of determining optimal policies, in large part because the required information about preferences and values is not available. Thus, a major concern of Chapter 8, which examines political processes for decision making, is how the processes generate information about individual preferences and weighs those preferences, explicitly or implicitly, to obtain a "preferred," or chosen, policy for the collectivity (community). Chapter 8 also evaluates the outcomes of political decision making. For example, does the process result in an efficient allocation of resources? Does it promote specified distributional objectives? In this evaluation, the chapter considers both the magnitudes and the distribution of the gains and the losses from political action. Of special interest is the question of whether one group is likely to lose (gain) continuously.

PART THREE

DECISION-MAKING TOOLS AND PROCESSES

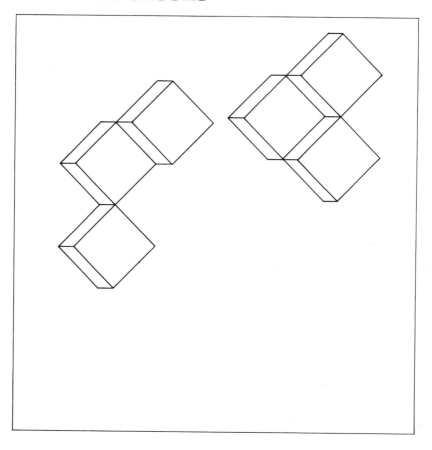

CHAPTER SEVEN

TECHNIQUES OF
ECONOMIC POLICY ANALYSIS

An efficient allocation of resources requires that social costs and benefits be balanced at the margin. In the preceding chapters we saw why such a balance may not be achieved with nongovernment institutions and mechanisms (markets, private cooperatives, clubs). We also saw that government action to improve resource allocation should be based on a calculation and weighing of the costs and benefits of that action. As a matter of fact, economists and other students of government have long urged that governments undertake such "benefit-cost" analyses. And the governments of virtually all modern nations have followed this advice to a degree, since they do conduct benefit-cost analyses in connection with some of their decisions. In the United States, the Army Corps of Engineers and the Bureau of Reclamation have used benefit-cost analyses since the 1930s to evaluate their projects (navigation, flood control, irrigation, etc.). In the 1960s, other federal agencies, most notably the Department of Defense, began to use benefit-cost and cost-effectiveness analyses and to develop programming, planning, and budgeting (PPB) systems, partly (perhaps largely) in response to a 1965 executive order by President Lyndon Johnson. Although these techniques were initially used in natural-resource development and military planning, they have come to be used in decision making about education and training, health and hospitals, transportation, and social welfare programs. These techniques are also used by some state and local governments.

In this chapter, we will look carefully at what is involved in benefit-cost analysis of both allocation and distribution policies, and we will appraise its usefulness. We will also discuss cost-effectiveness analysis and PPB systems.

If it should prove feasible to determine welfare-maximizing policies through an objective and scientific benefit-cost calculus, then, in principle, economic decision making could be left in the hands of technocrats. Even if a society does not wish to have decisions dictated by the outcomes of benefit-cost analyses, such analyses would still be useful in political decision making, as a source of information for individuals and their representatives. We shall see, however, that benefit-cost analysis of many, if not most, government policies is not feasible. Consequently, alternative mechanisms for obtaining information and making decisions are needed. In Chapter 8, we look at one class of alternatives, democratic political processes.

ELEMENTS OF BENEFIT-COST ANALYSIS

Government actions to provide public goods or adjust for externalities divert resources from one use to another, thereby affecting peoples' present and future welfare. Such *welfare effects* may be positive (benefits) or negative (costs). Benefit-cost analysis attempts to determine the net amount of the welfare effects — whether the diverted resources have greater value in their new use than in their former use.

More formally, benefit-cost analysis determines the present value, V, of the benefit and cost streams resulting from a particular government action, which we will hereafter refer to as a project. V is defined as

$$V = \sum_{t=0}^{T} \frac{B(t) - C(t)}{(1+r)^t}$$

The project's effects extend from the current period, $t = 0$, through future period T. For period t, the project's benefits and costs are $B(t)$ and $C(t)$, respectively. Projects that generate costs in the current period and benefits in future periods are called *investment* projects, in contrast with *consumption* projects, which generate benefits in only the current period. Traditionally, benefit-cost analysis has been used primarily for investment projects.

The benefits and costs of each period are discounted by the factor $1/(1+r)^t$, where r is the "discount rate." To obtain V, the discounted benefits and costs are totaled for all periods $t = 0$ through $t = T$. Benefits and costs that accrue in future periods are discounted to reflect the fact that future benefits are less valuable and future costs are less burdensome. In a subsequent section, we will discuss more fully the rationale for discounting and the problems met in defining and measuring the discount rate.

BENEFITS AND COSTS DEFINED

The benefit of a government project to a particular person is the amount that the person would be willing to pay to have the project undertaken. The cost is the amount that the person would require as compensation for the damages, losses, or other costs that the project imposes on that person.

Let us consider, for example, a project that consists of a dam on a river and a system of irrigation canals that provide flood control and irrigation to downstream property owners. Peter Bruno owns farm land downstream from the dam site. His annual profits average $5,000 without the dam. With the dam, his profits would average $6,000 per year because flooding is prevented and irrigation is provided for drought years. Assuming that these figures are accurate, Bruno would clearly be *willing* to pay up to $1,000 a year to have the dam, even though he would *prefer* to pay less or nothing. And the benefits of the project to Bruno are $1,000 per year. Stan Archer owns farm land upstream from the dam site. His profits average $4,000 per year without the dam. But with the dam, his annual profits would average only $3,600 because the backup of water behind the dam would flood his land and destroy his crop in one out of ten years. The cost of the dam to Archer is therefore $400 per year, the amount that he would require as compensation for the losses that the project imposes on him. This cost is the opportunity cost of the dam to Archer, that is, the value of what he must give up if the dam is built.[1]

The aggregate benefits of a project for a particular period, $B(t)$, are obtained by totaling the benefits accruing to all persons during the period. $B(t)$ thus shows the amount that all persons would be willing to pay for the favorable effects of the project (e.g., flood prevention, irrigation) that accrue during period t. $B(t)$ is the value of the package of goods and services that the project provides during the period. Similarly, $C(t)$ is obtained by totaling the costs that accrue to all persons during period t if the project is undertaken. These costs include the CCA necessary to decide on and carry out the project.[2] $C(t)$ is the aggregate opportunity cost of the project, the value of the

1 The calculations of benefits and costs in this example ignore the *risk reduction* that the project provides, a factor we discuss later in this chapter (p. 153).

2 Specifically included in the CCA are the costs of any benefit-cost analysis that may be undertaken. Also included are the compliance, administrative, and welfare costs of collecting the taxes required to finance the activity. These welfare (excess burden) costs are defined more fully in Chapter 9. For further discussion of how the welfare (excess burden) costs of taxation could affect government expenditure decisions, see Edgar K. Browning, "The Marginal Costs of Public Funds," *Journal of Political Economy*, 84, No. 2 (April 1976): 283–398. Browning estimates that in the United States the marginal welfare costs of taxes on labor income range between nine cents and sixteen cents per dollar of taxes collected. If these estimates are valid, they mean that "government expenditures must be at least 9–16 percent more productive than

FIGURE 7–1
ONE-PERIOD ECONOMIC BENEFITS OF A GOVERNMENT PROJECT

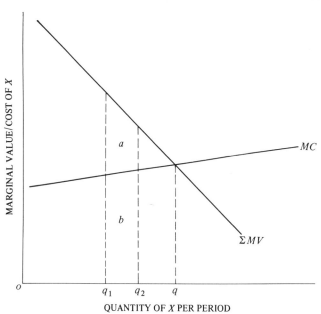

output that must be sacrificed in period t if the project is undertaken. If $B(t) > C(t)$, then the project provides a potential welfare gain to society for the period in question — there is a *social profit* from the project during period t if $B(t) > C(t)$.

Benefits and costs as defined here have the same meaning as the terms *value* and *cost* have in Chapters 3–5. For example, the benefit of a project that increases a community's supply of a public good from q_1 to q_2 during period t in Figure 7–1 is measured by areas a and b. The cost of the project is area b, leaving a welfare gain, or social profit, equal to area a, provided the CCA are incorporated into the MC curve.[3] With additional projects, the

private expenditures to produce a net welfare gain" (p. 283). Of course, that conclusion presumes that the dollar costs of resources used by government measure the value of the goods and services that those resources could have produced in private employment. Such may not be the case for the reasons discussed on p. 151 of this chapter.

3 The project might be installation of a smoke stack that reduces pollution from the municipal power plant. Or it might be the provision of an additional year of schooling for a community's children or the widening of some of the community's roads.

output of the public good can be extended further. If the projects have effects only in period t, then the efficient set of projects is that which maximizes the excess of benefits over costs. That would be the set that results in a public goods output of q in Figure 7–1. If the projects have effects in many periods, then the efficient set is that which maximizes V, the present value of the "properly" discounted value of present and future benefits and costs. We can now readily see the reason for employing benefit-cost analysis in government decision making: *It is a means of identifying the efficient level of government-provided goods and services.*

EFFECTS OF DISCOUNTING

Table 7–1 shows how discounting affects the values assigned to alternative projects. Projects A and B have the same initial cost, $150,000, but each has a different net benefit stream over the ten-year "life" of the project. For example, in the fifth year, project A yields undiscounted net benefits of $20,000 and project B, $40,000.[4]

Undiscounted net benefits are positive for both projects, and project B might seem superior to A since the "lifetime" undiscounted net benefits are $100,000 from A and $160,000 from B. However, discounting alters this picture in three ways. First, discounted net benefits are lower than undiscounted benefits, and they are lower as the discount rate is greater. Discounted net benefits from A total $61,330, $32,330, and $10,080 for discount rates of 5 percent, 10 percent, and 15 percent, respectively. The corresponding totals of discounted net benefits from B are $73,650, $15,070, and −$25,580. Second, discounted net benefits become negative if the discount rate is high enough. Project B's discounted net benefits are −$25,580 for a discount rate of 15 percent. Project A's discounted net

---

4 To make the example more concrete, let us say that project A is the purchase of a new bus. In the early years of its life, the bus yields relatively high (undiscounted) net benefits in the form of transportations services. However, as the bus ages, operating and maintenance costs rise and annual net benefits decline to $10,000 annually in the last five years of its life. After ten years, the bus becomes uneconomical to operate (it yields negative net benefits), so it is scrapped.

Let us say that Project B is the laying of an all-weather surface, such as cement, on several city streets that do not at present have a hard surface. The hard surface yields benefits in the form of more rapid and safer travel for the motorists who use the streets. Those net benefits rise as the city grows and traffic on the streets increases, reaching a peak of $60,000 per year in the seventh and eighth years. Net benefits (undiscounted) fall in the ninth and tenth years as the surface begins to break up and repairs have to be made. After ten years, the surface is sufficiently broken up that it is no longer economical to patch it; that is, repairing the old surface is so expensive that net benefits would be negative. It would be more economical to completely resurface the streets.

TABLE 7-1
EFFECTS OF DISCOUNTING ON PRESENT VALUE (IN THOUSANDS OF DOLLARS)

Year	Net Benefits of Project A				Net Benefits of Project B			
	Undiscounted	5%	10%	15%	Undiscounted	5%	10%	15%
0	-150.00	-150.00	-150.00	-150.00	-150.00	-150.00	-150.00	-150.00
1	60.00	57.12	54.54	52.20	2.00	1.90	1.82	1.74
2	50.00	45.35	41.30	37.80	3.00	2.72	2.48	2.27
3	40.00	34.56	30.04	26.32	5.00	4.32	3.76	3.29
4	30.00	24.69	20.49	17.16	30.00	24.69	20.49	17.16
5	20.00	15.68	12.42	9.94	40.00	31.36	24.84	19.88
6	10.00	7.46	5.64	4.32	50.00	37.30	28.20	21.60
7	10.00	7.11	5.13	3.76	60.00	42.66	30.78	22.56
8	10.00	6.77	4.67	3.27	60.00	40.62	28.02	19.62
9	10.00	6.45	4.24	2.84	40.00	25.80	16.96	11.36
10	10.00	6.14	3.86	2.47	20.00	12.28	7.72	4.94
V = sum of discounted net benefits	100.00	61.33	32.33	10.08	160.00	73.65	15.07	-25.58

benefits are positive for that discount rate, but they would be negative at a rate of 19 percent or more. Third, the ranking of the projects is affected by the magnitude of the discount rate. With no discounting or a discount rate of 5 percent, project B is superior to A, but the reverse is true for discount rates of 10 and 15 percent. In general, increasing the discount rate increases the rank of projects that have relatively greater near-term benefits (project A). That is, higher discount rates make "short-term" projects appear more favorable than "long-term" projects.

Since discounting complicates matters considerably, we might ask: Why discount? Why not use only undiscounted values of net benefits in making decisions? The answer, in brief, is that people are not indifferent about when costs and benefits accrue. They would rather have benefits sooner and costs later. We will discuss why this is so in the section on the discount rate.

USE OF PRESENT VALUE ESTIMATES

Once calculated, how is V used in decision making? When *all* benefits and costs are correctly measured and discounted, $V > 0$ tells us that the project is efficient — there is a potential welfare gain from undertaking the project. Conversely, $V < 0$ tells us that if the project is undertaken, some person(s) must lose. Therefore, if (1) V is correct and (2) the objective of society is economic efficiency and (3) there is no limit on the scale of governmental activity, then all projects for which $V > 0$ should be undertaken. However, if the scale of government is limited so that all projects for which $V > 0$ cannot be undertaken, government should undertake the *feasible* set of projects that has the greatest value. A set of projects is feasible if it is consistent with budgetary and other limits. For example, if there is no limit on the budget, both projects A and B should be undertaken, if the discount rate is 10 percent; and only project A should be undertaken if the discount rate is 15 percent. If the budget is limited to $150,000 so that only one project can be undertaken, then B should be undertaken if the discount rate is 5 percent, while A should be undertaken if the discount rate is 10 or 15 percent.

When there are several ways of achieving an objective — for example, several ways of building a dam and irrigation system — then each way can be considered as a separate project. Of this set of projects, the one with the greatest V will be the least-cost means of carrying out the given task. Thus, benefit-cost analysis can, in theory, be used to determine (1) whether achieving a given objective will promote economic efficiency and (2) the least-cost means of achieving the objective.

Of course, societies may seek objectives other than, or in addition to, economic efficiency, in which case the magnitude of V may not be the only factor influencing decisions. More importantly, the usefulness of V in decision making is limited by the uncertainty and differences of opinion about its magnitude that arise because the factual information used in its calculation is imperfect and because people have differing judgments about how income should be distributed.

BENEFIT-COST ANALYSIS: IMPLEMENTATION

We may think of government projects as sacrificing some goods and services (inputs) to create other goods and services (outputs). For example, the outputs of a dam on a river may include flood control, irrigation, electrical power, and recreational facilities. Among the inputs are the steel, cement, labor, etc., required to build the dam; the scenic, agricultural, and other values of the land flooded by the water behind the dam; and the loss of the flood plain environment and its associated wildlife and plant life. Similarly, national defense activities presumably increase the supply of "national security" or "freedom from foreign intervention," while decreasing the supply of other goods and services. To actually carry out a benefit-cost analysis, it is necessary to define, measure, and value the relevant inputs and outputs.

TYPES OF INPUTS AND OUTPUTS

In defining and measuring inputs and outputs, the basic question is how the project affects the supply of various goods and services. In this connection, it is helpful to think of the types of effects (inputs and outputs) that a project may have.

Inputs and outputs may be more or less directly related to the project, thus we have *direct* and *indirect* inputs and outputs. Electrical power and irrigation water are more directly related to the existence of a dam than, say, the quantity and quality of fish in the river. Similarly, inputs and outputs may or may not be *market-traded* — electrical power is, recreational facilities usually are not. They may be *tangible* or *intangible*. Increased agricultural production (wheat, cows, fruit) made possible by irrigation is tangible. Increased (or decreased) opportunities for recreation are intangible effects. Outputs may be *final* or *intermediate*. Electrical power used in the home is a final good because it is not used to produce other goods. Electrical power used by a factory is an intermediate good because it is used to produce other goods. Irrigation water is an intermediate good, while recreational opportunities are final goods. Inputs and outputs may *spill over* — accrue to persons residing beyond the jurisdiction of the decision-making government. A dam that is built by one state may control flooding in other states, providing an output (benefit) spillover. Or there may be a cost spillover if the lake created by a dam floods land in another state or if the irrigation water removed was previously used in other states.

Regardless of how the input and output effects of a project are labeled, they have a common element: They reflect a change in the availability (supply) of one or more goods or services. To be complete, benefit-cost analysis must evaluate all of the effects of a project or activity that take the form of changes in the available quantities of various goods and services. Such effects are termed *real*.

Pecuniary effects, in contrast, arise when the prices of market-traded goods and services change because of the project. A pecuniary cost occurs when, for example, marketing of the additional electrical power from the dam causes a fall in the price that other producers receive for their power. This cost is not real because what the producers lose in revenue and income, the consumers of electricity gain in lower electric power bills. Similarly, pecuniary gains (for example, the wage rates for engineers and iron and cement workers may rise because of the demands for such persons created by the dam project) are offset by pecuniary losses. Since pecuniary losses (gains) are offset by gains (losses), they reflect redistribution of income from one group of society to another, rather than a net loss (gain) to society. Therefore, they are not properly included in the benefits and costs of a project. Of course, pecuniary gains and losses are relevant in assessing the *distributional* (as opposed to efficiency) consequences of a project, a matter that we discuss later in this chapter.

VALUATION OF INPUTS AND OUTPUTS

The first step in the valuation of inputs and outputs is defining and measuring them. In some cases — for example, the electrical power from a dam — this is a simple task. But in many areas of government activity — defense, education, public health — outputs are difficult to define and measure. What does the U.S. Defense Department produce? National security? If so, how is that measured? And how many units of it are obtained when the missile force is increased by one missile? Schools "educate." But what is *education?* How is that measured? By scores on achievement tests? By the lifetime incomes of those educated? By adjustment to and acceptance of prevailing social mores? How much education is produced when an additional teacher is employed?

Inputs may also be difficult to define and measure. If the Grand Canyon is flooded when the Colorado River is dammed to provide water and electricity to California, what is lost? What is the input? How many units of it are lost?

Questions of that sort, which are inherent in defining and measuring project inputs and outputs, are obviously difficult. But they must be answered in the benefit-cost analysis of many government activities. And to the extent that they cannot be answered to the satisfaction of the members of society, benefit-cost analysis cannot be used, either as a mechanism of or an aid to decision making. Ironically and unfortunately, the areas in which defining and measuring inputs and outputs are most difficult are the areas in which there is the strongest case for collective decisions about resource allocation. This is not mere coincidence, however. Markets fail for basically the same reasons that benefit-cost analyses are either difficult or infeasible. Notwithstanding the difficulties, let us assume that inputs and outputs can be defined and measured so that we can consider the problem of assigning values to them.

Market prices as values   Some of the inputs and outputs of a project will be market-traded and will therefore have market values, or prices — electricity, cement, labor services, for example. Are the market prices the appropriate values?

Market prices are usually regarded as satisfactory measures of value for outputs that are market-traded, if consumer sovereignty is judged desirable and consumer choices are free of coercion. Acceptance of the principle of consumer sovereignty requires, in turn, acceptance of the existing distribution of income. If the existing distribution of income is judged unsatisfactory, then existing market prices, which reflect that distribution, are inappropriate guides to social policy because prices would likely be different if a satisfactory distribution of income prevailed. Apart from those qualifications, the major barrier to the use of market prices in valuing project outputs is that those outputs usually are not market-traded.

Inputs may be valued at market prices if those prices reflect the value of the goods and services that are lost (sacrificed) when the inputs are used for the project being analyzed. That is, the market price of the input must accurately reflect the value *to consumers* of products that can be produced with that input; the price of an input must be the value (to consumers) of its marginal product.[5] In addition, if the value of the marginal product of a given type of input is not the same in all of its uses, then the opportunity cost of the input (the value of the goods that are lost when the input is used for the government project) will depend on the use from which the input is drawn.

Market prices may inappropriately value inputs for a variety of reasons. For example, taxation of a commodity causes its price (value to consumers) to exceed the cost of the inputs used to produce it. Therefore, when a government project draws inputs from production of taxed commodities, input prices understate the value of the lost production. Similarly, the market

5 That statement presumes acceptance of the principle of consumer sovereignty, as we discussed in the preceding paragraph.

prices of inputs diverted from monopolized production may understate their opportunity cost because the prices of such products may exceed their input costs. On the other hand, government subsidy of the production of a commodity causes its price (value to consumers) to be less than its input costs, with the result that input prices overstate the value of the commodities lost when inputs are diverted from the production of subsidized commodities. The production or consumption of some commodities generate external costs (benefits). When a project draws inputs from the production of such commodities, the market prices of the inputs will overstate (understate) the value of the commodities given up. Also, when a project utilizes otherwise unemployed inputs (workers), the market prices of those inputs may exceed their opportunity cost.

Other approaches to valuation   How can values be assigned to inputs and outputs when market prices either do not exist or are inappropriate? Since the cost of an input (resource) used by a project is simply the value of the output (product) that could be produced with the input in its best alternative employment, the problem of valuing inputs and outputs is essentially a problem of valuing products. There is no generally satisfactory means of dealing with this problem. Instead, benefit-cost analysts have followed approaches that vary from situation to situation.

An obvious way to try to value outputs is through surveys that determine what people would be willing to pay for the outputs. This approach runs into the problem that people may not be able or willing to state how they value an output; they may not accurately reveal their preferences.[6] Therefore, economists have resorted to less direct means of valuation.

Project outputs may be intermediate goods that are inputs to the production of final goods. If so, the project output may be valued as the resulting increase in the market value of the final goods. For example, irrigation water used in farm production may not be market-traded and valued. But the value of the water is readily determined as the net increase in the value of farm production that it makes possible — the increase in the value of farm production, less the cost of the other inputs required for the production increase. Similarly, part of the value of flood control is the net value of the additional agricultural production that it makes possible. And the benefits of a highway can be partially valued at the saving in costs to the trucking industry made possible by the highway.

A project may sometimes reduce or eliminate costs that society must otherwise bear. If so, the magnitude of those cost savings provide a "lower limit" estimate of the benefits of the project. For example, the benefits of

6 Recall our discussion of this point in Chapter 4, p. 94.

pollution control projects are at least as great as the damages they prevent. Similarly, the benefits of a public program to vaccinate against a contagious disease (such as flu) may be partially measured as the savings in hospitalization and work-loss costs.

Projects often reduce risks — of flooding, accidents, loss of life. Such risk reduction has value apart from the implied prevention of losses (flood damages, etc.). Although intangible, risk reduction is no less a good or benefit than more tangible goods. To illustrate, suppose a dam prevents floods that cause crop losses of $1 million in one out of ten years, on the average. Suppose also that this is the only loss that the flood causes — there are no other damages to life or property. How much is the dam worth to the people whose property is subject to flooding? Presumably they would pay up to $100,000 per year for the dam's services in preventing crop losses.[7] But they would likely pay more because the flood prevention allows them to operate in a more certain environment. If they are willing to pay $110,000 per year, then $10,000 per year is the value of the risk reduction provided by the dam. These risk-reduction benefits are at least as great as the net cost of the flood insurance that the property owners no longer carry. This net cost, the difference between the premiums paid to insurance companies and the amount that the companies paid out in damage claims, is the amount that the property owners have been paying to reduce the risks associated with periodic flooding.

Similar reasoning helps to establish the value of the lives saved by a project. A person's initial reaction to the idea of valuing lives might be that life is "priceless" and that it is "hardhearted" to try to put a value on life. But is life in fact priceless? We implicitly put a price on life everytime we make a decision not to use resources so as to increase the life expectancies of some or all of our population. For example, suppose a highway between two cities can be built in either of two ways. Method 1 will cost $10 million less than method 2 because the former involves narrower traffic lanes, fewer traffic signals, and sharper curves. However, accident rates will be higher with method 1 than method 2. Over the years that the highway will be used, auto accidents will kill twenty more people with method 1 than with method 2. If society nevertheless chooses to use method 1, it is implicitly saying that the additional lives that will be lost are worth less than $500,000 each, on the average.

Of course, this reasoning only establishes that societies do, and in fact must, value lives either implicitly or explicitly. It does not tell us how we should go about determining how much a life is worth. One approach, an

7 The expected loss from flooding is the probability of flooding (.1) multiplied by the loss sustained if flooding occurs ($1 million).

economic approach, to valuing life is simply to say that the value of a life is that amount required to compensate all persons affected by the loss of a life for its loss. If undertaking or failing to undertake a particular project would result in the death of a particular person with a high degree of certainty, then valuing life would be fraught with emotion and difficult at best. The benefit-cost analyst would have to determine what those affected by a particular person's death would pay to save his or her life or require as compensation to endure the person's death.

However, most projects do not entail the loss of a life that is identifiable before hand. They instead result in a particular set of people being subjected to a greater or lesser risk of loss of life. Therefore, the value of a project's effects on life expectancies often may be defined and measured by the amount that affected persons would pay for the risk reduction provided by the project or would require as compensation for the risk increases implicit in the project.[8]

Governmental projects that provide transportation and recreation facilities; reduce air, water, and noise pollution; provide police and fire protection, etc., may affect property values. The change in property values caused by the project measures part or all of the discounted net benefits of the project. For example, the noise and air pollution generated by a municipal airport may cause homes located near the airport to have a lower market value than identical homes located elsewhere. If so, we may argue that, because people choose to suffer the damages in exchange for the lower housing price, the damages caused by the airport are less than or equal to this price differential.[9] Although this approach to measuring net benefits has been applied with some success, it does meet with some technical difficulties. And it seldom provides a complete measure of benefits and costs because they do not always affect property values.[10]

DISCOUNTING

Investment projects increase the availability of goods in future periods and therefore increase the welfare of persons living in those periods. But they

8 For further discussion of the problems of valuing life, see E. J. Mishan, "Evaluation of Life and Limb: A Theoretical Approach," *Journal of Political Economy*, 79, No. 4 (July-August 1971): 687–705.

9 Similarly, there is some differential in rent that would induce persons to live in rental housing near the airport rather than elsewhere. This differential is a measure of the damages suffered by the renters because of the airport.

10 See R. C. Lind, "Spatial Equilibrium, The Theory of Rents, and the Measurement of Benefits from Public Programs," *Quarterly Journal of Economics*, 87 (May 1973): 188–207; and the comments on that article in the August 1975 issue of the journal.

also reduce the availability of goods to persons living in the current period (period of investment). Investment projects thus reduce the current availability of goods in order to enhance their future availability.

As we noted earlier, it is customary to *discount* (assign less weight to) the future benefits and costs of an investment project. The main argument for discounting is that failure to do so would lead to acceptance of an investment project that merely increases the future availability of goods by the same amount that it reduces their present availability, thereby making some persons worse off (in their own judgment).[11]

Discount rate defined   The resources used in an investment project can be drawn basically from three sources: private investment, private consumption, or other government projects. Resources drawn from private investment would probably have earned a positive return. If so, a government project having a zero return must make some persons worse off than they would have been had the resources been invested privately. Indeed, a government project entails a welfare loss unless its social marginal rate of return (SMRR) equals or exceeds the SMRR on the investment that it displaces.[12]

To determine whether a project's SMRR equals or exceeds a particular rate, we discount the project's net benefits by that rate. For example, both projects A and B of Table 7-1 have a rate of return in excess of 10 percent because they have positive present values (V) when their net benefit streams are discounted at 10 percent. Therefore, both projects promote efficiency if they draw resources from investment that has only a 10 percent SMRR. But only project A meets this efficiency test if the alternative investment has a SMRR of 15 percent. These statements assume, of course, that all social benefits and costs were included when calculating the net benefit streams of the two projects.

If the resources used by a project do not displace private investment but, instead, reduce consumption, the project that simply returns its costs may decrease welfare because people appear to prefer present to future goods. They have positive time preference. One important reason for positive time preference is uncertainty about the future. For example, a person who is just indifferent between $100 now and $110 a year from now is said to have a

---

11 An example would be a project that costs $100,000 in 1978 and generates net benefits of $20,000 annually for the subsequent five years, 1979–1983.

12 The rate of return on either private or government investment is the discount rate for which the present value of the investment, V, is exactly zero. The rate of return thus calculated for the marginal unit of investment is termed the SMRR if *all* social benefits and costs are included in the benefit and cost streams that are discounted. The private marginal rate of return (PMRR), in contrast, may not reflect external benefits and costs — benefits and costs that do not show up in the market prices that are typically used in calculating private rates of return.

marginal rate of time preference (MRTP) of 10 percent per year. If those who bear the current cost of a government project through reduced consumption have a 10 percent marginal rate of time preference, the project must have a return over current cost of 10 percent per year if it is to compensate them for their deferral of consumption without making some persons worse off.

The conclusion to be drawn is that when a government project draws resources from the private sector, it promotes efficiency only if it has a positive present value (V) when its net benefit stream is discounted by the appropriate rate of discount, which is called the *social discount rate* (SDR). The SDR is either the SMRR of the displaced private investment or the MRTP of those whose consumption is reduced by the project. This conclusion presumes that benefit and cost streams and the discount rate are correctly measured.

Similarly, when a project draws resources from other government investments, the SDR should be the SMRR of the displaced government projects.[13] Or, if the displaced government projects are providing goods in only the current period, then the appropriate discount rate is the MRTP of those persons who must forgo these government-provided goods if the government investment project is undertaken.

While few would argue against discounting, there is no agreement about what the SDR should be. This is so for two reasons. MRTP and SMRR are difficult to measure. Also, some argue that the SDR should not be based on existing rates of time preference and rates of return, even if they are correctly measured. Let us consider these two problems in turn.

Measurement problems Discounting requires information about marginal rates of time preference and social marginal rates of return. Unfortunately, different measures of these rates may be obtained, depending on the source of the resources used by the project.

When a government project draws resources from consumption and is financed by borrowing, the MRTP of those persons who give up the resources used in the project is approximately equal to the interest rate on government bonds.[14] That is, since they are willing to lend to government at that rate, then that rate approximates the SDR because it is sufficient to compensate them for the goods they forgo in making the loan.

13 It is only when the government budget is fixed that undertaking one project displaces another government project. If the size of the budget is fully variable up and down, then we may always think of resources as being drawn from the private sector.

14 That statement is subject to qualification, as discussed in Mark V. Pauly, "Risk and the Social Rate of Discount," *American Economic Review*, 60, No. 1 (March 1970):195–198.

Determining the SDR is more complicated if the project draws resources from consumption by taxation rather than by government borrowing. In this case we have no obvious measure of the MRTP of those who give up the resources used by the project. When the tax falls on the poor, the MRTP may be fairly high, as indicated by the high interest rates that low-income persons pay on loans from consumer credit companies and "loan sharks." When the tax falls on higher income persons and, specifically, persons who lend money to government by holding government bonds, then the MRTP may be approximated by the interest rate on government bonds. Thus, a high SDR (20–30 percent) is more likely to be appropriate when projects are financed by taxing the poor rather than the rich.

When the government borrows to finance a project that draws resources from private investment rather than private consumption, is the SDR the interest rate on government bonds? Not unless this interest rate equals the SMRR on the displaced private investment, which is usually not the case. Some argue that the SDR exceeds the interest rate on government bonds in this case because of business taxes. To see why, let us suppose a business borrows at the same rate of interest as government, say 5 percent, to finance an investment.[15] To pay an interest rate of 5 percent *and* a property tax of, say, 2 percent, the business must earn a return on its investment of 7 percent. Thus, the PMRR on private investment may exceed the interest rate on government bonds.[16] And, it is argued, the appropriate discount rate also exceeds this interest rate.

However, this argument is not complete because the SDR is measured by the SMRR rather than the PMRR on the private investment that is displaced by the government project. The SMRR on private investment may not exceed the government bond rate even if the PMRR does. This is true for two reasons: First, the SMRR will be less than the PMRR to the extent that there are external costs associated with private production that are not reflected in private rates of return.[17] Second, government supplies goods and services to corporations that may offset, in part or in full, the taxes that corporations pay. Thus, unless we know how private rates of return are affected by external costs and benefits and government provision of services to producers, we cannot know whether the appropriate rate of discount exceeds or falls short of the interest rate on government bonds when the project is fi-

15 This statement assumes that lenders view government and corporate bonds as equally risky.

16 The PMRR may also exceed the interest rate on governments bonds because people view lending to corporations as more risky than lending to governments and therefore require a higher interest rate for loans to the former.

17 External benefits from private production would have the opposite effect, making the SMRR greater than the PMRR.

nanced by government borrowing. Neither can it be argued that the SDR is measured by the observed PMRR on displaced private investment. The same conclusions apply if the project is financed by taxation and draws resources from private investment.

Relevance of measured rates   Three other issues arise in determining the SDR, even in the absence of the measurement problems. First, people may be myopic — their MRTP may be "too high" — in that they will save less and consume more than is optimal *from their own point of view*. Second, investment, in effect, redistributes income from persons living in the current period (of investment) to persons living in future periods. There is no reason to think that a fair or equitable intertemporal (intergeneration) distribution of income will be achieved if the SDR is based on the *present* population's MRTP. Indeed, one might expect the present population to take too much for itself and leave too little for posterity. Conservationists argue in this manner, suggesting that projects that preserve resources (and income) for the future should be discounted at rates lower than the current population's MRTP. Third, and relatedly, some argue that distributional issues should be settled through political processes.

With respect to the problems of determining the SDR, two conclusions are inescapable. First, even if we think that the SDR should be based on actual marginal rates of time preference and return on investment, we may be unable to objectively and accurately measure such rates. Second, apart from measurement problems, we can question the suitability of observed rates on two grounds: (1) Consumers are myopic and (2) intertemporal equity in the distribution of income may require more or less investment than would be forthcoming if these discount rates were used. These conclusions in turn imply what, in fact, is the case: The choice of the SDR is a political decision.

UNCERTAINTY AND BENEFIT-COST ANALYSIS

Uncertainties arise at many points in benefit-cost analyses. Future consequences of policies and projects are far from predictable. (The expectations about the frequency and severity of flooding on which the analysis of a flood control project are based may or may not be realized.) Values can be assigned to inputs and outputs only with some, often unknown, degree of error. Discount rates can, at best, be imperfectly measured. Consequently, we often cannot plausibly assign a *single* present value to a project. There is, instead, a range of possible values, each corresponding to different future states of the world or different assumptions about the discount rate and the values of inputs and outputs. Uncertainty does not render benefit-cost analysis useless; indeed, the information about the *range* of possible effects (present values) of policies that may be generated through such analyses is helpful in decision making under uncertainty.

While there is likely to be some uncertainty about the outcomes of all projects, the degree of uncertainty may be greater for some projects than others. This raises the question of whether the degree of uncertainty should be an additional factor in the selection of projects. For example, projects X and Y may have the same *expected* present values, but the possible deviations from this expected value may be greater for project X than Project Y. Should we therefore favor Y over X? If so, should we also rank projects with less uncertain but lower expected present values over projects with more uncertain but higher expected values? Generally acceptable answers to these questions have not been developed. At this point, we can only say that such choices and rankings must be and are being made, either explicitly or implicitly.[18]

DISTRIBUTIONAL CONSIDERATIONS IN BENEFIT-COST ANALYSIS

Benefit-cost analysis, as we have explained it and as it is typically practiced, is concerned primarily with efficiency in resource allocation. However, distributional issues arise unless two conditions are met: (1) The existing distribution of income is satisfactory and (2) any changes in that distribution resulting from a project are negligible.

As we noted earlier, when the first condition is not met, market prices may be inappropriate measures of the value of outputs and the opportunity costs of inputs. Since market prices reflect the distribution of income, if income were redistributed to achieve a fair or satisfactory distribution, market prices might be significantly changed. And the present value of a project might be significantly different if its inputs and outputs were valued at prices based on the appropriate rather than the prevailing distribution of income. In addition, the cost of collective action may not be independent of how the gains and costs from the project are distributed.[19] In other words, we cannot rely on observed market prices for valuation of inputs and outputs if we think that the prevailing distribution of income should be significantly altered. And benefit-cost analysis of many, if not most, projects therefore will be impractical.

The second condition often will not be met. A project may provide employment to previously unemployed resources and it may affect the incomes received by particular resources (persons), whether employed or unemployed. Although pecuniary benefits and costs are not considered in the

18 For further discussion of uncertainty and benefit-cost analysis, see E. J. Mishan, *Cost-Benefit Analysis*, 2nd ed. (New York: Praeger, 1976), pp. 337–381.
19 See Chapter 4.

determination of a project's present value, they are quite relevant to an assessment of the project's distributional effects. Should benefit-cost analysis take account of these effects? If so, how? In particular, should a project that is inefficient by benefit-cost criteria nevertheless be undertaken if it improves (makes more equitable) the distribution of income?

To answer those questions, we must compare the costs of income redistribution by a tax-transfer mechanism with the costs of redistribution through government projects.[20] If the costs of operating a tax-transfer system are lower than the costs (welfare losses) implicit in accepting inefficient projects for distributional reasons, then the tax-transfer system is the preferred means of redistribution.[21] And decisions regarding a project should be based solely on efficiency criteria. In other terms, when deciding whether to undertake a project, its income distribution effects are relevant only if it is more costly to redistribute income via tax-transfer mechanisms than through the selection of projects that promote distribution objectives.[22]

COST-EFFECTIVENESS ANALYSIS

Cost-effectiveness analysis seeks to answer a more limited and less ambitious question than does benefit-cost analysis: What is the least-cost way of obtaining a given result (output)? Cost-effective analysis is more limited because it does not seek an answer to the questions: How much is the output worth? Is the result worth achieving? But, although cost-effectiveness analysis does not require that outputs (results) be valued, it does require that outputs be defined and measured and that inputs be defined, measured, and valued. The problems met in carrying out these latter tasks are the same as with benefit-cost analysis. An example of cost-effectiveness analysis would be comparing highway and mass-transit modes of transporting people into cities.

Because it is more limited than benefit-cost analysis in its objectives, cost-effectiveness analysis may be applied more widely in government decision

20 Examples of projects that might improve the incomes of the poor vis-à-vis the rich are educational and training programs for the disadvantaged and investment projects (power, irrigation) that increase employment and production in regions having high unemployment rates (Appalachia, Indian reservations).

21 An inefficient project is one having either a negative present value or a lower present value than forgone projects. The costs of operating a tax-transfer system include the costs implicit in the excess burden of taxation (see Chapter 9).

22 For further discussion of these issues, see Burton A. Weisbrod, "Income Distribution Effects and Benefit-Cost Analysis," in S. B. Chase, ed., *Problems in Public Expenditure Analysis* (Washington: Brookings, 1968); and U.S., Congress, Joint Economic Committee, "Collective Action and the Distribution of Income: A Conceptual Approach," in *The Analysis and Evaluation of Public Expenditures*, 91st Cong., first sess., 1969, pp. 177–200.

making. It is easier to determine whether missiles or bombers are the least-cost way of delivering a nuclear bomb to a given target than it is to determine whether having such capability is worth its cost.

PLANNING, PROGRAMMING, BUDGETING

Planning, programming, and budgeting (PPB) systems present government budgets in a way that makes it easier to evaluate expenditure proposals and compare alternative budgetary requests. PPB systems have been increasingly used by governments. They may or may not involve integral use of benefit-cost and cost-effectiveness analyses.[23]

There are several dimensions to PPB. First, government activities are defined according to programs. The programs may cut across government agencies, but typically they are defined within government agencies. For example, the U.S. Department of Health, Education, and Welfare has a broad program of education, which may then be grouped into classifications — "development of basic skills," "development of vocational and occupational skills," "development of academic and professional skills," etc. Within "development of vocational and occupational skills," subcategories include "improving the education of the general population," "improving the education of the disadvantaged," "improving the education of the handicapped."[24]

Second, the various programs of government are presented in terms of goals or objectives that are to be accomplished. This step requires government agencies to ask themselves what they are really trying to accomplish, and it widens the perspective of decision makers. For example, with the PPB approach, the purpose of a highway department is not to build highways, and the output is not miles of highways built. Highways are a means to an end, and goods and people can be transported by various means: highways, airways, waterways, railways, etc. PPB requires an answer to the questions: What are the goals of a transportation program? Does one mode of transportation accomplish those goals more effectively than another?

A third dimension of PPB is that of attempting to measure the output, or success, of government programs in terms of the stated goals. In measuring the output of transportation modes, we might want to know how each mode affects the level of pollution, reduces congestion, saves lives, reduces property damage, and displaces residents. In measuring the effectiveness of

---

23 For a discussion and evaluation of PPB, see Charles L. Schultze, *The Politics and Economics of Public Spending* (Washington: Brookings, 1968); Jesse Burkhead and Jerry Miner, *Public Expenditure* (Chicago and New York: Aldine-Atherton, 1971), chap. 6; Aaron Wildavsky, "Rescuing Policy Analysis from PPBS," in *Public Expenditures and Policy Analysis*, eds. Robert H. Haveman and Julius Margolis (Chicago: Markham Publishing Company, 1970).

24 See Burkhead and Miner, *Public Expenditure*, p. 188.

police protection, we might record the number and types of crimes, the value of lost property, and an index of the community's feeling of security.

The fourth and fifth aspects of PPB are those of determining the cost of the programs and projecting the costs over a number of years. The appropriate concept of cost is opportunity cost, as defined for benefit-cost analysis, and not money costs. Long-range planning is undertaken because budgetary commitments for one year imply budgetary commitments for future years. For decision making, it is relevant whether $20 million spent for a project today entails additional costs of $500 million or $100 million over a period of ten years.

Although PPB is superior to the conventional budgeting format, which simply states the cost of inputs used by various government agencies, it has limitations. There are problems with defining programs and deciding which government agencies should be responsible for administering the programs. Is West Point Academy an educational program, a national defense program, or both? Is housing assistance for veterans a veterans' benefit, national defense, or a housing program?

Problems also arise in defining goals, measuring output, and assigning costs to various programs. For example, what do we want an educational program to accomplish? Presumably we want an educational program to turn out a different person, but that is a very vague goal. Do we want to increase a person's lifetime earnings? Promote equality of opportunity? Improve citizenship? Enhance the quality of life? Some of those goals are not measurable, and analysts settle on more operational, but less interesting, measures of output, such as achievement-test scores and years of school completed.

Since the outputs of many government activities cannot be measured in terms of some common denominator, such as the dollar, it is difficult to determine the trade-offs among alternative uses of resources. How do we compare, say, "reduced crime" with "increased literacy" in deciding how to allocate resources between police protection and education? PPB cannot provide answers to such questions. The best it can do is improve analysis of program decisions. Ultimately, budgetary decisions are resolved through the political process, and the decisions reached may be influenced by PPB. Political decision making is the subject of the next chapter.

SUMMARY

Several techniques for discovering and evaluating the economic effects of government policies have been developed. And they are presently used in varying degrees by federal, state, and local governments.

The fundamental analytical framework is that of benefit-cost analysis, which makes clear what must be done if the economic effects of alternative plans are to be compared and evaluated. Benefit-cost analysis seeks an answer to the question of whether a particular activity is worth undertaking (does it produce aggregate welfare gains?) when it is undertaken at least-cost. Cost-effectiveness analysis trys to answer the more limited question: Given that a particular activity is to be undertaken, what is the least-cost means of doing so? PPB systems are frameworks for putting information in a form that is useful to decision makers. Both cost-effectiveness and benefit-cost analysis can be used as integral parts of a PPB system.

The main objective sought through the use of these techniques is efficiency in government. Unfortunately, they are costly to use. In particular, the information requirements of benefit-cost analysis are often so great as to make it either prohibitively costly or totally infeasible. And the cost and difficulty of benefit-cost analysis increases as the need for it increases — as the product of government activity becomes increasingly public in character. We are therefore often unable to determine whether a particular policy is or is not superior to other policies on efficiency grounds — efficiency criteria are not workable. That is, welfare-maximizing policies cannot be determined by a scientific benefit-cost calculus, and economic decision making cannot be left to technicians. There is always a trade-off between seeking policies that are consistent with efficiency (or other) criteria and the costs of doing so. This trade-off also arises in connection with political decision making, as we shall see in the next chapter.

SUPPLEMENTARY READINGS

Dorfman, Robert, ed. *Measuring Benefits of Government Investments.* Washington: Brookings, 1965.

Haveman, Robert H., and Margolis, Julius, eds. *Public Expenditures and Policy Analysis.* Chicago: Markham, 1970.

Mishan, E. J. *Cost Benefit Analysis.* 2nd ed. New York: Praeger, 1976.

Musgrave, Richard A. "Cost-Benefit Analysis and the Theory of Public Finance." *Journal of Economic Literature* 7 (September 1969): 797–806.

Schultze, Charles L. *The Politics and Economics of Public Spending.* Washington: Brookings, 1968.

CHAPTER EIGHT

DECISION MAKING THROUGH DEMOCRATIC POLITICAL PROCESSES

Individual preferences for private goods are revealed by market transactions as people each purchase the quantity of each good that they prefer, given their income and the prevailing prices. Each person's preferred quantity of a pure public good will also depend on what the taxpayer-voter perceives to be its price. But each person cannot freely adjust the available quantity to this preferred quantity, because the same quantity is available to all persons. That is, preferences for public goods cannot be revealed by allowing individuals to purchase their preferred quantity at a stated price. Instead, with public goods, there must be an agreement about the quantity that is to be supplied to all of the members of a community. And, unless cost-sharing agreements are already settled or constitutionally determined, the price or cost of the good to each person must be agreed upon. Such agreements require institutions or rules for making decisions. This chapter examines political processes for making decisions about public goods and their financing.

POLITICAL PROCESSES DEFINED

Political processes are basically mechanisms that translate individual preferences (rankings of alternatives) into social, or community, rankings and a social choice. Specifically, individuals and groups act through political processes to determine government budgetary and regulatory policies and thereby affect resource allocation and income distribution.[1] Political pro-

---

1 A contrasting view of the political process is that government is an entity with its own preference or welfare function.

cesses involve voting and activities variously characterized as campaigning, lobbying, negotiation, vote trading, and logrolling. Also, the operation of political processes and the implementation of political decisions require an administrative apparatus (a bureaucracy), the structure and staffing of which influences decisions.

In our analysis of political processes, we will be largely concerned with how the processes generate information about individual preferences and weight those preferences, explicitly or implicitly, to obtain a preferred or chosen policy for the community. The extent to which individual preferences are revealed through political decision making is of special interest because preferences regarding public goods are not revealed through market processes. Another concern is the evaluation of the outcomes of political decision making. Does a process result in policies that promote allocative efficiency? How does it distribute the gains and costs of government policies? Does this distribution promote specified distribution objectives? Of special interest is whether one person or group is likely always to lose. Individuals presumably attempt to secure welfare gains through their political activity, just as they do in their market activity. Does individual action through political processes therefore achieve those welfare gains that Chapters 3 and 4 show to be unobtainable through market processes?

Our focus will be on democratic processes, in which voting by the electorate on policies and for their representatives is a central element. Our analysis will first examine voting mechanisms, beginning with the case of direct voting on single issues and examining the consequences of alternative voting rules, such as unanimity and majority voting. Then we will look at the more realistic case of representative government. Finally, the analysis will indicate that decisions made through political processes are not determined solely by the votes of either the people or their representatives. Instead, the set of alternatives voted upon is greatly restricted by bureaucracies, technical advisers, committees, etc. For example, the standing committees in Congress often determine which issues are to be brought to the floor of Congress for a direct vote. Also, the alternatives selected through voting often leave a great deal of latitude to those charged with executing the decisions. Thus, voting usually just narrows the range of outcomes, after starting with an allocative set that has already been narrowed.

VOTING MODELS OF THE POLITICAL PROCESS

The most easily analyzed political processes are those in which voters follow some rule to select directly one alternative from a set of mutually exclusive alternatives. A voting mechanism consists of (1) a specification of who votes, (2) a procedure for determining the set of alternatives to be voted upon, and (3) a rule for choosing an alternative from that set. Our analysis assumes that everyone who is affected by a policy is eligible to, and in fact does, vote and that all feasible alternatives are considered.[2] In considering the question of how the winning alternative is to be determined, we will first look at the *majority* and *unanimity* rules in the relatively simple case of direct voting on single issues. Then we will treat the cases of multiple issue and representative voting, in which people vote on several issues at the same time or for representatives.

MAJORITY RULE

Although majority rule may be employed in making decisions on a variety of matters, the following analysis focuses on decisions about public goods.[3] To illustrate how the output of a public good is determined under majority rule voting, let us consider a three-person community, the members of which have the marginal value curves d_A, d_B, and d_C in Figure 8–1. Each person's preferred quantity of the public good X is that for which the person's marginal *tax price* equals his or her marginal value of X.[4] Marginal tax price is simply the amount by which a person's taxes increase when an additional unit of a public good is provided.

For the tax price to function as a true price in the determination of a person's preferred output, it must be perceived as such; that is, the person must recognize that his or her taxes vary in the indicated way as the output of the public good varies. For example, if the cost of X, shown by the MC curve, is shared equally among the three persons, then each person's tax price is $1/3\, MC$; A, B, and C prefer quantities q_A, q_B and q_C, respectively. However,

---

2 This is not to say that all *conceivable* alternatives are considered. The set of feasible alternatives is restricted by past decisions and the present state of affairs, while the set of conceivable alternatives may include "we could do this if we had not already done that" type of alternative, which would be feasible only if decisions were being made *de novo*.

   The alternatives that could be brought before the electorate are virtually limitless. Budgetary decisions alone require determination of the total amount, composition, and financing of government spending. The total amount of spending may vary over a wide range, and that total may be spent and financed in a variety of ways. Another set of issues may be termed *constitutional* — questions of how issues are to be decided and how choices are to be made. Because of the large number of potential issues to be resolved and because voting is costly, the set of alternatives actually placed before and voted upon by the people is narrowed in a variety of ways.

3 For a discussion of majority voting models, see James M. Buchanan, *Public Finance in Democratic Process* (Chapel Hill: University of North Carolina Press, 1967); and idem, *Demand and Supply of Public Goods* (Chicago: Rand McNally, 1968).

4 Recall from Chapter 4 that individuals' valuations of goods depend on their income; therefore, marginal value curves may shift as incomes change. More specifically, the curve applicable to a public good may depend on how the good is financed To simplify exposition, we assume a given initial distribution of income and that there are no income effects arising from the financing of the good. With these assumptions, the marginal valuation curves are stable.

FIGURE 8-1
PUBLIC-GOOD OUTPUT UNDER MAJORITY RULE: UNDERPRODUCTION

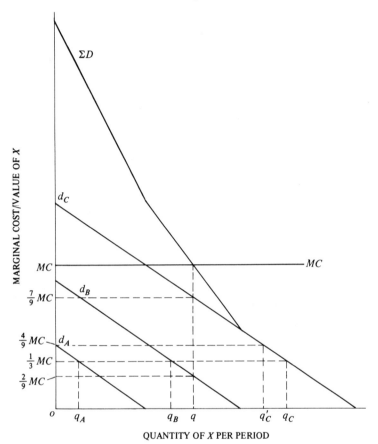

QUANTITY OF X PER PERIOD

because X is a pure public good, the same quantity must be supplied to all persons, and each member's preferences cannot be accommodated.

With majority rule, the common quantity will be q_B. Because B and C prefer q_B to any lesser quantity, q_B wins any election that matches q_B against any lesser quantity. When matched against any quantity greater than q_B, q_B also wins because A and B prefer q_B to any greater quantity. Thus, a majority of voters prefers q_B to any other quantity. This example illustrates the important and perhaps not surprising conclusion that majority rule leads to choice of the *median* preferred quantity.[5]

5 This conclusion is subject to the qualification that individual preferences must be "single-peaked," a condition we discuss more fully later in this chapter.

Economic efficiency The output selected by majority rule, the median preferred quantity, may or may not be the efficient quantity. The efficient quantity is the output for which marginal cost equals the sum of marginal values, assuming costs of collective action are zero at the margin. For the example in Figure 8–1, with equal tax shares and tax prices, the quantity selected by majority rule is less than the efficient quantity, q, which is determined by the intersection of the marginal cost and the sum of marginal values (ΣD) curves. However, the reverse may also be true, as Figure 8–5 shows (see p. 173).

By altering tax prices, each person's preferred quantity and the median preferred quantity may be changed. For example, in Figure 8–1, if C's tax share is increased to $^4/_9$ *MC*, while B's share is reduced to $^2/_9$ *MC*, their preferred quantities change to q'_c and q, respectively. And the median preferred quantity changes to q, the efficient quantity. Thus, the efficient quantity is chosen under majority rule if the median preferred quantity is the efficient quantity.

This example shows that if tax prices can be varied freely and there is enough information about individual marginal values, tax prices can be set so that the quantity chosen by majority vote is the efficient quantity. More generally, if marginal and average tax prices are set equal to each person's marginal valuation of the public good when the efficient quantity is supplied, then the efficient quantity will be unanimously preferred to every other quantity. Such taxation, which is termed *marginal benefit taxation*, results in selection of the efficient quantity by *any* voting rule.[6] For the example in Figure 8–1, marginal benefit taxation requires tax prices of 0, $^2/_9$ *MC*, and $^7/_9$ *MC*, for A, B, and C, respectively.

Unfortunately, the information required for marginal benefit taxation is not available, for reasons we discussed in the preceding chapter. Indeed, a major reason for decision making through voting mechanisms is that information about preferences is not otherwise available. Of course, the more homogeneous peoples' incomes and tastes are, the less their marginal valuations will vary. In the extreme case that incomes and tastes are identical, a system of equal tax prices will lead all persons to want the same quantity. This will be the efficient quantity if the sum of marginal tax prices, which equals the sum of marginal values, also equals the marginal cost of the good. In this case, the government budget is balanced at the margin.

Because marginal benefit taxation is costly if not impossible, some people are likely to be dissatisfied with the quantity provided. In the example in Figure 8–1, persons A and C are dissatisfied when tax prices are equal.

---

6 This statement presumes that people correctly perceive their tax price and vote their true preferences.

Moreover, this dissatisfaction may exist even if the efficient quantity is provided. Since the quantity of a public good cannot be varied among persons, some person will necessarily be dissatisfied unless tax prices are such that each person prefers the same quantity — unless there is unanimity about the quantity to be supplied.

Pareto improvements   Changes in resource allocation that increase the welfare of some persons without reducing the welfare of anyone are termed *Pareto improvements*. The notion of Pareto improvements presumes an existing status quo that will be maintained in the absence of an explicit decision to alter it. Will changes that represent Pareto improvements be chosen under majority rule? The answer might seem to be yes, since no one is made worse off by such a move. However, such is not the case. Although no one will prefer the status quo to any Pareto improvement, there may well be alternatives that a majority prefers to both the status quo and *any* Pareto improvement. Thus, a society that makes decisions by majority rule may reject policies that make everyone better off in favor of policies that harm some people.

Cyclical majorities   The fact that it may not lead to choice of the efficient quantity of a public good is not the only problem with majority rule. Majority rule may not produce stable, nonarbitrary decisions. The winning alternative may depend on the order in which alternatives are considered. For example, let us suppose that there are three voters, A, B and C, and three alternatives, X (a new wing for the city hospital), Y (a swimming pool for the high school), and Z (a new park). Each voter's ranking of the alternatives is displayed in Figure 8–2. Voter A ranks X first, Y second, and Z third. If Y and Z are voted on first, then Y (the swimming pool) wins. If Y is then matched against X, X (the hospital wing) wins. Since X is preferred to Y,

FIGURE 8–2
MULTIPEAKED PREFERENCES: CYCLICAL MAJORITY

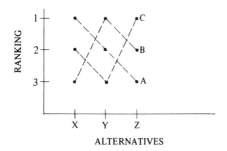

FIGURE 8–3
SINGLE-PEAKED PREFERENCES: STABLE MAJORITY

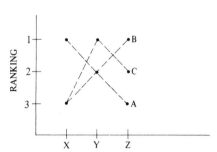

ALTERNATIVES

which is preferred to Z, X seems to be the preferred alternative. However, in an election against Z, X loses (the park wins). Thus, we have the problem that if X is chosen by the former sequence of voting, both B and C have an incentive to form a coalition to reverse the decision and have alternative X displaced by Z. The majority choice is thus arbitrary in that it depends on the order in which pairs of alternatives are voted upon; each of the three alternatives may be chosen if pairs are considered in the appropriate sequence. And the choice is not stable if it can be reconsidered, because no matter which alternative is initially selected, two voters (a majority) will always prefer a different alternative.

This *cyclical majority* problem does not always arise, as the case in Figure 8–3 illustrates. In that case, Y wins over X and Z, and Z wins over X regardless of the sequence of voting. Thus, majority voting produces a unique and stable ranking: Y over Z over X.

The two cases shown in Figures 8–2 and 8–3 differ in an important way: in Figure 8–3, the preferences are *single-peaked*. In the context of decisions about how much of a public good is to be supplied, preferences are single-peaked if each person prefers a particular quantity to either any lesser or any greater quantity. If the alternatives of Figures 8–2 and 8–3 are the amount of spending on, say, elementary education and X, Y, and Z denote low, medium, and high levels of spending, then the preferences of Figure 8–3 are clearly single-peaked. But in the cyclical majority case of Figure 8–2, person C prefers either high or low spending (X or Z) to medium spending (Y) and therefore does not have single-peaked preferences.[7]

The suitability of the majority voting rule clearly depends on whether

7 The classical works on cyclical majorities are Kenneth J. Arrow, *Social Choice and Individual Values* (New York: Wiley, 1963); and Duncan Black, *The Theory of Committees and Elections* (Cambridge: Cambridge University Press, 1958).

preferences are single-peaked for the classes of issues to be voted upon. For public goods decisions, preferences may indeed be single-peaked if the amounts of various public goods are separately determined. In Figure 8–1, each person's preferences are single-peaked. A's utility from the provision of X, as reflected by his or her consumers' surplus, increases as X is increased to A's preferred quantity, q_A, and decreases as X is increased beyond q_A. Thus, A's utility reaches a single peak at q_A. The utilities of B and C similarly peak at q_B and q_C, respectively. More generally, people's preferences regarding the quantity of a public good will be single-peaked if their marginal tax prices are each either constant or a constantly increasing or decreasing function of the amount of the good provided.

While preferences regarding budgetary decisions may be single-peaked, they need not be. For example, if person A's marginal tax price first rises and then falls as spending increases, as shown by the broken line in Figure 8–4, then his or her preferences will not be single-peaked. A's consumer surplus, an index of his or her welfare gain from the provision of X, clearly reaches two peaks.

Preferences also may not be single-peaked if expenditures for several functions are jointly determined, since the proportions of the total budget going to each function may change as budget outlays change.

Equity With majority rule, policies that favor the majority at the expense of the minority may be enacted. Redistribution may be direct, for example, taxing the rich to provide transfer payments to the poor. Or it may occur as public goods are provided, with the majority (minority) receiving goods having greater (lesser) value than their tax payments. In either form, the redistribution may or may not be regarded as fair.

UNANIMITY RULE

Rather than majority rule, a community might require that government policies receive unanimous approval. The output of a particular public good would then be that which is preferred by all persons to all other outputs.[8]

Unless all persons have the same tastes and incomes and therefore the same demand for a public good, unanimity requires that tax prices vary among persons. Moreover, people's marginal tax prices must each equal the individual's marginal valuation of the public good. For the example depicted in Figure 8–5, the quantity q will be unanimously preferred to all other quantities if A, B, and C face marginal and average tax prices of $\frac{1}{10}$ MC, $\frac{2}{5}$ MC, and $\frac{1}{2}$ MC, respectively. Unanimous agreement about the

8 The fundamental work on budgetary choice and the unanimity rule is Knut Wicksell, "A New Principle of Just Taxation," in *Classics in the Theory of Public Finance,* ed. Richard A. Musgrave and Alan T. Peacock (London: Macmillan, 1958).

FIGURE 8–4
TAX PRICES AND UTILITY PEAKS

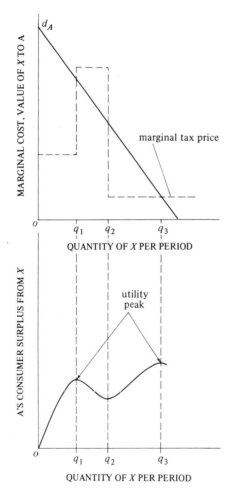

output of a public good is acheived by appropriately adjusting the tax prices people pay for a given quantity, while unanimity regarding output of a private good is achieved by appropriately adjusting the quantity supplied to a person at a given price.

Economic efficiency   In the example in Figure 8–5, the quantity selected by the unanimity rule was economically efficient. Is this generally the case? Yes. By definition, an inefficient quantity is one that in principle can be altered to the benefit of some and the detriment of none. Therefore, there is always an efficient quantity that the community will unanimously prefer to

FIGURE 8–5
PUBLIC-GOOD OUTPUT UNDER MAJORITY RULE: OVERPRODUCTION

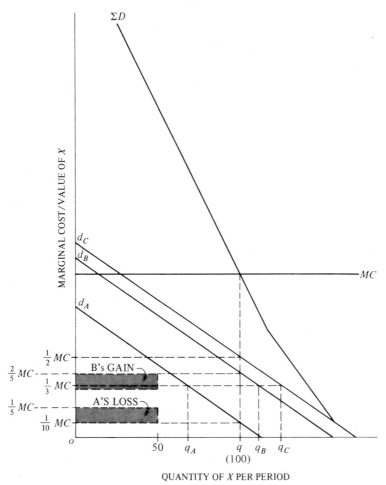

QUANTITY OF X PER PERIOD

any particular inefficient quantity.[9] And any quantity accepted under the rule will be efficient.

That conclusion loses significance once we recognize that there need not be unanimous approval of *any* alternative. One reason is that provision of a public good generates welfare gains that can be distributed in any number of ways. Therefore, a person may reject an efficient output in favor of an

9 This statement assumes that when a person is indifferent about a pair of alternatives, this indifference is interpreted as a vote in favor of, rather than against, each alternative.

inefficient one because the latter implies a more favorable distribution of taxes and, therefore, of the welfare gains from providing the good.[10]

To illustrate, in Figure 8–5, let us label as tax system 1 the case in which marginal and average tax prices for A, B, and C are $1/10$ MC, $2/5$ MC, and $1/2$ MC, respectively. With this tax system, when the efficient quantity of 100 is provided, persons A, B, and C enjoy a consumer surplus represented by the area above their individual tax-price line and below their marginal value curve. Let tax system 2 refer to the case in which A's tax price is set at $1/5$ MC for the first 50 units and $1/10$ MC for any additional units, while B's tax price is set at $1/3$ MC for the first 50 units and $2/5$ MC for any additional units and C's marginal and average tax price is $1/2$ MC. With tax system 2, the efficient quantity is still 100.[11] However, when the efficient quantity is provided, B's consumer surplus is larger (by the shaded rectangle) with tax system 2 than with system 1, while consumer surplus for A is smaller by the same amount with system 2.

With only one tax system, the efficient quantity was unanimously preferred to any other quantity. However, it is easy to see that A prefers a lesser quantity, say 80, under tax system 1 to the efficient quantity of 100 under tax system 2, because A enjoys a larger consumer surplus in the former case. The efficient quantity will not be unanimously preferred if it is provided by tax system 2. Similarly, because B prefers 80 units and tax system 2 to the efficient quantity and tax system 1, the efficient quantity will not be unanimously preferred if it is provided by tax system 1. Thus, when there is more than one tax system (more than one way of distributing the welfare gains from providing the good), then neither the efficient quantity, nor any other quantity, is unanimously preferred.

The conclusion we can draw is very clear: _No alternative will receive unanimous approval unless the alternatives are restricted to those that are consistent with a particular distribution of welfare gains._ That is, the distribution of the inframarginal costs of providing the public good, which is determined by the tax system, must be determined first; then the set of alternatives consistent with that distribution must be voted upon. In the preceding example, the distribution of the inframarginal costs of providing X differ between systems 1 and 2. Person A bears more of these costs under system 2 than system 1, while the reverse is true for B.

10 The net effect of government action might be welfare losses, as we noted in Chapter 4. If so, the problem remains, with the issue being how to distribute the net costs, rather than the net gains, of government action.

11 To simplify the geometric examples, we have assumed that the same marginal valuation curves apply with both tax systems. Since the two systems imply different disposable (after tax) incomes for A and B, this assumption means that marginal valuations are not affected by disposable income changes of the magnitude implicit in a change from one tax system to another.

We can state this conclusion differently: Distributional decisions, which entail choice among alternatives that differ in the amount of income and wealth assigned to one or more persons, always make some person(s) better off at the expense of others. Thus, distributional decisions are impossible under unanimity rule because *each* alternative will be inferior to at least *one* other alternative in the judgment of at least *one* person, who will therefore veto the alternative.

However, even if these distributional issues are settled, two barriers to unanimity remain. First, it is costly to define and vote on alternatives, each of which is a proposal to provide a specific quantity of a public good and to distribute the costs of doing so in a particular way.[12] These costs may more than offset any welfare gains from providing the efficient rather than the inefficient quantity that might be selected by another voting rule. The belief that such cost is very large underlies the frequently expressed judgment that with the unanimity rule it would be impossible to reach a decision.

Second, if the set of alternatives voted upon is open-ended rather than all-inclusive, a person may vote to reject his or her preferred alternative in a particular set, with the expectation that an even more favorable alternative will then be offered.[13] Such behavior, which is termed *strategic voting*, occurs because individual voters each see themselves as being able to block acceptance of any particular alternative. Therefore the problem of strategic voting can be eliminated by employing what Knut Wicksell has termed *relative unanimity* as the voting rule. For example, a 95 percent rule would likely eliminate strategic voting in large groups, because to block an alternative would require a blocking coalition of 5 percent of the voters. However, with smaller groups, the percent required for approval would have to be lower to prevent strategic voting — with less than ten voters and a 90 percent rule, one person could block, with less than five voters and an 80 percent rule, one person could block, etc.

Unanimity and the status quo   A common argument against the unanimity rule is that it would preserve the status quo. In the context of public goods decisions, the status quo might be a zero quantity or the presently provided quantity. This argument is not valid if acceptance of any alternative,

12 An efficient quantity can be defined only with reference to a specific distribution of both income and the costs of the public goods. Discovering this efficient quantity through a voting process requires consideration of *all* alternatives consistent with the specified distributional preconditions. Such wholesale consideration of alternatives is necessary unless the information about preferences that the voting is intended to supply is already available.

13 For example, in Figure 8–5, output q is efficient, and it is preferred to any other output when A, B, and C are charged tax prices of $1/10\ MC$, $2/5\ MC$, and $1/2\ MC$, respectively. But any one of the persons may vote against output of q, hoping to thereby gain (via a lower tax price for the same output or a greater output at the same tax price).

including the status quo, requires unanimous approval. With this interpretation of the unanimity rule, the status quo would be rejected in favor of at
least one alternative unless the status quo is itself efficient.

However, the argument is valid if unanimity rule is taken to mean that
only a limited number of alternatives will be voted upon; and, unless there
is unanimous perference for some alternative other than the status quo, the
status quo will be approved. This rule permits only Pareto improvements
from the status quo. There usually will be a number of Pareto improvements relative to the status quo. Some people will gain more with one improvement than with others; thus, there will not be unanimity about which
improvement to undertake unless the distribution of gains is settled prior to
voting. And the status quo may be chosen even though it is not unanimously preferred to all alternatives.

Voluntary exchange   The outcome under the unanimity rule can be
thought of as a *voluntary exchange*. The exchange of taxes for the public
good is voluntary in that all persons prefer the quantity supplied to any other
quantity (given their incomes and tax prices). And people each would willingly pay the taxes that they do pay rather than forego the good. For the example in Figure 8–5, A, B, and C are each willing to "buy" q units of X at
tax prices of $1/10$ MC, $2/5$ MC, and $1/2$ MC, respectively. Of course, the
police power of the state will nevertheless be needed to collect the taxes,
unless the availability of the good to each person is made dependent on the
person's tax payment.

The availability of the good can be made contingent on the payment of
taxes by each person if the decision rule is that a nonzero quantity of a
public good will be provided to the members of a community only if there is
unanimous approval of the quantity *and* people each indicate their approval
by paying an agreed upon tax price. With this rule, which is the basis of the
voluntary exchange approach, people each see their actions as affecting the
outcome (amount of X), and the free-rider problem is eliminated. The main
defects of this approach are the costs of reaching unanimous agreement
regarding the output of the public good.

Marginal values and income   We are by now well aware that decisions
about public goods are greatly complicated because people place different
values on successive units of a public good. It would therefore be helpful if
there were some observable indicator of the relative values that different people assign to public goods. Such may indeed be the case when differences in
marginal values reflect income differences. The marginal value assigned to
many goods — police and fire protection, parks, libraries — is likely to be
an increasing function of income. If so, then the range of preferred values

can be narrowed by making tax prices an appropriately increasing function of income. In Figure 8–5, the differences in marginal valuation schedules may reflect income differences, so that d_A, d_B, and d_C are representative of persons in low-, medium-, and high-income classes. If so, the range of preferred levels will be large if all persons are charged the same tax price. However, if the tax price is made an increasing function of income, then the range of preferred levels is likely to be narrowed. In particular, to narrow the range of preferred levels, tax payments should be progressive, proportional, or regressive with respect to income as the income elasticity of demand is greater than, equal to, or less than the price elasticity — provided that individuals' preferred levels differ only because their tax prices and incomes differ. More generally, the tax structure can in principle be manipulated to "squeeze" the distribution of preferred policies into a relatively narrow range.

WHICH VOTING RULE?

We have discussed two possible voting rules, majority and unanimity. But many more could be considered. For example, *qualified majorities* of three-fifths or two-thirds are sometimes used. Which voting rule should a community employ in making its decisions? Is there a "best" rule? Or, are some rules "better" than others? We could follow several approaches in trying to answer these questions, but economists would likely base their answers on comparisons of the equity and efficiency implications of alternative rules.

From the preceding analysis we know that any quantity of a public good that is in fact chosen under the unanimity rule will be an efficient quantity, provided that all alternatives are considered in the voting. In addition, if unanimous approval is required for change from a defined status quo, then only Pareto improvements will be approved, and no person's welfare will be reduced below its status quo level. In contrast, under majority rule the quantity chosen need not be efficient, and moves that are not Pareto improvements may be approved. These conclusions are the main arguments for the unanimity rule.

However, we also saw that the unanimity rule usually is not workable for reasons that we now briefly review. First, strategic voting may preclude a decision under unanimity rule.[14] Requiring less than unanimous approval

14 The problem of strategic voting is introduced when and because the free-rider problem is eliminated by requiring 100 percent, rather than a lesser percent, for approval. From the viewpoint of each person, the unanimity rule effectively reduces the group size to two, the person and all other voters. Each person's vote clearly has a potential influence on the outcome under unanimity rule, hence there is no free-rider problem. But there is an incentive and opportunity for strategic behavior.

of alternatives — relative unanimity or qualified majority — eliminates strategic voting because an alternative cannot be blocked by a single person or feasible coalition of persons.

Second, distributional decisions cannot be made under unanimity rule, yet such decisions are necessary to distribute the welfare gains (or losses) of government action and to determine whether the existing distribution of income is desirable. In contrast, rules requiring less than unanimous approval of decisions do permit redistribution and do not require that distribution issues be fully settled before voting on allocation issues. Of course, the capability for making decisions to alter the existing distribution of income is not desirable if the existing distribution is considered satisfactory.

Third, the costs of making decisions under the unanimity rule are high, so high, perhaps, as to prevent a decision from being reached. Such decision costs include the costs of defining and voting on alternatives, which include, in turn, the cost of obtaining information about alternatives and disseminating it to the voters; the voters' costs of assimilating such information; and the costs of actually casting and tabulating votes. Moving from unanimity rule toward majority rule reduces these costs primarily because the alternative set can be restricted, arbitrarily or otherwise.[15] For example, with majority rule, the set can include as few as two alternatives; yet one alternative will always be selected as socially preferred, except, of course, in the case of ties or indifference among alternatives. However, with unanimity rule, the alternative set must be at least large enough to include one alternative that everyone prefers to any other.

It is unclear what conclusion should be drawn from those arguments for and against unanimity rule. No voting rule appears to dominate others on either equity or efficiency grounds. Perhaps the least debatable conclusion is that strict unanimity is unworkable. Beyond this, it is an open question whether other rules, such as simple majority, are preferable to relative unanimity. The case for relative unanimity is strongest when distributional issues have been satisfactorily settled. Use of a rule other than relative unanimity enlarges the minority; some or all of the persons in this enlarged minority may be worse off than they would be under the relative unanimity rule. Does the reduction in decision-making costs obtained by employing a rule other than relative unanimity justify the welfare losses that may be generated for the minority? The answer is more likely to be yes if the minority does not always consist of the same persons. Surely it is more difficult to justify, say, simple majority rule if the same persons consistently make up the minority.

15 Rules that require less than a majority for approval, e.g., a plurality, do not always result in a choice. For example, if 40 percent is required, then in a three-alternative field, two alternatives could be approved. If the field is reduced to two alternatives to prevent this, then the plurality rule is not different from the majority rule.

In comparison to other rules, the relative unanimity rule would require more effort to discover voters preferences and to devise policies consistent with those preferences. The dissatisfied minority that would prefer an alternative to the chosen policy would thus be smaller. However, whether the agreement achieved would be worth its cost is open to question.[16]

MULTIPLE ISSUES AND VOTE TRADING

To this point, our discussion has assumed that only a single issue is being voted upon, although multiple-issue voting is a common practice. The most powerful argument for multiple-issue voting is simply the cost of doing otherwise. For example, it would be extremely costly for either the members of a community or their representatives to vote directly on every item of governmental spending. Thus, budgetary decisions are made for groups of expenditure items, e.g., national defense, health, education, and welfare.

Apart from questions of the costs of voting are the efficiency effects of multiple-issue voting and vote trading. With single-issue voting and no vote trading, the required consensus of voters is obtained by altering quantities or tax prices of public goods or both. However, the ability to alter tax systems and tax prices is limited. Multiple-issue voting and vote trading provide alternative means of gaining approval by allowing the losers on one issue to be compensated by gains on another. The forging of a platform by a political party or coalition is a familiar example of how these techniques may be used to promote consensus. Vote trading reflects the fact that compromise is typically necessary in political decision making.

To illustrate, suppose three projects affect three persons as shown in Table 8–1. Each project is efficient, since the net gain (sum across rows) is positive. Each project will be rejected by a majority if it is voted upon separately and there is no vote trading. However, A would willingly vote for projects 2 and 3 to assure acceptance of project 1; B would vote for projects 1 and 3 to assure acceptance of project 2; and C would vote for projects 1 and 2 to assure acceptance of project 3. Thus, with vote trading, unanimous approval of the three projects could be obtained. Alternatively, the three projects would be unanimously accepted if they were voted upon as an all-or-nothing package, which would be a multiple-issue vote.

---

16 The rules that are actually used for making collective decisions vary considerably. There are different rules for amending the U.S. Constitution, for overriding a presidential veto, for passing tax legislation, for impeaching a president, for building a school house, for convicting a person of a capital crime.

Although we have used equity and efficiency criteria in analyzing voting rules, there are circumstances in which other criteria may be more important. For example, suppose the effects of a decision are very risky, or possibly irreversible, or extremely unpopular and unenforceable. What voting rule is appropriate in such cases?

TABLE 8–1
PAYOFF MATRIX FOR THREE HYPOTHETICAL PROJECTS:
POSITIVE NET BENEFITS

Project	Net gain or loss (−) in dollars from project		
	A	B	C
1	100	−25	− 30
2	− 20	75	− 15
3	− 60	−30	200

Vote trading and multiple-issue voting are desirable for the example in Table 8–1 because they result in the acceptance of efficient projects that would otherwise be rejected. But such is not always the case, as Table 8–2 shows. None of the projects in that example are efficient. If voted upon separately and without vote trading, none are acceptable to a majority. However, A would gain $80 = $100 − $20 by agreeing to vote for project 2 in exchange for B's vote for project 1. B's gain on the exchange would be $20 = $75 − $55. Thus, with vote trading and majority rule, projects 1 and 2 could be accepted, even though the total gains to A and B ($100) fall short of C's loss ($110). Alternatively, C and B could trade votes, with C voting for project 2 in exchange for B's vote on project 3. With such an exchange, projects 2 and 3 would be accepted by a majority, and B and C would have net gains of $5 = $75 − $70 and $140 = $200 − $60, respectively. The total gains of B and C, $145, would fall short of A's losses of $155. Multiple-issue voting produces similar results. A package of projects 1 and 2 wins the approval of A and B, or a package of projects 2 and 3 wins the approval of B and C. In Table 8–2, which is representative of the "pork-barrel" phenomenon, vote trading and multiple-issue voting lead to the choice of inefficient alternatives under majority rule. However, none of the projects would be acceptable under unanimity rule.

Table 8–2 illustrates the Buchanan-Tullock argument that majority vote tends to result in excess public spending.[17] More generally, a majority of voters (or a majority of their representatives in the legislature) may form a coalition to implement projects (public expenditures) that serve their interests. If the costs of the projects are spread among all voters, then the members of the majority coalition will bear less than the full costs of their projects. Thus, a majority may approve projects for which the aggregate benefits are less than aggregate costs for all voters but for which aggregate benefits exceed aggregate costs for the majority. This is one reason why the overexpansion of output we referred to in Chapter 4 may occur.

17 James M. Buchanan and Gordon Tullock, *The Calculus of Consent* (Ann Arbor: University of Michigan Press, 1962), chap. 10.

TABLE 8–2
PAYOFF MATRIX FOR THREE HYPOTHETICAL PROJECTS:
NEGATIVE NET BENEFITS

Project	Net gain or loss (−) in dollars from project		
	A	B	C
1	100	−55	− 50
2	− 20	75	− 60
3	−135	−70	200

The two examples in Tables 8–1 and 8–2 clearly show the ambiguous efficiency implications of vote trading and multiple-issue voting. Inefficient alternatives may be accepted that would otherwise be rejected under majority rule. However, as the percent required for approval increases, it is increasingly difficult, but not impossible, for an inefficient alternative to gain acceptance. Thus, as the percent required for approval increases, vote trading and multiple-issue voting are more likely to facilitate acceptance of efficient alternatives that would otherwise be rejected.

REPRESENTATIVE VERSUS DIRECT VOTING

Decisions may be made by the electorate directly or by elected representatives of the electorate.[18] The major advantage of representative voting is that it is less costly than direct voting. Direct voting requires that each voter either become informed about the issue or vote in ignorance. The costs of informing voters includes: (1) the costs of obtaining information about policies, (2) the costs of disseminating information about policies to the voters, and (3) the costs to the voters of assimilating such information.

The first item is present with either direct or representative voting and is therefore not relevant to the choice between the two voting mechanisms. The second cost (disseminating information via government publications, newspapers, and television) is relatively slight given present-day means of mass communication and the economies of scale present in mass communication processes. Thus, it is the third item of cost that argues in favor of representative voting. It would simply be too time consuming for all voters to try to understand and evaluate the mass of information about government policies that is presently available. In addition, having fewer persons involved in voting reduces the costs of debating the issues and administering the voting system.

18 For an anlysis of the economics of political action in representative government, see Anthony Downs, *An Economic Theory of Democracy* (New York: Harper, 1956).

Representative voting may also facilitate vote trading, which, as we noted earlier, may or may not be desirable. With fewer people actually voting, the communication costs involved in arranging a trade are lower. There is also an incentive for representatives to arrange such trades, since their constituents are unlikely to have identical interests. Policies that favor one group of constituents may harm another. Therefore, representatives have an incentive to seek packages of policies that, on balance, produce net gains for all or a large enough fraction of their constituents to assure re-election. Representatives may act as "brokers" who arrange trades to benefit their constituents.

The main advantage of direct voting by the electorate is that all who are affected by the outcome can thereby express their preferences. With representative voting, some preferences may be disregarded and some information lost. The extent to which preferences are represented depends in part upon the number of representatives elected, the rules determining the eligibility of candidates, and the rules for determining the winner of an election. As the number of representatives increases relative to the population, it is perhaps more likely that different preferences will be represented. Diverse preferences are also more likely to be represented if candidates are chosen from among subsets of the population (candidate eligibility), such as occupational groups, age groups, and nationalities.

In fact, direct voting on political issues is rare in the United States, occurring most frequently in votes on local government bond issues. Typically, only a small minority of eligible voters participates in such direct votes. Voters apparently prefer to delegate most authority for decision making to elected representatives. The relatively high costs of direct voting apparently outweigh its advantages.

VOTER ELIGIBILITY AND PARTICIPATION

Efficiency and equity criteria are fundamentally concerned with the impact of government policies on the welfare of individuals. To achieve efficiency in allocation and equity in distribution, the political process must take into account the benefits and costs from government action that accrue to each individual. If voting is the basic means by which information about benefits and costs is generated, then each person who is affected by government should be allowed to vote. With democratic governments, this is essentially the case. The right to vote is extended to all persons, except those who are presumed to be either unaffected by a government's actions (because they reside outside its jurisdiction or are not permanent residents) or unable to evaluate the effects of policies (minors).

Unfortunately, as our analysis of voting mechanisms has shown, an equitable and efficient outcome is not guaranteed by the participation of all voters. One can hardly keep from concluding that matters are worse in the "real world," in which eligibility is restricted by a variety of means and participation is low.[19]

INCOME DISTRIBUTION AND POLITICAL EQUALITY

Inequality in the distribution of income may lead to inequality in political power even if "one person-one vote" applies. The main reason is that a political system requires resources to operate. These resources may be supplied by the relatively wealthy, giving them extra political power, especially in a representative system of government. There are basically two possible solutions to this problem: distribute income and wealth equally or publicly supply the resources needed to operate the process.

BUDGETARY PROCESS

The preceding discussion helps us to understand the role of voting in political decision making. But government tax and expenditure decisions are not determined solely by direct vote of either the electorate or their representatives. Instead, those decisions are made as government budgets are drawn up and carried out.[20] And the process by which tax and expenditure decisions are made is commonly termed a *budgetary process*.

The main participants in this process are the voters; the officials whom they elect (the president and members of Congress at the federal level and governors, mayors, councilmen, legislative representatives, etc., at the state and local levels); the various employees of government (the bureaucracy); and the lobbyists, consultants, etc., who provide information about and advocate or oppose particular policies. Tax and expenditure decisions are made by individuals, but most people participate in the decision-making process only as voters.

In discussing the budgetary process and the issues that arise in budgeting, we shall focus on the budgetary process of the federal government.

GENERAL PROCEDURE

The federal budget for each fiscal year is prepared initially by the executive branch of government. Government departments and agencies present preliminary budgetary requests to the Office of Management and Budget

---

19 Low voter participation can be expected in large-group decision making for the same reason that the free-rider problem arises. People each see the outcome as being independent of their own actions (votes) and therefore do not participate in collective decision making. This has lead to the suggestion that people be given a tax credit or some other financial incentive for voting.

20 In general terms, a budget is simply a plan for collecting and spending government revenues over some period. As revenues are collected and spent, goods and services are provided to the population and income is transferred among individuals.

(OMB), an agency responsible to the president. The requests contain memoranda justifying program proposals. The OMB reviews these preliminary requests and, after consulting with the president and advisers, submits guidelines to government departments and agencies. They use the guidelines and then present another round of budgetary requests to OMB, which reviews the requests, discusses and examines them with the agencies' personnel, and makes budgetary recommendations. The president reviews the final requests and submits the budget document to the Congress. The Congress evaluates the president's budget and authorizes spending and appropriates funds subject to presidential veto. The budget that is finally approved by both the president and the Congress usually differs from the budget initially proposed by the president.[21]

Governments change tax structures less frequently than they review and make spending decisions. One reason is that tax revenues increase with economic growth, so rising expenditure levels can be financed without changing the tax structure. Another is the difficulty of obtaining agreement about how the tax structure should be changed.[22] However, tax changes aimed at stabilizing the economy have been made in recent years. And it can be argued (see Chapter 17) that economic stabilization is best achieved by short-run adjustments in taxes, leaving government spending to be determined primarily on efficiency grounds. Tax legislation at the federal level must originate in the House Ways and Means Committee.

ROLE OF THE EXECUTIVE BRANCH

The government agencies of the executive branch constitute the major part of what is often called the "federal bureaucracy." In making their budgetary requests, the dominant concern of these agencies is probably the perpetuation and growth of the agencies themselves, rather than economic efficiency. The main reason for such behavior is that efficiency in government is difficult to measure and is not directly rewarded. In the private sector, the reward for efficiency is increased profits, which is prohibited in the government sector. Not being motivated to increase profits, government bureaucrats have an incentive to increase their power, prestige, and salaries by increasing the size of their operations. Cost savings that reduce appropriations prevent attainment of this objective. Thus, efficiency is likely to enter as a

---

21 For discussion of actual budget proposals in recent years and analyses of current issues in budgeting, see Barry Blechman et al., *Setting National Priorities: The 1976 Budget* (Washington: Brookings, 1975, and earlier issues in the series, which begins with 1971).

22 See Barber Conable, Jr., "Federal Tax Measures," in *Proceedings of the 69th Annual Conference on Taxation of the National Tax Association–Tax Institute of America* (Columbus, 1977). Conable suggests that the Tax Reform Act of 1976 was a package of relatively minor changes because major political forces could not agree upon substantive changes.

consideration in agency budget requests only to the extent that it calls for growth of the agency.

Similarly, agencies of the government have, at best, only weak incentives to take into account the effects of their budgetary requests on other government agencies or to determine whether their programs are "worth" more (or less) than other government programs. Such concerns are left to higher level government officials, such as cabinet secretaries, the OMB, and the president and advisers. The budgetary requests of government agencies are therefore appropriately tempered and adjusted by administrators whose views and perspectives are wider than the individual government bureaus and agencies.[23]

Of course, the elected members of the executive branch presumably wish to remain in office. To do so, they usually must "deliver" an attractive package of services to a majority of voters. The desire for re-election probably limits but does not rule out inefficiencies of the sort we have discussed because a majority of voters may prefer an inefficient policy over an efficient one.[24]

In addition to its role in making decisions, the executive branch also carries out and administers the programs and activities that have been decided on. Since programs and their objectives are often defined only in general terms, this administrative function can have important effects on the actual results of government policy. Indeed, members of the bureaucracy can thwart the intent of Congress and even the president as they administer programs.

ROLE OF CONGRESS

An individual representative of Congress cannot competently evaluate the entire federal budget. So members of Congress become specialists in certain aspects of the budget, such as defense, agriculture, and welfare, and they serve on subcommittees that prepare the appropriation bills for particular government agencies.

Prior to the Budget Control Act of 1974, the appropriation bills for the various government agencies were drafted by House and Senate appropriation subcommittees, with the subcommittee bills then going to the full appropriations committees and the House or Senate for approval. Differences between the House and senate bills were worked out in conference and reported to both houses. This procedure gave members of Congress little in-

---

23 For a theoretical analysis of bureaucratic behavior and suggestions for bureaucratic reform, see William A. Niskanen, Jr., *Bureaucracy and Representative Government* (Chicago and New York: Aldine-Atherton, 1971).

24 See p. 168.

centive to account for the effects of their actions on budgetary totals, revenue requirements, and stabilization policy. Each member might wish to limit total spending but nevertheless be reluctant to cut funds for projects of special interest in order to achieve a desired overall total.

In an effort to deal with this problem, the Budget Control Act of 1974 created House and Senate Budget Committees to control overall expenditure levels. These committees prepare and submit concurrent resolutions that set overall expenditure levels and revenue requirements for the coming fiscal year, as well as provide a breakdown of expenditures into general categories. The Congress must pass the first concurrent resolution by May 15 of each year. Congress then goes through the usual authorization and appropriations process. A second binding resolution, to be passed before the start of the new fiscal year (October 1), either confirms or modifies the target levels set by the first concurrent resolution. Legislation that raises expenditures above the ceiling or reduces receipts below the established floor cannot be considered unless a revised concurrent resolution is passed.

ADVOCATES AND LOBBYISTS

In addition to formal procedures for obtaining and evaluating information, such as benefit-cost analysis, political decision makers also receive information from persons who are affected by government programs. Various interest groups — manufacturers, farmers, labor organizations, consumers, the elderly, racial minorities, etc. — pay lobbyists, give testimony, and otherwise act to let decision makers know how particular programs may affect them. Such lobbying and advocacy activity is a source of information for political decision makers. In the past, Congress and the executive agencies relied much more heavily on interest-group information than they presently do. Indeed, interest groups may sometimes write the bills that legislators then sponsor, a practice that was not uncommon in the past and continues, to a lesser degree, in the present. Whether the information and assistance provided by interest groups improves decisions is likely to depend on the situation. However, legislators at all levels of government have reduced their dependence on interest groups as they have sought and gained expanded staffs and capabilities for independent research on the effects of their legislation.[25]

INCREMENTALISM

As we have seen, the budgets of the federal and other government units entail enormous expenditures. Altogether, government budgets in the United

25 For further discussion, see Charles L. Schultze, *The Politics and Economics of Public Spending* (Washington: Brookings, 1968).

States are in excess of 30 percent of GNP. The costs of evaluating in detail every expenditure would be prohibitive. The cost of making budgetary decisions is reduced considerably by making *incremental* decisions.

The government's budget in any fiscal year is best understood as largely a revision of previous budgets. It is not a completely new budget, but an extension of previous budgets. By and large, decisions about the budget are made marginally — whether to expand or reduce expenditures for various purposes. A significant part of the budget, estimated to be about 75 percent in 1975, is uncontrollable in that general program commitments have been made in the past that are unlikely to be changed.[26] Hence, the decisions are not whether highways will be constructed, the Social Security system will continue, or the Department of Defense will be dismantled. Rather, the decisions are whether expenditures will be increased or decreased for various functions. Although this approach reduces the cost of decision making, it discourages agencies from undertaking a comprehensive evaluation of their program, or major programs, and makes possible the survival of inefficient programs.

The incremental approach is in contrast to *zero-base* budgeting, in which government programs are comprehensively evaluated each year. In the extreme, zero-base budgeting means that each agency is assumed to start off the fiscal year with no budget and must justify its entire request. Zero-base budgeting is more costly than incremental budgeting.

Of course, not all decisions are incremental. When initially enacted, the Social Security program was not a marginal budgetary decision. Neither were the federal revenue sharing, space exploration, and federal highway programs. New programs may be very costly (such as Social Security), and they may represent radical departures from the past. Hence, the full social and economic consequences of the programs may be highly uncertain, and they are likely to require more analytical studies and stimulate more debate than incremental decisions. Once enacted, however, decisions about such programs tend to be incremental.

TAX EXPENDITURES

Tax incentives and subsidies, which give rise to what have been termed *tax expenditures*, are budgetary decisions and should be included in the budget along with other (direct) government expenditures. Tax rates have to be higher or other government expenditures have to be lower whenever "tax breaks," "loopholes," or "tax incentives" are given to any class of taxpayers. And the alternative to reducing taxes for any group of taxpayers is to give

26 For further discussion of budget controllability, see Blechman et al., *Setting National Priorities*, chap. 7.

them direct subsidies, leaving the tax structure intact. For example, if it is desirable to give industry X a subsidy of $100 million, the payment can be made directly to the industry rather than indirectly through tax reductions. Such direct subsidies would be included in the budget. In recognition of this, the Congressional Budget Reform and Impoundment Control Act of 1974 requires the OMB to submit annually a statement of tax expenditures. The sum of these expenditures amounted to about $92 billion under the federal income and corporation income taxes for fiscal year 1976.[27] Such information permits a more complete scrutiny of the budget and presumably improves decision making.[28]

IMPROVING THE BUDGETARY PROCESS

Recent years have seen a number of improvements in and suggestions for improving the budgetary process. Reliance on formal (benefit-cost or cost-effectiveness) analyses of programs and use of the PPB framework have increased, and further movement in this direction is widely advocated.[29] The budget format has been altered to include information on lending and tax expenditures. The planning period has been extended, with the budgetary implications of programs being projected three to five years into the future.

Although such improvement in the information available to decision makers may improve decisions, there is a limit to what can be gained through better information. Although budgetary decisions are not made directly or solely by voting, voting is the basic mechanism by which individual preferences are expressed. In the long run, improving the budgetary process (making budgetary decisions reflect preferences more accurately) may require changes in the mechanisms by which members of the legislative and executive branches of government are selected and the rules by which they reach decisions. This avenue for improving the outcomes of political choice is largely unexplored.[30]

27 *Special Analyses, Budget of the United States Government, Fiscal Year 1976*, and *Budget of the United States Government, Fiscal Year 1976*.

28 The tax expenditure budget is discussed in Stanley Surrey, *Pathways to Tax Reform* (Cambridge, Mass.: Harvard, 1973); and in Blechman et al., *Setting National Priorities*, pp. 184–189. Definition and measurement of tax expenditures requires either explicit or implicit definition of an "ideal" tax structure, a problem we deal with in Part Four.

29 For an assessment of budgetary policy in a particular area, see J. Nienaber and Aaron Wildavsky, *The Budgeting and Evaluation of Federal Recreation Programs* (New York: Basic Books, 1973).

30 See Niskanen, *Bureaucracy and Representative Government*, chap. 20.

SUMMARY

Resource allocation decisions are complicated and made costly by distribution issues because such issues must be settled either prior to or in conjunction with allocation decisions. A political process must therefore be able to resolve distribution issues, a requirement met by majority voting rules but not by unanimity voting. As we saw in Chapters 3 and 4, government's main advantage over other institutions for making allocation decisions is that it can employ the police power to resolve the distribution issues that always accompany allocation decisions. This advantage is lost with unanimity rule. However, other voting rules are deficient in that they permit the rejection of efficient projects, and even Pareto improvements, in favor of inefficient outcomes.

Voting processes can provide information about individual preferences. But the information is not without cost, and it usually is not sufficient to determine the efficient output of a public good. And, because decisions are made by what is termed a budgetary process rather than by direct voting, it is even more difficult to judge political decisions. Outcomes are, in fact, even more ambiguous than in the simple voting models we explored in this chapter. What we gain from the analyses of this chapter is not a blueprint for the design of a political process that makes decisions that are both equitable and efficient. Instead, we have a map of the pitfalls inherent in political decision making. Without the information about preferences that the political process is intended to reveal, we can neither design a system to achieve efficient allocation nor judge whether efficiency is the result of an existing system.

SUPPLEMENTARY READINGS

Arrow, Kenneth J. *Social Choice and Individual Values*, 2nd ed. New York: Wiley, 1963.

Buchanan, James M., and Tullock, Gordon. *The Calculus of Consent*. Ann Arbor: The University of Michigan Press, 1962.

Downs, Anthony. *An Economic Theory of Democracy*. New York: Harper, 1956.

Olson, Mancur, Jr. *The Logic of Collective Action*. Cambridge, Mass.: Harvard, 1965.

Niskanen, William A., Jr. *Bureacracy and Representative Government*. Chicago and New York: Aldine-Atherton, 1971.

Wildavsky, Aaron. *The Politics of the Budgetary Process*. Boston: Little Brown, 1964.

How government is financed determines the distribution among persons and, to a degree, the magnitude of the costs of government. In Part Four we deal with two basic questions: How should the costs of government be distributed? And what will be the distribution and magnitude of these costs if particular revenue measures are employed? Chapter 9 defines the main revenue alternatives — taxation, borrowing, sale of services, confiscation, and money creation — and discusses the main issues that arise in choosing among them. Chapters 10–15 describe the major taxes employed by U.S. governments and provide a comparative evaluation of them, using the equity and efficiency criteria presented in Chapter 9. Detailed discussion of the rationales for and consequences of government borrowing is deferred until Part Five, which deals with the stabilization activities of government.

PART FOUR

FINANCING GOVERNMENT

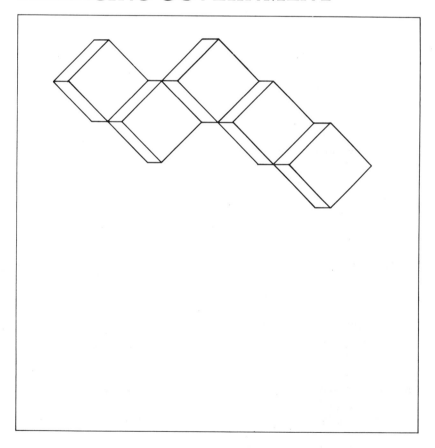

CHAPTER NINE

FINANCING GOVERNMENT: PRINCIPLES AND ISSUES

The preceding chapters have provided economic rationales for many government activities. Whether the actual activities of governments (federal, state, local) are based on these rationales is an open question. But regardless of why they are undertaken, government activities must be financed; that is, government must obtain control over the use of resources. The shift from private to government control of resource use will impose burdens, or costs, on some or all persons. Both the magnitude and distribution of these costs depend on how government is financed.

In this chapter, we will survey issues involved with financing, and we will examine in detail the reasons for and consequences of using various financing measures in subsequent chapters. In these discussions, we will not ask whether the government activities should be undertaken. Instead, we will take the fact of government as given and ask several questions: What are the alternative means of financing government? What are the costs of government? How does the manner of financing government affect the magnitude and distribution of governmental costs? What principles, or criteria, should guide the choice of financing measures? These principles are classified into two categories: equity criteria (How should the costs of government be distributed among persons?) and efficiency criteria (What manner of financing government conflicts least with efficient resource allocation?). Sometimes the method of financing that is preferable on equity grounds will likewise be preferable on efficiency grounds. But conflicts can arise, and financing decisions often involve equity and efficiency trade-offs.

THE ALTERNATIVES

Modern governments finance their activities by taxation, borrowing, and selling services. In addition, they may directly confiscate resources and create money. Finally, especially in time of war or other emergencies, resources and services may be contributed voluntarily by their owners.

SALE OF SERVICES AND CHARGES TO USERS

Some of the goods and services provided by government can be sold to finance their provision. In the United States and many other countries, government-provided postal services, parks and recreation facilities, transportation (subway and bus systems, bridges), housing, electrical power, irrigation water, etc., are financed in significant measure by either selling the service to users or charging them a fee. This mode of financing, in which government operates as an enterprise, clearly cannot be used to finance all government activities. Indeed, a major reason for governmental supply of goods is that the latter cannot be marketed (sold) because exclusion of nonpayers is costly if not impossible. In addition, redistribution activities obviously cannot be financed by a fee or charge paid by those to whom income is to be redistributed.[1]

Government enterprises can sometimes be operated at a profit, with the profit being a source of general government revenue. In the United States, government-operated utilities — water, electricity, sewage collection and treatment — are sometimes profit making, as are government-operated liquor stores, lotteries, and gambling activities. By and large, profits from government enterprises have been a relatively minor revenue source in nonsocialist nations. However, such profits are a major, if not the primary, source of general government revenues in socialist countries.[2]

TAXATION

Taxation is the use of the police power of the state to confiscate a generalized commodity: money. Taxation is not a voluntary exchange; it does not involve a *quid pro quo* by which taxpayers' receipt of particular commodities and services is dependent upon their payment of taxes.[3] Hence, services may

---

1 Those who receive income are not necessarily the only beneficiaries of income redistribution. As we noted in Chapter 6, the giver may also benefit.

2 Recall the related discussion of government monopolies in Chapter 3, p. 74.

3 In one sense, the payment of taxes is voluntary. A person pays taxes in exchange for freedom from prosecution and penalties for nonpayment.

FIGURE 9–1
CIRCULAR FLOW OF INCOME, SHOWING POINTS OF IMPACT OF TAXES ON
BUSINESS FIRMS AND PERSONS

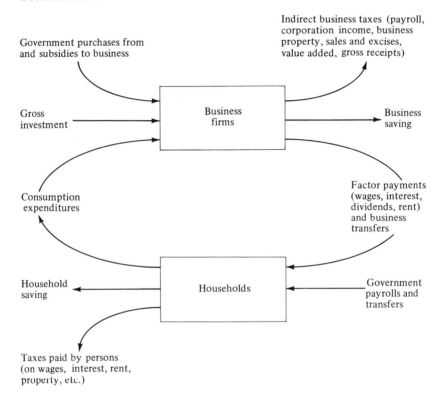

be financed through taxation when it is either impossible or undesirable to make availability of the service contingent upon payment of a specified fee, charge, or price. In addition, tax finance of cash and in-kind transfers makes possible the redistribution of income. Many types of taxes are levied. But all taxes have the common effect of reducing private money flows (of income or spending). Figure 9–1 shows the points of impact of the more common types of taxes.

BORROWING

To borrow, governments issue bonds in exchange for money. These bonds are promises to pay to the bondholder specified amounts of money at specified *future* dates. Borrowing does not directly employ the police power of the state, but government's ability to repay the bonds through future taxation is the reason that most government bonds have value and are marketable. The exceptions are revenue bonds that are not supported by government's taxing authority but, instead, are repaid from nontax revenues such as charges, fees, and rental receipts.

MONEY CREATION

National governments can create money, which can then be used to buy the resources that are wanted. The U.S. Treasury Department does not directly print new money to finance government spending. But the same effect can be achieved by the coordinated efforts of the Treasury and the Federal Reserve banks. This occurs when the Treasury sells new government bonds to finance government spending and the Federal Reserve banks simultaneously buy bonds with newly created money in the amount of the newly issued Treasury bonds. The effect is as if the Treasury had directly printed the money that it is spending.

CONFISCATION

Rather than confiscate the generalized commodity, money, government may confiscate particular commodities. For example, the military draft represents confiscation of labor. In contrast, with the volunteer army, government obtains cash through taxation, which it then uses to purchase the desired labor services. Eminent domain, which permits the government to condemn property for public use (highways, urban renewal), involves confiscation to the extent that the compensation paid to the property owners falls short of the amount that they would voluntarily accept for their property. Direct confiscation of resources is neither widely used nor widely advocated because it places the burden of government on those persons who happen to own the particular resources that are desired. With taxation, this burden can be spread more broadly and made independent of the types of resources that a person owns. Table 9-1 shows the extent to which various financing measures are used by U.S. governments.

NATURE OF GOVERNMENT COSTS

Several types of government costs can be distinguished: the *opportunity cost* of governmental resource use; the *administrative and compliance costs* of the mechanisms by which government is financed (the mechanisms by which government obtains control over resource use); and the *excess burdens* that

TABLE 9-1
SOURCES OF FUNDS, U.S. GOVERNMENTS, 1974-1975

	All governments	Federal	State	Local
1. Total revenue, own sources (billions)	$589.7	$360.5	$123.6	$105.7
2. Revenue sources as percent of total				
A. Individual income tax	24.4%	34.0%	15.2% }	2.5%
B. Corporation income tax	8.0	11.3	5.3 }	
C. Property tax	8.7	—	1.2	47.3
D. Sales and gross receipts tax	12.0	5.9	35.0	6.1
E. Insurance trust funds	17.1	22.3	14.5	2.1
F. Charges and miscellaneous	12.1	8.8	13.4	21.8
G. Utility and liquor stores	2.2	—	1.7	10.6
H. Other	3.1	1.7	8.0	2.1
I. Change in indebtedness [a]	12.3	16.1	5.7	7.6

a Row I is the difference in total indebtedness between 1974 and 1975, and it is included in row 1.

Sources: Rows A through H, U.S. Census Bureau, *Governmental Finances*, 1974-75; row I, U.S. Census Bureau, *Governmental Finances*, (1973-74, 1974-75).

result as individuals alter their economic decisions in response to government's financing of its activities. The latter two cost categories may vary with the type of financing, while the first does not. And choice among alternative financing measures may be based in part on differences in administrative and compliance costs and excess burdens.

OPPORTUNITY COST

Opportunity costs arise because government must obtain control over resources to carry out its activities. In a full-employment economy, the resources used by government would have been privately used to provide goods and services to some individuals. These individuals bear a burden measured by the value of the goods and services they forgo because of government's resource use. For example, to build a highway, someone must give up, and government must gain control over, the use of iron, cement, labor, machines, etc. This opportunity cost is not affected by the manner of financing government. It reflects a necessary and inescapable reduction in the availability of goods and services to some members of society; government activities cannot proceed without this cost being incurred.

In the case of government provision of goods and services, this opportunity cost may be defined as either the decrease in private-sector output that follows from government's use of resources or the corresponding decrease in real disposable income from private-sector sources. The burden, or cost, of government to a particular person is the person's loss of real disposable income.

Some government activities, usually labeled *transfer activities*, do not provide goods and services of the usual sort.[4] Instead, they transfer control over resource use by transferring income from taxpayers to specified persons. Like government's service-providing activities, these transfer activities entail a cost to those persons who give up control of resources, a cost that is measured by their loss of disposable income and the private-sector output that could be purchased with it. However, transfer activities need not decrease total private-sector output because the recipients of the transfers will demand and receive more private output. Thus, *the intent and the result of government transfer activities are primarily a redistribution of, but not a reduction in, private-sector output.*

ADMINISTRATIVE AND COMPLIANCE COSTS

Administrative and compliance costs may vary with the financing method. They include the flotation costs of government borrowing and the administrative, enforcement, and compliance costs of taxation. Administrative and enforcement costs include the government's costs of keeping records, auditing, prosecuting, etc. Compliance costs are the taxpayer's costs of keeping records, filling out tax returns, etc. Included in the latter are the costs incurred by taxpayers as they try to minimize their taxes. These costs are by no means trivial and are tangibly measured, in part, by the incomes of tax accountants and lawyers.

EXCESS BURDEN

With some financing measures, taxpayer burdens (welfare losses) may exceed the value of the output that could have been produced with the resources used by government. If so, there is an *excess burden*. In general terms, this excess burden reflects inefficiencies in the allocation of resources. The financing of government may cause inefficiencies if it distorts the

4 Redistribution of income and the results achieved — greater equality, political stability, etc. — are sometimes termed *public goods*, as we noted in Chapter 6.

relative prices of various products or the relative gains from the various uses of each resource and thereby alters private-sector economic decisions.[5]

For example, suppose a government highway project will directly use $30 million worth of steel, cement, labor, land, etc. This $30 million measures the opportunity cost of the resources directly used in the project because it is the amount that *must* be paid to the resource owners to attract the resources from their private-sector employments. However, the taxpayer burden of this project may exceed $30 million if it is financed by a tax that interferes with private-sector decision making. An *excise tax* on a single commodity, say blouses, would be such a tax because it makes blouses appear more costly relative to other commodities than is in fact the case. That is, an excise tax not only reduces real incomes, but also provides an incentive for taxpayers to use their income differently. In contrast, a *lump-sum tax* entails no excess burden because there is no action the taxpayers can take to alter this tax liability.[6] The taxpayers pay the same tax no matter how they spend their incomes or how much they work or save. The lump-sum tax collects revenue in a manner that does not in itself give taxpayers an incentive to alter their behavior.

As an illustration of how an excise tax makes taxpayers worse off than an *equal-yield* lump-sum tax, let us suppose that Lois Riley has $10,000 income if the highway project is not undertaken. To maximize her utility, she allocates this income as shown in column 1 of Table 9–2, buying 14 blouses at $10 each and 20, 1-pound steaks at $3 each.

If the highway project is financed by an excise tax of, say, 50 percent on blouses, Riley's disposable income is not directly decreased. However, the tax-inclusive price of blouses increases to $15, and they become more expensive relative to steaks and other goods. As a result, Riley spends less on blouses, more on steaks and other goods, as shown in column 2 of Table 9–2. Of her $90 expenditure on blouses, $30 goes to the government as the excise tax.[7]

---

5 Edgar K. Browning estimates that the total administrative, compliance, and excess burden costs arising from the collection of federal, state, and local taxes on labor income were about $19 billion in 1974, or about 6.6 percent of tax revenue. Of this total, about two-thirds was excess burden costs resulting from tax distortion of labor supply decisions. See "The Marginal Cost of Public Funds," *Journal of Political Economy*, 84, No. 2 (April 1976): 293.

6 A lump-sum tax is one that collects a specified sum from each person, with the amount not depending on any economic decisions that the person has made or might make. A lump-sum tax is, in essence, a tax on the existence of the person; it is also called a *head tax*.

7 This analysis assumes that the excise tax is shifted forward to the consumer and that the prices of goods other than blouses do not change. These are likely outcomes for a tax on a single commodity that is competitively supplied. In Chapter 13 we discuss the effects of excise taxes on prices more fully.

TABLE 9–2
EXPENDITURE PATTERNS AND EXCESS BURDEN

	Riley's income allocations		
		If the project is undertaken and financed by	
Items	If the project is not undertaken	Excise tax (50%)	Lump-sum tax ($30)
	(1)	(2)	(3)
Disposable income	$10,000	$10,000	$9,970
Expenditures for:			
Blouses	$ 140	$ 90	$ 120
	(14 blouses)	(6 blouses)	(12 blouses)
Steaks	60	77	57
	(20 lbs.)	(25²/₃ lbs.)	(19 lbs.)
Other goods	9,800	9,833	9,793
Dollar value of goods received (expenditures minus excise tax)	$10,000	$ 9,970	$9,970

If the highway project is undertaken and financed by a $30 lump-sum tax on each of the nation's one million taxpayer-citizens, including Riley, then her disposable income is directly reduced to $9,970.[8] Her income allocation in this case is shown in column 3 of Table 9–2.

With the excise tax, Riley ends up with $9,970 worth of goods, which is the same amount she has with the lump-sum tax, but less than the $10,000 worth that she had before the project. *However, the package of goods purchased under the excise tax is actually less valuable to Riley than the package purchased under the lump-sum tax, even though the two packages have the same tax-exclusive cost ($9,970).* How do we know this? Because with the lump-sum tax, Riley can purchase the excise tax package (6 blouses, 25²/₃ pounds of steak, and $9,833 worth of other goods), but she chooses not to do so. Instead, she purchases 12 blouses, 19 pounds of steak, and $9,793 worth of other goods. Therefore, Riley must be better off with the package of goods obtained under the lump-sum tax than with the package obtained under the excise tax. The difference in Riley's welfare level under the two taxes measures the excess burden of the excise tax.

Stated differently, the excise tax puts an excess burden on Riley because a change from excise to lump-sum taxation can make her better off without

8 The yield of the lump-sum tax ($30) has been set so that it collects the same revenue from Riley as would the excise tax because we wish to compare the effects on a person of two taxes that have the same yield.

reducing the revenue that the government collects from her. How? Suppose government initially collects $30 per year from Riley with the excise tax. Let government now collect the same $30 as a lump-sum tax. With this change, the price of a blouse returns to its original $10 level, and Riley is able to purchase an additional blouse by giving up the purchase of $3^{1}/_{3}$ pounds of steak. But her budget allocation under the excise tax is such that 1 blouse has the same value ($15) as 5 pounds of steak.[9] Therefore, an additional blouse has greater value to Riley than the $3^{1}/_{3}$ pounds of steak that she has to sacrifice to obtain it. And Riley can increase her welfare above the level prevailing under excise taxation by shifting some of her purchases from steak to blouses.

The excise tax generates an excess burden because it distorts prices so that they do not accurately reflect the economic costs of steaks and blouses; blouses are made to appear more expensive relative to steaks than is in fact the case. Excess burden may also arise if taxes distort the labor-leisure and consumption-saving choices, thereby affecting factor (labor and capital) supplies. Taxes may also induce uneconomic factor combinations — taxing labor inputs more heavily than capital inputs may cause capital-for-labor substitution. In each of these cases, excess burden arises because the system for collecting revenue causes the prices of some commodities to rise relative to the prices of other commodities or the incomes from producing some commodities to fall relative to the incomes from producing other commodities. These tax-induced changes in relative prices and incomes shift demands among commodities and reduce the supply of some commodities relative to the supply of others. Such changes cause a reallocation of resources that may be inefficient because the additional amounts of the commodities whose outputs are increased are less valuable than the amounts of those commodities given up to obtain them. If so, the value of goods available to the private sector has fallen by more than the amount of taxes collected.

TAX NEUTRALITY AND EXCESS BURDEN

A tax is said to be neutral if taxpayers cannot reduce their tax liabilities by altering their purchases or their sales of goods — that is, by altering their economic decisions. A lump-sum tax is neutral because it does not depend on any economic decisions of the person. A tax on money income is neutral except with respect to the labor-leisure choice and the choice between

9 If it were worth less, then she would buy 1 less blouse and use the $15 to buy 5 pounds of steak; if it were worth more, she would curtail her purchases of steak by 5 pounds and buy another blouse.

TABLE 9–3
CHOICE DISTORTION BY MAJOR TYPES OF TAXES

Tax	Choices distorted
Lump-sum	None
General income	Labor-leisure; present versus future consumption
General consumption	Labor-leisure
Excise (selective consumption)	Taxed versus nontaxed commodities; labor-leisure
Selective factor (tax on use of labor or capital inputs)	Taxed versus nontaxed inputs

present and future consumption. A proportional tax on all money expenditures for consumer goods is neutral with respect to the latter choice but not with the respect to the former. An excise tax is not neutral, as we saw in the Riley example.

Table 9–3 summarizes the choice-distorting effects of various taxes, and subsequent chapters discuss them in more detail. When a choice is distorted by a tax, excess burden results. The lump-sum tax is the only tax that distorts no choices.

Each instance of nonneutrality may lead to economic inefficiency and excess burdens *if resource allocation would have been efficient under neutral (for example, lump-sum) taxation.* Thus, economists often see tax system neutrality as a means of reducing or eliminating excess burden. But for several reasons, neutrality is not an objective to be pursued without qualification.

First, nonneutral taxes do not always alter choices. For example, an excise tax on a particular commodity, X, causes no output adjustment and no excess burden if the demand for X is perfectly inelastic. Also, if the resources used to produce X cannot be used elsewhere, then the supply of X is fixed and a tax on X does not change the equilibrium price and quantity. Instead, it simply reduces the incomes of factors employed in producing X. In both cases (inelastic demand and inelastic supply), the tax on X does not cause resource reallocation and, therefore, does not generate excess burdens.[10]

Second, nonneutrality may be desirable if there is a need for corrective taxation of externality generating activities, a topic we discussed in Chapter 5. Third, other secondary costs may be lower for the nonneutral system.

10 See Chapter 13, p. 298.

Finally, neutrality may conflict with equity principles, as we shall see in the next section.

EQUITY IN THE DISTRIBUTION OF COSTS

How should the costs of government be distributed? The answer to this question depends, in part, on whether government is transferring income or providing goods and services.

Government transfer payments to persons (Social Security, welfare, farm subsidies, etc.) redistribute income (and control over resources) from taxpayers to those who receive the transfer payments.[11] How such transfer payments should be financed depends on society's redistribution objectives. If the objective is greater equality in the distribution of income, then the transfer payments to low-income persons should be financed by progressive taxes that fall relatively heavily on high-income persons. Alternatively, if the objective is merely to provide a "floor" under the incomes of persons — to bring the income of all persons up to some minimum — then taxes need not be progressive in the upper-income ranges. Although opinions about society's redistribution objectives differ, many, if not most, people would support the ideas of limiting income inequality and providing a floor to incomes. Transfers financed by progressive income taxes would be basic mechanisms for achieving those objectives.[12]

To the question of who should bear the cost of governmentally provided goods and services, economists usually give two answers: Costs should be distributed according to (1) ability to pay or (2) benefits received.

ABILITY TO PAY

Government's use of resources to provide goods and services reduces the availability of other goods and services. Government thereby imposes a cost, or burden, on each person that is measured by the value of the other goods and services that the person must give up. Since this loss of goods and services is a loss of real income, a person's ability to pay (to bear the cost of government) should be related to the person's real income.[13]

---

11 This type of spending has been increasing rapidly, with transfer spending by all levels of government presently accounting for about 12 percent of personal income, in contrast to 1 percent in 1929. See Chapter 2, Table 2–3. About one-half of present federal spending is transfer payments.

12 For more discussion, see Arthur M. Okun, *Equality and Efficiency: The Big Trade-off* (Washington: Brookings, 1975), p. 102.

13 To say that a person bears a cost because of government is not to say that government imposes a welfare loss on the person, since the government's activities may also be of some

A person's real income is the value of *all goods and services accruing to the person from all sources* during a year, or some other period. Income defined in this way may be thought of as a measure of consumption possibilities. More specifically, the real income accruing to a person or family during some period is:

$$I = \frac{M - T}{P} + H + G$$

M is the money income accruing to the person or family from all sources, including cash transfers from the government. T is tax payments (other than sales and excise taxes that are paid at the time of purchase). P is an index of the prices paid for goods and services purchased in the market (it includes sales and excise taxes). H is the real value of commodities that people produce themselves or obtain in barter for goods that they have produced. And G is the real value of government-provided goods and services.[14] With these definitions $(M - T)/P$ is the real disposable income (the real value of the goods and services that can be purchased in the market place with after-tax money income).

M is measured *net* of the costs of generating it.[15] It includes money income from wages, interest, dividends, rents, capital gains, gifts, and inheritances, if we apply the broadest definition of income. The variables I, G, M, and H are stated as dollar amounts per period, usually per year. From the definition of real income, we can easily see that increased taxes *and* increased government provision of services (G) need not reduce real income. But government taxation and provision of services necessarily decrease, in the aggregate, the component of real income represented by private-sector output.

---

benefit. Instead, the sum of the two effects measures the net effect of government on the person's welfare.

14 A person's net payment to government is the tax payment minus the cash transfers received from government. In-kind income (G and H) increases a person's ability to pay, even though taxes are usually paid in cash, because in-kind income reduces the need to use money income to buy the particular goods and services it represents.

15 For example, a farmer may raise 1,000 bushels of wheat and sell it for $4 per bushel. The farmer's *net* income from wheat production is the *gross* income — $4,000 — minus the costs of fertilizer, seed, labor, gasoline, etc., that were incurred to produce the wheat. Similarly, wage earners often incur costs in the earning of income — costs of uniforms, tools, transportation to work, etc. The wearing out of factory machines and buildings in the production process is also a cost of generating income. And these costs must be subtracted from gross income to obtain net income. Since the costs of generating income reduce a person's ability to pay taxes, income taxes are usually levied on net rather than gross income.

Ability to pay also depends on a person's *need* for goods and services. Some expenditures are *nondiscretionary* if a particular standard of living is to be maintained. Thus, all income is not subject to taxation under the ability-to-pay principle. Instead, taxes should be levied only on *discretionary income* — income in excess of nondiscretionary expenditures. Nondiscretionary expenditures will depend on family or household size, as well as its other characteristics. So, in defining discretionary income and ability to pay, the question of what is the proper taxpaying unit — family or individual — also arises.

While many would agree with the general principle that ability to pay depends on income, defining the taxpaying unit and defining and measuring its income and nondiscretionary expenditures are major and continuing issues in tax and revenue policy formation.[16] We explore these issues more fully in Chapters 10 and 11.

BENEFITS RECEIVED

Another answer to the question of who should bear the costs of government is that those who benefit should pay. To make this principle operational, benefits must be defined and the amount of benefits accruing to each person must be measured. The benefit of a government-supplied service is the amount that the recipient would be willing to pay rather than go without the service. This is exactly the same notion of benefit employed in benefit-cost analysis (Chapter 7).

Recalling our discussion of benefit-cost analysis, we readily see that a major problem with benefit taxation is the difficulty in identifying beneficiaries and measuring their benefits. This has led to the suggestion that the *cost* of providing the service be taken as the measure of its benefit. For example, if the cost of a year of secondary education for a child is $1,200, then $1,200 is taken as the benefit of the service. Under benefit taxation, the child's family would be taxed $1,200. Of course, the actual benefits of the year of schooling to the child and others could exceed or fall short of this amount. And this cost-based approach to benefit taxation meets with the difficulty of allocating costs among the various persons served by government.

A second problem with benefit taxation is that it cannot be used to finance transfers, if transfers are based on non-Pareto criteria.[17] For example, the primary beneficiary of a welfare payment to a needy family is the family

16 For an excellent discussion of the concept and measurement of discretionary income, see *Report of the Royal Commission on Taxation*, vol. 3 (Ottawa: Queen's Printer, 1966), sometimes referred to as the report of the Carter Commission.

17 See Chapter 6.

itself. Financing the payment by a tax on the beneficiary (the needy family) would defeat the whole purpose of the government activity.

These problems notwithstanding, benefit taxation may be both feasible and desirable in some instances. The gasoline tax that is used to finance construction and maintenance of highways approximates a benefit tax.[18] And it is widely regarded as a fair tax for that purpose. Fees and licenses (for parks, autos, trucks, hunting, etc.) are also in the nature of benefit taxes when the proceeds are used to support the activity requiring the fee or license. Cities charge for sewage and garbage collection and, less frequently, for fire protection services; such charges approximate benefit taxes. Aircraft fuel taxes and landing fees are benefit taxes that support air transportation. Special property-tax assessments that pay for improvements (sidewalks, streets) to the taxed property are benefit taxes.

In each of these cases, an approximate form of benefit taxation is feasible because the persons benefiting from government services can be identified and a measure, albeit rough, of their use of the services is available. That is, the services provided are in the nature of private goods.

Benefit taxation to finance government-supplied goods that are public goods (nonrival consumption) is much more difficult. Since each member of the community receives the same quantity of the good, the basic problem is to determine how much each person is willing to pay for that quantity. If the good is a normal good, then the value that a person places on it will be an increasing function of the person's income. And benefits-received taxation would seem to call for an income tax, with higher-income persons paying a larger share of the costs of providing public goods than lower-income persons. But such reasoning does not tell us whether the income tax should be proportional, regressive, or progressive. Also, factors other than income, notably tastes, determine how much a person is willing to pay for a given quantity of a public good. We are therefore left with the conclusion that income taxation is not inconsistent with benefit taxation. But to define an income tax rate structure that approximates a benefit tax would require information about individual preferences that is not available.[19]

HORIZONTAL EQUITY

In its most general form, the principle of horizontal equity requires equal treatment of equals. Therefore, if equity requires the distribution of government costs according to ability to pay, then those having equal ability to pay

18 See Chapter 13, pp. 301–302, for further discussion of the gasoline tax.

19 See James M. Buchanan, "Fiscal Institutions and Collective Outlay," *American Economic Review* (May 1964): 227–235.

should bear equal shares of the costs of the government. If costs are to be distributed according to benefits received, then those receiving equal benefits should bear equal shares. In subsequent chapters, we shall see that the principle of horizontal equity is frequently violated by existing revenue systems.

VERTICAL EQUITY

How unequals should be treated relative to one another is the question of vertical equity. How should tax burdens be related to discretionary, or taxable, income? Should a person having, say, twice the taxable income of another person bear twice, more than twice, or less than twice as large a share of government costs? That is, should the tax (revenue) system be proportional, progressive, or regressive, respectively, with respect to income? If the ratio of tax burden to income is constant, then the tax system is proportional to income. If the ratio increases as income increases, the system is said to be progressive. It is regressive if the ratio falls as income increases.[20]

Many, if not most, people would oppose a regressive system of distributing government costs, especially if the system imposed significant burdens on those at the lowest income levels. Beyond this, there is no clear agreement on what would be a vertically equitable distribution of costs. For some, vertical equity would entail distributing the costs so as to achieve the greatest equalization of the distribution of income. For others, the appropriate distribution would be one that placed relatively heavy loads on the very rich and relatively light ones on the very poor, without necessarily maximizing the equalizing effects.[21]

INTERGENERATION EQUITY

Some government policies reduce consumption in the current period in order to increase consumption possibilities (income) in future periods. How should the cost of such investment activities be distributed? If the average

20 A tax may be related in some specific way to its base and related another way to income. For example, a general sales tax that is proportional to expenditures for the taxed items may be regressive with respect to income (see Chapter 13).

21 The issue of vertical equity arises in decisions about the progressiveness, or lack of it, of income tax rates as we discuss them in Chapter 10. In this chapter we are concerned only with equity in the distribution of the cost of government. We are not concerned with the distribution of benefits from government expenditures, except insofar as taxes are based on benefits received. The net burden of government (cost minus benefits) may be regressive, progressive, or proportional. See Chapter 23 for estimates of the distribution of this net burden.

income and standard of living continue to rise, as they have in the industrialized nations, the ability-to-pay criterion would require that future generations bear the costs of investments that enhance consumption possibilities of those generations. Such would also be the case under the benefits-received criterion.[22] However, if it is thought that future living standards will be lower than present standards, then the ability-to-pay rule would require that the cost of investments be borne by the present generation.

EQUITY AND COST MINIMIZATION

A reasonable rule in revenue system design would appear to be that of minimizing the secondary (administrative, compliance, excess burden) costs of financing any particular level of government activity. However, this rule cannot be applied without exception because the revenue system that minimizes the secondary costs may be undesirable in other respects. Most obviously, minimizing secondary costs may conflict with equity. Stated differently, efficiency in revenue collection may conflict with equity objectives.

For example, a lump-sum tax is neutral and would therefore cause minimal excess burdens. In addition, it would be a relatively easy tax to administer, enforce, and comply with. However, in the judgment of many it would not be equitable. It would not distribute costs according to ability to pay, unless all persons have equal ability to pay. In some instances, a lump-sum tax would appear to approximate a benefits-received tax in that some government-provided goods and services are distributed equally. However, the fact that people receive the same quantity of service does not imply that the service has the same value (benefit) to all persons. Thus, we cannot argue that a lump-sum tax is fair by the benefits-received principle, although it would seem to be more consistent with that than with the ability-to-pay principle.[23]

Similarly, while taxes on inelasticly demanded and inelasticly supplied products and factors cause no excess burden, such taxes usually are not equitable by either benefits-received or ability-to-pay criteria.[24]

22 We shall see later (Chapter 19) that borrowing is a means of transferring investment costs to future generations. The burden of an investment is always borne by the current generation in the form of reduced consumption in the period of investment. However, when the investment is financed by borrowing, the present generation may be compensated for lower present consumption with greater future consumption.

23 Of course, a lump-sum tax would tax persons according to the *average* cost of providing goods that are equally available.

24 A tax on salt (or blood transfusions) would be a tax on an inelasticly demanded commodity. A tax on either the market value or the rental income of land would be a tax on an inelasticly supplied factor. Some persons would see the former tax as inequitable, and the latter tax would be appealing to many on equity grounds.

We can cite other examples of equity-efficiency conflicts. For example, a proportional tax on consumption rather than income might promote saving and increase the supply of capital, as well as being neutral with respect to the choice between present and future consumption. But such a tax is more regressive with respect to current income than the income tax. Similarly, a highly progressive income tax might be favored on equity grounds, while scoring low on efficiency grounds because it is thought to discourage saving and labor supply by higher-income persons.

Finally, equity often requires taking account of the special circumstances of various taxpayers. But to do so may increase the complexity of the tax code and the costs of administering and enforcing it and complying with it. Thus, once again, equity is not a free good. At the same time, increasing the equity of the tax system (as the taxpayers perceive equity) may reduce tax evasion and therefore tend to reduce enforcement costs.[25]

INCIDENCE: THE ACTUAL DISTRIBUTION OF COSTS

In discussing the rules or principles for distributing the costs of government, we have been concerned with the question of who *should* pay these costs. Use of those rules to evaluate the equity of a revenue system requires that we also know how various revenue measures actually distribute the cost of government. That is, we must answer the question of who *does* pay if particular revenue measures are employed.[26]

At first glance this seems to be a relatively easy question to answer. Certainly, we can determine who actually sends the cash to the government treasury. This initial and direct effect of the tax payment itself is termed the *impact of the tax*. The impact of a tax is usually determined by the statute that authorizes the tax, which specifies who shall make tax payments and in what amount. But the story does not end there, because those who bear the impact of the tax may *shift the tax to others*. As a result the *incidence* of the tax, defined as "its effect on the distribution of real income among persons," may differ from its impact. For example, landlords will remit the property taxes levied on rental housing; thus, the impact of the property tax is on prop-

---

25 Taxpayers may reduce taxes by illegal or legal means. Illegal reduction of taxes (e.g. failing to report taxable income, claiming false exemptions, reporting illegal deductions) is called *tax evasion*. Legal reduction of taxes is called *tax avoidance*. For information about how the public views various forms of taxation, see Advisory Commission on Intergovernmental Relations, *Changing Public Attitudes on Governments and Taxes* (Washington: Government Printing Office, July 1975).

26 Our discussion of this question follows that of Richard A. Musgrave, *The Theory of Public Finance* (New York: McGraw-Hill, 1959), chap. 10.

erty owners. But owners may be able to raise rents to recover part or all of
the tax; thus, the tax is partially or fully shifted to renters and the incidence
of the tax is partially or fully upon renters.

More generally, incidence differs from impact because of adjustments of
market prices and incomes in response to the tax. That is, tax shifting occurs
when product or factor prices are adjusted *in response to taxes.* If we are to
conclude that tax shifting occurs, we must be able to explain why sellers (of
products or factors) will respond to the tax by raising prices. This explana-
tion must deal with the question: If it is in the sellers' interest to raise prices
in response to a tax increase, why was it not also in their interest to raise
prices *prior to the tax increase?* It is not enough, for example, simply to as-
sert that producers will raise prices and "pass on" the tax to consumers. We
must explain why the producers were not charging the highest possible price
before the tax increase.

Other complications arise in the assessing of incidence because the use of
tax revenues, as distinguished from their collection, necessarily causes other
changes. Specifically, when a tax is increased, the revenues gained must be
used to (1) increase government spending, (2) offset revenue losses from
decreases in other taxes, (3) increase government cash balances, or (4) retire government debt. The reverse changes must accompany tax decreases.

These uses of tax revenues affect the distribution of income in three distinct ways. First, the revenue used to provide goods and services or to make
transfer payments directly affects the distribution of income. Second, market
adjustments in prices and money incomes occur in response to the use as
well as to the collection of tax revenue. Finally, the use of revenue affects
aggregate demand, employment, output, and prices. Therefore, several concepts of incidence are frequently distinguished, each of which assumes and
includes the income distribution effects of a particular use of the tax revenues.

Absolute incidence refers to the case in which tax revenues are used to either reduce borrowing or add to government cash balances, with government spending unchanged. The collection and use of tax revenues reduce
aggregate demand. Lower aggregate demand leads to lower output or prices
and lower money incomes or both. Real incomes may or may not fall in the
aggregate, depending on wage-price adjustments and whether aggregate demand was excessive prior to the tax being levied. In Chapter 16 we treat this
case more completely.

Differential incidence refers to the case in which new tax revenues displace other tax revenues, with government spending unchanged. The dis-
placement of revenues from one tax with those from another is approximately but not necessarily dollar for dollar. Instead, the amounts are

calculated so that the level of aggregate demand is unchanged by the tax substitution.[27]

Budget incidence refers to the case in which new tax revenues are used to increase government spending, with other tax revenues and borrowing and cash balances remaining unchanged.

Recall the definition of real income: $I = [(M - T)/P] + H + G$. To determine the _differential_ incidence of two taxes, we have to determine

$$\Delta I \equiv I^a - I^b = \frac{M^a - T^a}{P^a} + H^a - \frac{M^b - T^b}{P^b} - H^b$$

for each taxpaying unit. The superscripts a and b indicate the values of M, T, P, and H prevailing with taxes a and b. Government services (G) drop out of the formula because they are assumed to be the same with each tax. The values of $T^a - T^b$ for the various taxpaying units will total zero unless one tax has a more deflationary effect on aggregate demand than the other. If there are no adjustments in M, P, and H when a change is made from tax b to tax a, then

$$\Delta I = \frac{T^b - T^a}{P^a}$$

and the differential incidence equals the differential impact. That is, taxpayers' real incomes are altered only if and as their individual tax payments are altered. This outcome is unlikely for most tax substitutions, but noting the conditions for equality of incidence and impact may help us to understand the concept of incidence.

For example, let us suppose that a proportional income tax is levied on workers employed in, say, the textile industry to provide public services that are distributed among all persons in society. The tax initially decreases the after-tax pay of the textile workers. If they make no adjustments in response to the decrease in their take-home pay and if the spending of the tax revenue by the government does not alter market prices and incomes, then the impact and incidence of the tax are equivalent. However, some adjustment is

---

27 The collection of a given amount of tax revenue with one type of tax may affect aggregate demand differently than the collection of the same revenue with another tax. For example, aggregate demand may be greater when a given amount of revenue is collected with income taxation rather than with sales taxation. If so, dollar-for-dollar substitution of one tax for the other would affect the level of output or prices or both.

likely, since the tax makes work in the textile industry less attractive relative to either work in other industries or the leisure time and home production activities that increase H. Workers are thus likely to shift from the textile to other sectors, and they may also reduce total hours worked and thereby increase leisure and home production.[28] The shift of textile workers to other industries would tend to raise the before-tax wages of the remaining textile workers and reduce the wages of other workers — money wages would increase in the textile industry relative to other industries. Thus, some of the burden would be shifted to workers in other industries. If labor is very mobile and homogeneous, then after-tax labor incomes would tend to be the same in all sectors (after market adjustments), even though the tax is levied in only one sector. That is, the textile workers would end up bearing no more tax burden (relative to their incomes) than any other workers.

The shift in labor increases the cost of labor relative to the cost of capital in the textile industry and reduces the cost of labor relative to the cost of capital in other industries. As a result, capital-labor ratios may change, and the owners of capital specialized to textile production may receive lower incomes, while the owners of capital specialized to other types of production may receive higher incomes.

A decrease in total labor supplied (and corresponding increase in H) would decrease after-tax money incomes $(M - T)$ in the aggregate or increase prices (P), the latter occurring because the lessened supply of market-traded goods would lead to higher money prices unless offsetting adjustments were made in the money supply. Also, the price of textile products would rise relative to the prices of other products, causing indeterminate changes in P and individuals' real incomes.

Market adjustments to the spending of the tax revenues to provide services may also occur. But they are unpredictable unless we know the nature of the government spending. A common assumption in tax incidence analyses is that the spending of revenue is neutral in that it does not alter market prices and incomes. Of course, such may not be the case. And market adjustments triggered by government's use of tax revenues may either offset or reinforce the adjustments to tax collection.

Several conclusions emerge from our discussion of tax incidence. First, market adjustments to a tax tend to shift the burden away from those from

28 Hours worked tend to fall because of the lower after-tax wage. However, hours worked tend to increase because workers now have to work longer to get the same after-tax income. These opposing effects of an income tax on labor supply are called the *substitution* and *income* effects, respectively. If the substitution effect dominates, labor supply is reduced and H increases, while the reverse is true if the income effect dominates. Which case prevails is an empirical question. For further discussion of this question see Chapter 10.

whom the tax is collected. Second, market adjustments may affect private-sector real income on either the income sources side, by affecting money incomes (M), or the income uses side, by affecting the prices paid (P). Third, equity judgments should be based on tax incidence rather than tax impact. The reason is that when market adjustments are taken into account, persons may make the same tax payments (bear the same impact) and yet have different tax burdens. Or persons may make different tax payments and have similar burdens. It is important to keep this third conclusion in mind as we try, in the following chapters, to assess the equity implications of various "tax preferences" or "tax loopholes."

EARMARKING

Tax earmarking occurs when taxes can be used only for a specified purpose. For example, federal gasoline taxes are earmarked for the Highway Trust Fund, which can only be used to finance highway and mass transit, the latter being a recent adjustment in the permissible uses of the funds. Earmarking links taxes and expenditures. It may therefore be a useful device for benefit taxation, in which case the rationale for earmarking would be that the taxes are payments for particular services. In other instances, earmarking is clearly not benefit taxation, as occurs when some fraction of a general tax, such as a state sales or income tax, is earmarked to support public schools, colleges, roads, or some other specific activity.

Earmarking is a controversial practice. Some argue that it introduces rigidities into budgeting, preventing revenues from being directed into the highest priority uses. That is, the "appropriate" amount of spending on a particular activity may be less or more than the amount of earmarked revenues. Most recently, this argument has been used to support the use of earmarked funds from the Highway Trust Fund to finance mass transportation rather than highways.

While the preceding argument is valid in some instances, a case can also be made for earmarking. As we noted earlier, earmarking may be useful as a device for benefit taxation. Also, by linking taxes and expenditures, earmarking may promote more efficient decisions. People are thereby made aware of both the cost of government activities and the uses to which their taxes are put. Relatedly, earmarking may be a means by which political bargains are guaranteed.[29]

29 For further discussion of these issues, see James M. Buchanan, "The Economics of Earmarked Taxes," *Journal of Political Economy*, 71 (October 1963): 457–469; and Charles J. Goetz, "Earmarked Taxes and Majority Rule Budgetary Processes," *American Economic Review*, 58 (March 1963): 128–136.

NEGATIVE TAXES

Transfer payments to individuals are essentially negative taxes. Such payments affect the distribution of income and the efficiency with which resources are used. Therefore, the effects of taxes and transfer payments can be similarly analyzed. That is, the same principles can be applied in evaluating both transfer payments and taxes.

In many instances, the effects of transfer payments on the incentives to supply capital and labor are unimportant because the transfer recipients are suppliers of neither labor nor capital. Indeed, their poverty is a reflection of their having few if any marketable resources. Many of the poor are elderly and disabled and therefore unable to supply labor. And virtually all the poor have such low incomes that they save little and are therefore unimportant as suppliers of capital. Only in the case of the working poor is there a potential adverse incentive effect. In this case, higher transfer payments may discourage labor supply, especially if the amount of the transfer payment is inversely related to the recipient's income.[30] However, evidence suggests that labor supply by primary earners (heads of households) is little affected by the receipt of transfer payments.[31]

Transfer payments that supplement the incomes of the poor may have a favorable effect on the supply of human capital by enabling poor families to enjoy better nutrition and medical care and making it possible for poor children to continue their schooling longer than they otherwise could.

TAXATION FOR SOCIAL CONTROL

Rather than being a means of financing expenditures, taxation may be used as a control device, with the revenues collected being incidental. Taxation to control activities that generate external costs is an example. Tariffs to limit imports are another example. Taxes levied for control purposes may be negative. That is, they may be subsidies — subsidizing activities that generate external benefits and subsidizing exports.

LIMITS OF TAXATION

Are there limits to the amount of taxes that can be collected from particular taxpayers? The answer depends on the alternatives to tax payment. If the alternatives are incarceration or fines, then the expected severity of such penalties must increase as the amount of taxes to be collected increases.

30 See Okun, *Equality and Efficiency*, p. 107.
31 See Joseph A. Pechman and P. Michael Timpane, eds., *Work Incentives and Income Guarantees: The New Jersey Negative Income Tax Experiment* (Washington: Brookings, 1975).

Thus, society's reluctance to employ very harsh penalties for nonpayment of taxes may limit the amount that can be collected. In addition, when taxes are dependent on taxpayers' decisions, taxpayers may alter their decisions to limit their tax liabilities. For example, income tax collections are limited because people can escape the tax by ceasing to engage in activities that generate taxable income.[32]

Limits may also arise because there are two other alternatives to paying a legislated level of taxes. One, taxpayers may be able to move their taxable activities outside the jurisdiction of the taxing government. Two, taxpayers may act through the political process to alter their liabilities.

Taxpayers would presumably take the first alternative only if they receive fewer net benefits from their present government's activities than they would receive from the governments of other nations or localities to which they could move. Of course, even if there are positive tax-benefit incentives to move to another government's jurisdiction, such movement would not occur if the costs of movement were sufficiently high.[33] Thus, a government's ability to tax is limited when its constituents can move beyond its jurisdiction. For example, city dwellers may move to the suburbs to escape relatively high city taxes. But this limit is not clear-cut and easily defined. Instead, it is likely to vary among taxpayers. And it depends on the behavior and decisions of other governments.

The second alternative, political action, would presumably be undertaken when the expected costs of action fall short of the expected gains from it. The gains and costs of political action are likely to depend on the political process and vary among taxpayers. The statutory and constitutional provisions governing taxation will clearly affect the costs of political action. Some people have louder political "voices" than others. Also, the equity of the tax burden seems likely to affect the expected gains from action. Redress is more likely to be obtained through the political process if tax liabilities are at variance with prevailing standards of equity. Again, we are left with a rather nebulous conclusion: The potential for political action to alter tax liabilities surely limits taxation, but the limit will vary among persons and with political institutions. Of course, the limits to taxation implicit in existing political institutions may permit taxation that is sufficiently oppressive to trigger revolution aimed at altering those institutions.

Rather than trying to reduce their tax liabilities through political measures, people may try to offset the taxes by increasing their before-tax

---

32 Of course, when people do adjust their decisions about resource allocation in response to taxes, the result is excess burden, as we discussed earlier.

33 In addition to the obvious costs of physically relocating, there may be costs in the form of reduced private-sector income and reduced amenities — climate, proximity to family, etc.

incomes. For example, large unions and large corporations may respond to higher taxes by seeking higher wages and prices. To the extent that they are successful, other taxpayers will bear a larger real burden or government will find the purchasing power of its tax revenues eroded by inflation. Such wage and price inflation generated by the responses of individuals and businesses to taxation may limit government's ability to tax (in real terms).

Our very general conclusion is that there are limits to the amount of revenue that a government can obtain from a given population. And the amount that can be obtained from a given taxpayer will depend on the political power of the taxpayer (his or her costs of political action) and whether his or her taxable activities can easily be relocated.

SUMMARY

How should government activities be financed? Entirely by taxation? If not, when should they be financed by borrowing, sale of services, or other means? What is the optimal revenue structure for government? Why? How government is financed determines both the distribution and the magnitude of the costs of government. And the answers to these questions therefore depend partly on how one thinks the costs of government should be distributed (principles of equity) and partly on how alternative financing measures affect the magnitude and distribution of government costs. Although what is fair or equitable is a widely debated issue, there can be no doubt that political decisions about taxation are strongly influenced by considerations of equity and fairness.

A system that distributes costs equitably may entail greater total costs than a less equitable system. Therefore, revenue system design normally encounters equity-efficiency conflicts. Resolving such conflicts may be difficult because a value must be placed on equity — that is, a trade-off rate between equity and efficiency must be determined, either explicitly or implicitly, as decisions are made. Also, revenue system design is complicated and consensus about what constitutes a good tax system is difficult to obtain because the incidence of a tax may differ from its impact and is difficult to determine.

The criteria for designing and evaluating revenue systems can be applied to individual elements of the system or to the system as a whole. The latter appears to be the more meaningful basis for evaluation. We are interested in the net, or overall, effects of the system on income distribution and allocation efficiency. However, to know how to modify the system if it is unsatisfactory, we must also know how the elements (various tax forms such as sales, property, and income) of the system differ in their effect on the economy. The question, What will be the effects of a partial or complete substitution of one tax for another? is important in revenue system design.

So we will, in the following chapters, examine the differential effects of alternative taxes, with each tax being compared to a bench mark tax — the proportional income tax. That is, we will determine the effects of collecting a given amount of revenue by taxes other than the proportional income tax.

SUPPLEMENTARY READINGS

Harberger, Arnold C. *Taxation and Welfare*, chaps. 1, 2. Boston: Little, Brown, 1974.

Musgrave, Richard A. *The Theory of Public Finance*, chap. 10. New York: McGraw-Hill, 1959.

Pechman, Joseph A., and Okner, Benjamin A. *Who Bears the Tax Burden?* chaps. 2, 3. Washington: Brookings, 1974.

Report of the Royal Commission on Taxation. Vol. 3. Ottawa: Queen's Printer, 1966.

CHAPTER TEN

INDIVIDUAL INCOME TAXATION

The individual income tax is the most important source of federal government revenue, and it is a growing source of revenue for state and local governments. Two broad questions arise in income taxation: (1) How should the tax base (taxable income) be defined? (2) At what rates should taxable income be taxed? In the first part of this chapter, we will suggest how these questions might be answered as we outline the main features of an "ideal" income tax. In the remainder of the chapter we will discuss the resource allocation and income distribution effects of a comprehensive income tax (CIT). In Chapter 11 we will compare and contrast this ideal tax with the U.S. federal individual income tax.

TAX BASE

A number of questions arise in defining and measuring the income tax base. What is income? Should all income be taxed? What subtractions (deductions) from income should be permitted? What is the taxpaying unit (individual or family)? Over what period should income be measured? In answering these questions, we will build on the discussion in Chapter 9 of the relationship between income and ability to pay.

DEFINITION OF INCOME

If the objective of income taxation is taxation according to ability to pay, we must define income comprehensively. Specifically, we must define a person's income for a particular period as the value of all goods and services accruing to that person during the period.[1] Income, as we are using the term, is *net* income; that is, the total of all income minus any costs of generating that income.[2]

Income, as we just defined it, derives from several sources and may take different forms. Income from the ownership of resources — capital, labor, natural resources — is *earned* income and can be classified as wages, salaries, profit, rent, interest, and dividends. Gifts and transfers are *unearned* income since people do not receive them for supplying productive services. Unearned income includes bequests, *inter vivos* gifts, private business transfers, and government transfers and subsidies. Capital gains and losses, changes in net wealth due to changes in asset price, are another form of income.[3]

Income, regardless of the source, may or may not take the form of cash. Examples of cash (money) income are: wages, social security payments, interest, an inheritance of cash, and gambling winnings.

An example of nonmoney income is leisure. When a person's time is exchanged for money income or used to produce products that are exchanged for money, the person is said to be "working." Otherwise, the person's time is said to be devoted to "leisure." The value of leisure-time activities is a component of income, even though such activities generate no money flows. Because leisure-time activities produce nothing that is exchanged for money, their value must be imputed. This imputed value is the money income that the person could have earned if the time had been used to generate money income rather than leisure. Other examples of nonmoney income are room and board received as partial payment for labor

1 This is basically what is referred to as the "Haig-Simons definition of income." See R. M. Haig, "The Concept of Income — Economic and Legal Aspects," in *Readings in the Economics of Taxation*, ed. Richard A. Musgrave and Carl S. Shoup (Homewood, Ill.: Irwin, 1959); and Henry C. Simons, *Personal Income Taxation: The Definition of Income as a Problem of Fiscal Policy* (Chicago: University of Chicago Press, 1938).

2 See Chapter 9, p. 203.

3 Asset prices may increase simply because of inflation — an increase in the general price level. Such inflation-generated increases in asset prices (capital gains) are not real because they do not increase the quantities of various goods and services that the asset owners can obtain in exchange for their assets. This has led some to suggest that inflation-generated capital gains should not be taxed as income. See Roger Brinner, "Inflation, Deferral and the Neutral Taxation of Capital Gains," *National Tax Journal*, 26, No. 4 (December 1973): 565–573. Against this view are the arguments that (a) our present tax system is based on money rather than real income; (b) there are other instances in which inflation generates an increase in money income and tax liabilities without there being a commensurate increase in real income; and (c) if the system is to tax real rather than money income from one source (capital gains), income from all other sources should be similarly treated — taxable income from all sources should be defined in real, rather than money, terms. For further discussion, see Arthur M. Okun, *Equality and Efficiency: The Big Trade-Off* (Washington: Brookings, 1975), p. 104.

services, the services of homemakers, home-grown vegetables, the value of government-supplied goods and services, a gift of real estate, appreciation in the value of an art collection, the rental value of owner-occupied homes, and the flow of services from consumer durables (automobiles, home appliances, etc.).

It is easy to see that income from some of these sources would be difficult to measure and tax. This does not mean that income from such sources is not appropriately included in a comprehensive measure of income. But it does mean that there is, in practice, a need to balance comprehensiveness against the costs and difficulties of administering and complying with an income tax. Partly for this reason, existing income taxes do not tax income from all sources, as we shall see in Chapter 11.

DISCRETIONARY INCOME, EXEMPTIONS, AND DEDUCTIONS

As we noted in Chapter 9, ability to pay taxes depends on a person's needs for goods and services as well as his or her income. That is, some expenditures are "nondiscretionary," and only when income exceeds the amount of nondiscretionary expenditures does the person have ability to pay taxes. In particular, at low-income levels, individuals and families have little discretion about the use of their income. If this view is accepted, discretionary income, defined as net income minus nondiscretionary expenditures, rather than net income, measures a person's ability to pay.

Nondiscretionary expenditures may be defined as those required to meet the biological, or "basic," necessities of life. In such case, nondiscretionary expenditures would be the "subsistence" income, the income required for the existence of the taxpayer. Or nondiscretionary expenditures may be relative and determined by cultural standards. Some have argued, for example, that incomes should not fall below some fraction, such as one-half, of the average or median income in the nation.[4] In any case, regardless of how discretionary income is defined, the tax base should be discretionary income rather than net income.

Discretionary income may be positive or negative. A taxpayer whose discretionary income is negative does not have enough income to cover nondiscretionary expenditures. If one of the purposes of the tax structure is to assure a tax-free income that is at least equal to the amount of nondiscretionary expenditures, negative discretionary income requires transfers (negative taxation).[5]

4 See Victor Fuchs, "Redefining Poverty and Redistributing Income," *The Public Interest*, No. 8 (Summer 1967): 88–95.

5 One of the original proponents of negative income taxation is Milton Friedman; see his *Capitalism and Freedom* (Chicago: University of Chicago Press, 1962).

To adjust income for predictable nondiscretionary expenditures, a particular amount of income can be exempted from taxation. The amount of exempt income should equal the amount of nondiscretionary expenditures for
the taxpaying unit. The exemption should therefore vary with the number of
persons in the taxpaying unit. It should also vary with other indices of need,
such as age and disability. In a family of four, a uniform per person exemption of $1,000 would exempt income of $4,000 from taxation.[6]

Not all nondiscretionary expenditures are reasonably predictable — for example, health care expenditures and expenditures necessitated by losses due
to weather, theft, fire, etc. For such nondiscretionary expenditures as these,
deductions or tax credits can be used. Or unpredictable expenditures can be
made predictable through insurance. Insurance premiums, rather than the
nondiscretionary expenditure itself, could then be deducted from income to
obtain discretionary income.

UNIT OF TAXATION

The unit of taxation under an income tax should be the family or unrelated
individual. One reason is that most families are decision-making units, with
each member's income being used for the benefit of the family as a whole,
rather than exclusively for the benefit of the family member who receives
the income. Also, a person's ability to pay taxes depends, in part, upon his
or her responsibilities to others. A person's immediate responsibilities are
her- or himself, members of the family, and others dependent on his or her
income. A practical argument for treating the family as the taxpaying unit is
that doing so eliminates the question of whether transfers and payments between members of the family should be taxed.

The question of how the taxpaying unit should be defined is essentially
the question of whether the income of family members should be pooled
and taxed as one or the income of each person should be taxed separately.
How this question is answered does not matter if income taxes are proportional to income and if the family's total taxable income is the same whether
the family is taxed as a unit or its members are taxed separately. In such
case, a family's total tax liability is the same regardless of how income is
divided among its members. But, with separate taxation of each family
member at progressive rates, a family's total tax liability is lower as the total
family income is spread more evenly among family members.

6 The exemption need not be a uniform amount per person. There is some evidence of
economies of scale to family size, in which case the size of the exemption would fall as family
size increased. See Harold M. Groves, *Federal Tax Treatment of the Family* (Washington:
Brookings, 1963).

ACCOUNTING PERIOD

Given a definition of income, over what period is it to be measured? One year? A lifetime? Clearly, of two people having the same current income, the one having a greater future and, hence, a greater lifetime income has a greater ability to pay. We can also observe that a person's income will be more variable as it is measured over shorter periods. Thus, many economists argue that income should be measured over a period longer than a year; or if it is measured annually, it should be averaged over several years in calculating taxes.

Averaging is particularly important with a progressive tax, since a person pays a higher tax if she or he receives the same amount of income at irregular rather than regular intervals. The result is horizontal inequity, with the person who receives income regularly paying lower taxes than the person who receives the same total income in bunches. One solution to this problem is to compute income taxes on the basis of lifetime income. Short of this solution, tax liabilities can be "smoothed" by averaging income over several accounting periods. One approach to averaging would be to cumulate income each year and apply a tax rate on the cumulated total each year. Taxes paid in previous years would then be subtracted from each year's tax calculations. In this way, persons with the same lifetime income pay the same tax no matter how irregular their income is.[7]

ACCRUED VERSUS REALIZED INCOME

People do not always receive income at exactly the same time that the income accrues (becomes due to them). Wage income that *accrues* daily as a person works is usually *received* weekly or monthly. Capital gains income *accrues* when an asset's market value rises above its purchased price, but this income is not *realized* until the asset is sold. As a result, the amount of income that accrues to a person during a year (or some other accounting period) may differ from the amount that the person receives during that year.

The accrual of income increases a person's command over commodities whether or not that income is realized in cash. The reason is that the person has the option of converting the accrued income into cash. So accrued, rather than realized, income is in principle the appropriate base for income taxation. However, in some instances, measuring accrued but unrealized income may be difficult, forcing taxation on a realized basis. Measuring the accrued capital gains (losses) from holding assets that are only infrequently traded is especially difficult. Fortunately, current market prices are readily

---

7 See William S. Vickrey, *Agenda for Progressive Taxation* (New York: Ronald, 1947).

available for many assets, such as publicly traded stocks and bonds, so that accrued gains (or losses) from holding such assets can be valued and taxed periodically. For other assets, accrued gains can at least be calculated at death, since the value of estates must be calculated for estate tax purposes. Any taxes due on accrued but unrealized gains can be spread out over several years to avoid forced liquidation. With this approach, all accrued gains are eventually taxed.

RATE STRUCTURE

Should tax rates on income be progressive, proportional, or regressive? Historically, attempts to justify progression have often assumed that the marginal utility of income declines as income increases. According to this reasoning, a tax payment of a given amount, say $100, imposes a smaller utility loss on higher-income persons than on lower-income persons. Minimizing the aggregate sacrifice of utility requires that the marginal rate of taxation increase with income. This *minimum aggregate sacrifice* argument for progression relies on the questionable assumptions that utility can be measured to determine tax rates and that, in fact, the marginal utility of income declines in a specified way as income increases.

Progression might be justified on other grounds. First, progressive taxes are a means of redistributing income from high-income to low-income persons. Government spending of a given amount and composition increases the real income of persons by the value of the government-supplied goods that each receives, while the taxes that each person pays decrease income. When such spending is financed by a progressive rather than a proportional tax, the real incomes of the poor are greater relative to those of the rich.[8] Progression may also be rationalized as a kind of insurance against unpredictable fluctuations in income. When income falls, tax liabilities fall more than proportionately, relieving individuals of some taxes when times are bad. When income rises, the reverse happens. The reduced taxes in low-income periods can be made up when taxpayers are in better economic circumstances. Third, when ability-to-pay taxation is defined as taxation in proportion to discretionary income, progression automatically follows.[9]

---

8 We discussed the arguments for and against reducing income inequality in Chapter 6.

9 Suppose $T = t(I - c)$, where T is income taxes, t is the tax rate, I is net income, and c is non-discretionary expenditures. From $T/I = [t(I - c)]/I$, it can be seen that T increases relative to I as I increases if c is constant. Progression results because a higher proportion of income is exempt from taxation at the lower income levels. Of course, progression could be increased by increasing t as discretionary income increases.

These are essentially ability-to-pay arguments for progressive tax rates. It is also possible to argue for progressive rates on the basis that the benefits received from government rise more rapidly than income. Benefits could rise more rapidly than income because high-income persons receive more services relative to their incomes than low-income people and because they place higher values on the services that they do receive. For example, police protection and national defense services may be largely for the benefit of high-income persons who have much to lose from either war or domestic criminal activity and who are willing to pay more than are the poor for such protection simply because they have higher incomes.[10]

While that argument is plausible, the reverse is usually held to be the case for the present mix of activities by U.S. governments. Therefore, it is commonly held that proportional or even regressive rates of income taxation would be required if the income tax is to be a benefits-received tax.[11]

ALLOCATION EFFECTS

A tax may have two kinds of effects on allocation decisions. An *income effect* arises if taxpayers alter their decisions in response to the tax-induced reduction in disposable income. A *substitution effect* arises if taxpayers alter their decisions in response to tax-induced changes in relative prices or in relative returns on alternative resource uses or in both. In this section we will examine these allocation effects of income taxation on taxpayer decisions about labor supply, saving, and investment.

In assessing the effects of the proportional income tax, we assume that the revenues are used to finance a predetermined amount of government spending. The allocation effects of the proportional income tax are then used as a bench mark, to which the effects of other taxes are compared. Such comparisons of the effects of alternative taxes is exactly what is needed in revenue system design, because we need to know whether substitution of one tax for another will improve the system. Thus, in this chapter we will compare the progressive income tax to the proportional income tax. In subsequent chapters we will compare each tax (sales, wealth, etc.) to the bench mark proportional income tax.

---

10 See W. J. Blum and H. Kalven, Jr., *The Uneasy Case for Progressive Taxation* (Chicago: University of Chicago Press, 1953), for further discussion of the issues of progressive taxation.

11 For a thorough and recent discussion of the problems of estimating the benefits from government and for estimates of the distribution of those benefits by income class, see Richard A. Musgrave, Karl E. Case, and Herman Leonard, "The Distribution of Fiscal Burdens and Benefits," *Public Finance Quarterly*, 2, No. 3 (July 1974): 259–311.

LABOR SUPPLY

A proportional income tax on all income (comprehensive income tax) has no substitution effect on the labor supply (labor versus leisure) decision because the value of leisure is included in comprehensive income. That is, the taxpayer cannot reduce his or her tax liability by working less because any decrease in income from labor supply is exactly offset by an increase in income in the form of leisure. However, the income effect of a proportional tax on *all* income will tend to increase labor supply as the taxpayer acts to offset the tax-induced decrease in the availability of market-traded goods.

Figure 10–1 illustrates the income effect on labor supply. In the absence of taxation, Al Deutch has a budget line *ab*. He can supply the maximum labor to obtain at most *oa* units of market-traded goods. Or he can supply the minimum labor to obtain at most *ob* units of leisure and self-produced goods. Or he can choose some intermediate mix. Suppose his utility-maximizing allocation of his total income is represented by point *e* — *oM* units of market-traded goods and *oL* units of other goods. With a proportional income tax on all income, his income is reduced by some amount, *a'a*, so that his budget line shifts in to *a'b'*. If market-traded and other goods are both normal, this reduction in disposable income entails a reduction in each type of good to a new utility-maximizing point, such as *e'*. At *e'*, total labor supply is greater than at *e*, and the amounts of both market-traded and other goods are lower, a reflection of the tax-induced decrease in disposable income.

In practice, income taxes are not fully comprehensive. They are, instead, levied on money income, thus excluding the value of leisure and self-produced goods from the tax base. When this is the case, a substitution effect is possible because people can reduce their income tax liability by increasing their leisure and reducing their labor supply. The tax lowers the price of leisure relative to the price of other goods.[12] This price reduction provides the taxpayer with an incentive to substitute leisure for work. Since the income effect may induce more work effort, and the substitution effect may induce less work effort, how a tax on money income affects work effort cannot be determined by a theoretical analysis.

To illustrate, in Figure 10–1, a tax on money income shifts Deutch's budget line to *a"b*. No tax is paid if he chooses no market-traded goods and supplies no labor. Therefore the maximum amount of leisure and self-produced goods is the same, *ob*, with or without the tax on money income.

12 The price of a person's leisure or leisure time activities is the value of the market-traded goods that the person must give up to engage in those activities. The value of the market-traded goods lost when a person takes an hour of leisure is the money income (after taxes) that the person could have earned if the hour had been devoted to work rather than leisure.

FIGURE 10–1
INCOME TAXATION AND THE LABOR-LEISURE CHOICE

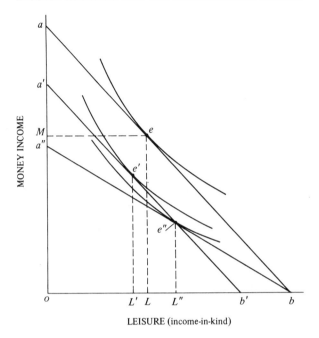

LEISURE (income-in-kind)

Tax liability mounts as Deutch supplies more labor to a maximum liability of $a''a$ when labor supply and market-traded goods are at a maximum. With this tax, his utility-maximizing labor supply is lower, point e'', than it was with the comprehensive tax, point e', even though the two taxes take the same amount of revenue from him. In this example, the imposition of a tax on money income reduces total labor supply from L to L''. This reduction is the sum of two effects: the income effect, which increases the labor supply from L to L', and the substitution effect, which reduces it from L' to L''. We can see that with differently shaped indifference curves, the total effect of imposing the money income tax could be to increase labor supply. Unless Deutch's choice is maximum leisure, the amount ob, then he is never worse off and may be better off (on a higher indifference curve) with the comprehensive income tax than with the tax on money income (market-traded goods) only. The welfare loss that may result from the taxation of money income rather than comprehensive income is another example of excess burden, as we defined it in Chapter 9.

Taxpayers will tend to supply less labor with a progressive tax on money income than with an equal-yield proportional tax. To illustrate, let us suppose Bernice Sommers earns $5 an hour and $10,000 a year and is taxed at a proportional rate of 20 percent, yielding $2,000 in taxes. Since her disposable income increases only $4 for each additional hour that she works, the marginal price of leisure is $4 per hour. With a progressive rate structure of, for example, 10 percent on the first $5,000 and 30 percent on the second $5,000, her total tax liabilities are still $2,000 at the same level of work effort. However, the marginal price of leisure falls to $.7(\$5.00) = \$3.50$ per hour. The income effect is the same under the two taxes because the tax yield is the same, but the substitution effect is more pronounced with a progressive income tax. Therefore, labor supply tends to be greater with a proportional than with a progressive tax.[13]

This analysis assumes that each taxpayer pays the same tax whether the tax is proportional or progressive, so the two taxes have the same income effects on labor supply. However, in the likely case that taxes are of equal yield in the aggregate, but not necessarily of equal yield for each person, then substitution of a progressive for a proportional income tax may change both the disposable income and marginal tax rate of some or all taxpayers. There are four possibilities:

1. Disposable income increases, marginal tax rate decreases.
2. Disposable income increases, marginal tax rate increases.
3. Disposable income decreases, marginal tax rate increases.
4. Disposable income decreases, marginal tax rate decreases.

Low-income taxpayers are likely to be in class 1, and high-income taxpayers are likely to be in class 3. For class 1 and 3 taxpayers, the income and substitution effects work in opposite directions; and there is no clear-cut effect on labor supply. Taxpayers in class 2 will supply less labor, while taxpayers in class 4 will supply more. Thus, the net effect of a change from proportional to progressive taxation on total labor supply cannot be determined a priori, unless tax yield (and disposable income) is unchanged for *each* person. All that can be concluded is that the two taxes are likely to differentially affect total labor supply.

The two taxes are also likely to differ in their effects on the supply of labor to various occupations. Compared to a proportional income tax, progressive taxation would tend to decrease labor supply to highly paid occupations and increase supply to lower paid occupations and occupations with large non-monetary rewards.

This analysis also assumes that taxpayers can freely adjust their labor

13 A tax that is equal in yield after adjustments in labor supply gives the same results.

supply. However, the effect of income taxes upon labor supply is limited by social and institutional decisions about the age that a person enters the labor force, the labor force participation rate of women (men), vacation time, the standard work week, overtime, second jobs, the retirement age, etc. In addition, there are strong nonmonetary factors associated with working that may make the supply of labor, or certain types of labor, highly inelastic (insensitive to money earnings).

Those rigidities help explain why studies of the effect of taxes upon labor supply indicate that the aggregate supply is not substantially affected by taxes. That general conclusion emerges from both statistical studies and studies based on interviews of individuals, usually highly paid, about their work response to taxes and their awareness of taxes.[14]

Thus, while it is possible that money income taxation may either increase or decrease labor supply, there is little evidence that it does either. Nor is there analytical or empirical support for the view that total labor supply would be greater (or lesser) with proportional rather than progressive taxation.

SAVING AND CAPITAL FORMATION

Savings are the source of an economy's capital. In real terms, people who save release resources from the production of consumer goods for the production of capital goods (or services). In some cases, the saving and investment occur simultaneously, as when families finance the education of their children. In other cases, the investors are not the savers. Given full employment of resources, the amount of saving determines the amount of investment that can take place.

Saving is essentially a trading of present for future consumption. The amount of such saving depends on the taxpayer's income and the price of future consumption, which is the amount of current consumption that must be given up to obtain a unit of future consumption. The price of future consumption is inversely related to the rate of interest earned on saving. A tax on income including interest income has income and substitution effects on

14 For an excellent review of the studies of the effects of taxation on labor supply, see George F. Break, "The Incidence and Economic Effects of Taxation," in *The Economics of Public Finance*, ed. Alan S. Blinder, George F. Break, Peter O. Steiner, Dick Netzer (Washington: Brookings, 1974), pp. 120–190. See also Lester C. Thurow, *The Impact of Taxes on the American Economy* (New York: Praeger, 1971); Arthur M. Okun, *Equality and Efficiency: The Big Trade-Off* (Washington: Brookings, 1975); Joseph A. Pechman and P. Michael Timpane, eds., *Work Incentives and Income Guarantees: The New Jersey Negative Income Tax Experiment* (Washington: Brookings, 1975); and Richard Goode, *The Individual Income Tax*, rev. ed. (Washington: Brookings, 1976), chaps. 3–4.

saving analogous to those on labor supply. However, the income and substitution effects on saving work in the same direction. The tax reduces disposable income and saving for taxpayers who have a positive marginal propensity to save (income effect). An income tax also gives taxpayers an incentive to reduce saving because it increases the price of future consumption relative to the price of present consumption by decreasing the after-tax return on saving (substitution effect).[15] Clearly, a proportional income tax unambiguously reduces saving.

Replacing a proportional with a progressive income tax that is equal-yield for each taxpayer increases each taxpayer's incentive to substitute current consumption for saving and would therefore tend to decrease total saving. The reason is that a progressive tax entails a higher marginal tax rate than the proportional tax, with the result that the reward for additional saving is less than with a proportional income tax.[16]

Replacing a proportional income tax with a progressive tax will likely change the disposable income of some or all taxpayers, even if the aggregate tax yield of the two taxes is the same. The possible changes are those listed on page 226. Class 1 taxpayers would increase their saving, and class 3 taxpayers would curtail their saving. The effects on taxpayers in classes 2 and 4 are ambiguous. Thus, the differential effect of progressive and proportional taxation on the total saving cannot be predicted without information about the number and behavior of taxpayers in each of the classes. Specifically, a proportional tax is unlikely to result in more saving than a progressive tax if saving is insensitive to the after-tax rate of interest. Available evidence on this issue is mixed, but private saving appears to be largely unaffected by the level and structure of income taxation.[17]

Nevertheless, it is frequently asserted that replacing the progressive U.S. income tax with a proportional tax would increase total saving. According to this view, increased saving by high-income taxpayers (class 3) would more than offset decreased saving by low-income taxpayers (class 1) because the marginal propensity to save is presumably greater for high-income than for low-income persons.[18] However, that assumption may not be valid if

15 The substitution is between present consumption and saving.

16 The reasoning is the same as that applied to the effect of progressive versus proportional income taxes on work effort.

17 See Break, "Incidence and Economic Effects of Taxation," pp. 191–202; and Goode, *Individual Income Tax*, chaps. 3–4. Break estimates that total saving is slightly lower under the existing federal income tax than it would be with a proportional tax. See also Colin Wright, "Saving and the Rate of Interest," in *Taxation of Income from Capital*, eds. Arnold C. Harberger and M. J. Bailey (Washington: Brookings, 1969).

18 On that assumption, one author estimates that replacing the present U.S. progressive income tax with a proportional one might raise household saving by less than 10 percent. See

families' saving and investment in human capital is taken into account. Specifically, parents save and invest as they make expenditures that enhance the income of children, and education spending by the general population has the same effect.[19] Such human investment expenditures are large segments in the budgets of low- and middle-income households. Taxes may cut into this kind of saving as well as other forms. When all forms of saving are considered, it is not clear how the marginal propensity to save varies with income. In particular, there is little evidence that the marginal propensity to save for investment in both human and physical capital increases as income increases.

Even if progressive taxation does result in lower saving than does proportional taxation, there remains the question of what is the efficient level of saving. Conventional analysis does not consider the external effects of saving-investment decisions. For example, if the progressive tax reduces saving more than the proportional tax, the lower rate of saving resulting from progressive taxation may be preferable on efficiency grounds if it reduces investment in those production activities that generate external costs and disinvestment elsewhere (say, deterioration in the environment, which is disinvestment in "natural" capital). The real income of society may be larger if certain kinds of investments are lower (e.g., strip-mining).

RISK TAKING

Saving and investment involve risks. Taxation, by affecting the risk of (distribution of returns from) investments, may affect saving and investment.

Risk-averse individuals require a higher rate of return if they are to invest in higher-risk, rather than lower-risk, investments. A proportional income tax reduces the reward to risk taking. And if risk is not also reduced, individuals may invest in less risky alternatives. However, risk is reduced if investment losses can be deducted from income in computing income taxes; i.e., if full loss offsets are permitted, the risk of investments is reduced. To illustrate, let us suppose an individual invests $10,000 with an expected return of 10 percent. A 50 percent income tax will reduce the expected return from $1,000 to $500. But the amount the investor stands to lose is also reduced, from $10,000 to $5,000. If the entire $10,000 is lost, it can be deducted against income for a tax saving of 50 percent or a net loss of $5,000. The net

Richard A. Musgrave, "Effects of Tax Policy on Private Capital Formation," in *Fiscal and Debt Management Policies* (Englewood Cliffs, N.J.: Prentice-Hall, 1963), pp. 58, 68.

19 Although there is a consumption component to some of these expenditures (parents, children, and the general population may derive current benefits from some of the expenditures), there is general agreement that there is an investment component as well.

return and risk are reduced in the same proportion. Whether these changes in risk and return will lead the taxpayer to shift investments from more risky to less risky assets is open to question.

With a progressive income tax collecting the same amount from each taxpayer, the marginal return on relatively risky investments is lower than with a proportional tax. The reason is that people who invest in riskier investments will have higher tax brackets when they win and lower tax brackets when they lose. That is, with progressive taxation and full loss offsets, the government's share of gains is greater than its share of losses. Thus, progressive taxation is less conducive to risk taking than proportional taxation. But it cannot be concluded on theoretical grounds that either tax reduces risk taking.[20]

Like the theoretical analyses, empirical evidence on the effects of taxation on risk taking is scanty and inconclusive. Also, it relates only to the influences of taxes on risk taking by individuals. Risk taking by corporations may be subject to different influences. Finally, there is the question of whether tax policy should be neutral with respect to risk taking.

INCIDENCE

In the preceding section we noted that factor supplies (labor and saving) appear to be little affected by income taxation; that is, they are fixed (perfectly inelastic). If such is the case, then a completely general and proportional income tax will be borne by the taxpayers on whom it is levied. The reason is that unless factor supplies are varied, no taxpayer can respond to the tax in such a way as to shift it by either lowering his or her tax liability or increasing his or her before-tax income. In this case, the tax incidence and impact are identical and the burden is proportional to income.

However, if income taxation does reduce saving, the reduction in total saving will in turn cause some of the tax that is levied on owners of capital to be shifted to suppliers of labor — if labor supply is inelastic. The reason is that with less saving and capital, the capital-labor ratio will be lower (workers will have fewer "tools") and the gross wage will be lower relative to the return on capital. Thus, workers lose not only by the amount of their tax payments, but also by the amount of this decrease in their before-tax income. Conversely, if labor supply falls while saving remains unchanged, the capital-labor ratio will be higher and the gross return on capital will be lower relative to the gross wage. And capital suppliers (savers) will bear a greater

---

20 For further discussion of this and other aspects of risk taking, see Martin S. Feldstein, "The Effect of Taxation on Risk Taking," *Journal of Political Economy* (September-October 1969): 755–769.

burden relative to their incomes than will labor suppliers. If both labor and capital supplies are variable, the net effect cannot be predicted without information about how the tax affects factor supplies and how those changes in factor supplies affect factor earnings.

Labor supply to some activities may be more elastic than to others. If so, there will be some tax-induced shifts in outputs and prices, which will affect real incomes. Similarly, capital supply to particular activities may be differentially affected by the tax, thus altering relative prices. Generally then, when factor supplies are variable in the aggregate or to particular sectors or both, real incomes of taxpayers may be altered on both the income sources and income uses sides. These effects are in addition to and may either reinforce or offset the direct effect of the tax payment on disposable income.

While these possibilities for shifting do exist, there is little evidence that either labor supply or saving are very elastic, as we noted earlier. So a conclusion that the incidence of a proportional income tax is approximately proportional to income is plausible and widely accepted. With fixed factor supplies, a progressive income tax is also borne by those upon whom it is levied, and the tax's impact and incidence are identical. Studies of tax incidence typically assume that such is the case.[21]

SUMMARY

If the intent of income taxation is to tax individuals according to their ability to pay, then taxable income should be defined as money and nonmoney income from all sources, minus nondiscretionary expenditures. That is, the income tax base should be what we have termed discretionary income.

Available evidence suggests that such a comprehensive income tax would be basically neutral in its effects on factor supplies. That is, total capital and labor supplies appear to be largely unaffected by existing income taxation and would presumably be even less affected by a more comprehensive tax. A progressive tax has a greater potential for affecting factor supplies than a proportional tax. The reason is that progressive taxation involves higher marginal tax rates and, therefore, stronger incentives for people to alter their economic behavior so as to alter their tax liabilities.

If broad-based income taxes do have little effect on total factor supplies, then those on whom the taxes are levied bear the burden — incidence and impact are identical.

A tax on discretionary income, comprehensively defined, would distribute

21 The most recent study to employ that assumption is Joseph A. Pechman and Benjamin A. Okner, *Who Bears the Tax Burden?* (Washington: Brookings, 1974).

government costs according to ability to pay and be neutral in its effects on allocation decisions. Nevertheless, two distinct problems arise. First, measuring income from some sources is difficult and costly, if not impossible. And, in practice, some comprehensiveness must be sacrificed to make the tax feasible and reasonably inexpensive to administer and enforce. Second, measuring discretionary income requires defining discretionary expenditures. But doing so in a way that meets widespread approval is likely to be difficult.

For both these reasons, income taxation based on the principles we outlined in this chapter will be difficult to implement. But that does prevent the principles from serving as useful guidelines or yardsticks for evaluating existing income tax systems. And we undertake such an evaluation in the following chapter.

SUPPLEMENTARY READINGS

Goode, Richard. *The Individual Income Tax*. Rev. ed. Washington: Brookings, 1976.

Report of the Royal Commission on Taxation. Vol. 3. Ottawa: Queens Printer, 1966.

Simons, Henry C. *Personal Income Taxation*. Chicago: University of Chicago Press, 1938.

————. *Federal Tax Reform*. Chicago: University of Chicago Press, 1950.

CHAPTER ELEVEN

THE UNITED STATES
INDIVIDUAL INCOME TAX

In this chapter we describe the U.S. individual income tax, note some of the more important consequences of departing from comprehensive income taxation, and make suggestions for closing the gap between "ideal" and "practice."

CONCEPT OF INCOME

The U.S. tax code defines gross income as "all income from whatever source derived. . . ." Specific sources of income are then listed as included in or excluded from the income tax base. Some sources included in our comprehensive definition of income are excluded by administrative and court rulings rather than by statute.

COSTS OF EARNING INCOME

Most costs of earning income are deductible from reportable gross income in determining net income: professional and union dues, operating an automobile, office space, travel, materials, etc. Controversial items have been moving expenses, business travel and entertainment, child care expenses, and education expenditures. There are rather liberal provisions for deducting nonreimbursed moving expenses for job-related moves. Taxpayers are allowed a tax credit equal to 20 percent of employment-related expenses for the care of children and other qualified individuals. The maximum credit is $400 for the care of one individual and $800 for two or more. Education expenditures may be deducted if they are required to maintain or improve skills in employment or are required by employers, regulations, or the law. The case for liberalizing provisions for deducting education expenditures is that they are a cost of earning income; not allowing their deduction discriminates in favor of investment in depreciable nonhuman capital. Education expenditures that increase income in future years should be treated as investment and amortized over some period of time.

The primary difficulty in determining which expenditures are to be treated as costs of earning income arises in distinguishing between costs and consumption. For example, education expenditures may be for enhancing income or for achieving a more satisfying current and future lifestyle. Travel may be business-related or for pleasure. In determining net business income, allowing for the costs of depreciable assets is a major problem.[1]

EXCLUDED INCOME SOURCES

The definition of income under the U.S. federal income tax laws does not conform to the comprehensive definition of income we developed in Chapter 10. We therefore discuss the main departures in this section.

Gifts and bequests   Gifts and bequests fall within our comprehensive definition of income, provided they are between members of different taxpaying units.[2] But they are not taxed as income under the U.S. income tax laws. Gifts and bequests are taxed under a separate tax, with the taxes being the liability of the donor and independent of the recipient's income. The effect of present law is to tax gifts and bequests at lower rates than other income.

Gifts and bequests presently are not taxed as income for two basic reasons. One is that there is debate about whether they should be so taxed.[3] The other is the practical problem of getting information about the transfers, especially when they are small in amount and between closely related persons.

The failure to treat gifts and bequests as income violates the principles of vertical and horizontal equity — if we accept the comprehensive definition of income as the appropriate basis for ability-to-pay taxation. Two individuals may receive the same bequest but have different incomes from other

1 In Chapter 12 we discuss the determination of net business income more fully.

2 For example, a bequest or gift from a father to a minor daughter would not be treated as taxable income to the daughter if the family is the basic taxpaying unit. However, when the daughter leaves and becomes a member of a different household, any assets she takes would be income taxable to that household. For a detailed discussion of this issue, see *Report of the Royal Commission on Taxation*, vol. 3 (Ottawa: Queen's Printer, 1966).

3 For arguments against the inclusion of gifts and bequests in taxable income, see Richard Goode, *The Individual Income Tax*, rev. ed. (Washington: Brookings, 1976), pp. 98ff.

sources. And an individual who receives a bequest of $10,000 will pay a different tax than a person who receives wages of $10,000.[4]

Government transfers Excluded from income taxation are government transfer payments, such as public assistance, Social Security, and unemployment compensation. Therefore, people who receive such transfers may pay lower taxes and have more disposable income than others who receive the same total income from working and other sources that are subject to taxation. Some people insist that this is not a problem because the transfer payments are so low, they should not be subject to taxation anyway. But that argument applies equally well to any source of income, as long as total income falls below the poverty level. Therefore, the appropriate policy would be to treat transfers as taxable income, with exemptions and personal deductions set to prevent taxation of incomes below the poverty line.

Part of people's Social Security receipts can be viewed as a return to them of their previous contributions to the Social Security system that have already been subjected to income taxation. If this view is accepted, then only Social Security payments in excess of an employee's contributions to the system should be taxed. The present exclusion of all Social Security benefit payments from income taxation is not justified because it discriminates against retirement income from private sources, which is taxable. With private pension plans, taxes are paid on the difference between the value of benefits and a person's contribution to the pension plan.

To put Social Security on the same basis as private pension plans, that portion of Social Security benefits that does not represent a return of a person's contributions could be included in taxable income. Alternatively, employee contributions into the system could be deducted from income and all Social Security benefits added to income.

The latter option is available to self-employed people and employees not covered by qualified employer pension plans. Such people can set up their own private retirement plans, subject to specified requirements, and deduct their contributions, which are subject to an annual limit, from their income.[5] These provisions tend to correct discrimination against people not covered by qualified employer pension plans. Contributions and interest

---

4 Some people advocate taxing gifts and bequests differently than income as a means of breaking up large fortunes and reducing inequalities in opportunity owing to the accumulation and transfer of wealth. Of course, to serve this objective, gifts and bequests should be taxed more heavily than other income. The opposite is in fact true. We discuss the taxation of wealth transfers in Chapter 15.

5 The Tax Reform Act of 1976 permits qualified husbands and wives to deduct contributions to a jointly or separately owned retirement account, up to a limit.

accruals on the accumulated funds are not taxed until pension benefits are received. This provision has the advantages of permitting interest to be earned on taxes that would otherwise be currently paid and deferring taxation until retirement, when people are generally in a lower tax bracket.

Interest on state and local securities   Interest earned on state and local government bonds is exempt from federal income taxation. If taxes are proportional to income, this exemption does not give any advantage to investors because the market tends to equalize after-tax rates of return on all investments of equal risk. At a proportional income tax rate of t, for example, market equilibrium requires $(1 - t)r = r_e$, or $r_e/r = (1 - t)$, where r and r_e are the yields on taxable and tax-exempt securities, respectively. With this relationship between yields, investors are indifferent between taxable and nontaxable bonds because they get the same *after-tax* return on either. In other words, with proportional taxation, market adjustments tend to eliminate the advantage of holding tax-exempt securities. And income taxation causes the same reduction in the incomes of the owners of both tax-exempt and taxable bonds.[6]

With progressive tax rates, on the other hand, investors are subject to different tax rates, and tax advantages exist for higher-income (upper-bracket) taxpayers. For example, if the market rates of return are such that $r_e/r = .6$, then investors having a marginal rate of taxation above .40 are better off with tax-exempt state and local securities than with taxable securities. However, the advantage to the high-bracket taxpayer is less than it might seem to be. To illustrate, let us suppose that Frank Tucher has sufficient income that his marginal tax rate is 70 percent; that is, he pays taxes of $.70 on each *additional* dollar of *taxable* income. He has $50,000 to invest in either taxable securities that yield 10 percent or tax-exempt securities that yield 6 percent. If he invests in the taxable securities, he receives pretax income of $5,000, which is taxable at 70 percent, leaving him an after-tax income of $5,000 - .7($5,000) = $1,500$. If he invests in the exempt securities, he receives a tax-free income of $3,000. The tax-exempt investment is clearly preferable. Tucher's gain from investing in tax-exempt, rather than taxable,

6 For example, suppose Keith Wratten and Sally Borish each have $10,000 to invest in bonds. Wratten buys taxable bonds that yield 10 percent pretax and 8 percent after payment of a 20 percent proportional income tax. With this 20 percent tax, the equilibrium *pretax and after-tax* return on the exempt bonds purchased by Borish would be 8 percent. Therefore they each receive an after-tax return of $800 on their $10,000 investments. There is horizontal equity because both investors are equally situated both before and after taxes are paid on their investment. However, there is the appearance of inequity because Wratten *pays* taxes of $200, while Borish pays nothing. Nevertheless, both investors bear equal tax burdens because market adjustments have caused Borish's earnings on her $10,000 investment to be $200 lower than she would have earned on a similar investment in taxable bonds.

bonds is $1,500. This gain is less than the amount, $2,100 = .7($3,000)$, that he appears to be saving by not paying taxes on his $3,000 of tax-exempt income. Market adjustments, by reducing the yield on tax-exempt bonds relative to the yield on taxable bonds, eliminate some but not all of the advantage of the tax exemption.[7]

With a progressive income tax, exemption of interest from state and local securities violates both horizontal and vertical equity principles. A person with investments in such securities may pay lower taxes than a person with the same investment in other assets, say a manufacturing of farming enterprise. And progressiveness in the tax structure is reduced to the extent that state and local securities are purchased by high-income groups.

The preferential treatment of state and local securities may encourage more investment (via lower interest rates) in state and local capital relative to private investments. And, for any given level of state and local borrowing, state and local taxes for debt service are lower. These effects are less objectionable if there is a bias against investment in state and local capital, since tax-free interest tends to correct this bias.

However, the exemption is inefficient in offsetting such a bias because it costs the federal treasury more in lost revenue than the state and local governments gain from lower interest rates. A direct interest subsidy of, say, 40 percent would be less costly to the U.S. Treasury and provide as great an interest saving to state and local governments. With this approach, the rate of interest on state and local securities would equal that of comparable taxable securities, and there would be no tax saving to bondholders and no horizontal and vertical inequities. The exemption could be eliminated at first on only new issues of state and local securities, with all such securities eventually being taxable. It would not be fair to repeal the exemption on outstanding bonds without compensating bondholders because they would suffer a capital loss as investors switched out of state and local securities.[8]

Imputed income from durables A major source of income that is excluded from taxation is *imputed income from the ownership of durable goods,* particularly automobiles and housing.[9] In addition, some of the costs of

7 We can readily see that if Tucher's marginal tax rate is 60 percent, his return on taxable bonds is $5,000 - .6($5,000) = $2,000$, and the gain from holding tax-exempt bonds is only $1,000. With a marginal tax rate of 50 percent, the gain falls to $500; with a marginal tax rate of 40 percent, the gain is zero. Of course, for people with a marginal tax rate below 40 percent, tax-exempt bonds are inferior to taxable bonds when $r_e/r = .6$.

8 For further discussion of these issues, see David L. Ott and Allan H. Meltzer, *Federal Tax Treatment of State and Local Securities* (Washington: Brookings, 1963).

9 Income is said to be imputed because it does not accrue in the form of a money flow. Its value must be estimated, that is, imputed. For example, the imputed gross income from owner-occupied housing is the rent that would be received if the house were rented.

generating such income may be deducted: mortgage interest and interest on consumer loans, property taxes, and gasoline taxes.

Table 11–1 illustrates the effects of those provisions. The Greco and Farrell families live in identical $40,000 houses, but the Farrells rent and the Grecos own their home. The families have identical employment income and net wealth and the same number of dependents and exemptions. The Farrells have invested $10,000 in bonds on which they earn 8 percent interest, while the Grecos have invested that amount in their home.

Both families have the same housing costs. The Farrells pay $5,400 per year in rent, which covers the property owner's costs of $2,200 — $1,400 for insurance, maintenance, and depreciation and $800 for property taxes — and provides an 8 percent ($3,200) return on the owner's investment of $40,000 in the house. The Grecos' outlays for insurance, maintenance, depreciation, and property taxes are the same — $2,200. They also have mortgage interest costs of $2,400 and an opportunity cost of $800 on the $10,000 that they have invested in their home. The opportunity cost arises because the Grecos could invest their wealth in bonds and earn 8 percent as the Farrells do.

The money incomes of the Farrells and the Grecos are $20,800 and $20,000, respectively. After allowing for exemptions and deductions, the Farrells have a taxable income of $18,300 and the Grecos, $14,300. They have tax liabilities of, respectively, $3,660 and $2,860 at a 20 percent tax rate. After housing costs and tax payments, the Farrells have $11,740 and the Grecos, $12,540. Even though both families live in identical houses and enjoy identical income circumstances, the Grecos have $800 more income after housing costs and taxes than the Farrells. The Grecos' income is higher by the amount of the tax savings from the exclusion of imputed income on the housing investment and the deduction of interest and property taxes [$800 = .2($800 + $2,400 + $800)].[10] Thus, homeowners are favored over renters, and in amounts that are very large in the aggregate. According to one estimate, the revenue loss to the federal government in 1970 by allowing the deduction of mortgage interest and property taxes was $5.7 billion, and the revenue loss from excluding net imputed rent was $3.2 billion.[11]

---

10 This example assumes competitive supply and pricing of rental units and that the real costs of providing similar dwelling units is the same whether the units are rented or owner-occupied. In reality, rents may in some areas exceed the competitive equilibrium level. Also, some tax provisions, primarily accelerated depreciation, may reduce tax liabilities for rental properties. Such tax savings could be passed on, in part, to the renter. So it is possible that a family could pay either more or less in rent than they would incur in *pretax* costs as owner-occupants of an identical dwelling. But the difference seems likely to be minor in most instances and unlikely to alter the basic picture given by the example in Table 11-1.

11 Richard Goode, *The Individual Income Tax*, rev. ed. (Washington: Brookings, 1976), p. 119.

TABLE 11–1
DIFFERENTIAL EFFECTS OF TAX TREATMENT OF HOMEOWNER AND RENTER

Item	Farrell family (renter)		Greco family (owner)	
Salary	$20,000		$20,000	
Interest income	800		0	
Net wealth	10,000		10,000	
Invested in bonds		$10,000		$ 0
Invested in home		0		10,000
Housing costs (total)	5,400		5,400	
Rent		5,400		0
Property taxes		0		800
Mortgage interest		0		2,400
Insurance, maintenance, and depreciation		0		1,400
Opportunity cost on investment in house		0		800
Money income	20,800		20,000	
Exemptions and deductions				
Mortgage interest		0		2,400
Property taxes		0		800
Other deductions and exemptions		2,500		2,500
Taxable income (money income less exemptions and deductions)	18,300		14,300	
Taxes (at 20 percent of taxable income)	3,660		2,860	
Income remaining after taxes and housing costs	11,740		12,540	

The differential tax treatment of homeowners and renters could be eliminated by taxing the net imputed income from owner-occupied housing. Mortgage interest and property taxes would not be separately deductible, since they are deducted in computing net imputed income. For the Grecos, net imputed income would be the rental value of their dwelling, minus the costs of supplying that dwelling to themselves: $5,400 minus $800 property taxes; $1,400 insurance, maintenance and depreciation; and $2,400 mortgage interest, leaving $800 net imputed income. Adding this to their $20,000 salary income gives them the same taxable income, $20,800 as the Farrells. With that adjustment in tax treatment, the two families would pay the same taxes and have the same income after taxes and housing costs — the tax law would be neutral with respect to the choice between renting and owning housing.

If the law is not changed to require taxation of net imputed income from owner-occupied housing, the inequities in the treatment of homeowners and renters could be reduced by disallowing the deduction of mortgage interest and property taxes. These are costs of generating the imputed income and should not be deductible as a cost when the income itself is not taxable.

That present tax treatment of homeowners and renters is horizontally inequitable is shown in Table 11–1. In addition, vertical inequity arises because higher-income homeowners may actually have more income after taxes and housing expenses than lower-income, home-renting families. The tax advantages presently accruing to homeowners favor middle- and upper-income families who own their homes over lower-income families who are unable to qualify for home loans and must rent.

Leisure and income in kind   Leisure is a form of income because it has economic value. Its value is at least as great as the income foregone by not working. To see why the federal income tax discriminates in favor of leisure activities, let us suppose that Jim MacDonald and Adrian Rogers both earn $10 an hour. MacDonald chooses to work twenty hours a week, while Rogers works forty hours. With a 20 percent tax on money income, MacDonald pays taxes of $40 a week, and Rogers pays $80. Yet both have identical opportunities and real income. The difference is that MacDonald chooses more income in the form of leisure; this additional leisure income must be worth at least $200 to him because he gives up $200 in money income to obtain it.

There are two ways, in principle, to eliminate that horizontal inequity: (1) Add imputed leisure income to money income for tax purposes, or (2) base taxes on wage *rates* rather than earnings. The main difficulty with the first approach is that of valuing leisure, the most practical alternative being to value an hour of leisure at the person's hourly wage rate. With the second approach, a tax factor would be applied to the wage rate, yielding the same tax revenue regardless of how many hours a person chooses to work. With a tax factor of, say, 8, a person who earns $10 an hour would pay $80 a week in taxes, regardless of hours worked. In such case, MacDonald and Rogers would be treated equally. And such a tax would not distort the choice between work and leisure. If a person decides to work longer hours and earn more money income, his or her taxes do not change. Among other problems, using tax factors would encounter the difficulty of estimating wage rates in the case of salaried persons. (Income from nonlabor sources, such as interest, profits, and dividends, would be taxed as it is at present.) Both approaches to allowing for leisure differentials require that voluntary leisure be distinguished from involuntary leisure arising from unemployment, forced retirement, and part-time work.

Activities such as gardening, mowing the lawn, and painting and repairing the house or car produce valuable goods and services — *income in kind*. A major source of income in kind is the services of homemakers. Income in kind is not taxed, due partly to the difficulty of estimating its value. Failure to tax income in kind discriminates against working in the marketplace, since money income is taxable. Permitting deductions for child care expenses incurred when working outside the house mitigates this discrimination.

Capital gains and losses   For tax purposes, realized capital gains (losses) are classified as *short term* and *long term*. Short-term gains are those realized from the sale of assets held for less than twelve months. Other gains are long term.

Taxes are based on *net* capital gains (capital gains minus capital losses). Net short-term gains are taxed fully as ordinary income. But only one-half of net long-term gains are included in the tax base. So the tax rate for long-term capital gains can be as low as one-half the rate for ordinary income.[12]

When capital losses exceed capital gains, the losses may be deducted in limited amounts from ordinary income, up to a maximum of $3,000. Such deductions reduce taxable income by the entire amount of short-term capital losses but by only one-half of long-term losses. The sum of short-term and long-term capital loss deductions cannot exceed the maximum in any single year. But capital losses that exceed the deductible maximum can be carried over to offset income in later years.

In addition, capital gains are not subject to taxation when assets are transferred as a gift or as a bequest. When assets are transferred by gift, capital gains that accrued prior to the date of the gift are taxable to the donee when and if the donee sells the asset. Capital gains are then calculated on the basis of the asset's value when the donor acquired it. Subject to some adjustments and a "fresh start" rule,[13] the Tax Reform Act of 1976 provides that capital gains realized from the sale of inherited assets be calculated on the basis of the asset's value when the *decedent* acquired the property. Thus with transfers by gift or bequest, accrued capital gains are taxed only if the asset is sold.[14] Of course, transfers by gift and bequest may be subject to gift and

12 The tax rate cannot exceed 25 percent of the first $50,000 of long-term capital gains, or 35 percent on gains in excess of $50,000. The excluded portion of capital gains is included in the base of the 15 percent tax on preference income (see p. 260). A special "roll-over" provision applies to capital gains on the sale of owner-occupied homes. See note 16, p. 244. Special provisions also apply to the sale of residences by persons over sixty-five.

13 The "fresh start" rule protects gains accrued before January 1, 1977, by stepping up the basis of estates to reflect their value as of December 31, 1976.

14 To illustrate, Juan Perez, Sr., has land that he purchased for $100,000 in 1977 and is now worth $200,000; thus there is a $100,000 accrued capital gain. Suppose he gives or bequeaths the land to his son. No capital gains tax is due until Juan Perez, Jr., sells the land. But, if the son sells the land for, say, $250,000, he must pay taxes on $150,000 of capital gains income — his capital gain is computed on the basis of the acquisition price of $100,000 his father paid.

estate taxes. But these taxes are typically small relative to the taxes due on the same amount of ordinary income.

These preferences mean that capital gains income is taxed at much lower rates than ordinary income, if it does not totally escape taxation. The result is both vertical and horizontal inequity. Persons with capital gains income pay lower taxes than persons with the same amount of ordinary income. Vertical inequities arise because high-income persons have relatively more capital gains income than lower-income persons and may therefore pay lower taxes. The progressiveness of the federal tax system is greatly reduced by the capital gains tax preferences. Table 11–2 shows the distribution by income class of realized capital gains and the accrued but nonrecognized gains transferred by gift and bequest. For the lowest income groups, excluded capital gains are less than 1 percent of income; for the highest income group, they are about 40 percent of income.

Capital gains preferences also greatly complicate the tax law and thereby increase taxpayer compliance costs. Tax accountants and lawyers spend their time and other resources seeking ways to convert ordinary income into capital gains income so as to take advantage of the lower tax rates.

Despite the inequities, it is argued that capital gains income deserves preferential treatment for other reasons. For one thing, capital gains income is irregular; with progressive rates, more taxes would be paid than if income were received in even installments. But this objection to full taxation can better be dealt with by either averaging income or taxing capital gains on an accrual basis. Gains accrue more evenly than they are realized. Present tax laws permit averaging.

Another argument is that some capital gains are due to inflation; taxation of such *money* gains is inequitable because the taxpayer who receives them would pay higher taxes but be no better off. But this problem is not unique to capital gains income. Adjustments for price-level changes, therefore, are appropriate not only for capital gains income but for other income.[15]

Favorable tax treatment of capital gains has also been defended as a means of lowering effective tax rates and increasing after-tax returns, thus providing individuals with an incentive to invest and increase economic growth. Whether such an incentive would be effective is open to question; there is little evidence that *total* saving is sensitive to the rate of return earned on the investment into which the saving is channelled. Even if a tax-induced increase in the rate of investment is forthcoming, its desirability is questioned by environmentalists and others. In addition, low taxes on

15 See note 3, Chapter 10. Even if all income is deflated by some *index*, some inequities would remain. An index is a weighted average of changes in selected prices. Not everyone is affected in the same way by a given set of price changes, but such is the presumption when adjustments for inflation (deflation) are made with a price index.

TABLE 11-2

REVENUE AND DISTRIBUTION EFFECTS OF THE 50 PERCENT EXCLUSION AND NONRECOGNITION OF GAINS TRANSFERRED BY GIFT AND AT DEATH, ESTIMATES FOR CALENDAR YEAR 1972 (MILLIONS OF DOLLARS)

Expanded AGI[a] class (thousands of dollars)	Expanded AGI[a]	Tax liability, present law		Excluded capital gains		Additional tax liability due to repeal of exclusions		
		Amount	Percent of expanded AGI[a]	Amount	Percent of expanded AGI[a]	Amount	Percent of expanded AGI[a]	Percent of present law tax
Less than 3	7,968	36	0.5	5	0.1	−1	[b]	[b]
3–5	27,610	475	1.7	55	0.2	7	[b]	1.5
5–10	145,033	7,655	5.3	988	0.7	168	0.1	2.2
10–15	216,483	18,843	8.7	1,831	0.8	414	0.2	2.2
15–20	180,340	19,354	10.7	2,004	1.1	578	0.3	3.0
20–25	109,886	13,301	12.1	1,743	1.6	595	0.5	4.5
25–50	142,941	20,707	14.5	5,199	3.6	2,383	1.7	11.5
50–100	41,178	9,672	23.5	3,957	9.6	2,372	5.8	24.5
100–500	31,355	9,241	29.5	6,006	19.2	4,278	13.6	46.3
500–1,000	4,360	1,324	30.4	1,423	32.6	990	22.7	74.8
1,000 and over	7,109	2,279	32.1	2,824	39.7	1,922	27.0	84.3
All classes	914,262	102,888	11.3	26,035	2.8	13,708	1.5	13.3

a Expanded AGI is the sum of adjusted gross income as defined under the Internal Revenue Code as amended through 1971 plus the following: 50 percent of realized capital gains, $17.1 billion; constructive realization of gain on gifts and bequests, $10.4 billion; exempt State and local bond interest, $1.9 billion; other preference income, $1.2 billion; dividend exclusion, $1.2 billion; interest on life insurance policies, $9.9 billion; homeowners' preferences, $15.5 billion; and transfer payments $79.8 billion.

b Less than 0.05 percent.

Source: Joseph A. Pechman and Benjamin A. Okner, "Individual Income Tax Erosion by Income Classes," in *The Economics of Federal Subsidy Programs*, Joint Economic Committee of the U.S. Congress, 1972, tables 2, 3, A–2, A–3.

capital gains provide an incentive to invest in sectors of the economy where capital gains are possible (cattle, timber, mining, real estate), even though these may not be the most productive areas for investment. In particular, present capital gains provisions favor investment in certain forms of natural and physical capital, but not in human capital. Finally, lower taxes on capital gains means higher taxes on other income, and the latter may also deter private investment. If other taxes are not higher because of the present treatment of capital gains, either government spending must be lower or government borrowing must be greater. Lower spending may mean lower government investment, while greater borrowing may lead to higher interest rates and lower private investment on that account.

Not only are the present low rates of capital gains taxation defended by that rationale, there also are arguments to further reduce capital gains taxes. Specifically, some argue that a lower rate of taxation would lessen the *lock-in* effect that occurs when the prospect of capital gains taxes discourages investors from selling assets on which gains have accrued and moving the funds into more productive investments. The counter to this reasoning is that the lock-in effect can be eliminated, not by taxing realized gains at a lower rate, but by taxing gains on an accrual basis. With accrual taxation, the owner cannot defer taxes by deferring sales, so there is no tax barrier to moving funds into more productive investments. The lock-in effect would also be greatly reduced by constructive realization and taxation upon transfer by gift or bequest. The prospect of a tax-free transfer of accumulated gains at death undoubtedly locks people into investments on which there are large accrued gains.[16]

An alternative to present capital gains taxation is to tax them in full as they accrue and to allow some loss offsets. The resulting expansion of the tax base would permit lower rates of taxation. If full taxation adversely affects investment incentives, the effect could be offset in part by lower tax rates and more generous loss offsets. Taxing on an accrual basis would also eliminate the lock-in effect.

This alternative has been objected to on the grounds that assets would have to be valued annually and imperfectly, that such valuation would be costly, and that some forced liquidations of assets would be necessary to pay tax liabilities. Of course, the increased costs of tax administration and compliance due to annual valuations would be offset to some degree by reduced costs in the form of taxpayers' efforts to convert ordinary income into capital gains income.

16 Others have argued for a tax-free "roll-over" as a means of eliminating the lock-in effect. Investors would be able to sell their assets without paying a tax on the gains so long as the funds are reinvested. Such proposals would convert the capital gains tax into a tax on consumption, not on income.

An alternative that involves a smaller departure from present practice would be to tax realized gains, gains at death, and gains at the time gifts are made. Table 11–2 shows the effects of this approach, which permits averaging to spread tax payments over time. Since all gains would eventually be taxed by this policy, inequities would be reduced and the lock-in effect would be lessened.

Dividend exclusion   Individual stockholders may exclude the first $100 of dividends received from domestic corporations ($200 for married couples filing joint returns). The purpose is to reduce the double taxation of corporate income. Double taxation is said to occur because income is taxed, first, under the corporation income tax and, again, as dividends under the individual income tax. This justification presumes that the corporation income tax is not shifted. If it is not shifted, the exclusion is an incomplete adjustment for double taxation since it applies only partially to dividend income. We discuss these issues more fully in Chapter 12.

Other omissions   Other omissions from taxable income include interest earned on life insurance policies, tax-free accumulation of income in retirement programs, and military housing and subsistence allowances. Also, some fringe benefits from employment, usually those that are in kind, are not taxed; an important example is employer-provided medical care, a particularly important item for military personnel.

EXEMPTIONS AND THE LOW-INCOME ALLOWANCE

Certain provisions of the income tax law free a minimum amount of income from taxation. Each taxpayer is allowed a basic personal exemption of $750 for the taxpayer and each dependent. A taxpayer is also permitted a $35 tax credit per exemption, or a credit equal to 2 percent of the first $9,000 of taxable income, whichever is higher.[17] In addition, a taxpayer is allowed a minimum standard deduction, or low-income allowance, of $1,700 for single persons and $2,100 for married couples. The low-income allowance is in lieu of the standard deduction or itemized deductions (see the sections that follow).

These exemptions, credits, and deductions can be viewed as approximate adjustments for nondiscretionary expenditures. Table 11–3 compares poverty-line incomes and the amount of income freed from taxation by these provisions under current and past laws.[18] Under the 1974 Individual

17 These credits were extended through 1977 by the Tax Reform Act of 1976.

18 The tax-free income provided by a tax credit is the taxable income that would produce a tax liability equal to the tax credit for the applicable tax bracket.

TABLE 11-3

MINIMUM TAXABLE LEVELS UNDER THE 1974, 1975, AND 1976 INDIVIDUAL INCOME TAX LAWS
COMPARED WITH ESTIMATED POVERTY LINES

Number in family (1)	1975 poverty line [a] (2)	1974 law [b] Minimum taxable level (3)	1974 law [b] Difference (4)	1975 law [c] Minimum taxable level (5)	1975 law [c] Difference (6)	1976 poverty line [d] (7)	1976 law [e] Minimum taxable level (8)	1976 law [e] Difference (9)	1976 law [f] Minimum taxable level (10)	1976 law [f] Difference (11)
1	$2,850	$2,050	$− 800	$2,564	$−286	$2,870	$2,700	$−170	$2,700	$− 170
2	3,470	2,800	− 670	3,829	359	3,683	4,100	417	4,100	417
3	4,253	3,550	− 703	4,793	540	4,513	5,100	587	6,270	1,757
4	5,442	4,300	−1,142	5,757	315	5,781	6,100	319	6,860	1,079
5	6,423	5,050	−1,373	6,717	294	6,824	7,075	251	7,450	626
6	7,226	5,800	−1,426	7,667	441	7,677	8,075	398	8,067	390

a Estimates by the Joint Committee on Internal Revenue Taxation.

b $750 per capita exemption; flat $1,300 low-income allowance

c $750 per capita exemption plus $30 per capita credit; low-income allowance of $1,900 for married couples and $1,600 for single persons.

d Poverty-line budgets for 1974 (U.S. Census Bureau, Current Population Reports, Series P-60, No. 102) projected to 1976 on the basis of the increase in the consumer price index.

e $750 exemption plus $35 per capita tax credit; $1,700 low-income allowance for single person and $2,100 for married couples.

f Column 8 plus earned income credit (10 percent of earned income up to $4,000 and reduced by 10 percent of earned income beyond $4,000). All income is assumed to be earned.

Source: Columns 1–6, George F. Break and Joseph A. Pechman, *Federal Tax Reform* (Washington: Brookings, 1975), p. 28. © 1975 by the Brookings Institution, Washington, D.C. Columns 8–11, authors' calculations.

Income Tax Law, minimum taxable income was below the poverty line for all classes of taxpayers shown in the table. For 1975 and 1976, the minimum taxable income was above the poverty level for all but one group of taxpayers.[19]

A more straightforward and accurate approach to adjusting for nondiscretionary expenditures would be to allow each family (taxpaying unit) a minimum deduction equal to its poverty-line income when computing its taxable income. Since poverty-line incomes are adjusted for changes in prices, the amount of the deduction would increase in periods of inflation.

An objection raised against the present system of exemptions and deductions is that, with progressive rates of taxation, the value of the tax reduction increases as income increases. For each $750 exemption, a family in the 14 percent marginal tax bracket receives a tax break of $105; a family in the 50 percent marginal tax bracket receives a tax reduction of $375. This feature could be eliminated by (1) having exemptions decline as income increases or (2) providing a uniform tax credit. To illustrate, a $750 exemption in the 14 percent bracket and $210 exemption in the 50 percent bracket would each provide tax relief of $105. A uniform $105 tax credit would achieve the same result. The present system of exemptions and credits is a compromise between these two approaches.[20]

EARNED INCOME CREDIT

The Tax Reform Act of 1976 extends through 1977 the earned income credit, which is granted to couples with children. It is equal to 10 percent of the first $4,000 of earnings minus 10 percent of earned income in excess of $4,000. When earned income equals or exceeds $8,000, the tax credit is zero. Any taxpayer with an income tax liability less than the credit receives a cash payment equal to his credit minus the tax that he owes. The purpose of this provision, which is a form of negative income taxation, appears to be to offset the Social Security taxes of low-income individuals and to increase their incentive to work.[21] But if that is its purpose, it is not clear why childless couples and individuals do not also receive the credit.

19 The results may be different for different classes of taxpayers not shown in Table 11–3, e.g., the aged.

20 For different views on deductions (exemptions) versus credits, see G. M. Brannon and E. R. Morss, "The Tax Allowance for Dependents: Deductions vs. Credits," *National Tax Journal*, 24 (December 1973): 599–610; and Thomas F. Pogue, "Deductions vs. Credits," *National Tax Journal*, 24 (December 1974): 659–662.

21 Richard Goode, *The Individual Income Tax*, rev. ed. (Washington: Brookings, 1976), p. 241.

The earned income tax credit raises the minimum taxable income levels of lower income families whose income is from earnings — for example, families with three, four, and five members (couples with one, two, and three children), as shown in column 10 of Table 11–3.

STANDARD DEDUCTION

Instead of the low-income allowance, the taxpayer may take the standard deduction or itemize deductions. We discuss itemized deductions in the next section. The standard deduction is 16 percent of adjusted gross income, up to a maximum of $2,400 for single taxpayers and $2,800 for married couples filing joint returns. The standard deduction simplifies tax compliance and administration in comparison to itemized deductions. But it fails to differentiate among taxpayers according to personal expenditures that reduce taxpaying capacity.

ITEMIZED DEDUCTIONS

Itemized deductions have been rationalized as a means of (1) allowing for the cost of earning income, (2) adjusting for unpredictable nondiscretionary expenditures, (3) promoting certain intergovernmental fiscal objectives, and (4) stimulating specified private expenditures. We will discuss these rationales in connection with major items that are deductible. Tables 11–4 and 11–5 show the amounts and distribution of the main categories of itemized deductions.

TABLE 11–4
PERSONAL DEDUCTIONS, 1973

Type of deduction	As percent of adjusted gross income	As percent of total deductions
Total deductions	21.7	100.0
Total itemized deductions	12.9	59.2
Taxes	4.7	21.8
Interest	3.8	17.7
Contributions	1.7	7.7
Medical expenses	1.3	5.9
Miscellaneous	1.3	6.0
Total standard deductions	8.9	40.8
Percentage deduction	3.3	15.2
Low-income allowance	5.6	25.6

Source: U.S. Internal Revenue Service, *Statistics of Income, 1973, Individual Income Tax Returns.*

TABLE 11-5
DISTRIBUTION OF PERSONAL DEDUCTIONS BY ADJUSTED GROSS INCOME
(AGI) CLASS, 1973 (THOUSANDS OF DOLLARS)

AGI class	Percent of total deductions	As percent of AGI
Less than 2	8.1	120.7
2–3	3.7	52.2
3–5	7.3	34.0
5–10	18.5	21.9
10–25	45.2	18.6
25–50	10.5	16.9
50–100	3.8	17.2
100–500	2.3	20.1
500 and over	0.5	27.2
All classes	100.0	21.8

Source: U.S. Internal Revenue Service, *Statistics of Income, 1973, Individual Income Tax Returns.*

Interest payments   When borrowed funds are invested to earn taxable income, interest payments are a cost of earning income and should be deducted from gross income. However, interest payments are presently deductible when the loans are for consumption spending or when the income
generated is not taxed. The latter occurs when an owner-occupied house or
a consumer durable is purchased with borrowed funds, but the imputed income is excluded from the tax base. In the case of housing, this deduction
favors homeowners over renters because homeowners are able to deduct part
of their housing costs.

State and local taxes   State and local taxes on income, sales, property, and
gasoline are deductible in computing federal income taxes. To the extent
that state and local taxes are payments for benefits received from government
services, there is no justification for this deduction any more than there is
for the deduction of private consumption expenditures. This reasoning applies particularly to the gasoline tax, which approximates a payment for
transportation services on highways and streets. Many local government services financed by the property tax also benefit property owners — police
protection, fire protection, neighborhood streets, and local education. The
property tax deduction for homeowners discriminates against renters, for the
same reason that the interest deduction discriminates against renters.

State and local income and sales taxes are less obviously related to the
benefits received from government services and, instead, cause some income
redistribution. The sales tax tends to be regressive, and the income tax may

be regressive, proportional, or mildly progressive, depending on the state or locality.

The deduction of state and local taxes reduces the progressiveness of the federal income tax, although it may encourage state and local governments to use more progressive taxes. A major argument for the deduction is that without it, the combined state, local, and federal tax rates on income could be too high and, perhaps, exceed 100 percent at the margin. Allowing the deduction of particular taxes discriminates against states that do not use them. This discrimination is a tool that can be used to induce states to employ a particular tax, say a progressive income tax, to qualify its citizens for the deduction.

Medical expenses Fifty percent of medical insurance premiums, up to $150 a year, are deductible from adjusted gross income. Out-of-pocket medical expenses are also deductible if they exceed a certain percent of adjusted gross income—medicines and drugs are deductible if they exceed 1 percent of adjusted gross income. Deductible expenses for medicines and drugs are added to doctor and hospital expenses, and this sum is deductible if it exceeds 3 percent of adjusted gross income.

The health insurance premium deduction may encourage some people to purchase insurance, but this effect is probably weak and may work in a perverse way. Lower-income taxpayers do not have a tax incentive to purchase health insurance because they utilize the low-income allowance or the standard deduction. Moreover, the incentive increases as taxable incomes and marginal tax rates increase, a feature that favors the higher income groups.

Personal medical expense deductions can be rationalized as an allowance for differences in taxpayers' nondiscretionary spending and ability to pay. A household has little control over the amount and timing of medical expenses that may at times be quite large and not covered by insurance. However, for people who employ a standard deduction and people with income too low to pay taxes, the medical expense deduction does not differentiate according to ability to pay. Two people with the same income claiming a standard deduction may not have the same ability to pay taxes because of a sizable difference in medical expenses. And poor people can deduct medical expense only if their incomes are at a taxable level.

An alternative approach would be a system of tax credits for medical expenses. A tax credit would be granted to individuals for a specified percentage of medical expenses incurred, with payment from the Treasury in the amount by which the credit exceeds taxes due, up to the full amount of the credit in the case of persons who owe no taxes. The amount of the credit as a percentage of expenses could increase as medical expenses increase and decrease with income. A deductible feature could also be incorporated, so only medical expenses in excess of the deductible amount would be used in computing the tax credit. A sliding-scale deductible could be tied to gross or taxable income, with the amount of the deductible varying directly with income. Such provisions would, in effect, provide national health insurance through the income tax system. That is not to say, however, that national health insurance is desirable or that it should be provided through the tax system. Rather, we are pointing out the consequences of introducing particular provisions into the law. This mechanism for providing national health insurance does have advantages. It is universal. It makes use of an existing administrative apparatus. Insurance coverage does not vary as a person moves or changes jobs. Claims for reimbursement are in effect filed with and processed by the Internal Revenue Service; false claims would meet with the same sanctions as any other effort at tax evasion. Schedules of permissible charges could be developed, if necessary, in much the same way that guidelines for depreciation and other deductions (such as state gasoline and sales taxes) have been established. Compliance might be strengthened because the administrative agency is the Internal Revenue Service, rather than another government agency or a private firm. Also, people would be responsible for paying their own medical bills and would perhaps be more concerned about cost than when their bills are paid by an insurance company.

Of course, several problems arise in this tax credit approach to health insurance. There would be a need for more frequent filing of income tax returns in those cases in which, because of either high medical expenses or low income, a person receives a net payment from the Treasury to offset medical expenses. This problem could be met by allowing taxpayers to file estimated tax returns on a monthly basis when they expect their tax credits for medical expenses to more than offset their income tax liabilities for the year. Tax refunds would then be payable on a monthly basis. Also, since some people would not have the resources to pay their medical bills and then file for the tax credit refund, it would be necessary to allow refunds based on *accrued* medical expenses.

Philanthropic and charitable contributions Contributions to certain religious, educational, charitable, scientific, literary, and other organizations may be deducted from adjusted gross income, subject to limits related to the taxpayer's income, the kind of property donated, and the type of organization receiving the contribution. The purpose of such deductions is to stimulate private spending for particular purposes. But the deductions also divert public-sector resources into the activities supported by the private contributions because the deductions are similar in effect to matching grants. If a taxpayer is in the 50 percent marginal tax bracket, a contribution of $1,000 reduces his or her tax liabilities by $500. The government must raise taxes or reduce expenditures by $500 to offset the tax loss. So taxpayers or individuals who benefit from government services match private contributions by the amount of the tax loss, $500 in this example. Also, the tax break, or the government's matching grant and the resulting reduction in the price of giving, increases as income and the marginal rate of taxation increases. Taxpayers who do not itemize deductions receive no tax break for contributions and therefore have no direct influence over which activities are to be supported by taxation.

The public at large helps to finance activities supported by private contributions. Thus, when the contributions are deducted in computing taxable income, equity and efficiency considerations suggest that the contributions finance activities that benefit the public, i.e., the charitable contributions should finance public goods or goods that have external benefits. Therefore, there is the question of how much control the public should have over the amount and composition of charitable expenditures. Presently, contributions are deducted largely by middle- and upper-income donors and therefore support activities preferred by those donors, although the government broadly defines the organizations that qualify for the tax deduction.

The activities presently supported by private contributions could be fully and directly financed by government. This approach would eliminate the present tax advantage to higher-income groups, but it would lead to more government control and, perhaps, reduce the diversity of supported activities. Diversity could be maintained and the advantages to the wealthy could be reduced by giving a tax credit for all charitable contributions. The credit would be some percentage of contributions. For example, a tax credit of 20 percent would give taxpayers a twenty-cent credit against taxes due for each dollar they give to designated activities.[22]

ACCRUED VERSUS REALIZED INCOME

U.S. governments tax income primarily on a realization rather than an accrual basis. In most instances, there is little lag between accrual and realization of income (e.g., wage and salary income), so either basis gives about the same results. But taxation of capital gains on a realized rather than an accrual basis does give very different results, as we noted above. According

---

22 It has been estimated that replacing the current charitable deduction with a 30 percent tax credit would increase total giving by 15 percent. But educational institutions and hospitals would lose about 20 percent of current gifts. See Martin S. Feldstein, "The Income Tax and Charitable Contributions: Part II — The Impact on Religious, Educational, and Other Organizations," *National Tax Journal*, 28, No. 2 (June 1975): 209–226.

to one estimate, only about 11 percent of accrued capital gains entered the income tax base (adjusted gross income) over the period 1946–1970.[23]

ACCOUNTING PERIOD

Taxes are accounted for on an annual basis, although periodic payments are made during the year on the basis of estimated annual income. Income may be averaged over five years if a person's income in one year exceeds the average income of the four preceding years by a certain amount. Reductions in income are not averaged. Very few taxpayers take advantage of this provision.

The present tax system would be more equitable if averaging were more easily and widely used. More effective averaging could be accomplished by providing for negative taxes (transfers) or the carry forward and back of unused exemptions and low-income allowances. When taxpayers' incomes are less than their exemptions and low-income allowances in any one year, they, in effect, lose part of the exemptions and allowances. Also, as we noted earlier, income could be cumulated annually, and taxes paid on the cumulated total each year. Taxes paid in previous years would then be subtracted from each year's tax calculations, and individuals with the same lifetime income would pay the same taxes.

TAXPAYING UNIT

In the United States, the basic taxpaying unit is the household — the people who live together and presumably pool their incomes. Households may consist of a single individual, married adults, parent(s) and children, and unrelated individuals when dependency can be established. There are different tax rate schedules for single persons, married couples filing a joint return, married couples filing separate returns, and heads of households. A single person pays more tax than a married couple with the same taxable income. The incomes of married persons may be combined, or they may be reported separately. Normally, tax rates are lower when income is combined. However, given the various rate schedules, marriage may increase the tax liabilities of two working persons who filed separate returns as single individuals. The tax on a head of household, e.g., an unmarried individual with dependents, falls between the tax on married couples and the tax on single individuals.

If exemptions and personal deductions adequately allow nondiscretionary

23 "The Effective Rate of the Capital Gains Tax," General Tax Reform, presented by James W. Wetzler, in panel discussions, 93rd Cong., 1st sess., U.S. Congress, House Committee on Ways and Means, February 1973, part 2 of 11, pp. 301–302.

expenditures, there is no justification for applying different tax rates to tax-paying units on the basis of whether they are single, married, or head of household. That is not to say there should not be differences in tax liabilities among taxpaying units, but the adjustment in tax liabilities is or can be made through exemptions and deductions. A single person or head of household has no greater taxpaying ability than a married couple with the same *discretionary* income.

The income of children is never reported by parents and is not reported by children unless it exceeds the $750 personal exemption. Even if a child reports income in excess of this exemption and claims the exemption, the parents may also claim the child as an exemption if they contribute over one-half of the child's support and he or she is under nineteen years or a full-time student. In other words, two exemptions may be claimed for children and students receiving income if parents provide more than one-half of their support. This provision discriminates against poor students whose parents cannot contribute the required support; only one exemption for the working student from the low-income family is claimed. Wealthy parents can also transfer property income to their children, which puts the income in a lower tax bracket, while continuing to claim the child as a dependent if they provide the required support. Such discrimination can be eliminated by pooling the income of children with the income of parents. And, if it is desirable to subsidize families whose children are adult but in school, there are ways of doing so that similarly benefit low-income and high-income families.

SIZE AND COMPOSITION OF THE TAX BASE

Table 11–6 shows that relatively little adjusted gross income (AGI) and tax payments come from the highest and the lowest AGI tax brackets. In fact, only 3.5 percent of the total paid in 1973 came from the lowest (below $5,000) and the highest tax brackets ($500,000 and above). Almost 30 percent was paid by the $15,000–$24,999 bracket, and about 80 percent came from the $5,000–$49,999 income range. The source of most income for tax purposes is wages and salary income, as shown in Table 11–7.

The distribution of tax liabilities by AGI class means that relieving the tax burden on the lowest income groups would be relatively inexpensive. For example, if income taxes on the groups below $4,999 were eliminated, the revenue loss would be $2.2 billion, or 2 percent of total taxes in 1973. At the other extreme, a doubling of the income tax in the $100,000 plus income classes would raise revenues by an amount equal to 8.2 percent of total income taxes in 1973. Hence, to raise substantial amounts of revenue from the very rich, there would have to be a significant increase in their tax base or tax rates.

TABLE 11–6
ADJUSTED GROSS INCOME (AGI) AND TAXES PAID BY CLASS, 1973 [a]
(PERCENT OF TOTAL)

AGI class	AGI	Taxes
Less than $2,999	0.9	0.2
$3,000–$3,999	1.6	0.7
$4,000–$4,999	2.3	1.2
$5,000–$9,999	17.7	12.3
$10,000–$14,999	23.5	19.5
$15,000–$24,999	29.4	29.7
$25,000–$49,999	13.5	18.4
$50,000–$99,999	4.7	9.5
$100,000–$499,999	2.5	6.8
$500,000–$999,999	0.2	0.7
$1,000,000 and over	0.2	0.7

a Preliminary.

Source: U.S. Census Bureau, *Statistical Abstract of the United States, 1975*, p. 234.

TABLE 11–7
ADJUSTED GROSS INCOME (AGI) BY SOURCE OF INCOME, 1973

Source	Percent of total
Wages and salaries	82.9
Dividends, interest, rents, and royalties	6.7
Business, profession, farm partnership	6.8
Sales of capital assets and property	2.1
Other	1.6

Source: Based on U.S. Census Bureau, *Statistical Abstract of the United States, 1975*, p. 233.

TAX BASE AND PERSONAL INCOME

Nearly all income that is defined for tax purposes in the United States is reported. To see this, let us compare the personal income (PI) series of the U.S. Department of Commerce with AGI.[24] The latest comparison by the Department of Commerce is shown in Table 11–8.

PI includes income not included in AGI, and AGI includes income not recorded in PI. When adjustments are made for those factors, AGI estimated from PI is $798.4 billion. As reported on tax returns, AGI was $746.6 billion (tax and nontax returns — rows 6 and 8 in Table 11–8). Hence, about 6.5 percent of taxable income was not reported, which can be

24 Personal income includes wage and salary disbursements, other labor income, proprietors' income, rental income, dividends, personal interest income, and transfer payments. It excludes personal contributions for social insurance.

TABLE 11–8

RELATIONSHIP BETWEEN PERSONAL INCOME (PI), ADJUSTED GROSS INCOME
(AGI), AND TAXABLE INCOME, 1972 (BILLIONS OF DOLLARS)

1. Personal income (PI)	944.9
2. *Subtract:* portion of income not included in AGI	211.6
a. Transfer payments	92.6
b. Other labor income	38.9
c. Imputed income[a]	50.8
d. Other	29.3
3. *Add:* portion of AGI not included in personal income	65.1
a. Personal contributions for social insurance	34.5
b. Net gain from sale of capital assets	16.8
c. Other	13.9
4. *Subtotal:* total adjustments for conceptual differences $(2 - 3)$	146.5
5. *Equals:* AGI of all individuals, estimated from PI $(1 - 4)$	798.4
6. *Subtract:* AGI on nontaxable returns	28.9
7. *Subtract:* Nonreported AGI	51.8
8. *Equals:* AGI on taxable returns	717.7
9. *Subtract:* deductions	142.8
10. *Subtract:* personal exemptions	128.3
11. *Equals:* taxable income	446.6

a Wages paid in kind, rental value of owner-occupied housing, food and fuel produced and
consumed on farms, value of interest to nonbusiness depositors in financial intermediaries,
holders of life insurance policies, and participants in noninsured pension funds.

Source: U.S. Department of Commerce, *Survey of Current Business,* vol. 55 (Washington: Government
Printing Office, 1975), p. 34.

accounted for by income that was below the legally reportable level, errors
in PI estimates, and tax evasion and avoidance.

TAX BASE COMPARED TO COMPREHENSIVE INCOME

How does AGI compare with our definition of comprehensive income (CI)?
Unfortunately, there are no estimates of CI, although some qualitative judgment can be made. Pechman and Okner have made an estimate of income,
called *adjusted family income,* that is more comprehensive than the series by
the Department of Commerce and is based on the department's national income series. *National income* measures income received by owners of factors of production (land, labor, capital). To arrive at adjusted family income, Pechman and Okner adjusted national income for transfer payments,
accrued capital gains, income not received by households, indirect business
taxes, and other items, based on data that were available for 1966.[25]

25 Joseph A. Pechman and Benjamin A. Okner, *Who Bears the Tax Burden?* (Washington:
Brookings, 1974).

In 1966 total adjusted family income was estimated at $721 billion (national income was $620.6 billion), and AGI was $470.3 billion. Hence, AGI was 65.2 percent of adjusted family income. After exemptions and personal deductions, taxable income was $364 billion, or 50.5 percent of adjusted family income.

Neither the national income series nor the concept of adjusted family income includes estimates of the value of leisure or most nonmarket activity (e.g., household work), items that would be included in CI. Nordhaus and Tobin provide estimates of the value of those forms of income for selected years between 1929 and 1965.[26] In 1965 the values of leisure and of nonmarket activity were estimated at $775.5 and $321.4 billion, respectively. If we assume that the ratio of adjusted family income to national income was the same in 1965 as in 1966, adjusted family income in 1965 was $657.7 billion. Adding the value of leisure and nonmarket activity to $657.7 billion gives $1,754.6 billion, a rough approximation of CI for 1965. In that year, AGI was about 24 percent of $1,754.6 billion. Although there have been some changes in the economy since 1966 (e.g., an increase in market employment by women), there has probably been no significant change in the relationship between AGI and our more comprehensive estimate of income.[27]

EXPANSION OF THE TAX BASE

Adoption of a comprehensive income tax base is very unlikely because of imputation problems, administrative difficulties, and political obstacles. But a broadened tax base could greatly increase the yield of the individual income tax without changing the tax rates. Alternatively, if the base were expanded, the same revenue could be obtained with much lower tax rates. The revenue loss from various provisions in the income tax law is shown in Table 11–9.[28]

---

26 Those estimates are in terms of current prices. Leisure includes time at restaurants and taverns; friend's or relative's home; games, sports, church; recreation at home; reading; and sleep during the hours of 6:00 A.M. to 11:00 P.M. See William Nordhaus and James Tobin, "Is Growth Obsolete?" in *Economic Growth* (New York: National Bureau of Economic Research, 1972), p. 47.

27 If all taxpaying units had the same ratio of nonmoney income to money income, exclusion of nonmoney income from the tax base would not matter. Inequities arise when the ratio of nontaxable income to total income is greater for some taxpayers than for others, as is surely the case.

28 For specific tax reform proposals, see George F. Break and Joseph A. Pechman, *Federal Tax Reform: The Impossible Dream?* (Washington: Brookings, 1975).

TABLE 11–9

TAX EXPENDITURES BENEFITING INDIVIDUALS UNDER THE
INDIVIDUAL INCOME TAX BY BUDGET CATEGORY, FISCAL YEAR 1978
(MILLIONS OF DOLLARS)

National defense	
Exclusion of benefits and allowances to armed forces personnel	1,260
Exclusion of military disability pensions	115
International affairs	
Exclusion of income earned abroad by U.S. citizens	135
Agriculture	
Expensing of capital outlays	440
Capital gain treatment of certain income	350
Natural resources, environment, energy	
Exclusion of interest on state and local government pollution control bonds	100
Expensing of exploration and development costs	150
Excess of percentage over cost depletion	300
Capital gain treatment of coal and iron ore	50
Capital gain treatment of timber income	100
Commerce and transportation	
Deductibility of nonbusiness state gasoline tax	880
Community and regional development	
Housing rehabilitation, five-year amortization	10
Education, manpower, and social services	
Exclusion of scholarships and fellowships	285
Parental personal exemptions for students aged nineteen and over	770
Deductibility of contributions to educational institutions	565
Deductibility of and credit for child and dependent care expenses	870
Health	
Exclusion of employer contributions to medical insurance premiums and medical care	5,840
Deductibility of medical expenses	2,870
Income security	
Exclusion of Social Security benefits	
Disability insurance benefits	430
OASI benefits for aged	3,460
Benefits for dependents and survivors	795
Exclusion of railroad retirement benefits	205
Exclusion of sick pay	55
Exclusion of unemployment insurance benefits	2,445
Exclusion of workers' compensation benefits	810
Exclusion of public assistance benefits	105
Net exclusion of pension contributions and earnings	
Employer plans	9,940
Plans for self-employed and others	1,535
Exclusion of other employee benefits	
Premiums on group term life insurance	835
Premiums on accident and accidental death insurance	75
Income of trusts to finance supplementary unemployment benefits	10
Meals and lodging	350
Employer contributions to prepaid legal expense plans	10
Exclusion of capital gains on home sale if over 65	70

Table 11–9 (cont.)

Excess of percentage standard deduction over low-income allowance	1,410
Additional exemption for the blind	20
Additional exemption for over 65	1,280
Retirement income credit for the elderly	440
Earned income credit	205
Veterans benefits and services	
Exclusion of veterans disability compensation	690
Exclusion of veterans pensions	35
Exclusion of GI benefits	200
General government	
Credits and deductions for political contributions	35
Revenue sharing and general purpose fiscal assistance	
Exclusion of interest on general purpose state and local debt	1,880
Deductibility of nonbusiness state and local taxes (other than gasoline and owner-occupied homes)	8,990
Interest	
Deferral of interest on savings bonds	625
Business investment	
Exclusion of interest on state and local industrial development bonds	110
Excess first-year depreciation	145
Depreciation on buildings in excess of straight line	
Rental housing	425
Other	175
Expensing of research and development expenditures	30
Expensing construction-period interest and taxes	140
Investment credit	2,205
Personal investment	
Dividend exclusion	480
Capital gain	7,360
Exclusion of interest on life insurance savings	1,995
Deferral of capital gains on home sales	935
Deductibility of mortgage interest on owner-occupied homes	6,030
Deductibility of property taxes on owner-occupied homes	4,995
Deductibility of casualty losses	380
Other tax expenditures	
Deductibility of charitable contributions (other than education)	5,475
Deductibility of interest on consumer credit	2,565
Maximum tax on earned income	855
Memorandum	
Combined effect of provisions listed above	
Capital gains	7,860
Exclusion of interest on state and local debt	2,090
Deductibility of state and local nonbusiness taxes	13,460
Deductibility of charitable contributions	6,040

Source: *Special Analyses, Budget of the United States Government, 1978.* Estimates are based on the tax laws in effect as of 31 December 1976.

MINIMUM TAX ON PREFERENCE INCOME

As an alternative to reducing or eliminating specific tax preferences (although some of this has been done), the Congress, in 1969, enacted a minimum tax on preference income. This provision was amended in the Tax Reform Act of 1976. The largest source of preference income is the one-half of long-term capital gains excluded from regular income. Before the Act, this accounted for about 85 percent of all reported preference income. Interest income from state and local government securities is not a preference income item.[29] A minimum tax of 15 percent applies to preference income if it exceeds an exemption of $10,000 or one-half of the regular tax liability, whichever is greater. To some reformers, this is too weak because of the low tax rate and the limited coverage of preference income. The minimum income tax is a second-best approach to tax reform because it only partially corrects for questionable income exclusions.[30]

TAX PREFERENCES AND HORIZONTAL EQUITY

Throughout the preceding discussion we have noted that particular provisions of the income tax laws, tax preferences, lead to horizontal inequities. In subsequent chapters we will make similar statements in connection with other taxes. However, such statements are subject to the qualification that market adjustments to taxes tend to reduce the horizontal inequities implicit in tax preferences.[31] The basic mechanism of adjustment is the tendency of resources (labor and capital) to move into activities and investments that generate income that is favorably taxed (taxed at relatively low rates). Such movement lowers the pretax income from favorably taxed activities relative to the pretax income from more heavily taxed activities. This movement reflects the tendency of resource owners to seek the highest return. With perfect resource (factor) markets and perfect mobility of resources, movement tends to continue until the *after-tax* return earned by each type of resource is the same in each of its uses. Then pretax income will be relatively low in resource uses that are accorded relatively favorable tax treatment. Therefore, tax payments will be lower in comparison to pretax income for those favored resource uses. But *tax burdens* will not vary between

29 Some other preference income items are accelerated depreciation, depletion charges in excess of cost, and itemized deductions (other than medical and casualty deductions) in excess of 60 percent of adjusted gross income.

30 For a discussion of alternatives to the minimum income tax, see Joseph A. Pechman, *Federal Tax Policy*, 3rd ed. (Washington: Brookings, 1977), pp. 118–119.

31 See Richard A. Musgrave, "ET(Equitable Taxation), OT(Optimal Taxation), and SBT(Second-Best Taxation)"; and Martin S. Feldstein, "On the Theory of Tax Reform," both in *Journal of Public Economics*, 6 (February 1976): 3–16 and 77–104, respectively. See also Feldstein, "Compensation in Tax Reform," *National Tax Journal*, 29 (June 1976): 123–130.

favored and nonfavored uses — there will be no horizontal inequities — because all resource owners will earn the same after-tax returns.

In our discussion of the exemption of interest on state and local securities (p. 236), we saw how such market adjustments reduce the advantage of holding those securities rather than others yielding taxable income. Similarly, in the example in Chapter 9 of a tax on the income of textile workers, we saw how market adjustments were likely to reduce incomes of persons other than the taxed textile workers, while reducing the burden of the tax on textile workers.

Such market adjustments are likely to mitigate, but not fully eliminate, horizontal inequities for several reasons. First, the required resource reallocations take place in time and usually cannot be made quickly; the horizontal inequity implicit in a tax preference is likely to depend on how long it has been legal. This fact is one basis for the often-stated view that "an old tax is a good tax." Second, whether the required resource reallocations will be made depends on the perceived permanence of the tax preference. Adjustments to a preference seem unlikely if its permanence is uncertain.[32] Given the continuing debate about and pressure for the elimination of many tax preferences, their permanence is surely uncertain. Third, resource reallocations may be limited by factor-market imperfections — legal and institutional barriers to particular resource uses.

Martin Feldstein makes a related point: Tax reform aimed at improving equity may itself create inequities as individuals adjust to the reforms. For example, as we noted above, eliminating the exemption of interest on *existing* state and local bonds in the pursuit of tax equity would cause a capital loss for current bond holders. Such loss might be regarded as unfair, since the bondholders purchased the bonds with the expectation that the interest would be tax-exempt. These short-term inequities could be avoided or mitigated by compensating for losses due to reform or by delaying reform until the market adjusts to the anticipated reforms.[33]

RATE STRUCTURE

The marginal statutory tax rates range from 14 to 70 percent on taxable income. The maximum rate on earned income (wages, salaries, professional income) is 50 percent.[34] The income brackets within which each rate

32 For example, the spread between the yield on tax-exempt state and local bonds and taxable bonds has narrowed in recent years, probably partly because the tax exemption is under steady attack by tax reformers. Bond buyers therefore are aware that the tax exemption may be eliminated as being greater than it was ten to fifteen years ago.

33 See Feldstein, "Compensation in Tax Reform," pp. 123–130.

34 A taxpayer must subtract all preference income from earned income before applying the maximum 50 percent rate.

TABLE 11-10
EFFECTIVE RATE OF INDIVIDUAL INCOME TAX BY ADJUSTED FAMILY
INCOME CLASS, 1966, UNDER MOST PROGRESSIVE INCIDENCE ASSUMPTIONS

Adjusted family income (thousands of dollars)	Effective tax rate (Percent)
Less than 3	1.4
3–5	3.1
5–10	5.8
10–15	7.6
15–20	8.7
20–25	9.2
25–30	9.3
30–50	10.4
50–100	13.4
100–500	15.3
500–1,000	14.1
1,000 and over	12.4
All classes	8.5

Source: Joseph A. Pechman and Benjamin A. Okner, *Who Bears the Tax Burden?* (Washington: Brookings, 1974), p. 59. © 1974 by the Brookings Institution, Washington, D.C.

applies vary, depending upon the taxpayer's filing status (e.g., single, married, head of household).

The effective rate of taxation on net income is below the statutory rates because of exemptions, personal deductions, and exclusions and other tax preferences. The effect of some of the tax preferences on tax rates is shown in Table 11–10. The data are for 1966 because that is the year for which the most comprehensive income measure is available. According to the estimates, the highest effective rate of taxation under the income tax is 15.3 percent, and effective rates become regressive after the $100,000–$500,000 income range. Table 11–10 does not include the value of leisure or household production in income. But even without those adjustments, it is clear that the effective rates of taxation are far below the statutory rates (14 to 70 percent at the margin).

SUMMARY

A comprehensive income tax is widely regarded as a suitable instrument for taxation according to ability to pay. It is suitable for differentiating among taxpayers, and it can be structured to achieve any degree of progressiveness. The incidence of the tax appears to fall on those who are legally responsible for the tax (its impact and incidence are approximately equal), so that the distribution of tax burdens is fairly predictable. The economic effects of an income tax are not altogether predictable, but there is no clear evidence that the tax has serious adverse economic effects.

The income tax, as it is structured in the United States, departs substantially from comprehensive income taxation as we defined it in Chapter 10. Some sources of income are taxed at preferentially low rates, taxpaying units with equal ability to pay are treated differently, and questionable deductions are allowed. In other cases, some deductions that are not presently permitted should perhaps be allowed (e.g., for some education expenditures). Most of the questionable provisions of the tax laws narrow the tax base, necessitate higher statutory tax rates, lead to horizontal and vertical inequities, and encourage the use of resources to take advantage of tax loopholes. To avoid such effects, the thrust of tax reform should be in the direction of broadening the tax base and allowing tax preferences only if there is an overriding social purpose to be served.[35]

SUPPLEMENTARY READINGS

Aaron, Henry J., ed. *Inflation and the Income Tax.* Washington: Brookings, 1976.

Break, George F., and Pechman, Joseph A. *Federal Tax Reform: The Impossible Dream?* Washington: Brookings, 1975.

Goode, Richard. *The Individual Income Tax.* Rev. ed. Washington: Brookings, 1976.

Pechman, Joseph A. *Federal Tax Policy.* 3rd ed. Washington: Brookings, 1977.

Simons, Henry C. *Personal Income Taxation.* Chicago: University of Chicago Press, 1938.

——. *Federal Tax Reform.* Chicago: University of Chicago Press, 1950.

Surrey, Stanley. *Pathways to Tax Reform.* Cambridge, Mass.: Harvard, 1973.

Vickrey, William S. *Agenda for Progressive Taxation.* New York: Ronald, 1947.

---

35 What constitutes an overriding social purpose is, of course, a value judgment. One might argue that the existence of the tax preferences is evidence that Congress has decided that the preferences *do* serve an overriding social purpose. But the tax provisions that are customarily labeled tax preferences are provisions about which there is continuing debate, even in Congress. So there does not appear to be a consensus that the provisions serve an overriding social purpose.

CHAPTER TWELVE

PARTIAL INCOME TAXES: CORPORATION INCOME AND PAYROLL TAXES

Income taxes may be either comprehensive or partial. We were concerned, in Chapter 10, with a comprehensive income tax. And, although conceptually the U.S. individual income tax falls within that category, in practice, it is not a comprehensive tax, as we saw in Chapter 11.

Some income taxes employed by government are not comprehensive, even in design. Instead, particular sources of income are selected for taxation. Two major instances are the U.S. payroll and the corporation income taxes. The former tax is levied on labor income, and the latter is levied on capital income.[1] In this chapter we will analyze the efficiency and equity effects of these two taxes.

CORPORATION INCOME TAX

Most countries (and some state and local governments) tax the net income of corporations as well as the net income of individuals. A corporation is a legal entity separate from its owners, the stockholders. The corporation pays a tax on its net income, while stockholders typically pay a tax on dividend income under the individual income tax. Dividends are not a deductible expense for the corporation. The owners of unincorporated businesses report their business income under the individual income tax.

1 The payroll tax can be viewed as a tax on human capital income and the corporation income tax as a tax on physical capital income. But even so, they are partial income taxes that are conceptually different from a comprehensive income tax.

The tax on corporate income applies to profit-making corporations. Religious, charitable, scientific, and other nonprofit organizations and associations are exempt from this tax. A small corporation may choose to be taxed as a partnership, in which case it pays no corporation income tax. But the full income of the corporation is then taxable under the individual income tax as income of the corporation's stockholders.

The federal corporation income tax rates are 20 percent on the first $25,000 of net income, 22 percent on the next $25,000, and 48 percent on net income in excess of $50,000.[2] Currently, the corporation income tax produces about 14 percent of the federal government's general revenues, ranking third in importance below the personal income tax and the payroll tax. Most state and some local governments also employ a corporation income tax, but it is a relatively minor source of their revenues (see Chapter 2). The tax rate is typically 4 to 6 percent, and a few states have progressive rates. The net income of a corporation doing interstate business is allocated to a state on the basis of the proportion of the corporation's sales, property, or payroll in the state. Some states use all three factors (giving each equal weight) in apportioning corporate income, and other states use one or two.

TAX BASE

The legal provisions relating to and the issues involved in determining the federal corporation income tax base are numerous and complex. We will discuss only the major provisions and a few of the problems.

In determining taxable income, corporations subtract from gross income the costs incurred in generating that income. The derivation of taxable income is shown in Table 12–1. The following provisions are particularly important:

1. Income from state and local securities is exempt from taxation.

2. Realized long-term capital gains are taxed at a maximum rate of 22 percent for corporations with net income below $25,000 and 30 percent for corporations with net income above $25,000. Capital losses are deductible only against capital gains.

3. Charitable contributions up to 5 percent of taxable income are deductible.

---

2 In addition to the basic rates, a minimum tax of 15 percent is applied to preference income of corporations in excess of $10,000 or regular tax liability, whichever is greater. Preference income includes the excluded portion of capital gains, depreciation on real property in excess of straight-line depreciation, depletion in excess of adjusted basis depletion, and bad debt deductions of financial institutions in excess of losses.

TABLE 12–1
DERIVATION OF CORPORATE TAXABLE INCOME

Total income
    1. Gross profit equals gross sales minus cost of goods sold
    2. Dividends
    3. Interest
    4. Rents
    5. Royalties
    6. Net capital gains (losses)
    7. Other income
Minus costs and deductions
    8. Compensation of officers
    9. Salaries and wages (not deducted elsewhere)
  10. Repairs
  11. Bad debts
  12. Rents
  13. Taxes
  14. Interest
  15. Contributions or gifts
  16. Amortization, depreciation, depletion
  17. Advertising
  18. Employee benefits (including pension, stock bonus, profit sharing, annuity plans)
  19. Other deductions
Equals taxable income (the sum of items 1–7 minus the sum of items 8–19)

4. For most corporations, operating losses can be carried backward three years and forward seven to offset taxable income in those years.

5. Generous provisions are made for the recovery of capital, and a tax credit is available for certain kinds of investment expenditures.

Items 1 through 3 are *general* features of individual income taxation, which we discussed in Chapter 11. Item 4 is a means of averaging income, another aspect of income taxation that we discussed in Chapter 11. Item 5 we will now discuss in more detail.

Depreciation   Capital assets (buildings, machinery, equipment, tools) generate both income and costs in future periods. One of the costs of using capital assets in production is *depreciation* — the decrease in the value of the capital during the production period. Depreciation occurs because buildings and machines wear out. Or, if they do not wear out in a physical sense, their economic usefulness declines because changing technology and input prices make them more costly to use than newer buildings and equipment.

To determine income, whether generated through the corporate or noncorporate sector, it is necessary to account for depreciation.

Depreciation charges are deducted from gross business income in obtaining taxable income. The charges are based on an assumed useful life of the capital asset and an assumption about how its value decreases in each year of its life; deduction of expenditures for capital assets are spread over the assets' estimated "lives." The Internal Revenue Service sets guidelines for the lives of about eighty broad classes of assets, and taxpayers may increase or reduce these lives by 20 percent.

For tax purposes, there are three general methods of allocating the cost of a capital asset over its life to determine taxable business income (corporate and noncorporate). These methods are illustrated in Table 12–2. The *straight-line* method can be used for all depreciable assets. But some kinds of assets can be depreciated at a faster or *accelerated*, rate. Two such faster rates, *double-declining-balance* and *sum-of-the-years-digits*, are shown in Table 12–2.[3] Using accelerated depreciation rules gives less taxable income

TABLE 12–2

THREE METHODS FOR DEPRECIATING A $1,000 ASSET WITH A TEN-YEAR USEFUL LIFE (ROUNDED DOLLARS)

Year	Straight line [a]	Double-declining-balance [b]	Sum-of-the-years-digit [c]
1	100	200.0	182
2	100	160.0	164
3	100	128.0	145
4	100	102.0	127
5	100	82.0	109
6	100	66.0	91
7	100	65.5	73
8	100	65.5	55
9	100	65.5	36
10	100	65.5	18
Total	1,000	1,000.0	1,000

a $1,000 divided by years of useful life.

b Compute straight-line depreciation each year against undepreciated balance and multiply by 2.

c Multiply 1,000 by the ratio of the remaining years of useful life to the sum of the years of useful life.

Source: George F. Break and Joseph A. Pechman, *Federal Tax Reform: The Impossible Dream?* (Washington: Brookings, 1975), p. 61. © 1975 by the Brookings Institution, Washington, D.C.

3 The methods in Table 12–2 are not uniformly applied to all assets. Special accelerated depreciation rules apply to certain categories of assets, such as pollution control devices.

during the early years of the asset's life and greater taxable income in the
later years. Hence, tax payments are lower in earlier periods and higher in
later ones.

Such tax deferral increases the present value of the income generated by
the depreciable asset. So it is advantageous to use accelerated rather than
straight-line depreciation; the gain from doing so is the present value of the
earnings on the deferred taxes.

Accelerated depreciation also presents advantages in connection with the
capital gains tax. For example, suppose a corporation uses the capital asset
in Table 12–2 for four years, with $590 claimed in depreciation charges
under the double-declining-balance method. For tax purposes, the value of
the asset (its *book value*) is then $410. Suppose the corporation sells the asset
for $700. With a market value of $700, the economic depreciation of the
asset has been only $300 ($1,000 − $700). With a tax rate of 48 percent,
economic depreciation would have reduced the corporation's taxes by only
$144 ($300 × .48), while the depreciation charges actually taken produced
tax savings of $283.20 ($590 × .48). Therefore, under accelerated depreciation, there is a net tax savings of $139.20 ($283.20 − $144).

With machinery and equipment, net tax savings is fully recaptured by taxing the capital gain (sales price minus book value, or $700 − $410 = $290) at
the full tax rate of .48, giving $139.20 in recaptured taxes. However, with
real estate property (buildings), the tax savings is only partially recovered, to
the extent that accelerated depreciation charges exceed straight-line depreciation. In the example we have used, accelerated charges exceed straight-
line depreciation by $190 ($590 − $400), so taxes of .48 ($190) = $91.20 are
recovered. The remainder of the capital gain is taxed at the capital gains tax
rate of 30 percent, giving a capital gains tax of $30 = .30 ($290 − $190). Al-
together, recaptured taxes amount to $121.20. This compares to full recap-
ture of $139.20, so the net tax saving is $18 from accelerated depreciation.
In the case of government-subsidized housing, the recapture of taxes may be
further reduced for each month the property is held for more than 100
months.[4]

Depletion allowances   Special provisions apply in the deduction of capital
costs in oil, gas, and other mineral industries. On economic grounds, the
cost of exploration, development, and drilling should be deductible over the
production life of the asset (the oil well or mine that is created) just as any
other capital cost. However, these costs can be deducted immediately, in effect allowing 100 percent depreciation during the first year of the asset's life.
This 100 percent depreciation is appropriate only if the outlays produce no

4 With the Tax Reform Act of 1976, recapture of depreciation in excess of straight line for un-
subsidized housing applies to post-1975 depreciation.

asset, as occurs when the well is a dry hole. Otherwise, the costs should be capitalized and deducted over the lifetime of productive wells or mines.

For many years, mineral-producing industries were allowed to deduct a specified percentage of gross receipts — a depletion allowance — in arriving at taxable income, with the total allowance not to exceed 50 percent of net income. Such depletion deductions did not preclude the deduction of nearly all capital expenditures actually made.[5] This percentage depletion has been eliminated for major oil and gas producers and is to be gradually reduced for small producers. Similar deductions for capital expenses and lower rate depletion allowances apply to other mineral producers.

Investment tax credit   In addition to depreciation charges, a business firm may credit against its tax liabilities a specified fraction of new investment expenditures for tangible personal property. Although the actual amount of credit is variable, the basic rate is currently 10 percent.

Investment incentives   As we have seen, the function of depreciation is to determine economic income. When tax depreciation is more (less) rapid than economic depreciation, income is under- (over-) taxed. Depreciation rules are nonneutral in their effects on investment incentives if the ratio of tax depreciation to economic depreciation is not uniform among industries, thereby encouraging more investment in those industries more favorably treated by the depreciation rules. And there is evidence of such nonuniformity.[6] Also, the special tax concessions granted to the mineral-producing industries may encourage greater investment in those industries.[7]

In addition to their function in accounting for economic income, depreciation rules, along with the investment tax credit, have been used as incentives to stimulate private investment by making such investment more profitable. Both measures are also intended to increase employment during recessions. Whether such is the result is open to question for two basic reasons. First, there is the question of whether these measures affect investment in plant and equipment. The second question is whether increased investment in plant and equipment increases the demand for labor or reduces labor demand through investment in automated equipment and labor-saving

5 For a detailed analysis of these provisions as they applied to oil and gas, see Stephen L. McDonald, *Federal Tax Treatment of Income from Oil and Gas* (Washington: Brookings, 1963).

6 See Robert M. Coen, "Investment Behavior, The Measurement of Depreciation, and Tax Policy," *American Economic Review*, 65 (March 1975): 59–74.

7 Preferential tax treatment is sometimes justified as an offset to existing inefficiencies in resource allocation or as a means of promoting national defense objectives. These rationales have been used to support depletion allowances. See McDonald, *Federal Tax Treatment of Income from Oil and Gas.*

technologies. Available evidence suggests that the depreciation and tax credit measures have relatively little effect on total investment and total employment. Their main effects appear to be revenue losses for the U.S. Treasury.[8]

ALLOCATION EFFECTS

How do a corporation income tax and a proportional tax on all income differ in their effects on resource allocation? Using a corporation tax to obtain a given amount of revenue means a higher rate of taxation of income from capital that is invested in corporations and a lower rate of taxation of income from other sources, primarily labor income and income from investment in unincorporated enterprises. Thus, substituting corporation for proportional income taxation would likely reduce the after-tax return to saving and increase the after-tax return to labor supply.[9] Incentives would thus be created for lower saving and greater labor supply.

Such substitution would also have income effects. People receiving a relatively small share of their income from investments in corporations would gain at the expense of those who receive a relatively large share of income from such investments. The former group (the gainers) would tend to save more and supply less labor, while the reverse would be true for the latter group (the losers). Depending on the balance of these opposing adjustments,

8 Tax incentives may simply change the composition of investment as well as (or rather than) increase aggregate investment. See Emil M. Sunley, Jr., "The 1971 Depreciation Revision: Measures of Effectiveness," *National Tax Journal*, 24 (March 1971): 19–30; Henry J. Aaron, Frank S. Russek, Jr., and Neil M. Singer, "Tax Changes and the Composition of Fixed Investment: An Aggregative Simulation," *Review of Economics and Statistics*, 56 (November 1972): 343–356.

For a review and appraisal of some of the studies of the effects of tax incentives on investment, see George F. Break, "The Incidence and Economic Effects of Taxation," in *The Economics of Public Finance*, ed. Alan S. Blinder, George F. Break, Peter O. Steiner, and Dick Netzer (Washington: Brookings, 1974), pp. 203–221; Carl S. Shoup, "Quantitative Research in Taxation and Government Expenditure," in *Public Expenditure and Taxation* (New York: National Bureau of Economic Research, 1972), pp. 23–29; and Lester C. Thurow, *The Impact of Taxes on the American Economy* (New York: Praeger, 1971), pp. 31–34. For a very readable discussion of what we know about the effects of the investment tax credit, see Bob Arnold, "Investment Tax Credit Has Had Little Impact On Economy So Far," *The Wall Street Journal*, August 11, 1976, p. 1.

9 The after-tax return on saving would not be reduced if incorporated and unincorporated enterprises could operate with equal efficiency. In such case, a tax on corporations would cause all enterprises to assume the unincorporated form, and the tax would yield no revenue. But that is not realistic because such a shift has not occurred despite high rates of corporate taxation. The after-tax return on saving is also unaffected if short-run shifting to consumers (buyers) or suppliers (primarily employees) or both is complete. As we will note later, complete short-run shifting cannot occur if corporations maximize profits.

the income effects of substituting corporation for proportional income taxation could either reinforce or counter the incentive effects. If they reinforce, thereby reducing saving and increasing labor supply, then saving would be lower and labor supply would be greater with corporation rather than proportional income taxation. If the income effects counter the incentive effects, labor supply and saving under the corporation tax may be greater than, the same as, or lower than they would under the proportional income tax. Clearly, the way in which corporate and proportional income taxes differ in their effects on saving and labor supply is an empirical question — a question for which empirical evidence is scant and conflicting.[10]

Even if corporation and proportional income taxation result in the same total supply of capital and labor, the corporate tax may cause a redistribution of total resources between the corporate and noncorporate sectors. This change in resource use would be inefficient if resources would be allocated efficiently between sectors with a proportional income tax. The reason is that a reduction in the supply of capital to the corporate sector increases the gross rate of return (gross of tax) on investment in that sector, while reducing it in the noncorporate sector. The higher *gross* rate of return in the corporate sector is a measure of the higher value that consumers place on the output produced, indicating that more of the good should be produced (if efficiency is the objective) relative to other goods. But private investors try to equalize *after-tax* returns over all investments; more of the highly valued output will not be produced because it is not profitable to do so.

In the following section we discuss these allocation effects further, since tax shifting results from tax-induced resource reallocations.

INCIDENCE AND EQUITY

There are three classes of individuals whose real incomes may be reduced by the corporation income tax. First, the income of *stockholders* may be reduced because fewer dividends are paid out or capital gains on common stock are lower. Second, the price of goods and services produced by the corporate sector might be increased, thereby reducing the real income of the *buyers* of those goods and services. Third, *suppliers* of labor and materials to

---

10 For discussion of the evidence regarding the effects of income taxes on saving and labor supply, see Richard Goode, *The Individual Income Tax*, rev. ed. (Washington: Brookings, 1976), chap. 3; and Break, "Incidence and Economic Effects of Taxation," pp. 180–203. Break (p. 194) suggests that saving might be as much as 5 percent higher or as much as 12 percent lower with corporation rather than proportional income taxation. There is little evidence to suggest that aggregate labor supply would be significantly different with one form of tax than with the other.

corporations may have their income reduced. If stockholders bear the burden, the tax is not shifted. If consumers bear the burden, the tax is shifted forward. If suppliers bear the burden, the tax is shifted backward. But regardless of whether and how it is shifted, the corporation income tax is borne by individuals, and not by some impersonal corporate entity.

How the tax burden is in fact distributed among these groups is an empirical question, the answer to which depends upon the structure of markets in which corporations buy and sell and the long-run allocation effects of the tax.

Short run   In the short run, capital resources cannot shift from one employment to another, and the total capital stock cannot change. If corporations are maximizing profits when a corporation income tax is imposed, and continue to do so, then the short-run burden of the tax is fully borne by the owners of the capital employed in the corporate sector. This is because there is a particular price and output combination that maximizes profits whether a tax rate applies to profits or not. For example, suppose a corporation maximizes profits at $100,000 with price $10 and output of 1 million units. A tax of 50 percent is imposed on profits, reducing after-tax profits to $50,000. This reduced level of profits is the maximum attainable with the tax because $100,000 was the maximum *before-tax* income. A higher price and lower output would only reduce profits, say to $95,000. This would leave after-tax profits of $47,500. Therefore, the corporation would not raise prices. Similarly, it would not be able to lower wages in order to shift the tax backward, because if profits were maximum before the tax, then costs, including labor costs, were minimum for the chosen output level. Also, when corporations maximize profits, the short-run incidence of a corporation income tax will be on the owners of capital employed by the corporations regardless of whether the corporations operate in competitive or noncompetitive markets.

However, corporations may not maximize profits — because it is socially unacceptable or because they fear antitrust action or have other objectives. If profits are not maximized, for whatever reason, a corporation income tax may result in higher prices because the tax is a stimulus to increase profits in order to restore after-tax income. Prices rise and consumers then bear a portion of the tax. Some of the burden also falls on labor if the corporation is paying wages above those necessary to obtain the desired quantity of labor. Such might occur if the corporation has monopsony power that it did not fully exploit before the tax.

Long run   In the short run, the burden of the corporation income tax can be shifted from the owners of capital employed by the corporations only if corporations are not maximizing profits. However, in the long run, the tax may be shifted to others because resources can move to untaxed sectors or the total supply of capital can change.[11] Consider first the case in which the total supply of capital is fixed but resources can move among sectors of the economy. Let X denote those sectors of the economy for which the corporate form of business organization is either required or highly advantageous, while Y denotes the other sectors.[12] Sectors X produce output x and sectors Y produce output y.

In the absence of a corporation income tax, capital owners would tend to earn the same gross and net returns on their capital whether it is employed by corporations or unincorporated firms.[13] Imposing a corporation income tax lowers the net return on capital employed by corporations. So capital owners have an incentive to move capital from sectors X to sectors Y.

As the supply of capital to X is reduced, the supply of commodity x falls, the price of x increases, and the gross rate of return to capital in X rises. The opposite occurs in sectors Y: The supply of capital increases, the price of commodity y falls, and the gross and net rates of return on capital in Y decline. These adjustments continue until rates of return *net of tax* are the same in the taxed and untaxed sectors. The incidence of the tax is thereby spread over all owners of capital; owners of capital in Y suffer a reduction in income as well as the owners of capital in X.

Although this analysis predicts that the corporation income tax reduces the return to all capital, the full burden of the tax does not necessarily fall on capital owners. For example, if sectors Y are relatively capital intensive (utilize less labor per unit of capital than sectors X), the demand for labor will fall. Labor demand falls because the labor released by X (as capital moves to Y) is more than can be absorbed by Y at prevailing wage rates. This general decline in the demand for labor causes labor income to fall relative to the income of capital owners. The reverse would occur if sectors Y are relatively labor intensive and X are relatively capital intensive.

In addition, the real income of individuals may be changed by the effect of the tax on relative prices. As we have seen, the tax causes the price of x to rise relative to the price of y. Whether individuals gain or lose as buyers depends upon the importance of x and y in their budgets.

---

11 The following analysis is based upon Arnold C. Harberger, "The Incidence of the Corporation Income Tax," *Journal of Political Economy*, 70 (June 1962): 215–240.

12 The corporate form is most advantageous when large concentrations of capital are required for production, as is the case with modern manufacturing.

13 Rates of return might differ because of risk differences, but they would otherwise be equal because capital can freely move between the corporate and noncorporate sectors.

This analysis does not tell us how the incidence of the corporation income tax varies by income class. If the tax falls entirely on capital, the tax is progressive because the amount of capital owned by persons typically is greater relative to their income if they are in higher rather than lower income classes. But the tax may be regressive if it reduces labor income or increases the relative prices of commodities that are relatively important in lower-income budgets.

To the extent that corporations shift the corporation tax forward or backward in the short run, because they were not maximizing profits, long-run resource shifting from the corporate to unincorporated sectors may not occur. If short-run shifting is complete, the relative profitability of investment in the corporate and unincorporated sectors is not affected. And there is no direct incentive for capital movement. However, capital and labor movements between sectors may occur because of relative price changes (with forward shifting, the price of x rises relative to the price of y) or because of wage changes (backward shifting means that workers earn relatively less in sector X and, hence, have an incentive to shift to sectors Y).

Resource movement from the corporate to the noncorporate sectors may be slight even if profit rates in the former are reduced. One reason is that, given the structure of capital markets, many individuals would earn a lower return or face more risk if their investments were in proprietorships and partnerships rather than corporate stocks. Also, the corporate form of organization may be more efficient primarily because it facilitates raising the large sums of capital needed for large-scale production. That is, with producing units organized as large-scale corporations, a higher rate of return on capital might be earned than if units were organized as smaller scale partnerships. For example, if the rate of return under corporate organization is 14 percent but is only 7 percent when production is undertaken by unincorporated firms, a 50 percent tax on profits in the corporate sectors would not influence the allocation of resources between the two sectors.[14]

In the long run, not only can resources move among alternative uses, but the total supply of capital can change as well. If the total supply of capital (savings) falls when the corporation income tax reduces the rate of return to capital, then real output will fall. Any such decrease reduces the real income of individuals as consumers, an income loss that is in addition to the loss they incur as suppliers of labor, capital, and land.

Empirical evidence on incidence and shifting   Although there have been a number of empirical studies of the incidence of the U.S. federal corporation

14 See Break, "Incidence and Economic Effects of Taxation," pp. 146–150, for a review of these arguments.

income tax, the question of its incidence remains unresolved.[15] However, it seems unlikely that the full burden of the tax falls on stockholders — the owners of the capital employed in the corporate sector — especially in the long run. Some shifting undoubtedly occurs because some corporations do not maximize profits. For example, regulated companies such as public utilities face limits on the profits they may earn. If such limits are effective, then a corporate income tax on such corporations is likely to lead to a request for and the granting of rate increases and higher utility charges. At the same time, full shifting is implausible because many corporations probably do strive to maximize profits. In the short run, then, they are unable to offset taxes by wage decreases or price increases. And their long-run ability to shift is limited because many firms would not forgo the advantages of the corporate form of enterprise simply to escape the tax. Finally, there is little evidence that the total supply of capital would be reduced substantially, thus shifting the burden to consumers.

Table 12–3 presents estimates of the incidence of the federal corporation income tax, by income class and under two incidence assumptions.

Ability to pay Can the corporation income tax be justified as an ability-to-pay tax? Is it horizontally equitable? In brief, the answer is no. If the tax is consistent with ability-to-pay or other equity principles, it must affect the distribution of individual income in a specified way. We have seen, however, that there are no definite conclusions about the incidence of the tax. If the tax is not shifted and is therefore borne by stockholders, it is both horizontally and vertically inequitable because it makes no allowances for differences in the ability to pay of various stockholders. Moreover, persons who supply capital to unincorporated businesses pay no corresponding tax, even though they may have equal or greater ability to pay than stockholders. That is, if the tax is not shifted, stockholders are taxed twice on their income, once by the corporation and once by the individual income tax, while owners of unincorporated businesses pay only the latter tax. If the tax is shifted, there is no double taxation of stockholders. But the tax remains unsatisfactory. If it is shifted forward to consumers in higher prices, it is, in effect, a variable rate excise tax. There is no reason that the burdens resulting

---

15 The difficulties with empirical studies are made clear in the following: M. Krzyzaniak and Richard A. Musgrave, *The Shifting of the Corporation Income Tax* (Baltimore: Johns Hopkins Press, 1963); John C. Cragg, Arnold C. Harberger, and Peter Mieszkowski, "Empirical Evidence on the Incidence of the Corporation Income Tax," *Journal of Political Economy* (December 1967): 811–822; and M. Krzyzaniak and Richard A. Musgrave, "Corporation Tax Shifting: A Response," and John C. Cragg, Arnold C. Harberger, and Peter Mieszkowski, "Corporation Tax Shifting: Rejoinder," *Journal of Political Economy*, 78 (July-August 1970): 768–777.

TABLE 12–3
ESTIMATED EFFECTIVE RATE OF U.S. CORPORATION INCOME TAX, UNDER
TWO INCIDENCE ASSUMPTIONS, BY ADJUSTED FAMILY INCOME CLASS, 1966

Adjusted family income class	Effective rate (%)	
(thousands of dollars)	Assumption 1 [a]	Assumption 2 [b]
Less than 3	2.1	6.1
3–5	2.2	5.3
5–10	1.8	4.3
10–15	1.6	3.8
15–20	2.0	3.8
20–25	3.0	4.0
25–30	4.6	4.3
30–50	5.8	4.7
50–100	8.8	5.6
100–500	16.5	7.4
500–1,000	23.0	9.0
1,000 and over	25.7	9.8

a One-half the tax is assumed to be borne by stockholders and one-half by property income in general.

b One-half the tax is assumed to be borne by consumers and one-half by property income in general.

Source: Joseph A. Pechman and Benjamin A. Okner, *Who Bears the Tax Burden?* (Washington: Brookings, 1974), p. 59. © 1974 by the Brookings Institution, Washington, D.C.

from the higher prices would be distributed according to ability to pay. And, if the tax is shifted backward, thus reducing incomes of employees and other suppliers, there is no reason for the pattern of burdens to be distributed according to ability to pay.

Benefits received   Do corporation income taxes pay for benefits received from government services? Benefit taxation of business is justified on grounds of efficiency, so long as the government supplies inputs into the production process that would otherwise have to be purchased from the private sector. If such inputs were not paid for (if they were supplied free to firms), marginal social cost would exceed private cost, and too much of the good would likely be produced.

It is unlikely that corporation income tax payments measure benefits received from government services. There is no a priori reason why benefits vary directly with corporation income, let alone with the particular tax rate on corporate income. Two corporations may receive the same benefits from government services but have different incomes and tax liabilities. Corporation income fluctuates with the business cycle as well as with shifts in demand, but the flow of government inputs does not fluctuate in the same way. (National defense protects business property whether corporate income is zero or positive.)

INTEGRATION OF CORPORATION AND INDIVIDUAL INCOME TAXES

There are two views about how corporate net income should be taxed. The current arrangement we discuss in this chapter is called the *separatist* approach, which is supported by several arguments. First, the corporation is an entity in itself, with a life of its own, distinct from that of stockholders. The corporation, therefore, has an ability to pay taxes. Second, if corporate income is not taxed separately, only dividends will be taxed; retained earnings will escape taxation. Third, if the corporate income tax burden falls on stockholders, the overall tax structure is more progressive than if the tax were repealed and replaced with a general income tax. Fourth, the tax is a levy for the benefits provided by the state to the corporation. And, fifth, a corporation tax is a means of controlling monopolies and the size of business firms.

Opposed to the separatist view is the *integrationist* view that corporate income is another form of income to individuals, which should be taxed as such if taxation is to be source blind. In this view, business firms, as such, have no ability to pay taxes. Only individuals pay taxes, in their capacity as consumers, workers, or capital owners. From the integrationist perspective, the corporation income tax is not a fair way of taxing individuals because, as we noted above, it taxes according to neither ability to pay nor benefits received. And it is not well-suited to controlling business size and monopoly. A corporation income tax applies to small as well as large corporations. And two firms of the same size may have different profit rates. A tax on some measure of size would be more appropriate.

If the integrationist view is accepted, how could the individual and corporation income tax be integrated? Basically, with an integrated system, stockholders are taxed as if they are partners receiving income from the corporation, an option that is presently available to small corporations. Under this method, all corporate net income, whether paid out in dividends or retained by the corporation, is assigned to shareholders and taxed at individual income tax rates. If continued, the corporation income tax would be treated as tax withheld from shareholder income.

For example, suppose a corporation's net income before corporation income taxes is $1 per share. A person holding 10 shares of the stock would therefore have $10 of corporate income, which the person would report as taxable income. If the person's individual income tax rate was 20 percent, the tax due on the corporate income of $10 would be $2. However, with a corporation income tax of 50 percent, $5 would have been withheld, and the person would be due a refund of $3. In contrast, if the person's individual income tax rate was 70 percent, $7 in taxes would be due the government, of which only $5 would have been withheld at the corporate level. So the person would have to make an additional $2 payment. In this way, the income accruing to persons who own corporations (stockholders) would be taxed the same as income from other sources.

With full integration, corporate income is taxed under the individual income tax whether it is paid out in dividends or retained in the corporation. Retained earnings add to stockholders' investment in the stock that they own. These retained earnings should be subtracted from the selling price of the stock in computing capital gains because they have already been taxed as income to the stockholder. Otherwise, income retained by the corporation will be taxed more heavily than that paid out as dividends. For example, suppose a person buys a share of stock for $30.00, holds it five years, and sells it for $40.00. Suppose also that annual income is $1.00 per share in each of those five years, of which $.50 is retained by the corporation and $.50 is paid out in dividends. The individual is taxed on the full income of $1.00 per share. When the stock is sold, the person's adjusted cost (adjusted basis) for computing capital gains is $32.50 — $30 for the original purchase price and $2.50 for the retained earnings on which taxes have already been paid. The capital gain is thus $7.50 when the stock is sold at $40.00.

When stockholders have to pay taxes on all corporate income, whether retained by the corporation or paid out as dividends, some stockholders may have to liquidate assets or pay the tax from other income sources. Stockholders might therefore pressure corporations to retain fewer earnings and thereby reduce a source of funds for corporate expansion. On the other hand, if the unintegrated corporation income tax causes resources to move from the corporate sector to the unincorporated sector of the economy, integration of the two taxes could reverse those capital flows and increase the supply of capital to corporations.

Other proposals for reform of the corporation income tax call for less than complete integration with the individual income tax. But whether complete or partial, integration of the corporation income tax with the individual income tax is appealing to those who believe that the corporation tax distorts the allocation of resources and distributes the tax burden capriciously and inequitably.[16]

16 For a number of articles dealing with integration of the corporation and individual income taxes, see the National Tax Association–National Tax Institute, "Symposium on the Taxation on Income from Corporate Shareholding," *National Tax Journal*, 28 (September 1975).

PAYROLL TAXATION

A payroll tax is a tax on wages and salaries. Like a corporation income tax, it is a partial rather than a comprehensive tax on income. It may be imposed on employees, on employers, or on both.

Payroll taxes accounted for about 30 percent of the U.S. federal government revenues in 1976. And these taxes have been the fastest growing source of revenue in recent years. The U.S. Social Security System is currently supported by a tax of 11.7 percent on wage and salary income, with one-half being imposed on employees and one-half on employers. The maximum tax base on wages and salaries is $16,500. Self-employed persons are taxed at a rate below the combined rate on employers and employees.

A payroll tax also finances unemployment compensation programs. State governments levy the tax, and it is credited against a federal payroll tax. The federal tax rate is now 3.4 percent, levied on employers, with a maximum tax base of $6,000 per employee.

Since federal payroll taxes finance particular programs, it might seem that such taxes should be analyzed only in conjunction with the benefits provided. But this would overlook the fact that we can change the method of financing these programs (Social Security and unemployment compensation). For example, federal income tax revenues rather than payroll taxes could finance Social Security. Indeed, there is substantial support for doing so. To evaluate such a change in financing, we must compare the allocation and distribution effects of the payroll and proportional income taxes without regard for the effects of the expenditures financed by the taxes. We make this comparison in the remainder of this chapter.

ALLOCATION EFFECTS

Payroll taxation, as it is practiced in the United States and in most other countries, differs from proportional income taxation in two ways. First, the payroll tax base includes only labor income (wage and salary); the income tax base also includes nonlabor income (rents, interest, dividends, etc.). Second, governments often levy payroll taxes on only that portion of a person's labor income that falls below some upper limit. For both reasons, the payroll tax base is smaller than the income tax base. Consequently, to provide a given amount of revenue, the payroll tax rate must be higher than the proportional income tax rate.

For example, if labor income is 75 percent of the income tax base, then to provide the same revenue, the payroll tax rate must be 33 percent ($1/.75 = 1.33$) higher. In addition, suppose that one-fifth of labor income is excluded from payroll taxation because only the first $16,500 of labor income is taxed. With this additional restriction, the payroll tax base is only

TABLE 12–4

MARGINAL AND AVERAGE TAX RATES UNDER PAYROLL AND PROPORTIONAL INCOME TAXATION

	Total labor income			
	Less than L		Equal to or greater than L	
Tax rate	Payroll tax	Income tax	Payroll tax	Income tax
Marginal tax rate on nonlabor income	0	t_y	0	t_y
Marginal tax rate on labor income	t_p	t_y	0	t_y
Average tax rate	$t_p\, x$	t_y	$(t_p\, L)/Y$	t_y

60 percent as large as the income tax base. And the equal-yield payroll tax rate has to be 67 percent $(1/.6 = 1.67)$ higher than the income tax rate.

To see the consequences of this higher tax rate, let t_y denote the tax rate applied to all income with the proportional income tax; L denote the maximum amount of labor income that is subject to payroll taxation; t_p denote the payroll tax rate applied to labor income below the limit L; and x denote the ratio of the person's labor income (W) to his or her total income (Y). That is, $x = W/Y$. For persons with labor income in excess of L, the marginal payroll tax rate is zero. The marginal tax rate on nonlabor income is zero with the payroll tax and t_y with the proportional income tax. The average tax rate under payroll taxation is $(t_p W)/Y = t_p\, x$ for the person whose labor income is less than L and $(t_p\, L)/Y$ for the person whose labor income equals or exceeds L. Table 12–4 summarizes these definitions.[17] As we noted above, $t_p > t_y$. And, since labor income can never exceed 100 percent of total income, $x \leq 1$.

Labor supply   How will equal-yield payroll and proportional income taxes differ in their effects on labor supply? The answer depends on the circumstances of the taxpayer.

For persons whose total labor income falls below the limit L, Table 12–4 shows that the marginal tax rate is higher and the after-tax return to additional labor supply is lower with payroll than with income taxation. Consequently, for those persons, the substitution effect is less favorable for labor

17 A marginal tax rate is the rate at which additions to income are taxed. With a payroll tax, additions to annual labor income are not taxed once the limit L is reached, and nonlabor income is never taxed. The average tax rate is simply the ratio of taxes paid to income received.

supply with the payroll than with the income tax.[18] However, if they have no nonlabor income, the income effect is more favorable to labor supply with payroll than with income taxation.[19] Thus, it is unclear which tax is more favorable to labor supply by persons who have no nonlabor income and whose labor income falls below L.

For some people with total labor income less than L, nonlabor income may be sufficiently large (and x sufficiently low) so that the average tax rate is less for payroll than for income taxation, that is, $t_p x < t_y$. If so, then both the income and substitution effects will be less favorable for labor supply under payroll taxation.

For people whose labor income equals or exceeds L, the substitution effect is more favorable for labor supply under payroll taxation.[20] The income effect will also be more favorable for labor supply under payroll taxation if income (Y) is sufficiently low that the average tax rate is greater under payroll than under income taxation (that is, Y is low enough that $(t_p L)/Y > t_y$). However, the differential income and substitution effects work in opposite directions if Y is large enough that $t_p L/Y < t_y$.

Both the income and substitution effects favor greater labor supply under payroll taxation (than under income taxation) only when total labor income exceeds L *and* total income is low enough that $(t_p L)/Y > t_y$. With L set at about the median family income, as it is presently for U.S. OASDHI taxes, the payroll tax provides a greater incentive to labor supply (than the income tax) for upper middle-income people who have little nonwage income.

Both income and substitution effects favor less labor supply only for people whose total labor income is less than L *and* the amount of nonlabor income is sufficiently high that $t_p x < t_y$. Such people would have primarily nonlabor income (rents, dividends, profits) and likely, although not necessarily, be high-income people.

As L becomes larger, the set of persons that would tend to supply more labor under the payroll tax than under the income tax shrinks, while the set

18 To illustrate, if w is a person's gross wage rate, then the person's net return from supplying an additional unit of labor is $(1 - t_y)w$ under the income tax and $(1 - t_p)w < (1 - t_y)w$ under the payroll tax. The *after-tax* income from labor is greater with income than with payroll taxation. That is, people with labor income below L have a greater incentive to substitute labor for leisure with payroll than with income taxation; the payroll tax has a more adverse substitution effect on labor supply.

19 That is, disposable income is less with payroll taxation because the average tax rate under payroll taxation is t_p, which exceeds t_y, the average tax rate under income taxation.

20 The reason is that the after-tax return for supplying additional labor is w under the payroll tax and $(1 - t_y)w$ under the income tax.

that would tend to supply less labor under payroll taxation increases. In the case that there is no limit to the labor income subjected to payroll taxation, no one would fall into the first set. Apart from these two sets, the differential labor supply incentives of the two taxes are ambiguous. Thus, it is not clear on theoretical grounds which tax provides the greater incentive for labor supply.[21]

The actual effects of taxes depend not only on the incentives that they offer but also on the response of people to those incentives. In Chapter 10 we noted that labor supply does not appear to be very responsive to taxation. The conclusion that emerges is that the differential labor supply effects of payroll and income taxation are unlikely to be an important concern in the choice between them because (1) the overall incentive effects are unclear, and (2) response to any incentives that exist seems likely to be weak.

Saving and investment   The marginal tax rate on the income from physical capital is zero under payroll taxation and positive under income taxation (see Table 12–4). So the differential substitution effects are such that saving and investment in physical capital (that generates nonlabor income) would tend to be greater with payroll taxation. The differential income effect also favors greater saving under payroll taxation by higher-income persons and persons who have relatively large nonlabor incomes. For lower-income persons whose income is largely from labor, the differential income and substitution effects are in the opposite direction, so that the total effect on saving is ambiguous.[22]

Investment in human capital typically yields a return in the form of labor income (wages, salaries, and the income of professionals such as doctors and lawyers). The return to such investment is taxed under both the income

21 A comparison of the payroll tax with a progressive income tax gives the same general conclusion about labor supply effects.

22 The income effects sum to zero in the aggregate, since the taxes are equal yield. Thus, one might conjecture that the differential income effects cancel. If so, the incentives for investment in physical capital are definitely greater with payroll taxation. In contrast, even with zero income effects, the differential effects on labor supply are still ambiguous.

In this chapter, we are concerned only with the effects of the payroll tax on saving. However, in the United States, the payroll tax finances specific programs, primarily the Social Security system. The effect of the Social Security system on saving, which consists of the combined effects of the payroll tax *and* Social Security benefit payments, is considered by Martin Feldstein, "Social Security, Induced Retirement, and Aggregate Capital Accumulation," *Journal of Political Economy*, 28 (September-October 1974): 481–495; Alicia Munnell, *The Effect of Social Security on Personal Saving* (Cambridge, Mass.: Ballinger Publishing Company, 1974); and Thomas F. Pogue and L. G. Sgontz, "Social Security and Investment in Human Capital," *National Tax Journal*, 30 (June 1977): 157–170.

payroll taxes. But the marginal rate of taxation on income from human capital investment depends on whether such income is above or below the taxable limit on payrolls. For people whose marginal income from such investment is below the taxable limit, the substitution effect suggests that the income tax is more favorable than the payroll tax. However, if the marginal income is above the taxable limit, the income tax is less favorable to human capital investment. Since there are individuals who fall in both income classes, the aggregate incentive effect is unclear.

The differential income effects may also be such that saving for investment in human capital is affected. In comparison to income taxation, payroll taxation tends to result in higher average tax rates for low-income persons and lower average rates for high-income persons. Hence, with payroll taxation, saving will tend to be lower by low-income persons and higher by high-income persons. If marginal saving is directed by low-income persons into investment in human capital and into investment in physical capital by high-income persons, then investment in human capital will tend to be greater with income rather than payroll taxation.

INCIDENCE AND EQUITY

The incidence of the payroll tax depends primarily on the elasticity of labor supply. With a perfectly inelastic supply of labor, the payroll tax reduces the after-tax wage rate by the amount of the tax; and the incidence of the tax is on the recipients of labor income. The reasoning is the same as we used to establish that the income tax will not be shifted if factor supplies (labor and capital) are perfectly inelastic. This is true whether the tax is collected from the employee, the employer, or both.

If there is some elasticity of labor supply, i.e., if some employees work less because of the tax, employers will tend to increase wages because the value of an additional worker (the value marginal product of labor) increases as the amount of labor used decreases. Such an increase in gross wages means either higher product prices or lower income to owners of capital or both. With elastic labor supply, part of the payroll tax may be shifted to buyers of products or to owners of capital or to both. However, since some laborers will work at lower wage rates than others, the supply of labor services will not be perfectly elastic; and the full burden of the tax will not be shifted.

The empirical evidence on the incidence of the payroll tax is mixed. One investigator concludes that the tax is borne by labor,[23] but this work has

23 See John A. Brittain, "The Incidence of the Social Security Payroll Tax," *American Economic Review*, 61 (March 1971): 110–125.

been challenged.[24] Another investigator concludes that the payroll tax does not reduce labor income, at least in the short run,[25] in which case, capital income may decrease or prices may rise or both may occur.

If the incidence of the payroll tax is largely on labor income, the tax violates the principles of horizontal and vertical equity. A person who receives labor income pays a higher tax than a person who receives the same amount of income from other sources. And two families with the same labor income may pay different taxes. Because the present tax applies to the wages of each wage earner and there is a taxable limit, a family with one wage earner who earns $20,000 pays less tax than a family with a husband and wife who each earn $10,000. Vertically, the tax is regressive because it does not apply to labor income above the taxable limit or to nonlabor income, which accrues primarily to high-income persons. In addition, there is no allowance for nondiscretionary expenditures through exemptions, deductions, or other mechanisms; and there is no differentiation among taxpaying units by other measures of need.

If the tax results in higher prices, with some prices increasing more than others, it amounts to a variable excise tax. If the tax is shifted to capital income, it may either reduce capital income or reduce capital formation and, hence, labor income.

Even if the payroll tax is not equitable as a source of general revenue, might it not be equitable as a means of financing Social Security benefits? If the tax reduces labor income, the answer is clearly no from an ability-to-pay perspective. Payroll tax financing of Social Security benefits would distribute the burden of caring for the old and disabled regressively. From a benefits-received perspective, the tax appears somewhat more equitable in that retirement and disability benefits are loosely related to a person's previous payments of Social Security taxes. But the link is weak indeed, and methods that would tie contributions more closely to benefits are clearly available — if such is desired. If the incidence of the tax is not on labor, the relationship between benefits received and taxes paid is even weaker. So the payroll tax is an inferior means of financing Social Security by either ability-to-pay or benefits-received criteria.

PAYROLL TAX REFORM

On the assumption that the payroll tax is regressive and horizontally inequitable as a general revenue source and as a means of financing Social

24 Martin S. Feldstein, "The Incidence of the Social Security Payroll Tax: Comment," and John A. Brittain's reply, *American Economic Review*, 62 (September 1972): 735–742.

25 Jane H. Leuthold, "The Incidence of the Payroll Tax in the U.S.," *Public Finance Quarterly* (January 1975): 3–13.

Security, it has been suggested that the present payroll tax be replaced, either partially or wholly, by the individual income tax. Failing this, the payroll tax could be modified by a system of exemptions or a minimum standard deduction to reduce taxes on the low-income groups. This reform would have to be coupled with an increase in the taxable limit or in the tax rate on payrolls or in both.[26]

SUMMARY

The corporation income and payroll taxes are discriminatory in that they are partial taxes, the former on income from corporate capital and the latter on labor income. Although the question of incidence remains open for both taxes, they are very likely horizontally inequitable. If the corporation income tax is not shifted, then dividends are taxed more heavily than other income. Also, all dividends are taxed at the corporate tax rate, even though corporate stockholders are likely to have different incomes. If the tax is shifted forward, it acts as a variable rate excise tax; if it is shifted to corporate employees, it is a variable rate tax on labor income. Similarly, if the incidence of the payroll tax is on labor income, the tax is regressive and horizontally inequitable as a general revenue source. The payroll tax is also inequitable as a means of financing retirement income because of the loose connection between taxes paid during working years and benefits received during retirement.

Both the corporation income and the payroll taxes may have different effects on resource allocation from the proportional income tax. But theoretical analysis does not tell us whether the effects are likely to be large or small. Empirical studies provide some estimates of the allocation effects of the two taxes, but the evidence is sometimes conflicting. On balance, there is little evidence that factor supplies differ greatly under either payroll or corporation income taxation from what they would be under proportional income taxation.

Among the more complex problems of taxation are those of determining corporate net income and depreciation allowances for capital goods. Although the function of depreciation is that of determining economic income, it has been used as a device to stimulate business investment and to favor investments of particular kinds. The investment tax credit has also been used as an investment stimulus, and the mineral-producing industries have been given special tax concessions.

26 See John A. Brittain, *The Payroll Tax and Social Security* (Washington: Brookings, 1972), Chap. 5; Joseph A. Pechman, Henry J. Aaron, and Michael K. Taussig, *Social Security: Perspectives for Reform* (Washington: Brookings, 1968); and Alicia H. Munnell, *The Future of Social Security* (Washington: Brookings, 1977).

On balance, it seems questionable that either equity or efficiency is served by taxing major components of income, as we do with corporate income and payroll taxation, rather than total income. This view is clearly inherent in those tax reform proposals that would either integrate the corporate and individual income taxes or displace payroll taxes with a broadbased income tax.

SUPPLEMENTARY READINGS

Brittain, John A. *The Payroll Tax and Social Security.* Washington: Brookings, 1972.

Goode, Richard. *The Corporation Income Tax.* New York: Wiley, 1951.

Munnell, Alicia H. *The Future of Social Security.* Washington: Brookings, 1977.

National Tax Association–National Tax Institute. "Symposium on the Taxation of Income from Corporate Shareholding." *National Tax Journal* 28 (September 1975).

Pechman, Joseph A. *Federal Tax Policy*, Chaps. 5, 7. 3rd ed. Washington: Brookings, 1977.

————; Aaron, Henry J.; and Taussig, Michael K. *Social Security: Perspectives for Reform.* Washington: Brookings, 1968.

Report of the Royal Commission on Taxation. Vol. 4. Ottawa: Queens Printer, 1966.

CHAPTER THIRTEEN

SALES AND EXCISE TAXATION

Sales taxes are levied on sales of products and services, with the tax typically being collected from the seller. They may be general, applying to all sales, or selective, applying to the sales of only specified commodities. Selective sales taxes are also called excise taxes. With sales taxation, the tax base is either all or a specified part of the sales of businesses. Such sales are generated as people or businesses use (spend) their income. Sales taxes are, therefore, taxes on *income uses*, in contrast with income taxes, which are on *income sources*.

Sales taxes can be used in their selective form to regulate consumption and production patterns — to discourage the activity that is taxed. In this case, revenue generation is not the primary purpose of the taxation; indeed, the more successful the tax is in discouraging the activity, the lower its revenues are. Selective sales taxes may also approximate user charges.

As a source of general revenue, sales taxes differ from income taxes in that they can favor particular uses of income with low or zero tax rates. Different allocation and distributional effects can thereby be obtained; in particular, consumption can be taxed while saving is exempted. Also sales taxation involves fewer collection points (taxpaying units), and the taxpaying units are more visible and less mobile than are individuals and families. Recordkeeping by businesses is likely to be superior to family recordkeeping, especially in underdeveloped countries where literacy rates are low. Thus, compliance may be less difficult and less costly with sales than with income taxation. Finally, sales taxes may not be an explicit and visible part of the purchase price; and they involve numerous small payments rather than a single large annual payment, such as may be required under property or income taxation. Thus, sales taxes may appear less burdensome to the taxpayer.[1]

1 With automatic withholding, the income tax is essentially similar in this respect. Of course, such indirectness and lack of visibility is not necessarily a virtue.

TABLE 13–1
STATE AND LOCAL GOVERNMENT SALES AND EXCISE TAXES, 1975
(BILLIONS OF DOLLARS)

Total	49.8
General sales and gross receipts	29.1
Selective sales and gross receipts	20.7
Motor fuel	8.3
Alcoholic beverages	2.1
Tobacco products	3.4
Public utilities	3.1
Other	3.9

Source: U.S. Census Bureau, *Governmental Finances, 1974–75.*

TABLE 13–2
ESTIMATED FEDERAL GOVERNMENT EXCISE TAXES, 1977
(MILLIONS OF DOLLARS)

Total	17.8
Alcohol	5.7
Tobacco	2.5
Manufacturers	0.1
Telephone and teletype	1.8
Gasoline	4.3
Other highway-related taxes	2.2
Airport and airway	1.1
Other	0.1

Source: *The Budget of the U.S. Government, Fiscal Year 1977.*

In this chapter we will first define the various forms of sales taxation and then discuss the economic effects of the forms that are commonly used in the United States. Tables 13–1 and 13–2 show revenues from various federal, state, and local sales and excise taxes. In 1975 sales and excise taxes accounted for about 14 percent of the revenues of all governments and 30 percent of the revenue of state governments.

TYPES OF SALES TAXES

Sales taxes differ in basically two ways. One is in the stage (or stages) of the production and distribution process at which they are levied. Several stages are commonly distinguished: retail or final sales, wholesale, and producer or manufacturer.[2]

2 See Carl S. Shoup, *Public Finance* (Chicago: Aldine, 1969), Chaps. 8, 9.

A *retail sales* tax is levied at the final stage. Retail or final sales of goods and services are sales to buyers who will not resell them. In contrast, with a *transaction,* or *turnover,* tax all of the sales revenue generated at every stage at which there is a market transaction is taxed. As with the turnover tax, a *value-added* tax is levied at each stage in the production and distribution process, but only on the value added at that stage. The value-added and retail sales taxes therefore have the same base if they are levied on the sales of the same products; they are alike in that they tax only once the total value represented by the final sale price of a product. The transaction tax base exceeds the bases of the retail sales and value-added taxes because the transactions tax may tax the same increment of value several times.[3]

The second way in which sales taxes differ is in the sales that are subject to (or exempt from) taxation. With a fully general sales tax, no sale of a commodity or service is exempt from taxation. However, in practice, sales taxes are not fully general, with some sales being exempted for a variety of reasons. Final sales of investment goods, such as buildings and machines, are typically exempted from retail sales taxation, making the tax basically one on consumption. Sales of necessities (food, drugs, clothing) are often excluded from retail sales taxation to make the tax bear less heavily on low-income persons. Sales by small businesses are exempted to reduce administration and enforcement costs. Sales of services by professionals (doctors, lawyers) frequently are not taxed. Some taxes, such as the tobacco, gasoline, and alcohol excise taxes, apply only to the sales of a single class of commodities.

Although the sales taxes presently employed in the United States and other countries are seldom exactly alike, they approximate one of the following types: fully general retail sales tax; retail sales tax on consumer goods, excise tax, value-added tax, and transactions tax. In the remainder of this chapter we will examine these taxes in sequence.

GENERAL RETAIL SALES TAX

A proportional tax on the final sales of all products and services, both consumer and investment goods, is equivalent in incidence and allocation effects to a proportional income tax, levied at the same rate. It does not matter whether a tax of a given rate, say 10 percent, is collected as income is received (income tax) or as it is used (sales tax).

This equivalence presumes, of course, that all income received is taxed

---

3 If production and distribution are a single rather than a multistage process, then value-added, retail sales, and transaction taxes have the same bases if they apply to the same set of products. See pp. 302–304 for a more detailed definition of transaction and value-added taxes.

and that all uses of income are also taxed. Such is virtually never the case in practice; sales and income taxes are never fully equivalent. In addition, equivalence requires that the income tax be levied on income gross of (rather than net of) depreciation charges if the sales tax is levied on sales of all investment goods. The reason is that such a sales tax applies to all uses of gross income including income used for replacement of depreciated capital.

RETAIL SALES TAX ON CONSUMER GOODS

Consumer goods are those that are "used up" in the period of purchase — those that quickly lose their value. In contrast, investment goods have value in future periods. Income that is received by a person or family but not spent on consumer goods is said to be saved. Hence, a tax on consumption taxes all uses of income except saving.

The retail sales taxes presently used by state and local governments in the United States approximate consumption taxes, although nonconsumption items are sometimes taxed. Therefore, we can obtain a fairly accurate picture of the economic effects of retail sales taxes by comparing the effects of proportional income and proportional consumption taxes.

SAVING AND INVESTMENT

People save either to increase their own consumption in future periods or to provide their heirs with greater income and wealth. The opportunity cost of such saving is the forgone current consumption. The gain from saving, either in terms of future consumption or bequests, is greater with a proportional consumption tax than with a proportional income tax because the interest income from savings is taxed under the income tax but not under the consumption tax. The consumption tax is even more favorable to saving if future consumption tax rates are expected to be lower than present rates (and vice versa). In the extreme case that a person is saving for perpetual accumulation, taxes on saving are postponed indefinitely under the consumption tax. For these reasons, the consumption tax has a more favorable *substitution* effect on saving than does the income tax; the incentive to save by *substituting* saving for current consumption is greater with consumption than with income taxation.

Consumption and income taxes also differ in their income effects. With total tax revenues the same under the two taxes, the tax rate on consumption must be higher than the tax rate on income because total income is greater than total consumption. As a result, people with relatively high consumption-income ratios pay a higher fraction of their income in taxes under the consumption tax than under the income tax. And, because of this *differential income effect*, such people will tend to save less under consumption than under income taxation. The reverse is true for people with relatively low consumption-income ratios. Most of the people in the former group will be low-income persons, while those in the latter group will be primarily high-income persons. Thus, the income effects of the consumption tax differ from those of the income tax in a manner that favors relatively greater saving by high-income persons and relatively lower saving by low-income persons. But the saving of many low-income persons may be near the feasible minimum, even with the income tax. If so, it cannot be lower still under a consumption tax. Therefore, greater saving by high-income persons under a consumption tax would likely not be offset by lower saving by low-income persons.

In short, the differential income and substitution effects of income and consumption taxation both favor greater saving under the consumption tax. Nevertheless, the fact remains that aggregate private saving does not appear to be responsive to changes in rates of return on saving and the distribution of disposable income.

More importantly, even if sales and income taxes do differ in their effects on aggregate private saving, it does not follow that these effects should be major factors in the choice between the two taxes. One reason is that any deficiency (or excess) of private saving can be offset by appropriate monetary and fiscal policy. Another reason is that there is no obvious and widely acceptable basis for saying that the saving rate under sales taxation is "better" than that under income taxation, or vice versa. That is, private saving and investment decisions may not be optimal in an efficiency sense.

That aggregate saving and investment are necessarily collective decisions is implicit in the fact that greater saving, taken by itself, reduces aggregate demand and thereby reduces output or the rate of price increase or both. Therefore, greater private saving does not automatically mean greater investment. Instead, a higher saving-income ratio makes possible a higher investment-income ratio only if there is a *collective* decision to maintain full employment and price stability with the appropriate mix of monetary and fiscal policies.[4] Only in this case is a consumption tax consistent with a higher investment-income ratio than an equal yield proportional income tax.

---

4 Less restrictive monetary policy must be followed with the consumption tax, while maintaining the same government budget deficit (or surplus). If the same monetary policy is followed under both consumption and income taxation, then the budget deficit (surplus) would have to be greater (lesser) for the consumption tax. The result would be that the higher *private* saving associated with the consumption tax would be offset in part or in full by reduced government saving. Modern governments attempt to manipulate aggregate demand and saving so as to limit unemployment and inflation. In Part Five we deal with this stabilization function of government.

LABOR SUPPLY

A consumption tax is usually regarded as regressive with respect to income. If such is the case, the differential income effects favor greater labor supply by low-income persons under the consumption tax. The reverse is true for higher-income (lower consumption-income ratio) persons. Thus, the differential income effects are in the aggregate ambiguous.

Turning to substitution effects, we cannot show that the return to additional work effort is generally greater under one tax than the other. Under some conditions, labor supply incentives may be greater with the consumption tax, but the reverse is also possible. Table 13–3 summarizes the differential income and substitution effects of proportional income and sales taxes.

PRODUCT MIX AND LOCATION OF ECONOMIC ACTIVITY

A proportional consumption tax provides no incentive for the substitution of one consumer good for another, as is also true for the proportional income tax. However, as we noted above, a consumption tax does provide an incentive to substitute investment goods for consumer goods. In contrast, with the income tax, peoples' tax liabilities are independent of how they spend their incomes.

In practice, sales taxes are virtually never equivalent to a fully general consumption tax; purchases of some commodities and services are exempted from taxation. A sales tax on consumption goods may therefore tend to shift resources into the production of the tax-exempt commodities and away from taxed commodities.

Similarly, sales taxation as practiced in the United States is not geographically uniform. Some states impose a sales tax, while others do not; and those imposing taxes do so at different rates. The resulting incentives are for resources to flow from high-tax to low-tax states. If resources do shift, prices will tend to be relatively higher in states with higher tax rates. And, because of the lower demand for resources in the higher tax states, the incomes of immobile factors will tend to be relatively lower. The movement of resources between states (or localities) is inhibited to some extent by the cost of moving and by the fact that other taxes may be higher if sales taxes are lower. Also affecting resource movements are the services provided by the governments.

DIFFERENTIAL INCIDENCE

If all income is spent on consumer goods, then equal-yield proportional income and consumption taxes have the same incidence. But all income is

TABLE 13-3
DIFFERENTIAL ALLOCATION EFFECTS OF PROPORTIONAL CONSUMPTION AND INCOME TAXES

Population group	Effects on work effort			Effects on saving		
	Income	Substitution	Combined income and substitution	Income	Substitution	Combined income and substitution
High consumption-income ratio — usually low income	Greater effort with consumption tax	?	?	Less saving with consumption tax	Greater saving with consumption tax	?
Low consumption-income ratio — usually high income	Less effort with consumption tax	?	?	Greater saving with consumption tax	Greater saving with consumption tax	Greater saving with consumption tax
All persons	?	?	?	Probably greater saving with consumption tax	Greater saving with consumption tax	Probably greater saving with consumption tax

not spent; some of it is saved. And high-income persons typically save a larger share of their income than do low-income persons. Consequently, both consumption and consumption taxes are typically a higher fraction of income for low-income than high-income persons. That is, while the incidence of the income tax is proportional to income, the incidence of the consumption tax is not. Instead, when compared to the income tax, the fully general consumption tax bears more heavily on low-income persons and less heavily on high-income persons.

We have noted that the supply of saving may be greater under the consumption than under the income tax. If so, a consumption tax leads to a higher ratio of investment to national income and a higher capital-labor ratio.[5] A higher capital-labor ratio means, in turn, that each worker works with more "tools" and receives a higher wage rate. It is thus possible that higher wage rates and money incomes may offset fully or in part the higher tax payments that low-income people (workers) make under the consumption tax. However, such people will necessarily be worse off with a consumption tax than with an income tax during those periods in which the capital that provides the higher wages is being accumulated. That is, all low-income workers in all periods cannot be better off (in terms of tax burden) with a consumption tax than with an income tax, although beyond some point in the future, workers may be better off.

The conclusion that the consumption tax is regressive requires another partial qualification. The regressiveness conclusion is usually supported with evidence that in any given year the consumption-income ratios of low-income households exceed those of high-income households. But when household consumption-income ratios are computed for longer periods (more than one year), the variation in the ratios is reduced. Indeed, for many families the *lifetime* consumption-income ratio approaches 1 — they consume all of their income. If this were true for all families then a proportional consumption tax would be proportional to lifetime income and, from this long-run perspective, would not be regressive.

As a matter of fact, lifetime consumption-income ratios do not appear to be significantly higher for low-income than for high-income persons. That is, lifetime consumption appears to be roughly the same proportion of lifetime income for all income classes. Proportional consumption and income taxes are approximately equivalent if a person's lifetime is taken as the appropriate period for evaluating the distributional effects of taxation. The two taxes are not strictly equivalent even under these conditions — the consumption tax will be relatively less burdensome than the income tax to those

---

5 That statement assumes that a higher saving-income ratio results in a higher investment-income ratio rather than in unemployment. That is, resources are assumed to be fully employed under either tax.

TABLE 13–4
EFFECTIVE RATES OF FEDERAL, STATE, AND LOCAL SALES AND EXCISE
TAXES, 1966

Adjusted family income ($ thousand)[a]	Effective rate of sales and excise taxation (percent)[b]
Less than 3	9.4
3–5	7.4
5–10	6.5
10–15	5.8
15–20	5.2
20–25	4.6
25–30	4.0
30–50	3.4
50–100	2.4
100–500	1.5
500–1,000	1.1
1,000 and over	1.0
All classes	5.1

a Adjusted family income is defined in Chapter 11, p. 256.

b The effective tax rate is the ratio of sales and excise taxes to income.

Source: Joseph A. Pechman and Benjamin A. Okner, *Who Bears the Tax Burden?* (Washington: Brookings, 1974), p. 59. © 1974 by the Brookings Institution, Washington, D.C.

who consume relatively more in the later years of their lives, while the income tax will be relatively less burdensome to those who consume relatively more in the early years of their lives.

In the discussion of differential incidence, we assumed that all income is included in the income tax base and that all consumption expenditures are taxed. In practice, taxes are never perfect. Unreported income and income in the form of bequests, gifts, and capital gains is either not taxed or only lightly taxed under existing U.S. income taxes. But the use of such income would be taxed with sales taxes. In contrast, income subject to income taxation would escape taxation under sales taxes if it is used to purchase tax-exempt goods and services. Thus, actual consumption or sales taxes may or may not be less progressive than actual income taxes. Table 13–4 presents estimates of the incidence of federal, state, and local excise and sales taxes that show such taxes to be regressive.

IMPROVING THE RETAIL SALES TAX

Proposals and policies to improve the sales tax, primarily to lessen its regressiveness, take several forms.

Sales tax rebate   The regressiveness of the retail sales tax can be reduced by giving a sales tax rebate to low-income persons, a mechanism used by a few states.[6] The rebate is a payment to each family or family member, which may decline in amount and even vanish as family income increases. In states that have an income tax, the rebate can be in the form of a tax credit — a reduction in income tax liabilities. If a person owes no income tax, or if the credit exceeds the income tax due, a cash rebate can be given equal to the difference between the credit and tax due. In states that have no income tax, a cash payment can be made to eligible families.[7]

Exemptions   Another means of reducing the regressiveness of the sales tax is exempting items that account for a large proportion of the expenditures of low-income persons. Thus, food expenditures are frequently exempted from sales taxation. Some states also exempt medicines and drugs, but this exemption is less directly aimed at aiding low-income persons.

As a means of reducing the burden of sales taxation on the poor, the rebate seems superior to exempting specified purchases. Exemption means greater revenue loss and higher tax rates because it applies to the purchases of both the poor and the rich, while only the poor need receive a rebate. With exemptions there are also problems in defining exempt items; for example, what constitutes food? Meals purchased in a restaurant? Candy? The rebate can also be structured to relieve all of the sales tax burden on the poor (if this is desirable), while food and other exemptions remove only part of the burden. For the rebate to be effective, all of the poor must file returns and receive a rebate, and this may require higher administrative costs. Exemptions also involve administrative and compliance costs because retailers such as grocers must separate sales into taxable and nontaxable categories.

Expenditure tax   An alternative to the sales tax is a personal expenditure tax, which has been tried in a limited way in Ceylon and India.[8] Under such a tax, people file returns, just as returns are filed under the income tax. The tax base is consumption expenditures, defined as "the difference between a family's income and the increase in net wealth during the year." A specified amount of consumption expenditures (based on the number of

6 Iowa experimented with and abandoned the tax credit. States using it include Colorado, Indiana, Nebraska, Hawaii, New Mexico, Vermont, and Massachusetts.

7 See James A. Papke and Timothy G. Shahen, "Optimal Consumption-Based Taxes: The Equity Effects of Tax Credits," *National Tax Journal*, 25 (September 1972): 479–487.

8 The expenditure tax is analyzed extensively in Nicholas Kaldor, *An Expenditure Tax*, 4th impression (London: Unwin University Books, 1965). See also Patrick L. Kelley, "Is An Expenditure Tax Feasible?" *National Tax Journal*, 23 (September 1970): 237–253.

TABLE 13-5

ILLUSTRATIVE CALCULATION OF TAXABLE EXPENDITURES FOR AN EXPENDITURE TAX

	Beginning of year	End of year
Total value of assets	$20,000	$21,000
Total liabilities	15,000	15,500
Net worth	$ 5,000	$ 5,500
Income for year (including capital gains, gifts, bequests, and imputed rent of owner-occupied housing)	$18,000	
Minus: change in net worth	500	
Equals: gross taxable expenditures[a]	$17,500	

a Expenditure taxes may, but they need not, provide for deducting other expenditures and allowances in computing "net" taxable expenditures. For example, expenditures on food and medicines might be exempted or a per-person basic deduction might be allowed.

persons in the family) or specified classes of expenditures can be exempt; and the tax can be proportional or progressive. Compared to a sales tax, the expenditure tax can be tailored more precisely to a taxpayer's economic circumstances. Table 13-5 shows how expenditures are calculated.

Although an expenditure tax may be preferable to a sales tax on equity grounds, it poses some conceptual and administrative problems. Tax returns have to show not only a person's income but also the change in his or her net wealth during the year; thus, the expenditure tax entails all the problems encountered in defining and reporting income. In addition, taxpayers have to keep account of and report changes in their assets and liabilities during the year, information which is available from the records people normally keep. The expenditure tax requires more recordkeeping than a sales tax but not a great deal more than an income tax. The number of taxpaying units is greater with an expenditure tax than with a sales tax, and the tax returns are more complicated. There is also the problem of distinguishing between consumption expenditures and investments, which is part of the general problem of measuring net wealth.

EXCISE TAXES

Excise taxes are levied on sales of a particular commodity or commodity group. Examples of excise taxes presently in use in the United States are those on the sales of gasoline, cigarettes, alcohol, and automobile tires. The tax may be a percentage of the selling price (*ad valorem*) or a fixed amount per unit of output.

ECONOMIC EFFECTS

Excise taxes tend to divert production from the taxed to the untaxed commodities, and they may therefore alter the mix of final products. In addition, if tax rates vary geographically, the location of either or both production and sales may be affected. However, since excise taxes usually are
levied on small sectors of the total economy, they have little effect on factor
returns and factor (labor, capital) supplies.

The burden of an excise tax falls on either the consumers of the taxed
products or the resources specialized to their production or both. The incidence and allocation effects of an excise tax depend on demand and supply
conditions for the product being taxed, as we now show more explicitly.

Suppose that an excise tax is levied on the sales of a product, X, that is
produced and sold competitively, with the tax being a fixed amount for each
unit sold. In Figure 13–1, the S schedule shows the marginal cost of producing commodity X in the absence of a tax. With the demand schedule D,
market equilibrium is at a price of p and output of q. With a tax of t per
unit, the marginal cost increases by t, and the marginal cost (supply) schedule shifts to S'. The tax causes equilibrium price to rise to p' and the equilibrium quantity to fall to q'. Some resources shift from the production of X
into the production of other goods as consumers shift expenditures. And the
price of X increases relative to the price of other goods.

The burden of the tax falls partly on consumers of X and partly on owners
of factors used to produce X. The price paid by the buyers, p', differs from
the price received by the sellers, p'', by the amount of the tax, which is also
the vertical distance between S' and S. The total revenue collected by government is $(p'-p'')q'$, or area $a+b+d+e$. Of that amount, consumers
bear a burden in higher prices equal to areas $a+b$ and suppliers bear a burden in reduced incomes equal to areas $d+e$. The total burden on consumers, their loss in consumer surplus, is area $a+b+c$, while the total burden on producers is their loss in producer surplus, area $d+e+f$. Thus,
producers and consumers lose more than government gains in revenue; the
amount of this *excess burden* is area $c+f$. The loss in producer surplus is
borne by the owners of the resources specialized to the production of X
because those resources have lower productivities and incomes in alternative
employments.

The extent to which the excise tax causes the price of X to rise (relative to
other prices) and resources to move out of the taxed industry depends on the
elasticities of the demand and supply schedules, elasticities that will vary by
type of commodity. At one extreme, demand may be perfectly inelastic —
the D curve may be vertical. If so, the price of the taxed good increases by
the amount of the tax, t, and no resources shift out of the production of X.
The tax burden falls entirely on consumers; the loss of consumer surplus

FIGURE 13–1
SHIFTING OF AN EXCISE TAX

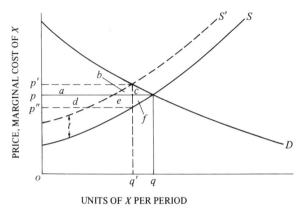

UNITS OF X PER PERIOD

exactly equals government's revenue gain — there is no excess burden. At another extreme, the supply may be perfectly inelastic, in which case the S curve is vertical and does not shift when the tax is levied. In this case, neither the quantity supplied nor the price paid by consumers changes. But the price received by the sellers changes by the full amount of the tax. The burden is fully borne by producers, and the loss in producer surplus exactly equals the gain in government revenue. Again, there is no excess burden.

As we move away from these extremes, the outcome changes. As demand elasticity increases (as the demand curve becomes less steeply sloped), the increase in consumer price is relatively smaller, and the reduction in output is relatively greater. As supply elasticity increases (as the supply curve becomes less steeply sloped), the increase in consumer price is relatively greater, and the decrease in output is relatively greater. Table 13–6 summarizes the various possibilities.

EVALUATION OF EXCISE TAXATION

Excise taxes are used for several purposes other than raising revenue. Judgments about the desirability of the distribution and allocation effects of excise taxes will often depend on the perceived purpose of the taxes.

Revenue source   One possible use of excise taxation is to raise general revenues. If the taxed items are consumed by high-income persons, tax burdens may be distributed progressively and in rough correspondence to ability to pay. But excise taxes on necessities distribute tax burdens regressively. So,

TABLE 13–6
EXCISE TAX EFFECTS UNDER DIFFERENT DEMAND-SUPPLY CONDITIONS

Demand and supply conditions	Effects of tax			
	Consumer price increase	Decrease in price received by producer	Decrease in output	Excess burden
Perfectly inelastic demand; supply not perfectly inelastic	Equals the amount of the tax	No	No	No
Perfectly inelastic supply; demand not perfectly inelastic	No	Equals the amount of the tax	No	No
Perfectly elastic supply; demand neither perfectly elastic nor perfectly inelastic	Equals the amount of the tax	No	Yes	Yes
Perfectly elastic demand; supply neither perfectly elastic nor perfectly inelastic	No	Equals the amount of the tax	Yes	Yes
Both supply and demand are neither perfectly elastic nor perfectly inelastic	Less than the amount of the tax	Less than the amount of the tax	Yes	Yes

excise taxes may or may not be vertically equitable, depending on what is the desired degree of progressiveness and on the type of commodities that are taxed. Whether or not they are vertically equitable, excise taxes are almost surely horizontally inequitable. Persons with the same incomes may have different consumption patterns and therefore may pay different amounts of taxes.

The conclusions that, as a general revenue measure, the excise tax may be regressive or progressive, and that the tax may be horizontally inequitable, implicitly assume that the full burden of the tax is on consumers. We have seen, however, that income recipients may bear part of the burden; therefore, to reach any firm conclusion about equity we would have to know the full incidence of the tax. It seems doubtful, however, that the burdens on income recipients, considered alone or in conjunction with consumer burdens, are equitably distributed.

As revenue measures, excise taxes may or may not involve large excess burdens, depending on demand and supply conditions (see Table 13–6). Therefore, they may or may not be superior on efficiency grounds to broad-based income and consumption taxes.

Regulation A second possible use of excise taxation is to regulate or direct consumption and production. It may be desirable for either efficiency or equity reasons to restrict the consumption of certain goods by imposing selective taxes. For example, excise taxes can be used to contract the production of goods that generate external costs, such as pollution. We discussed this approach to pollution control in Chapter 5. Taxes on the consumption of liquor may be similarly justified, since alcoholism generates external costs in the form of automobile accidents, broken families, etc. The more effective the tax is in curtailing the activity the less effective it is in generating revenue.

An excise tax greatly curtails the output of products for which demand is highly elastic, but it generates little revenue in the process. In contrast, excise taxes do not greatly affect the consumption and production of commodities for which the demand is highly inelastic. The revenues raised by taxes on externality-generating commodities can be used to finance corrections for the external cost. For example, the tax on alcoholic beverages can be used for programs to educate and reform drinking drivers or for the treatment of alcoholism.

Regulatory excises may also be levied for sumptuary reasons. That is, the taxes may be used to discourage what is judged by some members of society to be morally wrong consumption. This is sometimes given as the justification for taxes on alcoholic beverages and cigarettes, although more recently justification has been in terms of external costs. Such taxes are highly regressive and of limited effectiveness in curtailing consumption.

User charges Some excise taxes are thought to approximate a user charge. For example, taxes on motor vehicles and motor vehicle fuel approximate a user charge for highway services in that one pays the taxes only if one uses the services of a highway. These taxes are usually earmarked for highway finance. In contrast, payments of income or cigarette taxes are not a function of one's use of particular government services.

When a tax is a user charge, its distributional effects must be judged accordingly. For example, the gasoline tax is regressive in its incidence because gasoline purchases and taxes represent a larger fraction of income for low-income than for high-income people. However, if the gasoline tax is a user charge, this regressiveness is no more unfair than is the requirement that persons pay for their food. This latter requirement imposes a burden on people that is regressive, since lower income persons spend a larger share of their income on food than higher income persons. Similarly, taxes that approximate user charges need not entail allocation inefficiency, even though they may keep the taxed activity (for example, automobile travel) below the level that would prevail in the absence of the tax. Indeed, the tax may promote efficiency by forcing people to take account of the costs, including the costs of publicly provided services such as highways, that their production and consumption activities generate.

Of course, any real-world tax is unlikely to be a fully satisfactory user charge, as fuel taxes clearly illustrate. In Chapter 3 we saw that efficiency usually requires that the price of (user charge for) a good equal its marginal social cost. Present fuel and vehicle taxes do not meet this condition for several reasons. First, motor vehicles impose external costs on society in the form of air pollution. User charges should be great enough to cover (internalize) these costs. However, it is questionable whether fuel taxes are great enough in many circumstances to cover the marginal direct and external costs of highway use. Also, marginal pollution costs vary with both the time and place of driving; but fixed per-gallon or per-vehicle taxes make no allowance for such variation. Similarly, fuel taxes do not vary with traffic volume and, therefore, do not allow for congestion costs, which arise because congestion increases the marginal social cost of using the highways as it increases travel time and risks.[9] Third, some vehicles generate higher marginal costs than others. But a uniform fuel tax reflects this differential only if there is a one-to-one correspondence between costs generated and fuel consumed. Fourth, there is no assurance with the present system that the fuel taxes will be used to support the highways that are actually used.

OTHER SALES TAXES

Rather than being levied at the retail level, a sales tax can be levied at the manufacturer level, at the wholesale level, or at all levels of sales (transaction and value-added taxes).[10]

Taxes levied at the manufacturer or wholesale levels are usually less general than a retail sales tax. With taxes imposed at the manufacturer level, some sales go untaxed, depending upon how manufacturing is defined. (Is farming manufacturing? The services of a lawyer? Airline travel?) Excise taxes levied at the manufacturer level have an advantage over retail excise taxes because there are fewer points of collection and fewer administrative costs. For example, a tax on television sets might be levied on the manufacturer rather than on the retail outlet.

Both the wholesale and transaction taxes encourage vertical integration of businesses. To escape the wholesale tax, firms may attempt to sell directly at

---

9 Fuel taxes could be supplemented with another pricing system, such as tolls, that could be adjusted upward and downward with the volume of traffic flows.

10 For an analysis of various forms of sales taxes see John F. Due, *Sales Taxation* (Urbana: University of Illinois Press, 1957).

TABLE 13–7
ILLUSTRATION OF RELATION BETWEEN VALUE-ADDED, RETAIL SALES, AND TRANSACTION TAX BASES

Firm A		
Gross receipts from sales		$12,000,000
To households	$10,000,000	
To firm B of intermediate and capital goods	2,000,000	
Firm B		
Gross receipts from sales		$15,000,000
To households	$12,000,000	
To firm A of intermediate and capital goods	3,000,000	

retail. A transaction tax encourages firms to merge their operations rather than sell to each other and pay a tax. Both adjustments may lead to a greater concentration of economic power than would prevail with a retail sales tax. In addition, the effect of a transaction tax on relative prices depends on how many stages of sales a product passes through. Tax-induced price increases tend to be greater for goods that pass through many stages (transactions) than for goods that pass through few. Resources may be reallocated in response to the price changes, perhaps, if not probably, in a pattern that is less efficient than would be the case under retail sales taxation.

The base of a value-added tax[11] can be the same as the base of a general retail sales tax on consumer goods if value added is defined as gross receipts minus purchases from other firms and minus capital expenditures. This is known as the consumption type of value-added tax. Table 13–7 shows the identity of the tax bases; it assumes that each of the two firms in the economy illustrated sells its goods to households (consumption) and to the other firm. The goods that the firms sell to each other are intermediate goods and capital goods. With a retail sales tax on consumer goods, the tax base would be $22 million of sales to households ($10 million by firm A; $12 million by firm B). With a consumption-type value added tax, firm A would be taxed on value added of $9 million (receipts minus intermediate and capital goods purchases) and firm B would be taxed on $13 million. The value-added tax bases of the two firms sum to $22 million, which is also the retail sales tax base. The transactions, or turnover, tax base would be $27 million — the full amount of the sales by both firms.

11 Value-added taxation is used in most European countries and some developing countries. In the United States the tax has been proposed as a substitute for the federal corporation income tax, as an additional revenue source, as a source of federal revenue to reduce local property taxes, and as a business tax at the state level.

Two other types of value-added taxes are possible. One is the GNP type, in which case the tax base is gross receipts minus intermediate purchases only. The base is total final sales without regard for whether the products sold are consumer or investment goods. The other is the income type, in which case the tax base is gross receipts minus depreciation and purchases of intermediate goods.

For state governments in a federal system, a retail sales tax may be less complicated to administer than a value-added tax. Since goods sold at retail in a state often have value-added by firms outside the state, value-added must be allocated among states, which entails administration and compliance costs. The federal government does not have this problem. But a consumption type of value-added tax at the national level does have more points of collection (all stages of production) and more costs of administration and compliance than a retail sales tax (from only retail outlets). In addition, with a national retail sales tax, states and localities can integrate their retail sales taxes with the national one by using the national sales tax base and adding their own levy to the national tax levy. Such integration would likely reduce collection administration costs.

SUMMARY

The major forms of sales taxation in the United States are excise taxes and retail sales taxes. An excise tax may be used to correct for external costs, but as a revenue-raising device it treats equals unequally. And it may be regressive, depending on which sales are taxed and how the tax is shifted. Excise taxes may approximate user charges, to a greater or lesser degree.

The retail sales tax is relatively easy to administer, and it provides state and local governments with a revenue source that does not compete with the revenue sources of the federal government. It favors saving and is regressive relative to current income. This regressiveness can be reduced by broadening the tax base to include the sale of all services, many of which are presently exempt, and providing tax rebates to low-income persons.

A consumption based tax, such as the retail sales tax, is usually regarded as inequitable because it is regressive with respect to current income. But an alternative view is that people should be taxed according to what they consume of the national output. If this view is accepted and the sales tax is fully general, then it is vertically and horizontally equitable.

In fact, sales and income taxes are virtually never truly general. Therefore, theoretical arguments cannot establish that one tax would in practice be superior to the other on equity grounds. More specifically, a state sales tax with concessions to low-income groups may compare favorably to present state income taxes that typically reproduce the inequities of the federal income tax.

SUPPLEMENTARY READINGS

Due, John F. *State and Local Sales Taxation.* Chicago: Public Administration Service, 1971.

Kaldor, Nicholas. *An Expenditure Tax.* 4th Impression. London: Unwin University Books, 1965.

Shoup, Carl S. *Public Finance,* chaps. 8–10. Chicago: Aldine, 1969.

Sullivan, Clara. *The Tax on Value Added.* New York: Columbia University Press, 1965.

CHAPTER FOURTEEN

PROPERTY TAXATION

Wealth taxes are based on a person's wealth — the person's ownership of (claims on) real and financial assets. In the United States, the property tax is the main form of wealth taxation and the major local government tax. Other governments (federal and state) collect virtually no property taxes. In 1975, property taxes accounted for 82 percent of local government tax revenues; and 35 percent of local government general spending was financed with property taxes. Current debate about the incidence and economic effects of property taxation is lively, reflecting both the quantitative importance of the tax and the uncertainty about its effects.[1] In this chapter we will examine property taxation after a brief digression on the definition of wealth. In the next chapter we will look at other taxes on wealth and at wealth transfers.

WHAT IS WEALTH?

The real wealth of a nation is the value of the capital goods available for use by its citizens. These capital goods include machinery, buildings, inventories, land, human capital (skills), and natural resources. They have economic value because they can be used to produce goods and services in current or future periods or both. The value of this prospective flow of goods and services (income) determines the value of the capital good (asset) that generates it.[2]

1 Several publications discuss these issues thoroughly: George E. Peterson, ed., *Property Tax Reform* (Washington: Urban Institute, 1973); Henry J. Aaron, *Who Pays the Property Tax?* (Washington: Brookings, 1975); and Dick Netzer, *Economics of the Property Tax* (Washington: Brookings, 1966).

2 In a world of perfect certainty and perfect markets, the value of a real capital good will be the present value of the net income stream that it generates. For example, a capital good that is expected to yield $1,000 net income per year forever will have a value of $20,000 if the market

Real assets differ from *financial* assets, examples of which are common stocks and bonds issued by corporations, titles to property, and bonds and other evidences of debt issued by individual and government borrowers. Financial assets are claims on real assets and the income flows they generate. One person's financial asset is often another person's financial liability.[3] The distribution of financial assets tells us who owns the real assets of the nation. But, the value of these financial assets is not properly added to the value of real assets to obtain the nation's total wealth, since the nation's real wealth would remain even if all financial assets were to disappear.

In some cases, there is no explicit claim to real assets; that is, ownership rights are not established. Government "owns" a substantial part of the nation's wealth: parks, roads, courthouses, air force bases, etc.[4] Ownership rights to air and water are frequently not established. In other cases, the market does not operate to capitalize income streams generated by the asset because of institutional constraints or market imperfections. For example, the value of human capital can be estimated; but there is no market for human capital because human beings, unlike machinery and buildings, are not bought and sold on the basis of capital values.

A person's *net* wealth is the value of all of his or her assets, real and financial, minus the value of his or her liabilities. A person's net wealth usually differs from the value of the real assets (property) of which he or she is the legal owner. Hence, the tax bases of the net wealth and the real property taxes are distributed differently among persons. For example, suppose Mr. Perez buys a farm for $200,000 with $50,000 of his own money and $150,000 obtained as a loan from Mr. Archer. Both Archer and Perez have claims to the real asset, the farm. Ownership of the farm shows up as only $50,000 in net wealth for Perez; the remainder of the farm's value is part of Archer's net wealth. With a net wealth tax, Perez is taxed on $50,000 and Archer on $150,000. With a real property tax, Perez is taxed on $200,000 and Archer is not taxed. Moreover, if both taxes are employed, the value of the same real asset, the farm, is taxed twice.

PROPERTY TAX BASE

Property taxes are levied, usually at proportional rates, on the *assessed* value of taxable property. Although practice varies among states, taxable property

---

rate of return on investment is 5 percent ($20,000 = $1000/.05). In the case of owner-occupied housing, the flow of income is imputed (see Chapter 11, p. 237).

3 For example, if Mr. Perez obtains a mortgage from a bank to buy a house, the mortgage is an asset for the bank but a liability for Perez.

4 This real wealth of government is not a part of *privately* owned wealth, but government debt is a component of private net wealth.

TABLE 14–1
SOURCE OF PROPERTY TAX REVENUES BY TYPE OF PROPERTY TAX BASE,
U.S., 1972

	Amount (millions of dollars)	Percent of all property tax revenue
Nonbusiness		
Nonfarm residential realty	19,023	47.3
Farm realty	817	2.0
Vacant lots	320	0.8
Personalty	770	1.9
Total	20,930	52.1
Business		
Farm realty	1,860	4.6
Vacant lots	480	1.2
Other realty	9,170	22.8
Personalty	4,741	11.8
Public utilities	3,091	7.7
Total	19,270	47.9
Total	40,200	100.0

Source: Advisory Commission on Intergovernmental Relations, *Federal, State, Local Finances: Significant Features of Fiscal Federalism, 1973–74* (Washington: U.S. Government Printing Office, 1974).

is largely tangible real property: land, buildings, and structures. Personal property (household goods, machinery, automobiles) and intangible property (cash, stocks, bonds) usually are not included in the property tax base. And, when taxed, these forms of property are mobile and easily concealed, giving rise to evasion and high collection and enforcement costs. Table 14–1 shows the composition of the aggregate property tax base for 1972.

EXEMPTIONS

Property owned by federal and state governments and charitable, religious, and nonprofit organizations is usually exempted from local property taxation. The rationale for exempting government-owned properties is that one government should not tax another. The exemption of other property is usually viewed as a means of supporting the "socially worthwhile" activities of the property owning organizations (churches, educational institutions, hospitals, charities, etc.). It is also seen as a means of preventing government interference in religious activity. Some people question whether these activities should be favored by property tax exemptions.[5] And, even if it is

5 See Alfred Balk, *The Free List: Property Without Taxes* (New York: Russell Sage, 1971).

concluded that some support is justified, property tax exemptions may not be the best form of support. One alternative is direct subsidy of the activities that are judged to be socially beneficial. Compared to the hidden subsidies of property tax exemptions, visible direct subsidies permit more informed decisions about the subsidy of the activities in question. On the other hand, direct subsidy entails decision-making costs (How much aid for each organization?) and a greater government role in those areas where tax-exempt organizations are presently active. As another alternative to full exemption, organizations owning exempt property can pay charges and fees in lieu of property taxes for the services that they receive from government. This practice is becoming more common, but the fees and charges are usually less than the property taxes that the organization would pay.[6]

ASSESSMENT

Once it is decided which property is to be taxed, the value of the property must be assessed. The assessed value is usually defined as a fraction of market value. Property is rarely assessed at its full market value. Nationally, the assessed value averages about 30 percent of market value.

Market value may be estimated directly from the selling price of the property that has recently been sold. When a recent selling price is not available, selling prices of similar properties are used for assessment. For classes of property that sell very infrequently — industrial and commercial properties — other assessment techniques are used. Specifically, market value may be estimated by the replacement cost of the property or by capitalizing its income stream. With perfect capital markets, the market value of each property would equal the capitalized value of the income stream generated when the property is used as productively as possible. In practice, market value is often estimated by capitalizing the income flow associated with the property's current use. So property that is not in its most productive use, for example, idle land in an urban area, tends to be assessed at less than its market value. Observed selling prices tend to reflect the values of properties in their most productive uses.

Underassessment, which occurs when assessed values are less than market values, would not matter if all properties were underassessed by the same proportion. A lower assessed value would simply require a higher tax rate to raise a given revenue. But such is not the case in practice. Commercial and industrial properties tend to be assessed at lower fractions of market value

6 The federal government gives aid to local governments in "impacted" areas — where federal installations (military bases, offices) and their employees generate costs for local governments. This aid can be thought of as being in lieu of the payment of taxes on federal property.

than residential properties. Hence, the "effective" tax rate tends to be greater for the latter than the former.[7] Also, assessed value is commonly used as a measure of the fiscal capacity, or the relative wealth of a community, with some kinds of state aid being inversely related to fiscal capacity (assessed value). Thus, communities have an incentive to underassess their property more than other communities to qualify for more aid. Some states have tried to prevent this practice by requiring local governments to assess property at a uniform fraction of market value.[8]

TAX BASE VARIATION

The per capita value of taxable property varies substantially among communities. One primary reason for this variation is the uneven distribution of agricultural, commercial, and industrial property among communities. This variation in the fiscal capacities of local governments gives rise to nonuniformity of public service levels and effective tax rates, which may, in turn, affect location decisions and the equity with which the costs and benefits of government are distributed geographically. We say more about these effects in Chapters 20–22.

TAX RATES

For each tax district (county, city, school district), the tax rate is determined as the ratio of funds needed to total assessed property value. For example, if a tax district must obtain $1 million from the property tax to finance its chosen level of spending and if the assessed value of property within the government's jurisdiction is $50 million, then the tax rate is 2 percent on the assessed value of each tax payer's property. The tax payer's overall tax rate is the sum of tax rates levied by the various tax districts. In some cases, a maximum property tax rate is imposed on specific taxing districts by the state legislature or by vote of the citizens.

INCIDENCE: WHO PAYS THE PROPERTY TAX?

Before trying to determine who bears the burden of property taxes, let us first ask who might bear them. The taxes are levied upon and payable by the legal owners of property; the impact is upon property owners. And, unless the taxes can be shifted, the incidence is likewise upon owners. If shifted,

---

7 The effective tax rate is the ratio of the tax payment to the market value of the property.

8 For further discussion of the reasons for and consequences of underassessment, see Aaron, *Who Pays the Property Tax?*, chap. 4 and the studies cited there.

the burden may fall on the owners of other factors of production or on the consumers of products that require the services of property in their production.

Whether property taxes are borne by property owners or are shifted partially or fully to other persons is one of the more difficult and important questions in public finance. If the taxes are not shifted, then they are progressive with respect to current income because both property ownership and property income are concentrated in the higher income classes.[9] If the taxes are shifted to consumers, they are regressive with respect to current income because lower-income persons spend a relatively high proportion of their income on consumption. Thus, judgments about the equity of property taxation and the need for property tax reform depend largely on the incidence of such taxes. Until rather recently, studies of property tax incidence have concluded that the taxes on businesses and rented residential property are shifted to consumers and tenants, making the overall burden of property taxes regressive.[10] But this view is coming under increasing criticism.[11]

SHIFTING POSSIBILITIES

The impact of the property tax is on property owners. The tax will be shifted from property owners if the tax reduces the total supply of capital or causes individuals to change the use or location of capital.

Inelastic supply If the total supply of property is perfectly inelastic (fixed) and the tax is levied at a uniform effective rate, then the tax can not be shifted; its burden is on property owners.[12] When the tax is general, the same

---

9 See M. Mason Gaffney, "The Property Tax is a Progressive Tax," in *Proceedings of the Sixty Fourth Annual Conference on Taxation* (Columbus: National Tax Association, 1972). Also, if property taxes are capitalized, both current and anticipated future property taxes may be borne by those who own property at the time the property taxes are levied. We discuss tax capitalization on pp. 314–315.

10 See Dick Netzer, *Economics of the Property Tax* (Washington: Brookings, 1966); and idem, "The Incidence of the Property Tax Revisited," *National Tax Journal*, 26, No. 4 (December 1973): 515–536.

11 See Peter Mieszkowski, "The Property Tax: An Excise Tax or a Profits Tax?" *Journal of Public Economics*, 1 (April 1972). For an excellent survey of these and other studies, as well as a thorough discussion of the issues involved in property tax incidence, see George F. Break, "The Incidence and Economic Effects of Taxation" in *The Economics of Public Finance*, ed. Alan S. Blinder, George F. Break, Peter O. Steiner and Dick Netzer (Washington: Brookings, 1975).

12 That statement assumes that property owners are maximizing their money incomes at the time the tax is imposed. We discuss exceptions to this case on p. 314.

rate applies to all property in all uses, and owners cannot reduce their tax liabilities by changing property from one use or location to another. A fixed total supply means that owners either cannot or choose not to increase their before-tax returns on property by reducing its supply and making it more scarce relative to other factors of production. Under these conditions, property owners either cannot or do not take any action to reduce their tax liabilities or to offset the tax's effects on their disposable incomes.

If the tax is not fully general, as is surely the case, then some shifting can occur, even if the total supply of property is fixed. Shifting occurs if property owners can and do change property from high-tax to low-tax uses or locations or both. For such shifting to occur, property has to be "mobile" between uses and locations. For example, suppose that neighboring communities impose different effective tax rates on real property — 5 percent in community A and 10 percent in community B. Taken by itself, the difference in taxation gives property owners an incentive to relocate their property from community B to community A. Whether relocation occurs depends on how (1) the communities compare in other respects than taxation, such as provision of public services to property owners; and (2) difficult (costly) it is to relocate property. Some types of property cannot be relocated even in the long run — land, mineral deposits. But, in the long run, reproducible property, such as buildings, machinery, and inventories, can be relocated. If such relocation occurs, the supply of reproducible capital (property) in community B is reduced relative to that in A. This adjustment reduces the after-tax return to reproducible capital in community A and increases it in community B. So some of the burden of B's higher tax is borne by owners of the reproducible property located in A. Indeed, if reproducible property is sufficiently mobile, as it is in the long run, it tends to earn the same after-tax return in both communities. *That is, tax rate differentials do not lead to differential burdens for fully mobile factors.*

Movement of reproducible capital also reduces the capital-labor and capital-land ratios in B while increasing them in A, the result being higher incomes for immobile land and labor in community A and lower incomes for these factors in community B. Finally, the movement of capital may affect prices and therefore affect real income and tax burdens in a way that depends on how income is used rather than on how it is earned. Prices tend to increase in the capital-losing (high-tax) community and fall in the capital-receiving (low-tax) community.

Whether capital moves among locations or uses in response to property taxes depends on how tax revenues are used. Capital does not necessarily migrate to the location that taxes least. Instead, property location is also influenced by the supply of public services. Property owners may choose to locate their property in higher tax areas if the higher taxes make possible a greater supply of public services (roads, schools, police and fire protection).

Also, how the tax levied by a particular community affects the location of capital in that community depends on the taxes levied on other communities. For example, suppose community A levies a 2 percent tax on reproducible capital and all other communities do likewise. In this case, A's tax provides no incentive for capital to locate elsewhere because capital is similarly taxed no matter where it locates. However, if A is the only community levying a tax, there is a clear incentive for capital to locate elsewhere.[13]

Elastic supply   If the total supply of property is not perfectly inelastic, then burdens may be shifted even if tax rates are uniform. Such shifting occurs when the supply of reproducible property (capital) is decreased in response to higher taxes. Such a decrease means, in turn, lower capital-labor and capital-land ratios and lower total output (because fewer resources are available to produce goods and services). Thus, in the case of elastic property supply, property taxes may entail burdens (lower real disposable incomes) for people as consumers and as suppliers of labor and land.[14] Shifting possibilities under both elastic and inelastic capital supply are summarized in Table 14–2.

TABLE 14–2
SUMMARY OF SHIFTING POSSIBILITIES[a]

Form of property tax	Aggregate supply of reproducible capital is inelastic		Aggregate supply of reproducible capital is elastic	
	Capital is not mobile	Capital is mobile	Capital is not mobile	Capital is mobile
Effective rates are uniform across uses and locations	No shifting	No shifting	Shifting is possible	Shifting is possible
Effective rates are not uniform	No shifting	Shifting of differentials is possible	Shifting is possible	Shifting is possible

a When shifting is possible, it may be either partial or complete, depending on the demand and supply elasticities.

The conclusions in the table assume that property tax differentials are not accompanied by commensurate differentials in government provision of services to property owners.

13 See Aaron, *Who Pay the Property Tax?*, pp. 38 ff., for further discussion.

14 Recall that lower capital-land and capital-labor ratios mean lower rents and lower wages, respectively. Lower output means that some or all persons must have fewer goods and services available for their consumption, so they lose as consumers.

Short-run versus long-run shifting   Shifting requires adjustments in the stock of reproducible capital and its distribution among locations and uses. Since capital stock adjustments take time, the "short-run" incidence of property taxes must be on property owners. In some cases, the short-run adjustment period may be fairly long, as when a decrease in the existing stock of capital is required, which occurs only as capital depreciates. In other cases, the adjustments may occur quickly, as when an area is growing rapidly so that adjustment entails only an increase or decrease in the rate of growth of the capital stock.

Nonmaximizing behavior   Our discussion thus far has assumed that property owners maximize their income from holding the property. In particular, we have assumed that owners of business and rented residential property charge prices and rents that maximize their incomes. With this assumption, property owners are not able to offset a tax increase by raising prices or rents because they are already charging the income-maximizing price or rent.

But this assumption is not always valid, as when regulation of industries, such as utilities, prevents rents and prices from being high enough to maximize income (profit). So a property tax increase on regulated businesses, say electric utilities, would likely be used to justify higher electricity prices, resulting in the tax being shifted to consumers. Similarly, increased taxes on rental housing would likely be shifted to consumers if rent ceilings were in effect, because those ceilings would probably be increased. Property owners may not maximize income for other reasons than regulation — to discourage entry of competitors, fear of social disapproval, fear that competitors will not follow suit on a price increase. When prices and rents are less than maximum for any of these reasons, property owners may "pass on" their taxes to their customers. The extent to which prices and rents are restrained below their income-maximizing levels is an empirical question. But the general belief is that incomes are maximized by both competitive and purely monopolistic enterprises.

SHIFTING AND INCIDENCE ESTIMATES

Given the *possibilities* for shifting we have discussed, conclusions about the extent of *actual* shifting vary with the type of property.

Land   There is substantial agreement that property taxes levied on land are borne by landowners (not shifted), because the total supply of land is inelastic and land is not mobile between locations. Landowners cannot take action to offset their tax liabilities. Indeed, taxes on land tend to be capitalized into lower land value, causing current landowners to bear the full burden of present and anticipated future taxes.[15]

Landowners may in fact bear more than the full burden of the taxes levied on land because some of the taxes levied on property used in conjunction with land (buildings, machinery) may be shifted to landowners. Such shifting is most likely to occur if reproducible property is highly mobile or elastically supplied.[16] If property taxes are borne by landowners, and a significant fraction surely is, they are progressive, taxing higher-income persons more heavily than would a proportional income tax.[17]

Owner-occupied housing   The value of owner-occupied housing is another major component (more than 25 percent) of the property tax base. The incidence of taxes on such housing is commonly thought to rest squarely on homeowners because there is no one to whom homeowners can shift the taxes. The taxes cannot be shifted to consumers because the owners are also the consumers of the services of the property.

While there is agreement on who bears the taxes, there is dispute about whether the tax burdens are progressively distributed. Until recently, they have been regarded as regressive based on the assumption that the value of the housing owned by a family falls relative to the family income as that income increases. Critics of that view argue that the supporting evidence is inadequate. Although no definite conclusion has been reached, a reading of

15 To illustrate tax capitalization, let us suppose that the expected annual income from an acre of farm land is $100 after the deduction of all costs of generating that income (costs of seed, fertilizer, etc.) *except* taxes. Let us also suppose that investments of similar risk earn 10 percent after taxes. If this land is not taxed, then investors would be willing to pay up to $1,000 an acre for it because, at that price, they would earn as great a return on their investment as they could earn on alternative investments. In a competitive market, the price of land would be bid up to $1,000 per acre. Now suppose that a $20 per-acre property tax is imposed on land. To yield a 10 percent after-tax return, land would now have to sell for $800 per acre, since the after-tax income is $80 per acre. The tax would thus cause the price of land to fall to $800 per acre if the rate of return on competing investments remains at 10 percent. In this case, the tax would be fully capitalized; its burden would fall entirely on the owners of the land at the time the tax is imposed. To see why, note that for persons buying the land after the tax is imposed, an investment of $1,000 (1.25 acres of land) earns them an after-tax income of $100, the same after-tax income they would have earned with an investment of $1,000 (1 acre of land) before the tax was imposed.

16 A property tax on reproducible capital (buildings, machines, etc.) may mean that less capital is used with a given amont of land. For example, a smaller apartment building may be built on urban land, or less machinery may be used to farm agricultural land. If so, the gross rental incomes of landowners are lower because the capital-land ratio is lower.

17 For further discussion of the distribution of land ownership and its implications for property tax progressiveness, see Gaffney, "The Property Tax is a Progressive Tax."

available evidence suggests that the incidence of taxes on owner-occupied housing is unlikely to prove to be either highly regressive or highly progressive.[18]

Rental housing   The incidence of taxes on rental housing is in dispute, but full shifting to renters is regarded as unlikely. Land represents a significant share of the value of rented residential property. Taxes levied on land values are likely to be borne by landowners. In addition, property taxes levied on the value of residential structures are unlikely to be shifted fully to renters because such taxes will be levied on the reproducible capital represented by residential structures no matter where it locates. So mobility does not permit reproducible capital to totally escape property tax burdens. However, some of the burden of above-average taxes may be shifted to renters as capital moves out of the relatively high-tax areas, thereby reducing the supply of rental residences and increasing rents. At the same time, the supply of rental residences to low-tax areas may be increased, reducing rents and increasing the real incomes of renters in those areas. The net burden on renters in both high-tax and low-tax areas may be positive, but even so it seems highly unlikely that renters would bear even half of the total taxes levied on rented residential property.[19]

Nonresidential property   Agricultural, industrial, commercial, and other "business" properties are taxed. In principle, these taxes could be borne by the buyers of the products produced with the property. Or they could be borne by the property owners or other factor owners, primarily workers. But, it seems likely that a major share of these taxes is borne by property owners, for basically the same reason that taxes on rented residential properties are likely to be no more than partially shifted to renters.

Also, for these property taxes to be shifted to buyers (consumers), producers in high-tax areas must be able to sell at prices above those prevailing in low-tax areas. But such price differentials are not possible in many cases. Prices of farm products and other homogeneous materials such as petroleum products are determined in national markets. Since all producers of these products are subject to national competition, producers in a particular high-

18 For a review of the evidence, see Aaron, *Who Pays the Property Tax*, chap. 3. Offsetting the property tax burdens of homeowners is the favorable treatment they receive under the income tax laws, which allow property taxes and interest to be deducted from income without taxing the imputed income from home ownership. Also, some states have homestead exemptions, which exempt a specified amount of the assessed value of a home from taxation or give preferential treatment to older people or veterans.

19 In addition, tenants are probably favored somewhat by the liberal depreciation on apartment dwellings allowed under the federal income tax laws, which would tend to increase the supply of and reduce rents charged for apartments.

tax locality cannot charge more and thereby shift the burden to buyers. For such products, prices can differ between areas only by the costs of transporting the product from the low-price to the high-price area.

We can state that idea more generally: The price of a product sold in a high-tax area can exceed the price charged for the same product in low-tax areas *only* by the amount that it would cost the buyer to "import" the product from a low-tax area. Such importation may occur by having the product shipped from the low-tax area to buyers in high-tax areas; or the buyers may themselves move from the high-tax to a low-tax area. In some cases, the importation costs are low — mail-order purchase of high-value, low-weight items such as cameras and clothing. In other cases, they are high — housing, medical services, and other local services such as laundries, restaurants, and repairs. Property tax differentials may be reflected in price differentials in the latter but not in the former cases.

Table 14–3 presents estimates of the incidence of all property taxes on all classes of property.

TABLE 14–3

ESTIMATES OF PROPERTY TAX BURDENS AS A PERCENTAGE OF INCOME, 1966

Family income ($ thousand)	Property tax burdens as a percentage of family income		
	Traditional view [a] (%)	New view [b]	
		Case A (%)	Case B (%)
Less than 3	6.5	2.5	2.4
3–5	4.8	2.7	2.8
5–10	3.6	2.0	2.2
10–15	3.2	1.7	1.9
15–20	3.2	2.0	2.2
20–25	3.1	2.6	2.8
25–30	3.1	3.7	3.7
30–50	3.0	4.5	4.4
50–100	2.8	6.2	6.1
100–500	2.4	8.2	7.8
500–1,000	1.7	9.6	8.8
1,000 and over	0.8	10.1	8.7

a The tax on land is assumed to be borne by landowners; the tax on all structures is assumed to be borne in proportion to housing expenditures and consumption.

b The tax is assumed to reduce the average rate of return to all owners of capital, with land taxes being borne in proportion to property income in general (Case A) and in proportion to income from land (Case B).

Source: Henry J. Aaron, *Who Pays the Property Tax?* (Washington: Brookings, 1975), pp. 26, 47. © 1975 by the Brookings Institution, Washington, D.C.

ALLOCATION EFFECTS

Real property is capital. And the ownership, location, and use of real property reflects owners' decisions to employ their capital in particular ways. Taxation of property provides owners with an incentive to adjust the employment of their capital so as to reduce their tax liabilities and increase their real income. In response to property taxation, property owners may move their capital to investments that are not subject to such taxation. Or they may move investment into property that is taxed at a lower rate. Or they may reduce the total supply of capital by saving and investing less in all types of capital. In the preceding sections we saw how these adjustments alter the distribution of property tax burdens. In this section we will see how these adjustments may affect allocation efficiency.

As we noted above, if property tax rates are uniform and the total supply of capital (property) is fixed, then property taxation does not trigger resource (capital) reallocation.[20] But these extreme conditions are not met; tax rate differentials do exist. And resources may be reallocated in response to those differentials. Also, there may be some elasticity in the total supply of capital.[21]

Whether property-tax–induced reallocations of resource use prevent efficient resource allocation is an open question; we seldom know whether allocation would have been efficient in the absence of the adjustments. The usual assumption is that such reallocations are undesirable unless they can be shown to counter specific existing inefficiencies. That is, property tax rate differentials are assumed to generate excess burdens. Let us now look more closely at some of the adjustments that property taxation may trigger.

INTERINDUSTRY AND INTERAREA ALLOCATION

When property tax rates vary among industries and areas, reproducible capital will tend to move to the low-tax industries and areas. In addition, when tax rates on land depend on land use (depend on the industry in which land is employed), land may be changed from high-tax to low-tax uses. Some government units explicitly use low tax rates in an attempt to attract mobile, reproducible capital. *Tax holidays* for new industry locating in a particular

20 This statement assumes that the property tax revenues are not spent in such a way as to provide incentives for resource reallocation.

21 An elastic supply of capital is more plausible once we recognize that the savings of U.S. residents may be invested abroad as well as domestically. Even if the total amount of saving by U.S. residents is unaffected by the rate of return earned on that saving (as appears to be the case), the share of that saving invested in the United States — the domestic supply of reproducible capital — may be affected by U.S. taxation of capital (property). Why? Because higher taxes in the United States would make foreign investment relatively more attractive.

state or community are a common practice. While tax-induced changes in resource use undoubtedly occur, it is difficult to judge their magnitude and consequences for allocation efficiency.[22]

As an example of how interarea property tax differentials may cause inefficiency, suppose that some product, say textiles, can be produced at lower real cost in region A than in region B. Region A may have a real-cost advantage because of cheaper labor or power or because raw material or finished product markets are closer. In the absence of differences in taxation and public services, textile mills would be located in region A. However, if region A taxes the property of textile producers (their buildings and machinery) more heavily than B, all costs, taxes included, may be lower in B. If so, textile mills will locate in region B, and the *real* costs of producing textiles will be greater than they would be in the absence of the tax incentives to locate in region B. This real-cost differential measures the welfare loss (excess burden) generated by the property tax differentials.

INPUT CHOICES

Because a business can reduce its property tax liabilities by using less capital (property) and more labor to produce a given output, property taxation has been said to induce the substitution of labor for capital. Such substitution is inefficient *if* the cost-minimizing labor-capital mix would be chosen in the absence of property taxation.[23] But the substitution can occur in the aggregate only if the total supply of capital is reduced in response to the decrease in the rate of return caused by property taxation.

INVESTMENT IN PHYSICAL AND HUMAN CAPITAL

Property taxes apply to investments in physical capital but not to investments in human capital and may therefore tend to discourage the former investments relative to the latter. Also, a large share of property tax revenue is used to finance elementary and secondary education, which is to a large extent investment in human capital. So both the collection and use of property tax revenue tend to divert investment from physical to human capital.

This shift in investment is not necessarily inefficient. The rate of return on investment in human capital may be greater than that in physical

22 See L. G. Rosenberg "Taxation of Income from Capital by Industry," in *The Taxation of Income from Capital*, ed. Arnold C. Harberger and M. J. Bailey (Washington: Brookings, 1969), for estimates of the excess burdens resulting from the property taxes and corporation income taxes imposed on capital.

23 Such tax-induced change in input mix is not undesirable from the standpoint of businesses because it reduces their *money* costs. It is inefficient from the standpoint of society because businesses are not minimizing the value of the resources required to produce a given output.

capital.[24] By reducing the return to investment in physical capital and subsidizing investment in human capital, financing education by property taxes may result in a more efficient allocation of investment.[25]

HOUSING AND URBAN SPRAWL AND DECAY

Central cities seem to require higher public service levels than surrounding suburban areas, and there is evidence that effective tax rates are higher in some central cities than in the suburbs.[26] Unless public service levels are commensurate with the higher taxes, there is an incentive for marginal investments to be made in surrounding suburban areas rather than in the central cities, contributing to urban sprawl.

The property tax may also contribute to urban blight and decay because older buildings often are assessed at lower values than new buildings, even though their profitability is the same. There is, thus, less incentive to replace existing structures because doing so would increase tax liabilities. Similarly, it is cheaper to maintain facilities with labor-intensive methods than to remodel or rebuild, since the latter alternatives would increase tax liabilities.

The incentives that lead to urban decay and blight also lead to a substitution of other goods for housing. That is, to the extent that taxes on residential property are shifted forward, they act as excise taxes on housing.

IMPROVING THE PROPERTY TAX

The property tax has been and is likely to continue to be an important source of revenue. With this in mind, we will now consider some proposals to improve the tax.

TAX RELIEF FOR LOW-INCOME INDIVIDUALS

The property tax has been criticized for the burden it places on low-income, usually elderly, homeowners. To mitigate this effect, some states have

24 See Theodore Schultz, *Human Resources*, National Bureau of Economic Research, General Series 96 (Washington, 1972).

25 Also, other features of our tax system tend to counter that diversion of investment into human capital. Specifically, human beings cannot depreciate investments made in themselves, but physical capital is depreciable. Firms investing in physical capital may receive an investment tax credit, but not individuals who invest in themselves. So, when the overall tax and expenditure policies of federal, state, and local governments are considered, it is not clear whether investment in human or physical capital is favored by public policy.

26 Dick Netzer, *Economics of the Property Tax* (Washington: Brookings, 1966), pp. 74–75.

provided elderly homeowners with an income tax credit for a fraction of property taxes paid, with the amount of the credit usually varying inversely with income. A rebate is given if the credit exceeds income tax liabilities. In some cases, low-income elderly renters are also given a credit for a fraction of rental payments, on the assumption that renters pay part of the property tax.

LAND (SITE-VALUE) TAXATION

There are both equity and efficiency arguments for taxing land (site value) more heavily than structures and improvements (reproducible capital).[27] The equity argument contends that the rental return on site value is unearned — a gift of nature.[28] In addition, increases in site values are largely due to the investments and actions of individuals other than the owner and to inflation.[29]

On efficiency grounds, site-value taxation is advocated because it is neutral. The site-value tax is independent of how owners use their property, and it therefore does not act as a barrier to either the development of property or the maintenance and improvement of existing structures. In contrast, with the present property tax, property owners face increased taxes if they develop or improve their property. Thus, increasing taxes on site values in order to reduce taxes on improvements (reproducible capital) would tend to reduce urban sprawl and decay by favoring the development, improvement, and maintenance of property.

Changing to heavier taxation of site values would decrease land prices, perhaps imposing unfair capital losses on present landowners. This disadvantage could be lessened by making the shift a gradual one.

A barrier to complete replacement of present property taxes with site-value taxes is that the latter may not yield enough revenue, especially in urban areas.[30] Of course, this "revenue inadequacy" does not prevent a substantial

27 The site value of a property is simply the market value of the land in an unimproved state — its value in the absence of any improvements to the land itself and any buildings and structures on the land.

28 In contrast, labor income is earned by the sacrifice of leisure. And, because current consumption is sacrificed to supply reproducible capital, the return to such capital is earned. For further discussion, see Henry George, *Progress and Poverty* (New York: Doubleday, 1914).

29 The market value of a site depends on the use of surrounding land, transportation access, etc. So site value often increases because of public investments (the building of roads) and the private investments of others.

30 The rental income accruing to the site owner is the maximum amount of tax that can be extracted from her or him. If taxed more heavily, the site becomes valueless, and the owner will relinquish ownership rather than pay the tax. Such abandonment of property has occurred in a number of major U.S. cities.

shift away from the present form of property taxation to site-value taxation. Also, taxes on reproducible capital may be appropriate on efficiency grounds if they function as charges for services rendered to property owners. In such case, eliminating the taxes would have such services supplied free.

IMPROVED ASSESSMENT

A major criticism of the property tax concerns the way property is assessed — at varying fractions of market value, both within and across political jurisdictions. There are several ways that assessment can be improved.

Enlarging taxing jurisdictions would tend to reduce variations in the ratio of assessed to market value. For example, a metropolitan area taxing district with one assessment office would serve to reduce variations in assessment practices between the central city and surrounding suburban areas.

It might also be desirable for the state government to assess all industrial and commercial property, a class of property that is especially difficult to assess because of the infrequency of sales. Also, central state assessment would eliminate the tendency on the part of localities to underassess such property to attract business. Some states now centrally assess property such as railroads and public utilities that cuts across political jurisdictions.

Central assessment could be accompanied by central collection of taxes on commercial and industrial property, with the taxes being returned to localities on the basis of some measure of the proportion of property located in each locality. Or revenues could be allocated to localities on a per capita (or per student) basis. This approach would tend to offset variations in fiscal capacity among political jurisdictions. The per capita revenues would be the same for all localities, but the ratio of per capita revenues to property values would be higher for areas with low per capita property values than for those with high values.

One imaginative approach to improved assessment would be to have individuals assess the value of their own property, much as the income and sales tax bases are self-assessed. Self-assessment would be coupled with penalties for underassessment.[31]

SUMMARY

When property owners are not maximizing their incomes, they may shift taxes through rent and price increases. Even if they are maximizing incomes, shifting is possible under the conditions summarized in Table 14–2.

31 John D. Strasma, "Market-Enforced Self-Assessment for Real Estate Taxes," *Bulletin for International Fiscal Documentation*, September 1965, pp. 353–363, and October 1965, pp. 397–414.

While the table tells us when shifting is possible, it does not tell us when shifting will occur or how much of the tax may be shifted or to whom it may be shifted. We do see that shifting cannot occur if the supply of property is perfectly inelastic and if property is not mobile between locations and uses. But mobility between uses and locations does not lead to shifting if tax rates are uniform (independent of use and location). This last qualification is significant because virtually all property is subjected to some degree of taxation. Thus, all of the burden of the tax cannot be shifted by moving property between locations or uses even if such movement is possible; some tax burdens must be borne by property owners. When shifting does occur, property taxes act as do the excise taxes we discussed in Chapter 13, with incidence depending on demand and supply elasticities. Other factors being the same, shifting is more complete as the demand for the products produced with the property is more inelastic and as the supply of property (capital) is more elastic.

In terms of their actual incidence, property taxes have traditionally been viewed as regressive, in part because it has been thought that taxes levied on property other than land are shifted to buyers in the form of higher prices. But it has been recently argued and become more widely accepted that full shifting is highly unlikely. According to this new view, only above-average property taxes may be shifted. Even then, shifting occurs only if prices are not determined in national or wide-area markets. And the shifting process that produces price increases for some buyers also produces price decreases for other buyers.

Property taxes on owner-occupied homes probably are not distinctly progressive or regressive. Taxes on other property are unquestionably progressive insofar as they are borne by owners of land and property. Only that share of the property tax burden that is shifted to consumers is potentially regressive, and that share appears to be less than half of the total property tax burden. So, while the incidence of property taxes remains uncertain, they do not appear to be as regressive as they were once thought to be; indeed, they may be progressive. Moreover, the regressiveness that exists is with respect to current rather than permanent income. The shifted portion of property taxes is roughly proportional to consumption which, in turn, is proportional to permanent income.[32]

In short, from an equity perspective, property taxes are fairly attractive. Much if not most of their burden is probably distributed progressively with

32 Recall from Chapter 13, p. 294, that taxes on consumption need not be regressive. See also Aaron, "Who Pays the Property Tax?, pp. 27–32, for discussion of the effects of using current rather than permanent income to evaluate the regressiveness of tax burdens. Aaron (p. 45) also argues that these shifted burdens are positively related to family income because the higher tax areas, in which property taxes would have positive excise tax effects, are also the higher income areas.

respect to income. And, since many local government services benefit property owners, financing such services by property taxes is fair by the benefits-received criterion. All of this is not to say that property taxes could not be made more equitable by improved assessment practices and administration procedures.

From an efficiency perspective, property taxes have a potential for distorting decisions regarding land use and the distribution of reproducible capital among alternative uses and locations. But there is presently little basis for making a judgment about the welfare losses from such distortions. We can say, however, that making the effective rates of property taxation more uniform, both geographically and among uses, would likely lessen these distortions. Relatively heavier taxation of land and relatively lighter taxation of reproducible property would also reduce distortions.

SUPPLEMENTARY READINGS

Aaron, Henry J. *Who Pays the Property Tax?* Washington: Brookings, 1975.

Balk, Alfred. *The Free List: Property Without Taxes.* New York: Russell Sage, 1971.

Netzer, Dick. *Economics of the Property Tax.* Washington: Brookings, 1966.

Peterson, George E., ed. *Property Tax Reform.* Washington: Urban Institute, 1973.

CHAPTER FIFTEEN

TAXATION OF NET WEALTH
AND OF WEALTH TRANSFERS

While the main form of wealth taxation in the United States is the property tax, wealth transfers — gifts and bequests — are also taxed. In addition, net wealth taxation has been advocated, both as a new source of funds and as a replacement for property taxation.[1] What are the incidence and economic effects of these taxes? Can they be justified on traditional ability-to-pay or benefits-received principles or as a means of limiting inequality in the distribution of income? In this chapter we will consider these questions.

NET WEALTH

We defined net wealth in Chapter 14 as the difference between the value of a person's assets (land, stocks, bonds, cash, etc.) and the amount of his or her liabilities (loans and mortgages outstanding, accounts payable, etc.). Taxes on net wealth may be proportional or progressive, and they may exclude some minimum amount of wealth from taxation.

INCIDENCE AND EQUITY

The impact of a net wealth tax is on wealth holders. And, unless shifting is possible, impact and incidence are equal. If the tax is levied at uniform rates

1 Net wealth taxation is also referred to as *net worth* taxation. For arguments supporting net wealth taxation, see Lester C. Thurow, *The Impact of Taxes on the American Economy* (New York: Praeger, 1971), and Martin David, "Increased Taxation with Increased Acceptability—A Discussion of Net Worth Taxation as a Federal Revenue Alternative," *Journal of Finance*, 28, No. 2 (May 1973): 481–495.

throughout the nation, it cannot be shifted unless total saving and wealth (capital) are reduced in response to the tax. As we noted earlier, there is little evidence that aggregate saving is significantly influenced by taxation and that total saving would be reduced by a tax on wealth (accumulated saving).

The ownership of wealth (not including human capital) is highly concentrated (see Tables 15–1 and 15–2). Indeed, wealth is generally distributed progressively with respect to income (see Table 15–3). Therefore, if the net worth tax is not shifted, its burden is more progressively distributed than that of a proportional income tax. That is, in the absence of shifting, a net wealth tax will claim a greater amount of the income of the wealthy than an equal-yield proportional income tax. However, as Table 15–3 shows, the ratio of wealth to income is higher for people in the lowest and highest income classes than for those in the middle-income brackets. To make the net wealth tax uniformly progressive with respect to income, low amounts of

TABLE 15–1
CUMULATIVE DISTRIBUTION OF WEALTH, 1970

Percent of consumer units	Percent of wealth
11.4	2.7
17.9	5.6
29.9	11.6
47.9	21.8
60.0	29.7
82.1	48.7
96.3	71.7
100.0	100.0

Source: Data tabulated from Stanley Lebergott, *The American Economy: Income, Wealth, and Want* (Princeton, N.J.: Princeton, 1976), tables 14, 15, p. 246.

TABLE 15–2
DISTRIBUTION OF WEALTH BY INCOME CLASS, 1970

Income class (dollars)	Percent of total wealth	Percent of household units
0–4,999	11.6	29.9
5,000–9,999	18.1	30.1
10,000–14,999	19.0	22.1
15,000–24,999	23.0	14.2
25,000–49,999	17.1	3.2
50,000 and up	11.3	0.5

Source: Data tabulated from Stanley Lebergott, *The American Economy: Income, Wealth, and Want* (Princeton, N.J.: Princeton, 1976), tables 14, 15, p. 246.

TABLE 15-3
RATIO OF WEALTH TO INCOME BY INCOME CLASS, 1970 (DOLLARS)

AGI class [a]	Mean wealth [b]	Mean income [b]	Ratio of wealth to income
0–4,999	16,920	2,296	7.37
5,000–9,999	28,105	7,425	3.79
10,000–14,999	40,312	12,186	3.31
15,000–24,999	76,171	18,357	4.15
25,000–49,999	252,498	32,621	7.74
50,000 and up	1,116,482	87,431	12.77

a Adjusted gross income as reported to the U.S. Internal Revenue Service under the individual income tax.

b Wealth and income per tax return filed with the U.S. Internal Revenue Service under the individual income tax.

Source: Calculated from Stanley Lebergott, *The American Economy: Income, Wealth, and Want* (Princeton, N.J.: Princeton, 1976), tables 10, 13, pp. 242, 245.

wealth could be exempted from taxation, and the tax rate on net wealth could be made progressive.

Net wealth and benefits received   Is a person's net wealth an accurate index of her or his benefit from government-provided goods and services? Usually not; therefore, net wealth is not a suitable base for benefits-received taxation. Some services do benefit property owners and increase their net wealth — for example, roads, street lighting, police and fire protection. But other services — education, welfare, public health — benefit property owners only indirectly, if at all.[2] Also, when benefits do accrue to property owners, the benefits' magnitude is seldom closely related to the owners' net wealth. Instead, benefits may vary with the location, size, and use of property. And benefits may accrue to the renters rather than the owners of property.

Net wealth and ability to pay   Is net wealth a suitable index of ability to pay? How does it compare with income as an ability-to-pay measure? Income and wealth are related in that wealth (asset values) is a capitalized flow of income. If the relationship between net wealth and income were the same for all individuals, net wealth and income would be equivalent measures of ability to pay. For example, if Ellen Levine has net wealth of

2 For example, increased spending on public education may make a community a more desirable place to live and thereby increase the value of residential property. But this effect will depend on spending by other communities and the manner in which property values are determined.

$100,000 that yields income $10,000 per year, and Frank Tucker has net wealth of $50,000 that yields $5,000 per year, either net wealth or income would measure their relative ability to pay equally well.

But the relationship between available measures of income and wealth is not one-to-one for several reasons. First, income flows are not all capitalized at the same rate. Second, for income from some sources — particularly labor — there is a measureable money income flow but no corresponding asset value. That is, the income is not capitalized. Third, for some asset categories — consumer durables, owner-occupied housing — there is no readily measurable income flow, even though the asset is readily valued. In short, net wealth and income are not equivalent bases for taxation. In some instances, net wealth and income taxes may tax basically the same income flow. But in other cases, a net wealth tax may fall on income that would escape taxation under an income tax (such as income from owner-occupied housing). In other cases, an income tax may fall on income that would escape wealth taxation (labor income).

Both net wealth and income are clearly related to ability to pay. To be suitable bases for ability-to-pay taxation both would have to be adjusted for the taxpayer's circumstances — nondiscretionary expenditures. With such adjustment, it is not clear which is the more appropriate tax base. Of course, both could be used, and, as Martin David persuasively argues, the two bases would be complementary.[3] In particular, it can be argued that of two taxpayers with the same income and nondiscretionary expenditures, the one with the greater net wealth has greater ability to pay. Moreover, if the ratio of nontaxable income to wealth increases as income increases, a tax on net wealth could complement the income tax and increase progression of the combined taxes.

Taxation of both wealth and income does not always reduce horizontal inequities. For example, taxing net wealth in addition to income might seem to correct for the inequity of not taxing the imputed income from home ownership. But such is not the case because a net wealth tax increases the tax burden on individuals who rent and whose income is explicit and fully taxable. The homeowner pays less tax than the (equally situated) renter with or without a net wealth tax. Similarly, a net wealth tax reinforces, rather than offsets, the income tax's discrimination against saving.

Limiting inequality   Net wealth taxation is advocated as a means of limiting the concentration of wealth.[4] Wealth concentration can also be limited by progressive taxation of comprehensive income. But as we saw in Chapter

3 See David, "Increased Taxation with Increased Acceptability."

4 See David, "Increased Taxation with Increased Acceptability," p. 489.

11, the U.S. income tax is not comprehensive. Wealth taxation is superior to income taxation in this respect because, as we noted above, income and net wealth are only loosely connected. To control wealth concentration, net wealth may be taxed either on a regular, say annual, basis or only on transfer of wealth by gift or bequest. We discuss the latter method below.

ALLOCATION EFFECTS

With a net wealth tax, income is taxed only if it is saved and invested in physical capital or in financial assets, which are usually claims on physical capital. The net wealth tax is, then, neutral with respect to the labor-leisure choice, while the proportional income tax is not. Neither tax is neutral with respect to the consumption-saving choice. The income tax discriminates against saving by reducing the after-tax return to saving. The net wealth tax discriminates against saving because the amount of the tax depends on the amount of accumulated saving. The differential substitution effect of the two taxes on the consumption-saving choice is ambiguous. Whatever its direction, the effect on total saving is probably not significant, given the apparent insensitivity of saving to the rate of return earned on saving.

The net wealth and proportional income taxes will have different income effects. The net wealth tax places a greater burden on high-income individuals. The differential income effects of the two taxes could conceivably affect factor supplies, but there are neither analytical nor empirical bases for predicting the direction of such effects.

Thus, while net wealth and proportional income taxes could differentially affect factor supplies, the direction of such effects are presently unclear. And factor supplies appear to be sufficiently inelastic so that any effects are likely to be small. However, the direction of one effect on factor supply is clear: The net wealth tax provides a greater incentive for investing in human capital than does the income tax. Saving invested in human capital escapes taxation by the net wealth tax, provided it does not give rise to a financial asset. And the income from human capital is not taxed under the net wealth tax. Specifically, net wealth taxation is more favorable (than income taxation) to peoples' investment in their own education and training.[5]

USE AND FEASIBILITY

The United States does not employ net wealth taxes, although at least fourteen other countries have used such taxes. Objections against its use are that

5 For further comparison of wealth and income taxation, see Richard Goode, *The Individual Income Tax*, rev. ed. (Washington: Brookings, 1976), chap. 3.

TABLE 15-4

COMPOSITION OF TOTAL NET WEALTH, UNITED STATES, 1962

Class	Percent of total net worth
Home ownership	26.5
Other property of householders	11.2
Automobiles	2.8
Stocks	18.0
Marketable bonds	2.0
Liquid assets	11.4
Life insurance, annuities and retirement plans	6.1
Personal debt	−2.1
Miscellaneous	6.8
Business and profession net worth	17.3

Source: Lester C. Thurow, *Impact of Taxes on the American Economy* (New York: Praeger, 1971), pp. 130–132.

there are significant administrative problems in detecting and valuing wealth and that some people may be forced to liquidate their holdings to pay the tax. The latter problem may be serious for some individuals, such as low-income persons who own their home but have little money income. This problem could be overcome by exempting some minimum amount of net worth from taxation. For most people, the composition of net wealth can be altered in advance of tax payments to avoid severe problems of liquidation.

There remains the problem of valuing assets, which is also met in property taxation. Although the problems are not insignificant, Thurow estimates that most wealth is held in forms that can be assessed fairly easily; in fact, most of it is assessed under the property tax. The composition of net wealth in the United States in 1962 is shown in Table 15-4. According to Thurow, the most difficult item to assess is some fraction of business and professional net wealth. Personal property would also be difficult to detect and assess. This problem could be minimized, however, by exempting a certain amount of personal property from taxation, and property valued above the amount could be detected and valued through insurance records.[6]

WEALTH TRANSFERS

Wealth transfers occur as people make gifts during their lifetime and bequeath assets upon their death. The person making the transfer may be taxed according to the amount transferred. Or the person receiving the

6 See Lester C. Thurow, "Net Worth Taxes," *National Tax Journal*, 25, No. 3 (September 1972): 417–423.

transfer may be taxed according to the amount received. Current *gift and estate taxes* represent the former approach, while the *inheritance taxes* levied by some states on *heirs* represent the latter approach. Estate taxes are sometimes called *death taxes*. Wealth transfers can be taxed separately, as is current practice in the United States and other countries. Or gifts and inheritances can be taxed as income of the recipients as would occur with comprehensive income taxation of the sort we defined in Chapter 10. This latter approach taxes only wealth transfers between taxpaying units. Transfers within the unit, for example, between spouses, are not taxed.

CURRENT PRACTICE

With the Tax Reform Act of 1976, federal gift and estate taxes are levied at the same rates. Marginal rates range from 18 percent on the first $10,000 of the taxable base to 70 percent on amounts in excess of $5 million. The gift tax is computed by applying the tax rate to cumulated taxable gifts and subtracting gift taxes previously paid. Thus, taxes are based on the accumulated lifetime gifts and bequests of the donor, with the lifetime total of gift and estate taxes being about the same whether transfer is by gift or bequest.

A tax credit offsets part of the tax due on lifetime transfers. The tax credit is $30,000 beginning in 1977 and increasing to $47,000 in 1981. The credit means that taxes will not be paid until transfers exceed $120,666 in 1977 and $175,625 in 1981. Any part of the credit used to offset gift taxes is not available to offset estate taxes.

For estates in excess of $500,000, 50 percent of the estate may be bequeathed to a surviving spouse tax free. For smaller estates, up to $250,000 may be deducted for tax purposes, irrespective of the 50 percent limitation. There is also a deduction for gifts between spouses. The first $100,000 of gifts to a spouse is tax free, and 50 percent of gifts in excess of $200,000 is tax free.

Although gifts and bequests are taxed similarly, we should be aware of two differences. First, a donor may give up to $3,000 per year to *each* donee without paying gift or estate taxes. That is, *each* year a person can give $3,000 to *each* of any number of persons, with none of the transfers being subject to gift or estate taxation. Second, gift taxes paid on gifts made more than three years prior to death are not included in the gross estate when calculating the taxes due on lifetime gifts and bequests. Gifts made within three years of death are included in the gross estate (minus the $3,000 annual exclusion). For both reasons, combined gift and estate taxes can be reduced by making transfers as gifts rather than as bequests at death.

An estate tax differs from an inheritance tax. The estate tax is levied on the taxable value of the estate, whereas an inheritance tax is levied on the value of the estate inherited by each person. For example, with a taxable estate of $100,000, the estate tax is levied on $100,000, regardless of how it is divided among heirs. If the estate is equally divided between two individuals, an inheritance tax would apply to the $50,000 received by each heir and would be payable by the heirs. Inheritance taxes are most commonly used by state governments, with exemptions and rate schedules depending on the relationship of the heir to the deceased. Eleven states impose gift taxes. There is a limited credit of state estate taxes against federal estate taxes, a feature that was enacted to discourage states from competing for wealthy residents.

ALLOCATION EFFECTS

Unlike an income tax, wealth transfer taxes have no direct effect on income from labor and are therefore neutral with respect to the labor-leisure choice. However, taxes on gifts and bequests are not neutral with respect to saving because donors can avoid or reduce such taxes by increasing their consumption. An income tax also discourages saving by reducing the return to saving. Whether income taxation discourages saving more than taxes on wealth transfers do cannot be predicted. Similarly, wealth transfer taxes are likely to affect the distribution of income differently than an income tax. But how any such difference in income distribution may affect labor supply and saving is unknown.

INCIDENCE AND EQUITY

The main burden of wealth transfer taxes seems likely to fall on those making the transfers or the transfer recipients or both. These taxes can be shifted if the supply of savings and capital is reduced in response to them. But there is no evidence that such is the case; nor do wealth transfer taxes appear to differ significantly from a proportional income tax in their effect on saving.

Are existing taxes on wealth transfers fair? Gifts and inheritances fall within the comprehensive definition of income we developed in Chapter 10. Thus, taxation of gifts and inheritances as income to the recipient (or heir) is consistent with ability-to-pay taxation. However, current gift, estate, and inheritance taxes are imperfect as ability-to-pay taxes because the amount of such taxes does not depend on the ability to pay of the person who receives a gift or inherits part of an estate.

Another equity basis for taxation of gifts and bequests is that individuals should have the same economic opportunities, and those who receive gifts and inheritances are given greater opportunities than others. From this perspective, estate, gift, and inheritance taxes are means of reducing inequalities in the distribution of wealth and the opportunities and political influence that wealth permits.

SUMMARY

If there were a perfect correspondence between wealth and income, and if all forms of net wealth and income could be quantified, there would be no need for separate taxation of net wealth or wealth transfers. Either income or net wealth would measure ability to pay, and taxation of either base could reduce inequalities in the distribution of income and wealth.

In an imperfect world, it is not clear whether measurable net wealth or measurable income is a better measure of ability to pay. Income in this case would include gifts and inheritances. Complementing an imperfect income tax with an imperfect net wealth tax is a means of taxing income that escapes the income tax, but it may impose an additional tax burden on income that is fully taxable. If the tax laws permit an accumulation and concentration of wealth that is unacceptable, a net wealth tax can be used to reduce such concentrations. Wealth transfer taxes can accomplish the same result. This approach would be an alternative to a comprehensive income tax.

The incidence of a uniform net wealth tax is probably mostly on owners of wealth, and the incidence of wealth transfer taxes is probably on the donor, donee, or heir.

Net wealth and wealth transfer taxes are neutral with respect to the labor-leisure choice, but not with respect to saving. The net wealth tax favors investment in human capital more than does an income tax.

SUPPLEMENTARY READINGS

Pechman, Joseph A. *Federal Tax Policy*, Chap. 8. 3rd ed. Washington: Brookings, 1977.

Shoup, Carl S. *Federal Estate and Gift Taxes*. Washington: Brookings, 1966.

Thurow, Lester C. *The Impact of Taxes on the American Economy*, Chap. 7. New York: Praeger, 1971.

Governments are major demanders of goods and services and major employers of people. As such, governments affect aggregate demand for goods and services. And, in doing so, they may determine whether total demand exceeds or falls short of the goods and services that can be produced when the economy's productive capacity is fully utilized. When total demand falls short of capacity production (buyers want to buy fewer goods and services than the economy can produce), there is unemployment of people and machines; when it exceeds capacity, there is inflation. Intentionally or otherwise, the budgetary decisions of government affect aggregate economic activity and may either reinforce or dampen fluctuations and instability in aggregate private-sector activity. Hence, we now recognize that fiscal (budgetary) policies may serve a stabilization function.

Part Five examines this stabilization function of government, the basic purpose of which is to match aggregate demand with the existing productive capacity of the economy. In contrast, preceding chapters have looked at how government may directly and indirectly influence (1) an economy's capacity to produce as it (government) affects the supplies of labor and capital and the rates of technological change, and (2) the "mix" of goods and services produced with available capacity. Although both monetary and fiscal policy may be employed for stabilization purposes, Part Five deals only with fiscal policy. Chapters 16 and 17 present the rationale for and discuss the mechanics of fiscal stabilization. Chapter 18 looks at our experience with fiscal stabilization and reviews proposals for improving budgetary (fiscal) policy as a stabilization tool. Government borrowing and the accumulation of public debt are a consequence and key element of fiscal stabilization, so Chapter 19 examines the economic effects of public debt.

PART FIVE

FISCAL STABILIZATION

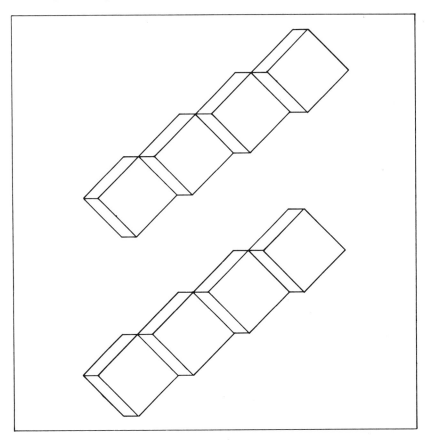

CHAPTER SIXTEEN

GOVERNMENT BUDGETS:
EFFECTS ON AGGREGATE DEMAND,
EMPLOYMENT, AND THE
PRICE LEVEL

As government spends to purchase goods and services, it directly affects aggregate demand (the total demand for the goods and services produced by the economy). As it finances its expenditures, primarily through taxation and borrowing, and makes transfer payments to individuals, government affects the demands of private spending units (households and businesses) and, hence, indirectly influences aggregate demand. Through these effects on aggregate demand, the fiscal (budgetary) policies of government may, in turn, influence aggregate employment, output, and the price level.

In this chapter we will analyze these effects of fiscal policy on the overall (aggregate) performance of the economy. We will first see how employment, the aggregate output of goods and services, and the price level depend on aggregate demand, given the economy's *capacity* to produce. Then we will see how fiscal policy affects aggregate demand. In Chapter 17 we will see how fiscal policy might be used to stabilize the economy by limiting unemployment and inflation, and we will explore some of the problems encountered in fiscal stabilization.

AGGREGATE DEMAND, UNEMPLOYMENT, AND INFLATION

At any point in time, the *capacity* of the economy to produce goods and services is limited by the supply of resources (land, labor, and capital) and by technology. In Chapter 1, we represented this limit by the production possibility curve (Figure 1–1, p. 6). We can also represent and measure this capacity limit by *potential* GNP (gross national product), the value of the annual (or other period) flow of goods and services that can be produced when the economy's capacity is fully utilized. Capacity can be so measured only with reference to a specific set of prices and a specific time. For example, in 1975 the U.S. economy could have produced an annual flow of goods and services (potential GNP) having a value of $1,369 billion in 1972 prices.

FIGURE 16–1
ACTUAL AND POTENTIAL GNP

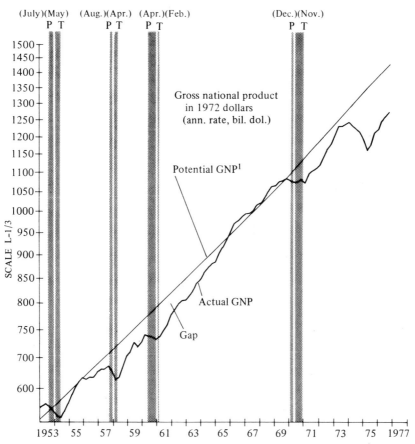

[1]Trend line of 3.5 percent per year (intersecting actual line in middle of 1955) from first quarter 1952 to fourth quarter 1962; 3.75 percent from fourth quarter 1962 to fourth quarter 1968; 4 percent from fourth quarter 1968 to fourth quarter 1975; and 3.75 percent thereafter.

Source: U.S. Department of Commerce, *Business Conditions Digest* (October 1976).

Corresponding to the flow of goods and services (output) is a flow of income. So the capacity of an economy can also be thought of as the income that is generated when all resources are fully employed. Since gross national income (GNI) equals GNP, potential GNP is a measure of the income that can be derived from full utilization of the economy's productive resources. The potential GNP (GNI) of the U.S. economy for recent years is shown in Figure 16–1.

Given the economy's capacity or potential for production, actual production depends on aggregate demand. Aggregate demand is the amount the various spending units (households, businesses, governments, and foreigners) are willing to spend on purchases of currently produced goods and services. It is customarily divided into four major components: consumption (C) and investment (I) demand of households and businesses; government demand for goods and services (G); and net foreign demand (X − M).[1] That is, aggregate demand is $Y \equiv C + I + G + (X - M)$.

The reason that actual production depends on aggregate demand is very simple: Goods and services will not be produced unless they are demanded — unless they will be purchased. When aggregate demand is less than potential GNP, actual production falls short of potential. Such was in fact the case in 1975 (as well as in many previous years) when, in 1972 prices, the actual GNP was $1,186 billion, which was $182 billion less than potential (see Figure 16–1). When aggregate demand exceeds potential GNP, the various spending units attempt to purchase more currently produced goods than the economy can produce, the likely result being a bidding up of prices and inflation (an increase in the price level).

Figure 16–2 illustrates the relationship of aggregate demand to output, the price level, and employment. Suppose an economy is in equilibrium (in the sense that total output of goods and services equals aggregate demand at prevailing prices) at output Y and price P in Figure 16–2a. Corresponding to this output are levels of employment of labor N in Figure 16–2b, and capital (not illustrated). What happens now if aggregate demand decreases (people want to buy less than is currently being produced at prevailing prices)? Real GNP falls and prices may fall slightly, moving the economy in the direction of point a in Figure 16–2a. Past experience suggests that wages and prices are highly inflexible downward, so the fall in prices is likely to be slight.[2]

1 For the United States, net foreign demand is the demand of foreigners for U.S. products, X, minus the demand of U.S. citizens for foreign products, M.

2 Robert Hall concludes that the main sources of inflexible wages are the government, regulated, and nonprofit sectors of the economy. Wage inflexibility may be transmitted to other sectors. Wage inflexibility leads, in turn, to price inflexibility. See Hall's "The Rigidity of Wages and the Persistence of Unemployment," in *Brookings Papers on Economic Activity*, vol. 2 (Washington, 1975), pp. 301–335.

FIGURE 16–2
PRICE, OUTPUT, AND EMPLOYMENT EFFECTS OF CHANGES IN AGGREGATE
DEMAND

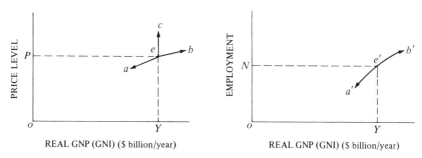

Accompanying the decline in GNP is a decline in employment of resources
toward *a'* in Figure 16–2b.

Alternatively, if the economy is in equilibrium at point *e* and aggregate
demand increases, prices or real GNP or both must also increase. If there is
excess capacity at point *e* (resources are unemployed), the main response is
an increase in real GNP — toward point *b* in Figure 16–2a. The corresponding movement of employment is toward point *b'* in Figure 16–2b.
However, if the resources of the economy are fully employed at point *e*,
then movement is toward point *c* in Figure 16–2a (prices rise while real
GNP remains unchanged). Since resources are fully employed, employment
does not change; the economy remains at point *e'* in Figure 16–2b.

To summarize, a decline in aggregate demand reduces real GNP and
employment (of labor and capital) while having relatively little effect on the
price level. An increase in aggregate demand increases real GNP and employment *if* there is slack in the economy (there is unused productive capacity), while putting relatively little upward pressure on prices. In contrast,
when the economy is operating at capacity, an increase in aggregate demand
increases prices and has little affect on real GNP and employment.

INCOME DETERMINATION: A SIMPLE CASE

To explain more fully the relationship between aggregate demand, on the
one hand, and output, employment, and prices on the other, let us consider
a very simple case. Suppose that government spending (G) and investment
spending (I) are fixed dollar amounts and that net foreign spending (X − M)
is zero. Consumption is thus the only category of spending (aggregate demand) that is endogenous (depends on economic conditions).

The main determinant of household consumption spending is the level of disposable personal income, which is GNP minus gross business saving minus net taxes. Net taxes are total taxes minus government transfers to persons. The present structure of the U.S. economy is such that disposable personal income and GNP are directly related. But the increase (decrease) in disposable personal income is less than the corresponding increase (decrease) in GNP because the sum of gross business saving and net taxes also increases (decreases) when GNP increases (decreases).

Consumption is directly related to disposable personal income, with the *marginal propensity to consume* (MPC) out of disposable income being less than 1. That is, consumption increases (decreases) when disposable income increases (decreases), but it changes by some fraction of the change in disposable income. Most estimates place the MPC between .7 and .9, with the short-run MPC being less than the long run.

Since consumption increases as disposable personal income increases, and personal income increases as GNP increases, consumption spending is an increasing function of the level of GNP (GNI). For example, suppose that disposable personal income increases by $.50 when GNP increases by $1.00 and that the MPC is .8. In this case, consumption increases by .8 ($.50) = $.4 for every $1.00 increase in GNP.[3] This relationship between consumption and GNP is depicted by the line labeled C in Figure 16-3.

We will discuss other factors that may influence consumption spending when we examine a more complicated and realistic model of income determination.

Aggregate demand for each level of GNP is the level of consumption spending forthcoming at that level, as given by the C schedule in Figure 16-3, *plus* the fixed amounts of government and investment spending, assumed to be $385 billion and $265 billion, respectively. For these assumptions, the equilibrium level of GNP is $1,800 billion; at that level consumption is $1,150 billion, which, with I and G of $650 billion, gives aggregate demand of $1,800 billion. At the equilibrium level of GNP, aggregate demand for goods and services (C + I + G) equals total production (GNP). This equilibrium point is represented geometrically in Figure 16-3 by the intersection of the aggregate demand schedule and the 45° line. At a lesser level of GNP, say $1,500 billion, consumption is $1,030 billion giving total demand of $1,030 + $265 + $385 = $1,680 billion — demand exceeds production by $180 billion. When demand exceeds production, order backlogs increase and inventories decline below desired levels, signalling producers to

---

3 The change in disposable income is equal to the change in GNP *minus* the changes in gross business saving and taxes. The example in Figure 16-3 assumes that gross business saving and net taxes increase by $.50 for each $1.00 increase in GNP, leaving a $.50 increase in disposable income.

FIGURE 16–3
INCOME DETERMINATION WITH FIXED LEVELS OF G AND *I*

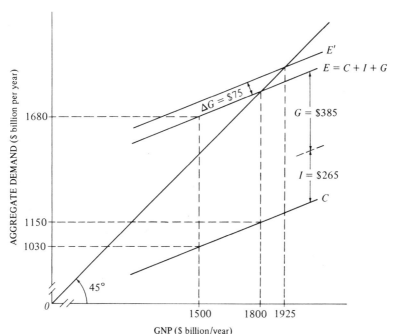

increase production. If producers have unused capacity, production and real GNP increase to meet the excess demand. If there is no excess capacity and production cannot be increased, prices tend to rise as buyers compete for a supply of goods and services that falls short of their total demands. In contrast, if GNP exceeds $1,800 billion, production exceeds demand. Inventories rise above desired levels and order backlogs shorten, signalling the need for less production; real GNP and employment fall until the equilibrium level of $1,800 billion is reached. Only at that level does production (GNP) equal demand, the condition that is necessary for the economy to be in equilibrium.

We can state the condition for equilibrium in the economy differently: Aggregate demand must equal aggregate income, since aggregate income measures the total value of the goods and services produced. Thus, when aggregate demand is more (less) than aggregate income, the various spending units (households, businesses, and governments) wish to buy more (less) than is being produced, and the economy is not in equilibrium. Aggregate income (GNI) is distributed among households, businesses, and governments: $GNI = DI + S_B + TX - TR$, where DI is disposable personal income accruing to households, S_B is gross business saving (income retained by businesses), and $TX - TR$ is taxes (TX) minus government transfers to persons (TR). $TX - TR$ is the *net* tax revenue of governments. Recall that we assume $(X - M)$ to be zero. Aggregate demand, then, equals aggregate income when $C + I + G = GNI = DI + S_B + TX - TR$. Household disposable income is allocated to consumption and saving: $DI = C + S_H$,[4] so we can write the equilibrium condition as $C + I + G = C + S_H + S_B + TX - TR$, or $I + G = S + T$, where S is business and household savings $(S_B + S_H)$ and T is net taxes $(TX - TR)$. The equilibrium condition, $I + G = S + T$, has a very simple meaning: Income that is generated from production and not spent on consumer goods, $S + T$, must be spent on other goods, $G + I$.

Fiscal policy influences the equilibrium level of GNP in our simple model in two ways. First, and most directly, government purchases of goods and services are a component of aggregate demand. Second, the disposable income and, hence, the amount of consumption spending corresponding to each level of GNP depends on the level of taxes and transfers. Higher personal taxes mean lower disposable income and consumption spending at each level of GNP, while higher transfers have the opposite effect. To better understand these fiscal policy influences, let us consider in sequence the effects of changes in government spending, taxes, and transfers.

CHANGES IN GOVERNMENT SPENDING

Let us suppose that in Figure 16–3 G is increased from $385 billion to $460 billion without any increase in taxes. That is, the increase in spending is financed by borrowing. The increase in G shifts aggregate demand upward from E to E'. The equilibrium GNP thus increases from $1,800 billion to $1,925 billion. What happens as a result of these increases depends on whether the economy's capacity is fully employed at the $1,800 billion level of GNP.

Consider first the case in which the economy's capacity was underutilized at the $1,800 billion GNP level so that the increase in G causes an increase in real GNP from $1,800 billion to $1,925 billion and no increase in price. Corresponding to this increase in real GNP is an increase in employment of labor and capital; the increase in aggregate demand increases utilization of the economy's productive capacity.

The ratio of the ultimate change in GNP to the initial change in government spending, $125 billion ÷ $75 billion = 1.67, is called the *multiplier*. The effect of the increase in G is multiplied because the initial increase in

4 This ignores private transfers to foreigners, usually a very small amount.

aggregate demand increases GNP and disposable income, which increases consumption, which again increases GNP, etc.[5]

What are the effects of the increase in G if the economy's capacity is instead fully employed at a GNP of $1,800 billion? Real GNP cannot increase; an increase in G and aggregate demand can only lead to a bidding up of the prices of the given amount of goods and services. Specifically, prices increase by $125 billion ÷ $1,800 billion × 100 = 6.94 percent, so that the goods and services that sold for $1,800 billion before the increase in G sell for $1,925 billion after the increase. The full-employment level of GNP becomes $1,925 rather than $1,800 billion. The increase in aggregate demand is thus satisfied by an increase in prices rather than an increase in output of goods and services.[6]

With GNP at $1,925 billion, consumption is $1,200 billion. However, with prices 6.94 percent higher, real consumption, measured in prices prevailing before the increase in G, is only $1,200 billion ÷ 1.0694 = $1,122 billion. Similarly, real investment spending is $265 billion ÷ 1.0694 = $248 billion; and real government spending is $460 billion ÷ 1.0694 = $430 billion. Although government spending has increased $75 billion in money terms, it has increased only $45 billion in real terms because the inflation resulting from the increase in G has reduced the purchasing power of each dollar by 6.94 percent. The $45 billion increase in real government spending has decreased real consumption by $28 billion and investment spending by $17 billion. The increase in real government spending has "crowded out" an equivalent amount of real private spending.[7] Recall that crowding out did not occur when capacity was underutilized. In that case, the real increase in government spending was greater ($75 billion versus $45 billion), real consumption spending increased by $50 billion, and investment spending was unchanged.

---

5 For a detailed derivation and discussion of the multiplier, see Thomas F. Dernburg and Duncan M. McDougall, *Macroeconomics*, 5th ed. (New York: McGraw-Hill, 1976), pp. 67–72.

6 Why does the increase in government spending cause only a limited increase in prices, instead of a continuing inflation? Basically, the *dollar* amount of aggregate demand rises less rapidly than prices and the *dollar* amount of GNP. When government spending is initially increased to $460 billion, aggregate demand immediately increases to $1,875 billion, which exceeds the existing GNP of $1,800 billion. As prices and GNP rise in response to this excess demand, the dollar amount of $G + I$ remains unchanged, by assumption. The dollar amounts of disposable income and, hence, consumption increase as prices increase, but by smaller amounts than GNP. Since the dollar amount of demand rises less rapidly than the dollar amount of production (GNP), production eventually catches up with demand. Inflation (price increases) ceases when excess demand is thus eliminated.

7 During actual periods of inflation, prices do not rise uniformly as our example presumes. However, the conclusion that the increase in real government spending crowds out an equal amount of real private spending remains valid.

FIGURE 16–4
EFFECTS OF A DECREASE IN G

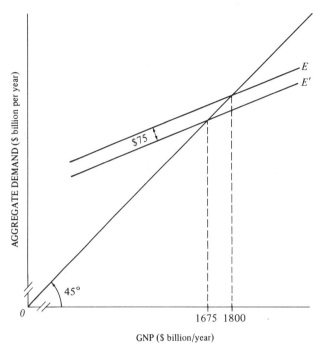

GNP ($ billion/year)

These two cases — the first being no increase in prices and the second being no increase in real GNP — should be viewed as polar cases. In practice, an increase in G is likely to increase both prices and real GNP, with the price increase being greater and the increase in real GNP being smaller as the economy's capacity is closer to being fully utilized. And some crowding out is likely to occur, but the increase in real government spending is fully offset by an equal decrease in private (consumption and investment) spending only when capacity utilization is very high, a state that has not existed in the United States since World War II.[8]

Figure 16–4 illustrates the effect of a decrease in G of $75 billion, with no change in taxes; hence, government borrowing falls by $75 billion. Since prices are inflexible downward, the decline in aggregate demand decreases real GNP and employment, with real GNP falling from $1,800 billion to $1,675 billion.

8 The discussion of the effects of increases in government spending and crowding out is simplified, since an increase in G entails an increase in borrowing, which may lead to higher interest rates. Higher interest rates, in turn, may reduce both C and I; real private output may be reduced by increases in both prices and interest rates when G is increased without increasing taxes. We discuss those effects on pp. 346–351.

CHANGES IN TAXES AND TRANSFERS

Personal taxes, such as income taxes, do not affect aggregate demand directly but, rather, via their effect on disposable income. To illustrate, let us look at Figure 16–5, where the consumption and aggregate demand functions of Figure 16–3 are reproduced. These functions are drawn for an implicit level of taxation. A change in taxes alters the consumption-GNP relationship. For example, suppose that taxes are reduced by $75 billion for each level of GNP, increasing disposable personal income by an equal amount. Higher disposable income means higher consumption, but consumption does not increase by the full amount of the increase in disposable income (the decrease in taxes). If the MPC is .8, then the $75 billion tax cut and corresponding increase in disposable income increases consumption by .8 ($75) = $60 billion. The consumption-GNP relation in Figure 16–5 thus shifts up to C' and aggregate demand increases to E'. Due to the multiplier, the increase in aggregate demand increases the equilibrium income from $1,800 to $1,900 billion.

From this point on, analysis of the effects of the tax cut and consequent increase in consumption and aggregate demand is the same as that for the

FIGURE 16–5
EFFECTS OF TAX CHANGES

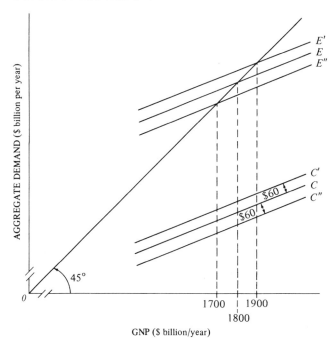

GNP ($ billion/year)

increase in government spending. If capacity is sufficiently underutilized at a GNP of $1,800 billion, then the tax cut will stimulate an increase in real GNP of $100 billion and very little increase in prices. However, if capacity is fully utilized, the tax cut will trigger price increases approaching $100 billion $\div$ $1,800 billion $\times$ 100 = 5.6 percent and no increase in real GNP. Thus, tax cuts and expenditure increases of equal amounts differ only in the *magnitude* of their effects on aggregate demand, employment, real GNP, and prices. A tax cut has a smaller expansionary effect than an equal (in dollar amount) increase in G because part of the initial tax cut is saved by households (20 percent when the MPC is .8) rather than being spent on consumption.

Similarly, tax increases affect aggregate demand, real GNP, and prices in the same fashion as decreases in G. The only difference is that a tax increase has a quantitatively smaller effect than an expenditure decrease of the same amount. To illustrate, in Figure 16–5 a tax increase of $75 billion for each level of GNP reduces consumption spending at each level of GNP by .8 ($75) = $60 billion if the MPC is .8, thus shifting the consumption-GNP relationship to C''. As a result, real GNP falls from $1,800 billion to $1,700 billion. In contrast, the $75 billion decrease in G reduced real GNP to $1,675 billion.

The multiplier for a change in taxes is smaller than, and opposite in sign to, the multiplier for an expenditure change. For the above examples, the government expenditure multiplier is $\Delta GNP/\Delta G$ = $125 billion $\div$ $75 billion = 1.67. The tax multiplier is $\Delta GNP/\Delta TX$ = $100 billion $\div$ − $75 billion = −1.33. Since the multiplier for changes in G is greater in absolute value than the tax change multiplier, an increase in G accompanied by an equal increase in T is expansionary. Conversely, a decrease in G accompanied by an equal decrease in T is "contractionary." That is, the *balanced-budget multiplier* — the multiplier for cases in which $\Delta G = \Delta T$ — is positive. For the example at hand, the balanced-budget multiplier is $\Delta GNP/\Delta G$ + $\Delta GNP/\Delta TX$ = 1.67 − 1.33 = .34.

Increases (decreases) in government transfers have the same effects as decreases (increases) in taxes because transfers are, in effect, negative taxes. An increase in transfers increases disposable income and consumption; a decrease in transfers has the opposite effect. The multiplier for changes in transfers is the negative of the tax change multiplier: $\Delta GNP/\Delta TR$ = − $\Delta GNP/\Delta TX$.

CHANGES IN PRIVATE-SECTOR DEMAND

Although our main concern is with the effects of government fiscal policies, we should be aware that changes in private investment and consumption demand may alter equilibrium income. If businesses decide to spend more (less) on investment at each level of GNP, then the aggregate demand schedule in Figure 16–3 shifts up (down) just as it does when government spending changes. Similarly, aggregate demand increases (decreases) when households decide to spend more (less) of their disposable income on consumption. The multiplier for such changes in private-sector demand is the same as the government spending multiplier. Changes in private-sector demand may be and often are a source of instability and therefore give rise to the need for monetary and fiscal stabilization.[9]

INCOME DETERMINATION: MONEY AND INTEREST RATES

In the preceding discussion we did not take into account some of the main factors affecting the various components of aggregate demand. In particular, interest rates affect both consumption and investment spending and some capital spending by state and local governments as well. Higher interest rates entail lower spending in these categories, other factors being the same. Private spending, particularly consumption spending, may also be affected by real balances, which are the purchasing power of the money and government bonds held by households and businesses. Spending tends to be directly related to these real balances. Both interest rates and real balances are affected in turn by the monetary policy of the Federal Reserve System (the Fed) and by government borrowing.

Our main concern is with fiscal policy. But it is important for us to know, in a very general way, how monetary policy affects aggregate demand because monetary and fiscal policies are to a degree substitute means of stabilizing the economy. The Fed controls the lending ability of commercial banks and, to a lesser extent, other lending institutions. In doing so, it affects interest rates and the money supply. Through restrictive monetary policy, primarily open-market sales of government bonds, the Fed can reduce the availability of credit, increase interest rates, and reduce the money supply. Thus, the Fed can reduce the C and I components of aggregate demand through restrictive monetary policy. With an expansionary monetary policy, usually achieved by the open-market purchases of government bonds, the Fed can increase aggregate demand.

The mechanics and issues of monetary policy are well discussed elsewhere.[10] Our purpose here is to note that the Fed may take monetary policy measures that either reinforce or offset the effects of fiscal measures (changes

9 For more discussion of the determinants of private expenditures, see Dernburg and McDougall, *Macroeconomics*, chaps. 4, 6.

10 Ibid., chaps. 7, 8, 9, 16, 19.

in taxation and government spending) on aggregate demand, employment, output, and prices. Therefore, unless otherwise stated, when we speak of the effects of fiscal measures, it is with reference to a given backdrop of monetary policy. That is, the stated effects are those that occur if the Fed does not alter its monetary policies in response to the fiscal measures being undertaken.

That is not to say, however, that fiscal measures do not affect interest rates; indeed, in the following sections we deal with such effects. More specifically, fiscal policies have monetary "feedback" effects that tend to dampen (reduce in magnitude) fiscal policy effects on aggregate demand. In the following sections we examine the effects of changes in government spending and taxes, taking account of these feedback effects.

INTEREST RATE EFFECTS

An increase in government spending tends to increase interest rates, thereby reducing private consumption and investment demand, for two reasons. First, as we noted above, increased spending with no change in taxes requires increased borrowing. Governments borrow by selling bonds. In doing so, they compete with private borrowers for funds, which usually increases interest rates (the price of borrowed funds) if monetary policy remains unaffected by the increase in spending and borrowing.[11] (Recall that we are assuming such to be the case.)

Second, as GNP rises in response to the increase in G, the demand for money for transactions increases. (Greater GNP means a greater volume of transactions.) Households and businesses try to obtain more money by selling other assets, primarily bonds. As they do so, bond prices fall and interest rates increase until people are satisfied with the available supply of money.

When interest rates increase for either of these reasons, the demand-expanding effect of increased government spending is less than it would be in the absence of such interest rate increases.[12] In other terms, an increase in G induces interest rate increases that tend to crowd out private spending. The magnitude of the crowding out depends on the interest elasticity of the

11 Borrowing results in the accumulation of debt. Hence, financing a spending increase of, say, $10 billion per year by borrowing rather than taxation means that the stock of debt inceases by $10 billion in *each* year that the higher level of spending is maintained. In Chapter 19 we examine the consequences of such debt accumulation.

12 Of course, these interest rate increases can be prevented by the Fed if it buys bonds on the open market to expand the money supply so that the increased demand for money can be met without an increase in interest rates.

transactions demand for money.[13] And it depends on the extent to which banks and other lending institutions are "loaned up" in the sense that they are either unwilling or unable to make additional loans to the government (buy its bonds) and acquire the bonds of the households and businesses that are attempting to add to their stock of money. If the lending institutions are fully loaned up, then government borrowing tends to drive up interest rates enough to crowd out an equal amount of private borrowing and spending, so that the increase in G causes little if any increase in aggregate demand. However, if lending institutions are not fully loaned up, government borrowing does not displace an equal amount of private borrowing and spending, although some crowding out is likely; and an increase in G generates a net increase in aggregate demand. This crowding out, unlike the crowding out we discussed in the preceding section, can occur even though the economy's productive capacity is not fully utilized.[14]

As a practical matter, U.S. lending institutions have never in recent years been loaned up in the sense we have discussed. Interest rate increases induced by an increase in government spending and borrowing would not, since 1930, have reduced private spending and borrowing dollar for dollar.

A decrease in government spending, given the level of taxation, decreases interest rates by the reverse of the above reasoning. Less spending means less borrowing and lower interest rates on that account.[15] Less spending also means lower GNP and a lower transactions demand for money and, hence, lower interest rates. The induced reductions in interest rates tend to stimulate private spending, thus partly offsetting the decline in aggregate demand created by the decrease in G. That is, private spending tends to "fill in"

---

13 Other factors being the same, a given increase in GNP causes a small increase in interest rates if the interest elasticity of the transactions demand for money is high, and vice versa. Hence, the crowding out of private spending is less the more interest-elastic the transactions demand for money is.

14 The extent to which lending institutions are loaned up may also be thought of as the *interest elasticity of the money supply*. It decreases as lending institutions become less willing (or able) to make loans and buy bonds. For a review of the literature dealing with crowding out, see Keith Carlson and Roger Spencer, "Crowding Out and its Critics," *Review of the Federal Reserve Bank of St. Louis*, 57, No. 12 (December 1975), pp. 2–17.

15 Lower spending, given the level of taxes, means a smaller government deficit or a larger surplus. A lower deficit means less *new* borrowing. A larger surplus means that the government is able to retire (repay) more of its previous debt. Increased repayment has the same effect on credit conditions and interest rates as decreased borrowing, because repayment of government debt releases funds to private borrowers. In short, when government decreases its spending while holding constant its tax collections, it increases the availability of funds to private borrowers, thus stimulating private spending that is based on borrowing.

some of the initial decline in aggregate demand caused by lower government spending. But filling in is unlikely to be complete. Thus, the decrease in G produces a net decrease in aggregate demand, but a smaller decrease than would have occurred in the absence of the interest rate effects.

Changes in net taxes, given the level of government spending, likewise affect interest rates.[16] An increase in net taxes tends to reduce interest rates because it reduces government borrowing and GNP. And the reduction in interest rates tends to reduce the demand-depressing effects of higher taxes. Conversely, a decrease in net taxes tends to increase interest rates; higher interest rates tend to counter the demand stimulus of the tax decrease.

REAL-BALANCE EFFECTS

The other monetary feedback occurs because fiscal policies may affect real balances. The real-balance effects arise if changes in government spending and taxes affect the price level.

If prices rise in response to the aggregate demand increase that results from an increase in G or a decrease in T, the purchasing power of the money and government bonds held by households and businesses declines. The *real* value of these dollar-denominated assets falls; that is, there is a decline in real balances. This is a decline in the real wealth of households and businesses, which may cause private demand, particularly consumption spending by households, to fall. To the extent that it does, the demand-stimulating effect of the increase in G or decrease in T is weakened.

The reverse occurs when the initial decrease in aggregate demand that follows from a decrease in G or an increase in T causes prices to fall. In this case, real balances increase because the purchasing power of a given stock of money and of government bonds is greater when prices are lower. This increase in real balances (real wealth) may stimulate private spending, thus partly offsetting the demand-depressing effects of the decrease in G or increase in T. However, because prices tend to be inflexible downward, the real-balance effect is likely to be a relatively weak offset to the decline in aggregate demand that results from a decrease in G or an increase in T (or any other source).

To sum up, changes in government spending and net taxes induce interest rate changes and real-balance effects, given that monetary policy is *not* adjusted in response to the fiscal changes. The interest rate and real-balance effects, in turn, alter private demand so as to *dampen* the *direct* effects of spending and tax changes. In other terms, these monetary effects of fiscal

16 Recall that *net* taxes may be increased by either increasing taxes or decreasing government transfers to persons, and net taxes may be reduced by the opposite actions.

policies tend to reduce the magnitude of the fiscal policy multipliers. More generally, these monetary feedbacks tend to dampen the effects of changes in aggregate demand from whatever source. However, they are unlikely to offset completely the basic fiscal effects. Hence, our conclusions in the preceding section, which did not consider interest rate and real-balance effects, hold: Increases (decreases) in government spending increase (decrease) aggregate demand, and increases (decreases) in *net* taxes decrease (increase) aggregate demand.

INCOME DETERMINATION IN AN OPEN ECONOMY

So far we have assumed that the economy is closed; that is, there are neither exports nor imports; so $X - M = 0$. Let us now consider the more realistic case in which there is foreign trade.

In very general terms, trade links the economies of virtually all nations, although the linkages are strongest when exports and imports are large relative to the size of the nation's economy (GNP). Because of these linkages, economies tend to move up and down together. An increase in aggregate demand in one country tends to spill over into other countries, increasing the demand for their production. Decreases in demand likewise spill over.

More specifically, when foreign trade is possible, part of any increase in aggregate demand, especially private demand for consumer and investment goods, tends to be met by imports—the purchase of foreign-produced goods and services. Imports represent a "leakage" of demand out of a country. Thus, with foreign trade, some of the increase in aggregate demand due to an increase in G (or decrease in T) is filled by foreign goods. And a fiscal change of a given amount has a smaller ultimate effect on domestic output, employment, and prices with trade than without it. That is, import leakages reduce the multiplier for changes in G and T.

Correspondingly, the fiscal (and monetary) policies of each nation affect aggregate demand, employment, and prices in other nations. The policies of large nations, such as the United States, have a greater international impact than those of smaller nations. For example, when the U.S. government increases aggregate demand in the United States by decreasing T or increasing G, it also increases aggregate demand in other countries. The reason is that U.S. residents buy more foreign-produced goods. Conversely, when the U.S. government takes restrictive fiscal measures, it decreases aggregate demand in other countries because U.S. residents import less. Because employment, output, and prices in each nation are affected by the policies of other nations, international coordination of stabilization policies would be useful and does occur to some extent. Indeed, economic conditions in small countries with large trade sectors, such as the Netherlands and the

United Kingdom, may be dominated by the policies of other countries, in which case stabilization objectives are unlikely to be achieved without the cooperation of major trading partners.

Although it reduces in absolute value the multipliers for fiscal changes, trade does not upset any of our earlier conclusions about the effects of changes in G and T. Trade, like the monetary feedbacks, merely dampens the effects of fiscal changes.

INFLATIONARY AND DEFLATIONARY GAPS AND THE POTENTIAL FOR FISCAL STABILIZATION

Historically, aggregate demand in the United States has fluctuated considerably from year to year for a variety of reasons: technological change, changes in economic conditions in other parts of the world, wars, changes in expectations of businesses and households, and variability in monetary policy and government spending and taxation. Whatever their source, demand fluctuations have meant that aggregate demand has often been excessive or deficient in relation to the economy's productive capacity. Capacity tends to change gradually and steadily, while demand tends to jump around.

When aggregate demand falls short of capacity (potential GNP) there is said to be a *deflationary gap*. In Figure 16–6 potential GNP is Y. But with aggregate demand as given by the E' schedule, the equilibrium level of GNP is Y' rather than the full-employment or potential level of Y. Unless demand is increased, GNP will fall below its potential by $Y - Y'$. An upward shift in the aggregate demand schedule to E is required to bring demand in line with the economy's capacity to produce. The magnitude of this required increase measures the deflationary gap. Such an increase in aggregate demand can in principle be achieved by increasing G or decreasing T or doing both.

An *inflationary gap* is said to exist when aggregate demand exceeds productive capacity, as shown by E'' in Figure 16–6. At prevailing prices, aggregate demand exceeds capacity by the vertical distance between E'' and E, which measures the inflationary gap. Unless it is eliminated, such excess demand leads to price increases (inflation), as we explained above. Excess demand can in principle be eliminated by decreasing G or increasing T or doing both.[17]

17 Eliminating inflationary gaps does not necessarily eliminate inflation because it is not always due to excess aggregate demand. There are other varieties of inflation, such as *cost-push*. Inflation that is not caused by excess demand may occur even when there is a deflationary gap or as the deflationary gap is closed. We discuss this problem, which greatly complicates stabilization policy, in Chapter 17.

FIGURE 16–6
INFLATIONARY AND DEFLATIONARY GAPS

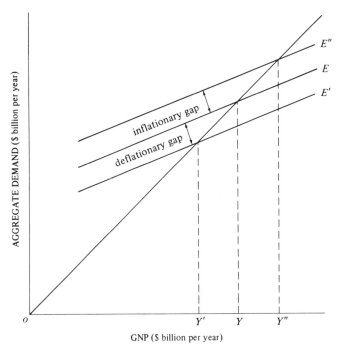

GNP ($ billion per year)

Thus, potential for fiscal stabilization (changing G and T to bring aggregate demand into line with capacity) exists when there is either a deflationary or inflationary gap. However, despite such potential, we cannot
conclude that the government should try to stabilize the economy with fiscal
policy if there are other adjustment mechanisms that automatically and
quickly eliminate inflationary and deflationary gaps.

Unfortunately, such is not the case. When a deflationary gap exists and
persists, we might expect that producers would reduce prices in an attempt
to sell more output and increase capacity utilization, while workers would
accept lower wages in order to reduce unemployment. In principle, such
downward adjustment of wages and prices may increase aggregate demand
in real terms via the real-balance effect. As prices decline the real wealth
represented by money and government bonds increases. Presumably, this
increase in real wealth would eventually cause people to spend a larger share
of their disposable incomes. For example, if prices, wages, and money
disposable incomes fall by 10 percent, consumption expenditures would fall
less than 10 percent because of the real-balance effect. Real consumption

expenditures, the total quantities of goods and services that people want to buy, would thus increase. In other terms, the real-balance effect tends to shift the aggregate demand schedule upward, thereby eliminating a deflationary gap.

However, relying on the real-balance effect to eliminate deflationary gaps is not an attractive policy for several reasons. First, as we noted earlier, downward flexibility of wages and prices has not been the rule. Adjustment via the real-balance effect would be, at best, a slow process, with much potential output being lost and the hardships of unemployment being borne during the lengthy adjustment period. Second, the real-balance effect on consumption spending appears to be relatively weak; hence large wage and price declines might be required to eliminate unemployment.[18] Apart from the time required for such price declines, other problems arise. In particular, the real burden of debt increases; debtors must pay off debts with dollars that are more and more difficult to earn because of lower wages and prices. Mortgages are foreclosed; homes, farms, and businesses are lost.[19] Finally, even if the real-balance effect would eventually eliminate a deflationary gap, *exactly* the same result can be achieved through an expansion of the stock of money and government bonds. That is, real balances can be increased either by decreasing prices with the stock of money and bonds being unchanged, or by increasing the stock of money and government bonds with prices being unchanged. The latter approach would work more quickly and not produce the distorting effects of large price declines.[20]

What about inflationary gaps? Will excess demand be eliminated in the absence of explicit, discretionary adjustment of G and T? The answer is yes, although inflation tends to be self-perpetuating to a degree. For example, inflation may breed expectations of future inflation, which may trigger hoarding and attempts to buy before prices rise further. Such *anticipatory* buying increases aggregate demand (relative to what it would have been in the absence of inflation), thus contributing to a fulfillment of inflationary expectations. Also, higher prices tend to lead to higher wages and costs, which justify higher prices, etc., causing a *wage-price spiral*.

---

18 Prices as measured by the Consumer Price Index declined by 22 percent from 1930 to 1933; yet unemployment remained high and the Depression persisted.

19 Mortgage foreclosures were a severe problem during the Depression of the 1930s and during most earlier depression periods experienced in the United States. The long period of declining prices that began in 1873 and persisted until the discovery of gold in Alaska in 1896 imposed large burdens on debtors, especially farmers, and led to pressure for monetization of silver and the fiery campaign rhetoric of William Jennings Bryan.

20 For further discussion of the real-balance effect, see Dernberg and McDougall, *Macroeconomics*, pp. 207–209, and Warren L. Smith, *Macroeconomics* (Homewood, Ill.: Irwin, 1970), pp. 330–333.

But there is a definite limit to that inflationary process *if* the money supply is not expanded in reaction to it. As we explained above, rising prices and money incomes increase the demand for money for transactions. With a given supply of money, an increase in the demand for money leads to higher interest rates, which curtail investment and consumption spending and aggregate demand. Also, with a given stock of money and government bonds, rising prices mean declining real balances and lower aggregate demand on that count.

In the example in Figure 16–6, the inflationary gap that exists when aggregate demand is given by E'' generates price and interest rate increases that tend to shift E'' down. At the same time, potential GNP increases in *money terms* as prices increase. Both adjustments occur until the inflationary gap is eliminated. In the new equilibrium, prices and interest rates are higher, the aggregate demand schedule is lower, and potential GNP is greater in money terms (because of higher prices) but not in real terms.

Even in the absence of restrictive fiscal policy, an inflationary gap is eliminated by higher prices and interest rates. Of course, the difficulty is that the gap is eliminated by inflation. Fiscal policies that reduce aggregate demand and eliminate the inflationary gap without allowing the inflation to run its course would seem to be more appropriate.

In sum, there are "automatic" mechanisms that tend to limit and eliminate inflationary and deflationary gaps. However, relying on such mechanisms can lead to long periods of unemployment and falling prices in the case of deflationary gaps and to inflation in the case of inflationary gaps. Moreover, the economy is subject to a continuing series of "shocks" (changes in aggregate demand) that generate inflationary and deflationary gaps. While each gap may eventually be eliminated by built-in adjustments, a series of demand-increasing shocks could generate a long period of inflation. Similarly, a series of demand-depressing shocks could generate a long period of unemployment. Or, if shocks are first deflationary, then inflationary, etc., then unstable, fluctuating economic activity occurs. This conclusion stands even though the U.S. economy currently has a number of built-in-stabilizers (to be discussed in the next chapter) that dampen fluctuations in aggregate demand. Hence, the economy is not inherently stable enough for us to conclude that fiscal stabilization efforts are unnecessary. However, the question does remain of whether there are workable mechanisms for fiscal stabilization. In Chapter 17 we will deal with this question as we examine the "how" of stabilization.

SUMMARY

For goods and services to be produced, they must be demanded (purchased). The total value of goods and services demanded by various spending units is called *aggregate demand*. When aggregate demand falls short of potential GNP, resources are unemployed; when aggregate demand exceeds full potential GNP, the price level increases.

Government influences aggregate demand as it raises revenue and makes expenditures. In principle, by appropriately adjusting its purchases (G) and its net taxes (T), government can match aggregate demand with potential GNP. When aggregate demand falls short of potential GNP, the appropriate fiscal policy is to reduce taxes or increase government spending. The opposite policy is appropriate when demand exceeds potential GNP.

Given the potential for stabilizing fiscal policy, there remain questions about its implementation and the proper mix of fiscal and monetary policies. We will explore those questions in the following chapter.

SUPPLEMENTARY READINGS

Dernburg, Thomas F., and McDougall, Duncan M. *Macroeconomics*. 5th ed. New York: McGraw-Hill, 1976.

Okun, Arnold M. "Potential GNP: Its Measurement and Significance." In *Readings in Money, National Income, and Stabilization Policy*, rev. ed., edited by Warren L. Smith and R. L. Teigen. Homewood, Ill.: Irwin, 1970.

CHAPTER SEVENTEEN

FISCAL STABILIZATION:
ISSUES AND PROBLEMS

Since the Employment Act of 1946, the use of fiscal policy to stabilize the economy has been a recognized function of the U.S. federal government. As we have seen in the preceding chapter, government's budgetary policy does affect aggregate demand. So there is clearly a potential for the use of fiscal policy to stabilize the economy.

While the basic idea underlying fiscal stabilization (the reduction or elimination of inflationary and deflationary gaps) is very simple, deciding on and executing stabilization policies turns out to be complicated — so much so that some have questioned whether discretionary fiscal policy can be used in a stabilizing manner.[1] In this chapter we examine the main issues and problems that must be confronted in designing and implementing stabilization policy, beginning in the next section with the definition of stabilization targets. We explore the problems of carrying out policies to achieve stabilization targets in subsequent sections. Finally, we consider the relative effectiveness of monetary and fiscal policies and discuss issues arising in the choice of a monetary-fiscal policy "mix."

STABILIZATION TARGETS

In very general terms, the object of stabilization policy is to match aggregate demand with potential GNP. However, that is not sufficiently specific to guide policy making — potential GNP must be defined more precisely. In

1 Some of the difficulties of implementing fiscal policy are discussed by Alan S. Blinder and Robert M. Solow, "Analytical Foundations of Fiscal Policy," in *The Economics of Public Finance* (Washington: Brookings, 1974), pp. 3–115.

doing so, we necessarily make an assumption about the degree or rate of labor force employment (unemployment) at which productive capacity is "fully" utilized. Also, the choice of a target unemployment (employment) rate for a specific period, say the coming year, carries with it the choice of an inflation rate, which is inversely related to the target unemployment rate. For this reason, stabilization goals are often stated in terms of inflation and unemployment rates, which, for a particular period, can be translated into a GNP target.

WHAT IS FULL EMPLOYMENT?

When is the capacity of the economy fully utilized? When everyone who wants a job is working? When there is a job for everyone who wishes to work, but not everyone is working because some people are moving between jobs? When unemployment does not exceed a specific percentage of the labor force? The first answer, which implies a zero-measured rate of unemployment, is unsatisfactory because some temporary unemployment is necessary in a dynamic economy. The demand for labor increases in some industries and falls in others as product demands and costs change. The temporary unemployment this produces is desirable. So, the second answer is perhaps the best — full employment occurs when there is a job available for everyone who wants a job (at prevailing wage rates).

However, the employment target has not been so stated in the United States, in part because we do not know the measured rate of unemployment for which the number of jobs would equal the number of job seekers.[2] Instead, "full" employment has been somewhat arbitrarily defined as when 96 percent of the labor force (those persons wanting to work) is employed. Thus, the potential GNP statistics given in Figure 16–1 assume that full employment and full capacity utilization occur at a 96 percent employment rate. In recent years some have redefined full employment to correspond with a higher overall rate of unemployment, usually 5 percent.[3]

---

2 Although a comprehensive measure of available jobs does not exist, there is evidence of an inverse relationship between the aggregate unemployment rate and job vacancy rates. See George L. Perry, "Changing Labor Markets and Inflation," in *Brookings Papers on Economic Activity*, vol. 3, ed. Arthur M. Okun and George L. Perry (Washington, 1970), pp. 411–441, for a study of labor market tightness.

Even with equal numbers of jobs and job seekers, there may not be a job for everyone who wishes to work because some people may lack *marketable* skills. When job seekers are unemployed because they do not have the skills required to fill existing vacancies or those likely to arise in the near future, the result is termed *structural unemployment*.

3 The main reason for redefining full employment is that the rate of inflation associated with a 4 percent unemployment rate appears to be greater today than it was fifteen or twenty years ago. Perry explains why such may be the case in "Changing Labor Markets and Inflation." He

WHAT IS PRICE STABILITY?

Like full employment, the concept of price stability is somew.
It does not mean that prices do not change but, rather, tha
average, of prices shows "little" if any change. In the Unit
Consumer Price Index (CPI), which is a regularly publish
average of the prices paid for consumer goods, is widely used to mea
price level (average prices). Other frequently used indices (averages) are ⎣
Wholesale Price Index (WPI) and the GNP deflator, the GNP deflator being
the broadest of the three indices as it is an average of the prices of all goods
and services included in GNP. Figure 17–1 shows the price movements of
recent years as measured by each of the indices.

From Figure 17–1 we can readily see that the rate of price change (degree
of inflation) experienced over any particular period depends on which price
index is used to measure the price level. One important issue, then, in
defining and measuring price stability, or the lack of it, is the choice of a
price index, which is, in turn, an implicit decision about the importance of
various price changes. If the CPI is used, then changes in wholesale prices
and the prices of investment and government-purchased goods are ignored
until and unless they are subsequently reflected in changes in the CPI. If the
GNP deflator is used, then changes in the price of each commodity is
weighted by that commodity's share in GNP; the importance of a change in
the price of a commodity is proportional to the commodity's importance in
GNP. The rate of change of the CPI is the most commonly used measure of
inflation, presumably because people are primarily concerned about changes
in the prices paid for consumer goods.

Regardless of which index is used to measure inflation, the target of
stabilization policy is usually stated as an *acceptable* rate of inflation. What
is acceptable varies among persons and over time and depends largely on
whether the inflation is correctly anticipated. People tend to plan on the
basis of what they expect the rate of inflation to be. If their expectations
prove correct, then the inflation does not disrupt their plans. If, however,

---

suggests that the changing composition of the unemployed portion of the labor force is a major
factor. The fraction of total unemployment accounted for by young, minority-group, and
women workers has been increasing, while the fraction accounted for by adult male workers has
been decreasing. That is, an aggregate unemployment rate of 4 percent implies a lower unemployment rate for adult male workers today than was the case fifteen and twenty years ago
and thus means a tighter labor market for those workers than it did in previous years. The
relatively greater demand for those workers leads, in turn, to relatively greater wage increases at
4 percent unemployment rate. See also, George L. Perry, "Unemployment Flows in the
U.S. Labor Market," *Brookings Papers on Economic Activity*, vol. 2 (Washington, 1972),
pp. 245–278; and idem, "Stabilization Policy and Inflation," in *Setting National Priorities: The
Next Ten Years*, ed. Henry Owen and Charles L. Schultze (Washington: Brookings, 1976), pp.
271–322.

FIGURE 17–1
PERCENTAGE CHANGE IN SELECTED PRICE INDICES

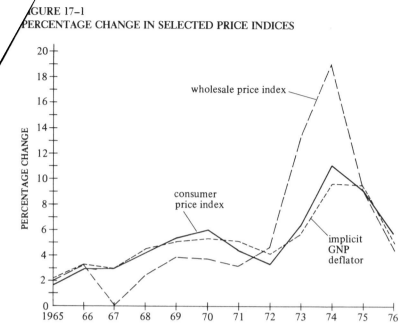

Source: Data from *Economic Report of the President*, 1976 and U.S. Congress, Joint Economic Committee, *Economic Indicators*, January 1977.

the actual inflation rate differs from the expected rate, plans are disrupted and adjustments must be made. Such adjustments may impose hardships that would not have occurred if the inflation had been correctly foreseen.

Presently, a 5 to 6 percent annual rate of increase in the CPI would probably be judged "acceptable" by most people in the United States, in part because plans have been made with the expectation that the rate would fall within that range. In contrast, *double-digit* inflation would probably be judged *unacceptable* by most. In other countries — for example, England, Brazil, Italy — double-digit inflation rates of 10–12 percent per year would probably be quite acceptable. What is satisfactory or acceptable depends on both past experience and what is thought to be feasible. The definition of full employment likewise tends to be conditional upon experience and feasibility.

FULL EMPLOYMENT–PRICE STABILITY CONFLICT

One reason, perhaps the main one, for the continuing debate about the definition and measurement of full employment and price stability is the belief

FIGURE 17–2
PHILLIPS CURVE

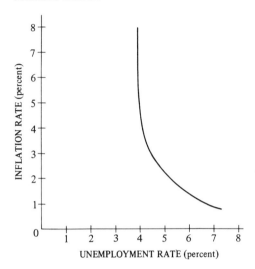

that a lower unemployment rate entails a higher inflation rate. This inverse relationship has come to be known as the *Phillips curve*, which is illustrated in Figure 17–2. Historically, there has indeed been such an inverse relationship, although it has been far from stable. In recent years, since about 1970, it appears to have shifted rightward, implying higher inflation rates at each unemployment rate.[4]

Moreover, virtually all estimates of the Phillips curve show inflation occurring even when there is no excess aggregate demand and employment is below the full-employment level (whether full employment is defined as 95 or 96 percent of the labor force). That is, the Phillips curve relationship implies that there are causes of inflation other than excess aggregate demand, some of which we discuss later in this chapter.[5] Inflation appears to

---

[4] A number of studies have estimated Phillips curves for the United States. See Otto Eckstein and Roger Brinner, *The Inflation Process in the United States*, Joint Economic Committee, February 22, 1972 (Washington: Government Printing Office, 1972); Perry, "Changing Labor Markets and Inflation"; and Robert J. Gordon, "Inflation and Recession in Recovery," in *Brookings Papers on Economic Activity*, vol. 1, ed. Arthur M. Okun and George L. Perry (Washington, 1971): 105–166.

[5] See pp. 376–377. That some inflation may occur even if there is no excess demand suggests that fiscal stabilization, which works by manipulating excess demand, cannot be completely effective in controlling inflation. We also discuss this point later in this chapter.

occur in modern economies such as the United States even though there is no inflationary gap of the sort we defined in Chapter 16.

The Phillips curve also implies a trade-off and conflict between unemployment and inflation. That is, a lower unemployment rate can be achieved *if and only if* we are willing to tolerate a greater inflation rate. We cannot enjoy simultaneously full employment and price stability if the latter is defined as a zero rate of increase in the price level. Instead, we must make a hard choice between the twin evils of unemployment and inflation. As we note earlier, selecting a target rate of unemployment carries with it the choice of an inflation rate. Debate results because people differ in their opinions about the relative seriousness of unemployment and inflation. Those who are more fearful of inflation prefer a higher target rate of unemployment than do those who are more concerned about the consequences of unemployment.

A number of economists, most notably Milton Friedman, have questioned the Phillips curve implication of a trade-off between unemployment and inflation.[6] Friedman does not deny that unemployment can be reduced *in the short run* at the price of a higher inflation rate. However, in his view, the economy tends toward a long-run equilibrium unemployment rate, a *natural* unemployment rate, which occurs when all labor markets are in equilibrium. The actual unemployment rate cannot be *permanently* lowered below this natural rate, and any attempt to do so will result in a continually *accelerating* rate of inflation. The basic reason for the acceleration is that workers require higher money wages once they recognize that prices are increasing at a higher rate (because of the measures taken to lower the unemployment rate). For employers to pay the higher money wages, prices must be still higher; higher prices lead, in turn, to demands for higher wages, etc. Thus, an attempt to hold the unemployment rate below its natural rate results in an upward spiral of wages and prices and an accelerating rate of inflation.

What are the implications of the *accelerationist view* of fiscal and monetary policy? Some argue that fiscal (and monetary) policies cannot permanently reduce unemployment below the natural rate. *These policies can only affect the rate of inflation.* Unemployment at the natural rate is just as consistent with a zero rate of inflation as with a positive rate. The goal of monetary and fiscal policy should therefore be price stability (zero inflation). There is no conflict, in the accelerationist view, between full employment (defined as the natural rate) and price stability. For those who are dissatisfied with the prevailing natural rate of unemployment, the appropriate policy is to try to reduce the natural rate.

6 Milton Friedman, "The Role of Monetary Policy," *American Economic Review,* 58, No. 1 (March 1968): 1–17.

Others question the accelerationist's policy recommendations for several reasons.[7] First, these *are* short-term trade-offs. Unemployment *can* be reduced during any particular period, say the coming year or two, with expansionary fiscal measures, with the likely result being a somewhat greater rate of inflation. Second, even though labor markets tend to a long-run equilibrium at the natural rate, they may not be in equilibrium at a given time. Fiscal and monetary policies may hasten adjustment to the long-run equilibrium, thereby reducing the hardships that unemployed workers bear during the period of adjustment. Finally, we do not know the natural unemployment rate. Is it 6 percent, 4 percent, or 2 percent? So the prescription of the accelerationists — do not try to force unemployment below the natural unemployment rate — is difficult to follow.

The debate we have just outlined is an important one, and one that is unlikely to be resolved or to die out in the near future. For present purposes, we will proceed on the assumption that fiscal and monetary policies can be used to affect both the unemployment and inflation rates, and we will examine the techniques and consequences of doing so.[8]

NEED FOR DEMAND GROWTH

Given a target unemployment rate, say 4 percent, potential (full-employment) GNP can be defined for each point in time. Because the labor force and labor productivity both tend to increase over time, potential GNP and the level of aggregate demand required to assure production at that potential also increase. Potential GNP grows at 3 to 4 percent per year; demand must grow at a similar rate to prevent the unemployment rate from either rising or falling. So stabilization policy must, in the final anlaysis, try to generate a *time path* of aggregate demand that corresponds to the time path of potential GNP. As the time path of aggregate demand is determined, so are the unemployment rates and inflation rates that prevail at each point along the path.

Achieving a full-employment time path of aggregate demand requires time paths of government spending and taxation that are consistent with full employment. The latter will clearly depend on the monetary policy being pursued during the period in question. So a fiscal policy to achieve full

7 James Tobin, "Inflation and Unemployment," *American Economic Review*, 62, No. 1 (March 1972): 1–18; and Arthur M. Okun, "Upward Mobility in a High-Pressure Economy," in *Brookings Papers on Economic Activity*, vol. 1, ed. Arthur M. Okun and George L. Perry (Washington, 1973): 207–261.

8 For additional discussion of the relationship between unemployment and inflation, see Thomas F. Dernburg and Duncan M. McDougall, *Macroeconomics*, 5th ed. (New York: McGraw-Hill, 1976), especially pp. 299–305.

employment cannot be defined without assumptions about monetary policy. We discuss this interaction of monetary and fiscal policy more fully below. But before doing so, we will examine a number of problems and issues that arise in the use of fiscal policy to achieve stabilization objectives.

BUILT-IN CHANGES IN FISCAL POLICY

Fiscal policy changes occur in basically two ways: (1) *Discretionary* changes are deliberate changes in expenditure programs and the tax structure that are decided upon by Congress and the president. (2) *Built-in* changes in taxes and expenditures occur in response to changes in economic activity, primarily the level of GNP and disposable incomes, with expenditure programs and the tax structure being unchanged. For example, an increase in transfers (a decrease in net taxes) caused by legislation that increases the benefits paid to each eligible recipient would be a discretionary change in fiscal policy. But an increase in unemployment compensation and welfare payments caused by a decline in GNP and disposable incomes and the concomitant increase in unemployment and the number of eligible persons would be a built-in change. Similarly, when GNP declines, personal incomes and corporate profits decline, causing income tax revenues and net taxes to fall. The reverse occurs as GNP increases. Built-in changes are "automatic," being induced by changes in economic conditions.

Built-in changes are primarily tax and transfer changes — changes in net taxes. Changes in purchases of goods and services, G, are largely discretionary. Figure 17–3 illustrates the relationship of the budget to economic activity, as measured by GNP. At a GNP of $1,000 billion, taxes would be $50 billion giving a deficit of $300 billion when government purchases, G, are $350 billion. As GNP increases beyond $1,000 billion, net taxes increase and the deficit declines, reaching zero at $2,000 billion. If GNP exceeds $2,000 billion, then there is a budget surplus.

STABILIZING EFFECTS

Built-in tax changes tend to stabilize the economy by moderating fluctuations in private demand for goods and services. The built-in tax decrease that occurs as the economy moves into a recession increases disposable incomes and consumption spending, thus making the fall in aggregate demand less than it would be in the absence of the tax decrease. The reverse happens as the economy expands: Tax revenues automatically rise, putting a brake on private spending (demand), thus moderating the expansion. In other terms, the federal tax system is an *automatic stabilizer*, which is defined as any feature of the economy that reduces in absolute value the change in aggregate demand that results from a change in GNP.

FIGURE 17–3
RELATIONSHIP BETWEEN GNP, TAXES, AND BUDGET DEFICITS

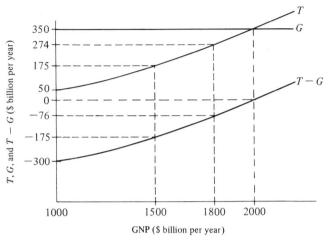

GNP ($ billion per year)

Reduced multiplier   Built-in tax changes reduce the need for short-term discretionary adjustments in fiscal policy by reducing the multipliers for changes in G and T, as well as private spending changes. In determining how much of a fiscal stimulus is needed to eliminate a deflationary gap, allowance must therefore be made for the fact that as GNP rises in response to the stimulus, taxes increase and some of the initial stimulus is lost. With built-in tax adjustments, a larger initial stimulus (increase in G or decrease in T) is needed to eliminate a deflationary gap of given size than would be needed in the absence of such adjustments. Conversely, when fiscal restraint is needed to eliminate an inflationary gap, the required initial restraint (decrease in G or increase in T) is greater because, as GNP declines in response to the restraint, net taxes also decline, offsetting some of the initial restraint.

GNP elasticity of taxes   Some taxes are more responsive to changes in GNP than others; that is, taxes differ in their *GNP elasticities*, where GNP elasticity is the percentage change in tax revenue divided by the percentage change in GNP. Revenues from a proportional income tax are less responsive to GNP changes (have a lower GNP elasticity) than a progressive tax levied on the same tax base. With a progressive rate structure, the average tax rate increases as GNP and, hence, the tax base (income) increase. In contrast with a proportional tax, the average tax rate does not change with changes in the tax base and GNP.

The corporation income tax is by far the most elastic (most responsive to changes in GNP) federal tax. Corporate income (profits) increases more rapidly than GNP when GNP is rising and decreases more rapidly when GNP is falling.

Both the federal individual and corporate income taxes have GNP elasticities in excess of 1, meaning that tax revenues rise more rapidly than GNP when GNP is rising, and fall more rapidly when GNP is falling. The GNP elasticity of consumption taxes tends to be close to 1, while the elasticity of payroll taxes is less than 1. Although any tax acts as an automatic stabilizer if its revenues change in the same direction as GNP (if its GNP elasticity is positive), higher elasticity taxes have a more stabilizing effect than lower elasticity taxes. This is important because the built-in stabilization provided by a tax system can be increased by increasing the importance of the more elastic taxes. At the federal level, this would mean increasing the share of revenues obtained from the income taxes and reducing the share obtained from the payroll tax.

FISCAL DRAG AND FISCAL DIVIDEND

In addition to moderating GNP fluctuations over the business cycle, built-in changes in fiscal policy have a secular effect. As GNP increases over time because of growth in the labor force and improving labor productivity, taxes tend to rise automatically and government spending in the absence of *discretionary* changes tends to remain at about the same level. Figure 17–3 illustrates that relationship. As the economy grows and GNP increases from $1,000 billion to $1,500 billion to $2,000 billion, taxes automatically rise from $50 billion to $175 billion to $350 billion. But G does not automatically change. Fiscal policy automatically becomes increasingly restrictive as the economy grows over time; the built-in, growth-induced tax changes exert a *fiscal drag*. Unless expansion of private-sector demand is sufficiently strong, this automatic restriction can cause reduced growth and stagnation.[9] This drag on the economy can be prevented only by *discretionary* changes in tax structure or expenditure programs or both.

Fiscal drag can also be viewed as a *fiscal dividend* that makes additional government spending and new programs possible without a change in tax rates or an increase in the government deficit. For example, in Figure 17–3, the fiscal dividend associated with the growth of GNP from $1,500 billion to $2,000 billion is $175 billion.

---

9 The stagnation of the late 1950s and early 1960s has been attributed to fiscal drag. For more discussion of the consequences of fiscal drag during that period, see Walter W. Heller, *New Dimensions of Political Economy* (New York: Norton, 1967).

FULL EMPLOYMENT VERSUS ACTUAL SURPLUSES AND DEFICITS

Built-in tax changes mean that in times of high unemployment the actual deficit is larger or the surplus is smaller than would be the case with lower unemployment and fuller utilization of the economy's productive capacity. For example, in Figure 17–3, suppose that full-employment (potential) GNP is $1,800 billion, at which the surplus, $T - G$, is −$76 billion. (To simplify terminology, we will use only the term *surplus*, with a deficit being shown as a negative surplus.) However, if the economy is operating at less than potential, say $1,500 billion, then the surplus is −$175 billion. Figure 17–4 shows the actual and full-employment surpluses for the U.S. economy for recent years.[10]

There are several reasons for distinguishing between actual and full-employment surpluses. First, any time that the full-employment surplus exceeds the actual, we know that fiscal policy is too restrictive to allow

FIGURE 17–4
ACTUAL AND FULL-EMPLOYMENT FEDERAL BUDGET SURPLUS

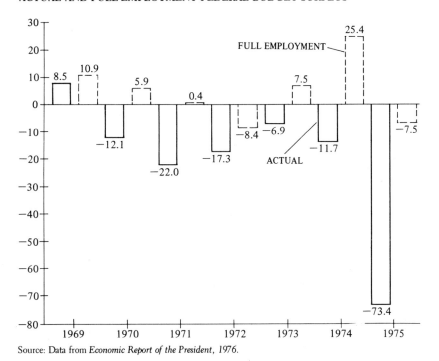

Source: Data from *Economic Report of the President*, 1976.

10 See Chapter 18, note 8, for reference to another estimate of the full-employment surplus.

achievement of full employment, given other conditions including monetary policy. If full employment is the objective of discretionary fiscal policy, such policy should try to assure that actual and full-employment surpluses are equal. And an index of the past success of fiscal policy is the extent to which such has been the case. From Figure 17–4 we can readily see that fiscal policy has seldom been fully successful in that sense.[11]

Second, when the full-employment surplus is decreased (by cutting taxes or increasing G) in order to eliminate a deflationary gap, the *actual* surplus will fall by less than the decrease in the full-employment surplus. The resulting expansion of GNP increases tax revenues. Indeed, it is possible (though not necessary) that a tax cut or increase in G that decreases the *full-employment* surplus will increase the *actual* surplus. To illustrate, let us suppose that in Figure 17–5 actual GNP is $1600 billion, $200 billion less than potential. The actual surplus is $206 billion − $350 billion = −$144 billion. G is now increased to $390 billion, decreasing the *full-employment surplus* from −$76 billion to −$116 billion. The increase in G expands aggregate demand and increases GNP and tax collections. With a multiplier of 2.5, GNP increases to $1,700 billion, taxes increase to $239 billion, and the actual surplus falls from −$144 billion to −$151 billion. The actual surplus falls by less than the full-employment surplus. However, with a multiplier of 4, GNP increases to $1,760 billion, taxes increase from $206 billion to $260 billion, and the actual surplus rises from −$144 billion to −$130 billion. With a multiplier of 5, GNP increases to $1,800 billion and the actual and full-employment surpluses coincide at −$116 billion. Whether a decrease in the full-employment surplus through a decrease in tax rates or an increase in G will increase the actual surplus is an empirical question, the answer to which is likely to vary from situation to situation. It is commonly argued that the tax cut of 1964 had such an effect.

Third, changes in the actual surplus do not signal discretionary changes in fiscal policy. For example, an increase in private-sector demand $(C + I)$ because of improved expectations will increase GNP and the actual surplus. But the increase in actual surplus does not indicate a more restrictive fiscal policy. Rather, it reflects the automatic increase in taxes that accompanies an increase in GNP. The full-employment surplus remains unaffected by

---

11 Although a comparison of actual and full-employment surpluses indicates how the budget affects employment and real output, it does not necessarily reflect what is happening to the price level. Inflation may occur whether the actual surplus is less than or equal to the full-employment surplus. From 1974 to 1975 the Consumer Price Index increased by 9 percent, but the estimated actual and full-employment surpluses were −$73.4 billion and −$7.5 billion, respectively. The unemployment rate was 8.3 percent.

FIGURE 17–5
EFFECT OF CHANGE IN FULL-EMPLOYMENT SURPLUS ON ACTUAL SURPLUS

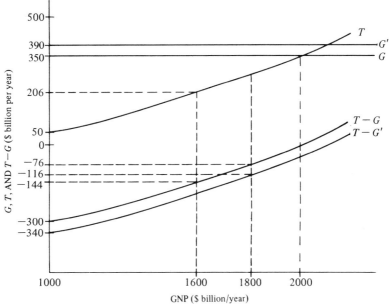

such a change in private demand. Therefore, to determine whether fiscal policy is becoming more or less restrictive, we cannot look at changes in actual tax collections and actual surpluses. Instead, we must look at how the full-employment level of taxation and surplus are changing.[12]

Correspondingly, we cannot judge whether fiscal policy has been expansionary or restrictive over a specific period by looking at how GNP changes over the period. GNP may not increase following a tax cut or expenditure increase that reduces the full-employment surplus because a change in

12 Changes in full-employment taxes and surplus are only approximate indicators of changes in the restrictiveness of fiscal policy. The various taxes and expenditure programs have somewhat different effects on aggregate demand (per dollar collected or spent). So some investigators have constructed "weighted" measures of the full-employment surplus, with each category of tax and expenditure being weighted in proportion to its effect on demand. In particular, changes in full-employment surplus do not reflect *balanced* changes in G and T. Yet, as we have seen in Chapter 16, balanced (equal) changes in G and T affect aggregate demand—the balanced-budget multiplier is positive. See Blinder and Solow, "Analytical Foundations of Fiscal Policy," for a discussion of the weighted full-employment surplus.

private demand, for example a decrease in investment, offsets the expansionary effect of the change in fiscal policy.

FISCAL POLICY LAGS

Aggregate demand cannot be immediately adjusted to a desired level through discretionary fiscal changes because such changes take time to implement. That required time, once the need for change is recognized, is called the *implementation lag*. For example, tax-structure changes as well as most expenditure changes must be authorized by Congress and then carried out by the appropriate executive agencies. Although the time required may vary from situation to situation, the implementation lag is likely to be several months, at a minimum, given current procedures for making tax and expenditure decisions. Once a fiscal change is implemented, time passes before the change has its full effect on aggregate demand; this passage of time is called the *response lag*. For example, following a tax cut, disposable incomes rise, but the full effect of higher disposable incomes on household spending is not felt immediately.

Given that the implementation and response lags are both positive, the need for fiscal changes must be predicted far enough in advance for the changes to have their desired effect on aggregate demand. That is, the *recognition lag*, the lag between the time at which a change in aggregate demand is needed and the time at which the need for such a change is recognized, must be negative. For example, if three months is needed to implement a change in taxes and another three months is required for the change to be reflected in an expenditure (aggregate demand) change, then the need for a tax change must be predicted six months in advance.

The need for a discretionary change in fiscal policy can usually be foreseen several months in advance; so the recognition lag is negative, at least in the sense that some people will foresee the need for change. However, discretionary fiscal changes are political actions; they cannot be dictated by technicians. There must be widespread recognition of the need for change. Unfortunately, by the time the need for change is widely recognized, it may be too late for effective action. The time required to gain support for a change can be included in the implementation lag or in the recognition lag. But regardless of how it is labeled, the time required to build a consensus is a factor limiting the timeliness and effectiveness of discretionary fiscal policy. Formula flexibility, which we discuss below, would greatly reduce this lag in changing fiscal policy.

Positive implementation and response lags mean that an economy that is off target or off course cannot be quickly returned to course. An existing excess or deficiency in aggregate demand simply cannot be eliminated. Indeed, action taken as long as a year in advance of a period in which a deficiency or excess of demand is expected (predicted) is unlikely to be fully effective in restoring demand to the desired level.[13]

WHICH FISCAL TOOL?

Built-in adjustments of taxes and expenditures, while helpful in stabilizing the economy, do not eliminate the need for discretionary changes in fiscal policy. The latter changes may be in tax structure, welfare-income maintenance programs, or expenditure programs that involve the purchase of goods and services, such as national defense and public works. In which area(s) of the budget should discretionary changes be made? Are changes in taxes more (less) suitable for stabilization purposes? Which taxes should be changed? In this section, we will consider these and related technical questions about discretionary fiscal policy.

TAX OR EXPENDITURE CHANGE?

Government purchases goods and services in order to provide national defense, highways, health services, etc. In doing so, it may promote efficiency, as we explained in Chapters 3–5. And in Chapter 16 we saw how purchases of goods and services, G, may be varied to stabilize the economy. But G cannot be varied to serve two masters: efficiency and stability. And a common view is that the amount and composition of G should be determined primarily by efficiency criteria on the assumption that the economy is at full employment. This view leaves the job of assuring full employment to discretionary and automatic adjustments in taxes and transfers. Government programs that are desirable on efficiency grounds are not cut back in order to curtail aggregate demand and reduce an inflationary gap. And inefficient programs are not undertaken simply to increase demand, provide employment, and reduce a deflationary gap.

As a general principle, this view that net taxes, T, rather than government purchases, G, should be varied for stabilization purposes seems fairly sound. However, there are several reasons why changes in G may sometimes be more effective in stabilization than are changes in T.

One is that changes in G can and usually do have a greater effect in

---

13 For further discussion of fiscal policy lags, see ibid., Milton Friedman, "A Monetary and Fiscal Framework for Economic Stability," in *Essays in Positive Economics*, 2nd ed. (Chicago: University of Chicago Press, 1959); and Albert Ando and E. Cary Brown, "Lags in Fiscal Policy," in *Stabilization Policies*, ed. Commission on Money and Credit (Englewood Cliffs, N.J.: Prentice-Hall, 1963).

some geographic areas than in others, while changes in T do not. This geographic focus is sometimes advantageous, sometimes not. For example, an increase in purchases of military aircraft may have its initial and major effect in Southern California, which is desirable if unemployment is relatively high in that area. More generally, stabilization policy is more effective when an increase (decrease) in G has its main impact in an area of relatively high (low) unemployment. Of course, when the reverse happens, the geographic focus of G changes is undesirable. Fortunately, it is often possible to adjust the composition of expenditure changes so that their geographic focus promotes rather than hinders stabilization.

Magnitude of response   Changes in G have a direct effect on aggregate demand because G is a component of demand. In contrast, tax changes directly affect disposable incomes and relative prices (in the case of changes in excise taxes) and only indirectly affect aggregate demand. Some of the change in disposable income resulting from a tax change is often offset by a change in private saving, rather than being reflected in a change in aggregate demand.[14]

In particular, a temporary change in income taxes and disposable income may have its main effect on current saving rather than current consumption expenditures. Higher (lower) taxes may lead mainly to lower (higher) saving rather than to lower (higher) consumption spending and aggregate demand. Such would indeed be the case if the permanent income hypothesis — that household consumption spending is a function of the permanent (long-run), rather than current, income of the household — is valid.[15] In any case, available evidence does suggest that the response of consumption spending to an income tax change is weaker and less rapid when the change is viewed as temporary rather than permanent.

Consumer expectations are also an important determinant of the response to tax changes. For example, if consumers expect economic conditions to worsen, they may save the increase in disposable income resulting from a tax decrease. Or they may meet a tax increase with a corresponding decrease in saving and little or no decrease in consumption spending if they expect boom conditions and higher prices. The effects of tax changes on business and household investment spending may also depend on expectations.

14 For that reason the multiplier for T changes is smaller in absolute value than the multiplier for G changes.

15 For a discussion of the various theories of how aggregate consumption is determined, see Milton Friedman, *A Theory of the Consumption Function* (Princeton: Princeton University Press for the National Bureau of Economic Research, 1957); and William H. Branson, *Macroeconomic Theory and Policy* (New York: Harper & Row, 1972), chap. 10.

Timing of response   The implementation and response lags differ for changes in G and T. If the lags are much shorter for discretionary changes in G than for changes in T, then we might opt for adjusting G, regardless of the consequences for economic efficiency. It is difficult to argue that such is usually the case, but the lags are sufficiently variable to be a factor in the choice of stabilization measures.

Tax rate changes must be legislated, usually after a fairly long process of hearings and deliberation.[16] The president and the executive agencies can vary the rate of government purchases somewhat in an attempt to stabilize, but only within the limits set by Congressional appropriations and obligational authority. If only relatively small discretionary changes are required, then the implementation lag is probably somewhat less for changes in G than for changes in T because the former can be made by the executive branch without Congressional action. However, if large changes are required, then Congressional action is necessary for changes in either G or T. Of course, implementation lags are not permanently fixed; instead, they depend on the decision-making processes of government. We discuss some proposals to shorten the lags later in this chapter.

Response lags, like implementation lags, are variable. The initial impact of changes in G is when private suppliers respond to changes in purchase orders. The response time (lag), which depends on the type of purchase, can be fairly long. For example, an increase in purchases of military equipment might have little near-term (within one year) effect on production because factories have to be built or modified or equipment has to be designed or tested. But response time to changes in G can also be short (three to six months), as would occur if previously planned construction projects (housing, roads) are implemented.

The response of consumption expenditures to a tax change that alters disposable incomes can be, and usually is thought to be, fairly quick (again, three to six months). But such need not be the case. Expectations may affect the timing as well as the magnitude of the response to tax changes. Any increase in spending because of a tax cut may be deferred when expectations are depressed; spending decreases in response to tax increases may be deferred if inflation is expected. Also, a tax change causes little immediate change in consumption if the latter depends on past disposable income as some theories imply.[17]

On balance, it is difficult to conclude that implementation and response

16 See Chapter 8, p. 183.

17 In some empirical studies, consumption is related to a weighted average of past income, with past income as a proxy for permanent (lifetime) income. See Dernberg and McDougall, *Macroeconomics*, pp. 79–80.

lags are, in combination, significantly different for changes in G than for changes in T. Rather, the lags are highly variable, depending on the type of tax or expenditure change and the economic and political environment in which the change is made.

Counterproductive effects   Tax changes may be counterproductive if either of two conditions hold. If government spending adjusts to the level of taxes generated by the existing tax system, an increase in net taxes generates a similar increase in G, thereby causing an increase rather than a decrease in aggregate demand. Conversely, if G falls by the amount of any decrease in T, then aggregate demand is reduced rather than increased by a tax cut. To the extent that G does adjust in this manner, tax changes are ineffective instruments of fiscal stabilization. Evidence against this automatic adjustment is that discretionary tax changes have been made without there being any immediate and corresponding change in G.

The second condition is that income tax increases lead to higher money wages, as workers seek to preserve their take-home, or after-tax, pay, while increases in consumption (sales) taxes lead to higher prices. If this condition is met, tax increases add to cost-push inflation by triggering wage and price increases, thereby worsening inflation. However, the cost-push effect is a one-time effect. The demand-depressing effect of a tax increase continues after the once-and-for-all upward adjustment of wages and prices. Over a number of periods, the net effect of a tax increase is a lower rate of inflation than would have occurred in the absence of the increase.

While there may be a tendency for tax changes to be counterproductive for the reasons we have just discussed, available evidence does not suggest that such is the case. Stabilization policy can still be based on the assumption that tax increases (decreases) reduce (increase) aggregate demand.

WHICH TAX CHANGES?

Given that stabilization policy is to rely primarily or importantly on tax changes, there is the question of which taxes should be changed: corporate income, individual income, payroll (Social Security and unemployment compensation), or excise taxes? Per dollar of tax change, the change in aggregate demand may be different for one type of tax than for another. And changes in the various taxes may have different effects on the composition of aggregate demand and output — for example, a decrease in corporate taxes may stimulate investment spending more and consumption spending less than would an equal dollar decrease in Social Security taxes.

In its fiscal stabilization efforts, the U.S. federal government has relied primarily on changes in individual and corporate income taxes. The investment tax credit has also been manipulated in an attempt to control the timing and magnitude of business investment in plant and equipment. Reductions of federal excise taxes have been a limited factor in previous efforts to stimulate demand.

While any tax change tends to affect private demand (consumption and investment spending), some tax changes have a greater effect on one component of demand than the other. Changes in Social Security and individual income taxes for low-bracket taxpayers have their main impact on consumption spending. In contrast, the main effect of changes in the corporation income tax and the investment tax credit (which is basically a negative excise tax on investment) is on investment spending. By varying the "mix" of tax changes, the relative magnitudes of the resulting changes in consumption and investment can also be varied.

While changes in corporate and individual income tax rates have been the main tools of fiscal stabilization, there has been considerable debate about how the rates are to be changed. One issue is the distribution of tax changes between high- and low-bracket and between corporate and individual income taxpayers. And tax reform issues, such as those we discussed in Chapter 11, have typically been interjected into the debate, even when stabilization has been the main reason for tax change.

The federal government has no broadbased tax on consumption spending. One argument for imposing such a tax is that it would be an effective stabilization tool. Varying the rate of taxation of consumption spending, especially consumer durables, could be very effective in controlling the timing, if not the magnitude, of such spending. Such a tax would work in the same way as the investment tax credit for spending on producer durables (plant and equipment). Indeed, for stabilization purposes, changes in a consumption tax credit would be as effective as changes in a consumption tax rate.[18]

18 For example, adding a 10 percent consumption tax or removing a 10 percent consumption tax credit effectively increases the price of consumer goods, thus deterring their purchase. If the tax change is expected to be temporary, the possibility for deferral is even greater. Conversely, a tax credit increase or a tax decrease encourages current consumption spending, especially if the change is temporary. In contrast to income tax changes, excise tax changes (achieved by changes in either taxes or tax credits on particular purchases—investment or consumption goods) are more effective in controlling demand when they are temporary.

The debate before enactment about whether to enact a change in consumption taxes is destabilizing. For example, public discussion of the possibility of an increase in a consumption tax aimed at curtailing excess demand is likely to increase *current* purchases as people try to buy before the tax increase goes into effect. This increase in purchases *adds* to inflationary pressures. In contrast, the debate before enactment about changes in income taxes is stabilizing.

COST-PUSH INFLATION AND
THE LIMITS OF FISCAL STABILIZATION

We have seen how fiscal policy may reduce inflation that is due to excess aggregate demand. Unfortunately, all inflation is not such *demand-pull* inflation. Inflation may also be of the *cost-push* variety.[19]

Cost-push inflation results from actions taken by commodity *suppliers* (rather than demanders, as in the case of demand-pull inflation) who are the owners of the factors of production (land, labor, and capital) used to produce the commodities. Cost-push inflation results when factor owners as a group demand more money income for producing a given output of goods and services than is being generated when that output is sold at prevailing prices. There is, in effect, an excess demand for income; income claims add up to more than 100 percent of the income being generated at prevailing prices. The demands for income can be met only by raising prices. Higher prices are likely to lead to demands for further wage-price increases, so the process of cost-push inflation tends to be self-reinforcing.

Of course, such cost-push inflation cannot continue indefinitely unless the money supply is expanded, as we discussed in Chapter 16. But experience shows that restricting the rate of monetary growth in order to control cost-push inflation causes unemployment. So monetary authorities face the unpleasant dilemma of either allowing the money supply to grow, thereby validating the excess income claims and cost-push inflation, or restricting monetary growth, thereby increasing unemployment. Similarly, restricting aggregate demand by fiscal policy in an attempt to control cost-push inflation is likely to lead to unemployment, while having little effect on the inflation.[20]

---

19 "Sector" inflation is another type of inflation that may occur even if there is no excess aggregate demand. Aggregate demand is usually distributed among various producing sectors so that some experience excess demand, while others face deficient demand, even though demand in the aggregate is neither deficient nor excessive. Prices tend to rise in the excess-demand sectors. If prices fall sufficiently in the deficient-demand sectors there is no problem. However, since prices tend to be inflexible downward, price increases in the high-demand sectors are not offset by price decreases in the low-demand sectors. The result is inflation (higher average prices). This inflation, which is due basically to sectoral imbalances in demand and downward inflexibility of prices, is similar to cost-push inflation in that it cannot be controlled by reducing aggregate demand, unless aggregate demand is reduced enough that *no* sector experiences excess demand. In this latter case, unemployment would surely be high. See Charles L. Schultze, "Recent Inflation in the United States," U.S. Congress, Joint Economic Committee, *Employment, Growth, and Price Levels*, Study Paper No. 1 (Washington, 1959).

20 As we noted earlier tax increases may contribute to cost-push inflation by increasing the wages and prices demanded by factor owners. Similarly, the increases in interest rates that usually accompany a more restrictive monetary policy are cost increases that may aggravate cost-push inflation. Of course, more restrictive monetary and fiscal policies do reduce

Both monetary and fiscal policies are ineffective in controlling cost-push inflation because they do not eliminate its cause: the excess income claims.[21] Control requires measures that limit income claims (demands), rather than measures like monetary and fiscal policies, which limit aggregate demand. An incomes policy that provides wage-price controls or guidelines for wage-price increases does strike at the cause of cost-push inflation. Other less radical and comprehensive measures, such as strengthening competition, have also been suggested.[22] For our purposes, it is sufficient that we note that fiscal measures cannot control cost-push inflation without affecting employment. Cost-push inflation occurs even when there is no inflationary gap, and any attempt to reduce such inflation by demand-restricting fiscal (or monetary) measures will cause an increase in unemployment.

However, cost-push inflation can be set into motion or accelerated by excess aggregate demand that causes prices to rise. Price increases caused by excess aggregate demand, in turn, trigger wage-price increases of the cost-push variety. So fiscal policy can prevent cost-push inflation that has its origins in previous episodes of demand-pull inflation.

INDEXATION

The difficulties in dealing simultaneously with the problems of unemployment and inflation, especially when the inflation is cost-push, have lead a number of economists to suggest indexation. Basically, *indexation* is the adjustment of the payments and receipts of businesses, households, and governments for price level changes. For example, wages would be adjusted upward in response to price level increases, with a 10 percent increase in the price level calling for a similar increase in wages. Such wage increases are called cost-of-living adjustments. Other transactions, between borrower and lender and between buyer and seller of goods and services, would be similarly adjusted. With perfect indexation, the distribution of *real* income and the allocation of resources would be unaffected by changes in the price level. The economy would thus be *insulated* from the effects of inflation; it

---

aggregate demand and demand-pull inflation. So tax increases and slower rates of monetary growth are likely to result in lower inflation rates when there is excessive aggregate demand (an inflationary gap). But such measures will have little effect on, and may even worsen, inflation when aggregate demand is not excessive.

21 More correctly, sufficiently restrictive monetary and fiscal policies might eliminate cost-push inflation. But in doing so, they would likely reduce aggregate demand to a point where the economy would suffer unacceptably high unemployment of workers and machines.

22 For further discussion of measures that may reduce cost-push inflation, see Perry, "Stabilization Policy and Inflation."

would be *inflation proof.* However, since indexation is costly, full insulation of the economy from the effects of inflation would be impractical.

Cost-of-living adjustments are now made in Social Security payments and in the pay of many workers and retirees. Further indexation is advocated by some, partly because it would reduce the incentive for wage and price increases in *anticipation* of inflation. Such increases tend to *cause* the inflation that they anticipate and are therefore an important reinforcing factor in any on-going inflationary process. But, others oppose indexation, fearing that it will make the economy more inflation prone. Their view is that as more and more people are protected from the consequences of inflation, the political support for anti-inflationary measures will diminish. That is, indexation, in the view of its opponents fails to the extent that it succeeds. There is yet no answer to the question of which of these views about the effects of indexation is valid.[23]

Included in complete indexation, and of special interest from a stabilization perspective, is the indexation of taxes. We have seen that tax collections increase (decrease) automatically when GNP increases (decreases). These built-in adjustments occur whether the change in GNP is real or simply the result of price changes. In particular, inflation can cause taxes to increase even though real GNP remains unchanged. Unless it is offset by a discretionary tax cut or an increase in government spending, this inflation-induced increase in taxes reduces *real* aggregate demand. Such reduction is appropriate if there is excess aggregate demand; it is the reason that the tax system operates automatically to limit excess-demand inflation. However, all inflation is not because of excess demand. Cost-push inflation may occur when there is unemployment. In that case, the inflation-induced decrease in real aggregate demand *increases* unemployment, unless it is offset by greater spending or a discretionary tax cut. The automatic tax increases caused by inflation are therefore two-edged swords: They are helpful in curtailing excess-demand inflation, but they may worsen unemployment when there is no excess demand and the inflation is of the cost-push variety.

For this, and a variety of other reasons, *indexation* of federal taxes has been proposed. Indexation would basically adjust tax brackets, exemptions, and deductions so that the tax liabilities of households and businesses would not depend on the rate of inflation.[24] With such indexation, inflation does

---

23 Some countries have employed indexation on a wide-spread basis; see Ronald Krieger, "Inflation and the Brazilian Solution," *Challenge*, 17, No. 4 (September-October 1974): 43–52.

24 For example, suppose a particular family's income increases from $15,000 to $16,500 during a year in which prices increase 10 percent. The family's real income is unchanged. However, with the progressive federal income tax, the family's *money* tax payment increases by more

not increase taxes in the manner described in the preceding paragraph. The tax system does *not* automatically limit excess demand inflation. Nor does it increase unemployment in periods of unemployment and (cost-push) inflation—that is, periods of "stagflation."[25] From a stabilization perspective, then, indexation has both advantages and disadvantages, the balance of which is unclear and subject to ongoing debate. For the present, we can only recognize the possible effects of indexation and note that many nations presently have indexed tax systems.[26]

RULES VERSUS DISCRETION

We have seen that discretionary changes in G and T can, in principle, be used to stabilize the economy. But we have also seen that problems arise in the implementation of discretionary fiscal policy. The more serious problems have been those of predicting the need for fiscal changes and uncertainty about the magnitude and timing of responses to those changes. Because of the difficulties, changes in G and T have sometimes been ineffective and even destabilizing. Therefore, some have suggested that discretionary changes in G and T be abandoned in favor of a budgetary policy governed by rules.[27]

Balanced-budget rules are one way of limiting discretionary changes. *Annual balance* — balancing each year's budget — is a rule that had wide acceptance forty to fifty years ago. Franklin Roosevelt pledged to balance the budget in his 1932 campaign for president. Since then many people have come to recognize that annual balance would be undesirable and, in today's economy, practically impossible. Also, annual balance can be achieved only by eliminating or offsetting (through discretionary changes in net taxes) the automatic stabilizing features of our tax-expenditure system, the main components of which are the federal and corporate income taxes and the welfare and unemployment compensation programs.

---

than 10 percent. Hence, its *real* taxes increase and its real disposable income falls, the likely result of which would be lower demand by the family for goods and services. In contrast, with indexation, the family's *money* tax payments would increase by only 10 percent, so its real taxes and real disposable income would be unchanged.

25 Indexation would similarly prevent *deflation* from reducing real taxes and thereby increasing aggregate demand.

26 For further analysis and discussion, see Henry J. Aaron, ed., *Inflation and the Income Tax* (Washington: Brookings, 1977).

27 See, for example, Milton Friedman, "Monetary and Fiscal Framework for Economic Stability"; and Committee for Economic Development, *High Employment Without Inflation* (New York, 1972).

While few argue for annual balance, there is support for less restrictive balance-budget rules. One alternative is that of *balancing the budget over the business cycle*, with the deficits of the recession years being offset by surpluses in high-employment years. A related rule, which has the greatest current support, is that of *balance in the full-employment budget*. On the surface, this has the appeal of reasonableness. But it implicitly asserts that when the economy is at full employment and the federal budget is balanced, there will be neither a deflationary nor an inflationary gap. While such may sometimes be the case, it is undoubtedly not true at all times. Indeed, in a number of preceding years the economy did not reach full employment even though the full-employment budget was in deficit. In all of those years, achieving full employment would have required larger full-employment deficits or larger budgets in total or easier monetary policy or some combination of the three.[28]

Full-employment balance is not appropriate because productive capacity grows rather steadily, while the nonfederal components of aggregate demand — the state and local government, private consumption and investment, and foreign components — are variable. Even if it is possible to offset these fluctuations in demand by variations in a *balanced* federal budget, doing so would entail large variations in federal purchases of goods and services and a violation of the rule that such purchases should be determined primarily by efficiency criteria.

So far we have said that balanced-budget rules are inappropriate because stabilization targets (full employment and price stability) cannot be achieved while following such rules. But some proponents of full-employment balance would reject this line of reasoning on the grounds that attempts to stabilize the economy through discretionary changes in G and T are as likely as not to increase instability. In this view, we cannot hit our stabilization targets dead center; we cannot fine-tune the economy; and stabilization objectives are in fact better served by adhering to the balanced-full-employment-budget rule and relying on automatic stabilizers. This pessimistic view of the potential for fiscal stabilization cannot be rejected out of hand. But we can note, in argument against it, that discretionary fiscal policy has had some successes and that our ability to forecast the need for and implement changes in fiscal policy has been improving.

A different argument for balanced-budget rules is that they foster fiscal

---

28 Recall that an increase in G accompanied by an equal increase in T yields a net increase in aggregate demand—the balanced-budget multiplier is positive (see Chapter 16, p. 346). So, in principle, a full employment level of aggregate demand can be achieved while balancing the budget *if* the budget (the level of government purchases) is sufficiently large.

discipline. According to this argument, deficits encourage and make possible excessive (inefficient) public spending. Presumably, surpluses would lead to "too little" public spending, although this latter point is seldom emphasized. But this argument is weak for two reasons. First, as we have seen in earlier chapters, especially Chapters 7 and 8, determining the efficient level of spending is difficult. And there is little reason to expect that the level that emerges from the political choice process is efficient, even if a balanced-budget rule is followed. Second, and more important, unemployment means inefficiency and welfare losses from private-sector activity. Inflation, especially at high rates, may also lead to inefficiency. Even if departures from the rule of full-employment balance (for stabilization purposes) lead to choice of inefficient levels of G, such departures may produce offsetting gains in the form of reduced unemployment and inflation. For example, if the economy had been operated at capacity during 1975, total output would have been about 15 percent greater than was in fact the case; output in the amount of about $230 billion (in 1975 prices) would have been gained if full employment had been achieved by discretionary monetary and fiscal policies. This is the gain that must be compared to any losses that result when the "fiscal discipline" provided by a balanced-budget rule is foregone so that discretionary changes in fiscal policy can be made.

Another approach to making fiscal policy less discretionary and more automatic is *formula flexibility*, which would employ legislated rules for changing G and T. Following this approach, Congress might pass a law requiring that income tax rates be (1) automatically decreased as the measured unemployment rate rises above some target level, say 6 percent; and (2) automatically increased as the measured inflation rate rises above some target, say 9 percent. Similarly, legislation could require changes in public expenditures, for public works and income maintenance, when unemployment and inflation rates pass some critical values.

Formula flexibility would substantially reduce implementation lags by reducing or eliminating the period for debate and consensus building that is required for discretionary fiscal action. But it is not clear that a quicker decision is a better one. More importantly, the information needed to decide upon discretionary changes is also needed to define the formulas for changing G and T. Indeed, formula flexibility assumes that this information is contained in the variables and parameters of the legislated formulas. If this assumption is valid, discretionary changes would be relatively simple matters with or without legislated formulas.

In sum, rules, whether balanced-budget rules or legislated formulas, are unlikely to generate a time path of aggregate demand that will fully achieve full employment and price stability targets. Whether discretionary changes that depart from such rules can do better is a question that can be answered only as we use and try to improve our capability for making stabilizing discretionary changes.

MONETARY VERSUS FISCAL POLICY

In the United States, monetary policy decisions are made by the Federal Reserve System's Board of Governors and Open Market Committee. The main tools of monetary policy are (1) open-market purchases or sales of government bonds, (2) changes in the discount rate, and (3) changes in the required reserve ratio for member banks. Through the use of these tools, the Fed (the label typically given to monetary policy makers as a group) directly affects the cost and availability of credit and the money supply and indirectly affects aggregate demand, employment, output, and prices. Thus, aggregate demand can be manipulated for stabilization purposes by monetary as well as fiscal measures. For demand expansion, open-market purchases of bonds, a lower discount rate, or a lower required reserve ratio can be used instead of or in addition to fiscal measures (increases in G, decreases in T). Conversely, open-market sales, a higher discount rate, and a higher required reserve ratio can be used, like decreases in G and increases in T, to contract aggregate demand.

While monetary and fiscal policies are substitutes, they are not perfect substitutes. They may affect the various components of aggregate demand differently. And, in particular situations, they may differ in their effectiveness as tools for controlling demand. The question therefore arises: When and to what extent is monetary policy to be used in stabilization? That is, how is the appropriate mix of monetary and fiscal policies to be determined? [29]

COMPOSITION OF AGGREGATE DEMAND

Both monetary and fiscal measures are general in that they are not aimed at controlling specific components of aggregate demand. Nevertheless, neither set of measures has a uniform impact on all demand components. Monetary measures affect aggregate demand by changing interst rates (changing the monetary price of borrowed funds) or changing the availability of loans at given interest rates. That is, monetary measures alter the ease with which buyers (households, businesses, governments, and foreigners) may finance

---

29 Our discussion of these questions is necessarily brief. For more detail, see Dernberg and McDougall, *Macroeconomics*, chaps. 7–9, 19.

purchases with borrowed funds. Borrowing finances a major share of consumer durable, investment (housing, buildings, plant and equipment), and state and local government capital expenditures. These categories of spending therefore tend to be sensitive to monetary measures. In contrast, tax rate changes affect aggregate demand by altering disposable incomes and therefore have a major impact on consumer spending for nondurables. Changes in G, of course, directly alter one component of aggregate demand.

A given level of aggregate demand can usually be achieved with a variety of monetary-fiscal policy mixes. A relatively restrictive monetary policy (relatively high interest rates, relatively low money supply and credit availability) may be combined with relatively unrestrictive fiscal policy (relatively low tax rates, relatively high disposable incomes and government purchases), and vice versa. The more restrictive monetary policy is (and the less restrictive fiscal policy is), the larger the consumption (C) share of aggregate demand will be. Conversely, the less restrictive monetary policy is, the larger the investment (I) share will be. Thus, a factor in the choice of monetary-fiscal policy mix is its effect on the composition of aggregate demand.

For example, when there is a deflationary gap with high unemployment of both workers and machines, expansion of capacity through investment is not needed. The main demand stimulus should be provided by a tax cut or an increase in G or both, rather than by easier monetary policy. However, when unemployment of labor is accompanied by high utilization of plant and equipment, then expansion of aggregate demand should be achieved, at least in part, by easier monetary policy so as to stimulate investment spending. When unemployment in the building and construction trades is high, easier monetary policy (lower interest rates) is also needed to stimulate the purchase and building of residences and other structures. Similarly, an inflationary gap that is largely due to excess investment demand is more effectively reduced by restrictive monetary measures than by a low-bracket tax rate increase or the curtailment of government employment.

While monetary and fiscal measures tend to have their main impacts on investment and consumption spending, respectively, such need not be the case. Consumer credit controls administered by the Fed can have a major effect on consumer durable spending, while investment tax credits, a fiscal tool, can affect investment spending.

RELATIVE EFFECTIVENESS

In most situations, a desired change in aggregate demand can be obtained by either monetary or fiscal measures. But in some circumstances, one set of measures will be more effective than the other. On the one hand, monetary measures tend to be ineffective in stimulating demand when (1) interest rates are already low; (2) the excess reserves of the banking system are high; and (3) the existing stock of housing, plant, and equipment is not fully utilized. The cost of credit is already low and reducing it further will be difficult; and any reduction that is achieved may have little effect on investment spending because present capacity is not fully utilized.[30] However, fiscal measures can work under these circumstances to bring about the desired change in aggregate demand.

On the other hand, fiscal measures are ineffective in stimulating demand when interest rates are high and the transactions demand for money has been reduced to its lower limit (the income velocity of money is at a maximum). Increases in G crowd out private spending by increasing interest rates, as we explained in Chapter 16. Decreases in T lead to higher disposable incomes and higher consumption spending. But because a higher volume of transactions cannot be carried out with the existing money stock, interest rates must rise enough and investment must fall enough to offset any increase in consumption, leaving total spending unchanged. In contrast to fiscal policy, monetary policy can in these circumstances be very effective in increasing aggregate demand.

These conditions under which monetary and fiscal measures are each ineffective in stimulating aggregate demand are polar cases, and the economy is unlikely to be at either extreme. The important conclusion, then, is that as the extremes are approached, one class of policy measures becomes increasingly less effective than the other. As interest rates and capacity utilization are lower, monetary measures are less effective than fiscal measures in stimulating demand. Conversely, the higher interest rates and capacity utilization are, the more effective monetary measures are in relation to fiscal measures.

Demand restriction can always be achieved by either monetary or fiscal measures *if* policy makers are willing to employ sufficiently high interest and tax rates and to reduce sufficiently government purchases. As a practical matter, demand restriction by both monetary and fiscal measures may meet with "political" limits — on interest and tax rates and on government spending.

The relative effectiveness of monetary and fiscal measures also depends on differences in the lags with which the measures affect demand. In comparison with fiscal policy, the implementation lag for monetary policy is short. Once the need for action is recognized (agreed upon) by the Federal Reserve Open Market Committee, the action can be quickly implemented. But the response lag is probably longer than with fiscal policy. Time is required for credit conditions to change in response to changes in monetary policy. More

30 In other terms, investment demand is interest inelastic.

importantly, plans for investment spending (for new houses, plants, machines) that are sensitive to monetary conditions cannot be altered quickly.

In short, because monetary and fiscal measures vary in their effectiveness, stabilization policy cannot rely solely on one or the other. Instead, a mix of monetary and fiscal measures is usually required, with the appropriate mix depending importantly on prevailing economic conditions.

ECONOMIC GROWTH

We have to this point taken as given the productive capacity of the economy and asked how fiscal and monetary stabilization measures might be used to assure full utilization of that capacity. Now we need to note that the choice of stabilization measures may affect the rate at which capacity grows. In particular, stabilization via relatively restrictive fiscal policy and relatively easy monetary policy is usually regarded as favoring economic growth. As we noted above, with such a policy mix, investment tends to be a larger share of aggregate demand and spending. The larger is the share of investment spending, the greater are the rates of physical capital formation and growth, other conditions being the same.

That traditional view overlooks the point that investment in human capital is also necessary for and conducive to economic growth. Because the consumption spending category includes much human capital investment, such investment may well be relatively greater with relatively easy fiscal policy and relatively tight monetary policy. That is, the monetary-fiscal policy mix that favors investment in human capital is probably opposite to the mix that favors investment in physical capital. Since both types of investment promote growth, it is unclear which policy mix best promotes growth. And the traditional view that growth is favored by a combination of relatively easy monetary policy and relatively tight fiscal policy can be questioned.

BALANCE-OF-PAYMENTS EQUILIBRIUM

In a system of fixed or partially fixed exchange rates, fiscal (and monetary) measures that expand aggregate demand for domestically produced goods also expand demand for foreign-produced goods (imports). Any inflation that occurs tends to turn both foreign and domestic buyers away from domestically produced products. For both reasons, expansionary measures tend to reduce net exports $(X - M)$, which means a smaller surplus or larger deficit on a country's balance of payments.[31] Conversely, restrictive measures tend

31 A balance of payments is a record of transactions with foreign nations. Purchases of goods, services, and assets from foreign nations and gifts and grants to them give rise to an outflow of foreign exchange. Sales to foreign nations and gifts and grants from them generate an inflow of foreign exchange. The deficit is basically inflow minus outflow.

TABLE 17–1

CONFLICTS BETWEEN DOMESTIC OBJECTIVES AND BALANCE-OF-PAYMENTS EQUILIBRIUM

	Balance-of-payments situation	
Domestic situation	Surplus	Deficit
Deflationary gap	No conflict	Conflict
Inflationary gap	Conflict	No conflict

to increase net exports and increase the balance-of-payments surplus (or reduce the deficit). Thus, measures that eliminate a deflationary gap and increase domestic employment and output may increase the balance-of-payments deficit. That is, the objective of domestic full employment conflicts with the objective of balance-of-payments equilibrium when a country has a balance-of-payments deficit. Similarly, measures to reduce inflation interfere with achieving a balance-of-payments equilibrium when the country has a surplus. No conflict arises when a country has a balance-of-payments deficit and an inflationary gap or a balance-of-payments surplus with a deflationary gap. Table 17–1 summarizes these conflict situations.

Some have suggested that the mix of monetary and fiscal policy can be adjusted to reconcile the conflict between balance-of-payments equilibrium and full employment and price stability. Specifically, if the economy has unemployment and a balance-of-payments deficit, expansionary fiscal measures can be combined with restrictive monetary measures to simultaneously increase aggregate demand and interest rates. The increase in aggregate demand reduces unemployment, while the increase in interest rates attracts foreign capital (encourages foreigners to buy U.S. assets). Conversely, an inflationary gap and a balance-of-payments surplus call for restrictive fiscal measures and expansionary monetary policy. The former measures reduce aggregate demand and the inflationary gap, while the latter reduce net capital inflow.

The main difficulty with this approach is that it often will not work. The United States has tried to reduce simultaneously its unemployment and balance-of-payments deficit through expansionary fiscal policy and restrictive monetary policy with some degree of success, most notably in the early 1960s. However, in small countries with large foreign-trade sectors, aggregate demand and interest rates tend to be determined by worldwide economic conditions (and the combined policies of other countries). For such countries, general monetary and fiscal policy measures tend to be ineffective in eliminating inflationary and deflationary gaps and balance-of-payments disequilibrium.

Flexible exchange rates offer another means of reconciling the conflict between stabilization and balance-of-payments objectives. Fully flexible exchange rates assure balance-of-payments equilibrium, freeing both monetary and fiscal measures for use in domestic stabilization. Since 1971, the United States and other major industrial nations have moved toward flexible rates. But the central banks of many nations continue to intervene in foreign exchange markets in an attempt to hold exchange rates within desired ranges.[32]

NEED FOR COORDINATION

We have seen how monetary and fiscal measures may either reinforce or counteract one another. For example, the Fed may respond to a tax cut with tighter monetary policy, thereby offsetting and frustrating an attempt by the Congress and the president to stimulate the economy. Or it may reinforce the effects of the tax cut with a policy of easier money. Clearly, there is a need for coordination of monetary and fiscal policies.

But such coordination is not automatic because different elements of the government have responsibility for the two policy areas. The Fed, an independent institution created by Congress, determines monetary policy. Congress and the president (and the executive agencies) formulate and execute fiscal policy. Historically, there has been a varying amount of communication between these two groups, and each has not always had accurate information about what the other was doing. More importantly, there has often been disagreement about what should be done. The Fed usually favors less expansionary policies than do the Congress and the president. Poor communication and conflicting views have tended to produce a "stop-and-go" stabilization policy. And there has been a secular increase in interest rates, in part because of the Fed's efforts to restrain aggregate demand when Congress and the president were unwilling to do so with fiscal measures.

The question of how better coordination can be achieved is a perennial one, and so is the related issue of the Fed's "independence." Those who wish greater coordination necessarily advocate a reduction in the Fed's ability to pursue an independent monetary policy of its choosing. While the need is clear, no satisfactory mechanism for coordination has been devised.

SUMMARY

The targets (objectives) of stabilization policy are usually said to be *low*, or *acceptable*, rates of unemployment and inflation. However, a nation may

32 For further discussion of flexible exchange rates, see Dernberg and McDougall, *Macroeconomics*, chap. 17.

not be able to keep its unemployment rate as low as it might like without experiencing "too much" inflation. Or unemployment may be too high if the nation tries to keep its inflation rate as low as it might like. So there is a trade-off between unemployment and inflation, known as the Phillips curve, that greatly complicates definition of these targets. In the United States, debate about the appropriate definition of stabilization targets is perennial and a source of delay and indecisiveness in policy making.

Given target unemployment and inflation rates, a GNP target can be defined for each point in time. The object of stabilization policy then becomes that of generating a time path of aggregate demand that corresponds to the time path of GNP. In principle, both built-in and discretionary fiscal changes can be helpful in keeping aggregate demand on a desired path. But a number of problems arise. Built-in changes in taxes and government spending occur quickly and continuously in response to changes in economic activity. These changes are stabilizing in that they reduce fluctuations in aggregate demand. They are helpful in that they cushion downturns and slow demand growth during booms. But the features of the tax expenditure system that give rise to these stabilizing built-in changes also create fiscal drag. Over time, as incomes rise because of real economic growth or inflation or both, net taxes also rise. This automatic long-run increase in taxes is called fiscal drag because it reduces aggregate demand. If not offset by demand growth from other sources, either increases in G or in private demand, fiscal drag gradually increases unemployment and reduces capacity utilization. Fiscal drag can also be reduced by periodic tax cuts.

Discretionary fiscal changes are necessary to eliminate fiscal drag. They may also be useful for moderating cyclical fluctuations. However, time is required to implement such changes (the implementation lag). And time is then required for the changes to have their desired effect on aggregate demand (the response lag). Therefore, undesired fluctuations in aggregate demand must be predicted six to eighteen months before their occurrence if they are to be offset by discretionary fiscal changes. The implementation and response lags, and the need for prediction that they imply, greatly reduce the usefulness of discretionary fiscal policy. Indeed, because of these lags, discretionary changes may sometimes, if not frequently, prove destabilizing.

The possibility of destabilizing fiscal changes has led to proposals that discretionary changes be abandoned in favor of rules, usually balanced-budget rules. The rule with the greatest current appeal is that of balancing the full-employment budget. The difficulty with these rules is that employment and price level targets will sometimes, perhaps frequently, be missed, especially if monetary policy is similarly shackled by a steady growth rate rule. The advantage of the rules is that discretionary policy may sometimes produce even worse results.

Formula flexibility and stand-by authority for the president to change taxes are often advocated as means of reducing implementation lags and the probability of destabilizing changes. If adopted, such measures would weaken the case for balanced-budget or other rigid rules. *But BB is a foolish paragraph when trying to operate the u at FE.*

Either government purchases or net taxes may be changed to achieve a desired change in aggregate demand. However, relying primarily on tax changes for stabilization allows government purchases to be determined on efficiency grounds. Thus, low-priority, low-value public projects ("leaf raking") need not be undertaken simply to assure full employment. And high-value projects need not be curtailed simply to reduce aggregate demand.

While fiscal changes can, in principle, limit demand-pull inflation, they are basically ineffective in controlling cost-push inflation. (The same is true for monetary measures.) The reason is that cost-push inflation is not due to excess demand; instead, it reflects pressures from the supply side on wages and other costs and prices. *GAD → MUE*

Both monetary and fiscal policies affect aggregate demand; hence, they are to an extent substitutes. But they differ in effectiveness. Fiscal policy is more effective than monetary policy in stimulating demand when interest rates are low and there is excess capacity. Fiscal policy is relatively ineffective in stimulating demand when interest rates and the income velocity of money are high.

Monetary and fiscal policies may also differ in their effects on economic growth and balance-of-payments equilibrium. These side effects on other economic objectives may be relevant when choosing between monetary and fiscal measures for stabilization.

Since monetary changes may either reinforce or offset fiscal changes, monetary and fiscal changes should be coordinated. At present, coordination is informal and varies with administrations because fiscal decisions are made by Congress and the executive branch, while monetary policy decisions are made by the Fed. Proposals for assuring greater coordination have been made. But no proposal has attracted sufficient support to assure its adoption.

SUPPLEMENTARY READINGS

Blinder, Alan S., and Solow, Robert M. "Analytical Foundations of Fiscal Policy." In *The Economics of Public Finance*, pp. 3–115. Washington: Brookings, 1974.

Friedman, Milton, and Heller, Walter W. *Monetary Policy vs. Fiscal Policy*. New York: Norton, 1969.

Lewis, Wilfred, Jr. *Federal Fiscal Policy in the Postwar Recessions*. Washington: Brookings, 1962.

Morley, Samuel. *The Economics of Inflation*. Hinsdale, Ill.: Dryden, 1971.

Okun, Arthur M., and Teeters, Nancy H. "The Full Employment Surplus Revisited." In *Brookings Papers on Economic Activity*. Vol. 1. Washington, 1970.

Perry, George L. "Stabilization Policy and Inflation." In *Setting National Priorities: The Next Ten Years*, edited by Henry Owen and Charles L. Schultze, pp. 271–323. Washington: Brookings, 1976.

CHAPTER EIGHTEEN

FISCAL STABILIZATION: THE RECORD

In the two preceding chapters we have examined the potential for and problems involved in fiscal stabilization. In this chapter we briefly review the record of fiscal policy in the United States, the central question being whether *discretionary* fiscal policy has in fact been helpful in stabilizing the economy.[1]

Figures 18–1 and 18–2 show unemployment and inflation rates since 1929. Seldom has either index been as low as we would like. But this fact alone does not mean that stabilization policy has been a failure. The relevant question is whether matters would have been worse in the absence of discretionary fiscal measures.

The results of the studies that have dealt with this question show a mixed record for decretionary policy. The automatic, or built-in, stabilizers have been effective but insufficient to keep the economy on a full-employment stable-price growth path.

EARLY STABILIZATION EFFORTS

Stabilizing fiscal policy was first advocated during the 1930s. The federal budget was indeed in deficit throughout the period, up to 8.6 percent of

---

1 Although our focus is on fiscal policy experience, stabilization policy is not the sole responsibility of the fiscal authorities. As we have seen, monetary policy may reinforce or offset fiscal policy. In reviewing the record of fiscal policy, we make judgments about the appropriateness of fiscal policy. But we cannot conclude that fiscal policy alone was responsible for success or failure in achieving stabilization objectives.

392

FIGURE 18-1
ANNUAL PERCENTAGE CHANGE IN THE CONSUMER PRICE INDEX

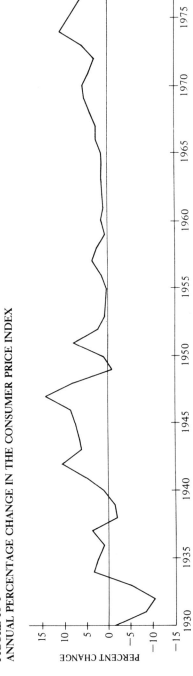

Source: Data from *Economic Report of the President, 1977*, and *Economic Indicators*, U.S. Congress, Joint Economic Committee, January 1977.

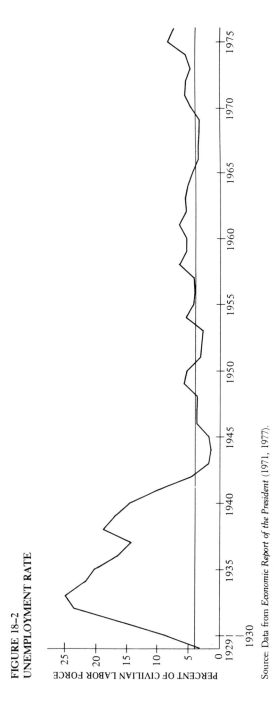

FIGURE 18–2
UNEMPLOYMENT RATE

PERCENT OF CIVILIAN LABOR FORCE

Source: Data from *Economic Report of the President* (1971, 1977).

GNP in 1931. Despite the actual deficits, there was a full-employment surplus in 1933, 1934, 1937, and 1938. Discretionary fiscal policy, as measured by changes in the full-employment surplus was highly variable.[2] The surplus decreased between 1929 and 1931, increased sharply from 1931 to 1933, and continued to oscillate throughout the decade. Moreover, the deficits and the federal budget were far too small to provide the needed stimulus. (Federal purchases of goods and services never exceeded 6.5 percent of GNP.) So the picture is hardly one of a concerted effort at "pump priming," as budget deficits came to be labeled. The 1930s did not provide a good test of the stabilization potential of fiscal measures because they were not consistently applied in the magnitude required to achieve noticeable results.[3]

EFFECTS OF WORLD WAR II

The increase in government demand for goods and services triggered by World War II provided the necessary economic stimulus to pull the economy out of the long depression. The demand increase began in 1939–1940, but the large increases in federal purchases came in 1941, 1942, and 1943. Purchases increased from $5.1 billion in 1939 to a peak of $89.0 billion in 1944, and the deficit increased from $2.2 billion to $54.5 billion.

Following that stimulus, unemployment was virtually eliminated and GNP increased 132 percent — from $90.5 billion in 1939 to $210.1 billion in 1944. In real terms, the increase was less — 72 percent. The increase in output was so great that real per capita consumption expenditures *exceeded* their prewar level *throughout the war*, despite the drain of goods and services into the war effort. Only in 1943 and 1944 did the components of GNP other than federal purchases fall slighty below their 1939 levels, by less than 5 percent in real terms. By employing the resources that were unemployed in 1939, the United States was able to fight a major war without forcing a decline in average real consumption.[4] This tremendous and rapid expansion of output and employment clearly and forcefully demonstrates the potential of expansionary fiscal policy.[5]

2 Discretionary changes alter the full-employment budget and result from Congressional and executive branch decisions to change taxes and expenditure programs.

3 For more detailed analysis, see E. Cary Brown, "Fiscal Policy in the Thirties: A Reappraisal," *American Economic Review*, 46, No. 5 (December 1956): 857–879.

4 Of course, there were shortages of particular goods. And the nation's stock of productive capital was allowed to deteriorate unless it was necessary for the war effort. But such capital deterioration as occurred did not prevent living standards from rising steadily following the war.

5 Monetary policy during World War II was also expansionary. From 1941 through 1945, demand deposits and currency increased by 123 percent.

POSTWAR STABILIZATION POLICY

Since the end of World War II, economic stabilization has been an important and widely supported economic objective. Evidence of this support is the Employment Act of 1946. While there has been no severe depression of the sort experienced in the 1890s and 1930s, there have been six recessions, the most recent one, 1974–1975, being the most severe.

Despite the mild character of the recessions, studies of the record of fiscal policy expose a number of deficiencies. Wilfred Lewis, Jr., in an evaluation of fiscal policy during 1946–1961, concludes that the automatic stabilizers were effective in limiting the severity of recessions. Such has also been the case since 1961. Figure 18–3 shows the induced federal deficit (the full-employment surplus minus the actual surplus). Changes in this deficit reflect the built-in adjustments of taxes and expenditures to changing economic conditions. These adjustments have clearly been stabilizing. The induced deficit has risen during and therefore cushioned downswings; and it has decreased during upswings.

Lewis finds that deliberate actions to counter recessions have usually been less helpful than the built-in adjustments (automatic stabilizers).[6] In a more recent evaluation, George L. Perry also gives low marks to discretionary changes in fiscal policy.[7] Perry uses changes in the high- (full-) employment surplus to measure discretionary changes in fiscal policy. Because of the response lag, which we discussed in Chapter 17, fiscal changes to limit recessions should be made prior to the beginning of the recession. That is, the full-employment surplus should be declining relative to GNP *prior* to the onset of a recession. Perry finds that such was the case only in the 1953–1954 recession. In the last three recessions, the full-employment surplus was increasing relative to GNP prior to the beginning of the recession. Thus, discretionary changes in fiscal policy tended to *reinforce* rather than offset the forces leading to the last three economic downturns.

In addition, discretionary changes often continued to be restrictive, the full-employment surplus continued to increase relative to GNP, during the recessionary downswing. In most instances, the full-employment surplus began to increase relative to GNP only after the recession had bottomed out. That is, discretionary changes in fiscal policy became expansionary only after the recovery from the recession was underway. Thus, discretionary

6 Wilfred Lewis, Jr., *Federal Budget Policy in the Postwar Recessions* (Washington: Brookings, 1962), p. 17.

7 George L. Perry, "Stabilization Policy and Inflation," in *Setting National Priorities: The Next Ten Years*, eds., Henry Owen and Charles L. Schultze (Washington: Brookings, 1976), pp. 271–322.

FIGURE 18–3
INDUCED FEDERAL DEFICIT (BILLIONS OF DOLLARS)

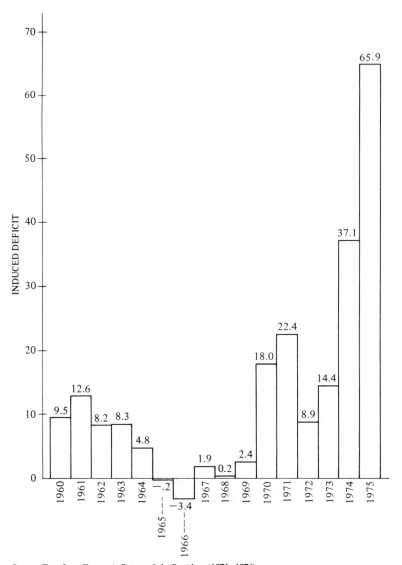

Source: Data from *Economic Report of the President* (1971, 1976).

FIGURE 18–4
FULL-EMPLOYMENT SURPLUS (BILLIONS OF DOLLARS)

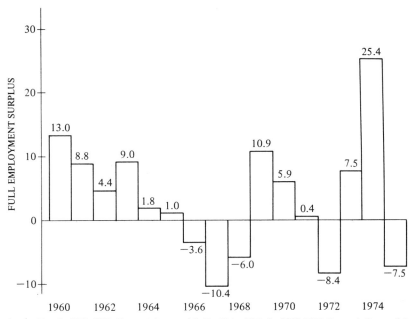

Source: Data for 1960–1968, *Economic Report of the President*, 1971; for 1965–1975, *Economic Report of the President*, 1976.

changes have reinforced the recoveries from recessions, but they usually have not moderated the downswings.

Discretionary fiscal changes aimed at curtailing inflation have been similarly tardy. In particular, restrictive measures to offset the sharp increase in government expenditures caused by the Korean and Vietnam Wars were too late to prevent substantial inflation.

Figure 18–4 shows the pattern of fiscal policy changes that gives rise to these conclusions.[8] Budgetary changes were expansionary through 1967:

8 The full-employment surplus figures in Figures 17–4, 18–3, and 18–4 are based on the potential GNP implicit in an overall unemployment rate of 4 percent. Lower estimates of potential GNP and the full-employment surplus are published in *Economic Report of the President*, 1977. The lower estimates use a variable full-employment rate that reflects changes in the composition of the labor force. However, as the report notes, the new estimates "have little effect on the period-to-period change in the full-employment surplus, which is the appropriate measure of the thrust of fiscal policy" (p. 77).

This re-estimation of potential GNP and the full-employment surplus reflects the on-going debate, referred to in Chapter 17, about how full employment should be defined.

The full-employment surplus declined from $13 billion in 1960 to −$10.5 billion in 1967. During the 1960s, this expansionary fiscal policy, dramatized by the tax cut of 1964, fueled a nine-year economic expansion.

The inflation rate began to rise in 1965 as the war in Vietnam escalated and private investment spending increased, partly in response to the investment tax credit. The president's Council of Economic Advisors saw a need for restrictive fiscal action as early as 1965, but it was mid-1968 before a 10 percent increase in federal income taxes, first requested by the president in January 1967, was enacted by Congress. The full-employment surplus increased from −$10.5 billion in 1967 to $10.9 billion in 1969, reflecting the widespread concern about the rising inflation rate. Unfortunately, because of the response lag, this fiscal restraint was too late to limit the inflation that was already underway. Indeed, this move probably worsened the economic downturn that began in the last quarter of 1969.

Expansionary measures were taken in response to this downturn; the full-employment surplus fell in each of the next three years (1970, 1971, 1972). Taxes were reduced by the Revenue Act of 1971, the investment tax credit was reinstated, and the wage-price freeze in 1971 was followed by two years of controls. While expansionary fiscal policy may have been in order in 1970–1971, it was clearly not needed in 1972. Yet from 1971 to 1972, federal government spending (full-employment level) increased 11 percent, and the full-employment surplus decreased. The overly expansionary fiscal policy of 1971–1972 was accompanied by easy money. But inflation was temporarily repressed by direct price controls.

The next two years saw a sharp reversal of fiscal policy, with the full-employment surplus rising from −$8.4 billion in 1972 to $25.4 billion in 1974. This fiscal restriction reinforced the economic downturn that began in late 1973.[9] At the same time, the removal of direct price controls in 1973 opened the door for previously repressed wage and price increases. Agricultural shortages, the oil price increases of the Organization of Petroleum Exporting Countries (OPEC), and the dollar devaluations of 1971–1973 added to upward pressures on prices. As a result, both unemployment and inflation rates reached record highs for the post-World War II period. A new term, *stagflation*, was coined to describe the unhappy outcome.

Tax-cut legislation was called for in January 1975 and enacted in April. Fiscal policy once again turned expansionary, with the full-employment

9 The sharp increase in full-employment surplus was due in part to the inflation. With progressive income taxes, inflation pushes income into higher tax brackets. So price and wage increases cause money income and tax revenue to rise even though real income remains unchanged. Real income fell in 1973–1974, but actual tax revenue continued to rise. Full-employment revenue and surplus increased even more sharply than actual revenue.

surplus declining from $25.4 billion in 1974 to −$7.5 billion in 1975. The economy bottomed out in the first quarter of 1975, just as the tax-cut legislation was being enacted. Again, the expansionary shift in fiscal policy came too late to moderate the downswing.

The overall picture, then, is one in which discretionary fiscal changes have been too late to be effective in moderating cyclical downswings and booms. Expansionary changes have strengthened recoveries that were already underway. Restrictive changes have come too late to prevent excess-demand inflation and have often cut short or weakened expansions, most notably in 1960.

What are the reasons for this lack of timeliness? One is that the need for action has not been clearly foreseen. Policy makers have lacked confidence in forecasts and therefore have been unwilling to take expansionary measures until the economy is clearly in a recession. Another reason is the fear that expansionary measures will lead to a higher rate of inflation if undertaken prior to a downturn. Indeed, restrictive changes (increases in the full-employment surplus) prior to downturns have undoubtedly been motivated in part by a desire to limit the inflation that usually accompanies economic recovery.

SUMMARY

Our brief review of the fiscal policy record in the United States clearly confirms that the federal government's budgetary policies can have a powerful effect on aggregate demand, employment, and prices. Built-in (automatic) adjustments in the federal budget have been stabilizing, causing the actual deficit to rise in periods of decline and to gradually decrease in periods of expansion.

The record of discretionary adjustments is much less impressive. They have typically reinforced economic recovery from recession troughs. But they have usually been too late to moderate downswings. Restrictive measures aimed at curtailing inflation have frequently cut short economic recovery or deepened the subsequent recession or both. In short, delays in making discretionary changes have reduced their effectiveness; in some instances, delays have been so long that the changes were destabilizing.

The lesson is clear: Discretionary fiscal changes must be more timely and more gradual. That is, discretionary changes must become more like built-in changes. Formula flexibility, discussed in Chapter 17, is one possible answer. Another would be stand-by authority for the president to make tax rate changes when a need is foreseen for either an increase or a decrease in aggregate demand. Over the years, other similar suggestions have been made for improving the timing of fiscal changes. None of the proposals is perfect;

but the need for a fiscal policy that anticipates and responds flexibly to changing economic conditions is clear.

The 1974–1975 downturn shows that sharp restrictions of aggregate demand and high rates of unemployment cannot be relied upon to hold inflation to acceptable levels.[10] Other means of controlling inflation, most likely an incomes policy, must be employed. And measures are needed to increase the productivity and employability of those members of the labor force who suffer the highest unemployment rates (the young, minorities, women). If successful, such measures would reduce the inflation rate associated with various overall unemployment rates: They would shift the Phillips curve to the left.

SUPPLEMENTARY READINGS

Lewis, Wilfred, Jr. *Federal Fiscal Policy in the Postwar Recessions.* Washington: Brookings, 1962.

Okun, Arthur M. *The Political Economy of Prosperity.* Washington: Brookings, 1969.

Perry, George L. "Stabilization Policy and Inflation." In *Setting National Priorities: The Next Ten Years*, edited by Henry Owen and Charles L. Schultze, pp. 271–322. Washington: Brookings, 1976.

---

10 Indeed, we can question whether inflation resulting from poor crops and agricultural shortages and from price increases by international cartels (such as the oil price increases by OPEC) can be prevented. To do so would require offsetting decreases in other prices, an unlikely outcome in view of the historical downward inflexibility of prices.

CHAPTER NINETEEN

GOVERNMENT BORROWING AND DEBT

Governments may finance spending by borrowing rather than by taxing, at least to a degree. In this chapter we will examine the reasons for and the consequences of government borrowing, a method of government finance that involves some of the more controversial and poorly understood issues in economics.

Borrowing differs from taxation in two major but related ways. First, as we have seen in Chapter 16, total demand for privately supplied goods and services is greater when a given level of government spending is financed by borrowing rather than by taxation. Second, borrowing distributes the cost of government differently than taxation, both among people living at a particular time and among people living at different times.

EFFECTS ON DEMAND, OUTPUT, AND PRICES

That tax and debt finance (borrowing) differ in their effects on output, prices and interest rates was implicit in our analysis in Chapter 16, and the following discussion is in part a review. But, since we did not directly compare the two methods of finance, we do so now. We will suppose that the amount and composition of government spending is fixed and look at the consequences of financing some fraction of that spending by borrowing rather than taxation.[1]

With borrowing (debt finance), businesses and households have greater

---

1 Unless otherwise stated, borrowing is presumed to be from domestic rather than foreign sources.

disposable (after-tax) incomes than they would with the equivalent amount of taxation. And so, there will be more demand for goods and services at the prevailing prices and interest rates with borrowing. At the same time, when government borrows, it competes with private borrowers, making private borrowing more difficult and costly and thereby decreasing the demand for goods that is based on borrowed funds.[2] The latter of these opposing effects is usually weaker. Therefore, aggregate demand for privately supplied goods and services is usually greater if government spending of given amount and composition is financed to a greater degree by borrowing. That is, increasing borrowing by, say, $10 billion per year and decreasing taxes by the same amount, while holding the level and composition of government spending constant, increases aggregate demand.

The effect of greater (or lesser) aggregate demand depends on the condition of the economy. If resources are fully employed, then output cannot increase; any increase in aggregate demand leads to higher prices and interest rates. More specifically, if there is full employment, then interest rates and prices must increase until real private demands are the same as they were before the debt-tax substitution. However, when labor and capital resources are not fully employed, greater aggregate demand can result in greater output of private goods and services. Experience shows that increases in aggregate demand typically have all three effects — greater output, higher prices, and higher interest rates — with the output effects being stronger and price effects being weaker as the degree of unemployment is greater.

Given these differential effects on aggregate demand, economic stabilization becomes an important consideration in the choice between debt and tax finance. Indeed, virtually all modern governments use a mix of tax and debt finance in their attempts to achieve full employment and price stability.

In a full-employment context, any increase in the output of government goods and services necessarily entails a decrease in the output of private commodities. The demand for private commodities must correspondingly be restricted. Tax finance restricts demand by reducing disposable money incomes. With debt finance, price and interest rate increases restrict demand. Thus, when resources are fully employed, taxation is a means of controlling inflation and distributing the costs of government differently than they would otherwise be distributed. Taxation is not necessary, but it may be desirable in comparison to its alternative.

If resources are not fully employed, increased government output need

2 This demand-decreasing effect of government borrowing can be offset if the Federal Reserve System expands commercial bank reserves enough that lenders can accommodate the government borrowing without reducing the availability of funds (at prevailing interest rates) to private borrowers.

not entail lower output of private commodities. And, in this latter case, debt finance of additional spending need not increase prices and interest rates. Indeed, when there is unemployment, the demand restriction implicit in tax finance of government expenditure increases is not appropriate, since expanded aggregate demand is needed to promote full employment.

Among the price increases that occur in response to the debt-tax substitution are increases in interest rates, which are the prices of borrowed funds and which affect the relative prices of current and future goods. The response of monetary policy makers to the debt-tax substitution may either reinforce or offset the interest rate increases that normally accompany the substitution. To the extent that monetary authorities ease credit, interest rate increases are relatively smaller and price increases are relatively greater.[3] The reverse occurs if the monetary authorities react by restricting credit. In any event, the debt-tax substitution may increase interest rates or prices or both and correspondingly reduce the real incomes of borrowers.

DISTRIBUTIONAL EFFECTS: CURRENT PERIOD

How do debt and tax finance differ in their effects on the distribution of income among persons living in the period during which the government spending and its financing are undertaken? To answer this question is to determine how the distribution of real income is changed if taxes are decreased by some amount and borrowing is increased by the same amount, with the amount and composition of government spending being unchanged. Of course, we are interested in the distributional changes that remain after all adjustments to the debt-tax substitution have taken place. The tax cuts of 1964, 1971 and 1975 are examples of such substitutions.

The debt-tax substitution initially increases the real income of persons by the amount of the tax decrease (borrowing increase). The increase in real income increases aggregate demand. As we noted above, if there is sufficient slack (unemployment) in the economy, the increase in demand can be accommodated without raising prices so that the real income gain from the tax cut is not eroded. And greater demand means greater output, and the employment of some previously underemployed persons, who thereby may gain real income. Thus, if there is sufficient unemployment in the economy, debt-tax substitution (a tax cut) may directly increase the real incomes of tax-

---

3 To ease credit, monetary authorities buy government bonds on the open market. Therefore, in this case, one agency of the government — the U.S. Treasury — sells bonds, while another agency — the Federal Reserve System — buys bonds. The end result is as if the government had financed its spending by printing money. Thus, financing expenditures by money creation is more expansionary than financing expenditures by borrowing from the public (individuals, businesses, commercial banks).

payers and indirectly increase the incomes of the previously unemployed, with there being a net gain in the aggregate.

In the case that the resources of the economy were fully employed before the substitution, the increase in the demand for goods and services that follows cannot be met. There is an inconsistency between what people demand in the aggregate and what the economy can supply. The inconsistency will be eliminated by adjustments in interest rates and the price level, which prevent real incomes from increasing in the aggregate and assure that aggregate demand is in balance with the supply capabilities of the economy.

Individuals may gain or lose from the combined effects of the tax decrease and the price and interest rate increases. For example, a person paying taxes of $1,000 on an income of $10,000 prior to the debt-tax substitution had disposable real income of $9,000 in current prices. Suppose now that taxes are cut to $910 by the substitution, leaving $9,090 instead of $9,000 after taxes. If prices rise exactly 1 percent as a result of the substitution, then the person neither gains nor loses. At that price level, $9,090 has exactly the same purchasing power as $9,000 previously had. If prices rise by more (less) than 1 percent, the person's real disposable income falls (rises) as a result of the debt-tax substitution.

This example shows that inflation functions as a tax when the share of debt finance is so large that inflation results. In this case, the burden resulting from the transfer of resources to government falls on those persons whose real incomes fall because of the inflation — persons whose money incomes increase less rapidly than prices. It seems unlikely that such inflation is more equitable than taxation as a means of distributing the costs of government. There is no reason to expect that those persons whose money income increases lag behind the rate of inflation are more able than others to bear the costs of government.

Our conclusion to this point is that debt-tax substitution in a full-employment situation has two opposing effects on individuals' current real incomes. Lower taxes mean higher real disposable incomes if prices remain unchanged. But the greater demand triggered by higher real incomes leads to price and interest rate increases that reduce real incomes. The end result may be a greater or lesser real income for any particular person and a changed distribution of real incomes among persons. Unfortunately, it is not possible to make generally applicable statements about how the distribution of income will be changed.

Stated differently, in a full-employment situation, the burden of government spending during the current period is the decreased availability of private goods. Tax finance reduces the availability of private goods to those persons whose real income is reduced by the tax — those persons and businesses who bear the incidence of the tax. Debt finance reduces the supply of goods to those persons whose real incomes are decreased by the higher prices and interest rates caused by debt-financed spending. The two sets of spending units will not be the same; hence, the differential effect of the two modes of finance.

DISTRIBUTIONAL EFFECTS: FUTURE PERIODS

Debt-tax substitution increases the stock of government debt. Therefore, there may be redistribution of income among persons in future periods as taxes are collected to pay interest and principle on the debt. In discussing these effects it is convenient for us to speak of two "generations": Generation 1 consists of those persons who receive income and pay taxes during period 1, the period in which the government borrowing and spending occurs. Generation 2 consists of persons who pay taxes and receive income in periods subsequent to but not during period 1.

INTRAGENERATION REDISTRIBUTION

Redistribution of income among members of generation 1 may occur as members of that generation are taxed to make interest and principal payments to bondholders (those members of generation 1 from whom the government borrowed). If people each hold bonds in proportion to their tax payments then there would be no net redistribution of income among members of this generation subsequent to period 1.

INTERGENERATION DISTRIBUTION

There may also be intergeneration redistribution as a consequence of the debt-tax substitution. Redistribution occurs to the extent that generation 2 is taxed to make interest and principal payments to bondholding members of generation 1. This transfer would not occur if the debt-tax substitution had not occurred. In this sense then, debt finance of spending undertaken by generation 1 during period 1 imposes greater costs on generation 2 than does tax finance of such spending. The burden of period 1 spending may be shifted in part to future generations. More specifically, any reduction in the availability of private goods and services that accompanies government spending in period 1 is borne by generation 1. However, with debt finance, interest and principal payments by members of generation 2 to the bondholders of generation 1 may partially compensate generation 1 for the reduced availability of goods during period 1. This result occurs even if the debt incurred in period 1 is "turned over" by borrowing from generation 2 to retire it. Of course, if the interest and principal payments are financed entirely by taxes borne by generation 1, then there is no intergeneration redistribution. Such is unlikely to be the case because generations of taxpayers overlap.

Associated with the tax collections required for principal and interest payments are excess burdens, which we defined in Chapter 9. Debt finance thus postpones the excess burdens of taxation so that they may fall in part or in total on members of generation 2. Although the magnitude of the excess burdens grows as the stock of debt grows, their significance probably increases primarily as debt and the taxes required for debt service increase relative to total incomes or GNP. Thus, a rising stock of debt does not imply an increasingly serious excess burden problem if the ratio of debt to GNP does not increase. In the United States, this ratio typically has not increased during peace time.

There is another way in which the debt-tax substitution may alter the distribution of income between generations. The substitution normally means higher interest rates during period 1. Higher interest rates may, in turn, decrease the investment share of private demand. If so, aggregate income in future periods will be lower with debt than with tax finance. This lower income reflects, in part, generation 1's decision to increase its current consumption at the expense of investment and its own future consumption. However, lower investment in period 1 may also lead to lower incomes for members of generation 2. If so, the real incomes of generation 2 are lower with debt finance than tax finance.

The view that investment will be lower with debt finance than with tax finance needs qualification. The higher interest rates associated with debt finance will indeed curtail investment that is based on borrowed funds. With tax finance, households will presumably curtail their lowest priority expenditures, some of which may be consumption (food, clothing) and some of which may be investment (a new house, or remodeling and repair of an old one; night school classes that would lead to a better job; preventive medical care). If households mainly curtail investment outlays then, contrary to the view expressed in the preceding paragraph, current investment and future incomes may be lower with tax finance than with debt finance; and, correspondingly, intergeneration burden transfers may be greater.

From the preceding analysis, we have an answer to a question of perennial concern: Who bears the burden of debt-financed government spending? A common view is that debt finance permits the present generation of taxpayers to shift the cost or burden of government to the taxpayers of future periods. Deficit spending burdens our children and grandchildren, so to speak. We can now see that there is an element of truth in this view. However, we must also keep in mind that under conditions of full employment, the total output of goods and services is at its upper limit. Thus, private purchases of goods and services must be lower if government purchases are greater — regardless of how government expenditures (purchases) are financed. The immediate burden of increased government spending, which is reduced availability of goods and services to households and firms, is necessarily borne in the current period. And burden transfer, which occurs only through the mechanisms discussed above, is unlikely to be complete.

JUSTIFIABILITY OF INTERGENERATION TRANSFERS

Suppose that debt finance does indeed place a larger burden on future generations than tax finance. Can such an outcome be justified? One answer is that if the benefits of the government spending accrue to members of future generations, as would be the case with capital expenditures for roads, parks, flood control, disease control research, etc., then it is appropriate that future generations also share the burden of the expenditures. If such burden sharing is achieved through debt finance, then debt finance of capital expenditures is appropriate, while debt finance of current expenditures is not.

Following this reasoning, it is often suggested that debt finance be used to finance capital projects, with interest and principal payments being determined by the timing of benefits. For example, suppose a new school building costs $1 million and will be used for twenty years. The benefits from the school are thus distributed over a twenty-year period. To similarly distribute the costs, the school could be financed by a $1 million bond issue with taxpayers paying in twenty installments, the sum of which would cover the principal and interest due on the bond issue.

If governments employ debt finance to implement such a "pay-as-you-use" policy, then we would expect the stock of government debt to be a reflection of the stock of government capital (roads, dams, school buildings, etc.) available to the nation; and growth in the stock of capital would imply and justify growth in the stock of debt.

Can the postwar growth in federal, state, and local government debt (see Table 19–1) be justified in the preceding terms? The stock of public capital has surely grown over the past thirty years. Whether it has grown more or less rapidly than the stock of debt is difficult to determine.

We have seen that when there is sufficient unemployment, debt finance may result in higher real incomes for the current generation, generation 1. There is then no need for investment and future incomes to be curtailed, to the possible detriment of generation 2. Indeed, generation 2 may benefit from the demand stimulus provided by debt finance if the result is a larger

TABLE 19–1
U.S. GOVERNMENT DEBT OUTSTANDING, SELECTED YEARS
(BILLIONS OF DOLLARS)

Year	Total	Federal	State and local
1940	63	43	20
1950	281	257	24
1960	356	286	70
1970	514	371	144
1975	765	544	221

Source: U.S. Census Bureau, *Historical Statistics of the U.S.: Colonial Times to 1957; Statistical Abstract of the U.S., 1974;* and *Governmental Finances, 1974–75.*

investment during period 1 and consequently larger incomes in future periods.[4] For this reason, it is generally accepted that debt finance is justified when it is required to stimulate aggregate demand enough to achieve full employment. Generation 2 is worse off only if it is taxed to make interest payments to generation 1, which does not result if government stimulates demand and increases employment by issuing debt that pays no interest (by printing money).

OUTSIDE DEBT

To this point we have assumed that the government borrows from domestic sources. When borrowing is from foreign sources, we need to modify the preceding analysis. With such external borrowing in lieu of tax finance, there need be no reduction of private demand to make room for government demand. Accompanying the loan from abroad will be an importation of goods and services, which will offset government's absorption of goods and services. In turn, when the foreign debt is repaid, goods and services are transferred to foreign countries.

Borrowing from foreign sources clearly transfers the burden to generation 2. None of the costs of expenditures undertaken in period 1 fall on generation 1 during that period. Instead, all of the costs fall on persons living in subsequent periods as they give up real resources to repay the foreign debt incurred in period 1. Some of the debt repayment may fall on generation 1, but some is also likely to fall on generation 2, with the latter's burden being greater, the longer the term of the foreign debt is.

4 The activities of the Works Progress Administration (WPA) and Civilian Conservation Corps (CCC) during the 1930s are examples of expenditures that stimulated demand and employment while contributing capital to future generations.

STATE AND LOCAL GOVERNMENT BORROWING

The need to assign costs to periods in which benefits accrue is particularly important in the case of state and local government spending. Because of population mobility, the population benefiting from capital spending by state and local governments is likely to differ substantially from the resident population at the time the expenditure is made. It would therefore be unfair to finance capital expenditures with a tax on the resident population at the time the expenditures are undertaken. Indeed, attempting to do so would likely inhibit such spending, to the detriment of future residents of the community. For this reason, debt finance has been advocated as a means of achieving pay-as-you-use finance of state and local government capital spending.

On the other hand, it has been argued that whether a local government's capital spending is debt or tax financed is of little consequence to its residents. The reasoning is as follows. Suppose a community undertakes a capital project, say a new sewage treatment plant. It can either pay for the project with a current property tax levy or borrow the money and repay it over a period of years with future property tax revenues. *If property taxes are capitalized* into property values, then property values will be higher with current tax finance than with borrowing. That is, people moving into the community will pay more for property if the capital project is tax financed rather that debt financed because they will not have the future tax liabilities associated with debt finance. The tax financed good is "free" to them. And the additional amount that they will pay for property will exactly equal the capitalized stream of future tax payments that would be required to retire the debt. So, with full capitalization of future property tax liabilities, current property owners would be indifferent to the form of finance. If the project is tax financed, they pay more taxes in the current period, but they are compensated with lower taxes and higher property values should they move before the benefits from the project are exhausted. With debt finance, current taxes are lower, but so are property values. The conclusion drawn from this reasoning is that if there is full capitalization of property taxes, future residents will bear the costs of services provided by current capital investments whether the investments are financed with current property taxes or with debt that is to be retired with future property tax revenues.

As a practical matter, the form of finance (debt versus tax) is likely to matter because full capitalization may not take place.[5]

---

5 See Wallace E. Oates, *Fiscal Federalism* (New York: Harcourt Brace Jovanovich, 1972), pp. 153–159, for a more complete discussion of these issues.

DOES DEBT HAVE TO BE REPAID?

Is there anything wrong with a continuously growing stock of government debt? Not necessarily. As we noted, a growing stock of debt may be justified if public capital is growing; and public capital would be expected to grow as long as population and per capita income are increasing.[6] Thus, we might expect the stock of debt to grow continuously over long periods in some societies.

Even if continuously growing debt is not justified in the preceding sense, it need not spell doom for the nation. The factor limiting government's ability to borrow is its ability to service and refund the debt. As long as new debt can be issued to pay the principal on existing debt and the interest payments can be made without having taxes so high that incentives are destroyed or significantly weakened, then the stock of debt is maintainable. And, in that sense, it is not too large. A number of economists have suggested that debt growth is not excessive if it does not exceed the growth of GNP (if the debt-GNP ratio does not increase). From Table 19–2, we can see that federal debt has not grown more rapidly than GNP over the last twenty years and that state and local government debt has. Of course, the fact that the growth of debt is bearable in that it does not seriously interfere with the functioning of or cause a collapse of the economic system tells us nothing about whether it is otherwise appropriate.

SUMMARY

Debt and tax finance have different effects on aggregate demand and, consequently, on prices, interest rates, output, and employment. Aggregate demand is greater as the share of spending that is debt financed is greater. Correspondingly, equilibrium output and prices and interest rates are directly related to the debt-financed share of spending. If that share of a given amount of government spending is sufficiently large, output approaches the capacity limits of the economy; any further increases in the share of debt finance result in price and interest rate increases.

Debt and tax finance also have differential income distribution effects, in part because of their differential effect on aggregate demand. With debt finance, members of the current generation gain because current tax liabilities are lower and money disposable income is higher. But they may lose if debt finance entails relatively higher prices and interest rates, higher future tax liabilities, or lower future real incomes (before taxes). How these various

---

6 As population grows, more schools, roads, etc., are needed. In addition, as the income accruing to a given population increases, it is likely that the population will want more goods of all types, including public capital goods.

TABLE 19–2
U.S. GOVERNMENT DEBT AS A PERCENT OF GNP, SELECTED YEARS

Year	All governments	Federal	State and local
1940	63.2	43.1	20.1
1950	98.7	90.2	8.4
1960	70.7	56.8	13.9
1970	52.3	37.7	14.7
1975	50.5	35.9	14.6

Source: Debt figures in Table 19–1 divided by GNP.

effects "net out" is difficult to say. The real incomes of members of future generations may also be differentially affected by debt and tax finance, with a likely but not necessary consequence being that members of future generations are worse off with debt than tax finance.

SUPPLEMENTARY READINGS

Dernburg, Thomas F., and McDougall, Duncan M. *Macroeconomics.* 5th ed. New York: McGraw-Hill, 1976.

Ferguson, J.M., ed. *Public Debt and Future Generations.* Chapel Hill: University of North Carolina Press, 1964.

Modern governments are virtually all multilevel, multiunit systems, such as the federal system in the United States. That is, government is decentralized to a degree in all modern nations. Chapters 20 and 21 explore the economic reasons for and the problems created by decentralization. The primary advantage of decentralization is that it permits and encourages diversity in providing public goods and services, which is desirable because people have different demands for public as well as private goods. At the same time, decentralization creates problems, most notably the spillover of benefits and costs from local and state government activities. Because state and local governments may either ignore or give little weight to the spillovers, their decisions may not be optimal from a national perspective. Also, diversity in the supply of some goods, such as education and justice, may be undesirable per se. Chapter 22 describes and evaluates various approaches to dealing with these problems and improving a federal system of government.

PART SIX

FISCAL FEDERALISM

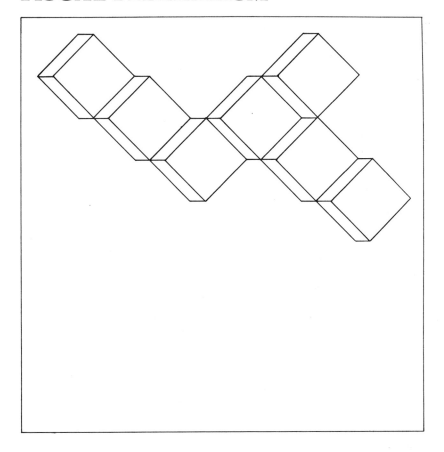

CHAPTER TWENTY

FISCAL FEDERALISM: PRINCIPLES AND PURPOSES

In virtually all modern nations, people are served by and subject to a number of governments. The United States has a multilevel, multiunit system of federal, state, and local governments. Are there economic reasons for such a system? Or should the economic (resource allocation and income distribution) activities of government be carried out by a single national government? The primary difference between *centralized* and *decentralized* government is that the latter permits policies to vary among geographic areas and their resident population groups. A basic question, then, is: Under what conditions is it both possible *and* desirable that governmental policies vary regionally?

In this chapter we will consider these questions. More specifically, we will consider the equity and efficiency rationales for decentralizing government's income redistribution and resource allocation functions. In Chapter 21 we will examine the problems that arise because the decentralization that has occurred has not been determined solely on economic grounds. In Chapter 22 we will examine the policies (grants-in-aid, revenue sharing, supplementary taxes, home rule, etc.) aimed at mitigating these problems. But before proceeding with the main tasks, let us look briefly at the structure of federalism in the United States and state more clearly what is meant by decentralized government.

STRUCTURE OF FISCAL FEDERALISM IN THE UNITED STATES

In 1902 local governments were dominant in our federal system in that they raised more revenues and had larger expenditures than either federal or state governments (see Table 20–1). Since then, the relative importance of federal

TABLE 20-1
CHANGING STRUCTURE OF FEDERALISM IN THE U.S.,
SELECTED YEARS (PERCENT)

	1902	1927	1940	1950	1960	1975
	Federal share					
Total expenditures	34.0	30.4	45.0	60.3	59.7	52.3
Civilian expenditures [a]	26.7	26.3	40.3	46.2	40.4	42.4
Total revenues from own sources	40	38	39	65	66	58
	State share					
Total expenditures	8.2	12.8	17.4	15.5	14.7	18.7
Civilian expenditures [a]	9.1	13.7	18.9	21.0	21.7	22.6
Total revenues from own sources	11	16	28	17	17	23
	Local share					
Total expenditures	57.8	56.8	37.6	24.2	25.6	28.9
Civilian expenditures [a]	64.1	60.0	40.8	32.8	37.9	35.0
Total revenues from own sources	49	46	33	18	18	19

[a] Other than for defense and international relations.

Source: U.S. Census Bureau, *Historical Statistics of the U.S.: Colonial Times to 1970*; and *Governmental Finances, 1974–75.*

and state governments has increased, with the federal government now being the dominant partner.

The increased relative importance of federal spending came about primarily because national defense and federal transfer payments to individuals have grown. The increased importance of both state and federal government reflects the increased interdependence and mobility of our society. Because of this interdependence, government policies have effects over larger geographic areas, and fewer decisions can be made on a strictly local basis.

Both state and local governments are receiving increasingly large shares of their total revenues from other governments (see Table 20–2), while the federal government receives virtually no revenues from other governments. Consequently, the federal government's share of revenue raised exceeds its share of spending (Table 20–1). Since 1902 the federal government's share of revenue raised has increased by 50 percent, while state governments' share has doubled and local governments' has fallen to slightly more than one-third of its 1902 level.

Table 20–3 shows the current intergovernmental division of responsibilities for major expenditure categories. The federal government is dominant only in national defense and related spending. State and local governments make the largest share of outlays in other categories. However, the

TABLE 20–2
INTERGOVERNMENTAL REVENUE OF STATE AND LOCAL GOVERNMENTS
AS A PERCENT OF TOTAL REVENUE, SELECTED YEARS

Year	State governments	Local governments
1902	4.7	6.1
1927	7.3	9.5
1940	12.2	24.7
1950	17.3	27.3
1960	22.7	27.1
1975	24.4	38.8

Source: Tables 2–13 and 2–14.

federal government's role is not fully measured by its direct outlays, because federal grants provide the revenues for and impetus to much state and local spending. For example, the federal government *directly* made only 31.0 percent of the outlays for public welfare in 1974–1975, but through grants it financed 52.8 percent of state and local outlays for that purpose (see the last column of Table 20–3).

Table 20–4 shows significant variation in the degree of state responsibility

TABLE 20–3
PERCENTAGE OF 1974–1975 EXPENDITURES ACCOUNTED FOR BY EACH LEVEL
OF GOVERNMENT[a]

Category of spending	Federal	State	Local	Percent of state and local spending financed by federal grants
Total expenditure	53.0	18.0	29.0	18.6
National defense and international affairs, postal service, and space research and technology	100.0	0	0	—
Education, total	7.5	24.1	68.4	10.2
Local schools	0	.9	99.1	—
Higher education	0	81.5	18.5	—
Highways	1.4	62.4	36.2	21.1
Public welfare	31.0	44.3	24.7	52.8
Health and hospitals	24.1	36.1	39.8	10.9
Insurance trust expenditures[b]	82.6	15.2	2.2	—

a Intergovernmental grants included at recipient level.

b Includes Social Security payments.

Source: U.S. Census Bureau, *Governmental Finances, 1974–75.*

TABLE 20–4

PERCENTAGE OF STATE AND LOCAL GENERAL EXPENDITURE FROM OWN
REVENUE SOURCES FINANCED BY STATE GOVERNMENTS, BY STATE,
1970–1971

State	Total general expenditure	Local schools	Highways	Public welfare	Health and hospitals
United States	52.7	43.3	74.5	76.1	51.5
Alabama	64.0	74.6	81.9	99.1	38.5
Alaska	78.9	86.8	72.7	100.0[a]	80.7
Arizona	59.2	47.5	85.8	95.7	38.4
Arkansas	57.0	54.2	93.2	62.2	44.1
California	47.6	37.1	74.0	68.9	36.1
Colorado	52.9	31.9	75.5	77.3	54.3
Connecticut	56.4	23.9	75.0	96.9	89.5
Delaware	69.9	76.3	78.7	100.0[a]	99.0[a]
Florida	50.9	61.7	79.5	96.7	33.3
Georgia	54.3	61.4	68.8	89.2	33.5
Hawaii	77.7	96.8[a]	53.7	99.6	96.7
Idaho	61.9	44.6	80.4	74.0	33.1
Illinois	51.1	36.6	85.9	94.3	62.0
Indiana	51.5	33.2	93.4	47.6	59.2
Iowa	50.5	28.9	73.4	74.5	27.5
Kansas	49.6	32.1	58.3	53.7	56.3
Kentucky	67.7	64.4	92.4	92.4	57.1
Louisiana	65.0	65.5	72.8	100.0[a]	72.5
Maine	60.7	34.7	65.2	89.0	84.3
Maryland	54.3	37.4	94.1	89.2	75.3
Massachusetts	50.0	26.4	62.0	100.0[a]	65.7
Michigan	52.8	43.0	80.6	88.6	55.0
Minnesota	54.9	48.1	58.1	46.4	44.0
Mississippi	65.4	66.3	75.2	99.0	30.4
Missouri	44.7	33.8	75.0	99.5	54.4
Montana	52.2	26.1	62.8	42.1[b]	63.1
Nebraska	44.2	20.1	57.6	73.4	40.9
Nevada	45.0	40.2	81.4	55.0	15.7[b]
New Hampshire	51.0	10.4[b]	62.7	67.9	82.1
New Jersey	43.1	27.5	66.5	73.3	42.7
New Mexico	74.9	74.5	91.2	98.2	37.4
New York	47.0	50.1	58.1	54.1	47.4
North Carolina	70.2	77.9	86.7	51.3	69.9
North Dakota	60.6	31.3	61.1	76.9	91.5
Ohio	42.9	29.8	79.7	90.8	44.0
Oklahoma	63.6	46.0	89.7	100.0[a]	55.9

TABLE 20–4 (*cont.*)

State	Total general expenditure	Local schools	Highways	Public welfare	Health and hospitals
Oregon	51.3	20.8	84.9	99.1	59.0
Pennsylvania	59.2	46.2	84.3	96.0	87.9
Rhode Island	64.7	37.1	56.4	100.0[a]	98.2
South Carolina	65.8	68.4	93.5	91.2	49.9
South Dakota	48.8	16.0	59.4	87.3	59.2
Tennessee	52.8	52.1	82.0	84.3	32.7
Texas	50.0	52.7	56.9	97.3	44.0
Utah	65.3	57.3	76.1	97.4	63.0
Vermont	72.8	35.2	76.1	99.5	97.0
Virginia	56.6	37.7	82.5	78.1	89.4
Washington	62.6	54.7	81.2	100.0[a]	54.8
West Virginia	71.3	56.7	94.7[a]	92.3	54.0
Wisconsin	57.2	31.7	51.2[b]	47.7	58.4
Wyoming	51.5	36.6	93.9	66.1	28.9

a Indicates state with largest state financed share
b Indicates state with smallest state financed share

Source: Advisory Commission on Intergovernmental Relations, *Federal-State-Local Finances: Significant Features of Federalism* (Washington: Government Printing Office, 1974).

for financing the major activities of state and local governments. On the average, states finance a larger share of state and local spending on public welfare and highways than on local schools and health and hospitals, with the degree of financing varying considerably among states. The states that finance a relatively large share of one activity do not necessarily finance a high share of other activities.

MEANING OF GOVERNMENTAL DECENTRALIZATION

A decentralized system is one in which groups within the total population are served by separate governments. Decisions regarding at least some government activities are made by such groups, rather than by the national population as a whole. Usually groups are defined as those persons residing within a particular geographic area.[1] Thus, decentralization implies that at least some government policies and activities may vary among regions of the

1 In some cases, however, the groups may be defined as those persons using a particular service, as in the cases of special taxing districts for flood control, irrigation, or drainage.

nation. In contrast, with a centralized system, there is a single government; policies do not vary among regions, and the same kinds and quantities of public goods and services are supplied in all regions.[2]

Decentralizing governmental decision making in a particular manner does not require that actual production of public goods and services and tax collection be similarly decentralized. For example, different levels of police and fire protection may be chosen by the several cities of a metropolitan area. Then each city could contract with the metropolitan area supplier for a particular frequency of police patrols and particular amounts of other police and fire protection activities.[3] Such an arrangement would permit economies of scale in the production of services without requiring that decisions be made by a single metropolitan area government.[4]

DECENTRALIZATION AND EFFICIENT RESOURCE ALLOCATION

The main economic rationale for decentralization is that many governmental activities do not affect the entire population of a nation; for example, providing services such as police and fire protection and air pollution control to a particular community. The main beneficiaries of such "local" public goods are the residents of the receiving community. This is not to say that no benefits accrue outside the community. But benefits diminish rapidly with distance from the community, as in the case of local parks which will be used more heavily by nearby residents than by people who reside at some distance. As shown in Figure 20–1, providing a particular local public good to community A affects only the residents of part of the nation — region L. The terms *locality* and *community*, which will be used interchangeably,

2 Of course, a single central government can attempt to tailor service levels to those desired by individual communities. To do so, decision making would in effect have to be decentralized, and there would have to be departments or divisions in the central government corresponding to the individual communities. These departments would have to perform essentially the same functions as would be performed by the community governments.

3 The Lakewood Plan in Los Angeles represents such an approach to supply of services in metropolitan areas. For discussion of this and other metropolitan area systems of government, see Robert L. Bish, *The Public Economy of Metropolitan Areas* (Chicago: Markham Publishing Company, 1971), Chap. 5.

4 Economies of scale in providing police and fire protection may arise, for example, because a central metropolitan switchboard and dispatch office are used, rather than there being a separate office in each city in the metropolitan area. Scale economies in tax collection are likely because the costs of collecting taxes are largely fixed. That is, collection costs per dollar of tax revenue are likely to be less if a state collects sales and income taxes on behalf of counties and cities within the state than if each city and county collects its own taxes. Such a system, while achieving economies of scale, does not prevent individual cities and counties from setting their own tax rates.

FIGURE 20–1
BENEFIT RANGE OF NATIONAL AND LOCAL PUBLIC GOODS

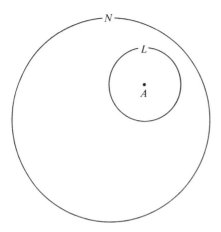

may refer to the area and population falling within the jurisdiction of any subnational (state, city, county) unit of government.

In contrast, a "national" public good is one that, once provided to the residents of one community, is equally available to all the residents of the nation — persons residing within the circle N of Figure 20–1. Once the output of a national public good is determined for one region, it is determined for all regions. The residents of the various regions cannot independently select the quantity of a national public good that will be available to them. There are very few examples of a national public good — national defense is the commonly cited example.

People who reside outside the benefit region of a local public good have little interest in the amount of that good provided. Moreover, other residents of the nation will not be affected if the residents of the region determine the amount of the good to be provided. In contrast, all residents of the nation may be concerned about the amount of the national public good provided to a particular region, because the amount provided to the nation is determined when the amount provided to any region is determined.

Both national and local public goods can be provided by either a single national government or a decentralized system of government. Which government structure is better from an efficiency viewpoint?

LOCAL PUBLIC GOODS

It is possible for the quantity of a local public good to vary among regions. If, for example, there is regional diversity in incomes and tastes, then the efficient quantity of the public good may also vary. Under such conditions, efficiency requires a system of government that permits different regions to have different amounts of local public goods. This reasoning underlies the view that decentralized government may be more responsive to people's demand than a single national government. Let us examine this view, first assuming a two-community nation with a fixed distribution of population between the two communities. Then we will consider the case of variable population distribution.

Fixed community size   In Figure 20–2, ΣD_A shows the marginal value that members of community A place on the X provided by their community. It is the vertical summation of the marginal value curves of the members of the community; it is a community demand curve of the sort we defined in Chapter 4. Let us assume that the boundary of each community corresponds exactly to the area within which the benefits from its provision of X accrue. Under this assumption, members of community B place no value on the X

FIGURE 20–2
EFFICIENT OUTPUTS OF LOCAL PUBLIC GOODS, TWO COMMUNITIES

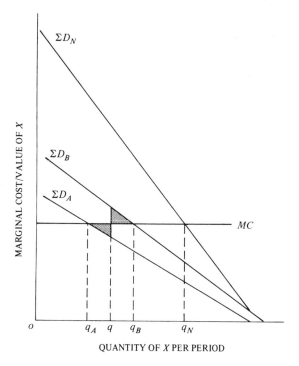

QUANTITY OF *X* PER PERIOD

provided by community A; and ΣD_A shows the marginal value of X to all persons of the nation (communities A and B). The curve ΣD_B is similarly defined and interpreted. The cost of providing X, shown by the MC schedule, is assumed to be the same in both communities, although the analysis would be the same if costs were different. (For the present we will ignore the curve ΣD_N.)

Given these value and cost schedules, q_A and q_B are the efficient quantities of X for communities A and B, respectively.[5] These outputs could conceivably be the same, in which case no welfare loss is associated with the nationally uniform output that would likely accompany national government provision of the public good. But it is surely more likely that the efficient quantities will differ because of intercommunity differences in tastes, incomes, and costs of the public good. Thus, achieving efficiency requires a system of government that permits communities to have different amounts of the good *if* demands or costs or both vary among communities.

While decentralized decision making is necessary for efficiency in the provision of local public goods, efficiency does not automatically follow. Each local government will provide the quantity that is efficient from a national viewpoint if (1) its jurisdiction corresponds to the area within which the benefits from the public good accrue, (2) the taxes that it collects are borne entirely by its constituents, and (3) it provides the quantity that is efficient for its own constituents. However, if providing the public good generates spillover benefits for residents of other localities, each local government tends to underestimate the value of the good to the nation as a whole and provide *too little* of it. Or, if some of the taxes collected by each government are borne by (exported to) residents of other localities, then each community bears less than the full cost of the public good that it provides and may therefore provide *more* than the efficient quantity.

For a national government to achieve efficiency in the supply of local public goods, it must act as a decentralized system of local governments. Stated differently, given a system of local government that meets the conditions we described in the preceding paragraph, centralization of decision making cannot increase the welfare of one person without reducing the welfare of another. Figure 20–2 illustrates the potential welfare loss if a national government provides local public goods. Community A prefers a lower level of X than community B. If the national government provides the same quantity to each community, then there will always be a potential welfare gain from decentralizing in order to provide the efficient quantity for each community. For example, if the central government provides q to both communities, then changing to a decentralized system that produces q_A and

5 This statement assumes that the CCA are zero at the margin and less in total amount than the welfare gains from such action.

q_B for communities A and B, respectively, will generate welfare gains equal to the two shaded triangles. It is possible to make the residents of both communities better off by such decentralization. Of course, some persons may, in fact, be better off with centralized decision making. But, if so, some person must be worse off.

Variable community size   In the preceding discussion we assumed a given population for each locality. However, population is mobile; a change in population distribution may change the benefits from and the costs of a given quantity of a public good. In Figure 20–2, movement of the population of community B to community A increases the marginal value of each quantity of public good provided by community A. Specifically, the curve ΣD_N, which is the vertical summation of the curves ΣD_A and ΣD_B, shows the marginal benefits of X to the now larger population of A. The reason is that X is a pure public good within the community; community A's output of X can be made available without cost to the population of community B if the latter moves to community A. Since the marginal value of X increases, the efficient output of X increases — from q_A to q_N. And the *per person* cost of providing a given quantity of the public good decreases.

These conclusions are in accord with our intuition. If several communities are so small in terms of population that each community can provide its current level of public services to additional people *without additional cost*, then increasing population density by moving the population of some communities into the remaining communities will reduce the aggregate and per person costs of providing a given level of public services. It is not efficient for small towns to provide as great a level of public goods as large towns.

Since the total and marginal benefits from a given quantity of a pure public good always increase when the number of persons in the benefit area (community) increases, and per person costs always decrease, benefits are maximized and per person costs are minimized when everyone in the nation resides in one benefit area (community). For example, if there are three pure public goods having benefit areas equal to (1) the nation's area, (2) one-half the nation's area, and (3) one-fourth the nation's area, then maximizing the benefits from and minimizing the per capita costs of given quantities of the three goods require that the residents of the nation live in one-fourth of the nation's area. Of course, population is not concentrated that way, for several reasons.

First, even if the per person costs of public services decline continuously as the number of persons in the benefit area increase, other costs may increase. With greater population density, housing costs may increase. The location of population and industry clearly affects transportation and production costs. Concentrating the nation's population into one benefit area probably would not minimize such *private* costs. Second, most public goods are not pure; instead, the amount or quality or both of a service available to each person in the community eventually declines as the community's population increases. The deterioration in quantity or quality of public services as population density increases is often termed *congestion cost*. Third, with only one community and one government, everyone must receive the same quantities of various public goods. However, as we noted earlier, if there are a number of government units supplying services, quantities can vary among communities and some diversity in tastes can thereby be accommodated.

From an efficiency viewpoint, community size and the distribution of a nation's population should reflect the balancing of several cost factors. On the one hand, the more geographically concentrated the population is, the lower the per person costs of providing *pure* public goods will be. But arguing against increasing population density are congestion costs and the higher costs of some private goods. In addition, the cost advantages of having fewer and more populous communities must be balanced against any welfare losses that occur because public service levels are less closely tailored to preferences.

NATIONAL PUBLIC GOODS

Our conclusion so far is that when individual preferences regarding government activity vary regionally, the welfare of individuals may be greater if local government, rather than a central government, provides local public goods. But this is not true for a national public good. If each local government acts independently to provide the quantity that maximizes the welfare of its own residents, then it will produce the quantity for which the sum of the marginal values to the members of the community equals the marginal cost to the community. The resulting supply generally will be less than the amount that maximizes welfare for the residents of the nation. The reason for this shortfall is that local governments acting independently may underestimate the value of national public goods; they may therefore undersupply those goods because they ignore the beneficial spillover effects of their actions on the residents of other localities. Thus, spillover effects and any resulting welfare losses are minimized when decisions about providing a national public good are made by the national government.

The argument supporting this conclusion is analogous to the reasoning in Chapter 4 by which we established that individuals acting independently may allocate too few resources to the production of public goods. More specifically, let us consider again the example of Figure 20–2, but supposing that X is now a national rather than a local public good. As before, ΣD_A is the vertical summation of the marginal value curves of the members of community A. Because X is a national public good, it is available to the members of both communities regardless of which community provides it. Thus, ΣD_A shows the value that the members of community A collectively place on each additional unit of X provided to the nation by *either* community. ΣD_B is similarly defined. Since each unit of X is available to both communities, the vertical summation of the two-community valuation curves, ΣD_N, shows the total value that all persons in the nation place on each additional unit of X.

When all persons in the nation are considered, the output of X for which the sum of marginal values equals marginal cost is q_N. This output is Pareto optimal (efficient) if the CCA are zero at the margin and less in total than the aggregate welfare gains from collective action. However, this output will not be produced by either community if they act independently.

If the two communities act independently in that they develop no means of sharing the cost of providing marginal units of X, then neither community will provide an additional unit of X if its value to the community's *own* members falls short of its cost. Community A will provide at most q_A of X because for outputs in excess of q_A, the cost of an additional unit exceeds its value to the members of A. Similarly, community B will provide at most q_B of X.[6] If community A provides q_A, then community B will provide only $q_B - q_A$. If community B provides q_B, then community A will provide nothing. Thus, there will be underproduction of national public goods if their provision is left to local governments and there is no mechanism for sharing their cost among localities.

The efficient amount (q_N) could be produced by cooperative action of the local governments, which would involve a joint decision about the quantity to be supplied and a sharing among the localities of the costs of producing the additional output.[7] Alternatively a single national government could produce the optimum. In any case, efficient provision of a national public good requires that the benefits accruing to all members of the nation be considered.

This analysis is not just applicable to the case of national public goods. It also applies to any case in which the benefits of public goods extend beyond

6 Since increasing output to q_A has the *potential* of increasing the welfare of each person in A, q_A may be termed the *independent adjustment optimum* for A. Similarly, q_B is the independent adjustment optimum for B. If B provides q_B, then A provides nothing, thus becoming a free rider. This prospect of a free ride may lead both A and B to wait for the other to act, in which case output may be zero. As we discussed in Chapter 4, the CCA and the distribution of gains and costs must also be taken into account in determining whether welfare gains in fact result from provision of those quantities.

7 For a discussion of the issues and problems involved in the formation of joint policies (alliances), see Mancur Olson, Jr., and R. J. Zeckhauser, "An Economic Theory of Alliances," *Review of Economics and Statistics* (August 1966): 266–279.

the boundaries (jurisdiction) of the government unit that determines the output. That is, the analysis is applicable to cases in which there are spill-over benefits, which occur because the range of interest (jurisdiction) of the decision-making government is less than the range of benefits from the goods provided by that government.

Because so little is known about actual government objectives and deci-sion processes, we cannot conclude from the above discussion that local governments *in fact* undersupply national public goods. Instead, we can conclude that they would do so if they acted independently to maximize the welfare of their residents. Local governments may in fact behave otherwise; and, if so, they may either oversupply or undersupply public goods with spillover benefits. Similarly, we cannot conclude that national governments will in fact supply the efficient (Pareto-optimal) quantity of national public goods because they may neither wish nor know how to do so.

PERFECT CORRESPONDENCE

From the preceding analysis, we might conclude that an ideal system (from the viewpoint of economic efficiency) would be to have a government's ju-risdiction coincide exactly with the area within which the benefits from and the costs of its actions accrue. A governmental unit would be created to pro-vide each public good (or set of public goods) having a particular benefit area. And each unit would finance its activities with taxes borne only by its residents. Thus, police and fire protection, education, transportation, and national defense might be provided by separate governmental units. Such a structure has been termed one of *perfect correspondence*. [8]

But a perfect-correspondence structure is not optimal because govern-ments are costly to create and operate. Once created, a particular govern-mental apparatus can be used to make a number of decisions. And scarce resources can be saved by reducing the number of governments and making decisions regarding several activities through the same government, even though the benefit areas of the several activities fail to coincide exactly with the government's jurisdiction. Such a saving is a plus for society. But it must be weighed against the welfare losses that members of society experience because the smaller number of governments is less able to accommodate diversity in individual preferences and because spillover of benefits and costs may lead to inefficient decisions by community governments. [9]

8 Wallace Oates introduces this concept in his book, *Fiscal Federalism* (New York: Harcourt Brace Jovanovich, 1972).

9 As we shall see in Chapter 22, the inefficiencies caused by lack of perfect correspondence and the resulting spillover of costs and benefits can *in principle* be prevented by an appropriately

As a practical matter, perfect correspondence would be unattainable because there is not sufficient information about the benefit areas of many public goods. And, more importantly, devising a tax system that confines tax burdens to the residents of a particular government jurisdiction is practically impossible in a highly integrated national economy in which population, goods, and resources flow freely across local government boundaries.[10]

PREFERENCE INFORMATION

If governments are to provide the quantity of a public good that is economically efficient from the perspective of their own residents, the preferences of the members of a society must be revealed in the decision-making process. In Chapter 4 we noted a number of barriers to such preference revelation.

While there is no reason to believe that local governments have perfect information about preferences, it is plausible that a decentralized system generates more accurate information about preferences for local public goods than does a centralized system. Indeed, a not inconsiderable advantage of decentralized government is that it is a means by which preferences may be revealed. More specifically, the more homogeneous are its constituents' demands for goods and services, the easier it is for the government to know what its constituents want. And when populations are clustered into demand-homogeneous groups and each group is served by a different government, government can provide efficient quantities of local public goods — the quantities that each group prefers.

In contrast, with heterogeneous populations, conflicting demands are expressed and the potential for catering to those varied demands is reduced. However, if population is not segregated into homogeneous groups, the existence of a number of local governments gives impetus to such segregation. People may "vote with their feet" and seek out the locality that provides the quantities of services that they prefer.[11] As they seek out the community that provides their preferred quantities, people express or reveal their preferences,

---

designed system of federal matching grants (and taxes in the case of cost spillovers). Unfortunately, such tax-grant systems are costly to design and administer; indeed, the information needed for doing so is seldom available.

10 That is, taxes are exported, a phenomenon we discuss in Chapter 21. Also, the governmental organization required for perfect correspondence is not unique. The subset of the nation's population that benefits from the supply of a particular local public good will depend on the point of supply. If we change the supply location (for example, locate a park differently), then the beneficiary population may also be changed. See Oates, *Fiscal Federalism*, p. 34.

11 The initial development of this notion is credited to Charles M. Tiebout, "A Pure Theory of Local Expenditure," *Journal of Political Economy*, 64 (October 1956): 416–424.

generating information that is not available if all local governments followed similar policies or if there is only a single national government.

When government is decentralized and the population is mobile, a government must, in effect, compete with other local governments for population and industry. It must follow policies that are as attractive as the policies of other governments to at least some population groups. There is, thus, an incentive to seek and respond to information about preferences, an incentive that is perhaps weaker with centralized government.

But decentralized government as a mechanism for revealing preferences is not without its disadvantages. In particular, since income, education, and, perhaps, race are important determinants of demand, preferences are most effectively revealed when communities are composed of individuals with similar income and education. Such clustering contributes to many of the problems we will be discussing in the next chapter, and, in the judgment of some people, is undesirable per se.

EXPERIMENTATION AND INNOVATION

A multiunit system of government facilitates and reduces the risks of experimentation. New programs can be tried in one locality without obtaining approval of national governing bodies. If the programs fail, the damage is limited; if they succeed, other localities can follow. In fact, many innovations in government have occurred in this way, first being tried in one or a few localities (or states) and spreading as other localities observe the success of the experiment.[12]

ECONOMIES AND DISECONOMIES OF SCALE

As the population or area within the jurisdiction of a government increases, the costs of making and implementing decisions may change. For example, decision making about the level of public services supplied to a given population and a given area may be more costly if the area is divided into two governmental jurisdictions, say two counties, rather than one. If so, decision-making costs decrease as the "size" of the governmental unit increases; there are economies of scale in governmental decision making. If the reverse is true, we say that there are diseconomies of scale. Scale economies and diseconomies, as well as the factors discussed above, are relevant in decisions about governmental structure. Other factors being the same, greater

---

12 New taxes are almost always introduced in this manner, such as state sales and income taxes. Other examples include merit systems for public employees, school financing systems, and recently, collective bargaining by public employees.

scale economies argue for greater centralization and vice versa. Evidence regarding scale economies in government decision making is sparse, although in many parts of the nation some decrease in the operating cost of government appears to be attainable through local government consolidation.[13]

DECENTRALIZATION AND INCOME REDISTRIBUTION

Governmental redistribution of income generally reduces the welfare of some persons.[14] If the government of a particular locality within a nation attempts to redistribute income from the rich to the poor, then the rich, who are made worse off, have a clear incentive to move to localities in which they are more favorably treated. And the poor have an incentive to move to the localities in which they achieve the greatest gains. Any population migration that does occur because of regional differences in redistribution policies is costly. And the result may be an inefficient spatial distribution of population and production.

Given free movement of population among localities, the local government that attempts greater redistribution from rich to poor than other localities drives out its rich residents and attracts poor from other localities. Each locality's redistribution activities are inhibited by the fear of losing its wealthy members and attracting the burden of the poor. Also, the members of each community know that as a single community they can have little impact on the national incidence of poverty and the aggregate distribution of income; any redistribution that takes place is determined largely by the aggregate actions of other communities. For these reasons, each community may elect to let other communities take care of the poor. Each community may choose a *local* policy that involves less redistribution than its constituents would prefer. And total redistribution by local governments may be less than the population of the nation would support if redistribution were carried out on a national basis. Stated differently, income redistribution approximates a national public good, which, as we saw, may be undersupplied by decentralized governments.

Finally, even if local governments do succeed in redistributing income, their policies may run counter to that of the national government. Local governments may choose to redistribute from poor to rich, while the national policy is the converse.

13 There are a number of empirical studies that provide evidence on the existence of scale economies. See W. Z. Hirsch, *The Economics of State and Local Government* (New York: McGraw-Hill, 1970), Chap. 8 and the studies cited there.

14 The exception is when the redistribution is Pareto-optimal, as we discussed in Chapter 6.

The above reasoning supports the traditional conclusion that primary government redistribution activities should be centralized. But Mark Pauly takes exception, noting that the distance between donor and recipient may influence the amount that the donor is willing to give.[15] That is, nearby poverty and its manifestations are more distasteful than "distant" poverty.[16] If so, the elimination or reduction of poverty is a local public good that may be more efficiently supplied by local governments than by the national government.

SUMMARY

With respect to efficiency, decentralization is most advantageous when (1) demands for public goods and services differ, (2) people with like demands congregate or would do so if communities were to offer different packages of public services, (3) public goods yield benefits over a geographic area less than the total nation, and (4) uniformity of public service levels is not an objective in itself. Whether any particular system of government, centralized or decentralized, dominates another on efficiency grounds is an empirical question. Some centralized systems may be more efficient in the provision of local public goods than some decentralized systems and vice versa.

Some might argue that in today's highly mobile society, everyone is potentially affected by the public service levels in *each* community and not just the community in which they reside; that is, there are no local public goods. For example, I am concerned about the police and fire protection services available in towns that I might visit or move to as well as in the town in which I live.[17] While that view cannot be dismissed as factually incorrect, the point of our analysis is that the benefits of some public goods diminish with distance from the point (community) of supply. Hence, everyone in the nation is not significantly affected by the level of provision of some public goods to communities other than their own. And, in deciding upon the degree of governmental centralization, a society must compare the welfare gains from having variety in service levels with the welfare costs of failing to consider the benefits or costs accruing to persons living outside the decision-making government's jurisdiction.

15 Mark V. Pauly, "Income Redistribution as a Local Public Good," *Journal of Public Economics*, 2, No. 1 (February 1973): 35–58.

16 For examples, see Ibid., pp. 37ff.

17 That is, people may have an *option demand* for goods and services provided by communities other than the one in which they reside. See Burton A. Weisbrod, "Collective Consumption Services of Individual Consumption Goods," *Quarterly Journal of Economics* (August 1964): 471–477.

The traditional view is that income redistribution activities should be centralized. However, an argument can be made for decentralized redistribution if the physical nearness of poverty is of concern to donors.

SUPPLEMENTARY READINGS

Bish, Robert L. *The Public Economy of Metropolitan Areas.* Chicago: Markham Publishing Company, 1971.

Hirsch, W. Z. *The Economics of State and Local Government.* New York: McGraw-Hill, 1970.

Oates, Wallace E. *Fiscal Federalism.* New York: Harcourt Brace Jovanovich, 1972.

Pauly, Mark V. "Optimality, Public Goods, and Local Governments: A General Theoretical Analysis." *Journal of Political Economy* 75, No. 3. (1970): 572–585.

Tiebout, Charles M. "A Pure Theory of Local Expenditures." *Journal of Political Economy* 64 (October 1956): 416–424.

CHAPTER TWENTY-ONE

ECONOMIC PROBLEMS
OF FISCAL FEDERALISM

The U.S. system of government has not been determined solely by economic considerations. Nor could it be. And even if economic factors were dominant in decisions that led to the present system, economic conditions have changed much more rapidly than has government structure. The current economic conditions would likely dictate a structure that differs importantly from the existing one. Therefore, government structure may limit achievement of efficiency and equity objectives. In this chapter we will identify a number of economic problems that arise because of the particular way in which our federal system of government is structured; in the following chapter we will look at possible solutions. Although we distinguish several separate problems, they are, in fact, related and often occur together and interact in their effects on equity and efficiency.

BENEFIT AND COST SPILLOVERS

The population and geographic areas affected by the policies of a particular government often do not coincide with its jurisdiction. That is, local government activities may generate costs or gains for people residing outside their jurisdiction. More importantly, local governments typically lack the ability and incentive to take account of such gains and costs in their decisions. Instead, they are likely to respond primarily or only to the wishes of their own constituents and ignore the spillover effects of their policies. The result may be that too few or too many resources are allocated to particular governmental activities, as we discussed above.[1]

In addition, spillover costs and benefits may create equity problems. Some of those who benefit from a good may not pay the costs of providing the good because they reside beyond the taxing jurisdiction of the local government. The reverse would be true for spillover costs.

Cost or benefit spillovers imply "spill-ins." If some of the benefits from each community's provision of public services spill over to other communities, benefits from the other communities' provision of public services must also spill in to some or all communities. Similarly, when there are cost spillovers, there are necessarily cost spill-ins. Won't these spillovers and spill-ins have offsetting effects on resource allocation? No, as an example readily shows.

Let us consider two communities that impose costs on each other. Community A imposes costs on its downstream neighbor, community B, by failing to treat the sewage dumped in the river that flows first past A and then past B. The costs arise because B has to spend more to treat the water it draws from the river for household and industrial purposes than it would if A employed a higher level of sewage treatment. Also, the value of the river for fishing and recreational purposes is reduced by A's failure to treat its sewage. Suppose these costs to community B amount to $1 million per year. Similarly B imposes air pollution costs on A because B does not filter the smoke from its municipal power plant and the prevailing winds are from B to A. The magnitude of these costs are, say, $750,000 per year. To eliminate the water pollution costs that it imposes on B, A would have to spend $1.5 million per year. Although A would benefit some from the reduction in water pollution, say $600,000 per year, the benefits to A alone do not justify the sewage treatment costs. Similarly, the benefits to B of filtering its power plant smoke are positive, say $300,000 per year, but less than the $1 million per year that the filtering would cost. If A and B decide independently on their respective pollution control projects, both projects will be rejected, even though there are reciprocal spillovers. That is, there are spill-in benefits for A (a $750,000 reduction in air pollution costs from community B's smoke filtering) and for B (a $1 million reduction in water pollution costs from A's sewage treatment).

But such rejection is inefficient because there is a potential welfare gain to both communities from undertaking both projects. Water pollution damages

---

1 See Chapter 20, pp. 424–426. Of course, such need not be the case if the decisions of various local governments are sufficiently coordinated. But such coordination would be tantamount to full centralization.

of $1.6 million per year would be prevented by spending $1.5 million per year on sewage treatment. Thus, if the costs of sewage treatment were shared, say $950,000 for B and $550,000 for A, both communities would gain more in reduced pollution costs than they would incur in increased sewage treatment costs. Similarly, both communities would gain if the costs of the smoke filtering were shared, say $275,000 for B and $725,000 for A, and the air pollution damages of $300,000 for B and $750,000 for A were eliminated.

This highly simplified example illustrates a very important point: The existence of cost and benefit spill-ins does not alter the conclusion that local governments, by looking only at the effects of their policies on their own residents, may fail to allocate resources efficiently when there are spillover costs or benefits from such policies.

TAX EXPORTING

Taxes levied by the government of one locality are often "exported" to the residents of other localities. Taxes are exported when persons who reside outside the jurisdiction of the taxing government bear part or all of the burden of the taxes — as tax-induced income reductions or as tax-induced price increases. For example, when a locality levies a property tax, nonresident owners of property may suffer reductions in after-tax rents; or if the tax is shifted forward, nonresident consumers may pay higher prices. A local sales tax is likely to be exported when nonresidents purchase products in the community. Tax exporting is most likely to occur when a locality can levy a property or production tax on industry that is owned by or sells primarily to nonresidents. Tax exporting also results from the deductibility of state and local government taxes in the computation of federal tax payments. For example, if your marginal federal tax rate is 25 percent, then a $1 increase in your tax payments to your state government reduces your federal tax payment by $.25 and your after-tax income by only $.75. The remainder of the $1 state tax burden is exported to federal taxpayers in general, who must now pay more taxes because you pay fewer. Or the burden is shifted to recipients of federal goods and services, if the decrease in your tax payments produces lower federal spending.

Tax exporting reduces the price of local public services to the members of the locality. They pay less than the full cost of such services since some of the costs (taxes) are exported to nonresidents. Therefore, the residents may spend too much from an efficiency viewpoint. In addition, there is the question of whether it is fair for nonresidents to share the cost of services enjoyed primarily by residents. Tax exporting tends to counter the effects of benefit spillovers and reinforce the effects of cost spillovers.

Tax exporting appears to be an empirically significant phenomenon in the United States. McLure estimates that for 1962 about 20–25 percent of all state and local taxes were exported to nonresidents of the taxing state. Not only is the average level of exporting significant, it varies significantly among states. Exporting rates ranged from 17 percent in South Dakota to 38 percent in Delaware in the short run, and from 15 percent in Maine to 35 percent in Delaware and Nevada in the long run.[2]

Exported taxes must, of course, be imported. Imported taxes reduce the disposable incomes of the residents of each locality. But tax importing, unlike exporting, is unlikely to alter the relative prices of private and public goods because the amount of imported taxes is unlikely to depend on how a community divides its total income between public and private goods. Tax importing, therefore, does not offset the incentive for substitution of public for private goods that tax exporting provides.

VARIATION IN FISCAL CAPACITY

Benefit and cost spillovers and tax exporting are not the only sources of equity and efficiency problems in a multiunit system of government. Several problems arise because the fiscal capacity — the resources available to a local government for support of its activities — is not uniform across localities.

HORIZONTAL INEQUITY

One problem caused by regional differences in fiscal capacity can be shown with a simple example. Let us suppose two communities have the same population and the same costs of public goods and that neither of the communities can export taxes. In community A, per capita income is $3,000, and in community B, it is $5,000; the two communities thus differ in their fiscal capacities. If each community spends the same amount per capita, say $500, per capita taxes will average $500/$3,000 = 16.7 percent of per capita income in the poorer community (A) and $500/$5,000 = 10 percent in the richer community (B). *Tax effort*, defined as the share of a person's income that is paid in taxes, will be higher *on the average* in the poorer than in the richer community. Yet service levels are the same, since spending is the same.

Moreover, if the two communities finance their spending with taxes that are directly or indirectly related to income, as are most taxes, then a person with a given income, whether rich or poor, will usually pay a lower share of

2 C. E. McLure, Jr., "The Interstate Exporting of State and Local Taxes: Estimates for 1962," *National Tax Journal* (March 1967): 49–77.

his or her income in taxes (have a lower tax effort) in the richer community. If taxes are proportional to income, then a person in community A pays 16.7 percent of his or her income in taxes, as opposed to 10 percent in community B. Among persons with the same incomes, those having high tax effort will have fewer public or private goods than those having low tax effort.[3] So the first problem growing out of regional differences in the distribution of income is one of *horizontal equity*: People with the same income but living in different communities will face different tax prices and either pay different taxes for the same public goods or receive different amounts of public goods for the same taxes. In other words, local governments may differ in the *fiscal residuals* they generate for people in essentially similar circumstances. A fiscal residual is the difference between the benefits received from and the taxes paid to the community government.[4]

Table 21–1 shows considerable variation among states in the indices of tax effort and fiscal capacity.[5] Generally, states with lower fiscal capacities have either higher tax effort or lower spending levels or both, an outcome that is consistent with the preceding example. Variation in tax capacity and effort among localities would presumably be even greater, although only limited data are available (see Table 21–2).

IMPOVERISHED GOVERNMENTS

The second problem arising from variation in fiscal capacity is that some governments may simply be too poor to provide what is regarded as adequate levels of public services. Table 21–1 shows that the states with low fiscal capacities usually do have low per capita expenditures, which are a rough measure of service levels. Whether those expenditure levels are "adequate" is an open question.

3 James M. Buchanan, "Federalism and Fiscal Equity," *American Economic Review*, 40 (September 1950): 583–597.

4 For our example, suppose that each person receives services costing $500 per year in either community A or B. Consider now the fiscal residual of a person who would earn $4,000 annually in either community and who values the government services received at exactly their cost of $500. With proportional income taxation, this person receives a fiscal residual of $500 − $400 = $100 in the richer community (B) and a residual of $500 − $667 = − $167 in the poorer community (A).

5 The data in Table 21–1 are not entirely satisfactory because they take account of neither tax exporting nor benefit and cost spillovers. Tax exporting affects both tax effort and tax capacity, while spillovers affect service levels obtainable from a given level of spending. Also, per capita expenditures do not accurately measure service levels because the per capita cost of providing a given level of service may vary among states and localities. For additional discussion, see Thomas F. Pogue, "Tax Exporting and the Measurement of Fiscal Capacity," in *Proceedings of the 69th Annual Conference on Taxation* (Columbus, Ohio: National Tax Association–Tax Institute of America, 1977).

TABLE 21-1

INTERSTATE DIFFERENTIALS IN FISCAL CAPACITY, FISCAL EFFORT, AND EXPENDITURES

State	Index of per capita income [a]	Index of fiscal capacity [b]	Index of fiscal effort [c]	Index of per capita expenditures [d]
Connecticut	125	110	98	108
District of Columbia	123	119	97	164
Alaska	119	170	110	255
New Jersey	118	106	97	98
California	116	120	107	126
New York	116	115	123	146
Nevada	114	172	81	134
Maryland	113	100	109	107
Illinois	112	105	99	97
Massachusetts	109	97	111	107
Washington	108	113	99	121
Hawaii	108	113	119	155
Michigan	108	99	109	103
Delaware	105	112	106	126
Ohio	103	96	86	79
Oregon	101	106	91	105
Colorado	100	106	97	102
Rhode Island	100	86	109	94
Florida	98	109	81	86
Indiana	98	91	99	79
Pennsylvania	98	87	104	92
Minnesota	97	100	113	110
Wisconsin	97	90	125	105
New Hampshire	96	99	83	85
Virginia	96	86	94	81
Missouri	95	92	85	84
Kansas	94	106	87	87
Arizona	94	106	98	99
Wyoming	93	146	85	129
Montana	93	103	90	104
Iowa	92	96	104	94
Nebraska	90	106	94	89
Texas	90	101	79	78
Vermont	89	85	123	117
Oklahoma	86	105	76	85
Utah	86	87	103	95
Idaho	85	92	98	88
Georgia	85	85	93	85

TABLE 21–1 (*cont.*)

State	Index of per capita income[a]	Index of fiscal capacity[b]	Index of fiscal effort[c]	Index of per capita expenditures[d]
Maine	82	79	105	88
North Dakota	79	108	94	99
North Carolina	79	81	91	73
Tennessee	79	80	88	78
New Mexico	78	105	92	98
Kentucky	78	80	92	79
South Dakota	77	94	104	99
Louisiana	75	102	88	92
West Virginia	75	76	94	86
Alabama	74	74	94	77
South Carolina	74	71	94	69
Arkansas	69	78	80	69
Mississippi	62	73	103	81

a State per capita personal income as a percentage of national per capita income, 1969.

b Per capita yield of state and local revenue system if all state and local taxes are levied at national average rates, expressed as a percentage of national average revenue yield (per capita); data are for 1970–1971.

c Actual per capita revenue as a percentage of per capita revenue capacity, 1970–1971.

d Direct general expenditures per capita (1970–1971), as a percentage of national average.

Source: Richard P. Nathan, *Monitoring Revenue Sharing* (Washington: Brookings, 1975), tables B-3, B-4. © 1975 by the Brookings Institution, Washington, D.C.

Measures to increase the fiscal capacity of a particular impoverished local government necessarily transfer resources from the residents of other localities and their governments. So it is not meaningful to say that all local (or state) governments are impoverished, since only the *relative* impoverishment of *some* governments can be reached by transfers. The resources available to all governments cannot be increased by transferring resources among persons or communities or both.

Of course, public-sector or government poverty in a particular community is accompanied by and reflects private-sector or individual poverty. A basic policy issue, then, is whether government poverty should be treated separately from individual poverty by, say, federal transfers to the governments of localities with relatively low fiscal capacities, or be dealt with by transferring income from relatively rich to relatively poor individuals. In Chapter 22 we will consider these questions.

TABLE 21–2
REVENUE CAPACITY AND EFFORT OF SELECTED CITIES, 1966–1967 [a]

City	Revenue capacity	Revenue effort
Seattle	165	110
Los Angeles	154	117
New York	152	133
St. Louis	136	93
Boston	129	93
Memphis	127	96
Chicago	125	85
Washington, D.C.	124	70
Cleveland	122	91
New Orleans	118	91
Pittsburgh	116	103
San Diego	110	112
Baltimore	100	111
Philadelphia	99	107
Columbus, Ohio	98	88

a Indices of revenue capacity and effort equal 100 if city has effort or capacity equal to national average. Revenue capacity is computed assuming all local tax bases are taxed at national average rates. Thus, the revenue capacity index of 152 for New York City means that its *per capita* revenue would be 152 percent of the national average per capita revenue if its tax bases were all taxed at national average rates. New York's revenue effort index of 133 means that the ratio of its revenues to its revenue capacity is 33 percent higher than the national average.

Source: Advisory Commission on Intergovernmental Relations, *Measuring the Fiscal Capacity and Effort of State and Local Areas*, M58R (Washington: Government Printing Office, 1972), table A-4.

INEFFICIENT LOCATION

Variation in fiscal capacity may cause a third problem. As we have seen, community governments can generate different fiscal residuals for people in similar circumstances. Location decisions may then be based, in part, on differences in fiscal residuals, rather than on differences in economic costs and productivities. The result may be inefficient location of economic activity and horizontal inequities. We discuss such inefficiency, which requires the mobility of population and resources between communities, below.

VARIATION IN COSTS AND NEEDS

Differences in fiscal residuals may arise because of variation in the costs of and the needs for public services, as well as variation in fiscal capacities. The main causes of interlocal differences in costs are the differences in climate, population size and density, and resource prices. Climate affects the costs of heating and cooling public buildings; building and maintaining roads, buildings, and other facilities; providing flood protection and sewage collection and treatment, etc. Resource prices may vary regionally because natural resources are not distributed uniformly and transportation is costly. For example, the prices of such materials as lumber, steel, fuel, and paper used by a government depend on the proximity of supply sources. Similarly, to attract labor, some communities may have to pay higher wages than others because of climate, isolation, living costs, or other factors.

Population size and density affect per person costs in several ways. The per person costs of roads, schools, and other facilities and services that must be distributed throughout a government's area of responsibility tend to be relatively high when the area is sparsely settled and the population is dispersed. For example, per capita costs of roads and schools are relatively high in sparsely settled states such as Wyoming and Montana. On the other hand, relatively high population densities may lead to congestion costs and relatively high per person costs of public services. So such costs for many local government activities tend at first to decline as a community's population increases and the high fixed (or overhead) costs of government are spread among more persons. But they may eventually rise as increasing population density generates congestion costs.[6]

Communities differ in needs because their population structures differ and some elements of the population require more public services and spending than others. For example, school-age persons, the poor, the elderly, and the disabled require more public services and spending (per person) than other population groups. Therefore, if the care of such groups is the responsibility of state and local levels of government, as indeed it is, then communities in which such groups are a relatively large fraction of the population have relatively high public service and spending needs.[7] Similarly, because schools are basically a state and local government responsibility, communities with a relatively large school-age population need to make relatively high outlays for public services.

Regardless of why they occur, community differences in public service costs and needs lead to differences in fiscal effort or the adequacy of service levels or both. High-cost communities generally have higher average fiscal effort and lower service levels (or both) than do low-cost communities, unless high- (low-) cost communities are also communities with high (low) fiscal capacities. Similarly, high-need communities generally have relatively

6 For additional discussion of factors affecting local government costs, see W. Z. Hirsch, *The Economics of State and Local Government* (New York: McGraw-Hill, 1970), chaps. 7, 8.

7 Those population groups may require relatively high outlays for housing, health care, and community services, as well as direct cash transfers.

high fiscal effort and relatively inadequate service levels, barring offsetting differences in fiscal capacity.

Cost and need differences may therefore have basically the same effect as do differences in fiscal capacity: Local governments may differ in the fiscal residuals they generate for persons of similar circumstances. However, cost-generated differences in fiscal residuals do not have the same equity and efficiency implications as do differences caused by varying fiscal capacities. Is it equitable to subsidize the governments and residents of high-cost localities so that persons with the same income will experience the same fiscal residual whether they live in high-cost or low-cost communities? Even if such subsidies are judged equitable, they may conflict with efficiency by taking away the incentives that the differences in fiscal residuals provide for the location of population and economic activity in the low-cost communities. That is, efficiency is promoted if the relatively high fiscal residuals available in low-cost communities attract population and economic activity to those areas and away from the high-cost communities.

In contrast, differences in fiscal residuals that arise because of need differences probably should be of concern on equity grounds. This is especially so when high needs arise because a relatively large fraction of the population is poor, elderly, or disabled. That is, it would be unfair in the judgment of many to place the full burden of caring for needy persons on the other residents of the communities in which the needy reside. Such differences in residuals should also be of concern on efficiency grounds, since they provide an incentive for the relocation of population and economic activity from high-need, low fiscal residual communities to low-need, high fiscal residual ones. Such relocation need not be consistent with the most productive use of resources and least-cost production. And it may aggravate the problem of disparate needs by further concentrating the needy elements of the population. [8]

Like low fiscal capacity, high costs and needs may result in inadequate levels of public services in some communities. In addition, even if service levels are not judged inadequate, they are likely to vary because of varying fiscal capacities, costs, and needs. [9] This lack of uniformity is not important for some services. But for others, most notably education, interregional differences are undesirable because they entail differences in opportunity. Table 21–3 shows that per pupil expenditures for elementary and secondary

8 Indeed, it can be argued that the central-city-to-suburb "flight" of industry and middle- and high-income families has been partly a response to such incentives.

9 These factors are not the only ones that may lead to inadequate or varying service levels. Communities may simply choose different levels because of differences in preferences or decision-making procedures. Also, choice may be influenced by spillovers and tax exporting, as we noted earlier.

TABLE 21-3
VARIATION IN PER PUPIL SPENDING AND SCHOOL TAX EFFORT, 1970

State	State average expenditure per pupil (1)	Per pupil expenditure of 95th percentile district as percentage of state average (2)	Per pupil expenditure of 5th percentile district as percentage of state average (3)	State and local school taxes as a percentage of personal income (4)
Alabama	438	119	84	3.8
Alaska	1,083	134	80	7.7
Arizona	766	219	72	5.7
Arkansas	534	118	61	3.9
California	922	136	55	4.5
Colorado	695	201	83	5.6
Connecticut	882	117	64	5.8
Delaware	793	104		6.0
District of Columbia	977	n.a.[a]	n.a.[a]	3.8
Florida	710	124	84	4.5
Georgia	600	100	70	3.9
Hawaii	851	64	51	5.5
Idaho	629	190	90	5.2
Illinois	803	160	74	5.3
Indiana	624	115	70	5.7
Iowa	890	115	73	6.0
Kansas	721	154	75	5.0
Kentucky	612	88	64	4.2
Louisiana	620	144	87	5.5
Maine	685	114	60	5.5
Maryland	882	93	77	6.2
Massachusetts	753	176	76	4.6
Michigan	842	106	64	5.8
Minnesota	883	92	57	6.2
Mississippi	476	132	73	4.5

State				
Missouri	714	119	55	4.3
Montana	822	309	76	5.8
Nebraska	527	258	74	3.9
Nevada	764	211	98	4.7
New Hampshire	692	118	54	4.6
New Jersey	963	115	60	5.1
New Mexico	724	133	69	5.8
New York	1,237	114	62	5.6
North Carolina	609	112	81	4.5
North Dakota	621	177	85	5.7
Ohio	680	123	72	4.4
Oklahoma	540	197	82	4.4
Oregon	891	168	63	5.9
Pennsylvania	876	168	78	5.2
Rhode Island	904	109	63	4.3
South Carolina	555	101	77	5.0
South Dakota	657	230	64	5.4
Tennessee	560	106	67	4.3
Texas	581	206	73	5.1
Utah	600	170	89	6.1
Vermont	934	101	46	7.4
Virginia	691	105	71	5.0
Washington	743	220	84	5.4
West Virginia	626	113	84	4.6
Wisconsin	875	111	67	5.7
Wyoming	810	472	84	6.0

a Not applicable

Source: Columns 1–3, *Review of Existing State School Finance Programs*, vol. 2, *Documentation of Disparities in the Financing of Public Elementary and Secondary School Systems — By State*, a Commission Staff Report submitted to the President's Commission on School Finance (1972), pp. 19ff. The figures in columns 2 and 3 have the following interpretation: In Alabama, for example, 5 percent of the school districts have expenditures that are 19 percent or more above the state average, while per pupil expenditures in 5 percent of the districts are less than or equal to 84 percent of the state average. Column 4, National Education Association, *Estimates of School Statistics, 1971–72* (1971–R13), table 9, p. 34.

education vary widely among and within states. Accompanying these expenditure variations are variations in the tax effort required for school finance. These differentials have triggered a significant shifting of the responsibility for financing schools from the local to the state level.[10] Yet disparities remain; and they have been the basis for a number of state and lower federal court decisions to the effect that the existing financing of public schools violates state constitutions or the U.S. Constitution. However, the U.S. Supreme Court ruled in its decision in *San Antonio Independent School District* v. *Rodriguez* that the Texas system of financing schools is not in violation of the Fourteenth Amendment of the Constitution.

MOBILITY, EFFICIENCY, AND EQUITY

Several problems arise because population and resources may move from one locality to another and governmental policies may create incentives for such movement.

RICH ENCLAVES AND POOR GHETTOS

We have seen that local government taxation and provision of services creates a fiscal residual for each person equal to the difference between the value of the services received and the taxes paid. If the residual is positive, the person experiences a net welfare gain from government activity. For a person having a given income, the residual is greater if the person resides in a richer rather than a poorer community because, as we saw earlier, the person pays lower taxes for the same services or receives more services for the same taxes. Clearly, the residents of poorer communities have an incentive to move to richer communities.

The incentive for interregional migration persists as long as communities differ in the fiscal residuals they provide for particular persons and classes of resources. Any resulting migration may or may not be desirable on efficiency grounds. Movement of people from the poorer to the richer communities may be economically inefficient if the people who move have greater productivity in the poorer community. The same is true for movement of other resources (capital).

If the tax structures and the costs of public goods do not vary among communities, then migration that equalizes fiscal residuals across communities

---

10 See Paul Cooper, "State Takeover of Education Financing," *National Tax Journal,* 24 (September 1971): 337–356; and Advisory Commission on Intergovernmental Fiscal Relations, *Financing Schools and Property Tax Relief: A State Responsibility* (Washington: Government Printing Office, 1973). For further discussion of school finance issues, see Charles L. Schultze, Edward R. Fried, A. M. Rivlin, and Nancy H. Teeters, *Setting National Priorities, The 1973 Budget* (Washington: Brookings, 1972), chap. 10.

will also equalize average incomes. However, migration is unlikely to continue until it equalizes average incomes because migration is costly; differences in fiscal residuals that are not large enough to offset migration costs will not be eliminated. Also, since people may earn higher incomes in some communities than others, they may not move to the community that offers the largest fiscal residual if it is one in which their income would be relatively low. Similarly, costs of private goods, such as housing, may vary among communities; and location decisions will take such costs into account. Indeed, fiscal residuals may become capitalized into property values. In which case they no longer provide an incentive for migration; the larger fiscal residual that a person would gain by moving to a particular community would be offset by the higher price of housing and other property.[11]

Finally, migration may not equalize average incomes across communities because each community has an incentive to block in-migration of people who generate more costs for the community than they pay in taxes. For example, if it costs $500 to make public services available to each new resident of a community, then tax payments by existing members of the community rise when another person comes into the community, unless the new entrant pays at least $500 in taxes. Since tax payments by low-income persons are usually smaller than those by high-income perons, communities have an incentive to block in-migration of relatively low-income persons by measures such as restrictive zoning.[12] This and other barriers lead to a segregation of persons into high- and low-income communities, which may be viewed as undesirable per se. Also, when those who move from the poorer communities are the relatively rich, then average income in the poorer communities falls, increasing both the tax effort of the remaining members of the poor communities and their incentive to move to richer communities. Thus, the migration of the relatively rich to the richer communities and the resulting increase in intercommunity differences in average income is a self-reinforcing process, if the poor are not also mobile.[13]

11 If it occurs, capitalization of fiscal residuals also eliminates the horizontal equity problem we discussed above because fiscal advantages (disadvantages) will be offset by higher (lower) rents and prices for property. All of the capitalized fiscal residuals, whether positive or negative, accrue to the owners of property at the time the tax and expenditure decisions become capitalized into property values.

12 The incentive for barring low-income entrants is even greater if welfare services are locally financed. Thus, pressures leading to segregated (by income) communities would be less with national welfare financing than with the current practice, which still places considerable burdens on local communities, despite recent shifts in welfare financing responsibilities to the state and federal levels.

13 The poor lack mobility because of economic barriers, primarily the relatively high cost of housing, to entry into rich communities.

TAX COMPETITION

Local government decision makers frequently fear that taxation of the incomes and activities of geographically mobile people and resources will cause them to move to other communities; they are therefore reluctant to tax them more heavily than do other communities. Indeed, local governments may try to keep their taxes relatively low so as to be competitive with other communities. The result may be relatively low benefit-tax ratios for owners of immobile resources. Such behavior is called *tax competition*.

The effectiveness of tax competition in attracting resources and population may be limited for two reasons. First, individuals and firms will look at both sides of the fiscal coin — tax levels *and* service levels — when making location decisions. Therefore, if government decision makers wish to compete with other communities they should try to provide larger fiscal residuals and not just lower taxes.[14] Second, other factors than fiscal residuals may be controlling in the location decisions of firms and people. Indeed, immobile factors such as land cannot relocate in response to tax differentials. Similarly, long-lived reproducible capital, such as factories, can relocate only in the long run.[15] Also, there is considerable evidence of worker reluctance to relocate in response to wage differentials.

However, fiscal residuals probably do influence some location decisions. And a community will gain (lose) those classes of population and resources for which it provides a fiscal residual that exceeds (falls short of) that provided in competing communities. Consequently, a community's tax and expenditure policies cannot depart very far from those of competing communities without affecting its resource and population base.

As we noted earlier, the migration of population and resources in response to fiscal residuals limits a single community's ability to redistribute

14 Henry J. Aaron provides one example of how and why communities might compete for population by offering high fiscal residuals to mobile persons. He suggests that communities may underprice and overproduce some goods, such as public education, in order to attract population. Such goods are, in effect, loss leaders. With a larger population, the community can spread the costs of providing other services among more persons, thereby lowering per capita costs to both old and new residents. This argument presumes that the community has excess capacity in some service areas so that they can be provided to a larger population without substantial additional costs. See Aaron's article, "Local Public Expenditures and the Migration Effect," *Western Economic Journal* (December 1969): 385–390.

For another example of how a desire to attract (or hold) industry may affect fiscal decisions, see Thomas F. Pogue and L. G. Sgontz, "Value Added vs. Property Taxation of Business: Effects on Industrial Location," *Land Economics*, 43 (May 1971): 150–157.

15 John F. Due finds little evidence that taxes are a significant factor in industrial location; see his article "Studies of State-Local Tax Influences on the Location of Industry," *National Tax Journal*, 14 (June 1961): 163–173.

income among its members unless other communities follow similar patterns of redistribution. Redistribution creates positive fiscal residuals for some elements of the population and negative residuals for others, and those who lose have an incentive to move elsewhere.

INFERIOR TAX OPTIONS

The possibility of population and resource migration in response to fiscal residuals also limits a locality's ability to use particular forms of taxation. Specifically, if people can alter their behavior or place of residence and thereby escape a community's tax levy *without* losing the services it provides, then the tax is not a suitable means of financing community services. For example, a city cannot employ a sales tax to finance its spending if its residents can easily take their trade to a neighboring city where there is no sales tax. Similarly, when residents can live outside the city while working in it and receiving its services, the city cannot employ income taxation unless neighboring communities do likewise.[16] Thus, when there is population and resource mobility, localities employ taxes that are similar in base and rate to those employed in other communities; or they employ taxes that fall on immobile resources, such as land and to a lesser degree, other real property. Communities are not free to innovate in applying taxes to mobile resources and populations. And they may not be free to employ taxes that are preferable on grounds of equity, administrative ease, and efficiency. Instead, there must be general application of taxes and "lock-step" movement of rates.[17]

For those reasons, local governments tend to rely heavily on property taxes and make relatively little use of sales and income taxes. (See Table 21–4, which shows that as the share of state and local revenue collected by the state government increases, the reliance on property taxes decreases.) That creates a problem if the property tax is regarded as inferior to the sales and income taxes. A common view is that the property tax contributes to urban decay and is regressive and relatively inelastic.[18] (However, as we saw

16 Cities do employ taxes that are called income taxes, for example New York City. But such taxes are more narrow in base than the federal income tax because they usually tax only income that is received from sources within the city. The tax base is primarily the payrolls of city employers.

17 Moreover, local governments are creatures of state governments. As such, they are commonly authorized to use only specified taxes.

18 Tax system elasticity refers to how much tax revenues rise in response to economic growth *without changes in tax rates*. The federal tax system is more elastic than most state tax systems, and the latter are more elastic than local tax systems. See Advisory Commission on Intergovernmental Relations, *Federal-State-Local Finances: Significant Features of Fiscal Federalism* (Washington: Government Printing Office, 1974).

TABLE 21-4
STRUCTURE OF STATE AND LOCAL TAX SYSTEMS

State	All state taxes, 1971–1972 Rank	All state taxes, 1971–1972 %	State individual income tax, 1971–1972	State general sales tax, 1971–1972	State and local property taxes, 1971–1972	Local income taxes, 1970–1971	Local general sales tax, 1970–1971	Average effective property tax rates, existing single-family homes with FHA insured mortgages, 1971	State as % of state and local revenue (from own sources) for local schools, 1970–1971
New Mexico	1	80.1	9.9	30.7	20.7	a	0.5	1.70	74.5
Delaware	2	79.3	28.0	—	17.2	1.6	—	1.26	76.3
West Virginia	3	75.9	12.8	12.3 b	20.8	—	—	.69	56.7
South Carolina	4	75.7	14.2	27.2	23.2	—	—	.94	68.4
Hawaii	5	75.5	23.3	29.5 b	19.1	—	—	.92	96.8
Mississippi	6	75.5	7.0	36.2	22.7	—	6.2	.96	66.3
Alabama	7	74.7	10.9	23.6	13.7	0.3	0.7	.85	74.6
North Carolina	8	74.4	18.4	16.6	25.1	—	—	1.58	77.9
Arkansas	9	74.3	11.4	23.4	23.9	—	—	1.14	54.2
Kentucky	10	73.6	13.4	27.2	20.9	5.5	—	1.27	64.4
Louisiana	11	70.7	6.7	17.8	18.3	—	9.7	.56	65.5
Alaska	12	68.4	26.2	—	23.3	—	6.5	1.61	86.8
Oklahoma	13	66.7	10.0	11.6	27.0	—	4.2	1.35	46.0
Georgia	14	65.3	13.1	23.2	30.8	—	—	1.44	61.4
Idaho	15	64.8	16.3	16.7	34.8	—	—	1.72	44.6
Washington	16	64.3	—	25.9 b	36.5	a	1.0	1.62	54.7
Utah	17	64.0	15.4	24.5	34.9	—	2.6	1.49	57.3
Florida	18	62.5	—	27.5	32.5	—	—	1.41	61.7
Tennessee	19	62.2	1.0	24.9	26.7	—	6.8	1.53	52.1
Pennsylvania	20	61.5	11.6	15.6	27.6	8.3	—	2.16	46.2
Vermont	21	61.1	17.8	8.3	38.3	—	—	2.53	35.2
Rhode Island	22	60.4	13.3	18.3	39.1	—	—	2.21	37.1
Arizona	23	60.2	9.6	22.7	38.6	—	5.4	1.65	47.5
Wisconsin	24	59.8	21.9	14.1	42.9	—	—	3.01	31.7
Virginia	25	59.6	18.3	13.0	28.2	a	4.3	1.32	37.7

26	Michigan	59.2	14.0	19.1	39.1	2.8	—	2.02	43.0
27	Minnesota	58.8	21.5	12.0	40.1	—	0.1	2.05	48.1
28	North Dakota	58.1	7.2	22.5	41.1	—	—	2.08	31.3
29	Texas	57.4	—	18.5	38.3	—	3.3	1.91	52.7
30	Maryland	57.2	20.6	13.1	31.9	9.3	—	2.24	37.4
31	Maine	57.1	5.8	21.2	43.3	—	—	2.43	34.7
32	Nevada	56.5	—	18.8	34.7	—	1.8	1.48	40.2
33	Wyoming	55.2	—	21.4	49.3	—	0.1	1.38	36.6
34	Iowa	53.1	14.2	15.3	46.2	—	—	2.63	28.9
35	Illinois	52.5	13.0	17.1	41.1	a	3.5	2.15	36.6
36	Missouri	51.9	12.6	18.2	37.2	3.1	0.8	1.79	33.8
37	Colorado	50.9	14.8	15.9	40.7	a	5.6	2.45	31.9
38	Connecticut	50.8	3.1	18.4	48.8	—	—	2.38	23.9
39	Kansas	50.7	9.2	17.3	48.7	—	—	2.17	32.1
40	Indiana	50.5	12.1	18.6	49.5	—	—	1.96	33.2
41	Oregon	50.2	24.8	—	48.0	—	—	2.33	20.8
42	Montana	49.7	18.5	—	50.4	—	—	2.19	26.1
43	Massachusetts	48.8	20.1	5.4	50.7	—	—	3.13	26.4
44	New York	48.4	17.4	10.6	36.7	3.6	6.9	2.72	50.1
45	Ohio	48.4	2.5c	16.5	43.0	7.4	0.4	1.47	29.8
46	California	47.9	13.1	14.3	47.6	0.1	3.9	2.48	37.1
47	Nebraska	46.2	7.8	14.5	50.3	—	1.0	3.15	20.1
48	South Dakota	42.5	—	19.4	53.8	—	0.7	2.71	16.0
49	New Hampshire	42.2	2.0	—	58.0	—	—	3.14	10.4
50	New Jersey	39.8	0.6	14.2	56.0	—	—	3.01	27.5
	U.S. (excluding D.C.)	55.3	12.0	16.3	38.8	1.7	2.4	1.98	43.3

a Less than 0.05 percent, not computed.

b Excluding business gross receipts.

c Based on collections for partial year. New tax effective 1 January 1972.

Source: Advisory Commission on Intergovernmental Relations, *Federal-State-Local Finances: Significant Features of Fiscal Federalism* (Washington: Government Printing Office, 1974), table A, p. 2.

in Chapter 14, its regressiveness is open to question.) Similarly, state tax structures are regarded as inferior to the federal tax structure because of the dominance of income taxes in the latter and sales taxes in the former.[19]

DUPLICATION OF EFFORTS

Even if state and local governments can and do employ the most desirable taxes on equity and efficiency grounds, there is bound to be duplication of administration and enforcement efforts. The costs of collecting a dollar of revenue will be greater if each city (or state) operates its own tax system than if there is only one national system. Stated differently, there probably are significant economies of scale in the collection of taxes.[20]

PRIVATE-SECTOR EFFICIENCY

For reasons we discussed above, fiscal residuals for mobile population and resources tend to equality across regions. But this equalizing process may result in an inefficient spatial distribution of population and private-sector activity. For example, North Dakota might tax an immobile factor, land, to create positive fiscal residuals for mobile manufacturing capital by providing services (roads, power, water, sewage treatment, etc.) to industry, the value of which are not covered by taxes on industry. It might therefore become profitable (from a private point of view) to operate steel mills in North Dakota, even though iron ore and coal have to be shipped into the state and the finished steel has to be shipped out. The inefficiency arises because of the needless use of resources in shipping raw materials and finished products. To prevent such inefficiency in industrial location, taxation should be according to costs generated. Taxes should reflect both the government's direct costs and the indirect or external costs occasioned by the presence of the industry.

The creation of such "competitive" fiscal residuals for mobile factors and population may also have inequitable distributive effects. In the example of

19 Those views are the basis for much of the current support behind general revenue sharing. We discuss revenue sharing and other approaches to the "inferior tax option" problem in Chapter 22.

20 Dick Netzer shows that the expenditures for financial administration as a percent of revenue collected decline rapidly as the size of the governmental unit increases. See his "State-Local Finance and Intergovernmental Fiscal Relations," in *The Economics of Public Finance*, ed. Alan S. Blinder, Robert M. Solow, George F. Break, Peter O. Steiner, and Dick Netzer (Washington: Brookings, 1974), p. 395.

North Dakota, landowners are made worse off, while any benefits from the policy are likely to accrue to immobile resources employed in the shipping industry. We cannot assume that such redistribution is desirable.

PUBLIC INVESTMENT

The conservation and public investment activities of governments provide goods and services to future members of a community. But intercommunity mobility may restrict such activity. For example, investment in a local park may be inhibited because the cost of the investment is borne by present residents, while benefits will accrue to future residents. Because of mobility, present and future residents will not be the same persons, and present residents may therefore not invest in the park. This type of investment generates benefits that spill over temporally rather than spatially. But the effect of the benefit spillover is the same: It tends to cause undersupply of some public goods.

That problem does not arise if the future residents can be made to "pay the bill" for goods and services generated by current investment outlays. Debt finance of local government investment is one means of doing so. Local governments do borrow to finance some investment spending, but some of those outlays are financed out of current taxes, in part because of limitations on local government's use of debt.[21]

SUMMARY

In a federal system, governmental resource allocation decisions may not be consistent with economic efficiency for several reasons. Benefit spillovers tend to cause governments to underprovide goods, and cost spillover and tax exporting tend to cause oversupply. Tax competition may result in an undersupply of services in general or in undersupply to nonmobile groups. But a summary statement about the combined effects of these conflicting forces is not possible; whether they result in systematic over- or undersupply of public services by local governments is not known. Instead, the conclusion must be that while we cannot assume that local government decisions will promote allocation efficiency, we also face significant difficulties in devising

21 See also Chapter 19, p. 409. This conventional view of the effects of local government debt finance has been questioned. For a full discussion of the issues, see Wallace E. Oates, *Fiscal Federalism* (New York: Harcourt Brace Jovanovich, 1972), pp. 153–161. For evidence that debt limitations do affect local government spending, see Thomas F. Pogue, "The Effect of Debt Limits: Some New Evidence," *National Tax Journal*, Vol. 23, No. 1 (March 1970): 36–49.

an alternative government structure that will do so. In particular, such statements as "local government services are generally inadequate" or "local governments face a financial crisis that prevents them from doing what is needed" are difficult to support either analytically or with data *if our objective in providing government services is allocation efficiency*. Such statements undoubtedly reflect, in part, the very human desire for more of everything.

Governments' effects on distributive equity are similarly difficult to judge in a federal system. That is, benefit and cost spillovers and tax exporting and importing make it difficult to determine the distribution of the costs and gains of government policies, whether such policies are considered individually or as a group.

SUPPLEMENTARY READINGS

Bish, Robert L. *The Public Economy of Metropolitan Areas*. Chicago: Markham Publishing Company, 1971.

Hirsch, W. Z. *The Economics of State and Local Government*. New York: McGraw-Hill, 1970.

Oates, Wallace E. *Fiscal Federalism*. New York: Harcourt Brace Jovanovich, 1972.

Pauly, Mark V. "Optimality, Public Goods, and Local Governments: A General Theoretical Analysis." *Journal of Political Economy* 75, No. 3. (1970): 572–585.

Tiebout, Charles M. "A Pure Theory of Local Expenditures." *Journal of Political Economy* 64 (October 1956): 416–424.

CHAPTER TWENTY-TWO

IMPROVING THE
FEDERAL SYSTEM

In Chapter 21 we discussed some of the economic problems of fiscal federalism: spillover effects, nonuniformity in tax capacity and effort and in service levels, tax competition, inferior tax options of local governments, and duplication of tax collection and enforcement activities. Many of these problems could be eliminated by centralizing political decision making and using a nationally uniform system of taxation. But such an approach has not proven popular because it would either eliminate federalism or greatly reduce the role and advantages of subnational governments. The more popular and widely used approaches have involved intergovernmental transfers, fiscal coordination, and regulation. In this chapter we will examine these policies, showing how they work and the problems met in implementing them.

INTERGOVERNMENTAL TRANSFERS

Many of the problems of federalism can, in principle, be mitigated by intergovernmental grants. And an apparent belief in the efficacy of grants has triggered a virtual explosion of intergovernmental transfers. Table 22–1 documents the recent growth in both federal and state transfers to other government units.

In general, the appropriate form or type of grant depends on the problem to be solved. So we next present a taxonomy of grant types. Then we show how grants may be used *in principle* to deal with the major problems we discussed in Chapter 21, and we ask whether grants can in practice live up to their promise. Finally, we look at the effects of grants on the distribution of income.

TABLE 22–1
INTERGOVERNMENTAL TRANSFERS, SELECTED YEARS
(BILLIONS OF DOLLARS)

Transfers by	1902	1927	1940	1950	1960	1970	1975
Federal government							
Education	.001	.010	0.154	0.369	0.950	5.844	8.959
Highways	—	.083	0.195	0.429	2.905	4.608	4.754
Public welfare	.001	.001	0.278	1.131	2.070	7.574	14.352
Total	.007	.123	0.884	2.371	6.994	23.257	49.628
State governments							
Education	.045	.292	0.700	2.054	5.461	17.085	31.110
Highways	.002	.197	0.332	0.610	1.247	2.439	3.225
Public welfare	—	.006	0.420	0.792	1.483	5.003	8.102
General support	.005	.098	0.181	0.482	0.806	2.958	a
Total	.052	.596	1.654	4.217	9.443	28.892	51.978
Local governments (to states only)	b	b	b	b	.209	.670	1.278

a Not available.

b Minor amounts.

Source: U.S. Census Bureau, *Historical Statistics of the U.S.: Colonial Times to 1970*; and *Governmental Finances, 1974–75*.

GRANT TYPES AND STRUCTURE

Table 22–2 lists the main types of grants. *Block grants* may be used for many if not all purposes; their use is relatively *unrestricted*. Few grants are totally unrestricted, but some, for example, federal revenue sharing grants, may be used to finance almost any activity of the recipient government. Block grants are also referred to as general grants. *Categorical grants*, on the other hand, must be used to finance a particular category of spending, such as school construction, training of law enforcement officers, or cash assistance payments to needy families. Use of categorical grant funds is very restricted. Categorical grants are also referred to as specific grants.

TABLE 22–2
TYPES OF GRANTS

Grant	Matching	Nonmatching
Block	Need related Not need related	Need related Not need related
Categorical	Need related Not need related	Need related Not need related

Within those two main classes, grants may be either *matching* or *non-matching*. With matching grants, the grantor government matches the recipient government's expenditures. For example, a 2-for-1 matching grant requires the recipient government to spend $1 on the aided activity for every $2 that it receives. Federal grants for interstate highway construction are 9-for-1 matching grants; the federal government pays 90 percent of the construction costs. Nonmatching grants do not require matching expenditures by the recipient governments.

Matching grants may be either *open-ended* or *closed-ended*. In the latter case, there is a fixed limit to the total amount that a given unit of government can receive. For example, a federal grant for special education might provide 2-for-1 matching up to a limit of $2 million per year per district. A district that spends $500,000 of its own funds annually would receive an annual grant of $1 million, a district that spends $750,000 would receive $1.5 million, etc. But all districts that spend $1 million or more would receive grants of only $2 million. With open-ended grants, there are no upper limits. Most federal and state matching grants are closed-ended.

Grant amounts may also be made dependent on the fiscal need or capacity of the recipient government, with the amount usually increasing with the fiscal need and decreasing with the fiscal capacity of the recipient. For example, the per person amount of the grant to each local government might be inversely related to the per capita income of the residents of the locality. Similarly, grants might be made dependent on the fiscal effort of the recipient government, as is the case with federal revenue sharing.

Table 22–3 shows the structure of intergovernmental transfers and the functions aided by existing grant programs. Most of the grants are categorical.

ADJUSTING FOR SPILLOVERS

In Chapter 21 we saw that local governments may ignore spillover benefits and costs when determining the output of a public good. They may therefore provide too little of a public good when there are spillover benefits and too much when there are spillover costs. One possible solution to spillover problems is a system of conditional grants. Other solutions include regulation by setting standards or performance levels, merger of or cooperation among governmental units, and a change in the level of government responsibility for the spillover-producing functions. The last two approaches can be thought of as means of "trapping" spillovers.

Figure 22–1 shows how a matching grant may be used to secure the efficient output of a good, say education, with spillover benefits. As we explained in Chapter 21, ΣD_A shows the marginal value that members of

TABLE 22–3
STRUCTURE OF INTERGOVERNMENTAL TRANSFERS, 1974–1975

Function aided	From federal to state and local governments	From state to federal and local governments	From local to state governments
Total ($ billions)	49.628 [a]	51.978 [b]	1.278 [c]
Percentage of transfers for			
Education	18.1	59.8	4.1
Highways	9.6	6.2	3.3
Public welfare	28.9	15.6	25.3
Health and hospitals	4.1	2.3	14.5
Natural resources	1.8	0.4	0.8
Housing and urban renewal	5.5	0.4	0.1
Air transportation	0.6	0.2	—
Other (except general revenue sharing)	17.0	15.1	52.0
General revenue sharing [d]	12.4		

a $35.451 billion to state governments and $14.177 billion to local governments.
b $.975 billion to the federal government and $51.004 billion to local governments.
c Full amount to state governments.
d $2.066 billion to state governments and $4.180 billion to local governments.

Source: U.S. Census Bureau, *Governmental Finances, 1974–75.*

community A place on units of public good X that are supplied by their local government. Because there are spillover benefits, people in other communities also value community A's production of X. ΣD_N shows the marginal value that all persons in the nation place on units of X provided by community A. When spillovers are accounted for, the optimal amount of X is q_A.

If community A maximizes the welfare of its residents, and ignores the benefit spillovers to nonresidents, it will produce only q'_A of X. It will not increase output from q'_A to q_A if it has to pay the full cost of doing so. However, community A would produce q_A if the unit cost of X were p_A. And the unit cost can be reduced from MC to p_A with a matching grant equal to $MC - p_A$. Then, q_A becomes the optimum output from the point of view of community A, which finances the provision of X with $p_A \times q_A$ of its own funds and $(MC - p_A) \times q_A$ in grant funds.

When output increases to q_A, the value of the additional output to all communities is the area $a + b + c + d$. The value of the additional output to community A is area $a + b$; the value to other communities is area $c + d$.

FIGURE 22–1
A MATCHING GRANT FOR EFFICIENT OUTPUT
OF A GOOD WITH SPILLOVER BENEFITS: COMMUNITY A

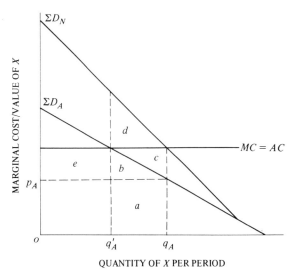

QUANTITY OF X PER PERIOD

The cost of the additional output is $a + b + c$, so that the net welfare gain to all communities is d.

Figure 22–2 repeats that analysis for another community, B. With a grant of $MC - p_B$ per unit of X, the price of X to community B is p_B, and output would be expanded to q_B. The value of the additional output to other communities is $h + i$ and the value to B is $f + g$. The cost of the additional output is $f + g + h$, so there is a net welfare gain to all communities of i. The total potential welfare gain from expanding output to the optimum in both communities is $i + d$, minus the CCA incurred in deciding upon and operating the grant program. In principle, the potential welfare gain can be distributed among individuals so that none are worse off because of the grants and some are better off.

Distribution of gains   Who, in fact, receives this welfare gain? To answer this question we must specify some mechanism for financing the grant. Suppose that there are only two communities and that the national government finances the matching grant payments to A by taxing it in the amount of areas $b + e$ and taxing community B the amount of area c (see Figure 22–1). The welfare of community B is increased by the area d, while community A

FIGURE 22–2
A MATCHING GRANT FOR EFFICIENT OUTPUT
OF A GOOD WITH SPILLOVER BENEFITS: COMMUNITY B

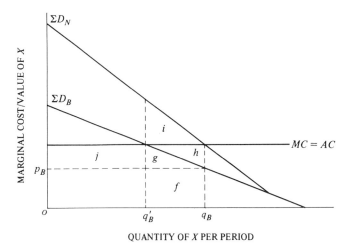

QUANTITY OF X PER PERIOD

is no worse off. Community A would pay the amount of area e, with or without the aid program, so its additional cost in extending output from q'_A to q_A is just equal to the benefit of the additional output, area $a+b$. Similarly, if the grant to B is financed by taxes on A of h and taxes on community B of $j+g$, citizens of B are no worse off, while community A gains in the amount of area i (see Figure 22–2).[1]

Does such a system of grants and taxes by the central government produce a Pareto improvement? Yes, in that community B gains d in Figure 22–1 and community A gains i in Figure 22–2. Those gains, however, assume that taxes and aid are distributed as we specified earlier. Another way to distribute taxes would be to collect taxes from each community equal to the aid that it receives: Figures 22–1 and 22–2 show that community A gains $h+i-c$, and community B gains $d+c-h$. The aggregate gains of the two communities, $h+i-c+d+c-h=i+d$, are positive. With this distribution of taxes, it is possible for one community, but not both, to lose. That outcome is generally true if the grant program succeeds in pushing output to the optimum.

1 This analysis assumes that the marginal value curves are not affected by the income changes implicit in the financing of the grants. If there are income effects, the basic conclusions are unchanged but the geometric illustration is more complicated.

Need for matching   The grant we have been discussing is a matching categorical type. It is categorical because it must be used to finance a particular
local expenditure. The matching provision reduces the price (unit cost) that
the local community must pay for X, which produces a substitution effect:
The local community will tend to substitute the public good for other goods.
With a matching grant, the local community cannot obtain grants unless it
spends funds from its own revenue sources. If the community reduces local
spending, it loses aid; and if the community increases spending, it receives
more aid. Hence, a local community has an incentive to increase the output
of local public goods.[2]

To obtain an efficient output of spillover goods, the matching grant
should be open-ended. That is, the amount of the grant received should
depend only on the matching provision and the recipient government's
spending; there should not be an upper limit to the amount of aid that a
government can receive. For example, if the matching grant is $MC - p_A$ per
unit of X, but the total amount of aid is restricted to some amount less than
$e + b + c$ in Figure 22–1, then the optimum of q_A will not be produced.

Variable matching   The matching grant need not match *all* local government expenditures; it need match only the marginal expenditures, those in
excess of q'_A or q'_B. That is, a *variable* matching grant can be used to induce the optimum outputs of q_A and q_B. The oMG schedule in Figure 22–3
shows the amount of a variable matching grant for community A. No
matching grant is needed to achieve expenditures of q'_A, the local optimum.
To expand expenditures beyond q'_A, the grant must equal (or slightly exceed
to provide a positive incentive) the difference between the cost of additional
output, MC, and the amount that the residents of A are willing to pay for
additional output, given by ΣD_A in Figure 22–1. The matching grant per
unit of output must rise as output is expanded beyond q'_A, as shown in
Figure 22–3, reaching a maximum of $MC - p_A$ at output of q_A. A variable
matching grant requires much smaller grant outlays than the constant grant,
which is $MC - p_A$ for the case at hand. But it also requires more detailed
information about a community's own demand and willingness to pay for
the good — the information incorporated into the curve ΣD_A in Figure
22–1.

Whether it is variable or constant, a matching grant induces an increase
in the output of X because it is a mechanism by which the *marginal* cost
of increasing the output from the local optimum, q'_A, to the national

2 Whether the grant will cause a community to spend more or less of its *own* funds on the
public good depends upon the elasticity of demand for that good.

FIGURE 22–3
A VARIABLE MATCHING GRANT

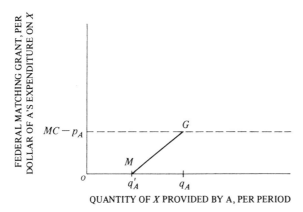

QUANTITY OF X PROVIDED BY A, PER PERIOD

optimum, q_A, may be shared. Such sharing is necessary because the local government does not receive the full amount of the benefits from, and therefore is unwilling to pay the full cost of, marginal units of X.

Nonmatching grants will not have this effect because they provide no cost sharing *at the margin*. For example, suppose the federal government provides such a grant to A equal to areas $a + b + c$ (in Figure 22–1), enough to pay for an expansion of X to q_A. However, community A is unlikely to increase its spending on X by the amount of the grant because it receives the same grant whether or not it increases X beyond q'_A. It can reduce expenditures on X from its own funds by the amount of the grant. Indeed, unless the grant exceeds $q'_A \times MC$, the amount required to fully finance the local optimum output of q'_A, we cannot be sure that the community will expand its output beyond the local optimum. Likewise, the only way of assuring provision of the national optimum, q_A, with nonmatching categorical grants would be for the grant to equal $q_A \times MC$. Then no local funds are necessary, and communities would spend the aid rather than go without it. This approach is more expensive, from the standpoint of national tax requirements, than a matching grant. With a matching grant, national taxes would only be $e + b + c$ (Figure 22–1).[3]

---

[3] Nonmatching grants may shift the marginal value curve because they entail an income effect, causing the community optimum and actual output of X to change. But since any shift in ΣD_A also means a shift in ΣD_N, the income effect will never cause the local optimum q'_A and national optimum, q_A, to coincide (Figure 22–1).

The change in local government spending induced by a nonmatching grant is likely to be

The conclusions of the preceding paragraph assume that local government decisions are based on a comparison and balancing of the marginal benefits and costs of an action *to the members of the community*. In such a case, allocation (expenditure) decisions cannot be altered through grants unless the grants alter marginal benefits or marginal costs, as they are perceived by community members. However, it is possible that local expenditure decisions are based primarily on the preferences of the local government bureaucrats and politicians, who may evaluate the benefits and costs of policies differently. In particular, the grant funds may be viewed as less costly than tax-collected funds (even though they could be used for tax reduction). If so, spending by the recipient governments may be greater even though there is no net income gain to the community and no change in the marginal cost of goods *to the members of the community*.

Cost spillovers   We have thus far dealt only with benefit spillovers. But we can readily extend the analysis to cost spillovers, which have the opposite effect. Taxes could be used by the central government to reduce the spillover-generating activity, a technique that we discussed in connection with pollution in Chapter 5. The policies used to adjust for spillover benefits can also be used to adjust for cost spillovers. For example, suppose community A disposes of sewage in a stream that damages the water quality to residents in community B downstream. Since the reduction in cost spillovers by community A can be viewed as a spillover of benefits to community B, the adjustments can be made with grants to rather than taxes on A.

Some qualifications   The preceding analysis shows *in principle* how grants may be used to achieve efficient resource allocation when spillover benefits (costs) cause local governments to undersupply (oversupply) public goods. In practice, grants may be very difficult and costly to implement. And the possibilities for improving efficiency are therefore much less than is suggested by our simplified analysis. Enormous information costs would arise in determining whether local communities over- or underproduce spillover goods and whether decision makers respond to corrective policies according to the

---

positive (negative) as the income effect is positive (negative). When federal grants to local governments are financed by national taxes, the income effect is the amount of the grant to the community minus the amount of additional federal taxes it pays to finance the grant program. Since total taxes from all communities equals total aid to all communities, one community's income effect cannot be positive without there being a negative effect for some other community. Income effects cannot be positive for all communities.

predictions of our model. These costs may be sufficiently high to prevent or significantly reduce possible welfare gains from corrective policies.

More specifically, our analysis assumes that local decision makers maximize the welfare of their citizens, which may not be a valid assumption because: (1) Marginal value and marginal cost schedules are not known; (2) political decision-making rules (such as majority rule) prevent the attainment of efficiency; or (3) other objectives of local communities, such as income redistribution, are more important than efficiency. If marginal value and cost schedules are not revealed or known, local and national decision makers have no way of knowing what is the efficient output. And public goods may be efficiently produced, overproduced, or underproduced. The same range of outcomes is possible under majority rule[4] or when nonefficiency objectives are pursued.

Even if marginal value and cost schedules are known, and welfare-maximization of the community is the objective of local decision makers, local governments may not be producing spillover goods inefficiently. If a community is able to finance goods with spillover benefits by taxing nonresidents, as well as its own residents, underproduction will not necessarily occur. So, in determining the amount of grants, tax exporting as well as benefit and cost spillovers must be taken into account. For example, in Figure 22–1, A's exporting of taxes to nonresidents may effectively lower the cost to community A from MC to p_A. The optimal amount of q_A would then be produced. In fact, tax exporting by community A may exceed or fall short of $MC - p_A$, so either underproduction or overproduction could occur.[5]

EQUALIZING TAX EFFORT, SERVICE LEVELS,
AND FISCAL RESIDUALS

Horizontal inequities are said to occur when indivduals in like circumstances are not treated equally under the fiscal systems of their local, state, and federal governments. Inequities occur if citizens in poorer communities pay a higher proportion of their incomes to finance a given level of public services than do citizens in wealthier communities. Accompanying such horizontal inequities are intercommunity differences in fiscal residuals that may lead to inefficient location decisions, as we explained in Chapter 21.

The example in Table 22–4 illustrates those conclusions. Suppose the federal system consists of two communities, A and B, with three groups of citizens in each community. Each community provides the same government services at an average cost per person of $1,200. Suppose each com-

4 See Chapter 8.
5 We discussed tax exporting in Chapter 21.

TABLE 22-4
ILLUSTRATION OF HORIZONTAL INEQUITIES IN A FEDERAL SYSTEM OF GOVERNMENT (DOLLARS)

Income class (1)	Number of citizens (2)	Income per citizen (3)	Cost of service per citizen (4)	Taxes with proportional rate, per citizen (5)	Fiscal residual [a] (6)	Additional tax (−) or transfer (+) to achieve equal tax burden per citizen (7)
Community A						
1	30	20,000	1,200	2,000	− 800	+800
2	50	10,000	1,200	1,000	200	−200
3	20	5,000	1,200	500	700	−700
Total	100	1,200,000	120,000	120,000		
Community B						
1	10	20,000	1,200	3,000	−1,800	+1,800
2	30	10,000	1,200	1,500	− 300	+ 300
3	60	5,000	1,200	750	450	− 450
Total	100	800,000	120,000	120,000		

a Fiscal residuals are computed as the per person cost of services provided ($1,200) minus taxes paid. The *value* of the services provided to a particular individual usually will not be equal to this average cost of services. However, if each person would receive the same services in either community, the differences in the fiscal residuals given in column 6 would be correct. For example, suppose that a person in income class 1 receives services valued at $1,500 rather than $1,200. Then the person's *true* fiscal residuals are $1,500 − $2,000 = −$500 in community A and $1,500 − $3,000 = −$1,500 in community B, rather than −$800 and −$1,800 as shown in column 6. However, the residual in community A minus the residual in community B is $1,000 in either case.

munity levies a proportional income tax to finance expenditures. Communities A and B would impose tax rates of 10 percent ($120,000 ÷ $1.2 million) and 15 percent ($120,000 ÷ $800,000), respectively, on each citizen. The tax payments by each citizen are shown in column 5, in Table 22–4.

That example shows that even with proportional income taxation, horizontal inequities may arise in a federal system of government. Horizontal equity is achieved *within each community* in that individuals within each income class pay the same taxes. Horizontal equity is not achieved *across communities* because to receive a given bundle of services persons in any given income class pay a higher proportion of their income in taxes if they reside in community B rather than in A. With each community using a proportional income tax, community A citizens pay a 10 percent tax, and community B citizens pay a 15 percent tax.

People also experience a difference in fiscal residuals in the two communities (see column 6). All people have a larger residual in A than in B and, thus, have an incentive to migrate to A. As we noted in Chapter 21, such migration may lead to inefficiency in the allocation of resources. And, if higher income persons are mobile while poor persons are not, migration makes the average income levels of communities even more disparate. For the present example, if only the members of income class 1 are mobile, then they will move from B to A, making B even poorer relative to A, and making fiscal residuals in B even lower relative to those in A. The migration-induced increase in the fiscal residuals in A strengthens the incentives for migration to A. And a vicious cycle of "the rich get richer and the poor get poorer" sets in, with either tax effort increasing or service levels decreasing or both in B. If all income classes are equally mobile, such segregation does not occur.

Taxation according to costs generated   These equity and efficiency problems do not arise if local communities tax individuals according to the cost of public goods provided to them. In the example in Table 22–4, this approach requires taxes of $1,200 from each person, and within each income class the proportion of income paid in taxes to support a given level of public output is the same. In A, citizens in income class 1 pay 6 percent of their income in taxes, and the like citizens in B do the same. Citizens in income class 3 in each community pay 24 percent of their income in taxes. It is true that *as a group* citizens in community B have a higher *average* rate of taxation than do citizens of A (15 percent versus 10 percent), but that is because there are more poor persons in community B. However, the poorer persons in community B do not, as individuals, pay a higher rate of taxation than the poorer persons in A. This method of taxation also eliminates incentives for interregional migration because fiscal residuals tend to be uniform across communities (zero for the example at hand).

One drawback to this form of financing is the difficulty of determining the costs generated by each person. Contrary to the example in Table 22–4, each person in a community usually does not receive the same services from government. Also, such policy may result in regressive taxation. That is, taxes may claim a higher proportion of the income of the lower income groups than of the higher, a result that many people would find objectionable. In other terms, taxation according to costs generated will promote horizontal equity, but it may create vertical inequities.

Geographically variable rates for federal taxes and transfers In principle, the national government can equalize fiscal residuals and eliminate horizontal inequities by taxing some individuals and transferring income to others. If local governments employ proportional income taxation, as shown in Table 22–4, a national tax-transfer scheme would restore horizontal equity by taxing community A citizens in income classes 2 and 3, $200 and $700 respectively; and community B citizens in class 3, $450. The taxes would then be transferred to community A citizens 1 and community B citizens 1 and 2 in the respective amounts of $800, $1,800, and $300 (see column 7). Such policy, if feasible, would result in regressive taxation.

Alternatively, the federal government might use geographically variable tax rates. To illustrate let us suppose the federal government is to raise $100,000 in revenues to finance an equivalent amount of expenditures. In Table 22–4, the sum could be financed by imposing proportional income taxes of 7 percent and 2 percent on the citizens of communities A and B, respectively. Since community A is imposing a 10 percent tax on income to finance local expenditures, its total tax bill (federal plus local) would be 17 percent. Community B's total tax rate would also be 17 percent, 15 percent local and 2 percent federal. Among other difficulties, this approach to promoting horizontal equity would meet constitutional obstacles in the United States.

Equalizing grants Equalizing grants have been by far the most popular approach to the problems under discussion. For the example in Table 22–4, when each community spends $1,200 per person and uses a proportional income tax, citizens of community A pay a 10 percent tax, and citizens of community B pay a 15 percent tax. To achieve horizontal equity and equalize fiscal residuals, the federal government could levy a 2 percent tax on the income of all citizens, yielding revenue of $40,000, which is transferred to community B as an unconditional grant. Community B then would have to impose a local tax of 10 percent to collect $80,000, which, combined with the $40,000 in grants, would finance expenditures of $120,000. In community A, a local tax of 10 percent would also finance expenditures of $120,000. Each citizen in each community would then be paying federal and local taxes of 12 percent of their income to finance a given service level of $1,200 per person.

The amount of an equalizing grant depends on the expenditure level for which horizontal equity is to be achieved. In the example in Table 22-4, a grant of $40,000 to community B is required to equalize the tax effort required to support an expenditure level of $120,000. To have equal tax effort in the two communities when spending is either $100,000 or $140,000 would require grants to community B of $33,333 and $46,667, respectively. This does not mean that the communities will or should spend at the levels assumed in determining the grants. Instead, the assumption is that each community should be able to reach some minimum expenditure level, and the tax rates required for that level should be uniform.

Problems with equalizing grants   At first glance equalizing grants appears to be a satisfactory way of achieving horizontal equity among local communities. Indeed, the preceding argument has been used to support the existing equalizing grant programs of federal and state governments. However, implementing such a policy can be difficult because the required information about the incomes and tax burdens of local communities is unavailable. Income data are usually available. But local (state) tax structures vary, and assumptions have to be made or knowledge gained about how taxes are shifted across borders and among income classes. For example, if the poor community B is a net exporter of taxes to community A, an equalizing grant to B may not be justified. The magnitude of the grant should, in principle, be adjusted for tax exporting. So tax exporting and importing and the variation in tax structures among subnational governments complicate and can impair the usefulness of equalizing grants in achieving horizontal equity.

To illustrate one of the problems, the example in Table 22–4 assumes that a proportional income tax is employed by both communities. Suppose, instead, that community A uses a proportional income tax and community B has a regressive tax. A regressive tax causes the tax burden as a proportion of income to increase as income decreases. If the federal government transfers income from A to B, and B uses the funds to reduce taxes across the board, the overall structure in community B will still be regressive. Across communities, individuals in the same income class will not pay the same taxes even with an equalizing grant. In community A, each person pays the same proportion of income in taxes. But in community B, that proportion falls with income. To accomplish horizontal equity, the grant would have to be used to realign tax burdens vertically, but this would be exceedingly complex when each community among thousands has its own tax structure.

When the costs of providing public services differ between communities, then equal expenditure levels will not result in equal service levels. Therefore, intercommunity differences in the costs of providing services must be considered in determining the grant amounts if the objective is to equalize the tax effort required for a given package of services. If such differences are accounted for, then the higher cost communities will receive relatively more aid than the lower cost communities, other things being equal. Whether subsidy of relatively high-cost communities is appropriate on efficiency grounds is open to question.

Another problem with equalizing grants is that they may reverse the income redistribution efforts of local governments. In Table 22–4, suppose the citizens of A wish to use a proportional income tax to finance expenditures that benefit low-income groups so that there is a net redistribution of income from the wealthy to the poor. If the national government imposes a tax on citizens of A to finance a grant to community B, the overall tax burden on the poor in community A may be greater than that preferred by the citizens of A. The preferences of the citizens of A are overridden.

Such a result is not objectionable if the federal government is the most suitable level of government to achieve redistribution objectives. However, local citizens may prefer to have some responsibility for redistribution policies. Local redistribution may be desirable if members of a local community are more concerned about the poverty of individuals closest to them, and local redistribution is effective to the extent that mobility costs inhibit the migration of persons in response to local redistribution policies.

IMPROVING REVENUE SYSTEMS

Grants have also been advocated as means of substituting federal (or state) taxes for local taxes, which is thought to reduce tax competition. And, federal (or state) taxes are thought to be more equitable and more efficiently collected than local taxes. When tax substitution is their only purpose, grants can be the block, nonmatching type, such as general revenue sharing, as it was enacted by the federal government in 1972. Of course, tax substitution can occur with any type of grant.

Tax substitution results if the federal grants are financed by higher federal taxes and the recipient governments use the grants to reduce local taxes rather than to increase local spending. Individuals then pay higher federal and lower local taxes. And, even if local governments increase their spending by the amount of the grants, there is a decrease in the share of local government spending that is locally financed. The relative importance of local taxes in the overall tax system is reduced.

It is questionable whether grants reduce tax competition. Unless all local spending is grant financed, local governments must obtain some revenues with their own taxes. They therefore have the option of keeping their tax rates relatively low in an attempt to attract industry and population. Of course, increasing the grant financed share of local government spending reduces the range over which local tax rates may be varied competitively.

REVENUE SHARING

Revenue sharing has received a great deal of attention in recent years. In the purest form of revenue sharing, the central government collects taxes and returns part of them to the local governments of the communities from which the taxes were collected. For example, the central government could collect an income tax and share with each community's government a uniform fraction of the revenue collected from residents of that community. However, federal revenue sharing, as provided for by the State and Local Fiscal Assistance Act of 1972, distributes funds on the basis of local population and fiscal effort and capacity, rather than in strict proportion to federal tax collections.

Can revenue sharing help solve the problems we have discussed? Shared revenues may be used by recipient governments to reduce their own taxes, increase spending, or both. But revenue sharing is not a cure for spillovers because it does not provide incentives for local governments to alter their spending on spillover-generating activities. That is, revenue sharing grants are not matching. Revenue sharing also does not reduce tax competition among localities because they are still free to manipulate their own tax structures for that purpose.[6]

Revenue sharing can, in principle, reduce disparities in fiscal effort and capacity. The federal revenue sharing formulas are such that local governments with low fiscal capacity or high fiscal effort receive relatively large per capita grants.[7] However, in practice, federal revenue sharing grants are not equalizing to any significant extent, partly because the grants are small and partly because of other factors in the distribution formulas. The present system is primarily a means of reducing reliance on local revenue sources either by directly substituting federal funds for local taxes or by expanding local spending without expanding local revenue. Revenue sharing permits localities to use more equitable taxes to finance any level of government

6 The sharing formulas do provide slight incentive for governments to increase their spending and therefore offset, to some extent, the pressures for tax competition.

7 For an excellent discussion of the revenue sharing formulas and their effects, see Robert D. Reischauer, "General Revenue Sharing: The Program's Incentives," in *Financing the New Federalism: Revenue Sharing, Conditional Grants, and Taxation*, ed. Wallace E. Oates (Baltimore: Johns Hopkins, 1975), pp. 62–90.

spending if the federal government's taxes are more equitable than local taxes. Administrative and enforcement costs are lower with revenue sharing than if the local governments were to employ independently the same tax as the federal government.

Revenue sharing has the disadvantage of separating the tax and expenditure decisions of local governments. Efficiency in local spending is unlikely unless decision makers are accountable not only for spending decisions but also for raising the revenue to finance the expenditures.[8]

INCOME REDISTRIBUTION AMONG PERSONS

As grants directly transfer income between governments, they indirectly transfer income among persons. Individuals gain disposable income if grants result in lower local taxes; they lose disposable income if grants are financed by higher federal taxes. Particular individuals and income classes may either gain or lose from the financing and distribution of intergovernmental grants; a person gains disposable income if his local taxes fall by more than his federal taxes increase and vice versa. The example in Table 22–4 illustrates this redistribution. The 2 percent federal tax imposes costs of $400 on persons in income class 1 in both community A and B, $200 on persons in class 2 in both A and B, and $100 on persons in class 3 in A and B. When the $40,000 of funds obtained from the tax are given to community B, citizens of B gain. In particular, for B to finance an expenditure level of $1,200 per person, persons in class 1 now pay taxes of $2,000 rather than $3,000; persons in class 2 pay $1,000 rather than $1,500; persons in class 3 pay $500 rather than $750. So, in community B citizens in class 1 gain $600; in class 2, $300; and in class 3, $150 from the grant program. In community A, people in class 1 lose $400; in class 2, $200; and in class 3, $100.

Individuals may also find their real incomes affected by changes in federal and local spending that take place because of grants. On the one hand, grants may be financed fully or in part by reduced federal spending for other purposes. That imposes real income losses on those persons who were beneficiaries of the foregone federal activities. On the other hand, when grants increase local government spending, some individuals gain real income from the expanded local activity.

---

8 For additional discussion of the role of revenue sharing in dealing with the major problems of federalism, see George F. Break, "Revenue Sharing: Its Implications for Present and Future Intergovernmental Fiscal Systems: The Case For," *National Tax Journal*, 24, No. 3 (September 1971): 307–312. Break argues that revenue sharing is not the best way of dealing with most of these problems, but it appears to be a politically acceptable second-best solution to many of them.

For a particular person, the four grant-induced changes (in federal taxes, local taxes, federal spending, and local spending) may be positive, zero, or negative in net amount. Generally, we do not know how intergovernmental grant programs redistribute real income among persons (that is, we do not know who is helped and who is harmed). Yet, such redistribution is surely an important consequence of grant programs, whether beneficial or harmful. And, since redistribution to achieve specific equity objectives is often a major reason for grants, we often cannot know whether grants serve their intended purpose.

INTERGOVERNMENTAL FISCAL COORDINATION

A second basic approach to the problems of federalism involves coordination of the revenue-raising activities of the several levels of government. Policies involving fiscal coordination include supplementary tax rates, tax credits and deductions, separation of tax sources, and home rule. We discuss these measures in turn.

SUPPLEMENTARY TAXES

The federal government may authorize either state or local governments or both to impose a tax on its tax revenue or tax base. The federal government then collects the tax and returns it to the state or local government. Similarly, state governments may allow local governments to levy supplementary ("piggyback") taxes on the state government tax bases. For example, cities may be allowed to levy a 1 percent sales tax that is on the same base as the state's sales tax and is collected at the same time. Or local governments may be permitted to impose a surtax on the income tax that the state collects from the residents of each locality.[9]

A few states currently impose a surtax on individuals' federal income tax liability, and this approach comes up for consideration periodically in other states. There are also a number of states where the local governments are permitted to impose a supplementary rate on the state government's sales or gasoline taxes. The state governments then collect the tax revenues and return to local governments their share.

Supplementary taxes do not avoid the problem of tax competition, but they may enable state and local governments to employ fairer taxes. Administrative and enforcement costs are reduced when collection authority

9 A surtax is a tax on a tax; with a local surtax levied on state income taxes, taxpayers' local income tax would be some percentage, say 10 percent, of their state income taxes.

rests with the higher level governments. Unlike revenue sharing, the use of supplementary taxes has the advantage of combining the expenditure and tax responsibilities of local government decision makers.

The Advisory Commission on Intergovernmental Relations has recently advocated greater local government use of sales and income taxes, but based on three conditions: (1) the state administers tax collection and enforcement, (2) limits are placed on the rates that can be assessed, and (3) the tax base within the state must be uniform. The most straightforward way of meeting these conditions would be for state governments to authorize local governments to levy supplementary taxes on the state sales and income tax bases.[10]

TAX CREDITS AND DEDUCTIONS

With tax credits, tax payments to one level of government are reduced by some fraction of tax payments to the other levels. For example, part of a person's local tax payments may be credited against his or her federal income tax liabilities.

A tax credit is similar in effect to a matching grant in that it reduces the marginal cost to the community of an increase in government spending. Suppose that taxpayers are permitted to credit 50 percent of their local income tax liabilities against federal income taxes. Then, when a person's local income tax increases by $100, $50 is credited against the person's federal income tax liability and he or she pays only 50 percent of the increase in local taxes. This credit is like a 50-50 matching grant. A tax credit differs from a *categorical* matching grant, however, because it provides matching funds for all categories of spending. A tax credit therefore cannot adjust for spillovers. A tax credit also differs from an equalizing grant because the implicit grant is not distributed on the basis of need or fiscal capacity. Another difference is that grants go directly to the local government, while the tax savings from the credits accrue to individuals. Nevertheless, a tax credit provides an incentive to local governments to increase spending because it reduces the cost of public goods to its taxpayers.

A tax credit may ease tax competition among subnational governments, since part of any tax increase is shifted to the federal government. But it does not eliminate tax competition. It will also not eliminate duplication of the tax collection machinery of overlapping units of government if each unit operates its own tax system. Such duplication is eliminated when the credit is used in conjunction with supplementary taxes.

10 For further discussion, see Advisory Commission on Intergovernmental Relations, *Local Revenue Diversification: Income, Sales Taxes and User Charges* (Washington: Government Printing Office, 1974), especially chaps. 3, 4.

Tax deductibility differs from a tax credit in that a deduction reduces federal taxes by reducing the federal tax base. If a person has an income of $10,000 subject to taxation at a 10 percent rate, a $1,000 deduction for local taxes paid would reduce the tax base to $9,000 and would reduce tax liabilities by $100.

Like tax credits, tax deductions are similar to a matching grant. However, the two devices affect the distribution of income differently. With progressive rates of federal income taxation, the tax deduction provides tax savings that increase as incomes increase. A tax deduction of $1,000 gives a tax saving of $150 to a person in the 15 percent marginal tax bracket and a tax saving of $500 to a person in the 50 percent marginal tax bracket. In contrast, with a tax credit, federal taxes are reduced by the same percentage of local tax payments, regardless of the taxpayer's bracket. In addition, the tax deduction does not benefit those taxpayers who do not itemize deductions but nevertheless pay federal taxes. A tax credit could apply to anyone who pays taxes. Neither the deduction nor the credit benefits individuals who do not pay taxes.

At present, virtually all state and local taxes are deductible in calculating taxable income under the federal income tax if the taxpayer chooses to itemize deductions. Also, the federal government allows a tax credit of (1) state estate taxes against the federal estate tax and (2) the state payroll tax for financing unemployment compensation against the federal payroll tax. The purpose of the estate tax credit is not to encourage state spending or to encourage the use of alternative taxes, but to eliminate competition among states for wealthy elderly residents who seek to reside where estate taxes are low. The purpose of the unemployment compensation tax credit is to induce states to adopt an unemployment insurance program, which all states have done, to avoid losing revenues that would otherwise be collected by the federal government.

SEPARATION OF REVENUE SOURCES

Historically, the three major levels of government in the United States have relied on different primary revenue sources: (1) income taxes and tariffs at the federal level, (2) sales taxes at the state level, (3) and property taxes at the local level. That separation of revenue sources is sometimes thought to be desirable because it prevents one level of government from pre-empting the revenues of another. For example, if the federal government should levy a sales tax of, say, 2 percent, it might prevent state governments from increasing their sales tax rates. Whether this view is valid is open to question. However, a desire to maintain separation of revenue sources is probably a factor inhibiting federal use of sales taxes and state use of property taxes.

HOME RULE

State governments presently limit the taxing powers of local governments, often restricting them to property taxes and often limiting property tax rates. *Home rule* would eliminate or reduce these restrictions and allow local governments to levy a wider variety of taxes, user charges, fees, licenses, etc. Home rule would not be effective in dealing with spillover problems, tax competition, and disparities in fiscal capacity and effort. However, allowing local governments greater flexibility in the collection of revenue could improve local tax systems in terms of equity and elasticity. Any gains from home rule could be more than offset by higher collection and compliance costs, unless the new local taxes (sales, income, gasoline, etc.) are centrally administered.[11]

OTHER SOLUTIONS

Other solutions to the problems of federalism that have been tried or proposed include: performance standards or requirements set by higher level governments; contracting between or merger of existing governmental units and greater reliance on fees and user charges at the state and local level. We will discuss each in turn.

PERFORMANCE STANDARDS AND REGULATIONS

One approach to achieving efficiency in the output of local spillover goods is that of having the central government require local communities to produce optimal amounts. With this policy, each community pays the full cost of output expansion. For example, the central government could simply pass and enforce laws requiring communities A and B to produce q_A and q_B in Figures 22–1 and 22–2. Community A would spend $MC \times q_A$ and incur a loss of c from its provision of X; B would be forced to produce q_B at a cost of $MC \times q_B$. Whether a particular community gains or loses depends on its gains from the output expansion in other communities. Community A is a net gainer if $i + h$ exceeds c; and B gains if $d + c$ exceeds h. Aggregate gains to communities A and B are positive $(i + d)$; hence, both communities cannot lose. Indeed, aggregate gains are the same with regulation as with matching grants, but regulation may distribute the costs of output expansion differently from grants.

More specifically, with regulation, each community bears the full costs of achieving the centrally specified outputs. However, if the cost distribution is

11 See Advisory Commission, *Local Revenue Diversification*, for more discussion of the problems of allowing local governments greater flexibility in revenue collection.

unacceptable, it can be changed by providing aid. For example, local schools that are required to meet curriculum standards set by the state government may be given lump-sum grants to finance the cost of meeting those standards.

Grants may be preferred to regulation not only for distribution reasons, but because they appear less coercive. In addition, regulation may entail greater enforcement costs than grants. With properly designed matching grants, communities voluntarily provide the national optimum. Compared to a system of granting funds to communities, an elaborate monitoring and enforcement system would be required to ensure that communities spend specified sums on numerous categories of expenditures. On the other hand, regulation does not require knowledge of how local governments make decisions. If the central government knows the optimal amount of local public goods, it can simply require that the optimum be produced. With grants, the central government must know both the optimum output *and* how local decision makers will respond to the grants.

GOVERNMENTAL MERGER AND CONTRACTING

Spillovers might also be accounted for by transferring the responsibility for producing goods with spillovers from local to central governments. If the central government knows and responds to local preferences and adjusts for spillovers, an optimal amount of public goods could be produced by centralizing decision making. Merger of, or cooperation among, subnational governments could have the same result.

A transfer of functions from local to central governments would be appropriate when locally produced goods convey largely national benefits, and there are economies of scale with centralized production and decision making. For example, each locality (state) could produce some level of national defense with the aid of categorical grants. But the grant program would have to be administered, decisions would have to be coordinated, and there would be numerous layers of political and bureaucratic decision making. Centralization could reduce the costs of such activities.

The same argument could be made for mergers between governmental units when locally produced goods have pronounced effects on surrounding communities, and tastes for the public good are fairly homogenous across political jurisdictions. However, it may be that merger and cooperation are appropriate only for particular functions, say, garbage collection. If so, forming a wholly new government from several local governments would produce some welfare losses because varying preferences for local public goods would be given less weight by the larger government body.

USER CHARGES AND FEES

User charges and fees may be based on costs generated or benefits received. In either case, this approach to financing is less likely than traditional taxation to create horizontal inequities and incentives for inefficient location of population and economic activity. With such financing, fiscal residuals are likely to be small and uniform across communities. Recall the example in Table 22–4.

Fees and charges are presently being used to finance in full or in part sewage collection and treatment, parking, airport facilities, highways, and recreational facilities. However, such financing is limited by the difficulty of identifying users and measuring the extent of their use. For example, how should user charges for the court system or police protection be determined?

In short, user charges and fees provide local governments with additional revenue options. When feasible, fees and charges are less likely than taxation to generate interregional differences in fiscal residuals and in the share of income paid in taxes.[12]

SUMMARY

We have discussed a number of ways of dealing with the problems of federalism that we identified in Chapter 21. Some policies, such as revenue sharing, may be partially effective in dealing with several of the problems. All the policies involve interaction between different levels of government — intergovernmental revenue transfers, fiscal coordination, or regulation. The interaction and coordination between government levels presumably has occurred and is occurring because of a desire to achieve specific efficiency and equity objectives, while retaining the multilevel multiunit federal structure of government.

For spillover benefits and costs, policy alternatives include matching grants (or taxes in the case of spillover costs); regulation of local government output; transfer of functions to higher government levels; and merger of, and cooperation among, existing units of government. The policies differ in their distributional effects and in their information requirements. But they are all similar in that, to a degree, they replace local with centralized decision making about the production of spillover goods. And, in all cases

12 For further discussion of user charge financing, see Advisory Commission, *Local Revenue Diversification:* chap. 5. Also see William S. Vickrey, "General and Specific Financing of Urban Services," in *Public Expenditure Decisions in the Urban Community*, ed. Howard Schaller (1963), pp. 40–87; and Selma Mushkin, ed., *Public Prices for Public Products* (Washington: Brookings, 1972).

except merger or cooperation, there is more control by the national government over the production of spillover goods, although grants give an appearance of less control. Grants permit local governments to choose output levels, but the national government changes the constraints (prices) that influence local choice.

Block grants, revenue sharing, and tax credits and deductions may, in principle, reduce disparities in fiscal capacity, effort, and residuals. Policies for improving the tax options available to local governments include block grants, revenue sharing, tax credits and deductions, supplementary taxes, and home rule. Tax competition may be somewhat mitigated by block grants and revenue sharing; but its basic cause — decentralized decision making about taxation — can be fully eliminated only by centralizing decision making. The duplication of tax administration and enforcement efforts can be reduced by supplementary taxes, revenue sharing, and block grants.

While there typically are several potential solutions for each major problem, by far the most common policy response has been an intergovernmental grant of one form or another. The result is a massive and growing system of grants that can be superficially rationalized as a response to the problems of federalism. And, in political debate and decision making, grant programs are often rationalized as means of achieving local government expenditures that satisfy national as well as local demands for spillover goods or as mechanisms for reducing or eliminating horizontal inequities.

But it is questionable whether grants are or can be effective in achieving those ends. The theory of matching grants assumes that each local government knows the benefits and costs of public goods and adjusts the benefits and costs at the margin to maximize the welfare of its citizens. At the same time, local decision makers presumably ignore the benefits and costs of local public goods to persons residing outside the community. If federal matching grants are to achieve efficiency, the federal government must know the community as well as the national benefits of local public goods; and local decision makers must respond to grants in a particular way. These assumptions may not be valid because (1) the required information is costly if not impossible to obtain, (2) nonresidents may be taxed to finance local public goods, (3) political institutions may prevent welfare maximization, and (4) welfare maximization may not be the goal sought by decision makers.

Similar difficulties are encountered in achieving horizontal equity with equalizing grants. To implement equalizing grants it is necessary to determine what expenditure levels to support and to have information about the distribution of income and taxes among thousands of communities. Horizontal equity may also require a change in the distribution of local taxes and expenditure benefits among individuals and a change in the overall tax effort of local governments. Equalizing grants do not provide for such redistribution.

Given those qualifications, it is questionable whether existing grant systems promote efficiency and equity. To justify a particular program on economic grounds requires more than the simplified arguments of the models we have examined. Enormous information costs are met in showing that particular grants systems can improve the allocation of resources or the distribution of income. What can be said is that grant programs spread the cost of local government activity over all taxpayers in a federal system, whether the distribution of the benefits and costs of the programs are known or desirable. It can also be conjectured that the widespread acceptability of grant systems does not rest on any demonstrated proof of their effectiveness in achieving efficiency and equity objectives. Instead, their popularity may derive from a misperception that grants offer "something for everyone" or "something for nothing."

SUPPLEMENTARY READINGS

Advisory Commission on Intergovernmental Relations. *Federal-State-Local Finances: Significant Facts of Fiscal Federalism: 1973–74.* Washington: Government Printing Office. The Commission publishes on a continuing basis data and analyses pertinent to the problems we discussed in this chapter.

Break, George F. *Intergovernmental Fiscal Relations in the United States,* Washington: Brookings, 1967.

Fried, Edward R., et al. *Setting National Priorities, the 1974 Budget,* chaps. 5–7. Washington: Brookings, 1973.

Heller, Walter W. *New Dimensions of Political Economy.* New York: Norton, 1967.

Maxwell, J. A., and Aronson, J. R. *Financing State and Local Government.* 3rd ed. Washington: Brookings, 1977.

Nathan, Richard P. *Monitoring Revenue Sharing.* Washington: Brookings 1975.

Schultze, Charles L.; Fried, Edward R.; Rivlin, A. M.; and Teeters, Nancy H. *Setting National Priorities, the 1973 Budget,* chaps. 9, 10. Washington: Brookings, 1972.

We have seen that government in the United States plays a large and pervasive role in economic decision making. We have also seen that a government role in many areas of decision making can be rationalized as a means of achieving equity and efficiency objectives. In Part Seven we ask whether the activities of U.S. governments do in fact serve these objectives. In doing so, we are also testing a particular hypothesis about why government exists and why it does what it does – the hypothesis is that governments came into being and continue to exist as mechanisms for achieving particular economic objectives.

Unfortunately, efforts by economists to determine whether U.S. governments promote efficiency and equity have been tentative and partial. Equity and efficiency criteria are not easily made operational. And the relevance and acceptance of any evaluative efforts are limited because people disagree about the economic objectives that should be sought and about their importance vis-à-vis other social objectives.

PART SEVEN

U. S. GOVERNMENT: CONSEQUENCES FOR EFFICIENCY AND EQUITY

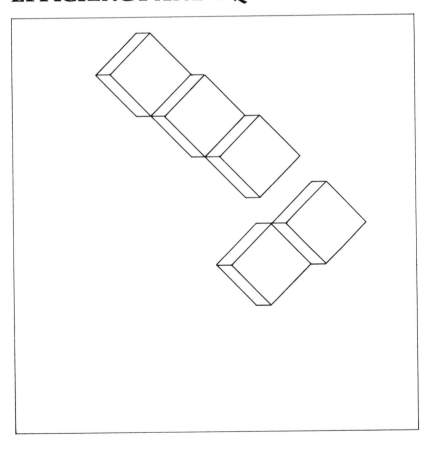

CHAPTER TWENTY-THREE

GOVERNMENT IN THE UNITED STATES: EQUITY AND EFFICIENCY

By any reckoning, government budgetary policies have major effects on resource allocation and income distribution in virtually all modern nations, including the United States. In this chapter we briefly summarize what we do (and do not) know about those effects: We do not know as much as we would like to know. But available information does allow us to make some tentative judgments about whether government does promote equity and efficiency objectives, which is an important question in its own right. And as we attempt to answer it, we make use of what we have learned in preceding chapters.

DISTRIBUTION AND EQUITY

The budgetary activities of federal, state, and local governments affect the distribution of income among persons in terms of both sources and uses. As they provide goods and services, governments directly determine the distribution of a major component of real income. And the financing of government activities alters both the distribution of disposable personal income and relative prices, thereby affecting the distribution of those components of real income other than government-provided goods and services.[1] In other terms, the various budgetary activities of U.S. governments entail benefits and costs, the former adding to and the latter subtracting from the real income of each person.

In the following sections we will first look at how benefits and costs are

1 Recall the definitions of real income and incidence we developed in Chapter 9.

distributed among persons in various income classes. Then we will see how subsidies and transfers benefit particular groups of persons, such as farmers, the poor, or homeowners. In the remainder of the chapter we will briefly evaluate these distribution effects and review some reform proposals.

DISTRIBUTION BY INCOME CLASS

Table 23–1 shows the net burdens (or benefits) of government expenditures and taxes as a proportion of income by income class if the 1968 fiscal system is (1) established in a setting without a fiscal system or (2) removed. On the average, the lower-income groups are net gainers (benefits exceed taxes) when the fiscal system is established, and they are net losers when the fiscal system is withdrawn. The reverse is true for the middle- and upper-income ranges. Although the estimates show a net redistribution in favor of the poor, they are subject to a number of qualifications.

In particular, as we know from preceding discussion, tax incidence is seldom a certain matter, and the allocation of benefits from government expenditures is even less certain. The estimates of Table 23–1 are averages for each income class, so particular individuals could experience substantially different income effects. Also, the estimates are for the direct effects of budgetary policies, and they therefore do not include effects of nonbudgetary policies, such as minimum wage laws, that may alter the distribution of income. Nor do they include the indirect effects of budgetary policies — the excess burdens and the economic growth effects of taxes and government spending.[2]

Nevertheless, these are the best available estimates of the overall redistribution effects of the budget policies of federal, state, and local governments. If the estimates are accepted, then we must conclude that government budgetary policies substantially alter the distribution of real income, making it more equal. For example, if the fiscal system had been withdrawn in 1968, individuals in the lowest income class would have lost 88 percent of their income, and people in the highest income class would have gained an amount equal to 13.5 percent of their income. Or, if we imagine a situation in which there is no fiscal system and one is then established, the estimates imply an average income increase of 1,333 percent for persons in the lowest income group and an average decrease of 11.9 percent for those in the highest group.

2 For further discussion of these problems, see Richard A. Musgrave, Karl E. Case, and Herman Leonard, "The Distribution of Fiscal Burdens and Benefits," *Public Finance Quarterly*, 2 (July 1974).

TABLE 23-1

NET BENEFIT OR BURDEN RATIOS RESULTING FROM ESTABLISHMENT OR REMOVAL OF THE FISCAL SYSTEM, 1968
(ALL LEVELS OF GOVERNMENT, ALL EXPENDITURES)[a]

	Total income bracket (thousands of dollars)[b]									
	Less than 4	4-5.7	5.7-7.9	7.9-10.4	10.4-12.5	12.5-17.5	17.5-22.6	22.6-35.5	35.5-92.0	92.0 and over
Establishment[c]	13.33	.354	.116	.010	-.038	-.076	-.087	-.090	-.084	-.119
Removal[d]	- 0.880	-.257	-.102	-.009	.040	.082	.095	.098	.091	.135

a The results are based on assumptions about tax incidence and the allocation of benefits from government expenditures that are explained fully in Musgrave, Case, and Leonard (see source note to this table). The benefits of general government spending are assumed to accrue to each person in proportion to the person's income.

b Total income consists of factor income to households, transfer payments, corporate profits before taxes and less dividends, employer wage supplements, imputed rent on owner-occupied housing, interest on insurance, other capital gains accruals and imputations.

c Numerator of ratio equals transfers plus real expenditure benefits minus taxes. Denominator equals total income minus transfers.

d Numerator of ratio equals taxes minus transfers minus real expenditure benefits. Denominator equals total income plus real expenditure benefits minus taxes. In considering both note that total income includes transfers.

Source: Portions of this table and excerpt from "The Distribution of Fiscal Burdens and Benefits," by Richard A. Musgrave et al. are reprinted from *Public Finance Quarterly*, Vol 2, No. 3 (July 1974), p. 298 by permission of the publisher, Sage Publications, Inc.

REDISTRIBUTION TO PARTICULAR POPULATION GROUPS

The fiscal activities of government may redistribute real income in a way that favors particular population groups, as well as particular income classes. Such redistribution is of course reflected in the estimates of Table 23–1. But it is of interest in itself because subsidies and preferences that favor particular groups are often the source of horizontal inequities.

Full discussion of the various ways in which particular population groups are favored by government policies would be a book in itself. However, the Joint Economic Committee has recently tabulated the budgetary effects and listed the beneficiaries of major federal subsidies and tax preferences.[3] The costs of the subsidies increased from $64.4 billion to $95.1 billion in the period 1970–1975 (see Table 23–2).

Federal subsidies are sometimes explicit cash payments; but in many cases they are implicit payments in the form of a reduction of tax liabilities (tax subsidies or tax preferences), loans at interest rates below the government borrowing rate, loan guarantees, goods and services provided at prices or fees below market value, government purchases of goods and services above market price, and government regulatory actions that alter particular market prices.[4]

The Joint Economic Committee concludes that the subsidies often redistribute income in a manner that favors middle- and upper-income persons. For example, "when housing subsidies are considered along with the direct housing programs for low-income people, the total effect is to provide more direct assistance to middle- and upper-income households than to low-income households. Moreover, all housing programs intended for low- and lower-middle-income households provide large amounts of help to a small fraction of eligible households and no direct help at all to the rest."[5] In addition, the subsidies generate horizontal inequities. For example, among persons of similar incomes, those with capital gains income pay lower taxes than those whose income is taxable at full rates; those who own homes pay lower taxes than those who rent similar residences, etc.[6]

Similarly, farm production controls and price supports are aimed at raising the incomes of farm families and increasing the viability of small

3 U.S. Congress, Joint Economic Committee, *Federal Subsidy Programs*, a staff study prepared for the use of the Subcommittee on Priorities and Economy in Government (Washington: Government Printing Office, 1974).

4 Ibid., p. 1.

5 Ibid., p. 3.

6 The bulk of housing subsidies accrue to homeowners. For a detailed discussion of federal housing policies and their beneficiaries, see Henry J. Aaron, *Shelter and Subsidies: Who Benefits from Federal Housing Policies* (Washington: Brookings, 1972).

TABLE 23–2
SUMMARY OF FEDERAL SUBSIDY COSTS (BILLIONS OF DOLLARS)

	Direct cash subsidies		Tax subsidies		Credit subsidies		Benefit-in-kind subsidies		Total order of magnitude	
	1970	1975	1970	1975	1970	1975	1970	1975	1970	1975
Agriculture	4.4	0.6	0.9	1.1	0.4	0.7			5.7	2.5
Food							1.5	5.9	1.5	5.9
Health	0.8	0.6	3.2	5.8			4.6	10.2	8.6	16.6
Manpower	2.0	3.3	0.6	0.7			0.1	0.1	2.6	4.1
Education	1.9	5.0	0.8	1.0	0.1	0.1	0.4	0.4	3.2	6.5
International	0.1		0.3	1.5	0.6	0.9			1.0	2.4
Housing	0.1	1.7	8.7	12.9	3.0	1.1			11.7	15.7
Natural resources	0.1	0.1	2.0	4.1			0.1	0.1	2.1	4.4
Transportation	0.3	0.6		0.1			0.2	1.7	0.5	2.3
Commerce	2.0	0.3	14.1	19.3	0.1	0.1	1.8	1.9	18.0	21.5
Other			9.4	13.1	0.1	0.1			9.5	13.2
Total order of magnitude[a]	11.6	12.3	39.9	59.7	4.1	2.9	8.8	20.2	64.4	95.1

a Individual items may not add to totals because of rounding error.

Source: U.S. Congress, Joint Economic Committee, *Federal Subsidy Programs* (Washington: Government Printing Office, 1974), p. 5.

owner-operated farms. In a recent study of those federal farm programs, Schultze concludes that they have generated higher returns to farming that in most circumstances have been translated into higher land prices. Thus, to a significant extent, subsidies have increased land rents rather than farm incomes.[7]

REDISTRIBUTION AND POVERTY REDUCTION

Some of the subsidies in Table 23–2 benefit low-income persons and presumably help to reduce poverty. In addition, state and local governments make transfers to the poor. Table 23–3 provides details about the various government programs that provide cash and in-kind transfers. The total amount redistributed in 1976 was about $331.4 billion. Social welfare expenditures rose from 3.9 percent of GNP in 1929 to 20.6 percent of GNP in 1976 (see Table 23–4).

All the transfers do not, however, accrue to poor persons. In 1973 about $100.7 billion, or 47 percent of total social welfare expenditures, were transferred to the lowest quartile in the income distribution. After taxes paid by that quartile, the net transfer was $78.2 billion, which was paid by persons in the upper three-fourths of the income distribution.[8]

TABLE 23–3
SOCIAL WELFARE EXPENDITURES UNDER PUBLIC PROGRAMS, ALL U.S. GOVERNMENTS, SELECTED YEARS (MILLIONS OF DOLLARS)

Expenditures	1929	1950	1960	1976[a]
Total	3,921.2	23,508.4	52,293.3	331,366.3
Social insurance	342.2	4,946.6	19,306.7	146,592.5
Public aid	60.0	2,496.2	4,101.1	48,945.6
Health and medical programs	351.1	2,063.5	4,463.8	19,192.5
Veterans programs	657.9	6,865.7	5,479.2	19,005.8
Education	2,433.7	6,674.1	17,626.2	86,425.5
Housing	—	14.6	176.8	3,127.8
Other	76.2	447.7	1,139.4	8,076.5

a Preliminary estimates.

Source: Alfred M. Skolnik and Sophie R. Dales, "Social Welfare Expenditures, 1950–75," *Social Security Bulletin*, January 1976, pp. 3–20; and idem, "Social Welfare Expenditures, Fiscal Year 1976," *Social Security Bulletin*, January 1977, pp. 3–19.

7 See Charles L. Schultze, *The Distribution of Farm Subsidies: Who Gets the Benefits?* (Washington: Brookings, 1971), especially pp. 31ff.

8 Edgar K. Browning, *Redistribution and the Welfare System* (Washington: American Enterprise Institute for Public Policy Research, 1975).

TABLE 23-4
SOCIAL WELFARE EXPENDITURES AS A PERCENTAGE OF GNP,
SELECTED YEARS

Fiscal year	Percent
1929	3.9
1950	8.9
1960	10.6
1976	20.6[a]

a Preliminary estimate.

Source: Alfred M. Skolnik and Sophie R. Dales, "Social Welfare Expenditures, 1950–75," *Social Security Bulletin,* January 1976, pp. 3–20; and idem, "Social Welfare Expenditures, Fiscal Year 1976," *Social Security Bulletin,* January 1977, pp. 3–19.

If we consider only the effects of government cash transfers and food stamps on the incidence of poverty, it is estimated that in 1971, 80 percent of the pretransfer poor received transfers and 43 percent were raised above the poverty level.[9] These figures suggest that government transfer programs are below the level required to eliminate poverty (as officially defined). And such is indeed the case. Recall from Chapter 6 that the number of poor remains at 24 million and the distribution of income remains highly unequal.[10]

Browning argues that these figures overstate the severity of poverty in the United States, largely because they ignore in-kind transfers. When cash transfers *and* all in-kind transfers are counted, Browning estimates that federal, state, and local governments transferred $33.6 billion to the poor in 1973. And the poor received $6 billion in income from their own sources, for a total of resources available of $39.6 billion. This compares to the $30.5 billion that would be required to raise each poor family to the official poverty line.[11] These figures do not mean that all families in 1973 were above the poverty level — transfers and other income are distributed unevenly among the poor. Nor do they mean that enough resources were allocated to

9 Michael C. Barth, George J. Carcagno, and John L. Palmer, *Toward an Effective Income Support System: Problems, Prospects, and Choices* (Madison: Institute for Research on Poverty, University of Wisconsin, 1974), pp. 24–31.

10 For further discussion, see Benjamin A. Okner, "Transfer Payments: Their Distribution and Role in Reducing Poverty," in *Redistribution to the Rich and the Poor,* ed. Kenneth Boulding and Martin Pfaff (Belmont, Calif.: Wadsworth, 1972), pp. 62–77.

11 Browning, *Redistribution and the Welfare System.* The $33.6 billion transfer to the poor does not include the benefits from state and local education expenditures. Browning assumed that official poverty-line estimates were established to account for this in-kind benefit.

the poor, since poverty-line definitions are arbitrary. Instead, in-kind transfers substantially affect income distribution and make poverty less severe than it seems to be when only cash transfers are considered.

STABILIZATION POLICY AND INCOME DISTRIBUTION

Fiscal measures aimed at stabilizing the economy affect both the distribution and the aggregate amount of income. People in the lower income groups are the big gainers from policies that decrease unemployment; their incomes and income shares typically increase. The reverse is true for policies that increase unemployment.

That the burdens of unemployment are borne disproportionately by lower income persons is shown in a study by Edward Gramlich. He finds that each 1 percent increase in the unemployment rate reduces the *average* incomes of poverty-line persons by about 4 percent in the case of blacks and about 3 percent in the case of whites. For persons having incomes equal to five times the poverty-line income, the average decrease in income is only 1 percent for each percentage point increase in the unemployment rate.[12]

Stabilization policies also affect income distribution by their effects on inflation. In the aggregate, the dollar gains and losses from inflation tend to cancel. That is, what one person loses because of higher prices, others gain in higher incomes. (Recall the related discussion in Chapter 1.) But particular persons or groups may be net losers.

While information about the redistribution effects of inflation is limited at best, two generalizations are widely accepted. First, unanticipated inflation transfers income from creditors to debtors. In particular, government, being a major debtor, gains from inflation as the *real* value of its debt declines. Second, people living on fixed incomes, retirees in particular, lose from inflation. Their losses are now limited because Social Security payments are adjusted upward to allow for increases in the cost of living. Inflation may have other redistributional effects, but they tend to vary from one inflationary episode to another.[13]

Since stabilization policies often affect both unemployment and inflation rates, as we explained in Chapter 17, their net effects on income distribution are difficult to determine. In recent years, stabilization policy has not prevented high unemployment rates. If a more expansionary policy had been

12 Edward M. Gramlich, "The Distributional Effects of Higher Unemployment," in *Brookings Papers on Economic Activity*, vol. 2 (Washington, 1974), pp. 292–336.

13 For further discussion of the distributional effects of inflation, see G. L. Bach, "Inflation: Who Gains and Who Loses?" *Challenge*, 17, No. 3 (July-August 1974): 48–55.

followed, the incomes and income shares of lower-income persons would have been higher. At the same time, lower-income persons might have either gained or lost, as a group, from any inflation caused by the more expansionary policy. They would have gained as debtors and lost as fixed-income recipients. It seems likely that lower-income persons would have gained on balance if stabilization policies had held unemployment rates down to 5 percent rather than the higher rates that have prevailed during the 1970s. Conversely, lower-income persons, as a group, tend to be hurt when inflation-fighting measures also increase unemployment. It is less clear that higher-income persons would also have gained from a more expansionary policy, since they lose less as a group from unemployment. But the *aggregate* gains from lower unemployment surely would have been positive, since lower unemployment means greater total income, while the main effect of inflation is a redistribution of income.

ALTERING THE REDISTRIBUTION EFFECTS OF GOVERNMENT

Overall, government budgetary policies appear to promote equality in the distribution of income (see Table 23–1). Whether the redistribution implicit in existing government activities is too great or too little is a matter of judgment. Certainly, many persons oppose the federal subsidies and tax preferences that appear to favor higher-income persons. In part, this opposition reflects a view that more redistribution and greater equality is needed. Also, the redistribution effects of current government budgetary activities often meet with disfavor because they do not eliminate poverty as it is officially defined and because people of similar circumstances are not similarly treated.

Dissatisfaction with existing income distribution and government's impact upon it has led to many proposals for change, most of which deal with government policies that have a direct effect on income distribution — mainly tax and welfare (income support) policies. And most proposals would simplify our tax and income support systems.[14] With simplification pushed to the limit, the tax base would be broadened by eliminating almost all tax preferences and deductions. And the income support system would become a nationwide negative income tax system. Additional simplification could be achieved by integrating the inheritance, gift, estate, and corporation income taxes with the personal income tax. Many reform proposals are not this dramatic, but most involve simplification to a greater or lesser degree. Our understanding of most reform proposals can therefore be improved if we look at the effects of extreme simplification and integration.

14 Milton Friedman has been a major advocate of that approach. See his *Capitalism and Freedom* (Chicago: University of Chicago Press, 1962).

TABLE 23–5

EFFECTIVE FEDERAL RATES OF INDIVIDUAL AND CORPORATION INCOME
AND PAYROLL TAXES UNDER CURRENT LAW AND UNDER FOUR REFORM
OPTIONS, BY COMPREHENSIVE INCOME CLASS, 1976 (PERCENT)

Comprehensive income class [a] (thousands of dollars)	Current law (1)	Option A (2)	Option B (3)	Option C (4)	Option D (5)
Less than 5	11.3	8.2	3.8	3.6	3.1
5–10	18.2	16.4	12.3	12.7	11.6
10–15	21.4	20.6	16.7	17.3	16.1
15–20	22.9	22.9	20.6	21.6	20.2
20–25	23.6	23.6	24.0	25.0	23.5
25–50	25.2	25.3	30.7	31.2	30.0
50–100	31.9	32.8	41.0	39.1	41.8
100–200	36.0	39.4	45.7	42.7	50.4
200–500	39.3	44.8	48.7	44.5	55.7
500–1,000	42.1	49.4	51.2	45.4	58.6
1,000 and over	41.9	52.1	51.9	44.5	58.3
All classes [b]	24.0	24.0	24.0	24.0	24.0

a Comprehensive income is adjusted gross income plus (1) the share of corporate retained earnings and the corporate tax allocated to individuals, (2) half of total estimated capital gains transferred by gifts or death, (3) excess of percentage depletion over cost depletion, and (4) interest on state and local government bonds.

b Includes negative incomes not shown separately.

Source: George F. Break and Joseph A. Pechman, *Federal Tax Reform: The Impossible Dream?* (Washington: Brookings, 1975), p. 126. © 1975 by the Brookings Institution, Washington, D.C.

As an example of extreme tax simplification, let us consider replacing the existing federal taxes on payrolls and individual and corporation income with a single tax on comprehensive income. A flat rate tax of about 24 percent on comprehensive income, as defined by Break and Pechman, would yield the same revenue as the three federal taxes (corporate and individual income and payroll).[15] That compares with effective rates that range, under present law, from 11.3 percent of comprehensive income for the lowest income class to 41.9 percent for the highest class (see Table 23–5). Of course, the average effective rate on taxable income as defined by current law would be much higher than 24 percent because taxable income is a much smaller tax base than comprehensive income as defined by Break and Pechman.

Besides leading to lower average tax rates, tax base broadening would make

15 The following estimates of tax rates are based on George F. Break and Joseph A. Pechman, *Federal Tax Reform: The Impossible Dream?* (Washington: Brookings, 1975). The estimates are for 1976, but similar figures would currently apply since the tax structure is basically the same.

TABLE 23-6
SUMMARY OF STRUCTURAL REVISIONS UNDER FOUR REFORM OPTIONS

Item	Option A	Option B	Option C	Option D
Capital gains				
Increase holding period from six months to one year	×	a	a	a
Eliminate alternative tax	×	a	a	a
Tax capital gains as ordinary income	...	×	×	×
Constructive realization of capital gains	×	×	×	×
Tax on preference income				
Reduce $30,000 exemption to $5,000	×	a	a	a
Eliminate deduction for taxes	×	a	a	a
Raise tax rates to one-half the ordinary rates (present base)	×	a	a	a
Personal deductions				
Eliminate state gasoline tax deduction	...	×	×	×
Eliminate separate health insurance premium deduction	...	×	×	×
Raise medical expense floor from 3 to 5 percent	...	×	×	×
Eliminate property tax deduction	...	×	×	×
Limit interest deduction to property and business income plus $2,000	...	×	×	×
Repeal percentage standard deduction and raise low-income allowance to $3,000	...	×	×	×
Treatment of married couples and single people				
Remove rate advantages of income splitting	...	×	×	×
Provide 10 percent tax credit (up to $1,000) for spouse with lower earnings	...	×	×	×

the distribution of tax burdens more progressive. Even a modest tax reform effort would increase progressivity (compare columns 1 and 2 in Table 23-5). More ambitious reform efforts would, of course, lead to even greater progressivity (see columns 3-5 in Table 23-5). Each of the reform options indicated in Table 23-5 is described in Table 23-6.[16]

16 Since publication of Break and Pechman, *Federal Tax Reform*, the Tax Reform Act of 1976 has broadened the tax base somewhat. For example, the first item on the list of reforms given in Table 23-6 (increase holding period from six months to one year) has been implemented. But most of the possible changes discussed by Break and Pechman have not been carried out.

TABLE 23–6 (*cont.*)

Item	Option A	Option B	Option C	Option D
Other provisions				
Eliminate percentage depletion	×	×	×	×
Eliminate deferral through DISCs	...	×	×	×
Eliminate deferral of income of foreign-controlled corporations	...	×	×	×
Eliminate dividend exclusion	...	×	×	×
Eliminate maximum tax on earned income	...	×	×	×
Repeal tax on preference income	...	×	×	×
Payroll tax				
Introduce $900 per capita exemption and $2,000 low-income allowance, with phase-out of $1 for every $2 of earnings (employee and self-employed only)	×	...	...	...
Introduce $900 per capita exemption and $2,000 low-income allowance; eliminate ceiling on maximum taxable earnings; raise tax rate by 1.7 percentage points (employee, employer, and self-employed)	...	×	×	×
Integration				
Tax all corporate earnings to share-holders at individual income tax rates [b]	...	...	×	×

a Revision not relevant because capital gains would be taxed in full.

b Tax-exempt organizations are assumed not taxed on their allocated share of corporate earnings.

Source: George F. Break and Joseph A. Pechman, *Federal Tax Reform: The Impossible Dream?* (Washington: Brookings, 1975), p. 128. © 1975 by the Brookings Institution, Washington, D.C.

There are, of course, less comprehensive proposals for tax integration and reform. And an important subset would shift part or all of the burden of financing the Social Security system from the payroll tax to the income tax. The main rationale for doing so is that the payroll tax is regressive. In the view of many, the need for such a shift is made more urgent by the rapid growth in Social Security outlays and the consequent rapid growth of payroll tax rates and revenues. Indeed, the payroll tax is the most rapidly growing federal tax. Since 1954 the percentage of federal revenues collected by payroll taxation has increased from 10.5 to 31.1 (see Table 23–7). Because the payroll tax is regressive, the growth in its importance means that the

TABLE 23-7
CHANGING STRUCTURE OF FEDERAL TAXATION, 1954 TO 1975[a]

Tax	Percentage distribution of taxes in fiscal year				
	1975	1969	1964	1959[b]	1954[b]
Individual income	44.8	48.4	46.0	47.3	43.2
Corporation income	14.7	20.4	22.2	22.3	30.5
Payroll	31.1	20.8	19.9	15.1	10.5
Estate and gift	1.8	1.9	2.3	1.7	1.4
Excise	7.6	8.4	9.7	13.6	14.4
Total	100.0	100.0	100.0	100.0	100.0

a Taxes are net of refunds.

b 1954 and 1959 include federal supplemental medical insurance, civil service retirement, other employee retirement which are excluded in other years.

Source: For 1975, *The Budget of the U.S. Government, Fiscal Year 1976*, p. 322; for 1954 and 1959, *Statistical Appendix to Annual Report of the Secretary of the Treasury on the State of the Finances for the Fiscal Year Ended June 30, 1969*, pp. 14, 17; and for 1964 and 1969, *Treasury Bulletin*, January 1972, pp. 2-3.

overall federal tax structure has become increasingly less progressive each year.[17]

Similar simplifications of the income maintenance system could be achieved with a universal negative income tax. The provisions and costs of one such program are summarized in Table 23-8. The net federal cost of the program ($17.8 billion for the marginal tax rate of .5) would require an increase in the average rate of taxation of comprehensive income of less than 2 percentage points (from 24 to 25.8 percent).

Of course, the floor-support levels ($4,800 for a family of four) are not particularly generous, given current price levels. Indeed, the poverty-line income for a family of four is more than $6,000 in 1977 dollars. But a negative income tax program with twice the federal budgetary cost of this example would raise the incomes of all poor persons above the poverty line, and require an increase in the average federal tax rate on comprehensive income of 3.5 percentage points (from 24 to 27.5).

There are many other proposals for broadening the federal income tax

17 For discussion of the possibilities for reducing reliance on payroll taxation, see Benjamin A. Okner, "The Social Security Payroll Tax: Some Alternatives for Reform," *The Journal of Finance* (May 1975): 567-578; U.S. Social Security Administration, *Reducing Social Security Contributions for Low Income Workers: Issues and Analysis* (1974); and Michael K. Taussig, "The Social Security Retirement Program and Welfare Reform," in *Studies in Public Welfare*, Paper no. 7, prepared for the use of the Subcommittee on Fiscal Policy of the Joint Economic Committee, 93 Cong., 1st sess., 1973, pp. 14-39.

TABLE 23–8

UNIVERSAL NEGATIVE INCOME TAX AND ITS ESTIMATED COST FOR FISCAL
YEAR 1976[a]

Family earned income (dollars)	Negative income tax payment for a family of four		Total family income (earned plus negative tax payment)	
	Marginal tax rate of .67	Marginal tax rate of .50	Marginal tax rate of .67	Marginal tax rate of .50
0	4,800	4,800	4,800	4,800
2,000	3,467	3,800	5,467	5,800
3,000	2,800	3,300	5,800	6,300
4,000	2,133	2,800	6,133	6,800
6,000	800	1,800	6,800	7,800
7,200	0	1,200	7,200	8,400
8,000	0	800	8,000	8,800
9,600	0	0	9,600	9,600

a Total estimated cost for the 1976 fiscal year is $21.1 billion for a marginal tax rate of .67 and
$27.1 billion for a marginal tax rate of .50. The net cost of the negative income tax would be
less if existing federal and state and local assistance programs are discontinued. Savings from
elimination of current federal and state and local cash assistance and food stamp programs
would be $10.3 billion and $2.4 billion, respectively, yielding a net cost of $27.1
billion − $12.7 billion = $14.4 billion for the case of a .50 marginal tax rate and a net cost of
$8.4 billion for a .67 tax rate. The net federal cost would be $17.8 and $11.8 billion,
respectively. These cost estimates also assume that for other family sizes, maximum cash
payments would be $1,600 each for the first two family members, $800 each for the third,
fourth, and fifth members, $600 each for the sixth and seventh, and $500 for the eighth. Those
maximum payments would be made only if family income were zero. Payments would be
decreased from the maximum levels by $.50 or $.67 for each $1 that the family earns.

Source: Edward R. Fried, A. M. Rivlin, Charles L. Schultze, and Nancy H. Teeters, *Setting National
Priorities: The 1974 Budget* (Washington: Brookings, 1973), p. 83. © 1973 by the Brookings Institution,
Washington, D.C.

base and simplifying and expanding the income maintenance system. But
the proposals just discussed illustrate several elements common to all
proposals. First, a universal income maintenance system that is generous
enough to eliminate poverty is going to be costly in a budgetary sense. Second, this cost could be financed without a large increase in the average rate
of federal income taxation if the base for income taxation is comprehensive.[18] However, if broadening the tax base does not accompany expanding

18 Recall that a program with a net cost of $35 billion would require an average rate of taxa-
tion of comprehensive income of 27.5 percent, while the rate would be 24 percent in the absence of such a program.

income maintenance programs, the average rates will increase much more.[19] Clearly, the feasibility of an improved and more generous income maintenance system is likely to depend on whether tax base broadening can be achieved simultaneously. Third, the budgetary cost of providing a given minimum level of income ($4,800 for a family of four in the above examples) increases dramatically as the marginal tax rate on income earned by the poor is deceased — $21.1 billion at a marginal rate of .67; $27.1 billion at .50; and $43.3 billion at .33.[20]

ECONOMIC EFFICIENCY

In Chapters 3–5 we saw how and why societies might use the mechanisms of government to promote efficiency in allocating resources. In this chapter we ask whether there is evidence that the budgetary policies of U.S. governments do promote efficiency. That such might be the case is plausible, since political leaders in their public statements and rhetoric express considerable concern about efficiency in government and the efficiency and productivity of our economy.

In Chapter 2 we became familiar with statistics outlining the size and growth of government in the United States. From them we do see that most of the goods and services provided by government are public goods, goods involving externalities, and goods that are probably produced under conditions of either decreasing cost or natural monopoly or both. Government thus appears to be operating in areas in which markets may fail and in which there is a *potential* for government to improve on the efficiency with which resources are used. However, the statistics do not tell us whether such improvement is the actual outcome of government actions.

To determine whether government is in fact promoting efficiency by providing a good or service, we must know whether its value exceeds its opportunity cost, the latter being the value of the forgone private-sector output. A summary measure of how government expenditures affect allocation efficiency would be the amount by which the total value of government-provided goods and services exceeds their opportunity cost. The opportunity costs should include the amount of excess burden generated by government tax and transfer activities. Without such a summary measure, we cannot

---

19 For example, an income maintenance program with a net cost of $35 billion would have, in 1975, required an increase of about 30 percent in the average rate of federal individual income taxation, given the tax base prevailing then.

20 See Edward R. Fried, A. M. Rivlin, Charles L. Schultze, and Nancy H. Teeters, *Setting National Priorities: The 1974 Budget* (Washington: Brookings, 1973), p. 83.

even conclude that welfare is greater with present government activity than it would otherwise be.[21]

DIFFICULTY OF MEASURING OVERALL EFFICIENCY

The information we require for a comprehensive efficiency evaluation of U.S. governments is not now available and, for reasons we discussed in Chapter 7, is probably not obtainable. What we do know are government's total purchases of goods and services, which have been about 20–22 percent of GNP for all U.S. governments. This amount measures the approximate opportunity cost of the resources used by governments in providing goods and services.[22] But it does not measure the value of the final goods and services provided. To value that output, we must know what people are willing to pay for the services provided — national defense, the judicial system and law enforcement, education, transportation, etc.

Because we know the approximate cost of government output but not its value, the value of government goods and services has come to be measured by their cost of production.[23] For example, the *value* of a highway or a civic center is taken as the *cost* of building it. But identifying value and cost that way is not accurate. For example, in Figure 23–1, the curve ΣD shows the value that all members of a nation place on each successive unit of a public good X. The S curve shows the marginal cost of the good.[24] Suppose that none of the good will be provided if it is not provided by government. If government provides q_1, the total value of the amount provided is area $a + b$;

21 We might be tempted to argue that the welfare gains from government are surely positive because the goods and services presently provided by government would not otherwise be provided. But that argument is false. Education, roads and other transportation facilities, police and fire protection, care for the poor, etc., surely would be provided at some levels through nongovernment institutions. National defense activities as we know them probably would not be provided in the absence of government. But, in the absence of government as we know it, large nation-states would not exist, and defense of the present type and scale would not be needed. Defense of the sort provided by the feudal lords of the Middle Ages might be provided instead.

22 Most of the purchases are *intermediate* goods and services that are used to produce the *final* services provided by government. For example, to provide police protection, government hires people (purchases labor), buys equipment (cars, radios, firearms), purchases or rents buildings, etc. These goods and services are used to provide the police protection, which is the final output. The costs of the intermediate goods and services, or inputs, *does not* measure the value of the final service or output.

23 This practice is followed in preparing the U.S. national income accounts, and they can never therefore show either a profit or a loss for government actions.

24 Recall our discussion and definitions of these curves in Chapter 4.

FIGURE 23–1
A MEASURE OF THE WELFARE GAINS FROM GOVERNMENT ACTION

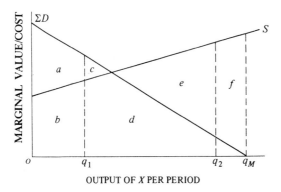

OUTPUT OF X PER PERIOD

and its total cost is area b. The welfare gain from government provision is area a minus the CCA. Government provision of X could result in a loss rather than a gain, as would be the case if q_2 were supplied. Then the net loss would be area $a + c - e$ minus CCA. Each good or service provided by government results in a *net* welfare gain or loss, as Figure 23–1 illustrates. The sum of the net gains and losses gives a measure of the *aggregate* welfare gains from government-provided goods and services. We can now easily see what information is needed to determine whether government provision of goods and services promotes efficiency.

IS THE PUBLIC SECTOR TOO LARGE?

A major unresolved issue in public finance and a subject of popular and political debate is whether resources are allocated optimally between the public and private sectors. Some argue that the public sector is too large, while others take the opposite view. That this debate continues is not surprising, given the difficulty of determining whether government in fact promotes efficiency.

One line of argument in this debate is that individuals may misperceive either the cost or the value of government output. For example, people may (mistakenly) think that their taxes are independent of how much government spends, because they each pay only a small fraction of the total taxes collected. Each person who thinks in this manner tends to demand additional public services until the marginal value of each service approaches its *perceived* marginal cost of zero. Such demands expressed through democratic decision making tend to push output to the point at which the marginal value of the good is zero, q_m in Figure 23–1. And, its total value may be less than its total cost, for example, if area $e + f$ exceeds area $a + c$.

Oversupply of public goods may also occur when the beneficiary and decision-making population does not pay the full costs of the goods. Expenditures for activities that have largely local benefits, for example, urban renewal and streets and roads, may be excessive if they are financed with taxes collected nationwide. We discussed the consequences of this *exportation* of taxes to nonbeneficiaries in Chapter 21.

Another argument suggests that the public sector is too small because individuals undervalue government output or exaggerate its cost. Advertising in the private sector and the social status identified with private consumption are cited as influences operating in this direction.[25] Still another argument takes a middle view that government tends to spend too much on activities that have an identifiable national purpose articulated by experts, while too little is spent on activities with net benefits that are real but remote and vague.[26] In particular, producers of such public goods and services as national defense, highways, and education, lobby and advertise in support of higher spending in these areas.

Even if individuals correctly perceive the value of and cost of government output, the efficient output may not be produced. We explained this with the political decision models in Chapter 8. With majority rule, the chosen quantity of a public good is that which is preferred by the median voter.[27] For example, in Figure 23–2, when each taxpayer is charged ⅓ MC for each unit of X, the median voter is B. For that equal-cost arrangement, the efficient output (q) is chosen. However, with a different cost-sharing arrangement or a different pattern of preferences, the chosen output might either exceed or fall short of the efficient output.

Even if efficient output is chosen and produced so that the public sector is neither too large nor too small in an efficiency sense, there may still be debate about the size of the public sector. Some people may be dissatisfied with the efficiency quantity. To illustrate, with equal cost sharing in Figure

---

25 Among economists, John K. Galbraith has been one of the more steadfast proponents of the view that government underproduces; see his *The Affluent Society* (Boston: Houghton Mifflin, 1958). For diverse views on this subject, see Edmund S. Phelps, ed., *Private Wants and Public Needs* (New York: Norton, 1962).

26 Harry G. Johnson suggests that, for these reasons, too much is spent for national defense and too little for public amenities and poverty relief. See his "The Economic Approach to Social Questions," in *Economics: Mainstream Reading and Radical Critiques*, ed. David Mermelstein (New York: Random House, 1970), pp. 15–23. See also, R. C. Amacher, R. D. Tollison, and T. D. Willett, "Budget Size in a Democracy: A Review of the Arguments," *Public Finance Quarterly*, 3, No. 2 (April 1975): 99–121.

27 See Chapter 8, pp. 168–169.

FIGURE 23–2
DETERMINATION OF PUBLIC-GOOD OUTPUT BY MAJORITY VOTE

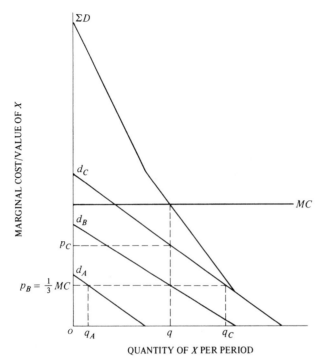

23–2, A prefers q_A to q and may therefore argue that X is overproduced and that the public sector is too large. In contrast, C prefers q_C to q and may therefore feel that the public sector is too small. In an efficiency sense, neither A nor C is correct. Those who would like more (less) of the public good produced would change their view if their cost share were increased (decreased). In Figure 23–2, the efficient output is unanimously chosen if A pays a zero price, B pays p_B and C pays p_C. This analysis suggests that debate about public-sector size may reflect distributional concerns, as well as (or rather than) efficiency concerns.

A third general reason for dissatisfaction with the division of resources between private and public government sectors is that some persons are offended by other people's tastes. Sally Borish may not like Lois Riley's tastes for private consumption; and Borish may think that Riley should give up her frivolous private consumption to finance more public services, for example to provide higher quality education. But this difference of opinion between Borish and Riley does not mean that resources are allocated inefficiently.

Although we have not exhausted the arguments surrounding the question of balance between the private and public sectors, we have said enough to show that the issue can not be resolved on the basis of a priori reasoning. However, a few empirical studies have attempted to determine whether the level of government expenditures satisfies efficiency criteria.[28] The results of these studies are generally consistent with the predictions of the majority-rule model of political choice. But no generalizations can be made about whether government spends too much or too little.

LESSONS OF PARTIAL EVALUATIONS

To say that we do not have and probably cannot obtain an overall measure of the efficiency effects of government activities, is not to say that judgments cannot be made about particular activities and practices. It is difficult to imagine how some services could be satisfactorily provided except through government mechanisms — the creation and enforcement of laws, property rights, and rules of exchange; other judicial services; national defense. Most people would probably believe that net welfare gains result from those government activities.

At the same time, casual observation suggests that particular goods or services are not worth their opportunity cost, or that a particular service can be provided at a lower cost. For example, all levels of government *subsidize* higher education in areas for which there is presently a *surplus* of trained people — elementary teaching and many areas of postgraduate education and training. Highway and air transportation is subsidized although their growth is responsible for much of the deterioration of the air quality of our cities. Farm price subsidies and production controls reduce food supply in a starving world and increase domestic food prices.[29] Price regulation keeps low-cost bulk carriers such as barges and railroads from effectively competing with higher cost trucks.[30] Entry into many professions and trades is

28 See Robin Barlow, "Efficiency Aspects of Local School Finance," *Journal of Political Economy*, 78 (September-October 1970): 1028–1040; T. E. Borcherding and R. T. Deacon, "The Demand for the Services of Non-Federal Governments," *American Economic Review*, 62 (December 1972): 891–901; T. C. Bergstrom and R. P. Goodman, "Private Demands for Public Goods," *American Economic Review*, 62 (June 1973): 280–296; L. L. Orr, "Income Transfers as a Public Good: An Application to AFDC," *American Economic Review*, 66 (June 1976): 359–371.

29 Production controls for a number of crops were removed in the middle 1970s because sharp increases in free-market prices reduced the need for supply restriction as an income-increasing device. But controls have since been reinstated.

30 See John F. Due, "The Railway Industry—Where Next?" *Challenge,* 19, No. 5. (November-December 1976).

restricted by government or government-sanctioned trade unions and professional organizations, thus reducing the supply and increasing the costs of the services provided.

More evidence along these same lines is provided by recent studies of federal subsidy programs undertaken for the Joint Economic Committee. The committee concludes that "many subsidies do not work well economically, they are often directed at outmoded or non-existent objectives, they redistribute income to the affluent, and in too many cases, their costs far exceed their benefits to society as a whole. . . . The studies made for this Committee have documented very clearly ways in which government subsidies prevent efficient market operations and increase prices."[31] Similarly, a staff report states that "with [defense] personnel costs running between $60 and $70 billion per year, it would be foolhardy to suggest that improvements in efficiency and productivity are not attainable."[32] The report then suggests changes in our national defense program that would produce savings of $2.6 billion in fiscal 1977, increasing to $18.7 billion in fiscal 1981. The report also notes possibilities for savings in other areas.

Other studies of government efficiency could be cited, some showing that particular government programs produce net benefits and some showing the opposite. But the examples we have already cited illustrate the point: Government budgetary policies may promote efficiency in some or many instances, but in many instances they do not.[33] How these pluses and minuses balance out is unclear.

There is one area, however, in which the efficiency implications of government policies are clear: economic stabilization. Demand expansion policies can, in periods of high unemployment, produce significant efficiency (welfare) gains. And failure to expand demand when there is unemployment prevents the attainment of an efficient allocation of resources. When labor and capital are unemployed, the economy is operating inside its production possibility frontier and, as we discussed in Chapter 1, resource allocation is not technologically efficient.

31 U.S. Congress, Joint Economic Committee, *Federal Subsidy Programs*, a staff study prepared for the Subcommittee on Priorities and Economy in Government (Washington: Government Printing Office, 1974), pp. 3–4. For the studies on which that staff report is based, see U.S. Congress, Joint Economic Committee, *The Economics of Federal Subsidy Programs*, a compendium of papers submitted to the Joint Economic Committee, 92 Cong., 2nd sess., 1972.

32 U.S. Congress, Joint Economic Committee, *An Economic Evaluation of the Current Services Budget, Fiscal Year 1977* (Washington: Government Printing Office, 1975), p. 32.

33 For discussion of some of the reasons why government policies may be inefficient and suggestions for improving decision making, see Charles L. Schultze, "The Role of Incentives, Penalties, and Rewards in Attaining Effective Policy," in U.S. Congress, Joint Economic Committee, *Economic Analysis and the Efficiency of Government*, part 3, Hearings of the Subcommittee on Economy in Government, September and October 1969.

One measure of the inefficiency associated with unemployment is the gap between potential and actual GNP, which we defined and discussed in Chapter 16. Figure 16–1 (p. 337) shows that this gap has been substantial throughout the 1970s. The resulting loss in output is large, about $600 billion (in 1972 dollars) for the years 1970–1976. That is, with resources fully employed, real GNP would have been larger during these years by an average of about $85 billion per year. As we explained in Chapter 18, the record of stabilization policy since 1946 has been far from perfect. The result has been inefficiency and a loss of production and income amounting to hundreds of billions of dollars by any reckoning.

SUMMARY

Available estimates of the overall redistribution effects of federal, state, and local budgetary policies show significant redistribution from higher income to lower income persons. Yet poverty persists, and the distribution of income remains highly unequal. The redistribution effects of government also favor particular groups, farmers, homeowners, educators, college students, etc., that are often in the middle- and upper-income classes.

Dissatisfaction with the prevailing distribution of income has lead to numerous proposals for "reform" and simplification of those government activities — taxation and income maintenance — that most directly affect income distribution. Tax reform proposals typically entail base broadening by closing loopholes — eliminating tax code provisions that are deemed vertically or horizontally inequitable. Whether such base broadening is indeed a move toward greater equity depends of course on one's values. But, whether justified or not, base broadening would greatly reduce the average tax rates required to obtain a given amount of revenue and increase the progressiveness of the tax system. And, in most instances, tax laws would be simplified, thus reducing compliance and enforcement costs.

Comprehensive tax reform may be more feasible politically than *piecemeal* reform. Closing only a few loopholes (piece-meal reform) is likely to make some people significantly worse off without noticeably reducing average tax rates. Those who are adversely affected will strongly oppose such reforms. In contrast, comprehensive reform would significantly reduce average tax rates, which would offset in part the losses of those persons who were favored by the eliminated tax preferences (loopholes). Political opposition to reform would thereby be lessened.

Proposals to reform our income ma ntenance (welfare) system typically aim at extending coverage to all person ;, including the working poor, and making the level of support more unifo m geographically either by a federal takeover of welfare or by federally mandated and finan ed minimum support levels.

The negative income tax illustrates most of the issues and elements of welfare reform proposals. A negative income tax would be fairly expensive in budgetary terms if it (1) provides a support level for all persons equal to their poverty-line incomes and (2) reduces benefits by $.50 or less for each dollar that the recipient earns. More generous income maintenance can be financed without large increases in *average* rates of federal income taxation only if the income tax base is broadened.[34] For that reason, tax reform may need to occur either before or along with the improvement of the income maintenance system.

In Chapters 3–6 we saw how the police power of the state, exercised through the institutions of government, might be used to promote efficiency in resource allocation and equity in income distribution. Although government need not be used to achieve those objectives, it is plausible that such would indeed be the case. That is, government may be used in modern societies to (1) secure a distribution of income and property rights that appears equitable to many if not most persons and (2) seek efficiency through resource reallocations that produce aggregate welfare gains for the members of the society. Alternatively, the powers of government may be used to promote special interests, as individuals and groups seek more at the expense of others and try to impose their will, regarding income distribution and other matters, upon others. If that view is correct, then government policies would reflect the struggles of persons having conflicting interests and the resolution, sometimes short-lived, of those conflicts through the exercise of the police power of the state.

The preceding brief survey of what we know about the effects of the U.S. government on efficiency and equity provides some support for both those views. However, it is not surprising that government is used in both ways. Once the police power of the state exists, and regardless of the reasons for creating the institutions of government that exercise and apply the power, individuals are likely to try to use the power for their own purposes. In some instances, the interests of many persons may be promoted by a particular government action. In the case that no one is hurt and someone is helped by the action, it is said to be a Pareto improvement. In other instances, the action may benefit few at the expense of many. The former cases are usually thought to be appropriate uses of the police power, while the latter are not. But in all cases government is being used to serve the interests of a person or persons.

We would like, of course, to be able to evaluate government's activities, distinguishing those that are desirable by economic (efficiency and equity)

---

34 Of course, more funds for income maintenance could also be obtained by reducing other categories of government spending.

criteria from those that are not. But such evaluation is often not feasible because economic criteria are difficult to make operational (they require information that is costly if not impossible to obtain). In addition, such evaluation, even if feasible, may carry little weight in policy making if the underlying equity or efficiency objectives are not widely accepted. Both the feasibility and the acceptability of economic evaluations are perhaps greatest when they show that *given* tasks can be accomplished with the use of *fewer* real resources.

How should we react to evidence that particular government policies fail efficiency and equity tests. A common reaction is that government *must* do better and that the perverse outcomes *ought* not occur, with the main prescription for improvement being a change in the personnel making the decisions. That is, a common view is that results will be different (better?) if different people make the decisions — if different people are elected to legislative and executive offices. While this view cannot be totally discounted, it fails to recognize that undesirable policy outcomes may be a reflection of the structure of the rules and procedures followed in the decision-making process. If such is the case, a change in and improvement of policy outcomes will require a change in the basic institutions of government — tax systems, electoral processes, legislative and executive roles, etc. Such institutional changes probably cannot be made unless the general population and electorate understand the roles that government might play in our economy, as well as the roles that it actually does play. It is this need that justifies the study of the subject matter of this book.

SUPPLEMENTARY READINGS

Amacher, R. C., Tollison, R. D., Willet, T. D. "Budget Size in a Democracy." *Public Finance Quarterly* (April 1975): 99–121.

Borcherding, T. E., and Deacon, R. T. "The Demand for the Services of Non-Federal Governments." *American Economic Review* 62 (December 1972): 891–901.

Boulding, Kenneth, and Pfaff, Martin, eds. *Redistribution to the Rich and the Poor*. Belmont, Calif.: Wadsworth, 1972.

Break, George F., and Pechman, Joseph A. *Federal Tax Reform: The Impossible Dream?* Washington: Brookings, 1976.

Browning, Edgar K. *Redistribution and the Welfare System.* Washington: American Enterprise for Public Policy Research, 1975.

U.S. Congress, Joint Economic Committee. *Federal Subsidy Programs.* Washington: Government Printing Office, 1974.

AUTHOR INDEX

SUBJECT INDEX

Ability to pay: and the corporation income tax, 275–276; and excise taxes, 299–300; and individual income, 202–204; and the net wealth tax, 327–328; and the payroll tax, 284; as a principle of taxation, 202–204; and the sales tax, 292–295; and wealth transfer taxes, 332–333

Adjusted gross income, 254–257

Aggregate demand: concept of, 336–339; and government debt, 401–403

Allocation of resources: see Resource allocation

Assessment, property tax, 309–310, 322

Averaging (taxable income), 221, 253

Balanced budget concepts, 379–382

Balanced budget multiplier, 346

Balance-of-payments, 385–387

Benefit-cost analysis: benefits and costs defined, 144–146; distributional considerations, 159–160; identifying inputs and outputs, 149–150; present value estimates, 148–149; and uncertainty, 158–159; valuation problems, 150–154. See also Dicounting

Benefit taxation: and the corporation income tax, 276–277; and excise taxes, 301–302; and the individual income tax, 223; and net wealth taxes, 327; and the payroll tax, 279, 284; as a principle of taxation, 204; and public goods output, 168

Bequests: see Wealth transfers

Budget balance: see Balanced budget concepts

Budget Control Act of 1974, 185

Budgetary process, 183; incrementalism, 186; and the role of Congress, 185; tax expenditures, 187–188, 258–259; zero-base budgeting, 187

Built-in stabilizers, 364–370

Capacity, fiscal, 435–444

Capital gains and losses: and the corporation income tax, 265, 268; and the

individual income tax, 241–245; and inflation, 242; and integration, 278; and investment incentives, 242–244; and the lock-in effect, 244; and tax reform, 244–245

Capitalization, tax, 314–315, 409

CCA (Costs of collective action): government vs. nongovernment, 98–99; and group size, 95; and pollution control, 111–114; and public goods supply, 88–99; and self-interest, 96; and voting rules, 178

Charges, 301–302, 475

Charitable contributions, 251–252

Collective action costs: see CCA

Communications costs, 111

Community size, 421–424

Comprehensive income, 217–219, 256–257

Constitution, United States, 29–30

Consumer sovereignty, 18–19, 78

Consumer surplus, defined, 55–56

Consumption: aggregate, 340; defined, 11

Corporation income tax: and ability to pay, 275–276; base, 265–270; and benefit taxation, 276–277; and capital gains, 265, 268; and depletion allowances, 268–269; and depreciation, 266–268; and equity, 271–277; incidence of, 271–277; integration with the individual income tax, 277–278; and investment incentives, 269–270; and investment tax credit, 269; and labor supply, 270–271; minimum tax, 265n.; rates, 265; and saving, 270–271

Costs: administrative and compliance, 197; of communications, 111; of enforcement, 93–94, 111; of excess burden, 197–200; of exclusion, 85–87, 94–95; of government, 69–71, 195–200; of information, 92, 111; marginal, 57–58; of negotiation, 92–93; of transactions, 111. See also CCA; Excess burden; Opportunity costs; Decreasing cost industries

Cost-effectiveness analysis, 160–161